Assaulted Personhood

Assaulted Personhood

*Original and Everyday Sins
Attacking the "Other"*

Craig C. Malbon

Hamilton Books

Lanham • Boulder • New York • Toronto • London

Published by Hamilton Books
An imprint of The Rowman & Littlefield Publishing Group, Inc.
4501 Forbes Boulevard, Suite 200, Lanham, Maryland 20706
Hamilton Books Acquisitions Department (301) 459-3366

6 Tinworth Street, London SE11 5AL, United Kingdom

British Library Cataloguing in Publication Information Available

Library of Congress Control Number: 2020945509

ISBN 978-0-7618-7243-6 (pbk. : alk. paper)
ISBN 978-0-7618-7244-3 (electronic)

∞™ The paper used in this publication meets the minimum requirements of American National Standard for Information Sciences Permanence of Paper for Printed Library Materials, ANSI/NISO Z39.48-1992.

To
Elroy W. Malbon (1915–2001)
Jordan J. ("Jordy") *Cohen*
John H. ("Jack") *Marburger, III* (1941–2011)
James H. Cone (1938–2018)

Contents

Acknowledgments   ix

Prologue   xi

1   On Being Human and Attaining Personhood   1

2   Personhood With Vulnerabilities in Soma (Body)   39

3   Personhood With Vulnerabilities in Psyche (Mind)   79

4   Special Challenges to Personhood in the 21st Century   131

5   America's Great "Original Sins"   215

6   Understanding Those Who Attack the Being of the "Other"   293

7   Prescriptions (Rx): Hard Truths, Contrition, and Metanoia   335

Epilogue   369

Index   377

About the Author   397

Acknowledgments

Based upon the Gratis Use Guidelines of the publisher, I gratefully acknowledge use of quotations from the Holy Bible, *New International Version*, *NIV* (2011), Grand Rapids, MI: Biblica, Inc., an imprint of Zondervan. For the rights to access without permission to quote under the Fair Use doctrine from the published works of the following authors: René Descartes, I thank *Bibliothèque nationale de France*; Michel Foucault, I thank Pantheon Books; Paul Monet, I thank Open Road Integrated Media, Inc.; Friedrich Wilhelm Nietzsche, I thank Cambridge University Press; and Henry David Thoreau, I thank Houghton Mifflin Comp. For the right of access to and permission to quote from the published work of Carl Sagan, grateful acknowledgment is made to Druyan-Sagan Associates, Inc. Cosmos Studios (Ithaca, NY).

I am especially indebted to several individuals whose insight, comments, and advice helped to shape this writing project. In particular I am indebted to the professional library staff at Columbia University, Stony Brook University, and the Marine Biological Laboratory without whose expert help and resourcefulness this project would not have been possible. I thank my colleagues in the Center for Medical Humanities, Compassionate Care & Bioethics at Stony Brook University: Stephen G. Post, John L. ("Jack") Coulehan, Brooke Ellison, Fr. Michael Vetrano, and Kevin Zacharoff. I also thank Andrew Flescher of the Program in Public Health at Stony Brook University. Through joint teaching and informal discussions, these talented folks enabled me to gain deeper insights about the topic of personhood. It is with thanks and humility that I acknowledge the students who have participated in my graduate ethics teaching. These fine graduate students, medical students, and physicians interrogated many of the topics related to personhood in class. I gained much from their learned insights. This research effort focused upon practical ethics for the 21st century enjoys the enthusiastic support of my two home departments (Pharmacological Sciences and Family, Population, & Preventive Medicine) and the Renaissance School of Medicine, Stony Brook University. I am deeply grateful for their continued support.

For the invaluable training at Union Theological Seminary in the City of New York from which I continue to benefit, I especially thank Euan Cameron, David Carr, Gary Dorrien, Roger Haight, Kelby Harrison, Brigitte Kahl, Janet Walton, and Cornel West. For mentoring in pastoral care I thank the Rev. Louis Tuleja (1930–2020), the Rev. Dr. Peter J. Vibert (retired), the Rev. Mary Barrett Spears, and Sister Patricia McDonnell, CSJ (Director of Pastoral Care, St. Catherine of Siena Medical Center, Smithtown, NY). For encouragement in the publishing process at Rowman & Littlefield I thank Neil Elliott (Acquisitions Editor), Brooke Bures (Associate Editor), and Becca Rohda Beurer (Managing Editor). For sustained deep discussion and interrogation of each topic of this writing project, I offer heartfelt thanks to the Rev. Dr. Hsien-Yu Wang (The Riverside Church in the City of New York).

Prologue

Ecce homo ("here is the man") sourced from the Gospel of John 19:5 re-counts the words of Pontius Pilate when he presents Jesus Christ, flogged, bound, and crowned with thorns to a hostile crowd just before the crucifixion of Jesus (2011). The German philosopher and public intellectual of 19th century Friedrich Nietzsche employed *Ecce Homo* as the title of his last original book (published in 1908), which he translated as *How One Becomes What One Is*. It is in the final chapter of that work, entitled "Why I Am a Destiny," in which Nietzsche captured the challenge of attaining full person-hood in the shadow of those who contest and assault it.

Elroy was a healthy octogenarian, who at 83 was diagnosed with a rapidly progressing dementia ascribed to Alzheimer's disease. Elroy still could drive his spouse to and from local and regional favorite places as well as play vigorously with his grandchildren. There was no doubt about his personhood. Yet his capacity and memory would suffer irreversible decline. One rightful-ly may ask, "what happened to Elroy's personhood over the three years of progressive dementia that culminated in his death?"

Gabby's life would be short by common measures. She succumbed to fetal death sometime after 28 weeks *in utero* (Malbon 2013). Her signs of life had passed, a grievous loss only to be confirmed by the obstetrician when quickening of poor Gabby could no longer be sensed by her mother. Two weeks later Gabby descended vaginally into this world, absent signs of life. Gabby's parents pleaded with the hospital chaplains for a baptism. As she gazed at the silent little girl cradled in her arms, Gabby's mom wondered how this little person could have lost personhood and been denied a blessing from God?

Irwin was in his late nineties and as spry as a millennial male. Stomach cancer would overtake his body, ravage his self-image, and isolate him within a deep depression. Other than clergy, some caring churchwomen, and a distant relative to whom Irwin relinquished his medical power of attorney, few could bring themselves to visit Irwin as he deteriorated. Closing his eyes for long periods during the day allowed Irwin to calibrate his feelings in response to such a harsh mixture of powerlessness, anger, and depression. Intentionally ignoring medical staff and visitors may have been his last attempt to express the remnant of his personhood, largely lost. Irwin must have wondered how the assault on his being, personhood, and independence had occurred? The perpetrators were many and their biting assaults were manifest in plain sight!

Elsewhere in a reproductive health clinic on Long Island an embryonic creation so valued and marveled by most, would succumb to a dilation and surgical curettage requested by a young pregnant woman. Absent a voice to declare personhood and without a proxy, this nascent life demands an answer to the question, who would defend his/her most basic human right of all people, in other words, the right not to be killed? What also of the rights of a pregnant woman who struggles daily, filled with economic uncertainty, food insecurity, and bereft of opportunities for her three small children? Who will advocate for this woman and for her need of a community in which her born and unborn children are certain to have available all the basic needs for their lives to flourish?

These real life narratives may horrify us. They prod us to gaze away from all too common daily assaults on personhood. Fundamental, age-old queries haunt virtually all aspects of our lives. When in development is personhood acquired or assigned? When in routine aging or accompanying physical/mental disabilities throughout life is personhood lost or discounted? There is no feature of our very lives that is more basic, personal, and important than our individual personhood. Yet we still grapple with the apparently "fluid" character of personhood illustrated by but a few examples. Has America arrived at a time when others feel empowered to assault the very concept of being human and personhood (Torchia 2008)?

Powerful narratives argue for, rather than against, the deep blessings of a robust, dependable, and bulletproof status for individual personhood. Jack lived a life that Teddy Roosevelt would have admired. As Teddy would have noted, Jack favored the "strenuous life". He was built like a mountain man, muscular, tall, broad shouldered and vital. He and his wife were raising five small children when, over a period of several months, Jack's life force seemed to be hemorrhaging from his body. The diagnosis was early and irrefutable. Jack was afflicted with amyotrophic lateral sclerosis (ALS or Lou Gehrig's disease), a progressive neurodegenerative disease that affects neurons in the brain and spinal column. As a pastor all too familiar with death and dying, I had witnessed the progressive deterioration of ALS victims, but Jack's situation was unprecedented. Although the average life expectancy following a diagnosis of ALS might span two to five years, Jack's robust vitality may have masked earlier symptoms. He was a friend, church member, devoted son, loving husband and father who relished all that life could offer. During his final months of rapid progressive loss of motor neuron function there was never a question about the status of Jack's personhood. Jack was a "Person in Full." He was able to embrace his diagnosis of inevitable total paralysis and respiratory failure with a grace that I seldom had witnessed. Surrounded by his children, loving wife, and tight knit family, Jack consciously declined heroic measures to sustain his failing respiration. Although moving in and out of consciousness due to anoxia and eventual comfort-care therapeutics, Jack had made sure that he would leave this world with his personhood fully and rightly "intact." Bathed in high levels of his body's own carbon dioxide and declining oxygen saturation, Jack passed, embraced in the deep love of his family and community; in other words, he remained a person in full until the end.

In my career I have been privileged to interact with, be mentored by, and befriended by people of great substance and accomplishment. Leading scientists, physicians, and theologians abound, yet not a single one escaped the vicissitudes of life. Racism, gender inequality, identity politics impacted their lives. Somehow (as we shall see) assaults on their personhood were overcome. Their narratives of successfully overcoming obstacles of enormous dimensions, suffering beyond most understanding, and daunting assaults on their personhood humble me. The most remarkable of all is my dear colleague Dr. Brooke Ellison. As both a medical scientist and pastor trained in chaplaincy I am intimately involved in the training of medical students not only in how drugs act (as a scientist), but also how the art of healing in medicine is founded upon medical ethics and compassion (as a pastor and chaplain). In this later capacity I met Brooke, a member of the medical humanities center, when it was her turn to bear witness to the 1st year medical students about her remarkable life. Her prior "unremarkable" life of an exuberant intelligent child took a grave turn when, at the tender age of 11, Brooke was struck by a car crossing a road on her first day of junior high school in 1991. The accident resulted in her being completely paralyzed from the neck down. In gripping words, Brooke bears witness to the medical students of the core value of life exemplified in the heroic struggle of Brooke and her mom Jean when confronting the obstacles to care for a quadriplegic child. Through adolescence and young adulthood, culminating with graduation *magnum cum laude* with a BS degree in cognitive neurosciences from Harvard, later a master's degree from Harvard's Kennedy School of Government, to faculty status at the Stony Brook University School of Medicine, Brooke (and Jean) overcame enormous obstacles. Even in the face of a life-threatening, life-changing traumatic injury and a follow-up that forced the realization of the enormous resources that would be needed for Brooke's life to flourish, Brooke and Jean would accept nothing less than the fullest personhood for Brooke.

In light of Brooke's unquestionable pursuit of full personhood, it is easy to overlook the dark seemingly uncaring side of our society that Brooke and Jean masterfully overcame by sheer will and goodness. We all applaud the successful multi-million dollar Coast Guard rescue of ill-fated novice sailors caught in avoidable storms, of ill-fated miners caught up in the inherent dangers of work thousands of feet below the sunlight, and of other such stories. Yet then how is it possible to overlook the fate of 12-year-old Deamonte Driver for whom a painful abscessed 6-year molar went largely ignored? His symptoms amplified through this inattention. A proper diagnosis revealed that this inattention provoked by an improperly treated abscess resulted in meningitis that then required a radical intervention, that is, brain surgery. Post-surgical intensive care therapy provided only a two-week respite for Deamonte's young life. He lapsed into a coma and died under hospital care. Who denied the personhood of Deamonte Driver? Who overlooked his prolonged pain and suffering caused by lack of access to basic dental care? Who permitted the abscess in his jaw to progress to meningitis and a death sentence? Was the personhood of Deamonte contestable on some grounds that seem obvious in hindsight, but overlooked at that time? When a child of color is raised in a challenging socio-economic environment or circumstance well outside of his/her control and suffers in the margins of our society, can we explain our lack of valuing his/her being? When infant and toddlers of immigrant families are forcibly separated from their parents at our Southern border, can we explain the moral basis for such a horrific outcome? These all-too-common images of brutality leveled at the "least of us," can neither be ignored nor forgotten. Although seldom cast in the proper context, these examples drill down into our souls and provoke difficult complex questions about our sense of personhood. Is it only familial (e.g., "me and my own"), or community-based identity politics, or tribal (i.e., nation of origin), or faith-based religion (i.e., behold U.S. State Department Muslim "ban" mentality), or race, etc. that decants our empathy for the least of us? Would these horrific outcomes occur if these "others"—that is, oppressed people of color, nationality, race, ethnic and gender categories—had not been deprived of their fullest personhood? Does not being human render all *Homo sapiens* deserving of such basic human rights?

In this book we shall be confronted, made aware of, and wrestle with the topic of assaults on being human and the more challenging concept of full "personhood." Excellent general resources support us as we interrogate personhood assaulted by abortion (Malbon 2013), ageism (Ayalon 2018), infanticide (Tooley 1983), vulnerabilities of the body (*soma*) and of the mind (*psyche*) (Joseph 2016; Pfeiffer 2007), intellect (Kittay and Carlson 2010; Kittay 2019), disabilities (Shapiro 1994; Smart 2009), drug dependence (Sederer 2018) and the opioid crisis (Newton 2018), Jim Crow laws (both old and "new) (Alexander 2010), forced incarceration (Anderson 2008), modern day slavery (Scarpa 2008), LGBTIQ sexuality and gender identity (Mogul, Ritchie, and Whitlock 2011), rampant identity politics (Fukuyama 2018; Brown 2018; Russell-Cole, Wilson, and Hall 2013), racism (West 1994; Wallis 2016; Dorrien 2018), and frank xenophobia (Dunbar-Ortiz 2014). In the common everyday landscape of the sick, dying, and incapacitated (Mosher 2018) shall we be shocked and dismayed, enraged and engaged, challenged by long-overdue self-discernment about the sanctity of personhood in 21st century America? Reading and pondering the contents of this book is designed to afflict the comfortable through the telling of painful truths. But this is not a book of judgment, it is a book that invites self-awareness, repentance and contrition, seeking and offering forgiveness, and a change of heart best termed "*metanoia*."

The very act of writing this book, confronting these all-to-common ethical and moral issues affecting all of our daily lives personally catalyzed a painful but necessary metanoia. We shall encounter "two original sins and a plethora of everyday sins" that America cannot escape and must confront. Contested being human and assaults on personhood pervade our lives. We as a nation grow dull to the acute suffering of others, discounting our moral principles and foreclosing on the future of the nation in the world. To achieve the goal of this reading and yield to metanoia we must confront squarely the issues of contested personhood. Is simply being human, justification for full personhood? Who assigns and who assaults personhood? Once assigned, is personhood subject to discount or withdrawal? Under what circumstance of birth, infirmity, physical and/or mental disability, or disease will the subconscious, ill-informed decision-making about who we are or wish to be reflect upon our own everyday assault on the "other" and their personhood? Do we have the stomach to unearth, receive, and validate our present-day complicity in and culpability for two original sins and a plethora of every day assaults on personhood that degrade the very notion and nature of what it is to be a human being with full personhood?

REFERENCES

2011. *The Holy Bible containing the Old and New Testaments*. New International Version. Grand Rapids, MI: Biblica, Inc., an imprint of Zondervan.

Alexander, Michelle. 2010. *The new Jim Crow: Mass incarceration in the age of colorblindness*. New York, NY; Jackson, TN: New Press, distributed by Perseus Distribution.

Anderson, Elijah. 2008. *Against the wall: Poor, young, Black, and male, the city in the 21st century*. Philadelphia, PA: University of Pennsylvania Press.

Ayalon, Liat. 2018. *Contemporary perspectives on ageism*. New York, NY: Springer Berlin Heidelberg.

Brown, Austin Channing. 2018. *I'm still here: Black dignity in a world made for whiteness*. New York, NY: Convergent Books.

Dorrien, Gary J. 2018. *Breaking White supremacy: Martin Luther King Jr. and the Black social gospel*. New Haven, CT; London, UK: Yale University Press.

Dunbar-Ortiz, Roxanne. 2014. *An indigenous peoples' history of the United States*. Boston, MA: Beacon Press.

Forman, James, Jr. 2017. *Locking up our own: Crime and punishment in Black America*. New York, NY: Farrar, Straus and Giroux.

Fukuyama, Francis. 2018. *Identity: The demand for dignity and the politics of resentment*. New York, NY: Farrar, Straus and Giroux.

Joseph, Monica A. 2016. *Discrimination against the mentally ill*. Santa Barbara, CA: Greenwood, an imprint of ABC-CLIO, LLC.

Kittay, Eva Feder. 2019. *Learning from my daughter: The value and care of disabled minds*. New York, NY: Oxford University Press.

Kittay, Eva Feder, and Licia Carlson. 2010. *Cognitive disability and its challenge to moral philosophy*. Chichester, West Sussex, UK; Malden, MA: Wiley-Blackwell.

Malbon, Craig C. 2013. *Abortion in 21st century America*. North Charleston, SC: CreateSpace Publishing.

Mogul, Joey L., Andrea J. Ritchie, and Kay Whitlock. 2011. *Queer (in)justice: The criminalization of LGBT people in the United States*. Boston, MA: Beacon Press.

Mosher, Lucinda. 2018. *Personhood, illness, and death in America's multifaith neighborhoods: A practical guide*. London, UK; Philadelphia, PA: Jessica Kingsley Publishers.

Newton, David E. 2018. *The opioid crisis: A reference handbook*. In Contemporary world issues. Santa Barbara, CA: ABC-CLIO, LLC.

Pfeiffer, Mary Beth. 2007. *Crazy in America: The hidden tragedy of our criminalized mentally ill*. New York, NY: Carroll & Graf Publishers.

Russell-Cole, Kathy, Midge Wilson, and Ronald E. Hall. 2013. *The color complex: The politics of skin color in a new millennium*. New York, NY: Anchor Books.

Scarpa, Silvia. 2008. *Trafficking in human beings: Modern slavery*. Oxford, UK: Oxford University Press.

Sederer, Lloyd I. 2018. *The addiction solution: Treating our dependence on opioids and other drugs*. New York, NY: Scribner.

Shapiro, Joseph P. 1994. *No pity: people with disabilities forging a new civil rights movement*. New York, NY: Times Books.

Smart, Julie. 2009. *Disability, society, and the individual*. Austin TX: Pro-ed.

Tooley, M. 1983. *Abotion and infanticide*. London, UK: Oxford University Press.

Torchia, J. 2008. *Exploring Personhood: An Introduction to the Philosophy of Human Nature*. Lanham, MD: Rowman & Littlefield Publishers, Inc.

Wallis, Jim. 2016. *America's original sin: Racism, White privilege, and the bridge to a new America*. Grand Rapids, MI: Brazos Press.

West, Cornel. 1994. *Race matters*. New York, NY: Vintage Books.

Chapter One

On Being Human and Attaining Personhood

INTRODUCTION AND DEFINITIONS

"*Cogito, ergo sum*," penned by René Descartes (1596–1650 CE, Descartes 1637), appeared first in French in the *Discourse on the Method*. This Latin philosophical proposition crafted by Descartes, translating to "I think, therefore I am," remains foundational in our epistemology (i.e., study of how we come to know something) of "self," which is a proper starting point for exploring "personhood" in the twenty-first century. If explored for more than four centuries, does the concept of "self" or "personhood" require further explanation? Is there a need and purpose for yet another book on "personhood"? Currently the U.S. Library of Congress lists >4,000 books and the Web of Science >4,000 articles on the topic of "personhood." This abundance reflects the rich dimensionality of "personhood." In view of the existing largesse of articles, reviews, and opinions, is there need for one more? In my life as a biomedical scientist (Moxham and Malbon 1996; Malbon 1997; Sivaraman et al. 1997; Liu et al. 2001; Ahumada et al. 2002; Wang and Malbon 2003; Malbon 2005, 2007; Bertalovitz et al. 2016), ethicist (Malbon 2013), chaplain, and ordained minister I frequently encounter issues targeting personhood. Being one of the first labs in New York to be authorized and supported by the National Institutes of Health (NIH) to employ human embryonic stem cells to investigate questions about early human development (Okoye, Malbon, and Wang 2008), we deeply considered the inherent ethical dilemma before embarking in human stem cell biology. What, one asks, is the "status" of stem cells harvested from discarded human embryos (McLaren 2007; Sugarman 2008; Blendon, Kim, and Benson 2011; Neaves 2017)? Precious human cells dividing in a Petri dish, are they legitimate targets for

1

probing new approaches with which to tackle human disease? Or, does their use constitute a serious violation of an embryo's "personhood"? Ultimately we were provided with human embryonic stem cells (H7 line) sourced from discarded embryos and licensed through WiCell Research Institute in Madison, WI. We researched early embryonic development employing these stem cells, seeking knowledge about cell-derived factors (e.g., Wnt ligands) that guide the cell fate of embryonic cells. Such information has proven invaluable in the efforts to steer undifferentiated stem cells to highly differentiated cells such as pancreatic and organ-specific cells that one day might replace the need for organ transplant. Our work was supported by the National Institute of General Medical Sciences, NIH (Bethesda, MD) and by the NYSTEM stem cell science program of institutional development funds from the State of New York.

Before we embarked on this line of research, the laboratory members posed many queries about ethical principles raised in anticipation of such investigations. Questions central to the discipline of medical ethics often distill to what constitutes a human being, a person, and fully ensouled person (Jeeves 2004)? Is an anencephalic neonate congenitally lacking cerebral hemispheres and a large part of the skull and with only hours to live to be accorded the same level of personhood as a healthy newborn baby? Chaplaincy takes one to an environment replete with suffering and dying. What qualities of life constitute true "personhood"? Are the unconscious, comatose, or the deeply forgetful any "lesser" persons than the average human being? Should the status of one's personhood justify or limit expensive chronic or end-of-life care in the face of limited healthcare resources? As a pastor I encounter the everyday stark dimensions of personhood in a congregation of human beings seeking spiritual guidance and growth in the face of disappointment, suffering, loss, and limitations. Who decides about the personhood of another human being? Is personhood an irrevocable human right, what ethicists term a "negative right," that is not subject to action of another person or group? When our loved ones lose capacity (i.e., in the medical context, a person's ability to make decisions about their health/healthcare) or battles a chronic debilitating disease, are they or are we (or maybe the courts) best suited to interrogate issues of their personhood? Are circles of family and personal friends free from conflicts of interest or the best informed to render end-of-life decisions for another person? These queries are but a few of the gritty topics about personhood that need an airing.

Personhood: on Being Human

Refining our definition of "personhood" is a complicated task. Much more than simply the "status of being a person," personhood includes dimensions of culture and philosophy as well as politics and the law. Properties often associated with personhood are agency, self-awareness, and possession of human nature, rights, and duties. Even if a definition of the properties of personhood can be agreed upon, knotty issues abound. When and how does personhood arise? Who can acknowledge or grant personhood? Is personhood a constant state, spanning from the fertilized egg to the very last breath of life? Or can personhood be discounted, lost, or suspended if one or more of its many properties are in decline or entirely absent? Lastly, if these properties can be ascribed to non-human primates (e.g., chimpanzees and gorillas), lower species (e.g., dolphins, Border Collies, and pain-sensing cephalopods), or perhaps supercomputers (e.g., Summit) trained to learn and to create smart "artificial intelligence" (AI), does the world of personhood expand beyond *Homo sapiens*?

What perspective should we adopt towards defining "personhood"? If restricted to the burning moral question of personhood in abortion, for example, America (i.e., the United States) might seem a reasonable launching point for our exploration (Malbon 2013)? Clearly the moral question of abortion provokes anthropological, philosophical, and theological questions about the personhood of an embryo or fetus. Yet, adopting such a narrow dataset on abortion as foundational for interrogating the multifaceted, multidimensional definition of "personhood" can be justified. Such a starting point may interrogate when personhood is assigned, but would fail in illuminating when personhood can be discounted or rescinded, if ever? Should the perspective for interrogating personhood be restricted to issues confronting only the "Western world"? Although neither global nor universal, such a point of demarcation would capture much of the ethos of 21st century America as well as the Western culture from which and with which it evolved. Compromising on and focusing upon the traditions of the Western world in general and America in particular enables us to trace several important threads in our moral thinking about personhood.

The influence of Greco-Roman classicism, Renaissance, Romanticism, and moral norms created by migrations of people linked historically to the eventual Western world is not exhaustive, but will provide a solid foundation for current 21st century American thinking. Not unexpected, foundational principles of Judeo-Christian traditions emerge and will play a dominant role in shaping a Biblical approach in the United States (Hauskeller 2011). Although employed widely to interrogate the topic of personhood in the Western world, the biblical warrant on personhood must be expanded to include other world religions. Importantly, moral questions about the personhood of the embryo and fetus, of those with disabilities and limitations of "norms" are posed by a Western world that clearly caters to what Stephen Post terms "*hyper*cognition" and performance (Post 2000). *Hyper*cognition, that is, the ability to perform complex mental functions seemingly beyond the average human, will play an outsized role in our evaluation of the status of personhood for many human beings (Post 2000). This decidedly global question of personhood, deserving of serious and broad moral consideration, impacts being human in every nation, culture, and people. The aging, those with physical disabilities and/or mental limitations and failings, those for whom a procreative event is not safeguarded and welcomed by society, those unconscious and those who are dying all will call the question of what it means to be human, a person, and to what degree one is a "person" in the fullest medical, legal, and anthropological definition. The journey to American determination of personhood will take us back to the ancient pillars of philosophy and more pertinently to the very founding of the American republic. In so interrogating America's shaping of personhood and explaining the current day assaults on it, we will encounter two great "original" sins. The first aimed at indigenous Native Americans in the land. The second aimed at African/African Americans shackled by slavery. My thesis is that these two "original" sins are the headwaters that fuel the plethora of assaults on personhood that plague everyday American society in the 21st century.

Personhood, from Socrates to Nietzsche: Socrates, Plato, and Aristotle

Philosophers have grappled with defining "personhood" and the nature of the "soul" for millennia (Torchia 2008). Prior to Socrates (469–399 BCE), the greatest transition in philosophy was displacement of an existing mythical view of the cosmos to ideas that could survive interrogation by rational and naturalistic arguments (Torchia 2008). Eventually, however, atomists shrank discussions to a binary cosmos consisting either of atoms or void (Cartledge 1999), a perspective that alienated those searching for greater clues as to the nature of the body (in Greek, "*soma*") versus the mind (in Greek, "*psyche*") of human beings. The liberal aspect of the itinerant intellectual Sophists (5th century BCE) engendered a cultural and moral relativism that provoked a backlash of healthy skepticism of atomist theories (Dillon and Gergel 2003). Such skepticism would benefit a second great transition, this one to humanism, catalyzed by Socrates (circa 470–399 BCE). Emphasis on the good of human life and its agency in a natural world provided the energy to drive Socrates and his method into the realms of the nature of morals, the soul, and personhood (Morrison 2011). No longer constrained by myths or divine apology, Socrates placed key questions in the vice of unyielding dialectic conversations aimed at rooting out false premises and weak thinking. What was the nature of human being? What was it in "personhood" separating human beings from animals? What was the seat of the intellect and soul?

Socrates' chief disciple Plato (~425 to ~347 BCE) would succeed in merging earlier mythical Greek elements with Ionian speculation, providing a platform on which to interrogate Socrates' powerful dialogues on the human condition. For Plato there was no contest to questioning superiority in metaphysical dualism, in other words, psyche *versus* soma (Loose 2018). The soul and its rational capacity were superior to the body as well as to the soul's lower irrational parts. Left unresolved by Socrates and Plato at that time was the basis of the immortal, immaterial properties of that part of the soul, relegated by both to the head. The mortal, impermanent fate of the lower aspect of the soul and its attendant body seemed more addressable. Socrates posited that it was acquisition of this intellectual rational thought-bearing soul that made human beings unique in creation (Goetz and Taliaferro 2011). The source of the envisioned persistence of the soul after death as well as its emergence in human development revisit us today in much the same way as we ponder the nature of personhood, especially in terms of abortion on the one hand and either capital punishment or physician-assisted suicide on the other.

Aristotle (384–322 BCE), like Socrates and Plato, valued most highly the fusion of philosophy and scientific efforts, a pursuit that human beings were uniquely equipped to accomplish with intuitive reason, intellect, and inquisitiveness (Aristotle ~350 B.C.E). The theory on how we gain knowledge, termed "epistemology," was essential to Aristotle's proposal on the nature of the human psychology. His goal was to interrogate the "soul," proceeding from how we perceive it to the basis for it. Sensory perception was the window on knowledge. A priori assumptions about human nature clouded the acquisition of data. Aristotle valued most highly personally observable data as prime substrate for his search for intelligibility and meaning. It is the quality of this discernment of first principles upon which Aristotle ascribes wisdom. The pursuit of universal knowledge exceeded the boundaries of mere descriptions of material composition and form, as exemplified in the arts. The nature of causality included a good dose of "teleology." Aimed at deciphering the end goal or purpose, teleology (or "*telos*") seeks to explain a phenomenon in terms of the purpose that it fulfills in a broad sense, rather than how the phenomenon arises. Plato's dismissal of the soma as no more than a necessary material output for the soul's employ was untenable to Aristotle. Confounded by Plato's immortal property of a soul, unlinked to the body, Aristotle forged a new proposal in which the soul-soma construct is shown to be necessary for the "perfection" of a human being, integral in both its potential and actualization. Personhood was a property available only through the soul-soma union in the perfection of animal life into being human. This emphasis on "perfection" clearly points to a model with a theological endpoint. Persistence of the soul in the absence of a living soma seemed problematic to Aristotle, as it does to many theologians. Opening the aperture of the query, Aristotle offered that the persistence was not of the soul per se, but rather of the human species that expresses the soul. As the seat of intellect, rational thought, and intuitive genius, the Aristotelian soul shared many attributes to those described by the Sophists, Socrates, and Plato.

Augustine of Hippo and Thomas Aquinas

The advent of Christianity added an important element to the evolving concept of personhood. The spiritual world of the ancient Greeks was replete with cults and a well-developed mythology (Burkert 1979). Classical Greek philosophy provided the early Christians with rudimentary tools with which the new faith, narratives and doctrines, and spirituality could be interrogated and better understood. The New Testament offered both new possibilities towards spiritual understanding as well as frank challenges to the dualism prefigured by Socrates and Plato on the soul *versus* body. Augustine of Hippo (354–430 CE), who lived in the mid-Patristic period (100–787 CE), wrestled with and sought harmony between evolving Christian dogma and the very nature of human beings, in other words, personhood (Augustine and Dods 2009). The Trinity (i.e., the Creator, Redeemer, and Sustainer) offered a vast cosmos of spirituality available to Christian believers (Augustine and Matthews 2002). Augustine had to coalesce the unity of the human soul and body as elaborated in the Scriptures with the continuing controversy as to whether or not the Platonic dichotomy of soul over body was of merit. Minimally Aristotelian thought could offer the possibility that the soul guided the soma towards intellectual perfection. The early Christian Church (30–325 CE) would adopt a theology in which the pursuit of humankind should be to seek "perfection" in spirituality aimed at union with Almighty God. In this manner the soul took on a more expansive role not only in elevating humans by seeking virtue (i.e., Aristotle's Nicomachean ethics), but also in guiding humans towards holiness and sanctification in God. When viewed as a divine gift to human beings alone, the fused soul and soma of the New Testament created considerable obstacles to any further dissection or expanded analysis of dualism, as did Aristotelian thought. Manichaeism evolved in Persia as per the writings of the prophet Mani (216–276 CE) (Widengren 1965). This line of thought provided a dualistic cosmology, of a cosmos struggling between the good spiritual light versus the evil dark material world.

Augustine's conversion from harsh dualistic Manichaeism to unity and harmony of Christian belief was made possible by a strong influence of Neoplatonists and Patristic scholars. Augustine viewed this harmonious union of soul and body as the unique "person/persona" that advanced well beyond the inability of Platonic/Neoplatonic thinking towards explicating the person as *individual*, not *type* (Copleston 1985). Foundational to arriving at this discovery, the personhood exemplified by Christ as divine (spiritual) and human (soma-like) facilitated Augustine's discernment of the unity of human soul and body in the overarching context of the personhood of Jesus Christ. Included in personhood was not only body and soul, but also an acceptance of the existence of "free will" in humans, bequeathed by a Creator and deeply burdened by the fallenness of human beings. This fallenness, I shall argue, is the primary driving force for assaults on personhood and for contesting being human. The ability of humans to discount the "other" as less than "self" and thereby contest the personhood and moral value of the "other" will be encountered again and again in our investigations of assaulted personhood.

Medieval Christian thought on the topic of personhood would emerge 800 years after Augustine, in the work of Thomas Aquinas (1225–1274 CE) (Chesterton 2009). Aquinas was a dominant figure in philosophy, theology, the law and in advancing reason-based "natural" theology (Besong 2018) during a time of great rediscovery of the metaphysics, philosophy, and the ethics of Aristotle. Initiated by the earlier work of Augustine, the question of personhood, soul, and soma began a migration of aspect from Athens to Jerusalem and to a decidedly Christian perspective lensed through Aristotelian and Augustinian philosophy. Aquinas would expand the aperture of the interrogation of personhood and on being human beyond Christianity itself (Aristotle and Thomas 1951). He would argue for discernment about God, the human condition, and divinity, first and foremost by reason. His foundational views on being human would benefit from his deep theological faith and discernment, yet never would escape them. If you wanted to interrogate personhood, success would not rest solely on either faith or reason, but by application of *both* faith and reason in tandem. Aquinas, liberated from the suffocating disputations of science and reason in the arena of the Church, relished and embraced a *sacra doctrina*. *Sacra doctrina* can be translated to "holy interrogation," "sacred analysis," or "sacred science." This "sacred science" offered by Aquinas was not a substitute for reason and for philosophical interrogation. Rather, Aquinas realized two things: there are limits to the power of philosophical analysis (at least operationally, though likely only limited by current human capabilities) and that even within the limits of well-reasoned faith the knowledge of God required *sacra doctrina* of divine revelation (Hause 2018). For Aquinas, the God revealed in the Book of Exodus (3:14) as "I AM WHO I AM," would remain ineffable, a transcendent fusion of essence and existence into one.

The topic of personhood invites theological interrogation. For what purpose was the essence of human existence? Only by interrogating the nature of human existence would the worth and potential of the individual alone be revealed. For Aquinas, as for Augustine, divine creation of human beings with soul and soma supplanted the metaphysical dualism of material (physical) and immaterial (spiritual) reality that plagued earlier philosophers. Aristotle developed a concept of "hylomorphism." This concept posits that a table was not merely a composite of atoms but rather was a collection of atoms whose form (i.e., as a table) provided function. This observation piqued Aquinas' curiosity. Informed by Aristotle's hylomorphism extending beyond atoms/matter to the essence of things through their form, Aquinas enriched the domain of what personhood included to topics of essence, the image of God, and the dignity of God's earthly creatures. Like Augustine, Aquinas cast the personhood of human beings in the model of Christ Jesus, a composite of divine (spiritual) and human (soma-like). The power of the Trinity was its co-dwelling, "perichoretic" relationality of a Creator, Redeemer, and Sustainer all in one. Human beings were relational by design, coming together and finding their greatest worth in *Sanctorum Communio*, what Dietrich Bonhoeffer would term a "sacred communion" within the body of *Christ Risen* (Bonhoeffer 1963). In the example, *sacra doctrina* interrogates the nature of the Trinity, Incarnation, and Resurrection to lens further into the nature of individual personhood, human value, dignity, and purpose (Rolnick 2007). In searching for what distinctively powers personhood, Aquinas would point to intellect, curiosity, and the gift of free will. These attributes were essential to establishing the potential and real worth of being human. The high value that American society places on *hyper*cognition evolved from these early efforts of philosophers and theologians aimed at defining "personhood." Today more than any other time in history, the combined quality of intellect and high-speed mental performance has emerged as a major criterion by which to measure the relative "value" of a person.

What Aquinas did not address is to what extent does a diminished intellect, curiosity, and free will discount the personhood of any individual? If dignity and status of humans depend upon relationality with God, what of the *hypo*cognitive individual, the unconscious, and the disabled who cannot meet such lofty goals of performance for consideration of their status as people (Post 2000)? Will their very being be contested on the grounds of substandard performance and/or potential, even within their likeness and image of God, *imago Dei*? Does either a human embryo *in utero* or a elderly person actively dying have the capacity of reason, self-discernment, and self-determination to "qualify" for full or even discounted personhood in Aquinas' way of thinking? How about today? Whether it is *sola scriptura* or *sola doctrina*, Aquinas benefitted from a Christocentric model based in the holy and ineffable. Yet, Thomas Aquinas remained burdened with theological blinders that precluded his explicating a theory of personhood that can accommodate all the children of God, the greater as well as the lesser. If human beings are to occupy the vaulted position of creatures made in the image and likeness of the Creator, how can personhood of any human be contested to be as anything less than full?

Descartes, Locke, Hume, and Ryle

The advent of the 17th and 18th centuries was characterized of expanding scientific gains. On the continent, earlier towering figures such as Nicolaus Copernicus, Johannes Kepler, and Galileo, cast a long shadow onto the doorstep of what would eventually be the Age of Enlightenment (Berlin 1970). Many thoroughgoing Christian mathematicians, physicists, and theologians, like Isaac Newton (Iliffe 2017), viewed the cosmos as created by God and as such propelled forward by a "*telos*" of the purposeful will of God for human beings. Human existence, in this context, was actualization of God's will here on Earth. Out of this mélange of theology, science, and psychology would arise several philosophers who again would wrestle with the issue of personhood, not so much in our narrow discourse of what constitutes "personhood," but rather in the formidable and unresolved issue of the nature of the soul. Earlier efforts that produced a dualistic explanation of soul *versus* soma, in other words, theological *versus* atomistic, would be cast aside. A more rigorous eye would be turned to delving into the "mind-body" relationship, to the psychology of the "self." René Descartes (1596–1650), referred to as the father of Western philosophy, first considered epistemology itself, that is, how we know of our very existence and garner information on other things (Dodd and Zardini 2014). Famously, Descartes is quoted, "I think, therefore I am". To Descartes, the "soul" and the "mind" were one in the same. He sided with Augustine in supporting "I" as the "soul," a break from Aquinas. He rejected teleological arguments, either divine or otherwise. His natural philosophy paid little attention to dissecting corporeal substance into matter and form, as did Aristotle and others. Descartes viewed the body mechanistically as an extended corporal machine, whereas the mind, he proffered, was composed of some substance (?) that was both non-extended and "thinking in nature," fused in some manner (?) to the machine of the body (Urban 2018). Lacking any shape, form, or not even occupying space, the soul remained indivisible, a sort of nebulous "mission control" that was simultaneously conjoined with the body, but yet not part of it spatially. Descartes relied upon anecdotal data on "phantom" limbs (i.e., a sensation that an amputated, missing limb is still attached) and neuroanatomical analysis of the pineal gland (i.e., a small endocrine gland in vertebrate brains that produces melatonin controlling circadian rhythm 24-hour cycles), to cobble together a model of the soul (Goetz and Taliaferro 2011). With respect to the pineal gland, it apparently escaped Descartes attention that although clearly lacking a soul by his criteria, lower vertebrates (e.g., reptiles, amphibian, and fish) do possess pineal glands! In all fairness, interrogating the phantom limb by Descartes reflects his awareness of the complexity of proprioception (i.e., awareness of positional movement of the body) and what would later be described as "neural networks" active in conscious thought (Schmidhuber

2015). Later, Nicholas Malebranche (1638–1715) and Arnold Geulincx (1625–1669) would be dismissive of Descartes' Cartesian attempts to describe the soul and its interaction with the body machine (Malebranche, Jolley, and Scott 1997; Geulincx et al. 2006). Unfortunately, these two philosophers would revert to theological invocations that God alone synchronizes the physical and mental efforts of human beings. These theological apologists afforded no advance over the hypothesis of Descartes that they so readily discredited.

Whereas Descartes would conclude that a person is a unified, thinking, non-extended mental "substance," John Locke (1632–1704) would argue to the contrary that a "person" couldn't be a "substance" whatever. What creates the "person" (or for Locke, the "self") is the consciousness experience. Proposed as properties of personhood, consciousness and the capacity for rational thinking and for self-awareness were overarching for Locke as well as his predecessors (Locke and Cranston 1965). Locke noted that if a prince and a lowly cobbler were to exchange their physical bodies, each would retain their prior personal identity regardless of bodily attachment. The immaterial property of a person's thinking and rational being might echo earlier notions of the "soul," embraced often in a theological sense. Locke rejected this notion of the "self" being the long sought after "soul." For Locke the key element is consciousness. He proposed that consciousness is a master control of the person, exerting its guidance over time and continued existence. Integral to Locke's concept of a "person" was not only consciousness and rational thinking, but also a functional memory (Locke and Phemister 2008).

Locke would posit that we persist as persons only as far back as our memory serves us, operating through a stable framework of consciousness whose content is dynamic (Sheridan 2010). For Locke, people who are deeply forgetful may only exist as persons in the moment. By Locke's reasoning, the near absence of long-term memories for such unfortunate individuals as patients with Alzheimer's disease would diminish or preclude their "personhood." Prescient to a later discussion of contested human being for those who commit crimes, Locke offers that God would have mercy and forgive the criminal whose mind cannot recall the crime committed. Although making progress in prefiguring neural networks and the complexities of consciousness as "self," Locke was not without critics. Joseph Butler (1692–1752) rightly critiqued Locke's absence of the very body that preceded the development of the mind and consciousness, that is, there is an essential linkage between soma and psyche. The person must be a body, have substance, and support the very properties of personhood that Locke's proposals demand (Butler 1889). Butler also prefigures that such a tight set of criteria to fulfill personhood argues that loss of personhood may be envisioned whenever one's memory or rational thinking becomes impaired (Denise, White, and

Peterfreund 2008). Later, Thomas Reid (1710–1796) noted that Locke had oversimplified the various elements of what constitutes and enables human being. In particular, Reid objections included: Locke's notion of consciousness being rather stable is as odds with human experience; memory cannot be cast as simply an extension of the conscious state; and, input other than that of the self-consciousness (e.g., testimonies of others about us) do shape our person and self-identification (Cuneo and Woudenberg 2004).

David Hume (1711–1776) approached the concept of self-becoming-human as an empiricist (Hume 2004). He rejected "notions" such as the "mind," "soul," and other shorthand for the complexity of person and personal identity. Freed from these shackles, Hume set forth a "scientific" approach to interrogating what constitutes a person based primarily on sensory perceptions of the self (Pitson 2002). By definition, such an approach values perceptions by the self that leave unanswered the very nature of the self (Waldow and ebrary Inc. 2009). Forced to mentalistic descriptions, Hume saw no evidence of self as a persistent "substance" at the core of a person. More like an ever-moving window of experiences (i.e., consciousness?) that summates in the most recent perceptions, Hume's "personhood" displays little persistence and is clearly not immutable. Hume does little to differentiate the relative contributions of perceptions versus those of ideas, suggesting that perceptions are ephemeral even if constantly reinforced. Tending to lean into physicalism (i.e., the doctrine that the real world is composed entirely of the physical world), Hume rightly sought a biological source rather than mythology about what constitutes personhood. Yet, he was able to move personhood from mythology to biology, leaving it rather untethered in the absence of a more complete knowledge of complex neural networks grounded in biology. Hume's writing may strike the reader as the height of irony. Hume seems in search of a "self" (i.e., person) whom he cannot find (Dicker 1998). What he found was only perceptions "by self," not "of self."

Gilbert Ryle (1900–1976) would critique the lack of clarity about both Descartes' and Hume's linkages between immaterial consciousness (i.e., their so called "self") and the bodily behaviors under its control (Ryle 1949). Ryle's Official Doctrine (i.e., dogma) of the "Ghost in the Machine" would lay bare the gaping holes in their proposals. Ryle would plumb the depths of the "inner" and "outer" experiences that had been considered almost two separate domains of mind and body (Glombicek and Hill 2010). For Ryle the observable properties of person were largely behavioral, whereas Hume's experiences were largely restricted to sensory perception. In a post-modern world, employing either Hume's or Ryle's criteria may preclude some individuals from being human or having full personhood. Yet postmodern thinking will find more congruence with Ryle's thinking than Hume's, even though Hume's empirical methods added much to modern psychology. This dichotomy harks back to dualism and early observations of Augustine and others, but with a difference. Sharply viewed by Ryle, he proffered that there can only be a "metaphorical dualism," as the mind and the body act and have physical interfaces that force us to approach them as a fusion. Even our primitive understanding of neural networks, artificial intelligence, and memory compel us accept that the "soul" is immaterial, but yet the necessary product of a soma on which the soul remains absolutely dependent. Personhood clearly must be founded in the soma. No matter how rudimentary our understandings of the human brain, there is no doubt that the sum total of the ancient concept of the "soul" is to be understood in the totality of molecules signaling and storing information in the human mind (i.e., brain-based, not mythology). To what extent consciousness, rational thinking, and memory weigh in the assignment of personhood in part or *in totem* for 21st century America requires further interrogation (Koch 2019).

Friedrich Nietzsche

In pursuit of systems by which "personhood" may be ascribed (e.g., virtue ethics for Greek citizens, *imago Dei* for Christians, relationality for Abrahamic theology, and others) the input of Friedrich Nietzsche (1844–1900) may seem off base. Nietzsche was an influential 19th C philosopher whose contributions will come into play as we proceed towards understanding contested personhood in modern times. Shaped by his reading of German philosophers Arthur Schopenhauer (1788–1860), Friedrich Albert Lange (1828–1875) and composer Richard Wagner (1813–1883), Nietzsche lifted up human will as the essential component of the psychology of human being (Kaufmann and Nietzsche 1968). He was dismissive of the view that free will (as well as unconsciousness) was inherently evil in a theological sense, rather accepting them as simply human and of input. In critiquing the Christian religion (but not Christ), Nietzsche cast off the chains of dogma and doctrine as sophomoric and poorly critiqued (Nietzsche, Horstmann, and Norman 2002). He regarded the whole edifice of the Christian church's value system and morals to be patently false. Christian values preached by Jesus with regard to compassion and sacrifice for the "least of us" was weak-minded, according to Nietzsche. Humans should stand on their own two feet and vigorously interrogate aspects of faith and morality rather than bow down to them in soft-minded deference. His view of personhood thus can be best understood as boldly "selfhood unbridled." The limits on personhood were at best self-delimiting with the extreme manifestation being the independent and self-defining "*übermensch*" (i.e., "Overman" or "Superman"). Such "super human" beings constituted the very apex of human achievement and having reached this zenith had no need of rules and morals. Perhaps we can rehabilitate Nietzsche's 19th century definition of "selfhood" and aim towards a non-uniform set of creative and inclusive characteristics for the *übermensch* that exists in all human beings? Such high aspirations exist for all human beings, regardless of their true gifts that may be valued differently by either subjective or societal criteria as espoused by Nietzsche. His notion was that people should be empowered to formulate their own values. Can this proposal be adapted to accommodate all people? Such inclusivity of all human beings within an ongoing Creation, however, would have been anathema for Nietzsche. His primary goal was to insure the evolution of humankind by placing it firmly in the hands of solely the *übermensch*, not common *volk* or *menschen*.

Ironically, Nietzsche's thinking becomes most relevant in anticipation of a later search for the source that empowers those individuals who contest the personhood of "others." For Nietzsche, the *übermensch* himself/herself was outside of critique, but fully endowed to critique the very being of *all* others. The faculty by which a human decides on and initiates an action is the "free will" for Nietzsche. Since pre-Socratic times, philosophers have wrestled with the human will and its role in personhood and psychology. Nietzsche, unlike Schopenhauer, viewed free will as positive and essential in human evolution and history. More precisely, Nietzsche lifts up a powerful desire of human beings to dominate, over their own inner weaknesses, over other people, and over their environment. This "will-to-power" proposal, as made clear in "On the Genealogy of Morals" published in 1887 (Nietzsche and Samuel 2006), is the asymmetry of the power dynamic between the master versus slave morality. In congruence with the *übermensch* concept, Nietzsche argues that the will-to-power was not a simple aspect of human psychology, but rather a unifying principle deeply connected with efforts aimed at dominating other peoples, to biological principles of domination by the fittest (although Nietzsche did not support Darwin's theory of evolution), and a thoroughgoing principle underlying the cosmos. In "Thus Spake Zarathustra" (Nietzsche and Kaufmann 1995), Nietzsche penned, "Wherever I found a living thing, there found I Will to Power; and even in the will of the servant found I the will to be master". Nietzsche's thinking about personhood and the will-to-power which dominates the determination of who is deserving of full personhood became more obvious as the modern world was displaced by postmodernism.

Assaulted Personhood in a Postmodern World

A current 360° scan of our Western world clearly supports the notion that the context for interrogating assaults on personhood is "postmodernity." Lost is the modernist view of self-actualized, self-referent human beings capable of reshaping their lives (and the world) through socially progressive thinking and action. Postmodernists viewed such notions as silly and uncritical extensions of Enlightenment beliefs that are woefully out of date. Not so much was self-worth about who one is, but rather how one behaves. In modernist thinking, intrinsic self-worth was a dominant theme. It was inclusive in perspective, seeking only to identify through research those obstacles to human flourishing. Postmodernism chips away at the very heart of intrinsic self-worth and replaces it with criteria upon which personhood is judged as worthy for a given individual (Cahoone 2003). This is not a new perspective. Both Plato and Nietzsche would argue for setting a high bar for bestowing personhood and for robust efforts aimed at contesting personhood for the least of us. Such matter-of-fact determinations about being human "in-full" generated a paradox. In the postmodern world, personhood granted to members of *Homo sapiens* alone by modernists now also could be bestowed to supercomputers like Summit that supports artificial intelligence (Service 2018), to robotic beings programmed to "ape" human emotions (Nijssen et al. 2019), to some higher-functioning animals other than humans (Versace et al. 2018), and even to extraterrestrial visitors (Kwon et al. 2018), if they exist.

Based upon this brief introduction to "personhood," what would be the leading criteria to establishing personhood in the postmodern world of 21st century America? Not unlike the dualists Aquinas and Descartes, higher order intellect, rational thinking, and the river of consciousness were the narrow gate of assigning the status of "person" to a member of *Homo sapiens*. For Locke and Hume, both sensory perception in the conscious world and knowing that one is thinking (even that of an AI supercomputer) seemed to insure that personhood would be assigned only to those fittest with regard to cognition. The modern world likewise valued powerful intellect, but failed to adequately address the biases of culturally conditioned thought. Moral and ethical prescripts, hierarchal cultural norms, and values that were unshared had no voice for modernists. The nihilism replete in Nietzsche's work and extended to Samuel Beckett (1906–1989) had a postmodern currency that modernistic introspection was incapable of addressing (Beckett 1971; Hasan and Beckett 2002; Beckett, Lawlor, and Pilling 2012). The postmodern movement fueled assaults on personhood and enabled a critique of being human itself. Attacks on the permanence of personhood and on theological canons as a source for interrogating morality were commonplace.

Modernism largely had equated personhood with the simple act of being human. Modernists viewed this perspective as hopeful and inclusive by design. Personhood would be classified as a "negative" right. A negative right was one that was bequeathed by the divine or ultimate being, one that could not be withdrawn or discounted by mere mortal human beings. In the postmodern sense, personhood was no longer a negative right. A subjectively measured label, affixed by others and granted fully to but a worthy few, personhood was commodified by postmodernists. Assignment of personhood was no longer unconditional, a negative human right, or granted for life.

Personhood was to be assigned in real time, subject to discount or to withdrawal should the individual fail to meet prescribed subjective criteria. Additionally, the theological canons operating for millennia would no longer be valued as revelation of the divine, but rather simply a reflection of a quaint bias of a special interest group whose values could not be defended nor proclaimed to the critical thinkers of postmodernism. As we shall see, the empirical hard-line thinking of the postmodernists would come to haunt dogmatics of modernist thinking now viewed with a jaundiced eye as simple hypocrisy. How is it possible for a patient in either a persistent or permanent vegetative state (PVS) to be considered a human worthy of full personhood? Should a multi-cell stage human embryo, 2-days post implantation, be considered a person, or merely a parasitic entity for a pregnant woman? For the postmodernists, would the PVS patient be ranked a "0" on a personhood scale of 0 (absent personhood) to 10 (highest ranking)? Would the embryo deserve a rank of 10/10? Will critical thinking reveal biases that render such determinations as incommensurable? Are we now unable to find a common set of values or even descriptors on criteria for personhood? In America, perhaps we have morphed into "moral strangers," that is, people unable to communicate on such lofty moral issues without acrimony and name-calling.

HISTORIC ROOTS OF CONTESTING PERSONHOOD

Ancient Roots

The roots of people contesting the personhood of the "other" are ancient and remain robust. In virtually all cases, the perpetrator who first was empowered to cast judgment upon to what extent another human being is to be considered worthy of personhood is the *patriarch* (Kaufman 1987). Culturally often considered as the male head of a family, tribe, nation, or empire, the patriarch is a position most well known in sacred books and theology. The Greek term for "patriarch" translates best as "chief, father, or head of a family." The social and political structures of "patriarchy" that exert dominion, oppress, and exploit women, children, and slaves are historical and nearly universal. From the Ancient Near East (~3000 BCE) to everyday 21st century America domination of women, children, "lesser" peoples and societies by men remains deeply rooted. The Ancient Greeks reinforced the ideas that women were inferior to men in all categories, except childbirth and child-rearing. Religious dogma has largely perpetuated this line of oppression. Feminist and womanist scholars have lifted up the toxic byproducts of patriarchy in the modern world (e.g., oppression, objectification, and exploitation of women), leveling right criticism at religious dogma, biological theory (i.e., essentialism), and self-perpetuating social structures aimed at oppressing women. "Power-and-Control" exerted by men over women includes sexual abuse, spousal abuse (i.e., spouse as property), income disparity among equals according to gender, and so forth. In America, only when placed in the shadow of the 1840's work of Elizabeth Cady Stanton and Susan B. Anthony that powered the passage of the 19th Amendment to the U.S. Constitution (i.e., guaranteeing women's right to vote) in 1920, do the fuller dimensions of male domination and patriarchy in the U.S. come into focus.

In the Abrahamic religions, Abraham, Isaac, and Jacob are referred to as the patriarchs of Israel (Faley 2003). Fast-forward to the 21st century and the designation of heads of the Catholic autonomous churches as patriarchs is no coincidence. The label denotes authority, power, and status whether in reference to Athens, Jerusalem, or Rome. Historically, patriarchal societies display male dominance in a variety of ways, through expression in religious, economic, social, political and legal dimensions of everyday life (Plessis, Ando, and Tuori 2016). In many such societies property and title are inherited by patrilineal tradition (Grenholm and Patte 2005). As such, much of the human substrate of ancient times (e.g., women, slaves, children) was commodified, then considered property, largely devoid of personhood, or certainly devoid of full personhood, although exceptions did exist.

From a historical perspective, patriarchal property included women (especially widows) and children (especially orphans), men of lesser standing in a society who may lack citizenship (whether it occurs in ancient Greek society and in modern 21st century America), education, economic status, and freedom (pointedly, "slaves"). The course of human development is replete with interventions by patriarchs in contesting, judging, and assigning personhood as a means of power and control, sustaining the dominance of male heads of families, tribes, nations, and empires. Later we shall interrogate the legacy of the long history of patriarchal rule that freely contests the being human of the "other" and how it has impacted our thinking and actions in 21st century America (see chapters 4–6).

The terms "personhood" versus "ensoulment" needs disambiguation as we progress through aspects of early human development and the very status of human life. Perhaps the most important difference is the extent to which one can assault, contest, or discount personhood versus the soul of another. In spite of all-or-none judgments about personhood, the discounting of a persons' status has a long history in America. Notable is the 1787 U.S. Constitutional Convention grappling with the issue of how slaves would be counted in determining a state's population (with respect to representation and taxation). A "Three-Fifths Compromise" was reached challenging potential political dominance of the Southern States who had the largest population of slaves. The compromise was simple. For the census the slaves would be included, but counted only at 3/5ths the value of a freeman (i.e., largely White, patriarchal, entitled men of the ruling class). Ancient Greeks were more restrictive with assigning personhood. It was an all-or-none proposition, a binary approach to achieving personhood. If you were a woman, or a man less than 30 years of age, or a male lacking education, economic status, or somehow otherwise lacking in the credentials for citizenship, you were denied personhood. Conquered peoples (whether men or women) were not entitled to personhood in the truest sense in most ancient cultures.

The assignment of personhood from a theological perspective has been changing (although not evolving) for millennia. Absent the anatomical certainty of sonograms and CT scans, patriarchs of the Church assigned not "personhood" *per se*, but rather ensoulment. For the early Church, a soul was divined as arising at the first point of quickening; in other words, when a pregnant woman detects movement of a fetus (Goetz and Taliaferro 2011; Malbon 2013). Remarkably, the boundaries for quickening and ensoulment were not the same for male versus female fetuses. The unique feature of this theological determination was that the soul was deemed to be wholly indivisible. One could not possess 1/5 or 3/5ths of a soul. Ensoulment became a binary assignment. Either you had a soul or you did not. Yet assignment of ensoulment was not conflated with assignment of personhood. An unborn fetus may have been ascribed a soul, but few would consider it to have personhood in the social, cultural, and especially legal sense (Malbon 2013). From the standpoint of patriarchy, in the absence or presence of a soul, unborn fetuses (whether of family or of owned slaves) were mostly considered an asset, a property, a commodity that might have future value, but perhaps not yet. In 21st century America, the moral conundrum of ensoulment versus personhood is repeatedly encountered, not just in terms of an unborn fetus, but even into very late stages of human existence. Suffice it to say, ensoulment remains binary and once assigned is considered irrevocable. As the stages of human living progress, from conception to death, this tension between the moral questions of ensoulment, persistence of the soul, and the assignment versus status of "personhood" will be encountered. Are fertilized human eggs prior to implantation morally equivalent to a neonate? Can people diagnosed as suffering in a persistent vegetative state possess a soul, but not full personhood? Do the deeply forgetful or intellectually impaired suffer loss of all or part of their personhood as well as their souls? On what basis will the status of personhood be evaluated, and by whom?

Understanding the Concept of "Otherness"

At the core of contesting personhood are concepts such as "other," "otherness," and "not self." To understand how one migrates to a position of superiority (i.e., as briefly described above for the power, control, and status afforded to men by patriarchy) requisite for contesting personhood of people, the phenomenon of human experience of "self" and the "other" must be grasped. Throughout our lives we acquire a mental picture of ourselves based not only from our own experiences in life, but also from internalization of input from those about us. Post neonatal life, the infant "self" begins to discriminate the mother as "other." Later stages in normal child development include individuation and recognition of "self" from "other." This constitutes the roots of formation of self-image, which can create some anxiety initially (Mahler, Pine, and Bergman 1975). Outside of this inner realm and psychology of self that supports our self-image are images of the "other"; in other words, the sum total of all remaining human beings with whom our lives intersect. Georg Wilhelm Friedrich Hegel (1770–1831) articulated the essential nature of the "other" as complementing the evolution of the self-image (Rauch, Sherman, and Hegel 1999). Edmund Gustav Albrecht Husserl (1859–1938) proffered that "*inter*subjectivity," the psychological relationality among people, required the "other" in order to apprehend the "self" in contrast (Tymieniecka et al. 1977). Lacking the inner component of self-awareness in self-image, humans default to reliance upon sensory perception, simple conscious awareness of other human beings. Emmanuel Lévinas (1906–1995) was critical of the manner in which the "other" was diminished to a simple object of the consciousness in opposition to the self. He viewed "*alterity*"—in other words, the fullest dimension of "otherness" beyond simple sensory perception—to extend to a transcendent state that was both perplexing yet attractive to "self" (Lévinas and Poller 2003). Lévinas' focus was on the examination and detailed comparisons that humans make in confronting the "other." The analysis should be thorough and neutral, seeking the richness of differences between self and other. Early childhood differentiation of "self" from "other" usually is focused about the infant-mother axis and does include initial anxiety. Throughout development, the ability to identify "self" *versus* "non-self" will remain key. Cues first from mother and family, later cohorts and tribes enable humans to assess benefit and risk of other-than-self interactions. This added dimensionality does not reduce, however, the anxiety of "self" when confronted with the "other," a being who is clearly other than the self as well as other than self's circumscribed tribe or group. Herein is where the anxiety provoked by the other's mere existence stimulates "self" to challenge the worth and personhood of the "other." Although attributable to simple ignorance, the angst of self in the face of other is a universal response. Ultimately, anxiety within the self emerges and targets the very personhood of the "other," seeking to decant this fear by assaulting the source of the anxiety and loathing.

Whether the result of the perpetual U.S. War on Terrorism (commenced in 2001 in response to the 9/11 attacks) or the confrontation of U.S. society with Mara Salvatrucha (i.e., MS-13) gang members in the suburbs of Long Island, the stimulus (i.e., otherness) and response (i.e., contested personhood) is an autocatalytic angst that ramps up anxiety, mistrust, fear and hatred. Once personhood is assaulted, derivative actions follow. The anxiety of self in the face of an "uncertain" other will provoke tribal coherence of self to outnumber the other (e.g., as often observed in protest marches organized for the Alt-right), to declare the other as strange and villainous (e.g., post 9/11 negative depictions of people of color in general and Muslims in particular), and to marginalize and sequester the "other" away from tribal self (e.g., incarceration to immigrant internment facilities or to Guantanamo Bay, Cuba). Of course there are rare conditions when personhood and essential rights can be withdrawn with good cause; for example, either an epidemic or a pandemic (e.g., the 1918 Spanish flu or 2019 COVID-19) requiring quarantine of suspected infectious patients. Yet in most contexts the purpose of contesting another's being human often is not so altruistic. Fear of the "other" always succeeds in generating suspicion and anxiety for the "self." The antidote to this poison of fear is denying personhood of the other. As exemplified in the genocide and displacement of indigenous Native Americans and the debasement and horrific treatment of African and African American slaves (see Chapter 5), intense fear of "other" was the innate, irrepressible response of "self." This fear-fueled hatred was essential to the ultimate goal of assaulting the personhood of these "other" peoples, declaring them "subhuman" and not "self." Dehumanization provided the warrant for the dominant White patriarchy to declare indigenous Native Americans as well as African and African American slaves and their descendants as "beings under dominion" of [White] men, an often cited "biblical warrant" extracted from Genesis 1:26 of the Hebrew Bible.

Who are the Gatekeepers of Personhood?

The nature of the "gatekeeper" of personhood demands interrogation. Gatekeepers are those who sit in judgment of a person's value. A brief treatment of ruling class patriarchy then and now, provided above, yielded some overarching clues. Yet, the "gatekeepers" (as we shall label those who make such decisions on personhood) are much more varied. Their considerable power and control over the "other" often is layered. In ancient times the kings and rulers took (or were given) authority on the fullest range of assignment of personhood (Fishbein 2002). Their authority extended from the fetus that grows in the womb of an indentured slave to the life and death decisions over close associates and officials whose only access to personhood was through unwavering fealty to the head. Although monarchal and representative governments may appear to have blunted local patriarchal authority in assigning personhood, their governments even in modern times are replete with examples of such power and control (Dubber 2005). More common today are special interests groups whose platforms (narrow or wide) may include intentional assignment of full (e.g., for a human embryo) and discounted (e.g., for an anencephalic neonate) personhood according to their preferences. Pro-life groups active in the United States and elsewhere provide a ready example. For the pro-life group, the unborn embryo or fetus is assigned full personhood and deserving of legal status (Malbon 2013). A pregnant woman may be denigrated to non-personhood based upon a decision to seek an abortion (Malbon 2013; Haugeberg 2017). Pro-choice groups likewise may be viewed as advancing the fullest personhood of a pregnant women and proclaiming abortion to be a "human right" (Harrison 1983; Malbon 2013). Yet, pro-choice groups often seem to ignore the presence of a pro-creative event (i.e., pregnancy and living fetus), avoiding discussion of personhood status of a nascent life while lifting up the legitimate, seemingly competing interests of the pregnant woman (Sanger 2017).

Perhaps religious teachings can facilitate discussion of personhood by canon or dogma? The first such theological assignment was made by Boethius (477–524 CE), a 6th century philosopher, *magister officiorum* of the Roman Empire, and senator. Thomas Aquinas credits Boethius with offering *naturae rationabilis individual substantia*, which translates as "an individual substance of a rational nature" (Thomas, Hibbs, and Thomas 1999). Augustine and the church patriarchs had been wrestling with the idea of "person" within the doctrine of the Trinity in Christian thought. Boethius ventured further to define in simple terms the basic property of personhood that has largely survived even today. He challenged full personhood of a person when high-level cognition is uncertain, for example, as are the deeply forgetful (Post 2000). Boethius' person included two Christian elements. The first essential element was possession of a "rational" soul. The second prerequisite, affirming the belief that every person was created *imago Dei*, required one to be cast in the shadow of the human nature of Christ. Edicts of theological sources (e.g., the Ten Commandments, the teachings of Jesus of Nazareth, the Holy Qur'an of Islam, etc.) and of philosophical sources (e.g., the analects of Confucius and Pali Canon of Buddhism, etc.) often include prescriptions for virtuous living by which loss of personhood (or even worse the "soul") can be avoided. Failure to abide within such strict doctrinal boundaries, however, can result in formal *ex*communication and even loss of one's *soul* through damnation. Issues about assigning personhood in 21st century America are often cut short of deep interrogation. The validity of moral positions often is disguised in church or theological dogma as if the matter is "settled," that is, closed for discussion. Such theological gatekeepers will be encountered repeatedly in a myriad of assaults on personhood found in 21st century America.

The judicial arm of representative governments often is assigned as arbiter of questions of personhood status. In Western law the tradition may seem a reversal of the aforementioned theological doctrines. For example, a "person" by legal definition might be ascribed rights (e.g., human rights) and duties. Recognized as a legal "person" those with rights and duties are afforded protection. In the U.S., controversies about personhood are constantly raised in opposition to long-standing patriarchy, particularly that embraced by White Anglo Saxon Protestant colonists who seeded America with English common law. Recent history of legislative efforts in the Federal Courts reflects earlier efforts to afford women equal rights to vote, under the 19th Amendment to the Constitution (1920). The Supreme Court decision in *Reed v. Reed* (404 U.S. 71, 1971) found that the 14th Amendment of the U.S. Constitution also applies equally to women with regard to the Equal Protection clause. Women and other vulnerable populations have relied heavily upon rulings of the judiciary to remedy assaults on their personhood aimed to withdraw rights protected by the state as well as by the U.S. Constitutional (Thomasma, Weisstub, and Hervé 2001). The 14th Amendment likewise afforded the rights of citizenship to Black men in the United States. Although slavery was abolished in the United States in 1865, we shall see that the fight for full personhood for people of color continues in our times.

Children, largely considered minors and not legally designated as "persons," are a vulnerable population holding an ambiguous claim to personhood. Remarkably, state and local laws in the U.S. permit corporal punishment of children by parents absent legal protection for these minors (Fitz-Gibbon 2017). Ironically, protecting corporal punishment persists at a time when both Federal and state legislatures march in robust support of protecting the unborn and neonate (e.g., U.S. Born-Alive Infants Protection Act, 2002). Populations confined to jails, prisons, and immigrant detention centers are highly vulnerable to denial of full personhood. At a rate of >700 individuals incarcerated per 100,000 people (and certainly not inclusive), the U.S. tops the list of nations that incarcerate their people. As noted, the post-Civil War South enacted Jim Crow laws to discount the advances in personhood, such as voting rights, for the Black people achieved through the 1865–1877 Reconstruction Era in the U.S. (Alexander 2010). Although many Jim Crow practices were abolished, the disproportionate incarceration of people of color in the U.S. continues to deny full personhood to more than three million people (Alexander 2010). Adding to this startling number are those "illegal" immigrant populations who are now "detained" in facilities throughout the U.S. Currently, the immigrant populations seeking domicile in the U.S. is composed of people of color, migrating from mostly South American nations. In 2020, the lives of these immigrants and undocumented immigrants in the U.S. are extremely vulnerable to exploitation and criminal apprehension. The lives of millions of these people in the U.S. are in constant turmoil. The April 2018 the Justice Department unveiled a new "zero tolerance" policy intended to ramp-up criminal prosecution of people seeking to enter the U.S. illegally. Unauthorized immigrant parents were being criminally prosecuted and separated from their children. This harsh and traumatic separation of children from family revealed the pervasive and unbridled effort of a U.S. administration seeking to demonize all immigrants. There was no differentiation of those entering illegally from those legally seeking political asylum in the U.S. Separating young children and infants from their parents was employed as a "deterrence" for border crossings in the U.S. for any reason. The most recent data available in the 2018 Global Slavery Index, reports that more than 400,000 Americans remain locked in "modern" slavery in the United States! In this case, the Federal judicial rightly has demanded an end to such egregious assaults on personhood, especially when manifest in separation of immigrant parents from young children. Although vulnerable populations continue to be familiar targets of assaults on being human worldwide, at least in the U.S., some judicial protections have been afforded to the most vulnerable among us. Regrettably, justice is often too slow or intentionally delayed, unable to redeem these fragile lives. Vulnerable immigrants are readily denied justice and due process for political theater. The administration of the 45th president repeatedly panders to right wing conservative groups that enjoy support from White nationalist and White supremacists.

Persistent Challenges to Being Human

Globally and for time immemorial, personhood has been under continual assault. In a global sense, many ethnic conflicts involving the loss of life, liberty, and pursuit of happiness are simple national or tribal efforts to delegitimize the personhood of the "other." Ethnic conflicts such as those in the Balkans, Chechnya, Darfur, the Gaza Strip and West Bank, India, Indonesia, Israel, Rwanda, South Sudan, and Sri Lanka are deadly conflicts based in tribalism or nationalism that dehumanizes the adversary, enabling a clear conscious for the death and destruction that follows for the "other," a nonperson (Wells 2015, Rudolph 2015). These all too human behaviors have been subject of many recent articles that seek to identify why and how such abject de-personhood can arise and take a firm hold on otherwise law-abiding citizens. Historically, the claims of self-sovereignty of indigenous peoples are the primary target for assaults on their personhood (Dunbar-Ortiz 2014). Absent personhood, autonomy, and deprived of agency, indigenous peoples are targets of oppression, loss of property and liberty, and in the extreme the victims of overt genocide (Totten 2018). Remarkably, human rights violations of an individual "other" can capture global interest, as in the case of the detentions of Nelson Mandela (Bodden 2019) and Liu Xiaobo (Yu and Hsu 2015). Yet, ethnic conflicts that can result in genocide involving loss of hundreds and thousands of human beings can operate hidden in plain sight (Cohen 2007). Intervention by the courts to protect victims may be tepid or too late to preserve personhood and attendant human rights (Jasinski 2017).

Plainly, efforts aimed at contesting the personhood of a designated "other" have commonalities in basis and methodology. In discounting the human being, relegated to the label of "other," the aggressor seeks to objectify the "other." In so doing, the targeted ones are robbed of personhood and viewed as merely "objects" and labeled as "other," lacking autonomy and self-determination. This *modus operandi* remains the primary tool employed to deprive indigenous peoples in America (and elsewhere) of their lands and freedoms (Dunbar-Ortiz 2014). The aggressor may claim that the objectified "other" lacks capacity, strength, and intellect. Espoused by the aggressor, these false "deficiencies" that are assigned as character flaws of the indigenous populations become the basis for degrading their personhood and justifying their subjection to the dominion by the White ruling class. The aggressor further may discount the suffering of the "other," recalibrating experiences and feelings experienced by the "other." The mass suffering of displaced indigenous Native Americans, enslaved Africans and African American slaves and their descendant is deemed false, of lesser, little, or no worth. Searching oneself, these declarations and methodologies should feel familiar. We too navigate everyday life's controversies among people whose "otherness" we can easily detect based upon their race, color, creed, sexual orientation, socio-economic status, physical or mental disabilities, and so on. Yet, we feign empathy for the "other," while all too ready to deny knowledge of and complicity in the great foundational "original" sins that fuel everyday assaults on personhood and on being human in 21st century America. The Rev. Dr. Martin Luther King Jr. once remarked upon the arc of a moral universe being long, but always curving toward justice. This prophetic thought encourages us towards a path aimed at addressing our individual and corporate culpability for foundational "original sins" as well as derivative everyday assaults on personhood in America.

ASSAULT ON PERSONHOOD IN 21ST CENTURY AMERICA

Who Are the Victims?

What of the victims of these perpetrators who assault personhood? Who are they? How broad is this scourge in 21st century America? The spectrum of victims of contested personhood in America is broad, but only the general landscape can be introduced herein. In-depth analyses of vulnerable populations and the basis for assaults on their personhood will follow, embracing those with vulnerabilities in body (see Chapter 2) and mind (see Chapter 3), as well as those that are especially challenged in today's American society (see Chapter 4). Interrogating the situation in the U.S. begs the question if the U.S. provides a paradigm for countries in the Western world engaged in assaulting personhood at home and abroad? The answer is a decided "yes" and it can be proclaimed with good reason. In virtually every instance of contested personhood underpinning ethnic and social conflicts in the world, the U.S. has an obvious hand, even though it may demure from publically declaring that such is the case.

Well into the second decade of the 21st century, we note ethnic and social conflicts that represent textbook cases of "self" versus "other" in which personhood of the "other" has been heavily discounted or extinguished entirely. Sweeping West from Afghanistan and Iran, through the Arabian Peninsula (e.g., Iraq, Syria, Lebanon, the West Bank, Gaza Strip, Israel, and Yemen), across the Northern Africa and the Sahel "coast" (i.e., Egypt, Libya, the Sudan, Chad, Mali, Burkina Faso) to Southeast Asia (e.g., Myanmar) and the Philippines, brutal and deadly ethnic conflicts rage. U.S. foreign policy often has underwritten participation or intervention by American interests in each of these theaters of conflict where assaults on personhood close out the most fundamental negative human right of personhood, that is, not to be killed! Closer to home, conflicts about migration of peoples seeking political asylum rage between the U.S. and Mexico. The current day migration of peoples, displaced largely from the Northern Triangle of South America, is a raw source of ethnic and racial conflicts both outside and within America. Inside the United States, the Southern Poverty Law Center lists nearly 1000 hate groups, including active Ku Klux Klan groups, neo-Nazi groups, and gangs like MS-13 whose manifestos target vulnerable populations in and seeking to come to America (Southern Poverty Law Center 2018).

What threads of contested personhood are found within the fabric of such global and American gatekeepers? The grid pattern necessary for this landscape has no hard boundaries. Rather, these assaults globally have soft and overlapping boundaries. Personhood often is contested in such a manner that the victims are placed in double or triple jeopardy. Is it these gatekeepers' intention to protect someone's personhood? If so, then whose personhood will be protected and whose will be withheld? More often than not, these gatekeepers intentionally seek to protect personhood of "self," while insuring loss of personhood of "other" on the basis of a least one or more criteria (Third World Women's Alliance 1971–1980). Dominant in the U.S. landscape are judgments against the "other" made by patriarchy (typically the White ruling class) on the basis of race, skin color, ethnicity, religious beliefs, and/or sexual orientation (Ore 2019). Ironically, these criteria reflect the very history of a country that has benefitted enormously by waves of fresh new immigrant populations to our shores. However, as each new wave of immigrants washed ashore, two responses were typically catalyzed: anxiety and exploitation. In the 21st century, America displays heightened angst in response to the very act of immigration itself, not necessarily aiming at a specific group of individuals. Declarations that the U.S. is "full" are commonplace, even during periods of increased aging out of seniors and declining fertility rates of the White ruling class. At a time when there are more than 50 million refugees seeking domicile outside of their home countries worldwide, both the nation of origin (especially if from a predominantly Muslim country) and the citizenship status of immigrants take on overly inflated significance for the ruling class gatekeepers.

Being a woman, a person of color, and a person seeking political asylum from a South American or predominantly Muslim country creates formidable obstacles to exercising rights guaranteed by U.S. Constitution for asylum. The jeopardy of gender extends far beyond the usual patriarchal discrimination against women. Gender "identity" with reference to peoples self-ascribed as members of the LGBTQ+ community has been advanced as a new threat to civil order to the ruling class (Lau 2018). Sexual orientation, a persistent pattern of romantic and/or sexual attraction to "others," likewise continues to be a source of fierce discrimination (and violence) in the work place and in virtually every other dimension of human living in the U.S. today (Neacsu et al. 2018). In addition, personhood can be degraded through ageism (Ayalon 2018). This assault on personhood would seem paradoxical, especially as the population of middle and late-stage adults swells in the aftermath of the Baby Boomer generation. The fullest dimension of disabilities, whether physical or psychological, can become substrates for discounting one's personhood. Vulnerabilities can provoke denial of employment, biased discussions limiting access to healthcare for the infirmed, to preclusion from adequate end-of-life care for the dying (Smart 2016; Smart 2018). Lower on the scale of criteria for contesting human being are possession of a criminal record (even for those whose sentenced time "has been served"), being incarcerated in the penal or immigration systems (while awaiting justice), and dependence on drugs (both licit and illicit), alcohol, or other addictive substances (Alexander 2010). More subtle, yet potent discriminators are colorism (e.g., shades of color that favor whiteness) (Russell-Cole, Wilson, and Hall 2013), physical anomalies (e.g., obesity and baldness) (Brownell 2005), and aspects of "attractiveness" when deemed absent in a specific individual (Hamermesh 2011). These criteria, triggers for contesting personhood, show some variance in their social application over time and context. Some metrics (such as race, skin color, and religious affiliation) have played dominant roles in the depersonalization of the "other" since the founding of the U.S. Other criteria (e.g., immigration status and country of origin) wax and wane in their impact on assignment of personhood based upon desires to exploit "otherness" for economic and/or political gain, or both.

Something Old, Something New, Something Borrowed, and Something Blue

Like the old wedding rhyme, the assaults on personhood in our time stem from something old, something new, something borrowed, and something blue. In 21st century America we cannot but acknowledge that we readily adopted the same "old" biblical warrants for conquering people and indenturing their services (and lives) as slaves. For the indigenous Native Americans, in the land as the first Paleo-Indians for more than 30,000 years, their genocide, criminal mistreatment, dispossession and the assaults on their personhood constitute an "original sin" (Banner 2005). The rationale for explicating this harsh, inhumane treatment of "people in the land" emerged almost two hundred years after the assault started (Dunbar-Ortiz 2014). The Discovery Doctrine, a U.S. ploy to usurp lands heretofore occupied by the indigenous Native Americans for more than 30 centuries, was based upon a very "old" logic containing in a 1493 Papal Bull *Inter Caetera (Banner 2005)*. Assault on American indigenous peoples offered harsh critiques of their cultures, fueling more than five centuries of oppression and exploitation (see Chapter 5)! Suffice it to say, elevated levels of domestic violence, alcohol abuse, and depression on tribal lands are best understood as a toxic byproduct reflecting back to colonial oppression and depersonalization aimed at Native Americans (Dunbar-Ortiz 2014). Our untoward behavior aimed at the "other" is of our own making and not new. Later we shall explore possible paths to truth and reconciliation for our "old" original sins, that is, transformation not of laws but of hearts.

In 1501 Spanish settlers brought African slaves to Santo Domingo (DR). Less than 150 years later, slavery had been introduced to colonial North America, first legalized in the Massachusetts Bay Colony and the Plymouth Plantations in 1641. Proponents would declare that slavery was a "necessary evil" and "positive good" for America (Liston 1972, Morgan 2005). President Abraham Lincoln issued the Emancipation Proclamation at the end of the second year of the bloody Civil War. This "emancipation" and a Reconstruction period that followed lifted up the plight of freed slaves giving them for the very first time a political voice. The eventual "new" backlash to enlivened Black voting was enactment of Jim Crow laws that enforced racial segregation in the South (Tischauser 2012; Fremon 2015). The Civil Rights Act of 1964 and the Voting Rights Act in the following year sought to overcome these "new" legal barriers, including Jim Crow laws that deny African Americans equal rights under the 15th Amendment (Alexander 2010). As we develop this theme of "original" sin of slavery fueling 21st century racism and assaults on personhood in upcoming chapters, the writings of American philosopher and public intellectual Cornel West (b. 1953) will emerge as a compelling prophetic voice. In *Race Matters*, West offered a breathtaking rebuke of America. The U.S. was viewed as a racist ,White patriarchal nation with a dark history of oppression and exploitation that supports White supremacy (West 1993). No human enterprise in the entire history of the republic has both depersonalized and deprived personhood from so many Americans than White supremacy operating in plain sight in the United States, both then and now (Dorrien 2018). Later we shall encounter the "new" Jim Crow and its legacy in a nation still steeped in racism (Alexander 2010). In her book *The New Jim Crow: Mass Incarceration in the Age of Colorblindness* (2010) Alexander lifts up what is "new"; in other words, a systematic 21st century oppression and social control of Black bodies through a commercialized, industrial-scale penal system and court-enabled incarceration of millions of African Americans (Alexander 2010).

Much of the resistance and resilience of Black Americans to structural oppression was "borrowed" from their four hundred year legacy of suffering. The pulse of Black resistance was palpable and brought to voice in Black spirituals and the blues (Cone 1991b), by the Civil Rights movement and towering intellectuals such as Martin Luther King Jr. and Malcolm X captured in *Martin & Malcolm & America* (Cone 1991a, 1997), in *Dietrich Bonhoeffer's Black Jesus* (Williams 2014), in *The Souls of Black Folks* (Du Bois 1903), in *The New Abolition (Dorrien 2015)* and in countless other responses to the shackles of oppression by a White ruling class supremacy and its inescapable "guilt" captured in *Breaking White Supremacy* (Dorrien 2018). In Chapter 5, I proffer that such assaults perpetrated against Africans, African Americans and their descendants as well as this unresolved guilt of White America constitute an "original" sin, foundational to the American empire.

The roots of contested personhood in the U.S. (as elsewhere) are varied but clearly "borrowed" from diverse and pervasive forces in the world. One cannot escape the observation that when there is no apparent "other" to counterbalance the "self," self will then create an "other" in response to some fundamental anxiety that permeates human interactions (Tymieniecka et al. 1977). Social groups that by history and genetics are clearly quite homogenous, for example, can create hierarchical systems by which to discriminate within the same narrow population. Religious fervor, skin color, education, and wealth are well-known criteria by which human populations can rank-order themselves. Caste systems, levels of religiosity and adherence to religious dogma, as well as factors such as colorism, lookism, and enhanced ethnicity have a long history of creating hierarchy into which the "self" can relax within the embrace of like/like-minded folks. Peddling unfounded criticism and racist assaults on the personhood of those labeled "other" has long provided a cathartic vent for fear and anxiety of the threatened "self." The caste system of India as well as the British colonial regime (e.g., the "Raj") operating in the Indian colony provided well developed and adaptable models for contesting personhood to the point of a fine art (Rangari 1984). Unsatisfied with the preceding Indian caste system, the British Empire Rajs promoted even more broad and rigid caste systems for systematizing various social/cultural norms (and anxieties) among India's populace. All of these efforts in the "colonies" operated openly to contest the personhood of the "other," robbing him/her/them of rights that would be considered today as inalienable, negative "human rights" (Jaffrelot 2005).

Colonization of the New World brought with it creation of a civil-religious hierarchy in Mesoamerican communities. These dual roles in civil (e.g., judges) and religious (e.g., clergy) added additional gravitas to the judgments passed down on who were to be considered "self" as compared to "other." Along with civil and religious authorities were economic realities of power and control that can enforce (and benefit from) assaulting the personhood of the "other." This merger of power and control in the theological/judicial fusion clearly is "borrowed." Ancient Greek, Hebrew, and Roman societies employed power and control as well as divine warrant to manage those peoples who by conquest became "non-person" property under their dominion. In the U.S. in particular, waves of the immigrant "other" were held up to comparison to existing landed selves and deemed threatening to the fabric of law, order, and freedoms of current citizens. In the 19th century for example, landed "British" Protestants in America were deeply challenged by waves of European Roman Catholic peoples who they characterized as barbarians, adherents of the anti-Christ, obedient to the authority of the Pope (Farrelly 2018). Nativist movements have emerged throughout the history of the U.S. Some were aimed at newly immigrant Chinese and later Japanese groups. These movements fueled fear and trepidation through xenophobia, labeling the interlopers as less than human, unworthy of personhood (Knobel 1996). In the 20th century, more than 100,000 Japanese Americans within the U.S. were forced to relocate to concentration camps during World War II (Robson 2014). In the 21st century we have the Tea Party slogan of "Amnesty for Millions, Tyranny for All." With more than 40 million immigrants, most of whom are legally admitted to the U.S., the U.S. would seem an odd place for such depersonalization of new immigrants to gain traction (Railton 2019). Cries warning of diluted national identity, disease-carrying (e.g., HIV and later COVID-19) "invaders," immigrant-based criminal activities, economic loss and instability, as well as unsubstantiated claims of creating an increased welfare load still provoke robust tribalism, nativism, and nationalism in the U.S., as well as in the global theatre of Europe, the Mideast, and Africa. The 2016 U.S. presidential election (Meacham 2018) and the 2016–2020 Brexit movement aimed to exit the UK from the European Union (Jordana et al. 2019) revealed an unmistakably robust xenophobia. There is a deep anxiety globally in the landed citizenry to waves of new immigrant classes now crashing upon their shores and hovering at their borders. Harsh "anti-immigrant" sentiment was critical to the outcomes of both of these political tests of the inclusivity of the civilized nations of the "modern" global world.

Personal Reflection: Pastor Paul B., a Troubled Soul

Paul B. was a remarkable fellow. He was the progeny of immigrants who came to Ellis Island from the poverty and hopelessness of Central Europe. Although devoid of formal training beyond a compulsory 6th grade of public schooling, Paul's parents provided him both the ethos for education and doggedness that would propel him to be the first college-educated family member. Paul's *alma mater* was not some publically supported two-year community college, but rather Yale University. Perhaps it was early theological interests ignited at Yale that eventually would change his trajectory from medical or graduate training to Westminster Theological Seminary and ultimately onto Called ministry in the Reformed Church. What would evolve, as the most remarkable aspect of Paul's thinking, was a robust nativist response, enlivened in response to the 2016 national election. No longer the learned theologian and ordained preacher ministering to the poor, Pastor Paul became an adherent to a "New" Gospel, a gospel advanced by Fox News! Now, the "least of these" for Paul was not the suffering immigrant from worn-torn Afghanistan or Yemen, but the least economically privileged parishioners of his mostly middle- and upper class church that he served in Connecticut. In some way, deeply felt insecurities from his hardscrabble past certainly were neither dead nor resolved for Paul. As clergy member and pastor, I found his remarkable anti-immigrant and xenophobic "new voice" startling to say the least! His new politics were received as startling, especially to those who were familiar with Paul's immigrant roots and early life. Paul's assault on immigrant personhood squarely aimed at the "least of us"; in other words, those not at all unlike his former self, accustomed to the poverty encountered living on the margins of South Boston. This unexpected change in Paul's "worldview" was decidedly "something blue" for me. He was a friend, a mentor, who like me had pastored several small congregations. The congregations that I served were not unlike Paul's own "flocks." He had given up on the Good News, preferring rather to preach the "Prosperity Gospel" and to view faithfully the nation through the lens of Fox & Friends.

The strategies that were employed by Pastor Paul, as revealed in our head-to-head conversations about national politics, were neither unique, nor timely, nor innovative. The methodologies that the good pastor employed now were derivative of the Labeling Theory. This theory has two major elements. The first posits that the behavior and self-identity of people can be influenced by terms employed to label them, much like a self-fulfilling prophecy. The second judges "deviance" not to be inherent (such as a vice like gluttony), but rather as a character or property of a negatively viewed,

minority group of "other" with whom one interacts (Becker 2018). This
theory explicates how the behaviors of minorities may be labeled or assigned
as "deviant" by a dominant ruling class. Appearing in public without a tee
shirt, that is, bare chested, could be labeled as "deviant." By such labeling,
deviations from "normal," no matter how trivial, become a self-fulfilling
prophecy for "deviance." If members of the "other" chew tobacco to the
abhorrence of the dominant culture, then as a class the "other" can be labeled
"deviant." Simple association can be employed to ensnare even a non-tobac-
co user. Indirect labeling "well, I am sure that he chews at home" is sufficient
to garner a label as "deviant." Such negative views are employed with intent
to stigmatize members of minorities, labeling them with powerful negative
attributes. Negative labels can impact not only their perceived social status,
but also their own social identity and self-image.

Casting aspersions upon an individual or group can damage one's self or
collective image. Bereft of suitable tools of resistance and resilience, the
labeled "other" can suffer deep and long lasting loss of self-image and in its
place find self-loathing emerging. Recently I overheard the conversation of a
family of immigrants from Mexico remarking about the frequency of their
arrests on the streets of South Texas. One family member painfully suggests
a reason, "it must be in our blood!" Such self-loathing is a product of long-
standing structural oppression, labeled with negative minority stereotypes,
for example, wetbacks, shiftless, criminal, and ignorant. Such assaults on
personhood can be particularly toxic when fueled and amplified by identity
politics. Discussion of the changing "face of America" (e.g., the increasing
numbers of people of color in the U.S.) on Fox News provokes anxiety and
fear in the dominant White ruling class. The election of the first man of color
to the U.S. Presidency in 2008 provoked widespread "White fragility," a
termed coined by Robin DiAngelo (DiAngelo 2018). The fact that minorities
make up almost half of U.S. births is trumpeted by right-wing media as a
"call-to-arms," a dog whistle for racists, White nationalists and supremacists.

Pastor Paul's ecclesiastic approach to his like-minded Christians also
adopted strategies derivative of Game Theory (Han 2013). This theory and
its derivative Evolutionary Game can be employed to shape outcomes in
social settings. According to these theories, formalized social contracts in
which political "norms" of collective "selves" are concocted and then employed to justify the metering out of pre-assigned values of personhood to the
"other." Evolving versions of Game Theory often reflect on attempts of
collective "selves" to recover norms from traditions that specifically give the
"self" an edge over the "other" (Stanish 2017). Such strategies seek to optimize the situation of a collective of ruling "selves" at whatever necessary
expense of the lesser "other."

Pushback by the White ruling majority against Black Americans with
regard to progress on Civil Rights and Voting Rights came in the form of the

New Jim Crow (Alexander 2010). In this stage of his life Pastor Paul viewed the world as a zero-sums game in which gain by the "other" was not to be welcomed, but rather feared as threatening to a privileged *status quo* of a "landed aristocracy." The central thrust of Game Theory for Paul was contesting the "being human" of the "other," whenever it challenged the preferred "being White." Exploiting the disadvantaged and burdened least of us, the "other," was not *un*Christian, but rather a reaffirmation of the biblical warrant in which the lesser comes under the dominion of the greater. Insuring an upper hand in dealing with perceived (or real) threats embodies in the "other" was necessary to preserve the treasured *status quo* of Paul and his like-minded congregation. The moral instability of the minorities then was viewed as justification for unprovoked police brutality, not the other way around. The good pastor was blind to the very same oppression and exploitation that his parents, like many recent immigrants, suffer under the boot of the White ruling class in America. *Hyper*violence aimed at people of color, divergent religious faiths, and differing sexual preferences by local police, state and federal authorities constitute a public demonstration of the extent to which the White ruling class seeks protection of privileged status. His sermons valued the "old" traditions, law-and-order and banished the ugly truths of impoverished people of color who would resist assimilation to the character preferred by their oppressors.

Paul knew well the most common and oldest foils employed to assault personhood in the "other" were divine "selection" and biblical warrant. He often preached from the Hebrew Bible, especially from Genesis, wherein his weapons of choice were readily available. The Genesis story (1:26–28) included the warrant for those chosen to "have dominion/subdue" the fish of the sea and over the birds in the air and over every living thing that moves upon the earth (v. 28). Clearly the benefits of contesting the being human of the "other" degrades full personhood and subjugates the "other" to the dominion, by the ruling class as per the biblical warrant in the last verse. Beyond biblical warrant, contractual theology that has influenced Christian dogma over two millennia was a central dogma for Paul during the run-up to the 2016 presidential election. Constantine the Great (272–337 CE) employed contractual theology at the Battle of Milvian Bridge (312 CE). The emperor asked God for a biblical warrant ensuring success in an effort to gain an upper hand against his foe Maxentius. According to Constantine's perspective, the "prayer" was answered on the battlefield! In the contractual sense, the Constantine's victory at Milvian was repaid by the creation of the Holy Roman Empire. Within this "Holy" empire, not unlike others, is the operating principle that anything but "self" would be declared "other." Only through submission and obedience to dominion assigned to Constantine by God was the "other" to be managed. This contractual theology is the very core of the prosperity gospel and others reaching back to Genesis for biblical warrant. Adherents of the prosperity gospel sense a contractual link to exist between financial blessings and physical well-being as gifts from God and making forward payments for faith and financial support of religious efforts. This buying a "stairway to heaven" through materialism and contract, not faith, seemed acceptable to Paul.

Well-read in the Classics and U.S. history, Paul likewise became an adherent to the myth of American exceptionalism. Paul knew well that virtually all world religions include dogma that can be hijacked to provide a divine warrant to justify assault the personhood of the "other." Now the immigrant "other" created in Paul only fear and trepidation, rather than unconditional love and blessings. As validated by his right-wing media, the "Discovery Doctrine" became the bedrock of Paul's new sense of justice. Bequeathed to the White ruling class of the Colonial period of American history and ascent to the American Empire, the doctrine struck Paul as a biblical warrant. He tossed aside as spurious, claims of indigenous Native Americans to ancestral lands and of their deep spirituality, although reflecting more than thirty centuries of richly diverse and spiritually deep oral traditions. According to Paul, the U.S., like the Greek, Roman, and Imperial rulers of history that aligned their power with the gods, must embrace again an Almighty God that had not heard the lamentations of millions of immigrant peoples here in America who suffered and died at the hand of that "City on a Hill" (Dunbar-Ortiz 2014; Brickhouse 2015). Paul bristled at my progressive views espoused about the discovery doctrine and American empire. The fact that world courts and religions resoundingly rejected the Doctrine of Discovery as a violation of human rights and misinterpretation of biblical warrant was not the point to him. For Paul, a Christian Protestant minister, there was little doubt that God had elected some to rule and "others" to serve, but always within the dominion of a White ruling White. For me, the sad reality that Paul and I had become "moral strangers" was a painful outcome. Looking back, it was not my beloved friend that had changed, but rather it was me. My seminary training, chaplaincy, and pastoral experience had transformed me!

In America today, racism and subjugation of the "other" are the first derivatives of the two "original sins" that we shall interrogate in detail later. Conquest narratives decorate our lives in books, journals, news, and social media. As captivating as these conquest myths strike the average American today, they deserve a deeper interrogation. As we progress through an in depth interrogation of the question of personhood in the 21st century we will encounter these criteria both individually (e.g., race, color, religion, ethnic origin, sexual identity, etc.) as well as in synergistic combinations of double and triple jeopardy (e.g., an immigrant Muslim woman of color) in which risk to personhood can and often leads to violence, subjugation, and yes even death. Criteria employed in 21st century America all too frequently in day-to-day efforts aimed at labeling and assaulting the personhood of the "other" includes: race; color; gender; sexual orientation/preference; religious affiliation; age; and our starting points, disabilities of the body (soma, Chapter 2) and mind (psyche, Chapter 3).

REFERENCES

Ahumada, A., D. C. Slusarski, X. Liu, R. T. Moon, C. C. Malbon, and H. Y. Wang. 2002. Signaling of rat Frizzled-2 through phosphodiesterase and cyclic GMP. *Science, 298*(5600): 2006–10. doi: 10.1126/science.1073776.

Alexander, Michelle. 2010. *The new Jim Crow: Mass incarceration in the age of colorblindness.* New York, NY; Jackson, TN: New Press, distributed by Perseus.

Aquinas, Thomas. 1951. *Commentary on Aristotle's* De anima (Kenelm Foster and Sylvester Humphries, trans.). New Haven, CT: Yale University Press.

Aquinas, Thomas and Thomas S. Hibbs. 1999. *On human nature.* Indianapolis, ID: Hackett Pub.

Aristotle. c. 350 BCE. *Aristotle's On the soul (*De anima*)* (J. A. Smith, trans.). The Classic Archive. Cambridge, MA: the MIT Press (retreived February 16 , 2016).

Augustine, and Marcus Dods. 2009. *The city of God.* Peabody, MA: Hendrickson Publishers.

Augustine, and Gareth B. Matthews. 2002. *On the trinity* books 8–15, Cambridge texts in the history of philosophy. Cambridge, UK; New York, NY: Cambridge University Press.

Ayalon, Liat. 2018. *Contemporary perspectives on ageism.* New York, NY: Springer Berlin Heidelberg.

Banner, Stuart. 2005. *How the Indians lost their land: Law and power on the frontier.* Cambridge, MA: Belknap Press of Harvard University Press.

Becker, Howard Saul. 2018. *Outsiders: Studies in the sociology of deviance.* New York, NY: Free Press, an imprint of Simon & Schuster, Inc.

Beckett, Samuel. 1971. *Samuel Beckett.* Björnstjerne Björnson, Pearl Buck and Ivan Bunin, Nobel Prize library. New York, NY: A. Gregory Publishers.

Beckett, Samuel, Sean Lawlor, and John Pilling. 2012. *The collected poems of Samuel Beckett: A critical edition.* London, UK: Faber and Faber.

Berlin, Isaiah. 1970. *The age of Enlightenment: The eighteenth century philosophers.* Freeport, NY: Books for Libraries Press.

Bertalovitz, A. C., M. S. Pau, S. Gao, C. C. Malbon, and H. Y. Wang. 2016. Frizzled-4 C-terminus Distal to KTXXXW Motif is Essential for Normal Dishevelled Recruitment and Norrin-stimulated Activation of Lef/Tcf-dependent Transcriptional Activation. *J Mol Signal, 11*(1). doi: 10.5334/1750-2187-11-1.

Besong, Brian. 2018. *An introduction to ethics: A natural law approach.* Eugene, OR: Cascade Books, an imprint of Wipf and Stock Publishers.

Blendon, R. J., M. K. Kim, and J. M. Benson. 2011. The public, political parties, and stem-cell research. *N Engl J Med, 365*(20): 1853–6. doi: 10.1056/NEJMp1110340.

Bodden, Valerie. 2019. *Nelson Mandela.* 1st edition. ed, Odysseys in peace. Mankato, MN: Creative Education.

Bonhoeffer, Dietrich. 1963. *The communion of saints: A dogmatic inquiry into the sociology of the church.* New York, NY: Harper & Row.

Brickhouse, Anna. 2015. *The unsettlement of America: Translation, interpretation, and the story of Don Luis de Velasco, 1560–1945s.* New York, NY: Oxford University Press.

Brownell, Kelly D. 2005. *Weight bias: Nature, consequences, and remedies.* New York, NY: Guilford Press.

Burkert, Walter. 1979. *Structure and history in Greek mythology and ritual.* Berkeley, CA: University of California Press.

Butler, Joseph. 1889. *The analogy of religion, natural and revealed, to the constitution and course of nature.* London, UK: G. Bell and Sons.

Cahoone, Lawrence E. 2003. *From modernism to postmodernism: An anthology* (expanded 2nd ed.). Malden, MA: Blackwell Pub.

Cartledge, Paul. 1999. *Democritus* (The Great Philosophers series). New York, NY: Routledge.

Chesterton, G. K. 2009. *St. Thomas Aquinas.* Dover books on Western philosophy. Mineola, NY: Dover Publications.

Cohen, Jared. 2007. *One-hundred days of silence: America and the Rwanda genocide.* Lanham, MD: Rowman & Littlefield Publishers.

Cone, James H. 1991a. *Martin & Malcolm & America: A dream or a nightmare.* Maryknoll, NY: Orbis Books.

———. 1991b. *The spirituals and the blues: An interpretation.* Maryknoll, NY: Orbis Books.

———. 1997. *Black theology and Black power.* Maryknoll, NY: Orbis Books.

Copleston, Frederick C. 1985. *A history of philosophy.* New York, NY: Image Books.

Cuneo, Terence, and René van Woudenberg. 2004. *The Cambridge companion to Thomas Reid.* New York, NY: Cambridge University Press.

Denise, Theodore Cullom, Nicholas P. White, and Sheldon Paul Peterfreund. 2008. *Great traditions in ethics.* Belmont, CA: Thomson Wadsworth.

Descartes, René.1637. *Discours de la méthode pour bien conduire sa raison et chercher. La vérité dans les sciences, plus la dioptrique, les météores et la géométrie* (in French). Paris, FR: Bibliothèque nationale de France Gallica.

DiAngelo, Robin. 2018. *White fragility: Why it's so hard for White people to talk about racism.* Boston, MA: Beacon Press.

Dicker, Georges. 1998. *Hume's epistemology and metaphysics: An introduction.* London, UK: Routledge.

Dillon, John M., and Tania Gergel. 2003. *The Greek Sophists.* London, UK; New York, NY: Penguin.

Dodd, Dylan, and Elia Zardini. 2014. *Scepticism and perceptual justification* (1st ed.). Oxford, UK; New York, NY: Oxford University Press.

Dorrien, Gary J. 2015. *The new abolition: W.E.B. Du Bois and the Black social gospel.* New Haven, CT: Yale University Press.

———.2018. *Breaking White supremacy: Martin Luther King Jr. and the Black social gospel.* New Haven, CT; London, UK: Yale University Press.

Dubber, Markus Dirk. 2005. *The police power: Patriarchy and the foundations of American government.* New York, NY: Columbia University Press.

Du Bois, W.E.B. 1903. *The souls of Black folk.* Chicago, IL: A. C. McClurg & Comp.

Dunbar-Ortiz, Roxanne. 2014. *An indigenous peoples' history of the United States.* Boston, MA: Beacon Press.

Faley, Roland J. 2003. *Biblical profiles: Contemporary reflections on Old Testament people.* New York, NY: Paulist Press.

Farrelly, Maura Jane. 2018. *Anti-Catholicism in America, 1620–1860.* Cambridge, UK; New York, NY: Cambridge University Press.

Fishbein, Harold D. 2002. *Peer prejudice and discrimination: The origins of prejudice* (2nd ed.). Mahwah, NJ: L. Erlbaum.

Fitz-Gibbon, Jane H. 2017. *Corporal punishment, religion, and United States public schools.* New York, NY: Springer Berlin Heidelberg.

Fremon, David K. 2015. *The Jim Crow laws and racism in United States history.* Berkeley Heights, NJ: Enslow Publishers, Inc.

Geulincx, Arnold, Samuel Beckett, J. A. van Ruler, Anthony Uhlmann, Martin Wilson. 2006. *Arnold Geulincx Ethics: With Samuel Beckett's Notes.* In *Brill's Studies in Intellectual History.* Leiden, NL; Boston, MA: Brill.

Glombicek, Petr, James Hill, editors. 2010. *Essays on the concept of mind in early-modern philosophy.* Newcastle upon Tyne, UK: Cambridge Scholars.

Goetz, Stewart, and Charles Taliaferro. 2011. *A brief history of the soul.* Malden, MA: Wiley-Blackwell.

Grenholm, Cristina, and Daniel Patte. 2005. *Gender, tradition and Romans: Shared ground, uncertain borders* (Romans through history and cultures). New York, NY: T&T Clark.

Hamermesh, Daniel S. 2011. *Beauty pays: Why attractive people are more successful.* Princeton, NJ; Oxford, UK: Princeton University Press.

Han, The Anh. 2013. *Intention recognition, commitment and their roles in the evolution of cooperation: From artificial intelligence techniques to evolutionary game theory models* (1st ed.). New York, NY: Springer Berlin Heidelberg.

Harrison, Beverly Wildung. 1983. *Our right to choose: Toward a new ethic of abortion.* Eugene, OR: Wipf and Stock Publishers

Hasan, Ira, and Samuel Beckett. 2002. *Samuel Beckett, wordmaster: Waiting for Godot: text with critical commentary.* Karachi, IN: Oxford University Press.

Haugeberg, Karissa. 2017. *Women against abortion: Inside the largest moral reform movement of the twentieth century.* Urbana, Chicago, IL: University of Illinois Press.

Hause, Jeffrey. 2018. *Aquinas's Summa theologiae: A critical guide.* New York, NY: Cambridge University Press.

Hauskeller, M. 2011. Believing in the dignity of human embryos. *Hum Reprod Genet Ethics, 17*(1): 53–65.

Hume, David. 2004. *An enquiry concerning human understanding.* Dover philosophical classics. Mineola, NY: Dover Publications.

Iliffe, Rob. 2017. *Priest of nature: The religious worlds of Isaac Newton.* New York, NY: Oxford University Press.

Jaffrelot, Christophe. 2005. *Dr. Ambedkar and untouchability: Fighting the Indian caste system.* New York, NY: Columbia University Press.

Jasinski, Michael P. 2017. *Examining genocides: Means, motive, and opportunity.* London, UK; New York, NY: Rowman & Littlefield International.

Jeeves, Malcolm A. 2004. *From cells to souls, and beyond: Changing portraits of human nature.* Grand Rapids, MI: W.B. Eerdmans.

Jordana, Jacint, Michael Keating, Axel Marx, and Jan Wouters. 2019. *Changing borders in Europe: Exploring the dynamics of integration, differentiation, and self-determination in the European Union,* Routledge / UACES contemporary European studies. Abingdon, Oxon, UK; New York, NY: Routledge.

Kaufman, Michael. 1987. *Beyond patriarchy: Essays by men on pleasure, power, and change.* Toronto, CN; New York, NY: Oxford University Press.

Kaufmann, Walter Arnold, and Friedrich Wilhelm Nietzsche. 1968. *Nietzsche: Philosopher, psychologist, antichrist.* New York, NY: Vintage Books.

Knobel, Dale T. 1996. *America for the Americans: The nativist movement in the United States.* New York, NY; London, UK: Twayne Publishers: Prentice Hall International.

Koch, Christoff. 2019. *The feeling of life itself: Why consciuosness is widespread but can't be computed.* Cambridge MA: The MIT Press.

Kwon, J. Y., H. L. Bercovici, K. Cunningham, and M. E. W. Varnum. 2018. How will we react to the discovery of extraterrestrial life? *Frontiers in Psychology, 8.* doi: ARTN 2308 10.3389/fpsyg.2017.02308.

Lau, Holning. 2018. *Sexual orientation and gender identity discrimination.* Leiden ND; Boston MA: Brill.

Lévinas, Emmanuel, and Nidra Poller. 2003. *Humanism of the other.* Urbana, Chicago, IL: University of Illinois Press.

Liston, Robert A. 1972. *Slavery in America: The heritage of slavery.* New York, NY: McGraw-Hill.

Liu, T., A. J. DeCostanzo, X. Liu, Hy Wang, S. Hallagan, R. T. Moon, and C. C. Malbon. 2001. G protein signaling from activated rat frizzled-1 to the beta-catenin-Lef-Tcf pathway. *Science, 292*(5522): 1718–22. doi: 10.1126/science.1060100.

Locke, John, and Maurice William Cranston. 1965. *Locke on politics, religion, and education.* New York, NY: Collier Classics Books.

Locke, John, and Pauline Phemister. 2008. *An essay concerning human understanding.* Oxford, UK; New York NY: Oxford University Press.

Loose, Jonathan. 2018. The Blackwell companion to substance dualism. In *Blackwell companions to philosophy.* Hoboken, NJ: Wiley Blackwell.

Mahler, Margaret S., Fred Pine, and Anni Bergman. 1975. *The psychological birth of the human infant: Symbiosis and individuation.* London, UK: Hutchinson.

Malbon, C. C. 1997. Heterotrimeric G-proteins and development. *Biochem Pharmacol, 53*(1): 1–4.

———. 2005. G proteins in development. *Nat Rev Mol Cell Biol, 6*(9): 689–701. doi: 10.1038/nrm1716.

———. 2007. A-kinase anchoring proteins: Trafficking in G-protein-coupled receptors and the proteins that regulate receptor biology. *Curr Opin Drug Discov Devel, 10*(5): 573–9.

———. 2013. *Abortion in 21st century America.* North Charleston, SC: CreateSpace Publishing.

Malebranche, Nicolas, Nicholas Jolley, and David Scott. 1997. *Dialogues on metaphysics and on religion.* Cambridge, UK; New York, NY: Cambridge University Press.

McLaren, A. 2007. A scientist's view of the ethics of human embryonic stem cell research. *Cell Stem Cell, 1*(1): 23–26. doi: 10.1016/j.stem.2007.05.003.

Meacham, Jon. 2018. *The soul of America: The battle for our better angels.* New York, NY: Random House.

Morgan, Kenneth. 2005. *Slavery in America: A reader and guide.* Athens, GA: University of Georgia Press.

Morrison, Donald R. 2011. *The Cambridge companion to Socrates.* Cambridge, UK; New York, NY: Cambridge University Press.

Moxham, C. M., and C. C. Malbon. 1996. Insulin action impaired by deficiency of the G-protein subunit G ialpha2. *Nature, 379*(6568): 840–4. doi: 10.1038/379840a0.

Neacsu, Dana, David Brian Holt, Margaret Butler, Iain W. Barksdale, American Association of Law Libraries, and American Association of Law Libraries. 2018. Social Responsibilities Special Interest Section. In *Sexual orientation, gender identities, and the law: A research bibliography, 2006–2016.* Getzville, NY: William S. Hein & Co., Inc.

Neaves, W. 2017. The status of the human embryo in various religions. *Development, 144*(14): 2541–3. doi: 10.1242/dev.151886.

Nietzsche, Friedrich Wilhelm, Rolf-Peter Horstmann, and Judith Norman. 2002. *Beyond good and evil: Prelude to a philosophy of the future.* Cambridge, UK; New York, NY: Cambridge University Press.

Nietzsche, Friedrich Wilhelm, and Walter Arnold Kaufmann. 1995. *Thus spoke Zarathustra: A book for all and none.* New York, NY: Modern Library.

Nietzsche, Friedrich Wilhelm, and Horace Barnett Samuel. 2006. *On the genealogy of morals.* Oxford, UK: Oxford University Press.

Nijssen, S. R. R., B. C. N. Muller, R. B. van Baaren, and M. Paulus. 2019. Saving the robot or the human? Robots who feel deserve moral care. *Social Cognition, 37*(1): 41–56. doi: 10.1521/soco.2019.37.1.41.

Okoye, U. C., C. C. Malbon, and H. Y. Wang. 2008. Wnt and Frizzled RNA expression in human mesenchymal and embryonic (H7) stem cells. *J Mol Signal, 3*(16). doi: 10.1186/1750-2187-3-16.

Ore, Tracy E. 2019. *The social construction of difference and inequality: Race, class, gender, and sexuality.* New York, NY: Oxford University Press.

Paquette, Robert L., and Mark M. Smith. 2010. *The Oxford handbook of slavery in the Americas.* Oxford, UK; New York, NY: Oxford University Press.

Pitson, A. E. 2002. *Hume's philosophy of the self.* London, UK; New York, NY: Routledge.

Plessis, Paul J. du, Clifford Ando, and Kaius Tuori. 2016. In *The Oxford handbook of Roman law and society.* Oxford, UK: Oxford University Press.

Post, Stephen Garrard. 2000. *The moral challenge of Alzheimer disease: Ethical issues from diagnosis to dying.* Baltimore, MD: Johns Hopkins University Press.

Railton, Ben. 2019. *We the people: The 500-year battle over who is American.* Lanham, MD: Rowman & Littlefield.

Rangari, Ashok D. 1984. *Indian caste system and education.* New Delhi, ID: Deep & Deep Publications.

Rauch, Leo, David Sherman, and Georg Wilhelm Friedrich Hegel. 1999. *Hegel's phenomenology of self-consciousness: Text and commentary*. New York, NY: State University of New York Press.

Robson, David. 2014. Understanding American history. In *The internment of Japanese Americans*. San Diego, CA: ReferencePoint Press.

Rolnick, Philip A. 2007. *Person, grace, and God, Sacra doctrina*. Grand Rapids, MI: William B. Eerdmans.

Rudolph, Joseph R., Jr, editor 2015. *Encyclopedia of modern ethnic conflicts* (2nd ed.). Santa Barbara, CA: ABC-CLIO.

Russell-Cole, Kathy, Midge Wilson, and Ronald E. Hall. 2013. *The color complex: The politics of skin color in a new millennium*. New York, NY: Anchor Books.

Ryle, Gilbert. 1949. *The concept of mind*. Chicago, IL: University of Chicago Press

Sanger, Carol. 2017. *About abortion: Terminating pregnancy in twenty-first-century America*. Cambridge, MA: The Belknap Press of Harvard University Press.

Schmidhuber, J. 2015. Deep learning in neural networks: An overview. *Neural Networks, 61*: 85–117. doi: 10.1016/j.neunet.2014.09.003.

Service, R. F. 2018. Design for US exascale computer takes shape. *Science, 359*(6376): 617–8.

Sheridan, Patricia. 2010. Continuum guides for the perplexed. In *Locke, a guide for the perplexed*. London, UK; New York, NY: Continuum.

Sivaraman, V. S., H. Wang, G. J. Nuovo, and C. C. Malbon. 1997. Hyperexpression of mitogen-activated protein kinase in human breast cancer. *J Clin Invest, 99*(7): 1478–83. doi: 10.1172/JCI119309.

Smart, Julie. 2016. *Disability, society, and the individual*. Austin, TX: PRO-ED, Inc.

———. 2018. *Disability definitions, diagnoses, and practice implications: An introduction for counselors*. New York, NY: Routledge.

Southern Poverty Law Center. 2018. *Active hate groups in the United States in 2017*. Montgomery, AL: Southern Poverty Law Center.

Stanish, Charles. 2017. *The evolution of human co-operation: Ritual and social complexity in stateless societies*. Cambridge, UK; New York, NY: Cambridge University Press.

Sugarman, J. 2008. Human stem cell ethics: Beyond the embryo. *Cell Stem Cell, 2*(6): 529–33. doi: 10.1016/j.stem.2008.05.005.

Third World Women's Alliance (U.S.). 2018. *Triple jeopardy: Racism, imperialism, sexism*. New York, NY: Third World Women's Alliance.

Thomasma, David C., David N. Weisstub, and Christian Hervé. 2001. International library of ethics, law, and the new medicine. In *Personhood and health care*. Dordrecht, NL; Boston, MA: Kluwer Academic Pub.

Tischauser, Leslie Vincent. 2012. Landmarks of the American mosaic. In *Jim Crow laws*. Santa Barbara, CA: Greenwood.

Torchia, J. 2008. *Exploring personhood: An introduction to the philosophy of human nature*. Lanham, MD: Rowman & Littlefield Publishers, Inc.

Totten, Samuel. 2018. *Dirty hands and vicious deeds: The U.S. government's complicity in crimes against humanity and genocide*. North York, Ontario, CN: University of Toronto Press.

Tymieniecka, Anna-Teresa, International Husserl and Phenomenological Research Society, Société philosophique de Fribourg., and Schweizerische Philosophische Gesellschaft. 1977. Analecta Husserliana. In *The self and the other: The irreducible element in man*. Dordrecht, NL; Boston, MA: D. Reidel Pub. Co.

Urban, E. 2018. On matters of mind and body: Regarding Descartes. *J Anal Psychol, 63*(2): 228–40. doi: 10.1111/1468-5922.12395.

Versace, E., A. Martinho-Truswell, A. Kacelnik, and G. Vallortigara. 2018. Priors in animal and artificial intelligence: Where does learning begin? *Trends in Cognitive Sciences, 22*(11): 963–5. doi: 10.1016/j.tics.2018.07.005.

Waldow, Anik, and ebrary Inc. 2009. David Hume and the problem of other minds. In *Continuum studies in British philosophy*. London, UK; New York, NY: Continuum.

Wang, H. Y., and C. C. Malbon. 2003. Wnt signaling, Ca^{2+}, and cyclic GMP: Visualizing frizzled functions. *Science, 300*(5625): 1529–30. doi: 10.1126/science.1085259.

Wells, Maureen. 2015. *Ethnic conflicts and global interventions* (Terrorism, hot spots and conflict-related issues). New York, NY: Novinka.

West, Cornel. 1993. *Race matters.* Boston, MA: Beacon Press.

Widengren, Geo. 1965. *Mani and Manichaeism,* History of religion. London, UK: Weidenfeld and Nicolson.

Williams, Reggie L. 2014. *Bonhoeffer's Black Jesus: Harlem Renaissance theology and an ethic of resistance.* Waco, TX: Baylor University Press.

Yu, Jie, and H. C. Hsu. 2015. *Steel gate to freedom: The life of Liu Xiaobo.* Lanham, MD: Rowman & Littlefield.

Chapter Two

Personhood With Vulnerabilities in Soma (Body)

THE EMBRYO, THE FETUS, AND ABORTION

The Basics of Emerging Life

Historically, few topics generate more heated debates than those upon the question of the morality of the act of abortion (Malbon 2013). Early descriptions of methods employed to abort a fetus were recorded more than 7000 years ago. Chinese folklore literature describes the use of abortifacient medicinals that provoke premature expulsion of an unborn fetus. The use of mechanical injury, abdominal massage, and abortifacients in ancient times was no less contested than in modern times. The Hippocratic Oath (400 BCE) forbade the use of abortifacients, although some argue that it was only the method, not the abortion per se, that was forbidden (Veatch 2012). Modified by local history and culture, the new Hippocratic "Oath" has now become a "pledge"; that is, it is no longer taken as a solemn oath before God (Miles 2004). The 2017 version of the pledge adopted by the World Health Organization focuses more upon the physician honoring the autonomy and dignity of the patient, but remains subject to local amendment. In fact, the Hippocratic Pledge as applied today has no legal status, has no uniform verbiage promoted by the American Medical Association, and can be appropriated and modified by state medical ethics boards. Thus in the 21st century, America has no national medical canon that takes a position either for or against abortion.

An embryo is an early stage of development of a multicellular organism, whether a starfish, great white shark, or human being. Since humans reproduce sexually (as opposed to asexually) the embryo typically represents the product of a fertilization event of a female egg by a male sperm that generates the zygote. In human development, the multicellular expanding zygote is considered embryonic from the point of fertilization to the beginning of the third month of a nine-month gestational period (Carlson 2018). At about 8 weeks of development the embryo is about 3/4 inch (18 mm) in length, has a beating heart whose beats are detectable by Doppler fetal monitoring, and displays spontaneous limb movements in ultrasound imaging. The moment in pregnancy when a pregnant woman can detect fetal movements in the uterus, termed "quickening," occurs much later. From the 10th week of development onward the developing human is termed a "fetus." At this age in development all major structures are formed and will grow and further develop (Larsen et al. 2001).

Critical in our biological analysis of human development is the issue of viability of the fetus, especially as it relates to gestational age versus likelihood of survival outside of the womb, in other words, that would occur in a "premature" birth (Behrman, Butler, and U.S. Institute of Medicine 2007). A fetus weighing less than half a kilo (17.6 ounces) rarely survives premature delivery. At 21 weeks of development about 20–35% of fetuses do survive. The survivability of the fetus increases dramatically throughout the subsequent weeks of development. At weeks 22–23 of development, survival climbs to 50–70%. By 25–27 weeks of development more than 90% of such "preemies" will survive. The long-term survival of preemies as well as the amount of neonatal intensive care required to support a preemie is inversely proportional to developmental age at delivery. It is important to keep these landmarks and survival rates in mind with regard to our discussion of personhood in the "early termination of pregnancy," in other words, a more politically-sensitive euphemism for "abortion."

Abortion is often defined as the early and deliberate termination of a pregnancy, most often performed during the first 26 weeks of human development (Malbon 2013). This definition, however, does not include the involuntary expulsion of a fetus from the uterus by natural causes before it is capable of surviving independently, termed a "miscarriage." In other words, in the former case the abortion is "induced," whereas in the latter case the abortion was "spontaneous." Today, intentional abortion is primarily performed using abortifacient drugs that medically stimulate a premature expulsion of the fetus. For early 1st trimester use, either mifepristone (an anti-progestin) in combination with misoprostol (a prostaglandin analog), or a prostaglandin in combination with methotrexate (for up to 5 weeks of development), or a suitable prostaglandin alone will provoke an abortion. These so-called "medical" abortions offer significant advantages to the pregnant woman over surgical procedures, but are thoughtfully prescribed only up to 5 weeks of embryonic development (Malbon 2013). At up to 13 weeks of development, the embryo can be surgically aspirated by suction, a procedure termed "manual vacuum aspiration," MVA, or "mini-suction."

Early in pregnancy, dilation of the cervix is not a prerequisite for mini-suction abortion. Alternatively, for abortion of a fetus up to 13th week of development, dilation and curettage (D&C) is performed, surgically scraping the fetus from the uterine wall. In situations of fetal development from 13–26 weeks, the cervix must be fully dilated and the fetus evacuated (D&E) (Malbon 2013). After 14 weeks of development, the alternative procedure intact/intrauterine dilation and extraction (IDX) is possible. The IDX procedure had been a target for a Federal ban since 1995. IDX requires the surgical decompression of the head of the fetus before evacuation is possible. Federal law had intentionally mislabeled the surgical procedure as a "partial-birth abortion," a concoction of the Pro-Life National Right to Life Committee activists whose moniker is not medical, but rather highly confusing. Yet, the Partial-Birth Abortion Ban Act was passed by Congress and signed into law by President George W. Bush in 2003. In response to the cases of *Stenberg v. Carhart* (2001) and later *Gonzales v. Carhart* (2007), the U.S. Supreme Court voted to uphold the 2003 ban. Euphemistically termed "induced miscarriage," this typically late termination of pregnancy (TOP) abortion procedure prematurely induces labor in 11-week or older fetuses and requires the coincident killing of the fetus. Such killing is required in late TOP procedures. In late stages of fetal development in which viability outside of the womb is high, although not guaranteed, the death of the fetus prior to extraction is unavoidable. It is important to state unequivocally that from a strict biological standpoint, the embryo/fetus constitutes "life" within the spectrum of early human development (Nilsson et al. 2009). With this absolute certainty about a fetus being "alive" in mind let us wrestle with the most fundamental question at the core of the moral question of abortion, when does being human commence?

When Does "Being Human" Commence?

Essential in efforts to characterize development, we must interrogate what constitutes personhood and ask when does "personhood" arise in development? In this case, the query is aimed squarely at the very beginning, asking when does being human commence? At least three primary levels of analysis exist: the biological; the neural; and the theological. The question most often posed is, when does "life" begin? This is a seemingly straightforward question in a strictly biological context, or is it? Above, one possibility was offered. Human "life," in a common sense context, commences with fertilization of the female-derived egg with male-derived sperm, resulting in a viable zygote. Life commences at the start of the patterned embryogenesis and development common to human experience. Yet, the query "when does life begin?" is a bit more complex to answer. A more foundational response is in order. Life as we know it commenced approximately 3.8 billion years ago. The fundamental paradigm of life on Earth is based in the blueprint encoded in double-stranded DNA and founded operationally on the process of DNA replication (Alberts 2019). When DNA is replicated, each strand of an existing DNA acts as a template for the generation of a new strand. The new strand thus replicated is complementary to its single-strand template. In this context the question "when does life begin?" is answered simply, in other words, life emerged "once, approximately 3.8 billion years ago." Answering the derivative query "when does the life of a specific human individual commence?" will demand additional contextual background. Herein we only can answer that life arises when a viable zygote emerges that encodes a *specific* potential individual. There can be no question about the validity of this more precise answer. It hangs upon the knowledge that our concern is never about a *generic* person, but rather is focused upon the emergence of an *individual* human being, in other words, a unique "one-of-a-kind" human product of on-going creation itself.

We may ask, is this response just wordsmithing, offering more precision, or more obfuscation? The question that truly captivates is not when does a human being arise, but rather when does "being human" commence? In judging "becoming human," what criteria would we insist upon about the developing zygote to render a verdict on "being human" rather than simply being alive? Is existence itself enough to warrant being human? Is patterned growth and development enough to fulfill the label of human being? What do we really mean when we speak of "coming into being"? The more likely responses to this query point us from the biological towards an interrogation of the neural. Which properties associated with being human extend well beyond simply existing? Whether we draw upon the wisdom of the ancient Greeks, early Church patriarchs, and the great minds of the medieval age and Renaissance, or from current day experts and specialists (see Chapter 1), the properties of "being" human are certain to include certain capabilities, functions, and sensory perception that we equate with normal, well-functioning *adult* members of *Homo sapiens*. These properties highlight the role of "consciousness" within the act of being human. Certainly we recount the values placed upon consciousness and thinking as requirements for personhood in Ancient times. Less precise are the neural definitions sought to explicate "sentience," that is, the capacity to perceive one's environment, pain or injury, suffering or pleasure. The complex, seemingly ineffable states of human sentience constitute our "consciousness."

Defining "consciousness" can be challenging (Koch 2019). We noted earlier that for different philosophers and ethicists the term "conscious" can be multifaceted and complex in character (Kind 2018). The simplest is the notion that consciousness is a state of being "awake." We can expand this definition to include not only being awake, but also being aware or cognizant of one's surroundings. Further, full consciousness for some experts includes not only awareness of one's surrounding, but also the elliptical answer that consciousness is being awake and conscious of one's surroundings as well as aware of one's being and of the mind itself in the world (Brooks and Mehler 2017). In moving from the biological to the neural, concerning the mind and sensory perception of one's surroundings and oneself, our understanding of "being human" remains outside of our own mental grasp. We started our interrogation of being at the one-cell zygote stage. Yet would any of these functional criteria been met by zygotic human life? Some may still quite rightly argue that the embryonic zygote is a human being (Malbon 2013). This line of reasoning confounds assignment of personhood and of being human at stages from fertilization, to implantation, to early fetal development. The same criteria will confound us when interrogating the late stages of *in utero* life as well as when considering the personhood of fully formed adult individuals who lack one or more of the above criteria explicated as required to fulfill the state of being human. This challenge should not and must not dissuade us from the fullest interrogation of all stages and conditions observable in a human life, from the embryo, to the fetus, to the neonate, up to an including advanced stages of adulthood. We may conclude that in 21st century America, personhood as well as the very act of being human are contested routinely for individuals spanning the entire condition of human existence. These assaults on personhood extend well beyond depersonalization of the "other," well into the discounting of human being to the level of subjugation and even sometimes to death. Clearly for the embryonic and developing human being, the most fundamental negative right protected under the U.S. Constitution—the right not to be killed—appears to be at risk. Legally, the precarious nature of the unborn life hangs upon not the determination of life per se, but rather upon the determination of personhood and perhaps the concept of *ensoulment*.

Discussion of soul *versus* soma, mind *versus* body and the four millennial history of "dualism" actually expands the aperture of the core questions. When do we commence being human? When are we assigned personhood? Historically speaking, this question of personhood and when it commences *in utero* for humans was posed long before current vantage points of biological and of advanced neural functioning of humans existed. The primary force driving the question of being human *in utero* earliest was strictly confined to the realm of theology. Philosophers and theologians recognized the immaterial character of the human "soul" and yet, for theological purposes, needed to be able to assign when a soul emerged in a human being (Malbon 2013). This emergence of a soul is termed the process of "ensoulment." The moral question about the practice of abortion would be an important driving force in ascertaining personhood in the developing embryo/fetus. The theological influence of the Abrahamic religions would need to reconcile the notion of ensoulment with prescripts declaring that killing by volition for any reason was a "mortal" sin. In most situations, committing a mortal sin would condemn the violator to *ex*communication from the Church and to eternal damnation. Basically, theologians were asked to answer a simple question. When would an abortion be considered a simple medical procedure (i.e., before ensoulment of the embryo/fetus) in contrast to the sin of murder (i.e., ascribed to the willful killing of an ensouled person)? From a strictly legal perspective, the embryo/fetus has few rights, but ensoulment offered the ticket to a seemingly greater level of personhood. This rudimentary and incomplete level of ensoulment was assigned not to indicate personhood, but rather to insure that if an abortion was performed, it could be declared as murder.

Early Church fathers, absent anatomical information from dissection and the detailed imaging of the 21st century, defaulted to their best guesses on onset of ensoulment. For centuries, the demarcation of personhood, as limited as it was for a fetus in those times, was assigned to the first perception of "quickening." Once a pregnant woman perceived movement of the fetus within the womb, so-called "quickening," by definition of the times, ensoulment of the *in utero* being had occurred. Of course, this definition of ensoulment could put the fetus at risk; in other words, only the pregnant woman was empowered to establish if and when quickening had occurred. That such a declaration would preclude the woman from obtaining an abortion created a potential conflict-of-interest in disclosing quickening by a woman seriously contemplating an abortion. We must keep in mind that up until the 1950s and the advent of effective oral contraceptives, abortion was truly the single most effective means of reproductive control. Prior to the advent of oral contraceptives, only abstinence, physical barriers (e.g., condoms and diaphragms) and abortion were available for women (and their partners) seeking to avoid unwanted pregnancies. For nearly two millennia, papal encyclical letters of the Catholic Church have stipulated that abortion is a mortal sin and that this position is "unchanged and unchangeable." This strict position on abortion as anathema to the Church indeed has not changed. In a 2016 apostolic letter, however, Pope Francis extended indefinitely the power of Catholic priests to forgive women who have had abortions.

Personhood: *In utero* Development and the "Other" Life

Returning to the criteria necessary for assignment of personhood in the fullest sense (e.g., consciousness, capable of being aware of one's surroundings and of one's own being, etc.) we readily perceive the continuing challenge of assigning personhood to the unborn. In the modern era of sonograms, CT-scans, and other imaging capabilities that reveal detailed anatomical development, the status of these higher order sensory functions in the fetus remains enigmatic. If we hold fast to criteria such as perception of the self, the taking of the first breath, demonstration of sight recognition, and other perceptions we are left to guess work about the status of the most of such developmental and sensory landmarks. Well-intentioned efforts to ascertain when a fetus has sufficient higher-order neural function to support the perception of pain are understandable. Unfortunately, the precise time in development when pain perception arises remains controversial. Results from studies aimed directly at probing this question in the human fetus are not without criticism (Malbon 2013). In light of such studies, one wonders if the argument has distilled down to a premise that perception of pain alone connotes ensoulment? Are we confusing theological matters with those of medical science and with a good deal of unfounded speculation? Or are we simply struggling with the knowledge that abortion results in the termination of a human life, ensouled or not!

In its essence, the theological position on the morality of abortion cannot easily accommodate a "grey zone" for people and institutions facing the dilemma of either encouraging or denying a pregnant woman the right (or medical need) for an abortion. Should the Church not take into consideration the medical and emotional status of a pregnant woman? As many bystanders would agree, the right to obtain an abortion for a morally legitimate reason should remain a free choice. What has ensoulment to do with the decision anyway? What conditions could activate the so-called, "universal rule of exceptions" for abortion (Malbon 2013)? This rule refers to numerous cases in which the right to an abortion was upheld although clearly contrary to dogmatic political and theological assumptions on the sanctity of life promulgated by the Church. The reason that we must interrogate the sanctity of life is this, the question of abortion rests upon the knowledge that it centers on the sanctity of *two* lives, not one. Acceptance that two bona fide lives are involved (i.e., the embryo/fetus as well as that of the pregnant woman) remains central to the moral dilemma (Harrison 1983). Recognition of a nascent life as also a "being" was a tough nut to swallow for earlier feminist pro-choice supporters. This truth is a hard truth for anyone interrogating the morality of abortion. Yet if we ignore the life of the pregnant woman, we align ourselves with patriarchal forces that have oppressed the reproductive rights and voices of women for millennia. Early waves of feminism sought to focus the debate surrounding abortion on the rights of women first, almost to the point of considering the *in utero* life as "parasitic." Beverly Harrison (1932–2012) was a Christian theologian and feminist theorist of social ethics who challenged the notion that the embryo/fetus has no rights (Harrison 1983). Pro-choice activists should concede, Harrison proffered, that there are *two* lives in the equation of every abortion decision. Harrison would argue that, once said, women's rights must not be relinquished to the male dominant culture, but rather that there exists a "preferential option" for the pregnant women in which the life of a fetus is not paramount over that of the woman (Malbon 2013). Abortion even may be misconstrued to pit two lives against each other, rather than embracing the intimate relationship between the pregnant woman and a developing fetus. Does the personhood of a developing life need to be discounted? Is contesting the personhood of the pregnant woman the single option? Are both potentials on equivalent moral standing?

Pro-life activists, assigning personhood (and often ensoulment) to the single cell zygote, embryo, or fetus, deny the pregnant woman personhood. Paradoxically, pro-life activists are displaying the very act that they profess to disdain in those advocating for the "other" life; in other words, the life of the pregnant woman whose personhood pro-life activists are assaulting. Pro-lifers argue that there is no choice to be rendered by the pregnant woman! From a standpoint of human rights, it could seem that pro-life groups are arguing for "coercive childbearing!" But yet, to ignore the fact that a human zygote is most likely to be birthed, live and develop into a conscious human being deserving of personhood in full, remains untenable for either pro-choice or pro-life activists. Pro-life activists challenge the pro-choice position endorsing abortion on the grounds that "a woman who chooses abortion can always have another baby." This position may appear true, but it is false and misleading. What remains absolutely true is that an abortion terminates a specific pregnancy, that is, a unique, embryonic life is lost forever. A future pregnancy cannot rescue the termed fetus. Rather, a future pregnancy following an abortion will constitute the creation of another new life, but one different from that of the life lost to early termination of the prior pregnancy. These positions on the morality of abortion highlight the fact that in 21st century America, the topic is "thick" and cannot be reduced to a few sound bytes on either side of the debate. A hard-and-fast set of rules regulating such a monumental and difficult decision will never lend themselves to a paper-thin patina of process ethics. In the abortion calculus, the personhood of both lives is contested (by different groups) and seemingly only one will be granted full personhood. This is true with one overarching exception. If it is a human right for a woman to have the legal option for an abortion and then she choses against this option, then clearly both lives rise to full personhood. This outcome, I offer, would be the pinnacle of ethical decision-making. If a woman is denied the right to choose abortion, then this precious deliberative outcome is precluded. In such a situation, all outcomes must be considered "coercive" and largely consistent with age-old and pervasive patriarchy. Having no choice cannot and should not be misunderstood as "ethical," it is most certainly not!

Careful analysis of recent historical data on the number of abortions performed annually reveals a clear downward trend in the number of elective abortions performed in the U.S. The basis for the decline is not obvious and likely is multifaceted. Our favored outcome on the moral question of abortion would retain absolute free choice by the woman and yet find the number of abortions performed each year declining nearly to zero. Simply on the basis of medical necessity in which a therapeutic abortion is unavoidable (often permitted as necessary under the moral position of St. Thomas Aquinas' "double-effect"), we must accept that not all abortions can be avoided. Medically necessary abortions (e.g., in response to ectopic pregnancies, etc.) would constitute a vanishing small number of abortions performed today, less than 1%. Yet, an operational need of "zero" elective abortions in the continued presence of the legal right to seek an abortion would remain the ultimate goal for the fullest personhood status of all lives concerned.

What strategy could possibly deliver on such a grand proposal? Although untested, the solution that I offer is simple and virtually infallible (Malbon 2013). It requires foremost an absolute national commitment of all people to nascent life, or more precisely, to "all" nascent lives. The challenge then is this, for American society to commit itself to the welcoming of *all* pro-creative acts (i.e., pregnancies) and to the life-long flourishing of *all* lives. Such a commitment for flourishing would not be rendered null and void at the moment of live birth. It is often said that the sanctity of life professed by pro-life activists seems to terminate at birth of a child. Yet, for the grand proposal to succeed, this pledge must extend from birth throughout the entire life span of each new life. If life is sacred at conception, is it not sacred from the womb to the tomb? If American community embraced each and every pregnancy offering a pledge to provide the support necessary for that new life to flourish from womb to tomb, there would be little need for abortion, excepting medical exigencies that place the mother's life at risk, such as severe infection, heart failure, severe preeclampsia, and ectopic tubal pregnancy. When supported by the fullest resources available in community aimed at insuring a flourishing life for all pro-creative events, the need and desire for abortion, I offer, would disappear. This outcome would not violate, but rather support the goals of both pro-life and of pro-choice activists. The pledge would align well with the theological underpinning of most communities of faith.

In researching the topic of abortion almost a decade ago, as a chaplain and counselor, I seldom encountered a pregnant woman for whom the moral dilemma of abortion was not thick with heart-wrenching discernment and deep emotion (Malbon 2013). For those women whom I interviewed, the dominant theme in their seeking an abortion was nearly always economic uncertainty. Then it was the aftermath of the Great Recession driving many of economic decisions for families. The financial legacy of the Great Recession, now overlaid by the Great Lockdown caused by the COVID-19 pandemic, continues to fuel fear and trepidation to those considering the economics of additional child bearing. The stock markets may bounce back, but for those on the underside of economic life in America (i.e., those who are absent adequate living wages as well as base wealth), the aftermath of Great Recession and Great Lockdown in the economics of their lives is still a cause for grave concern. Although a decade later, the COVID-19 pandemic of 2019/2020 again threatens the lives of the food-insecure, shelterless, working poor, and unemployed in ways reminiscent of the aftermath of the Great Recession. Yet, a community with a strong unwavering commitment to fully assist in a pro-creative event and life that follows would nearly obviate the need for abortion, even in such challenging economic circumstances. Made today, such a long-term commitment to the flourishing of all pro-creative events and the lives to follow would essentially eliminate the need for elective abortion (Malbon 2013). Pro-life activists, I argue, fail to adequately understand or empathize with pregnant women that face uncertain futures for their children in 21st century America.

For the embryo and fetus, but to a lesser extent the toddler, the absence of full personhood status can be ascribed to a lack of reaching "full" development, individuation and legal emancipation. For *Homo sapiens*, toddlers remain in development for more than a decade. What contributes to contesting the personhood of these, the "least of us," includes a utilitarian argument termed the "time-relative interest." Consider the case in which a 3-year-old toddler and a 70-year-old adult both are diagnosed with terminal conditions and have less than three months to live. Most would consider the case of the toddler as compared to the older person to be more depressing, since the toddler normally might have had 80 more years ahead by actuarial data. The older person, in contrast, might have less than 10 years available on average. This case displays a "time-relevant interest" for the toddler over the interests of the older person. Yet, commonly we do not extend a time-relative interest to an embryo/fetus marked for a possible abortion. Why is this so? The answer is based upon the notion that for the toddler, much less so for the fetus, attachments to the community are already significant in valuing the personhood (or "potential" personhood) of the 3-year old. The so-called "prudential unity" to the community is far weaker for a fetus, much stronger for a toddler. The older person would have the greatest prudential unity, but in this case the potential benefit already has been largely consumed by a 70-year-old adult. The potential is apparent but untapped for a toddler, yet seemingly limitless although essentially viewed as absent for the case of a fetus? Thus, assaults upon the personhood status of the unborn fetus generally go unchallenged. Paradoxically, assaults occur in spite of the potential of a rich full >80-year life span. Later we shall revisit the important relationality of the community (i.e., "time-relevant interest") and its impact of the deliberations aimed at contesting personhood under conditions outside of those encountered in the simple timeframe of conception, birth and early childhood.

Stillbirth, Personhood & the Personhood Movement

Germane to the discussion of personhood in the context of human development is a paradoxical phenomenon that plagues the medical specialty of obstetrics. The personal struggle for a woman over the moral dilemma of elective abortion is nearly uniformly minimized by pro-choice and perhaps embellished by pro-life activists (Malbon 2013). Proclaiming closure on the biological/theological dilemma of the morality of elective abortion is not so easily accomplished. Establishing when personhood *versus* ensoulment occurs in the developing zygote is equally problematic. Yet, it seems we all can agree that abortion clearly terminates the life of a specific human individual. Death *in utero*, however, can occur under several other circumstances outside of elective abortion, including death in the absence of intent or deed (Cunningham and Williams 2010). If *in utero* death of a fetus occurs at or before 18 weeks of development, the fetus is medically termed to have "miscarried." The woman whose pregnancy ceases in this manner may describe the loss as having suffered a "miscarriage." Other descriptors such as "spontaneous abortion" and "pregnancy loss" would be equally definitive. A "live" birth can occur in this early time frame, although death of the fetus usually occurs shortly after. When death occurs within the 18th to 26th weeks of development, the event now is medically termed a "stillbirth." A birth event occurs, but the stillborn displays no signs of life (Cunningham and Williams 2010). Although associated with complications of pregnancy such as preeclampsia, birth defects, poor health or infection of the mother, the causes for stillbirth can remain unclear (Spong 2011).

In American society there is a tendency to differentiate "fetal-loss" from "child-loss" even if medically speaking the outcome is the same, that is, cessation of a nascent life. With our measuring stick of personhood, it would be hard to argue that abortion (whether elective or spontaneous), miscarriage, stillbirth, and child-loss result in the death of a more or less developed "person." Is the status of personhood equivalent in each of these cases of untimely death? The emotive product and guilt associated with the sum of these losses would suggest that all women who suffer child loss are deserving of societal compassion, empathy, and understanding for the difficult and often tragic outcome (Schroedel 2009).

Medical advice often highlights the need to extend empathy and counseling to the victim of a spontaneous abortion or stillbirth. Yet, no clear similar directive can be found for patient care involving a woman who has just undergone an elective abortion for a fetus that may well fall within the range of miscarriage and stillbirth events (Cunningham and Williams 2010). This tendency to minimize suffering attendant to child-loss on account of elective abortion echoes a patriarchal, perhaps misogynist, theme. Such harsh indifference to the emotive side of losing a child, even if lost to a desperate personal situation and unwelcoming future for the unborn, targets the vulnerable and yet courageous woman who accepts the option of a legal and medically supervised termination of pregnancy (Malbon 2013). To preclude the very fullest compassion and understanding from any one of these victims of child-loss, yes even if the loss is by intent, is to contest the fullness of the personhood both of the mother and nascent life. Stigmatizing a woman who is capable of making a decision of such gravity and anathema to her very being is an assault on her personhood. Pope Francis shames the many that cast the first stone upon the woman courageous enough to spare the future of her existing children and family to seek an abortion for an unwanted pregnancy.

The landmark Supreme Court decision of *Roe v. Wade* provoked a vigorous public debate about our primary topic of personhood and when it is assigned. The Personhood Movement (e.g., Personhood USA) sought to avoid the biological, neural, and theological levels of complexity, simply proclaiming that fertilization was the moment at which full personhood commenced in human development (Farnell 2012). Such a proclamation generated many moral, legal, and practical considerations for Americans wrestling with the question of the morality of abortion. Justices of the U.S. Supreme Court recognized the Pandora's box of legal issues that would arise if the fertilization "event" were afforded legal status by the Bill of Rights (Boonin 2019). The human rights of pregnant women under the same Bill of Rights would suffer, especially in cases of rape, incest, ectopic pregnancy, and loss of the privacy of a pregnant woman deemed to be essential to making such a grave personal decision unfettered by activists of all types. Predictably, during the Obama administration, women's rights and the pro-choice advocates enjoyed a welcomed respite from anti-abortion forces (Greasley and Kaczor 2017). The ascent of the Trump administration in 2016 changed the calculus markedly. Fetal rights and pro-life advocates now rightly proclaimed and enjoyed a greater voice and the upper hand (DeKeseredy and Currie 2019). Opponents of abortion rights view changes in the make-up of the Supreme Court justices attendant to the Trump administration as a prime opportunity for newer conservative (some would offer "patriarchal") jurists to shift the balance of the court towards overturning *Roe v. Wade*. By mid-2019, the tide already had turned towards states' rights *versus* Federal rights. The conservative pro-life states were winning the contest hands down with respect to the question of abortion. The result was an unrelenting avalanche of state laws replete with spurious restrictions aimed at closing abortion clinics rather than protecting the health of pregnant women. With a new conservative majority, the Supreme Court was viewed as leaning towards permitting further restrictions upon the rights of pregnant women in America. For many of these women, the least of us, this judicial turmoil was impacting their ability to deliberate on one of the hardest of personal decisions; in other words, whether or not to seek an early termination of an unexpected pregnancy. It was the intent of pro-life activists that the barrage of newly enacted state restrictions challenging the very existence of abortion clinics in America eventually would provoke an appeal aimed to reach the level of the Supreme Court. Would this strategy work? Would calling of the question of the legal and moral basis of *Roe v. Wade* provoke its repeal? Would not investing time, effort, and resources towards the "grand bargain" offered above to solemnly pledge to secure the birth and futures of all procreative acts in America achieve the same goal? Though compassion and empathy rather than indifference and harsh judgment, *Communio Sanctorum* in moral solidarity can embrace all procreative acts and pledge support for life from womb to tomb.

THE NEONATE/INFANT: A "PERSON" OR ONLY A "PROXIMATE" PERSON?

Striving to Come into Being

Birth is universally recognized as a landmark event signaling the successful traverse of a human developing from *in utero* existence to "life in the world." Yet, for the newly born, "personhood" is neither full nor guaranteed. Is personhood to be granted to a live birth premature fetus (perhaps born at 22–24 weeks of development, weighing less than a kilo in mass), yet withheld from a fetus approaching possible termination in the mid second trimester (weighing 0.5 kilo)? There is no overarching difference between the biological and structural elements of development of these two fetuses, except their expected viability *ex utero*. Survival *ex utero* is about 20–35% of babies born at 21 weeks, rising to more than 90% four weeks later (Wilburn 2014). At best, creating a dividing line between "persons" and "not-yet-persons" based upon such data would be arbitrary. Properties more complex than simple mass and potential viability for achieving personhood have been debated since ancient times. Successful development of consciousness, some level of sensory perception of the world about, and eventually "knowledge of self as being" are acquired later. Thus, the status of personhood for the neonate/infant can rest precariously on rather subjective criteria. No matter how rudimentary the accomplishments of a neonate with respect to the criteria established by others for personhood, the preponderance of data on human development suggest that with additional development and maturation, a neonate will develop through a normal childhood. Six million years of evolution led up to the appearance of modern humans (i.e., *Homo sapiens*) about 200,000 years ago. The robustness of human longevity (more than ~80 years of age) reflects the benefits of this evolution and supports the conviction that in the absence of extraordinary outside intervention, most live births today will continue to live for about eight decades or more. This expected longevity of human beings is precisely why it is important for us to interrogate neonatal life, seeking to ascertain how personhood should be evaluated in neonates. With this robust potential to become a fully-fledged adult member of the species, how can the most fundamental of all human rights—the right not to be killed—be withheld in neonatal human development? More to the point, endowed genetically with the full potential to develop into an adult human being, how can a neonate/infant be deprived of this most fundamental right of full personhood?

The neonatal period (technically speaking only the first 28 days of *ex utero* life) is precarious, especially if spent in an incubator of a neonatal intensive care unit (NICU). Preterm birth, birthing-related asphyxia, infections, and birth defects lead a daunting list of potentially fatal outcomes in the first month of *ex utero* life. Beyond the first month is the period of infancy, extending to the first birthday. Childhood is commonly considered to commence with birth, lasting in legal terms until emancipation of the individual at 18 years of age in the U.S. Operationally, infancy (derived from the French term for "lacking speech, *l'enfant*) routinely extends beyond the neonatal phase for 2–3 years. Hallmarks of this important period of development are acquisition of speech, ambulation, and control of the bowels. "Toddler" may replace "infant" at the moment independent ambulation becomes routine. In spite of the criteria that we apply to humans at any age that are meant to reflect gains in personhood (e.g., cognition, speech, ambulation, bowel control, etc.), progress in early childhood is clearly only proximate and limited with respect to those goals. This raises the issue of whether or not personhood status is achieved only when some mixture of advanced capabilities are achieved? Or is gaining personhood all-or-nothing? On the other end of the age spectrum (i.e., late adulthood), we shall revisit personhood status and note the failure to fulfill more fully these same criteria can lead to assaults on personhood status, discounting or revoking it entirely for the aged and/or infirmed. The danger is this, lacking a legal voice and the ability to defend itself in sophisticated cognate terms, the infant remains at risk to lose the most fundamental right that many associate with birth itself, that is, the right not to be killed. When challenged, life-and-death decisions about neonates/infants most often default to parents or to their legal guardians. This concrete legal morass rightly should correct our initial assessment that *ex utero*, neonates/infants are freed of the dangers of being killed. Today our society largely assigns both normal as well as neurologically or physically impaired neonates/infants as "non" persons, beings but clearly lacking in personhood.

Striving for Full Personhood

It has been offered that every potential person has a *prima facie* claim to the benefits of full personhood, especially the negative birth right to not being killed (Tooley 1983). The premise is that virtually all humans eventually will acquire full personhood and the human right and legal benefit of a right to live. It might be argued that any member of *Homo sapiens*, by birth, has entered upon a developmental pathway that virtually guarantees eventual full personhood, so on what grounds could personhood be contested (Steinbock 2011)? If potentiality grants provisional personhood, then abortion, contraception, or abstinence might seem equally morally wrong. These claims can seem farfetched in a time of oral contraception, legal abortion, and condoms (Sumner 1981). If potentiality is accepted for membership in the species, why do we continue to see situations in which neonate and infants are striving for personhood against great odds? Some would argue that an infant never achieves personhood! Lacking achievement of the criteria discussed above (e.g., consciousness, sense of self, etc.), the infant may be declared undeserving of personhood, deserving only recognition of a potential for *eventual* personhood later in development (Singer 2011). Examples of unassigned, contested, or failed personhood aimed at "the least of us" are global in scope, not confined to the U.S., the Western world, or so-called "modern" world. The numbers are staggering for loss of neonates/infants owing to their lack of perceived personhood status and of negative rights associated with being human. As such, these the least of us lacking personhood become targets for oppression, abuse, and exploitation as discussed earlier exploring the topic of "patriarchy."

A few examples of the scale of assault on the "least of us" will help to inform our perspective. *Gendercide* is the devaluation and loss of female neonates/infants in response to preference for male heirs (Berlatsky 2014). Analysis of the disequilibrium between male/female ratios (i.e., ideally 1:1) in a population opens a window into the prevalence of gendercide, the practice of selective killing of one or the other sex. By such calculations it is possible to estimate that gendercide was widespread in China, eliminating tens of millions of female infants and/or neonates (United States Congressional-Executive Commission on China 2016). Application of the "one-child" policy at a time when sex determination *in utero* by imaging technology was not available provoked widespread female infanticide or "*femicide.*" In China, the one-child policy was so extensive, that in 2020, disequilibrium of female/males has resulted in 40+ million more men than women under the age of 20. Abortion and infanticide provoked by the one-child policy may have resulted in several hundred millions of child losses over the four decades of the policy. South, East, and Central Asian countries also display gender disequilibrium that cannot be readily explained except through femicide aimed at infants, neonates, and children. Patriarchal and patrilineal societies that favor male heirs place great pressures on selection of male-only progeny (Howe and Alaattinoglu 2019). Currently, in places like China and India, screening in pregnancy is employed to identify and selectively abort female fetuses. In the U.S., expensive reproductive technology permits a different approach, that is, selecting sperm in the hope of favoring those carrying a "Y" over and "X" chromosome based upon the lesser mass of a sperm with the considerably shorter Y chromosome. Zygotes can be prepared using selected sperm. Three days later zygotes can be accessed again, cells being screened for sex status using fluorescent dyes. The DNA dyes enable a search for embryos with the tinier XY than XX chromosome pair. The procedure eliminates the need for a later stage abortion. Thus the Petri dish essentially becomes the site of culling female embryos for destruction, prior to implantation (Brysk 2018). This protocol is not unlike that which happens when IVF is employed for infertile couples. Once successful implantation of multiple fertilized eggs has been achieved, a selective multi-fetal "reduction of embryos" is performed. The reduction is therapeutic, aimed at avoiding high-risk multiple births (e.g., as exemplified by an "octo" mom). In all of these cases, embryos, neonates, infants, and children of female gender must strive for personhood, faced with a daunting set of challenges aimed at their demise. In an environment meant to silence these "lesser voices" as well as the voices of advocates who may truly display no conflict-of-interest and seek only to protect the negative rights of females, the obstacles are many. For female neonates and infants, the negative right to not being killed can be lost and nascent lives forfeited.

Neonatal Euthanasia and Infanticide

Above we pondered if by merely "being," all members of *Homo sapiens* were entitled to personhood? Further we queried assignment based upon either current or potential fulfillment of criteria that includes consciousness, awareness of surroundings, self-awareness, as well as acquisition of social and moral attributes. The argument that personhood is to be considered all-or-nothing, either a full person or not a person at all, avoids the complexity of evaluating criteria and assigning personhood. Gendercide (particularly femicide) and gender-selective reproductive techniques alone require discernment about morality, just as does elective abortion. Such cases, which challenge our criteria and definitions of what constitutes personhood, offer little moral certitude. Another challenging situation is presented when a neonate is born lacking a major portion of the brain and skull. Such "anencephalic neonates" display a neural tube defect that precludes the normal formation of the brain (i.e., a brain lacking the telencephalon) and skull. With few exceptions, the anencephalic neonate will survive little more than a few hours or days postpartum. This case represents an extreme in which the self-limiting viability seems to avoid the more troubling questions about neonatal/infant euthanasia. Parents and medical caregivers of newborns with the most bleak of futures often must confront moral questions at the heart of personhood, in this case advocating for the voiceless, the very least of us (Walters 1997). For parents and caregivers the question of personhood of their patient children may not be fully resolved upon diagnosis of an *in utero* malformation. When confronted with a live birth and no real hope of a "life," how are the parents to view the status of personhood for the affected child? During such difficult times of moral discernment, parents of such children also may be confronted with plaintive requests for organ donation aimed to sustain the lives of other children (Caplan, McCartney, and Reid 2015). Infants are sometimes viewed to be in a "probationary" period in which entry into the community of persons must be earned through fulfilling the expected potentials of the species, especially with regard to cognition. For newborns with profound delays in cognitive and physical development even the progressive matter of "degrees criteria" (i.e., attaining some, but not all of the milestones for development) and true potentiality may set the bar too high for personhood. If the bar is set with simple conception, quickening, fetal heartbeat, and/or live birth, on what moral grounds would the personhood of anencephalic neonate be denied?

The moral issue associated with *euthanasia* ("*eu*" = good + *thanatos* = death) emerges in many cases involving children presenting with lethal birth defects (such as anencephaly) and terminal childhood diseases (such as certain brain cancers). These are heart rendering and knotty moral issues for parents and caregivers. A categorical imperative for moral law in the spirit of Immanuel Kant might argue that life is of immeasurable value and ending life should be forbidden (Kant, Gregor, and Timmermann 2012). This imperative might seem acceptable to those who may be experiencing reasonable health. Yet, my experiences in chaplaincy would argue that such a moral imperative is unworkable. Neonatal ICU scenes of incubator-tethered infants in pulmonary distress for whom death is near will transform the observer. Similarly, the experience of being with people suffering intractable pain, who ask the chaplain to pray with them for a speedy death are not to be forgotten. Additionally, such a moral imperative offered above would rob a patient of autonomy, especially a child. Hastening death by voluntary withdrawal of nutrition and hydration may seem appalling to most, yet in reality can be a godsend for those in the throws of unremitting pain. For the newborn whose very best prognosis (even with extraordinary medical intervention) will be limited to a life of hours or days filled with fruitless struggle and certain death, interrogation of the morality of euthanasia remains ever so murky.

For neonates who medically are deemed profoundly defective we still argue for the four pillars of medicine: autonomy, beneficence, non-maleficence, and justice (Klugman 2016). How do we judge the application and success of such lofty goals for the least of us destined for suffering and lives cut short? Euthanasia for infants, neonates, and young children by definition cannot be voluntary. Their lack of full-fledged personhood rightly renders them wards of parents and caregivers. Herein the double dilemma is non-voluntary euthanasia. Non-voluntary euthanasia is a form of euthanasia employed when the patient is a child or may be otherwise unable to give informed consent. I have assisted many fraught parents wrestling with questions concerning moral justification for euthanasia. The most common questions were what are "standard" criteria of selection for voluntary euthanasia (or non-voluntary euthanasia in the case of a child) and how such a morally challenging decision will be made? Their base challenge aims at questioning the inalienable right of a "fully" human person to not be killed (Moreno 1995). It relates to an incomplete individual, a legal nonperson (i.e., a child) whose potential now may be either nonexistent or grim at best. Even when the decision to passively euthanize a severely compromised newborn seems justified, the question of who becomes responsible for the actual decision remains. Parents, attending physician, and caregivers are invited and welcomed into these deeply troubling conversations. No matter how the decision may be made to move forward, in the end it is the voiceless newborn, lacking in the credentials of personhood, whose life will be terminated. For those who remain—in other words, the "survivors"—the issue of contested personhood and euthanasia fuel common feelings of profound guilt that the survivors will take to their own graves.

For some people, moral issues surrounding abortion, infanticide, and child euthanasia are simply nonstarters. There are those for whom such acts are anathema and profoundly immoral. Interrogating these particular moral questions remains irresolvable if the aim from the outset is to generate some simple hard-and-fast "rules." When so promulgated, hard-and-fast rules make unnecessary the very act of deliberation. Arguing that the extension of the existence of a suffering moribund fetus or neonate to give to it a "fuller" life, strikes me as disingenuous. Procrastination only stalls the inevitable and in doing so, may add to the suffering of a nascent being. In the U.S., the "fuller" future is a field of moral landmines. It is a society that has supported original sins, waged chronic conflicts and wars elsewhere to maintain American empire, and promotes a neoliberalism that continues to exploit, oppress, and enable more loss of human lives both at home and abroad. Is extending the existence of a moribund fetus or neonate to enjoy this "fuller" life really morally acceptable? The palpable abhorrence to infanticide based upon gender or economic struggle is understandable, but perhaps only in places where all procreative acts (i.e., pregnancies) would be fully embraced. Under China's former "one-child" policy, the birth of a daughter as the only child, placed the entire family's future in jeopardy and at odds with millennia of tradition and of patrilineal flow of estate and wealth (Anderson, Beaman, and Platteau 2018). Submitting to the one-child rule when that child is female was viewed as putting at risk generations of accumulated assets and insured the need for an expensive dowry (Fong 2004). Yet, can we turn our moral eyes away from the image of a parent intentionally killing a female child in response to such harsh legal realities?

The unborn and infant both suffer in most situations from the lack of assigned personhood. Considering the possible overlap between a late-term abortion and infanticide, why do people generally find the latter more repulsive than the former? From a moral standpoint, it has been argued that *infanticide* is more moral than abortion. American philosopher Michael Tooley (1941–present) challenged the philosophical rigor with which the moral dilemma surrounding abortion often was cast (Tooley 1983). Commonly held views (in the Western world) on abortion, infanticide, and killing of non-human animals provoked Tooley to posit the conclusion that it would be far better and more morally correct to opt out of abortion and rather promote birth with the goal that only in early childhood could one make the best moral judgment about the quality of an individual. Embedded in this logic is the notion that setting aside abortion, thereby delaying the judgment to wherein infanticide or child killing remained the only options, was morally justified. This practice would be enforced for only those fetuses whose potential to develop into fully fledged adult human beings seemed seriously in doubt (Tooley 1983). Thus rather than contesting personhood in the absence of data, Tooley proffered that the proper course was to "wait and see." Opting out of abortion thereby forced a binary outcome of life/death for the toddler, who was intentionally spared earlier from abortion on account of insufficient data. Noted earlier, prudential unity with community is far greater for a toddler than for a first-trimester fetus. This greater prudential unity of the toddler makes Tooley's logic difficult for most people to understand, let alone, stomach, although the logic of the argument is compelling from his perspective. From my perspective, this approach again seeks a hard-and-fast rule for a complicated and thick moral dilemma. It may benefit from rigorous thinking, but seems from my perspective to be off the mark for serious interrogation of personhood in early childhood.

The German philosopher Max Scheler (1874–1928) offered a profound moral insight, encapsulated in the term "moral solidarity." This concept finds the greatest utility when we are confronted with issues contesting the personhood of the fetus, infant, and/or toddler as well as those interrogating the unknown potential for a nascent life to develop into full personhood in a society (Moore 1982). Scheler (Scheler and Stikkers 1980) and later Malbon (Malbon 2013) lifted from such discussions of morality the inescapable role and responsibility of society may play either enabling or precluding the practices of abortion and infanticide. Moral solidarity (Scheler) or *Communio*

Sanctorum (Malbon) provide a perspective that all members of a community bear some responsibility for social conditions that enable abortion and infanticide. If deprived of personhood and made vulnerable to killing, fetuses aborted and neonates euthanized constitute a sin that extends responsibility beyond an individual perpetrator (or group) to a shared guilt among *all* members in community. Scheler argues that within the concepts of community and of shared responsibility every member must claim his/her own culpability for all lapses in moral judgment and action. Malbon suggests that in a responsible "community of saints," all pregnancies would be both welcomed and flourishing insured throughout the newborn's entire lifespan. Both of these ethicists make abundantly clear that a "faceless community," silent on issues of social and moral content, are not truly in community. By definition, they lack moral solidarity. Abortion and infanticide may be the initial topics that call for moral solidarity, but so also would waging war, use on anonymous killing drones by remote control, acceptance of neonatal euthanasia, as well as adoption of capital punishment. In due time we shall visit each of these other topics and ascertain who is assaulting the personhood of the "other"? Additionally, we shall interrogate the grounds on which these perpetrators make such judgments.

Savior Siblings for "Spare Parts"?

The pace of medical advances in the 21st century, especially in regard to reproductive technology, has been nothing short of impressive. Many advances target the infertile couple and those who wish to establish the "genetic health" of a zygote/embryo prior to implantation. As with all advances in medical technology, ethical concerns abound and deliberations always trail rather than lead discussion of the morality of new capabilities that impact human life. From the standpoint of both assigning and contesting personhood, one medical "advance" that poses a conundrum of moral issues revolves about what has been termed the intentional creation of "savior siblings." Currently, by use of tissue typing in conjunction with preimplantation genetic diagnosis (PGD), doctors can select a human embryo for implantation based upon the results of prior screening. In this case embryos are selected for a very unique and specific function. The embryos selected are poised to become a "savior sibling." Savior siblings are a brother or sister capable of donating life-saving tissue to an existing child with a life-threatening disease (Whitehouse 2010). Tissue typing provides screening for an embryo with human leucocyte antigen (HLA) compatibility to the existing sibling. The screen is essential to insuring that the donated tissue from the "savior" sibling, once transplanted to his/her older "recipient" sibling, will not be rejected by the recipient's immune system.

German philosopher Immanuel Kant promoted the idea that a human being has intrinsic value in and of itself. Kant would argue that such value in a cognate, self-discerning, intellectual adult would be cause enough for full undeniable personhood (Kant et al. 2012). Further he offered that rational human beings should always be treated "as an end" in herself/himself. For Kant, regarding human beings "as a means" to something else was immoral. This term "means-to-an-end" refers to any action (i.e., the means) performed for the sole purpose of achieving something else (i.e., an end) has guided decision making in medical ethics. The important element here is the term "sole" which implies that a savior sibling would be created solely to save the older sibling. Frankly speaking, it would seem impossible to most people to believe that the addition of another child within a family unit would be contested on such grounds. Even if additionally created to save a sibling, would not the new child fully integrate into the family unit and be of worth independent of circumstances associated with his/her procreation?

Commodification of human life is anathema to ethics and moral standards almost universally (Smith 2015). Turning a human life, whether an embryo, infant or toddler simply into a ready source for scarce compatible tissues would seem abhorrent. There are at least three counterarguments to the Kantian worry about commodification as we apply it to creating savior siblings. First, as mentioned, the notion that a savior sibling would not be welcomed fully into the family as any new child on his/her own merits seems a stretch. Some might argue that in completing a family unit, the addition of a new child who also can act as a savior sibling might be expected to enhance rather than diminish the savior sibling's standing in the family. Yet, if poorly explained, savior siblings later might question in their own heart if the impetus for their creation was traditional rather than solely utilitarian in nature? Failure to adequately address this quandary might well provoke psychological unrest and depression for the savior sibling as she/he grows. Yet, in the broadest sense, some utilitarian goals for a pregnancy may be as innocuous as avoiding an "only" child family, intentionally enlarging a family, or simply providing for an heir.

A second counterargument proffers that the intrinsic value of any effort aimed at actually saving an existing child from a certain death cannot be underappreciated in the moral sense (Pence 2015). Preserving human life is always a noble cause. Children dying from any number of diseases that theoretically can respond to hematopoietic stem cell transplantation are candidates for transplant from an HLA-compatible savior sibling. Diseases addressable by preimplantation genetic diagnosis, such as beta-thalassemias, Fanconi anemia, and Diamond-Blackfan anemia, can be avoided by the selection of a proper savior sibling from the pool of HLA-compatible zygotes. This dual selection model of identifying the proper savior sibling also provides a real "benefit" for the eventual savior sibling, that is, precluding the child from the suffering or falling prey to a deadly disease. The derivative benefit of providing a cure for a sibling with the fatal disease again gains moral worth as the saving of a precious human life. More than 60% of Americans approve of PGD selection in identifying savior siblings (Bayefsky and Jennings 2015).

A third counterargument is the well-worn excuse that technology in medicine will always advance in front (and not behind) of the moral questions that it provokes. In the absence of clear moral guidelines, the default aimed at banning a technological advance invokes the worry of a creating a "slippery slope" (Walton 1992). According to this logic, failure to adequately address the morality of PGD and selection of savior siblings will create a slippery slope leading to "designer" babies, an outcome feared by many ethicists for a variety of good reasons (Walton 1992). One can recall the application of the slippery slope argument against *in vitro* fertilization (IVF), a technique whose utility and application to infertile couples today is lauded and virtually uncontested. Some would question the morality of "tinkering" with life under any circumstances, although likely not to argue against heart transplants and use of artificial joints. In some cases an antagonist to such advances in reproductive technologies proclaim a theological position that if created in the image of God (i.e., *imago Dei*), humans should not become substrates for editing the Creator's plan.

Does creation of savior siblings herald a new dawn in human evolution, the creation of "designer babies"? This term has a very negative connotation, speaking to trivialization and commodification of human life, editing a human being for one's personal taste? The end point of "creating" specific designer babies is a misnomer. As made clear by the protocol for savior siblings, it is a selection process seeking some specific trait. When the trait is sought to prevent disease, the ethical perspective may be troubling, but is not considered trivial. Are designer babies on that "slippery slope" of ethics to which we often refer, just beyond savior siblings? Beyond selection, however, is true editing of human genes, made possible by employing the powerful CRISPR-Cas9 genome editing capability (Doudna and Sternberg 2017). Some might welcome and embrace the capacity to edit the human genome of a zygote for eye color, hair color, adult height, and so on, in preparing an embryo for implantation. Even simpler technologies, like gestational surrogacy in which a woman offers her womb to carry the pregnancy of another woman to term, are not without some dire moral outcomes (Twine 2015). Recently, a surrogate mother was left with one of a pair of twins who was diagnosed with Down's syndrome while *in utero* (Crockin and Jones 2010). Who becomes responsible when such reproductive advances go amuck? The moral solidarity (Scheler and Stikkers 1980) and *Communio Sanctorum* (Malbon 2013) arguments offer that in a society that enables, permits, or does not preclude the use of such technologies, the moral burden of any untoward outcome (i.e., a human life rendered "defective" on no account of its own) must be shared fully and wholeheartedly among all members of the community. To insure lifelong flourishing of all procreative events in community and with moral solidarity remains an overarching goal for any ideal American society.

Finally, we can neither ignore nor escape the moral responsibility for the "death" of the countless human zygotes/embryos consumed by the PGD screening process. This dilemma is focused on the same moral question germane to elective abortion, to embryo reduction that is standard in IVF treatments, and quantitatively of greater import to the PGD selection process seeking a disease-free, HLA-compatible donor savior sibling. Discarding healthy, but HLA-incompatible (and therefore unsuitable) embryos is killing under our most restrictive definition regarding when life and personhood commences, that is, fertilization. Data derived from actual case studies collected and analyzed for nine couples whose children suffered from anemia/leukemia the number of viable embryos consumed (i.e., killed) in the quest of the "right" ones are startling. In sum, the PGD screening and implantation resulted in five successful pregnancies, but consumed 171 embryos, discarded for lack of suitability. Even if one argues that perhaps 50% of the embryos may have carried the defective gene afflicting the older sibling, 65 viable human embryos were discarded in a plan that yielded five successful pregnancies. So once again, the equation of human loss *versus* human gain forces us to assess what number of human embryos would be too many to sacrifice (i.e., destroy) in pursuit of a single suitable savior sibling embryo? Is discard of 1, 5, 10, 50, or 100 embryos too great a moral sacrifice in the search for a single savior sibling? Perhaps even with a heavily discounted personhood, viable human embryos in sums of hundreds must surely constitute at least one full personhood "equivalent"? When speaking strictly about procedures that abort *in utero* or destroy *in situ* (in a Petri dish) healthy human embryos of normal fertile women, the notion that having another child absolves one of the moral consequences of the selection process consuming many viable embryos is fallacious. Although it is true that a normal fertile woman may become pregnant in the future, the child later produced is not the same child as the embryo/embryos destroyed and discarded earlier in the selection process. Each embryo would yield a unique and valued human being, but not the same human being.

In the last sections we confronted a variety of assaults waged against being human for perhaps the "least of us," that is, the embryo, the fetus, neonate, infant, and toddler. These representatives of early stages in human development all constitute life, which we accept as commencing with fertilization. The quest for defining when personhood commences plagues the interrogation of assignment and weighing of personhood at each of these stages of human life. Ensoulment is a theological concern that speaks also to the issue of personhood. In the cases discussed above, full personhood is almost never assigned to the early developmental stages of being human. Rather, pregnant women, parents, and legal guardians constitute the primary defenders and advocates of record for human rights of these "lesser beings" that we would expect to strive autonomously towards full personhood, if each had a robust voice advocating for their unfulfilled lives. To the extent to which these protectors share the belief that the human right not to be killed is intrinsic to all human life called into being or to the extent to which these individuals may harbor silent conflicts of interest that might benefit discounting the personhood status of their "wards" remains troubling and morally ambiguous. In the next section we exit the early stages of development that conclude with emancipation. We extend the analysis of assignment of personhood to those fully adult human beings whose vulnerabilities can be considered only of body (soma). Historically, physical disabilities place a being's personhood status at risk for discount and perhaps even denial. Lacking full personhood, such potential victims remain in jeopardy for loss of their intrinsic rights to freedom, to flourishing, and perhaps to not being killed!

THOSE WITH VULNERABILITIES

All Human Beings Possess Imperfect Soma

The manner in which we interact with others often reflects on our assignment of the personhood of the "other" based in part on their physical being. In a world of Facebook, Snapchat, Instagram, Zoom, and camera phones, detailed physical being has never been so accessible. Such widespread visual access may reveal features that we like as well as those we dislike and would rather not share, concealed by intent. Vulnerabilities both of a physical nature, involving the "soma" as well as of a mental nature, involving the "psyche," can seriously impact the assignment of personhood by others. According to the U.S. Census Bureau, in 2010 (United States Bureau of the Census 2010), more than 55 million people self-identified as persons with physical and/or mental disabilities. About 50% of these self-reported disabled people considered their disability to be "severe." Exploring disabilities that provoke others to discount or revoke full personhood in children and adults, we shall for the sake of discussion dissect the vulnerable population into two groups: persons with physical disabilities (i.e., those with disabilities in the soma/body) and persons with mental disorders (i.e., those with disabilities in the psyche/mind). This separation at times will be revealed to be imprecise and artificial, owing to disabilities (e.g., Parkinson's disease) in which a progressive, degenerative neural disease provokes a loss of a physical capability or where a physical injury to the brain (e.g., traumatic brain injury) results in a loss of mental function. Irrespective of where the lesion occurs (soma, psyche, or both) persons with such vulnerabilities clearly are marginalized in the U.S. They are forced to accept and to occupy a status of discounted personhood. For centuries, people with physical vulnerabilities were deemed "invalids," derived from the Latin term *invalidus*, coupling "*in*" meaning lacking with "*validus*" meaning strength. Thankfully this pejorative term is no longer employed to further stigmatize those with imperfect soma.

Our current interrogation, much like it was for zygotes, embryos, and fetuses, is designed to pinpoint situations in which the personhood of physically disabled/vulnerable people is contested and employed to assault their personhood. The goal is to identify who is making the judgment on personhood status and on what basis the being of a vulnerable human is contested. The physical complexity of the human being guarantees almost an infinite number of deficiencies, limitations, and imperfections in an exhaustive listing. Therefore we must limit the number of examples to be interrogated. An exhaustive treatment of physical disabilities simply is not possible. Although the treatment cannot be expansive, commonalities emerge among the many bases employed to assault personhood. A Gestalt emerges in which the depersonalization of people with disabilities/vulnerabilities reveals how assaults on personhood stigmatize, penalize, and marginalize the vulnerable in 21st century America. In the case of human beings with early, less fully developed soma (e.g., embryos and infants) there existed no "before" and "after" for comparison of fledgling personhoods. All such beings were deemed absent of conscious awareness and cognate capabilities expressed by the adult. For individuals with physical disabilities and vulnerabilities, this is not the case. For these adult victims often there is a "before" in which their lives were thankfully unremarkable and then an "after" characterized by the disability, viewed in sharp contrast to their earlier being. Disabilities can be acquired virtually at any time in life, including *in utero* (Garland-Thomson 2017). Many are acquired in childhood as well as adulthood. Disabilities and vulnerabilities of the soma often fall within a broad spectrum of severity. They can range from life threatening (e.g., congestive heart failure and cancer), to the cosmetic (e.g., birthmarks, obesity, and general appearance), although equally painful for the vulnerable beings so victimized. Through better understanding of the criteria upon which full personhood of a person with disability/vulnerability of soma may be challenged, we gain insight into our own personal judgments. This effort begs us to answer how do we gauge "personhood" of others? How well are we prepared to internalize the suffering provoked in victims of disability/vulnerability when we discount their personhood, even if only subconsciously? We must accept our own guilt, complicity, and culpability to judge the personhood status of the "other." We encounter these "victims" in our everyday lives. Our own culpability as well as the suffering created in response to our discounting of the being human of the vulnerable "other" truly is universal and all too often overlooked in daily life.

Vulnerabilities in Body (Soma)

People with physical disabilities, by U.S. legal definition, have a physical impairment, medical disorder, condition, or loss that affects the body (Garland-Thomson 2017). Within this definition is a wide spectrum of medical targets including cardiovascular (e.g., congestive heart disease), circulatory (e.g., stroke), digestive (e.g., Crohn's disease), developmental (e.g., spina bifida, dwarfism, acromegaly, Prader-Willi syndrome), endocrine (e.g., diabetes), genitourinary (e.g., kidney failure), hemic (e.g., sickle cell anemia), immune (e.g., AIDS), lymphatic (e.g., lymphedema), musculoskeletal (e.g., osteoarthritis, amputations, multiple sclerosis, paralysis, Proteus syndrome, short stature), reproductive (e.g., precocious sexual development, birth defects, sexually transmitted diseases), respiratory (e.g., amyotrophic lateral sclerosis, asthma, cystic fibrosis, tuberculosis), sensory perception (e.g., blindness, hearing loss), spinal cord injuries (i.e., leading to partial or near total paralysis), and skin (e.g., ichthyosis, severe burns, albinism). Many of these conditions and diseases disable their victims in obvious ways that affect mobility, force reliance on external equipment, shorten life-span, and degrade the quality of life (Garland-Thomson 2017).

Some physical disabilities are less debilitating, can be overcome, and may be easier to conceal visually. Sight impairment, hearing loss, and well-managed cardiovascular diseases are good examples. Disabilities/vulnerabilities that require use of crutches or of a wheelchair or of bottled oxygen, in sharp contrast, are nearly impossible to conceal. Some "cosmetic" vulnerabilities disfigure one's appearance and place an enormous burden on the victims who suffer from public encounters with people lacking tact and compassion. Birthmarks, burns, craniofacial malformations (e.g., cleft palate/lip), keloids, obesity, neurofibromatosis, severe acne, and vitiligo (i.e., absence of skin pigment in white patches on the body, including skin and hair) constitute the most common examples (Patzer 2008). Beyond these explicit conditions are the challenges of a society that values "beauty." The nature of perceived beauty is a complex determination weighing an amalgamation by the beholder of the age, gender, color, body size and shape, and everything from the symmetry of one's face to the color of one's eyes in the object person in question (Rodrigues 2018; Patzer 2008). Human beings constantly take cues and signals from their exterior and interior world that shape views of what constitutes "beauty" (Berry 2007). To the extent that our value system on beauty is out of touch with that of society-at-large or within our own community of friends often creates problems of "self" in our body image (Berry 2008). Consider the possible reception a man would receive upon returning to a high school 30-year reunion as bald, weathered faced, and scaling in at 140% of his ideal body weight? Our responses to the "other" versus "self," even when we too are diminished by vulnerabilities and age, reflect a value system at work internally, even if subconsciously. Our determinations of what constitutes beauty can and do discount, challenge, or assault person-hood of the "other" in subtle as well as significant ways.

Tom B. was a 23-years-old, second year medical student actively engaged in training at a medical school in New York City. Twenty-something students in training engage in learning "medical humanities," encouraged to make use of small group discussions to broach tough topics. Issues such as death and dying, giving good patients bad news, and gauging physician empathy are discussed in a variety of contexts. One session aimed at uncovering how students' personal experiences may color/shape their patient-physician relationships going forward. A question was posed to the members of a small group. Would you share with the group an experience in your past with regard to medical care that remains very much "with you"?

Tom, well known to be shy, was a diligent and gifted medical student. Tom never sought to draw attention to himself in class, so it was remarkable when he volunteered first off to share an experience within the safe space of the small group. With grave reluctance, proportional to the deep suffering he was about to share, Tom commenced. When Tom was twelve he often worked along with a group of townspeople clearing saplings and brush from a wooded lot near his church. His duty was to pick up the small boughs raining down from the guys using chain saws working above him. Their task was to reduce the canopy of trees later to be felled. Tom would haul the larger boughs away from the base of the tree so that they could be dimensioned with a chain saw on the ground. Working late into the afternoon, Tom sought to make up time before sunset would call an end to their afternoon activity. He asked one of the young men with a chain saw to bisect a large limb that he had hauled over. Rather than take the time to secure the limb against the ground, Tom encouraged his friend to make the cut while he held the bough aloft. Tom had put himself in harm's way, facing the blade of an active chain saw. Towards the end of this dangerous stunt the chain saw bucked, the limb snapped. The blade struck Tom's lower face and jaw. The blade cut through his cheek, lacerated his jaw and removed several teeth. Tom was evacuated to a local hospital emergency room, suffering a disfiguring but non-life threatening set of facial injuries. The injury would be dressed, but required eventual reconstruction and plastic surgery. Within his small group, Tom shared the vivid recollection of his first visit to a plastic surgeon, a very sad day. Tom overheard a few comments about his "disfigured" face as his mother consulting with the surgeon. At the elevator on the floor of the doctor's office, Tom's mother ran into a community acquaintance. As if Tom was not even present, the "friend" exclaimed how unsightly

Tom's facial wound was. "He had such a beautiful face. Now look at him," said the friend. "Yes," his mother agreed. "We are hoping that this surgeon can do something with this ugly scar." Tom's wound now extended from his face to his persona, to his very self-image, a wound that had persisted long after the physical scars had healed.

Tom may not have recollected the actual words in that exchange, but the content was clear. Tom wept forcefully as he relived that incident among his classmates. A decade later, after cosmetic surgeries and his eventual growth of a beard, Tom remained deeply wounded. His suffering demeanor brought tears to all eyes. Tom shared with the group that successful plastic surgery and growth of his beard had never overcome the shock and sadness of that incident. The incident assaulted his personhood at a tender age, when he was especially vulnerable about his appearance. He assigned some of his shy demeanor to the aftermath of his accident. His "disability," though now largely hidden, still was shaping his life. He volunteered that this disability left him feeling "damaged" and no longer "whole." The discussion that followed was empathetic, cathartic for Tom, and informed us all about the linkage among perceived beauty, physical vulnerabilities, and inner personhood. Perhaps Tom's desire to become a fine surgeon was a healthy "growing edge" towards a career provoked by his physical disfigurement and daily reflection?

Personhood and Experience of the Physically Challenged and Vulnerable

Who then contests the personhood status of the physically challenged and vulnerable? Quite frankly we all do. Confronting a disabled individual, we often draw back with apprehension and alarm simply because we see the person as "other," certain that the person is not "self." Most often the vulnerability may in no way be physically disabling, for example, a disfiguring craniofacial malformation, a prominent blood-red birthmark, of a remnant scar carrying with it a painful memory. Lacking exposure to the physically disabled, however, makes us particularly uncomfortable in their presence and may rob us initially of our empathic core. We may view the victim more as their disability rather than a person. A discounted personhood often is established by what may be lacking rather than that which is present. A person with a disabled body is sometimes viewed as "incomplete," never fully a person. With no visible history of "before" an injury or loss, physically disabled people may become locked in time to the event provoking the disability. With more experience, or "conditioning," typically most of us develop greater ease and comfort and less distress in subsequent interactions. Anyone who has cared for a loved one who becomes wheelchair-bound due to injury or simple aging will recall the first time they visited a skilled nursing home replete with people using wheelchairs. Within a few months of visits, we are conditioned to the sight and use of the wheelchair. With new-found ease we now can look beyond the contrivance of the wheelchair, seeing rather the person. Only with conditioning, do the physical anomalies seemingly vanish. Apprehension is transformed to empathy and understanding.

In a large medical center, I encounter several staff people who are suffering from disfiguring neurofibromatosis (NF). NF is a genetic disorder often characterized by the appearance of café au lait (patches of light brown skin) spots, fleshy bumps, and benign tumors. Such facial tumors can be disfiguring and their appearance disquieting to the first-time viewer. In hospital elevators, visitors can be startled by the appearance of staff people with NF, while staff familiar with their colleagues are comfortable and interact effortlessly with the victims of this disease. Years ago on a flight to Tel Aviv, I was seated in business class next to a man in his late twenties and his travel companion. This young man was suffering from an extraordinary overgrowth of his skull and soft tissue on the right side of his head. Typically, men's ears average about 6.0 cm in length, 2.0 cm in width. The passenger seated next to me displayed a right ear approximately 30 cm in length, 15 cm in width. The mass of this poor fellow's skull combined with an overabundance of soft-tissue precluded him from speaking. He had great difficulty to breathe normally. Truthfully I was shocked initially by his appearance. I recognized immediately that he was likely suffering from Proteus Syndrome, the result of a developmental mutation of the AKT1 gene. His travel companion discussed with me if I would be uncomfortable seated next to this man for the long flight to Israel, but I was not so inclined. I could not but wonder about the suffering of one with a normal mind and spirit, yet burdened with such a challenging craniofacial anomaly? To most I suspect he was viewed not as a person, but first and foremost as a character like the "Elephant Man." I shall never forget either this tortured fellow or the suffering he must have endured as a consequence of this profound physical anomaly.

Situations like the above reveal the ability of a physical anomaly to provoke anxiety. Our response to the anxiety is to withdraw, reflecting a first-impression judgment. In so doing initially we degrade the personhood of the victim. Generating frank anxiety and absent any exposure to such anomalies, physical vulnerabilities can create the "other." In 1989, I was invited to meet with then president of Boston University, Dr. John Silber. I initially was taken aback where upon meeting at the side of his desk Silber, in a short-sleeved shirt, outstretched his right hand, an appendage that was malformed. Since birth, Silber had suffered with a withered right forearm and rudimentary hand. It seemed to me that Silber was keen to observe my reaction to this physical deformity. I just as brazenly secured his right arm above the elbow and shook his left hand with vigor, admiring his ability to reach over the

divide of a physical anomaly to make me comfortable. We got along famously, and I grew to deeply admired Dr. Silber. It was a learning experience for
me. I was glad to observe a master of skilled communication decant my
apprehension and replace it with true affection for the man.

Aside from such rare individuals as John Silber, frankly speaking, many
people with physical disabilities are subjected to marginalized existence in
the U.S. Vulnerable people are talked down to, talked over, or ignored as if
their personhood has been revoked. Chaplains, for example, are trained to
seat themselves at eye-level or slightly below eye-level when communicating
with someone bound in a wheelchair. Most often the reality of such communication is quite different. Standing over a wheelchair-bound person, people
often carry on conversations talking down to or over the wheelchair-bound.
We discount personhood, operating as if the physically vulnerable are not
part of the conversation or actually not present at all! Examples of our disregard for the full personhood of the physically disabled/vulnerable among us
are all too numerous. Walk through any shopping mall in America and check
it out. What is a typical response of the physically disabled? Distress, anxiety, and avoidance seem a common response. This response depersonalizes
someone suffering with a physical burden, such as a missing limb or pronounced limp. The disabled person may feel stigmatized. Their gifts of an
active mind, valuable experiences in life, and a good heart can be inadvertently delegitimized or intentionally ignored. They are labeled as "other."
Furthermore, some perpetrators of discounted personhood fear being
"lumped in" with the disabled. Honestly, many people feel very uncomfortable in the company of the disabled. Some caregivers, friends, or relatives
express feelings of awkwardness when accompanying someone with a no-
ticeable physical anomaly in public. Ignoring and distancing oneself from a
disabled person becomes a prime defense mechanism. Avoidance seeks to
minimize drawing attention, attention provoked by association in public with
someone trying to manage life with an obvious disability. Such discounted
being and contested personhood can eclipse the fact that a withered hand,
amputated limb, or café au lait spots is only that, a loss or condition endured
by another being who in the broadest sense remains a "person-in-full."

Following an amputation of a foot, or the onset of pulmonary disease, or
simple aging does not the corpus remain largely intact? The necessary presence of crutches, of a portable oxygen generator, or a walker simply reflects
physical vulnerabilities, nothing more. If we can achieve moral solidarity or
enter *Communio Sanctorum*, we can avoid or overcome our seemingly innate
bias towards the disabled, made "other." We can see them properly as folks
who have suffered bad brute luck, that is, as the old adage notes, "bad things
happening to good people." In a moral society with true solidarity, those who
may be wounded in a myriad of ways bodily should be embraced with
extravagant welcoming. Have they not suffered enough! We need to see

these strangers as moral friends, in community, as "self," not "other." The physically disabled/vulnerable simply strive to be afforded their fullest personhood, our acceptance, and unconditional love. Those challenged with drug addiction (explored in chapters 3 and 4), suffering COPD from chronic smoking, or cirrhosis of the liver from alcoholism should remind us that these unfortunate folks are suffering the loss and illness. Their current limitation is just physical, not a character flaw deserving of shunning from the community. When we contest the personhood of the disabled we are not in *Communio Sanctorum*. For our purposes, *Communio Sanctorum* is not a theological construct, but rather as a simple, universal concept of community. It is a community in which all are in covenant with each other, all are "self," share in moral solidarity, and embrace all with love and respect. Who among us does not long to be in true community, in which all are equal, grounded in unconditional love and in responsible moral inclusion and solidarity?

In the real 21st century world, physical disabilities/vulnerabilities provoke assaults on personhood across America. American history and experience bears out this sad fact. The Americans with Disabilities Act of 1990 (ADA) was a national response to our own shortcomings in caring for the disabled, aimed at affording full civil rights to Americans with a variety of disabilities (Bakaly and Schneiderman 1990). The ADA covers both physical (soma) as well as mental (psyche) disabilities. This expansive civil rights legislation demanded reasonable accommodation and accessibility for the disabled in terms of employment (Title I), public entities and transportation (Title II), public accommodations and commercial facilities (Title III), telecommunication (Title IV), and in other areas, such as freedom from coercion and retaliation (Title V). Like most well-intentioned legislation, the ADA yielded great success in many areas. Yet, "soft" discrimination of the folks with disabilities persists. Discounting the personhood of people with disabilities continues. Discrimination based upon physical disability, race, color, and gender, continues to operate *sub rosa*. In day-to-day interactions, assaults and contestation of the personhood of the physically disabled/venerable extract a very high emotional and psychological toll on these victims. Life with a disability is challenging enough. In spite of the ADA, physical vulnerabilities will provoke "otherness." Thus the physically disabled remain marginalized and their personhood the target of fresh assaults. Damage to the inner self can provoke self-loathing and abject suffering that can extend well beyond a physical disability.

Being Fully Human in an Imperfect Soma

What are the consequences of contested personhood for people with physical disabilities? Those who contest the fullest personhood of the disabled contribute to marginalization and discrimination, humiliation, harassment, and intimidation of folks with imperfect soma. When we do nothing to support those victims of such assaults who choose to make a complaint aimed at such discrimination we are out of community. When we equate physical disability with mental deficit, the self-image of the vulnerable is damaged beyond that attendant to a physical disability. When we talk to the disabled in louder than normal voice and employ slower speech patterns, we create or reinforce the false notion that their physical disability limits their mental capacity, which is very rarely the case. "Talking down" to someone constitutes a real time assault on his or her personhood. Not uncommon also is the behavior of infantilizing the disabled. We only reinforce a disability by offering a narrow range of activities that may largely lay outside of their current capabilities. By doing so, we overlook the largely "whole" person who simply suffers with a physical loss, anomaly or limitation. Acting as if the disabled are "helpless," caregivers contribute to infantilizing the people for whom they care. Denigrating the physically infirmed may include assault on their self-image as a sexually mature being, treating them as if they are "proto" asexual human beings. Even terms of endearment employed in caring for children, like "honey" and "sweetie," are inappropriate in assisted-living domiciles in which adults with physical limitations reside. Yes, they may need assistance to overcome the physical impairment, but they are not "proto" human beings. Does suffering a disability mark a retreat to a childlike, prepubescent existence? Do not we demean the personhood of the disabled by highlighting the disability, rather than lifting up the greater being of one who merely is "making do" with the bad brute luck a physical vulnerability?

Seeking full personhood and voice for those of us inhabiting an imperfect soma is not a luxury awarded to the privileged that view themselves as more perfect or normal than their wards. It is an effort aimed at fulfilling our moral obligation to love and to respect all members of *Homo sapiens*. Tens of millions of Americans self-report to be physically disabled. Are we purposefully forgetting that we all inhabit less than perfect bodies? It is not simply a question about to what degrees are we all "disabled"? We need to embrace all people and avoid reinforcing the "deficit" versus the wholly normal "remainder" of the person! Extensive interviews of the physically disabled demonstrate conclusively that irrespective of the degree of true disability, the disabled often self-label using phraseology like "less than whole . . . not a whole person . . . only a half person" (Lindemann 1981). Callous language directed at the disabled shape their self-imagery, their inner well-being. The loss of confidence in one's general health is commonplace for the disabled and alone can be a cause for serious concern. Loss of the ability to largely control one's environment as well as one's soma, common in rehabilitation hospitals and settings, is a well-known trigger for depression and, on occasion, other psychological disorders (Marini and Stebnicki 2018). I have observed that the infirmed with mobility problems often view the life of a wandering but free shelterless person on the streets with great envy. At least the homeless are deciding how to cope with the problems confronting their lives, that is, they are enjoying autonomy. The life of a homeless person often seems to the immobile as preferential to a secure life of constant devaluation of self, demoted to a mere existence as a ward at the mercy of the decision making of others. True autonomy, even if limited, can be a cathartic to the depression provoked by apparent loss of control of one's life. Is it so difficult to understand the hopelessness of physically disabled folks created by confronting a world of disinterested "strangers" and "caregivers" who may subconsciously and inadvertently discount their full humanity? The personal gifts and blessings that remain beyond a disability remain to be fully embraced. A path forward from despair needs to focus on these blessings that remain, not on what has been lost. Hopelessness will remain a formidable threat to the well-being of the physically vulnerable. Encouraging an outlook that uplifts the potential for greater independence and towards a goal of a return to full personhood can help the healing and recovery process.

There are many compelling narratives about hope of the physically disabled overcoming enormous odds. The life of Brooke Ellison is not the only one but is the most compelling narrative to which I bear witness with unbridled admiration. The narrative that Brooke currently offers to medical and graduate students as well as to the world of the physically disabled and vulnerable is an inspiring story of trauma, resilience, and recovery. At the age of eleven, Brooke was hit by a car while walking home from her first day of junior high school. Paralyzed from the neck down and suffering quadriplegia as a result of traumatic injury, Brooke (under care from her mother Jean) went on to graduate from high school with high honors. Harvard accepted her for baccalaureate training. She graduated *magna cum laude* with a BS degree in cognitive neurosciences and later earned an M.S. degree in public policy from Harvard's Kennedy School of Government. Stony Brook University awarded Brooke a PhD in 2015. She now sits on the faculty of the medical school and teaches. Dr. Elison lectures about the challenges of physical disabilities and also advocates politically for greater support of embryonic stem cell research. Stem cell therapy for spinal cord injuries remains for Brooke an essential work in progress. I often recommend medical students, physicians, and healthcare workers to attend her lectures. In advance I suggest that they view the 2005 movie of the week for broadcast television on Brooke Ellison's journey towards autonomy in the face of catastrophic physical loss (Carlo-Simpson and Reeves 2005). When these folks finally meet Dr. Ellison, attend her classes, and listen to her advocacy for stem cell research the response is uniformly one of admiration and love. Recently, Brooke Ellison published an insightful essay on how her vulnerabilities in soma shaped her thinking as a medical ethicist. It is a powerful narrative worth a deep reading and contemplation.

APPENDIX 1: FURTHER NOTES

*Text in italics are callouts to places within the chapter.

Historically, few topics generate more heated debates than those upon the question of the morality of the act of an abortion. "Our prime purpose in this life is to help others." This quote is attributed to His Holiness Tenzin Gyatso, the 14th Dalai Lama (b. 1935). The basic message is not unlike that contained in the first and major precept of the Oath of the Hippocratic Corpus, the oath that has been recited as early as the fifth and third centuries (BCE) by virtually all students upon entering the Calling to be a physician (Cavanaugh 2018). In Latin, the oath's first intention is *"primum non nocere."* translating into "first do no harm." Such phrases call attention to the underpinning of moral solidarity in *Communio Sanctorum*. Our covenant with each other is there is no "other," only "self" in true community. Accordingly, we certainly first should do no harm to each other.

Death in utero can occur under several circumstances outside of elective abortion, including death in the absence of intent or deed. One rightly might query why the issues of abortion, stillbirth, infanticide, and so on, are included here? Certainly normal pro-creative events (from conception), zygotes, embryos, fetuses, neonates, and toddlers historically and time immemorial constitute a highly vulnerable group to assaults on their personhood assignment (and lives). Although technically lacking any disability or deficit, these human lives are simply nascent, lack emancipation, and remain outside of the boundaries of humans benefiting from full personhood. *Thus their disability is simply the vulnerability of not being fully developed and absent of voice* (Malbon 2013). At each of these stages of normal human development there exist those who could and do discount their personhood. The basic negative human rights of virtually all human beings to not be killed can be denied or withdrawn from the not fully developed. We delved into the practices of abortion, gendercide, femicide, infanticide, and similar assaults on personhood that target the "least of us." Inclusion of developing beings and their ongoing vulnerabilities to assault is both proper and timely for any discussion of threats to being human and assaults on personhood.

Discussion of soul versus soma: this discussion extends from the earlier discussion of the evolution of the concept of a "person." Recall the discussion about "dualism" in which there is professed to exist both a body ("soma") as well as a mind ("psyche"). The dualism theories were not fully capable of explicating the complexity of how neural networks operate. Although accepting that neural networks require the soma, dualism remains unable as yet to readily explain human properties such as consciousness, thinking, and self-awareness. For a timely and insightful treatment of the topic of consciousness and neural network, see the recent work of Christof Koch (Koch 2019).

The theological influence of the Abrahamic religions would need to reconcile the notion of ensoulment with prescripts declaring that killing by volition for any reason was a "mortal" sin. Since the landmark U.S. Supreme Court decision of *Roe v. Wade*, the conditions that provoke *ex*communication and eternal damnation with respect to elective early termination of a pregnancy have heightened. Simply supporting a woman's choice to decide whether abortion is a morally permissible act or not has been declared a mortal sin, in and of itself (Malbon 2013). The act of voting for a candidate that even favors a pro-choice stance on abortion has been declared a case of moral complicity that places in jeopardy the eternal salvation of the voter's soul. The Reverend Bishop Thomas J. Paprocki (Springfield, IL) has declared that Catholics who publically support pro-choice views on abortion will be denied Holy Communion (see Bunson, Matthew. 2019. "Bishop Paprocki: Communion Prohibited to Pro-Abortion Illinois Catholic Lawmakers." Kansas City MO: *National Catholic Reporter*, published online June 5, 2019 at: https://www.ncregister.com/daily-news/bishop-paprocki-communion-prohibited-to-catholic-lawmakers-who-voted-for-il [accessed April 30, 2020]).

The foundational position of the Roman Catholic Church (and other conservative orthodox world religions) on abortion indeed has not changed. During the "Jubilee of Mercy" year (commencing December 2017), Pope Francis in a letter to the Church called upon clergy to greater empathy for women who have had abortions, declaring theirs an "agonizing and painful decision." Pope Francis declared that all priests would be empowered to "absolve the sin of abortion" for those who seek forgiveness with contrite hearts. Yet overall the position of the Church on elective early termination of pregnancy remains "unchanged and unchangeable." Over centuries this position of the Church on abortion appears to be monolithic, yet the universal "rule-of-exceptions" clearly applies even to this seemingly "unchanged and unchangeable" dogma (Malbon 2013). For further analysis of the views of Pope Francis on women who have abortions see: Boorstein, Michelle and Sarah Pulliam Bailey (2015), "Pope Francis Emphasizes Forgiveness for Women Who Have Abortions," Washington DC: *The Washington Post,* Acts of Faith, published on September 1, 2015 at: https://www.washingtonpost.com/news/acts-of-faith/wp/2015/09/01/pope-francis-to-allow-all-priests-to-forgive-women-who-have-had-abortions-and-are-contrite/ (accessed April 30, 2020).

People with physical disabilities, by U.S. legal definition, have a physical impairment, medical disorder, condition, or loss that affects the body. People with physical disabilities, as defined by the U.S. legal definition in the ADA are heterogeneous as are the disabilities that they suffer. A comprehensive list of possible physical disabilities/vulnerabilities manifest in the complex and incompletely understood human body renders any attempt at being exhaustive a fool's errand. Thus there is no intention to afford to the reader an exhaustive and detailed survey of physical disabilities and vulnerabilities. Rather, the focus interrogates how those seeking to discount "being human" and to assault "personhood" can exploit physical limitations of the "other." A category of people who lack a perfect soma would include *all* human beings. Excellent sources are cited in the text with which the reader can extend their knowledge of physical disabilities in a more detailed manner.

Are inherent differences in the physical soma to be considered deficiencies, anomalies, or gifts? Defining physical disabilities/vulnerabilities is not at all straightforward. Technically speaking, one could consider physical attributes such as those attendant to race, ethnicity, gender, pigmentation, and other physical characteristics as bases for assaults on personhood. These physical differences provoke assaults simply on the basis of a victim be labeled as "other," someone who presents unlike "self." These physical differences often are adaptations that evolve to sustain life in a harsh environment. Variations of the density of skin pigmentation are perhaps the best example. Yet, increased pigmentation of the skin continues to provoke fear and anxiety of the White ruling class dominant in 21st century America, as it has since the 17th century colonial period of the founding of America. Such fear can provoke assaults on personhood and denial of basic humans rights. Once labeled as "other," people of color are subjected to oppression and exploitation by the dominant White ruling class (see Chapter 5). Challenges posed to indigenous Native Americans and to Africans, African American and their descendants by the dominant White ruling class deprived these people of color of being human. Discrimination and labeling of the "other" fuels both assaults on their personhood as well as subjugation. In order to better understand how the synergy of xenophobia and racism of populist politics in 21st century America powers assaults on the personhood of people of color, we first must explore in detail the nature of the "original sins" initiated in the 17th century. The American empire was founded and thrived due in large part to its two "original" sins.

The life of Brook Ellison is not the only one, but the most compelling to which I bear witness with unbridled admiration. The made-for-television movie *The Brooke Ellison Story* was broadcast originally in 2005. The documentary interrogates the challenges to the spirit that accompany disabilities to the soma. Dr. Ellison's narrative matures, offering more insights into the extraordinary spirit of Brooke and her mother Jean. Recently, Dr. Ellison published a compelling essay on how her vulnerabilities in soma shaped her thinking as a medical ethicist. The essay is part of *Project Muse* and can be viewed here: Ellison, Brooke (2019) "The Patient as Professor: How My Life as a Person With Quadriplegia Shaped My Thinking as an Ethicist," *Perspectives in Biology and Medicine* 62:2 Baltimore, MD: The Johns Hopkins University Press, released 2019 at: https://muse.jhu.edu/article/728491/pdf (accessed April 30, 2020).

REFERENCES

Alberts, Bruce. 2019. *Essential cell biology* (5th ed.). New York, NY: W.W. Norton & Company.

Anderson, Siwan, Lori A. Beaman, and J. P. Platteau. 2018. *Towards gender equity in development* (1st ed., UNU-WIDER studies in development economics). Oxford, UK: Oxford University Press.

Bakaly, Charles G., and Martin Schneiderman. 1990. *The Americans with disabilities act.* Englewood Cliffs, NJ: Prentice Hall Law & Business.

Bayefsky, Michelle, and Bruce Jennings. 2015. *Regulating preimplantation genetic diagnosis in the United States: The limits of unlimited selection* (Palgrave series in bioethics and public policy). New York, NY: Palgrave Macmillan.

Behrman, Richard E., Adrienne Stith Butler, and Institute of Medicine (U.S.). Committee on Understanding Premature Birth and Assuring Healthy Outcomes. 2007. *Preterm birth: Causes, consequences, and prevention.* Washington, DC: National Academies Press.

Berlatsky, Noah. 2014. *Gendercide* (Opposing Viewpoints series). Farmington Hills, MI: Greenhaven Press, an imprint of Gale, Cengage Learning.

Berry, Bonnie. 2007. *Beauty bias: Discrimination and social power.* Westport, CT: Praeger Publishers.

Berry, Bonnie. 2008. *The power of looks: Social stratification of physical appearance.* Aldershot, Burlington, VT: Ashgate.

Boonin, David. 2019. *Beyond Roe: Why abortion should be legal-even if the fetus is a person.* New York, NY: Oxford University Press.

Brooks, Alasdair Mark, and Natascha Mehler. 2017. *The country where my heart is: Historical archaeologies of nationalism and national identity.* Gainesville, FL: University Press of Florida.

Brysk, Alison. 2018. *The struggle to end violence against women: Human rights and the dynamics of change.* New York, NY: Oxford University Press.

Caplan, Arthur L., James J. McCartney, and Daniel P. Reid. 2015. *Replacement parts: The ethics of procuring and replacing organs in humans.* Washington, DC: Georgetown University Press.

Carlo-Simpson, Judy and Christopher Reeves. 2005. *The Brook Ellison story.* T.V. Movie-of-the-Week; color video and sound recording, DVD; 90 min. Culver City, CA: Sony Picture Home Entertainment.

Carlson, Bruce M. 2018. *Human embryology and developmental biology* (6th ed.). St. Louis, MO: Elsevier.

Cavanaugh, Thomas A. 2018. *Hippocrates' oath and Asclepius' snake: The birth of the medical profession.* New York, NY: Oxford University Press.

Crockin, Susan L., and Howard W. Jones. 2010. *Legal conceptions: The evolving law and policy of assisted reproductive technologies.* Baltimore, MD: Johns Hopkins University Press.

Cunningham, F. Gary, and J. Whitridge Williams. 2010. *Williams obstetrics* (23rd ed.). New York, NY: McGraw-Hill Medical.

DeKeseredy, Walter S., and Elliott Currie. 2019. *Progressive justice in an age of repression: Strategies for challenging the rise of the right.* New York, NY: Routledge.

Doudna, Jennifer A., and Samuel H. Sternberg. 2017. *A crack in creation: Gene editing and the unthinkable power to control evolution.* Boston, MA: Houghton Mifflin Harcourt.

Farnell, Brenda. 2012. *Dynamic embodiment for social theory: "I move therefore I am."* New York, NY: Routledge.

Fong, Vanessa L. 2004. *Only hope: Coming of age under China's one-child policy.* Stanford, CA: Stanford University Press.

Garland-Thomson, Rosemarie. 2017. *Extraordinary bodies: Figuring physical disability in American culture and literature.* New York, NY: Columbia University Press.

Greasley, Kate, and Christopher Robert Kaczor. 2017. *Abortion rights: For and against.* Cambridge, UK; New York, NY: Cambridge University Press.

Harrison, Beverly Wildung. 1983. *Our right to choose: Toward a new ethic of abortion.* Boston, MA: Beacon Press.

Howe, Adrian, and Daniela Alaattinoglu. 2019. *Contesting femicide: Feminism and the power of law revisited.* Abingdon, Oxon, UK; New York, NY: Routledge.

Kant, Immanuel, Mary J. Gregor, and Jens Timmermann. 2012. *Groundwork of the metaphysics of morals* (revised ed.). Cambridge UK: Cambridge University Press.

Kind, Amy. 2018. *Philosophy of mind in the twentieth and twenty-first centuries: The history of the philosophy of mind.* New York, NY: Routledge.

Klugman, Craig M. 2016. *Philosophy: Medical ethics.* Farmington Hills, MI: Macmillan Reference USA, a part of Gale, Cengage Learning.

Koch, Christof. 2019. *The feeling of life itself: Why consciousness is widepread but can't be computed.* Cambridge, MA: The MIT Press.

Larsen, William J., Lawrence S. Sherman, S. Steven Potter, and William J. Scott. 2001. *Human embryology* (3rd ed.). New York, NY: Churchill Livingstone.

Lindemann, James E. 1981. *Psychological and behavioral aspects of physical disability: A manual for health practitioners.* New York, NY: Plenum Press.

Malbon, Craig C. 2013. *Abortion in 21st century America.* North Charleston, SC: CreateSpace Publishing.

Marini, Irmo, and Mark A. Stebnicki. 2018. *The psychological and social impact of illness and disability* (7th ed.). New York, NY: Springer Publishing Company.

Miles, Steven H. 2004. *The Hippocratic oath and the ethics of medicine.* Oxford, UK; New York, NY: Oxford University Press.

Moore, James F. 1982. Max Scheler's principle of moral solidarity a bridge between two ideas of God (PhD thesis). Chicago, IL: University of Chicago.

Moreno, Jonathan D. 1995. *Arguing euthanasia: The controversy over mercy killing, assisted suicide, and the "right to die.* New York, NY: Simon & Schuster.

Nilsson, Lennart, Lars Hamberger, Mark Holborn, and Anne Fjellström. 2009. *A child is born.* London, UK: Jonathan Cape.

Patzer, Gordon L. 2008. *Looks: Why they matter more than you ever imagined.* New York, NY: AMACOM.

Pence, Gregory E. 2015. *Medical ethics: Accounts of ground-breaking cases* (7th ed.). New York, NY: McGraw-Hill.

Rodrigues, Sara. 2018. *On the politics of ugliness.* New York, NY: Springer Science+Business Media.

Scheler, Max, and Kenneth W. Stikkers. 1980. *Problems of a sociology of knowledge.* London, UK; Boston, MA: Routledge & K. Paul.

Schroedel, Jenny. 2009. *Naming the child: Hope-filled reflections on miscarriage, stillbirth, and infant death.* Brewster, MA: Paraclete Press.

Singer, Peter. 2011. *Practical ethics* (3rd ed.). New York, NY: Cambridge University Press.

Smith, Malcolm K. 2015. *Saviour siblings and the regulation of assisted reproductive technology: Harm, ethics and law.* Farnham, Surrey, UK; Burlington, VT: Ashgate.

Spong, Catherine Y. 2011. *Stillbirth: Prediction, prevention, and management.* Chichester, West Sussex, UK; Hoboken, NJ: Wiley-Blackwell.

Steinbock, Bonnie. 2011. *Life before birth: The moral and legal status of embryos and fetuses* (2nd ed.). Oxford, UK: Oxford University Press.

Sumner, L. W. 1981. *Abortion and moral theory.* Princeton, NJ: Princeton University Press.

Tooley, M. 1983. *Abotion and infanticide.* New York, NY; London, UK: Oxford University Press.

Twine, France Winddance. 2015. *Outsourcing the womb: Race, class and gestational surrogacy in a global market*. New York, NY: Routledge, Taylor & Francis Group.

United States Bureau of the Census. Geography Division. 2010. *2010 population distribution in the United States and Puerto Rico*. Washington, DC: U.S. Census Bureau.

United States Congress Executive Commission on China. 2016. *Gendercide: China's missing girls*. Hearing before the Congressional-Executive Commission on China, One Hundred Fourteenth Congress, second session, February 3, 2016. Washington, DC: U.S. Government Publishing Office.

Veatch, Robert M. 2012. *Hippocratic, religious, and secular medical ethics: The points of conflict*. Washington, DC: Georgetown University Press.

Walters, James W. 1997. *What is a person?: An ethical exploration*. Urbana: University of Illinois Press.

Walton, Douglas N. 1992. *Slippery slope arguments*. Oxford, UK; New York, NY: Clarendon Press & Oxford University Press.

Whitehouse, Beth. 2010. *The match: "Savior siblings" and one family's battle to heal their daughter*. Boston, MA: Beacon Press.

Wilburn, Josiah. 2014. *Fetal development: Stages of growth, maternal influences and potential complications*. New York, NY: Nova Biomedical.

Chapter Three

Personhood With Vulnerabilities in Psyche (Mind)

MORAL PERSONHOOD AND "MENTAL ILLNESS"

The "Inner" Self

Perhaps Henry David Thoreau best captured the significance of the inner world of the human mind, "Not till we are lost, in other words not till we have lost the world, do we begin to find ourselves . . ." (Thoreau et al. 1932). The "psyche" and the "mind" are synonyms for the "inner self" where the mental self resides. It also is the seat of vulnerabilities of the mind that target the afflicted with degraded and sometimes lost personhood. Few people are more vulnerable in 21st century America than those diagnosed with "mental illness." The complexity of the human mind is laid bare by the myriad of ways in which mental illness is expressed (American Psychiatric Association DSM-5 Task Force 2013). Pathologies occur in thought (e.g., autism spectrum disorder, attention deficit disorders, delusions, insanity, waning cognition in the elderly), mood (e.g., depression, bipolar disorders), anxiety (e.g., PTSD, generalized anxiety disorders, obsessions, etc.), pervasive psychoses (e.g., perfectionism, lack of empathy, narcissism), and hybrid or blended psychopathologies (e.g., complex trauma, panic disorders, personality disorders, addictions including cocaine, opioid, and alcohol, eating symptoms). In 2010, more than 40 million people in the U.S. were diagnosed with some form of mental illness (Whitaker 2010). The classification is imprecise for many disorders. Some people display more than one pathology whereas others may display relatively mild forms of mental illness that require little or no intervention for them to blend into the community. Unlike various obvious physical disabilities (e.g., amputation), mental illness can and is often masked by those afflicted, in order to avoid being placed in a vulnerable state with a label. Contested personhood is a formidable, ongoing and pervasive obstacle both for those suffering from mental illness as well as for their family, caregivers, and advocates. An expansive treatment of this complex and knotty issue of mental disabilities/vulnerabilities is not attempted. Rather, examples are discussed as emblematic of the challenges to personhood encountered by those with mental disabilities/vulnerabilities. The goal simply is to lift up common modalities of how personhood is assaulted, challenged, and often denied for these who are "the least of us," deserving of compassion, care, and love. Importantly, we shall explore the seemingly paradoxical situation of people with mental illness contesting their own personhood and why this occurs.

The "Other" With Intellectual Disabilities

Cognitive ability is highly valued in our current society. In fact, *hyper*cognition is sought after and rewarded in many large and small ways (Post 2000). From elementary school to the very bastions of *hyper*cognition, for example, the ivory towers of academia and gilded towers of industry, we reward intellect with certificates of achievement, for example, the very common "my child was high honor student of the month at . . ." bumper stickers, Nobel prizes, and lucrative careers. Such recognition is not misplaced, but often we fail to recognize that virtually all human capacities can be evaluated (maybe imprecisely at times) in metrics and placed on a simple graph with the "x" (horizontal) axis extending rightward from the apparent absence of the capacity (i.e., folks with profound deficits in intellect) at the origin to the extraordinary upper limits on the right-hand end (Freedman, Pisani, and Purves 2007), a position occupied by such luminaries as Leonardo Da Vinci, Stephen Hawking, John Nash and Albert Einstein.

The "y" (vertical) axis is simply the number of individuals in the general population, each person positioned at his/her own intelligence quotient, plotted upon the horizontal "x" axis (Figure 3.1). The distribution of intelligent quotient (i.e., IQ) scores for the general population then is plotted vertically on the "y" axis, the greater the number of individuals the higher the upper edge of the plot. Such a plot (i.e., a Wechsler intelligence plot) displays a "bell-shaped" curve, wherein the 95% cohort of individuals is found in a range of IQ values of 70 to 130. Nearly 70% of the population is found in the interval of IQ scores of 85 to 115. More to the point, less than 0.1% of the population displays IQ above 145; less than 0.1% of the population displays an IQ below 55! Keep in mind that IQ score is but one metric of human performance, that is, measured intellect. Such bell-shaped curves are not the exception, but rather the norm for virtually all metrics of human performance. The bulk of us populate the mid-region (IQ scores between 85 and

Bell-shaped "normal" Distribution of Intelligence

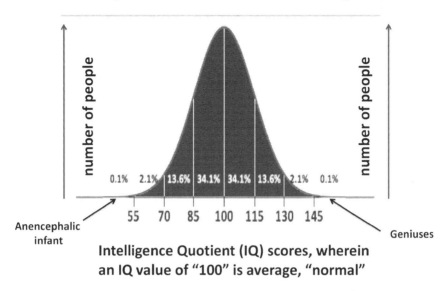

Figure 3.1. Example of Distribution Plot for Human Performance: Intelligence according to IQ Score. Note that the plot, by definition, includes all people. The "X" (horizontal) axis represents the IQ scores of all individuals. The "Y" (vertical) axis is the number of the individuals in the population plotted against their corresponding IQ score. The "normal" distribution for human population versus any metric of performance often appears as shown. This is a "bell-shaped" curve. The midpoint in the center of the "X" axis identifies the "normal" or "average" IQ score (i.e., 100). The population with IQ scores from 85 to 115 constitutes 68% of the population. The population with IQ scores from 70 to 130 constitutes 95% of the population. Both the left (lower IQ scores, less than 70) and the right (higher IQ scores, greater than 130) constitute the extremes of human performance with regard to the metric of intelligence, as measured by the IQ score. The important concepts depicted in this kind of plot are as follows: every person is included (i.e., the plot is inclusive), the bulk of the population appears about the center of the bell-shape, and there always exist "outliers" on the extremes of the low (anencephalic infant) and high (geniuses) ends of the metric, herein IQ scores. Thus, this plot is a graphic depiction of inclusivity and normal distribution of population for virtually any parameter (e.g., height, weight, intelligence, etc.). Created by the author.

115) with the remainder occupying either ends of the metric, tailing off towards the right (highest scores) and left (lowest scores). Perhaps the most important feature to remember, intrinsic to such a plot, is that *all* members of the population are represented. There are no members of the group that exist

outside of this mathematical treatment. Thus, by design, the graph is absolutely *inclusive*, that is, there is no "other," only "self" in this population.

Philosophers and ethicists alike grapple with the concept of "personhood." Society generally seeks expert guidance on how to properly view personhood, not so much for those of us in the mid-range of a "normal" bell-shaped curve (IQ range of 85 to 115), but mostly for those individuals who place at either tail end of the distribution. Goods and services required to insure the proper care and ability of any life to flourish in community also vary when confronted with those who populate either tail-ends of the graph of IQ score. Individuals at either end may have greater than average needs. Often the challenge for professionals is justifying to society at large investments of social resources to target these people with "special" needs. Therefore, let us begin by discussing populations that reside at the extremes on both ends of the IQ graph. At the left-hand extreme margin, for example, would be placed an anencephalic infant. Lacking higher brain structures, such an infant would require enormous medical resources to survive, even if only for a short period. Individuals with extremely low IQ scores (located on the far left of the x-axis, with IQ scores below 55) are relatively rare (demonstrated by the small number of people on the y-axis, much less than 0.1%, Fig. 3.1). Some philosophers/ethicists would argue that in such cases of extreme deficit of intellect individuals lack virtually all the criteria commonly accepted for personhood status (Singer 2011, 2016). In the absence of conscious, rational awareness of their surroundings and of their own being, these vulnerable members of *Homo sapiens* are labeled "defective," precluding them from full person status or from personhood at all. Lacking personhood, those who occupy the left-hand extreme (Fig. 3.1) of IQ score are often categorically denied human rights. Such very low IQ scores rob them of personhood and in some cases rob them of the most basic human right, that is, the right not to be killed! If we accept "defective" labeling for these the "least of us," the least of us morph from "self" into "other." These vulnerable human beings are intentionally differentiated, labeled and separated from "self" and community. Such a community response reflects the absence of moral solidarity and is not *Communio Sanctorum*.

In sharp relief, we generally assume that those "gifted" ones who populate the right-hand extreme edge of the IQ score graph are declared true "geniuses," with IQ scores of 160 or greater. These persons, in the fullest sense, are much like Nietzsche's *übermenschen*. Yet, simple-minded assumptions may lead us to grossly incomplete understanding of the situation. Take the remarkable case of John Forbes Nash, Jr. (1928–2015). Nash was an American mathematician, who made fundamental contributions to game theory and decision-making in complex systems (Nash 2016). His work was recognized with many prizes, not the least of which would be the Nobel Prize in Economic Sciences awarded to Nash, John C. Harsanyi and Reinhard

Selten in 1994. Yet, as illuminated in the biography, *A Beautiful Mind*, Nash suffered from and was treated for profound paranoid schizophrenia, requiring his institutionalization on several occasions (Nasar 1999). Was the cost to society to properly treat John Nash justifiable based upon his periods of brilliant lucidity? Was Nash's intermittent lack of thought grounds by which to assault, challenge, or discount his personhood? Likewise, would the physical disability of noted cosmologist Stephen Hawking, that is, early-onset progressive motor neuron disease also known as amyotrophic lateral sclerosis (ALS), and the considerable cost of attendant care preclude this brilliant fellow from full personhood? Would late stage ALS be grounds to challenge, discount, or deny Hawking's personhood by birthright? Does end-stage ALS (a disability/vulnerability of soma) deny a victim personhood and the human right of not being killed? Individuals displaying thought deficiencies and the ethical queries encountered in the high-cost treatment and care of these vulnerable populations can challenge the very notions of personhood status. The bell-shaped plot of IQ score (Fig. 3.1) will be revisited as we interrogate how personhood status is assigned. Whether or not personhood based upon IQ score alone is all-or-nothing and whether or not the assignment of personhood is final and irrevocable will challenge our notions of justice and care. Keep in mind that as the extraordinary intellectual individuals on the extreme right-hand edge of our IQ plot, victims of mental illnesses and vulnerabilities of the mind on the left-hand extreme are human beings, included in the rich diversity displayed by inclusive community.

Fragile X Syndrome & Autism Spectrum Disorder

The causes of intellectual impairment are many, reflecting the complexity of the functioning human mind and the many genes, environmental factors, and injuries that can damage such an intricate network of neurons. Injuries, that is, traumatic brain injury (Ashley 2018) and anoxia from near drowning (Wilson, Winegardner, and Ashworth 2014), typically are postnatal and can lead to profound intellectual disability in otherwise normal individuals. Identifying a likely genetic basis for intellectual disabilities has benefitted by the availability of newer techniques of molecular biology, such as rapid whole-genome sequencing (which incidentally required several years to sequence the very first human genome), analysis of chromosomes (thread-like molecules that contain hereditary information), and genomic microarrays (Kulkarni 2014). About 20% of the mental anomalies appear to be cytogenetically visible abnormalities of chromosomes. Another 20% of anomalies can be ascribed to submicroscopic copy number variants, in which normal genes are over represented. Single-gene defects constitute another major cause of intellectual disability. A single mutation of the FMR1 gene, for example, has been determined to be the physical basis for fragile X syndrome (Willemsen and Kooy 2017). The presence of the FMR1 gene is essential for normal cognitive development (i.e., translational control in synaptic plasticity) as well as for female reproductive function. In fragile X syndrome, cognitive, physical, and behavioral abnormalities can vary according to the individual's sex, age, degree of gene mutation (i.e., elongation of CGC repeats in the gene), mosaicism, and degree of gene silencing (Willemsen and Kooy 2017). Individuals (i.e., parents) at increased risk of carrying a permutation or full mutation of FMR1 gene typically are afforded preconception and/or prenatal screening to assess the risk of fragile X syndrome in an offspring (Van Herwegen and Riby 2015). In spite of reports speculating as to linkage(s) between intellectual disability and FMR1 that first appeared more than 20 years ago, the details of how such mutations (i.e., an abnormality in genetic repeats and gene silencing) lead to the global changes in intellectual capacity remain obscure. With animal models of fragile X syndrome being exploited and new capabilities for interrogating and editing genomic DNA at hand, continued progress is likely. The story of the FMR1 gene perhaps is paradigmatic of how formidable will remain fully understanding the formation of normal human thought and intelligence. Large clinical studies of affected individuals with gene-based intellectual disabilities and proper controls will be needed to fully validate candidate genes and their influence on intelligence. Beyond single-gene mutations are the role of polygenic (multiple genes) that together contribute to acquisition of or loss of intelligence (Goldstein and Reynolds 2011). It should be clear from research on fragile X syndrome, attributed to a single gene mutation, that advanced techniques of pre-conception and prenatal screening for polygenic (i.e., multiple genes)-based disabilities in intelligence offer even more formidable challenges to those seeking to assess the risk of any potential disorder of intellect in an offspring.

In the constellation of disorders that can alter human intellectual development is autism spectrum disorder (ASD). ASD displays a frequency of about 2.7%, or about 1 in every 59 for 8-years old children (Goldstein and Ozonoff 2018). It is a developmental disorder that disrupts communication and behavior of affected children (Omnigraphics Inc. 2018b). The symptoms of ASD can be detected in the first two years of life. With similarity to the plot displayed in Fig. 3.1, a histogram plot of ASD quotient scores within the general population reveals that indeed it is a "spectrum" disorder. The wide variation of the severity of the many, but not uniform, symptoms of individuals of ASD observed in the general population can be plotted (see Fig. 3.2). In this instance, the Autism-Spectrum Quotient (AQ) scores for 500,000 individuals in the general population are displayed as a histogram (Ruzich et al. 2015). AQ scores with values of 0–11 indicate few autistic traits. AQ scores of 11–21 are the averages scores for the general population. Values of 20–25 indicate above average autistic tendencies. AQ values of 26–31 indicate people who may likely display borderline ASD. Values in the range of 32–50 are strongly indicative of individuals in the general population who display ASD. Overall, the plot reveals that a significant percentage of the general population display weak, strong, or very strong indications of ASD. Thus, this simple plot of ASD character in the general population provides a visualization of how complex spectrum disorders appear clinically when graphed in this plot. Intellectual disability in ASD is really a cognitive deficit that may be so subtle that it cannot be claimed an intellectual disability at all. High functioning autism and Asperger's syndrome (folded into ASD in 2013) include many individuals with "normal" intelligence and yet who display some anomalies within social communication (Rausch, Johnson, and Casanova 2008). ASD may manifest itself in some people with very narrow deficits in, for example, learning abilities, but otherwise display absence of significant deficit in intelligence (Amaral, Dawson, and Geschwind 2011). By design, plots of intelligence of the general population (Fig. 3.1) include *all* people, including those with some ASD traits and other with a probable diagnosis of ASD (Fig. 3.2). IQ scores of individuals with ASD are contained within and overlap with the plot of IQ scores of the general population (Fig. 3.1). From these data, it can be concluded that learning disabilities of many sorts may include a role of intelligence. Keep in mind, however, that alterations in intelligence are not pathognomonic features of ASD.

There is little doubt that children and adults with ASD are victims of discrimination, challenging the dimensions of their personhood (Graham 2008). Questioning the personhood status of children and adults with ASD is not new, but advocacy in recent years has done much to reveal and confront those who contest the personhood of people on the ASD. Human beings are composites of a complex array of interacting skills, gifts, and yes, limitations. Using a narrow metric to contest the being and personhood of the "other" reflects negatively upon the perpetrator and not upon their victims. Educational opportunities geared to ASD children, development of their latent skills, and recognizing the intrinsic worth of these children, as we commonly would for all children, have enjoyed greater public understanding and support due to advocacy by parents, caregivers, and those who care about social justice for all. Children with ASD do not grow out of vulnerability to discrimination. Rather they become adults who rarely escape such victimization, especially that encountered in the workplace (Booth 2016). There are several powerful narratives of overcoming assaults on personhood by those with ASD (Grandin 2011; Myers 2019). The assaults on the individual personhood as well as their families include crushing economic burdens associated with societal and family costs associated with care of ASD people. This will become a recurrent theme upon which healthcare insurers contest personhood. These attacks are not hidden, but rather happen in plain sight. Denial of proper coverage, these families suffer in ways that can degrade the

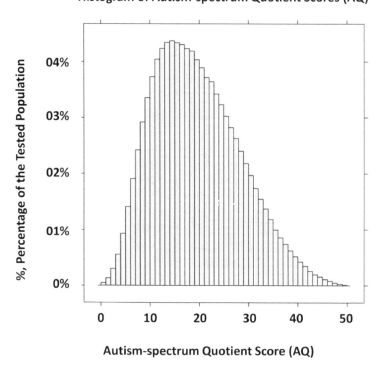

Figure 3.2.   Histogram of Autism-spectrum Quotient Scores (AQ) displayed for a population of 450,394 people in the UK. The AQ test (consisting of 50 questions) was designed to investigate whether adults of average distributed intelligence (i.e., IQ scores from 85 to 115) display symptoms of autism spectrum disorder (ASD). This represents a large data set obtained from nearly half a million adult respondents who, by definition, are considered to possess "average" intelligence. The plot is reminiscent of the bell-shaped curve shown in Figure 3.1. The "X" (horizontal) axis represents the AQ scores of all individuals. For AQ scores, the value 16.4 is accepted as the mean, average value. The "Y" (vertical) axis is the percentage (%) of the tested population plotted against their corresponding AQ score. The plot clearly shows that the distribution of AQ scores is bell-shaped for a large population of adult individuals selected at random and by definition of "average" intelligence. Most human qualities display this same bell-shaped curve. The key determinant is inclusivity, i.e., the plot includes all people. The data show that all people can be related visually within a bell-shaped plot in which all are "self." Selecting out and eliminating people labeled as "other" is not permitted. These data were adapted from the following free and open access journal article: Ruzich E., Allison C., Chakrabarti B., Smith P., Musto H., et al. (2015) Sex and STEM occupation predict autism-spectrum quotient (AQ) scores in half a million people. *PLOS ONE, 10*(10): e0141229, free and open access to article and data from https://doi.org/10.1371/journal.pone.0141229 (accessed on April 30, 2020).

financial status of the entire family. Severe uninsured financial burdens can yield significant and life-long impact on the health-related quality of life for both the ASD people as well as their families and caregivers.

Visualization of bell-shaped depictions (Figs. 3.1 and 3.2) plotting various human traits, properties and performance *versus* population numbers provide insights in the very nature of being human. Generally, in a plot of any human trait, whether height, weight, or intelligence, we readily accept as fact that we can find ourselves, *all* of us, somewhere on the plot. Reflecting upon the profound meaning of such a plot is necessary, as it will reveal visually and numerically our individual connectedness to all other people. We should challenge ourselves to strive to accept *all* members of the fullest community of *Homo sapiens*. All of our unique character, gifts and limitations plot as "bell-shaped" curves wherein inclusivity is guaranteed. All of the people with ASD plot as a bell-shaped curve within the boundaries of the larger, bell-shaped curve of human intelligence (i.e., IQ plot in figure 3.1). All are present and counted. The broad middle core constituting 70% of the population as well as the extreme ends of such plot reveals visually our deep connectivity to one another! We all are contained in the plot, within an array of human beings. Keep in mind that intelligence is only one dimension, one of many criteria of being human. We all are endowed with gifts beyond intelligence that also shape the persons that we are and can become. If inadvertently we examine a single dimension of a person (e.g., height, weight, intelligence, etc.), we only will "see" that dimension. Searching for the fullest person in the "other" requires us to open the aperture of our shared time and empathic engagement. When we see all "other" as "self" in community, we are embracing truly being human, inclusive of humanity's rich diversity and broad spectrum of gifts and blessings (Solomon 2012).

Prader-Willi Syndrome and Down Syndrome

Prader-Willi syndrome (PWS) and Down syndrome (DNS) are important topics to explore in regard to vulnerabilities in psyche, especially those along the dimension of intelligence. People with Prader-Willi syndrome generally display intellectual impairments as well as a constellation of behavioral anomalies such as gross hyperphagia (i.e., marked overeating due to an extreme impairment of the satiety response), deficiencies in pituitary function, obesity, and type-2 diabetes (Whittington, Holland, and Prader-Willi Syndrome Association. 2004). This genetic disorder occurs in one out of every 15,000 live births. PWS results from a genetic aberration in chromosome 15 (15q11–q13) complement. Human cells have 23 pairs of chromosomes, 22 pairs of autosomes as well as one pair of sex chromosomes, 46 chromosomes in all per cell. In most cases of PWS the father's chromosome 15 is deleted, defective, or silenced, whereas the remainder of patients with PWS have two copies of chromosome 15, both copies derived of maternal origin (Höybye 2013). In the absence either of known risk factors or typical Mendelian genetic patterns of inheritance, diagnostic screening for PWS in preconception and prenatal developmental stages currently is not possible. About 95% of PWS children have lower than average intelligence (IQ < 85), coincident with varying degrees of learning disabilities rooted in deficiency in spoken language, although not in either reading or vocabulary. In spite of this IQ deficit, some children with PWS can display robust visual organization and perception. The complexities of brain dysfunction in PWS have been employed to challenge the notion of full personhood for some affected individuals (Jeeves 2004).

Brain deficiencies, injuries, or congenital lesions no doubt shape our personhood, but can they discount, assault, or deny personhood? The financial burdens and quality-of-life concerns for PWS children mirror the earlier discussion about ASD children. Life-long disabilities of psyche can incur a crushing emotional and financial burden to parents and caregivers, especially when health insurers contest the notion of full personhood of affected individuals. Indeed, PWS children can be compromised with respect to intelligence and do often display significant behavioral problems. The PWS cohort, not unlike the ASD cohort, still occupies their places on the bell-shaped curve of human intelligence (Fig. 3.1). Surprising gifts and attributes can be overlooked when limiting the focus to perceived intelligence alone.

One of the most common chromosomal abnormalities found in humans is trisomy (i.e., harboring a third additional copy of a chromosome) 21, or Down syndrome (DNS). This extra genetic material results in overexpression of some portion of chromosome 21 gene complement. In the U.S., about 1 in every 700 live births annually is diagnosed with DNS, with its prevalence annually increasing (Skallerup 2008). Older mothers are more likely to have a child with DNS. In the U.S., the increased prevalence of DNS may reflect an increasing delay in childbearing for women who choose to wait until later in life to start a family. Most individuals with DNS display intellectual deficits considered to be either mild (i.e., IQ 50–69) or moderate (i.e., IQ 35–50). DNS children who present as "genetic mosaics" expressing two different and variable genotypes in a single individual display a somewhat lower intelligence deficit (Pueschel 2006). People with DNS display physical characteristics that are pathognomonic for the syndrome, for example, small chin, a flat and wide face, short neck, and short stature (Mendez 2017). Survival of people with DNS is reduced, with a life expectancy of about 50 years, as compared to ~78 years for non-DNS people. Less than 60 years ago, the life expectancy of DNS children in the U.S. was only 10 years! Integration of DNS children into caring communities that offer advances in medical treatment aimed at the unique deficits of DNS may explain this remarkable increase in longevity (Jacob and Sikora 2016). Those with the requisite learning to attend high school display graduation rates of 40%! Disabilities of people with DNS, however, are not confined to measured intelligence. For example, congenital heart defects are found in 50% of DNS babies. Older adults with DNS display increased risk of dementia.

Assaults on the personhood status for people with DNS deserve special consideration. Perceptions about people with DNS offer important insights into potentials and limitations in assigning personhood and how these perceptions of personhood can change with time. Due to its prevalence as well as the means of early diagnosis *in utero*, DNS presents a thick dialectic on human reproductive rights. Available genetic tests (e.g., through amniocentesis of chorionic villus sampling) coupled with the possibility of early termination of the pregnancy of a DNS child *in utero* creates a difficult moral dilemma for expectant parents (Kaposy 2018). In the U.S. the hard facts are that early termination rates for pregnancies with a diagnosis of DNS is >60%. Termination rates in Europe overall and for some populations within the U.S. exceed 90%! With regard to contesting the personhood for a fetus with DNS, a 2011 report revealed that when non-pregnant people were asked about terminating their own fetus if diagnosed with DNS, 23–33% said "yes." Pregnant women whose fetus were screened positive for DNS, in contrast, eventually said "yes" for therapeutic abortions in 89–97% of the pregnancies. What factors might dominate the decision to welcome rather than to abort a fetus with DNS? As a chaplain, I am sure that one overarching factor is how medical professionals respond to and present the diagnosis of DNS to the parents. Will healthcare professionals embrace the pregnancy offering balanced information on what the life of a child with DNS might be in 2020 going forward? Would they paint a bleak picture of the financial and emotional expenses that might be incurred by a family "burdened" with a DNS child? There is no doubt that when confronted with a fetal diagnosis of DNS and the knowledge that the current longevity of the child would extend beyond their own lives, parents would rightly ask out of concern (Knauss and Martina 2016; Kaposy 2018), "who then will care for my child?" One wonders if it is even possible to enter such a painful dialectic without confronting impossible guilt. Prospective parents know far more about their DNS fetus than do most parents do who are expecting a child assumed to be absent DNS. Courageously, some choose DNS rather than early termination of the pregnancy, shedding new light on ethical evaluation of prenatal testing technology as informative, but not necessarily decisive with regard to the abortion option (Kaposy 2018).

If assignment of moral personhood rests upon criteria of consciousness, perception of surroundings, perception of self, intelligence, reasoning, active memory, and so on, then overly emphasizing a disability in intelligence alone as the sole justification for assaulting the being for children with DNS would be wrongheaded. People with DNS mature and many of these parameters initially viewed as deficits show marked improvement and may respond well to the challenges of increased autonomy desired by DNS adolescents and young adults (McFarlane 2014). As self-awareness and cognitive empathy emerge so does moral behavior based in empathic engagement (Prasher and Prasher 2014). For children and adults with DNS, community is essential. Modeling and developing empathic engagement for folks with DNS most readily evolves in community, especially within communities that display moral solidarity with the "least of us." Family and/or group settings encourage greater social engagement and model compassion, pro-social behavior, and a moral agency, qualities not limited by intellectual disability observed in most DNS children.

Advocacy for human rights for people with DNS takes two forms. The first emphasizes what's wrong with aborting fetuses screened positive for DNS *in utero* (Kaposy 2018). Some may view this position as simply pro-life or right-to-life, but its application to the case of a fetus with DNS prompts a stark moral question (Solomon 2012). Aborting a child diagnosed with DNS assaults personhood, denies the negative right of the nascent life to not be killed. The inclusive community in moral solidarity, our *Communio Sanctorum*, upholds diversity and pledges solemnly to support the flourishing of *all* members, life-long. Pushing against these positions rightly, however, is the human rights of the pregnant woman and family whose emotional and financial concerns, which are quite real, cannot be discounted as either insignificant or unethical (Malbon 2013). The second theme in advocacy of personhood in DNS is simply that there is social good to bringing a child with DNS into this world (Kaposy 2018). Capable of engaged compassion, moral agency, and full participation in family, groups, and community, people with DNS in 21st century America can expect to enjoy fuller and happy lives. In a world that values *hyper*cognition, advocacy of personhood on behalf of people with DNS might seem bold and wildly unjustified to some. Yet, time spent among people with DNS who are thriving in their 3rd and 4th decades of life today would make a compelling case for their robust and uncontested personhood!

Not all philosophers and ethicists support this bold proposal for affording individuals with intelligence disability uncontested personhood (Singer 2011). John Rawls' revised *A Theory of Justice* (1999) offers a Kantian perspective on how distributive justice might benefit from social contracts. Rawls believes that society should optimize liberty, but not at the expense of all other members. In the face of inequality, Rawls recommends that distributive justice must be capped and restricted. Distributive justice is to target only social and economic inequalities. His notion of justice seems to preclude some of the very least of us from personhood and human rights. Protecting the personhood of those with vulnerabilities in psyche follows the dimension of caring, not social or economic inequalities. Eva Kittay sees justice as demanding of inclusivity (Kittay 2001, 2019), much like *Communio Sanctorum* (Malbon 2013). Caregiving in family, modeled about the mother-infant relationship, views the needs of the "other" as self, not to be discounted either by the dimensions of the need or by the competing needs of the caregiver (Kittay 2001; Kittay and Carlson 2010; Kittay 2019). Much like the case for the infant, those with deficits in intelligence or other aspects of psyche are in need of demanding care. They cannot reciprocate, requiring advocates who can give voice to their needs. If restricted to fairness and reciprocity, justice has no place for dependency or lovingkindness (Kittay 2019). Cognitive disabilities morally compel us to care and to act for those who need. Embracing those with intellectual vulnerabilities will help us to get right with our innermost values and the ethics of care (Kittay 2019). Our concept of *Communio Sanctorum* is untenable if covenant is broken for the truly dependent, who are unable to reciprocate for our care (Malbon 2013). *Communio Sanctorum* is untenable if the least of us with the direst needs for care are walled off from our hearts and not included with our community. There can be no moral solidarity in a community that picks and chooses who either is worthy for membership or whose burdens are too great to be shared within community. Thus, the strident position of some ethicists may be based upon solid logic (Rawls 1999; Singer 2011) but absent loving-kindness and deep caring will remain untenable for others (Kittay and Carlson 2010; Kittay 2019; Malbon 2013).

Contesting personhood of people with intellectual disabilities can originate from either the "topside" or from the "underside" of life. From the topside refers to those who contest full personhood of the "other" from their own ethereal privileged position of relative *hyper*cognition. Dwelling in the right-hand extreme of our plots of IQ, these *hyper*cognates are uncomfortable and unfamiliar in the fuller territory of the bell-shaped curve that depicts all human beings relative to IQ measurement (Singer 2016). Yet they fail to observe that both extreme tails of the curve (right-hand as well as left-hand reaches, Fig. 3.1) are "aberrant" by definition, deviating from the "norm" or "normal type." Both cohorts being labeled "aberrant," how would one justify discounting the one (left-handed extreme) while embracing the other (right-handed extreme)? Ethicists, striving to make strong the dependence of personhood status around cognition alone, have problematized the very notion of the "norm." In this specific case, from the underside refers to those who come at the issue of personhood and intelligence from a false "ethical" position around "speciesism." Speciesism is the ethical position that humans have some innate greater value than non-human primates. This position challenges the so-called "animal rights" movement and its core belief that some or all animals should be afforded the same consideration or rights as human beings. Their position often is employed to advance rights for non-human primates or more broadly for *all* animal towards attaining "personhood."

Speciesism, in contrast, makes the broad assumption that humans are superior to all "beasts" (Ryder 1998; Armstrong and Botzler 2008; Singer 2006). This proffered superior position of humans is then employed to justify exploitation of their dominion over all other animals and *sub*humans, echoing the Creation narrative in the Book of Genesis (refer to Chapter 1). Tongue and cheek support for speciesism has become a straw man for some ethicists who intentionally adopt the speciesism mantra that human beings are human based solely upon their innate superior intelligence (and perhaps derivative *hyper*cognition). The binomial nomenclature and taxonomy, *Homo sapiens*, (i.e., Latin translating as "wise man"), is often employed to justify speciesism on ethical grounds and simultaneously to contest full personhood for the cognitively disabled. These assaults on the personhood of the cognitively disabled by those arguing around speciesism (Singer 1975) must be pushed back and viewed askance ethically. For the label *Homo sapiens* was assigned only to extant members of subtribe Hominia, who by some subjective classification were labeled to be of "superior" intelligence. By adopting such abject discrimination on the basis of intelligence, ethicists in this group lumped those with disabilities/vulnerabilities of the mind into the category of "beasts!" Labeling people with a deficit of intellect as "beasts" can and does provoke severe repercussions. As "beasts," these people are deprived of full personhood, negative rights, and at times the fundamental human right not to be killed!

We refuse to enter into such a sham taxonomic trap in which members of *Homo sapiens* who display lower intellect will be assigned the same "personhood" as non-human primates, lower species, and other "beasts" (Kittay and Carlson 2010). The ethicists that argue against granting full personhood to the intellectually impaired would have us believe that assigning people with cognitive disabilities full personhood would require us also to grant similar status to non-human primates, dolphins, Australian sheep dogs and other animals displaying intelligence! Simply put, their notion is that if all humans (regardless of intelligence) are guaranteed the right not to be killed and then so to must all higher functioning *sub*human animals! This "logic" is best viewed with a jaundiced hermeneutic of suspicion. The numbers of non-human and lower species killed by intent by society (>70 billion annually) reveals how specious is such a declaration. Although some philosophers/ ethicists truly may seek to stem the flow of enhanced rights of non-human animals from a perspective of *Homo sapiens* (Machan 2004), the argument can and does flow in the reverse. Seeking to contest the personhood of the intellectually impaired on the basis of their perceived equivalence to non-human species, I proffer, should be a non-starter in ethics. It is no coincident that those who use DNS in their logic purportedly around speciesism often are adherents to same earlier philosophers like Kant, Rawls, and others, who valued rational capacity as the essential foundation of moral personhood. In terms of René Descartes logic, these ethicists would prefer perhaps, "I think less/not, therefore I am less/not." When superior cognitive capacity is used as a moral gauge of personhood status, equal value of all human life will no longer be guaranteed. Such thinking makes those with any measurable intelligence deficit vulnerable, robbing the right not to be killed from those who in this narrow dimension of human function may be truly considered to be "the least of us" (Kittay and Carlson 2010).

The disability rights movement and growing interest in disability studies have raised to the public square many issues encountered by those with vulnerabilities in thought, psyche, and body. The movement should provoke all of us to question the historically lax responses of society to the real obstacles confronting the disabled (Failer 2002; Vaughn 2003; Kittay and Carlson 2010; Kittay 2019). For people with DNS, many obstacles persist even today that challenge their full personhood. DNS can provoke early termination of a pregnancy, restriction of DNS people to actively engage in the community, and obstruction of their human desires for love, companionship, and even marriage. How can we justify assaults on the personhood of people with DNS that deprive them of "life, liberty, and pursuit of happiness" guaranteed to all in the Bill of Rights of the U.S. Constitution? How dare we? Recognizing, receiving, and validating the deep suffering of the marginalized and oppressed with mental vulnerabilities are good first steps in overcoming our long-term stigmatization of those with such disabilities, especially those of intelligence.

I would rather argue from an entirely different perspective, however, aimed at working towards inclusive community. From the technologies guiding early diagnosis of DNS to the improved and improving interventions made available to parents with DNS children for a brighter future, we must admit that we make these investments because these children are part of, not outside of, our community. If we truly embrace every pro-creative event (i.e., every pregnancy and birth) in a community with a lifetime commitment to the flourishing of each and every life, more pregnant women faced with a positive diagnosis of DNS, I speculate, would make their best moral decision. It is not enough to advocate only for the birth of children diagnosed with DNS. We must advocate for the fullest lives of people with DNS, from the womb to tomb. Few of us could fully envision the quandary and heartache of parents wondering about the care of their children with disabilities who will likely out-survive them? If we are to be in moral solidarity with all members of our community, our *Communio Sanctorum*, then all children are our concern. The unconditional love that supports family and community must know no boundaries. To initiate a comparison between a child with an intellectual disability and that of a non-human animal violates our moral solidarity and degrades any hope for *Communio Sanctorum*.

Fetal Alcohol Spectrum Disorder & Fetal Valproate Syndrome

Aside from genetic-based diseases that are either inherited or emerge spontaneously in humans and affect thought, there are environmental insults that can compromise the intellectual potential and capacity of children. In these cases, the children can be considered innocent victims of bad brute luck. In the Old Testament Book of Judges (13:3–4) the narrative of the birth of Sampson offers the injunction, "[3]The angel of the Lord appeared to her and said, 'You are barren and childless, but you are going to become pregnant and give birth to a son. [4]Now see to it that you drink no wine or other fermented drink and that you do not eat anything unclean.'" In the mid-20th century, a linkage emerged between *in utero* exposure to alcohol consumed by pregnant women and a range of physical and mental disabilities with lifelong implications for the children's development. Fetal alcohol exposure then was shown to cause brain and growth problems that mostly are irreversible. Earlier diagnosed and termed "Fetal Alcohol Syndrome" (Abel 1981), the symptoms and conditions associated with prenatal alcohol exposure have expanded and are included within the newer terminology, that is, Fetal Alcohol Spectrum Disorder or FASD (Rodger and Gowsell 2014). Much like the moral dilemma of abortion, FASD also involves both the nascent life as well as that of a pregnant woman. FASD impacts the personhood and future of both the mother as well as the child who suffers from FASD. These assaults on personhood in FASD occur in succession. The first assault targets the pregnant woman who consumes alcohol. Often she may consume alcohol toxic to the unborn out of shear innocence, not knowing that at the time she is pregnant. Yet absent early knowledge of the pregnancy, women who give birth to children subsequently diagnosed with FASD can and have been prosecuted criminally (Clarren, Salmon, and Jonsson 2011; Jonsson 2018). Challenge to the autonomy of the unknowingly pregnant mother, following the aftermath of a child failing to develop properly, especially cognitively, may lead years later to a criminal indictment of the mother (Jonsson 2018).

Absent from the accusatory nature of FASD with regard to the pregnant woman is the fuller understanding of alcoholism and the factors that promote widespread alcohol abuse and addiction in American culture (Watkins 2012; Watson and Zibadi 2017). Based upon my pastoral experience with chemically dependent people, I can swear to the greater challenge of understating more fully the widespread addiction to alcohol. Although my Clinical Pastoral Education included training about addiction, including alcohol use disorder (see DSM-5), I greatly underestimated its prevalence in the general community. Unremarkably, alcohol abuse displays high comorbidity with mental illness. As a society we must remind ourselves that alcohol abuse like any other addiction is a medical condition, not a flaw in moral character! Criminal indictments based upon evidence of FASD are rarely successfully. Paradoxically the failure in prosecution appears to reflect personhood status of the injured party, that is, a fetus, infant or neonate that we have shown earlier to be largely devoid of voice. The very personhood of the aggrieved party, that is, a child suffering with FASD, is contested and declared to be nil by the defense put forth to spare the mother. In its severest form, FASD leads to not only intellectual and cognitive disabilities, but also physical disabilities and social/behavioral issues (Kerins 2015; Sharma 2017). Once again, if in moral solidarity with all members of a community that welcome pro-creative events, *Communio Sanctorum* must assume responsibility for those conditions that provoke alcohol abuse, especially when the addiction targets pregnant women. Even when the scientific data are without question, American society is reluctant to embrace medical advice favoring abstinence from alcoholic beverages, especially for women not practicing safe sex during their childbearing years. Various pundits will proffer that it is a matter of degree only, that is, perhaps a few drinks daily in moderation will not be harmful in pregnancy? The now well-documented toxic effects of alcohol and the toll of alcohol abuse on society should heighten our sense of moral solidarity in community. We should actively seek to reduce these well-known risk factors for both mother and child. Finding satisfaction in criminalizing common behaviors and assaulting personhood of those who need help rather than harsh judgment is a no-win situation. Offering those struggling with alcoholism (also known today as alcohol use disorder) unconditional understanding, love, and support is nuclear to a health community in moral solidarity.

Fetal valproate syndrome (FVS), in contrast to FASD, is a rare disorder that places the lives of either a pregnant mother who suffers from epilepsy, her offspring, or both, at risk. Valproic acid (known in the U.S. as Depakote) is an effective mood stabilizer (e.g., for treatment of bipolar disorder), a seizure medication that effectively manages patients with epilepsy, and also a drug prescribed to treat migraines. Poorly managed patients with epilepsy have seizures and historically (since ancient times) have been stigmatized for the "falling down" sickness. At therapeutic levels for managing epilepsy of a pregnant woman, however, valproic acid *in utero* can provoke lowered IQ, learning disabilities, autism spectrum disorder, attention deficit disorder, spina bifida, and congenital malformations in a developing fetus (Gupta 2017). The first trimester of *in utero* development is the most sensitive to these untoward effects of valproic acid. During this period of human development spinal cord, heart, skeleton, muscles, and genitals are rapidly developing. Although seemingly a straightforward approach to avoid these untoward side effects, cessation of valproic acid may not be an option. Seizures provoked by the absence of valproic acid therapy may be equally damaging to the fetus and potentially lethal for both the pregnant woman as well as the fetus *in utero*. Again we are confronted with a moral dilemma and two possible bad brute outcomes. Should their children display FVS in later development, mothers who require valproic acid therapy to survive typically suffer great shame. The challenges of raising a child with FVS are considerable and often cause great emotional suffering and a lasting sense of guilt for the mother. Children who develop FVS post exposure *in utero* can display a myriad of birth defects. Some defects are profound, provoking a clear and lifelong challenge to the personhood status of the affected child. The mother, in turn, may be severely ostracized, marginalized for making a poor "choice," when only two poor, brute bad luck "options" were available to her. Fully informed of such challenges, *Communio Sanctorum* accepts that even the best management of the mother with valproic acid may inflict injury on mother, fetus, or both. It responds with understanding and empathy, ready and willing to absorb the human and financial losses within the community.

Clinical Research Trials and the Intellectually Disabled

Assaults on personhood often are employed to diminish or eliminate the human right of autonomy. Ideally, autonomous behavior is the ability to act intentionally with understanding and absent of outside controlling influences. For most people, autonomy constitutes self-determination. For Immanuel Kant, autonomy requires rationality, the capacity to determine one's own destiny. For the intellectually disabled, the criterion of rationality and how it is appraised constitute grave threats to their personhood and human rights. The intersection of patient autonomy for the intellectually impaired with opportunities to participate in clinical trials is replete with thick ethical concerns. Whether or not people with intellectual disabilities should participate in clinical research remains a contentious and "hot button" topic in ethics. The fulcrum of the controversy weighs the rights to autonomy versus avoidance of exploitation and of maleficence of intellectually impaired participants in clinical trials (Emanuel 2008). "First do no harm" is the core of nonmaleficence, a pillar of medical ethics. The central question distills to whether or not the intellectually impaired should participate in clinical research at all? Do they have the capacity to fully understand the real risks and benefits of a clinical trial? How is true "informed consent" insured in a population of individuals who have varying degrees of intellect? If intellectually impaired people cannot provide "informed consent," how will clinical trials of potentially beneficial new drugs and protocols that could someday benefit them go forward? Developing clinical trials that aim to balance the risks and benefits of participants who in this case may lack capacity at times and under certain situations is a tall order in therapeutics aimed at people with vulnerabilities of the mind.

Clinical research presents a multitude of ethical dilemmas that require real life decisions in advance in order to protect the patients (Lynch 2019). Unfortunately there exists many examples of exploitation of patients in clinical research. Virtually all of these horrific occurrences required a necessary first step, that is, denying or discounting the personhood of the patient subjects so as to render them as a "means rather than an end." Immanuel Kant declared that employing humans as a means to an end was patently immoral. Kant admonished that each person is an "end-unto-her/him selves" and is not to be "exploited" as they have inherent worth. Recall that we cannot readily apply Kant's logic to our current topic of clinical trials, around personhood and participants with mental disabilities/vulnerabilities. Kant employed the criterion of "rational" as absolute for application of this logic. Rational human beings cannot be treated as a means to an end! How about those of us suffering from mental illness who may display varying degrees of rational thought? Are we no longer protected under the umbrella of this logic of Kant's? Recent history of cases in which participants were denied both autonomy and personhood make clear that clinical research can skirt around true informed consent. Children incarcerated at the infamous Willowbrook State School for intellectual disability suffered such a clear case of exploitation and abuse (Lynch 2019). Children as well as adults suffering with developmental disabilities routinely have been subjected to abuse, deprived of their full personhood. The last decade has been replete with stories from the U.S. and abroad of children who become "wards of the state" only to be mistreated, sexually abused, deprived of human rights and in some circumstances killed. For our purpose of discussion it might seem best to conclude that exclusion of the intellectually impaired from clinical research is the best moral outcome. Yet, blanket exclusion of people with such disabilities from research paradoxically may be unjustified and unfair, amounting to another form of discrimination. Rather, I offer that the overarching issue in allowing for participation in clinical research should be, whose interest is being served by participation of this individual (Emanuel 2008)?

Clinical research may provide therapeutic modalities and benefits only available to participating patients. Research can offer benefits and hope to the intellectually disabled as well as to their families, seeking to participate in furthering understanding about the disability and possible therapeutics. Contesting the autonomy of the intellectually disabled can effectively bar them from participating in any research, even clinical research that may be invaluable to them as well as to others. On the other hand, the history of abuse of this cohort as patients is clear and their vulnerability to manipulation must be carefully weighed (Emanuel 2008). A core concern regarding potential patients for clinical research who have mental disabilities is that of "capacity." Capacity is the ability to make well-informed decisions, not just medical ones. Yet for clinical research, the real question around "informed consent" is whether or not someone whose capacity (i.e., intelligence in this case) may be limited in making decisions about clinical research should participate? This concern gains gravitas when a protocol poses real, potentially severe risks to their health and well-being. Among the cohort of the intellectually disabled, individuals who lack capacity, including some who have never been deemed competent, are the most at risk for exploitation. By default, their participation in clinical research, which may or may not include medically invasive procedures, is left to a surrogate decision-maker (Müller and Schaber 2018). Within the boundaries of clinical research that may provide a clear and direct benefit to the subject, that is, participants with intellectual disability, even never-competent individuals, would seem worthy of deep consideration of their individual risks versus benefits. Non-therapeutic research, in which the participants gain no clear or direct benefit, require the very highest bar for ethical participation (Emanuel 2008). Yet, within a limited capacity to understand and to give informed consent, intellectually disabled patients can exercise altruism and display understanding of the value of increased knowledge that might result from clinical research (Müller and Schaber 2018). Precluding those with adequate capacity to consent participation in clinical research then rightly diminishes their personhood. For the intellectually disabled, well-reasoned analysis of the participant's desire and of the real risks *versus* benefits to the individual (i.e., informed consent) and to society, is both proper and moral, befitting the expression of their rights as persons.

Are we empowering the never-competent individuals with profound intellectual disability to greater personhood when we enroll them into research protocols that have no clear or direct benefit to them and may involve medically invasive procedures? It is one thing to encourage participation of the intellectually disabled in non-therapeutic research to which they consent on altruistic grounds, yet quite another to have a surrogate decision-maker do so for a never-competent ward. Is there any basis for consent in this case? Ethically speaking, it is possible to conclude that if the individual was competent that he/she would likely consent to participation on the same altruistic grounds (Müller and Schaber 2018). Would not we all agree about that which is truly altruistic? Yet, we cannot ignore a basic conflict-of-interest. When some real level of discomfort or pain might accompany a protocol, is it just and proper to have someone else decide that such participation in the clinical trial is justified by altruism alone? Those familiar with the need to obtain blood samples of patients with dementia know well how traumatic the procedure can seem to someone who understands at best only the immediate physical insult and not the necessary reasoning behind it. Others might argue that through participation in research both competent as well as never-competent individuals provide some social benefit to all. This supposition may well be true in some cases. Such justification rests upon a tenuous proposal that non-consenting individuals with intellectual disability "owe" something to the society that they inhabit. Is a *quid pro quo* to be established by others for those protocols that may inflict pain or discomfort on the participant, in this case someone with diminished capacity? From a standpoint of person-hood, suggesting that individuals with diminished capacity truly owe a "debt" to society flies in the face of basic morality. Consider the human right to merely exist, to enjoy free will and autonomy, to thrive, and to be pro-tected by negative rights that preclude suffering unnecessary pain at the hands of the "other," is this the basis for a "debt" owed to society-at-large by the least of us? Do those with intellectual disabilities incur such a contractual debt to society by just existing?

Two subtle points seem worthy of further consideration. First, only a trained physician can assess capacity. "Competence" (or legal capacity), in contrast, is the purview of a judge. The discussion above might be miscon-strued to suggest that "capacity" as well as the related "clinical competence" is a well-defined property that can be readily and accurately assessed. This belief could not be further from the truth. Determination of both capacity and competence often are contested vigorously and with good reason. Second, how well can we insure full comprehension and true informed consent by any participant in a clinical protocol, let alone a person with some intellectual disability? Based upon my own experience in hospital settings in which acute and/or serious medical protocols are being presented to a patient with clear capacity, I only can offer that the real-life trauma in the moment often chal-lenges achieving full comprehension and true informed consent. The alien environment of a hospital, the complexities of the protocol/procedure being discussed, and the duress and human frailty in the moment make full under-standing of risk *versus* benefit almost impossible in some cases. When a potential participant in a clinical research protocol is intellectually disabled, the burden of assessing full comprehension and achievement of an adequate threshold of "informed consent" demands both sincere beneficence and non-maleficence by medical providers, families, and caregivers. Absent intellec-tual capacity and autonomy, the patient remains at grave risk of assaulted personhood. Though diminished in the single dimension of measured intelli-gence, individuals retain the innate right to full personhood. In covenant with each other, *Communio Sanctorum* (our all inclusive community) protects the rights of the least of us, offering unconditional support for the human rights of all (Malbon 2013). This quality is essential to the fabric of moral solidarity and foundational to inclusivity in community.

MENTAL DISORDERS: CREATING THE "OTHER"

Mental Health and Vulnerabilities in the U.S.

In 2016, the prevalence of diagnosed mental illness in the U.S. approximated >2.4 million living within the schizophrenia spectrum, >6.1 million living with bipolar disorder, >16 million living with major depression, and >42 million living with anxiety disorders. The economic, social, and personal impact of mental illness (not including intelligence deficit) are staggering. More than $200 billion in wages are lost annually to mental illness claims. The concurrence of mental health in concert with an addiction disorder is >10 million lives. More than a quarter of 0.5 million homeless adults staying in shelters in the U.S. suffer from a serious mental illness. About a quarter of the 2.3 million adults incarcerated in U.S. prisons, jails, and detention centers have a recent history of a mental health condition. It is unquestionable that members of each of these groups afflicted with poor mental health are stigmatized and marginalized in America. Taken together this domain of mental illness constituted *in toto* the greatest single threat to personhood and to individual human rights facing the U.S.!

Although there are clear similarities in the assaults on personhood for those with physical and intelligence disabilities, the situation for people with mental illness are far more complex and often more challenging to address (Hales et al. 2014). First, the onset of mental illness (e.g., in cases of depression, anxiety disorder, etc.) can be so gradual and subtle that illness can progress without diagnosis and of course without necessary treatment. Even early or first-time psychosis is preceded by changes in thought and perceptions that can appear so gradually that signs and symptoms can be difficult to differentiate from behaviors deemed within the range of normal in adolescents. Second, some forms of mental illness, unlike most physical and intellectual disabilities, are temporary, can self-extinguish or be effectively treated by various types of self-medication. Mental illness can vary in severity, can be temporary or prolonged, and may well respond to appropriate treatment (Black and Andreasen 2014). Third, the symptoms of mental illness may wax and wane. The illness experience can be impacted by interactions with other people, with society-at-large, and within the local environment (e.g., workplace or school). Finally, unlike most of the disabilities discussed above, many mental illnesses are of unknown etiology (Hales et al. 2014). Even in the absence of an etiology, certain factors (i.e., triggers) such as stress can initiate and/or amplify an episode of mental illness. Labels of "mentally ill," "depressed," "schizo," and others stigmatize affected individuals. Labeling, in turn, can provoke assaults upon or outright denial of the personhood of the mentally ill. Such contested personhood can result from routine social pathologizing of ordinary sadness, mislabeling it as "depression."

Vulnerabilities of people with mental illness have an added dimension that is lacking from those with disabilities discussed earlier. Our focus has been upon those in community and society itself that contest being human of the "other." Confronting the world with any disability can be daunting. The disabled encounter people in the external world who actively or passively stigmatize, marginalize, and discount the very being of the disabled. With mental illness we encounter a new dimension, that is, the "inner self" of those with mental illness with which they themselves must contend (Rose 1996). As we examine various forms of mental illnesses and the assaults on personhood derivative of a diagnosis, commonalities emerge about this "inner self" that deserve mention. A definitive psychiatric diagnosis can be the gateway to understanding and treating a mental illness for concerned family and friends. But often the affected individual receives a diagnosis very differently. A diagnosis of "mental illness" almost indelibly impacts the individual's own sense of self, that is, their own perceived personhood. The individual now must contend not only with the interruption of their lives to accommodate the diagnosis (and sometimes new derivative limitations) as well as the treatment, but also must amend their own self-narrative with this new information, that is, they now are certifiably "mentally ill," suffering with a mental disorder (Rose 1996). Typically we build our own narratives based upon inter- and intrapersonal interactions that concern our physical, mental, and social well-being. Diagnosis of mental illness shakes the foundation of our narrative. It must be amended to accommodate a new label that is heavily laden with stereotypes, stigmata, and years of interpersonal interactions with people also considered to be suffering from "mental illness." As we shall see, this intrapersonal dimension of the "inner self" can reinforce the negative input from others. It can dramatically affect our self-laden personhood and how we now look at ourselves being human in light of a diagnosis of mental illness.

Personhood and Disorders of Anxiety, Mood, and Psychosis

Anxiety is a fact of life, perhaps especially modern day life in the U.S. (Omnigraphics Inc. 2018a) If suffered only in the short-term, exaggerated worry, tension, and anxiety may not be a cause for alarm. When generalized anxiety, however, becomes chronic, exaggerated, and with little or nothing seemingly provoking it, the condition is labeled as a "mental disorder." Anxiety disorders is a broad classification and includes panic disorder, social anxiety disorder (or phobia), obsessive-compulsive disorder (OCD), and post-traumatic stress disorder (Hales et al. 2014). Although obvious when poorly controlled by medications or rituals that may temporarily calm the individual, anxiety disorders often are not readily detected by casual friends and strangers, but rather by loved ones and close confidantes. Partners of affected individuals and family members often suffer the public absence of a person dealing with an anxiety or phobia that precludes one or both from social gatherings or events (Russo, Coker, and King 2017). Frustration and anger with such occurrences is not surprising. Thoughtful and constructive anger of a partner or family member should be directed at the situation, not *ad hominem,* at the individual suffering from an anxiety disorder (Russo,

Coker, and King 2017). Already shaken by the inability to live life to the fullest, the individual with an anxiety disorder may be hypersensitive to criticism aimed at an already damaged sense of self. Personhood in this unique situation is in the hands of loved ones as well as the afflicted one, to be either rehabilitated or torn down. The inability to participate in social or other events might lead to the anxious individual being ostracized, which too can damage one's fragile personhood even further. In a community with moral solidarity, the existence of such anxiety disorders would not be hidden but rather shared, openly and without guilt. As part of a community, the member suffering from an anxiety disorder should be entitled to greater consideration, understanding, and empathy. For the anxious person, "self" is fragile. An empathetic supportive community is a proven path to greater self-esteem and confidence for the anxious. Anxiety disorders, like those of mood and of psychosis often are chronic in nature (Balinson 2018), best addressed by a therapeutic community that embraces the solidarity of all as "self," with no "other" (Woo and Keatinge 2016).

Mood disorders also are quite common in the U.S. About 10% of adults report having suffered from a mood disorder in the prior year. Among the category of "any mood disorder," the prevalence is 50% higher for females than males. As age advances from the bracket of 18–29 years to 60+ years of age, the prevalence of severe mood disorders increases from ~4% to ~13%. Yet nearly a quarter of all adults will experience in their lives a mood disorder that requires professional treatment (Muneer 2018). Mood disorders include *major depressive disorder* that is prolonged and persists with extreme sadness, *bipolar disorder* that is characterized by periods of great sadness (depression) and exuberant happiness (mania), *seasonal affective disorder*, depression derivative of medical illness, and depression induced by substance abuse or medication (DeRubeis and Strunk 2017). The onset of these depressive disorders can be insidious and professional health care often is first sought when the emotions begin interfering with work, relationships, or other aspects of one's personal life. With time, certain depressed individual can be diagnosed readily, even by the layperson. Interacting with an individual with depression can be exhaustive in itself and often leads to consequential marginalization or shunning of the affected person (Muneer 2018). This marginalization and shunning by others challenge the personhood of the individual who may already have turned to self-loathing in a depressed state, which only further fragments their self-image. People suffering from depression sense this challenge and often respond by avoiding interaction with other people. In the work place, isolating oneself can reduce productivity and community. At home, interactions with friends and family alike can suffer when depression affects a member of the family unit. These avoidance defense mechanisms are damaging to a depressed person. At the extreme they can provoke loss of a job, marital breakdown, and mounting interpersonal pressures. Fractures to one's personal life can trigger further depression, highlighting both the chronic and the cyclic properties of some forms of depression. Depression and mood disorders in general are associated not only with feelings of sadness, but also with hopelessness, helplessness, and general irritability (Muneer 2018). Each of these facets of emotion affects both the inter- and intrapersonal sense of personhood and in cases often reinforces the negative emotions that pervade mood disorders. We note again that individuals suffering from depression are challenged from without, that is, by those who assault their personhood, as well as from within, that is, at their own hand. Therapeutic engagement aimed to restore personhood and self-image requires intervention aimed at healing the inner self as well as the external "self," best embraced and nurtured by a beloved community in moral solidarity.

Certain forms of mood disorders display a complex, non-monogenic inheritance pattern or predisposition for risk that can be shared by other family members. Bipolar disorder is a prime example of such patterned shared risks (Soares and Young 2016). In the U.S., more than 6 million adults suffer from bipolar disorder, a disease characterized by dramatic and unpredictable mood swings between depression and mania (Vieta, Reinares, and Martinez-Aran 2019). Bipolar disorders are classified into four groups, each of which involves significant changes in mood, energy, and activity. The changes swing from highly elated moods and energized episodes (i.e., mania) to periods of acute sadness and hopelessness (i.e., depression). Seldom suffering mania or depression alone, people suffering bipolar disorder fall upon a broad spectrum of individualized forms, some readily apparent, others more subtle. Commonly accompanying these cardinal symptoms of bipolar disorder are hallucinations and delusions (Vieta, Reinares, and Martinez-Aran 2019). Owing to few clear boundaries with regard to clinical presentation, the term "bipolar spectrum disorders" has gained greater acceptance. Risk for chemical dependence, abuse of licit and illicit substances, attention-deficit/hyperactivity disorder (ADHD), and anxiety disorders is greatly increased in individuals diagnosed with bipolar disorder (Hales et al. 2014). The onset of the disorder is insidious, especially if the symptoms present subtly, typically occurring during adolescence and early adulthood (Singh 2019). Narratives of those suffering from bipolar disorder and of their family capture the challenges that exist in daily life and speak of the challenges to *inter*personal as well as *intra*personal dimensions of personhood. Self-reporting reveals that affected individuals often recognize the damage to personhood that results from aggressive and violent behavior, cognitive impairment, and psychotic events seemingly beyond their control. The response to such lowered self-esteem can be periodic loss of executive control of impulses that leads to drug/alcohol abuse, overspending, high-risk behaviors, delusion of grandeur, and uncontrolled irritability (Rothman-Kerr 2019).

Bipolar disorders largely can be treated pharmacologically as well as through a variety of therapies, for example, cognitive, interpersonal, group support (Ketter and American Psychiatric Association 2015). In spite of improved healthcare for people with bipolar disorders and the mandate of the Americans with Disabilities Act, people with bipolar disorders suffer from marginalization, unfulfilled employment potential, and the stigma of mental illness. In my clinical experience, the situation encountered by people with bipolar disorder can be very disheartening and challenging. Public empathy for forms of mental illness is not uniform. Bipolar disorder promotes social behaviors that can provoke a desensitization of people's empathy for someone struggling with this particular chronic mental illness. Often nicknamed "bi's," "bipolars," "manics/maniacs," or "manic-depressives," these people suffer from stereotypes advanced by the media with a heavy negative connotation. Whereas society may have moved beyond making fun of people with intellectual disabilities, the outward manifestations of poorly managed bipolar disorder provide a caricature largely promoted in the media. Although pitching no potentially therapeutic drugs overtly, direct-to-consumer television advertisements depict bipolar disorder-associated behaviors that most affected people would wish not to expose. The advertisement usually points to a website, which then pitches the drugs being hawked as effective in treatment. One could consider this a "public service announcement" or a shameless example of "disease mongering." Whichever your take, such ads commodify the person struggling with bipolar disorder.

As observed for others with mood disorders in particular, the internal frustration and sense of shame that can pervade their being (even when well-managed) can be amplified and deepened by being ostracized in school, workplace, or social gatherings (or by the mass media). Paradoxically, these same individuals display many qualities of compassion, creativity, and affability that can seem to go unnoticed. Whom do we blame for this deep discounting of personhood suffered by those with bipolar disorders? Truthfully, we all share the blame. Outbursts in public by people with bipolar disorder only reveal a person in an acute crisis, someone who we may never know otherwise. We can become guarded in our response to them, seeking avoidance rather than engagement. Yet, working through the anxiety of strange episodic behaviors of the "other" we may be surprised to discover a person within, not unlike our "self." Suffering under an undue burden from the "outside" as well as the "inside" does not preclude maintenance of full personhood! Many people with bipolar disorder can do well, be gainfully employed, and have a family within a community of support that can assist in their regimen of necessary medications and routine of psychotherapy (Mondimore 2014). If we are to offer true moral solidarity to individuals with bipolar disorder, we must educate our community in advance about such mental illness before an encounter. Prepared with understanding that this is just another medical condition with challenging manifestations, the community can learn to prepare for and embrace the situation when it comes along. Forewarned that embracing those with bipolar disease will require patience, compassion, unconditional love, medical and psychological management promotes more favorable outcomes for the victim and the community. Promoting the dignity of personhood for someone struggling with mental disease is a hallmark of inclusive community, in moral solidarity regarding the worth of all people.

Schizophrenia is the most common functional psychotic disorder. It is a chronic and severe brain disorder that generally affects both mental function and behavior (Marcsisin, Gannon, and Rosenstock 2017). As a "psychotic disorder," it is characterized by an inability to think clearly, to display sound judgment, to communicate well, to behave appropriately, and to comprehend reality (Hales et al. 2014). *Schizophreniform disorder* includes these same symptoms but typically only lasts for a period of 1 to 6 months. *Schizoaffective disorder* is the presence of schizophrenia in tandem with a mood disorder (e.g., depression and/or bipolar disorder). The break with reality and presence of delusions and hallucinations over a lifetime makes schizophrenia extremely challenging to manage. Although far from clear, environmental factors (e.g., psychoactive/psychotropic drug use) and genetic susceptibility towards the disorder (e.g., 50% risk for an identical twin with a sibling diagnosed with schizophrenia) are triggers for the emergence of schizophrenia (Hales et al. 2014). Schizophrenia is diagnosed most often in people in their late teens to early 30s (Black and Andreasen 2014). In my own experience working with families trying to cope with a schizophrenic member, the disorder emerged most often during the first semester or year of university with/without exposure to common drugs of abuse.

Developmental changes in the frontal cortex, culling of specific cortical neurons in maturation, and endocrine agents are likely involved in the timing of emergence of schizophrenia. People suffering from schizophrenia display both positive presenting symptoms (e.g., hallucinations, delusions, hyperactive thinking) as well as negative absent symptoms (e.g., flat emotions, poor social functioning, disorganized thinking, impaired attention, working memory, and executive function) (Marder and Chopra 2014). Lifelong therapy often involves a combination of psychotherapy, antipsychotic and anti-tremor medications, and well-managed healthcare services. In this situation, the positive role that community can play in promoting the well-being of these burdened souls is enormous. Working with homeless individuals, who may suffering from some form of schizophrenia, one comes to see church-affiliated community as a major default support group for these afflicted. Understandably, family patience and resources can be exhausted by aberrant and often offensive behaviors that can accompany schizophrenia. The exhaustion of maintaining a family with a member suffering from schizophrenia can tax and break the back of any family, no matter how dedicated and loving. Remarkably, presence of family and an overabundance of unconditional love during the early emergence of schizophrenia can be the best tool aimed at avoiding lifelong and deteriorating human interactions that often result in homelessness.

With regard to personhood, schizophrenia may represent an extreme, demonstrating the profound influence of inner-self *versus* the outer world on the victim's sense of well-being and personhood. It is a case in which "self" and "other" dwell in one person, confronting each other internally at great cost to personhood. In many cases, the appearance of both the negative and positive symptoms heralds a decline in personhood that often can result in degradation or complete loss of self-image (Harris 2019). Family, friends, and society may pull back from affording understanding, embracing odd behaviors, overlooking offensive actions, and intervening empathetically with people suffering from schizophrenia. Outsiders function more like mirrors. They can reflect what is going on in the inner-self of the person suffering from schizophrenia. The individual, in turn, also is able of critiquing his or her own "self." The social response to the person suffering in schizophrenia itself may act as a trigger, provoking further negative reinforcement to the ongoing loss of self. To the outside world, the loss is interpersonal aimed at the afflicted. For the afflicted, the most damaging revelation of the loss of self emanates from the changed, inner world of the self. The inner world of the self is sometimes referred to as "ipseity," the quality of being oneself (Tsuang, Faraone, and Glatt 2019). More accurately ipseity can be described as *deep* selfhood. Loss of ipseity is not only as a loss of self, but a loss of selfhood to the world. Aspects of selfhood can be transformed into external objects as viewed by the afflicted. The afflicted may become aware of a loss of the sense of "being there" in the world. It seems to them that their very presence is slipping away (Tsuang, Faraone, and Glatt 2019). Thus, in our analysis of personhood and the nature of being, schizophrenia may present as the very extreme of loss of personhood. In this difficult case, the afflicted individual can contest the being in their inner self and provoke a complete loss of ipseity. Recovery of personhood to any significant extent becomes nearly impossible as the disorder progresses in many individuals. These observations of people with schizophrenia provide a powerful insight into how the "*inter-*" and well as "*intra-*" personal assessments of self-operate to constitute personhood in normal individuals. Depersonalization by the "other" alone, like self-provoked loss-of-self by itself, is capable of degrading personhood. Paradoxically, in schizophrenia, the ultimate source of contested personhood becomes the self. The example of schizophrenia reveals in a compelling way the existence of two interacting poles guiding selfhood and ipseity, one created by the "other," a second created by "self."

Disorders of Eating, Impulse Control, and Personality Disorders

As noted above, challenges to being human and fulfilled personhood can arise from without, from the "other," and sometimes from within, from the "self." Complex mental illnesses can be dominated by contested being from inputs from the either "self" or "other," or from a dynamic hybrid of both forces. It may shock most to learn that of all mental illnesses, eating disorders show the highest mortality (Mehler and Andersen 2017). Prominent eating disorders, such as anorexia nervosa, bulimia nervosa, and binge-eating disorder, are severe psychiatric syndromes whose causes are far from definite, but may include social, cultural, psychological, and biological factors (Wade 2017). Nearly 30 million people in the U.S. suffer from eating disorders, with women constituting the largest percentage in all three disorders. Approximately 10 million women are diagnosed with anorexia nervosa. In addition to death through malnutrition, 1 in 5 deaths of people with anorexia nervosa is by suicide. Nearly half of all people suffering from anorexia nervosa, bulimia nervosa, or binge-eating disorder have a comorbid mood or anxiety disorder (Abraham 2016). In anorexia patients, anxiety disorders co-present along with obsessive-compulsive disorders and social phobia. Substance abuse disorder, usually alcohol, also is comorbid with bulimia and with binge eating (Hales et al. 2014).

Understanding the complex interplay between "self" and "other" in personhood of someone with an eating disorder is a challenge. It is likely that input from the "other," such as culturally dominant notions of appearance, shape, body, and personhood itself, act in synergy to enable the ultimate expression of an eating disorder. These inputs and those from the inner self lead to self-constructs aimed at ameliorating the tension between perception (which can in some people be very much distorted) and reality. In my own experience, limited to young women with anorexia nervosa or binge-eating disorder, the "other" seemed to be seizing control of their lives, demanding submission or at least some accommodation. In the absence of a significant inner voice with which to counter such demands, the control of "self" could only be achieved by dramatic, self-injuring behavior. In one case a young, well-nourished woman reluctantly submitted to marriage to an eligible young medical student, only to be crushed by patriarchy of the husband (demanding sexual submission) and in-laws (demanding grandchildren). Over the course of six months, this well-nourished young woman lost more than 50 pounds of body mass. Eventually she was diagnosed with a severe case of anorexia nervosa. In a second case, a young woman living at home and sexually abused by a step-father displays the symptoms of anorexia nervosa that trimmed away most of her body fat, including the fat normally deposited during the development of secondary sexual characteristic as an apparent push back to sexual advances. Emerging with this drive to an asexual body shape was a paradoxical behavior. The young woman donned sexually revealing clothes as a response, presumably aimed to disappoint her aggressor with display of her new asexual body morphology. Both of these young women displayed the emergence of anorexia as a "last-defense," a desperate act aimed to diminish the sexual being within them. In some cases young women suffering from anorexia nervosa starve themselves to the point of seeking, literally, to disappear (Zanetti et al. 2014). The untrained layperson draws the erroneous conclusion that the anorexia simply is a "metabolic disease," one characterized by wasting away. In fact, it is a profound eating disorder in which the inner "self" is left to contend with a perceived negative body image through starvation. Herein personhood is assaulted by "self." The "other" is quite unaware of the basis for the lack of eating, owing the weight loss simply to a poor appetite or to intentional dieting. Consequently the "other" can team up with "self" to exacerbate the suffering through misguided advice on eating and a total lack of compassion for a potentially life-threatening disorder.

Hospitalization may be required to address the long-term management of eating disorders (Anderson, Murray, and Kaye 2018). Taking weeks or months to manage in a hospital setting, anorexia nervosa displays a constellation of emerging challenges. In seeking to ameliorate suffering, chaplains are trained to invite open discussion of the issues, embracing the shared suffering, receiving and validating the suffering consuming their frail victims. Hospitalized victims suffering from anorexia nervosa often respond to this strategy well, almost relishing in the diagnosis of being a *bona fide*, legitimate "anorexic." Commonly plagued initially with misdiagnoses, patients afforded a clinical diagnosis of anorexia nervosa can view the diagnosis as an achievement, a demonstration to the world that they truly are suffering from a clinical problem, that is, a real "win." Acquiring membership within a therapy group of people suffering from an eating disorder also may be cathartic. Members can benefit emotionally in this type of refuge, that is, a high-affinity group of well-wishers all displaced to the margins of everyday life, as live-in patients at a specialty clinic that cares solely for adolescents with anorexia nervosa. All members demonstrate solidarity against an outside world to which they are reacting. Paradoxically such a group experience may inadvertently trigger negative thoughts in response to "seeing one's self in others." The experience may reveal uncomfortable truths not initially sensed or understood about an individual's state. Seeing one's self in others may provoke further painful insights. The realization that the trained staff also may now see additional problem areas in a given individual provokes added anxiety. Being known as an "illness" rather than a "person" can provoke depersonalization on one hand, yet on the other hand many offer reassurance derivative of being in full solidarity within a tight group with a common diagnosis.

Eating disorders, particularly anorexia nervosa, constitute the extreme response to loss of control and basic human existence. Loss to the "other" who seeks to control one comes first. Later, after internalization, loss to "self" dominates. The initial goal of this self-inflicted loss is to provoke the apparent disappearance of one's sexual identity, especially in women victims of sexual abuse. Ultimately the victim's assault on self seeks to achieve the very real disappearance of one's own existence. The fallacy herein is an expectation that by taking acute control of one's body shape and mass, one can achieve autonomy and fuller personhood. Unfortunately, this overvaluing of body shape and mass distorts their perceptions of self. Ultimately, the way in which a person experiences his or her own body/shape deeply impacts their sense of personhood. So once again, the interplay either within the inner self in responding to depersonalization or loss of human rights (e.g., hospitalization is a loss of freedom) provokes a marked reordering of perceptions of one's own body. Added to this burden are the interpersonal interactions in an uncomfortable manipulative world overly concerned with image, appearance, what constitutes beauty and sexual attractiveness, as well as "lookism." Successful therapy may include hospitalization for short-term intense treatment. Over the long term, the therapeutic strategy will hinge upon access to a community that embraces the healing process through care and unconditional love. This is found within *Communio Sanctorum.*

Personality is the complex combination of qualities that form each person's distinctive character. In 21st century America, "personalities" of great development are valued and often touted as "celebrities, VIPs, stars, luminaries," and so forth. Psychologically speaking, personality is viewed as a way of thinking, a way of feeling and expressing emotion, and the ways in which we behave. A person's personality typically changes only modestly from the sandbox to the tomb, that is, it has consistency. Yet, some personalities appear to involve thinking, feeling, and behaving in ways society and cultures view as aberrant, that is, "not-normal." People suffering in this manner are diagnosed and labeled as having a "personality disorder." People suffering from personality disorders seldom seek treatment for the complex disorder driving the psychopathology. Rather, they seek treatment for the depression/anxiety frequently comorbid with personality disorders. In the U.S., approximately 10% of the general population suffers from personality disorders (Livesley and Larstone 2018). Though seemingly vague and imprecise, the classification of personality disorders falls into clusters with similar overarching symptoms (Livesley and Larstone 2018). Cluster A disorders present as odd, bizarre, and eccentric and may include paranoid, schizoid, and schizotypal personalities. Cluster B disorders present as dramatic and erratic, including antisocial, borderline, histrionic, and narcissistic personalities. Finally, cluster C disorders present as anxious and fearful, including avoidant, dependent, and obsessive-compulsive personalities (Hales et al. 2014).

What these disorders have in common are inner experiences, behaviors, and beliefs that deviate from social, behavioral, and psychological norms in their cultures. In some cases, the personality traits may offer a paradoxical advantage to the person. The best example is the apparent selection process for CEOs/political leaders in which executive narcissistic personality disorders may prove quite beneficial to the eventual success of their victims (Gabbard, Crisp, and American Psychiatric Association 2018; Frank 2018). Narcissistic personality types demand the fullest of personhood on the grounds of their seemingly supernatural and often delusional capabilities. Particularly with individuals displaying the narcissistic executive disorder, it is the "inner" voice that dominates, filters, and pushes forward that which is self-aggrandizing, while pushing back the voice(s) of the "other(s)" that are not *in sync*. Personhood is both a "means" and an "end" for the narcissist. Most of these personalities form in response to early inadequacies (perceived or real) and becomes an armament with which to confront the slings and arrows of the "other." Childhood disabilities that can cause assaults on the victim's sense of personhood, reemerge in narcissism to drive forward increased armament, often accompanied by rash and chaotic proclamations as to the now near divine-like attributes of the once former "victim." As if some great effort to punish all "others" who are the naysayers, the narcissist develops a personhood no longer subject to the world around them. Like Nietzsche's *übermensch* or superman, people suffering with narcissistic personality disorders consider the rules and laws that protect society from aberrant behavior as not applying to them (Schmahl, Phan, and Friedel 2018). Yet, it is the seemingly impervious nature of the narcissist's personhood, rendering it impenetrable to critique, that often foreshadows a rise to power and control both in politics and in the boardroom of many Fortune 500 corporations. In politics of 2020, notable figures have emerged onto the global stage who all display classic signs of executive narcissistic disorder, each fueling authoritarian delusions of grandeur in their sphere of influence.

Borderline personality disorder, in contrast to narcissism, is a severe mental disorder characterized by heightened instability in mood and behavior, with attendant challenges to self-image, social interactions, and overall functioning (Stanley and New 2018). The intensity of moods, depression, and behavior, in the absence of proper impulse control strain relationships and place the individual at risk for self-destructive tendencies, including attempted and successful suicide. Borderline personality types suffer from assaults on personhood, both in relation to an outer world that seems abnormal to them and in response to an inner world that includes periods challenging their already low self-worth and their mental stability. Whereas the narcissist puts on a formidable armor of undeserved vainglory to insulate her/him from the realities of the life they invade, the borderline personality frets with anxiety and depression about a threatening world in which unconditional love seems as unattainable as self-loathing seems unavoidable. Whereas the narcissist is always telling the "other" how wonderful and brilliant he or she is, the person suffering from borderline personality is continually in pursuit of an answer to the question, "am I of value?" Friends and family within the sphere of a person suffering borderline personality are literally "walking on egg shells" with respect to the victim's constant search for affirmation of self-worth. This ceaseless search for self-worth is manifest in all interpersonal interactions. Persistent queries aimed to titrate support for intrinsic self-worth and personhood by the person with borderline personality are accompanied by ever increasing testing in search of external affirmation. "If you loved me, you would do X," becomes the mantra for those seeking to affirm continued love and support in the face of often escalating demands. For friends and family, this pursuit by one suffering from borderline personality disorder becomes exhausting, seemingly hell bent on seeking to unearth a feared exception to the affirmation of worth and love. Violation of true unconditional love and support is met by a partial violent dissolution of personality and collapse of personhood. Herein, the inner voice of the victim, the "self," is the least robust, constantly seeking affirmation by the outer voices of the "other." The person suffering with borderline personality disorder exemplifies personhood that by the dominant role of personality can never achieve robustness, but only can exist on the "borderline." Thus their borderline personality disorder confines them to a "borderlands existence" in a tenuous place marginalized both by the inner as well as by the outer world. Provision of patience and unconditional love in the face of daunting and repeated assaults derivative of borderline personality disorder defines the invaluable therapeutic role that covenantal community can offer in tandem with psychiatric drug treatment and structured outpatient dialectical behavior therapy.

Although differing from more severe form of schizophrenia (see above), *schizoid* and *schizotypal personality disorders* share the same challenges to establishing and maintaining interpersonal relationships. Many who suffer from one or more of these disorders express increased paranoia and attendant reduced expression of emotions, diminished pleasure, and deflated motivation in their lives (Sperry 2016). Both personality disorders, however, lack the hallucinations and delusions prominent in true schizophrenic individuals. Whether or not these personality disorders are part of a spectrum that can expand to the full-blown psychoses of schizophrenia is the focus of active debate (Sperry 2016). People with such disorders are often grouped into clusters. Cluster A individuals are victimized by assaults on their personhood largely derivative of the powers of dominant society. They feel at the mercy of the "other" who may view their eccentric and odd behaviors as strange and perhaps at times menacing. People in cluster B often display very dramatic, emotional, and unpredictable thinking. Aberrant thinking may be coincident with signs and symptoms of other disorders discussed above. Cluster C individuals present to society as overly anxious and fearful. Everyday interactions for such victims can be formidable obstacles to fulfilled personhood and good mental health. Those suffering with dependent personality disorder display a severe and pervasive psychological dependence on others, lacking the self-confidence to make even the most trivial of decisions without extraordinary reassurance from the "other." Similarly, obsessive-compulsive personality disorder includes the same challenge to making everyday decisions, especially when broken order or rituals threaten the structure and orderliness of the individual's personality and perceived existence. Confronted with respected authority, these individuals often will submit. Authorities that they do not respect will be resisted. Forming meaningful interpersonal relationships is challenging for individuals who suffer from dependent and obsessive-compulsive disorders. These strains on relationships often result in marginalization of the victims and fragmented personhood. Self-abnegation of those suffering in cluster C may be viewed as an "inner voice" of selfhood. Renouncing one's self, however, provides a pervasive and powerful assault on personhood.

Although only the briefest of surveys of this complex area of abnormal psychology, these descriptors capture the tension and interdependence of the inner voice, the ipseity, of "self" *versus* the voice of "other" captured in daily interactions, culture, and society. In the absence of persistence and stability of a "normal" personality, the victims of contested personhood live challenging, seemingly impossible lives with attendant great suffering and marginalization. Unconditional love in abundance with attendant patience and understanding may be the best therapeutic environment for these suffering souls. Only a community steeped in moral solidarity and covenantal inclusivity can provide for the best opportunity of flourishing of those with fragmented, distorted, and incomplete personalities.

Post-Traumatic Stress and Regaining Personhood

Stress is an unavoidable fact of life and it creates suffering. Stress can produce positive outcomes, such as focus, renewed attention, the power to overcome challenges (Hobfoll 1998). In this way, short-term moderate stress can be beneficial to most people. When stress becomes chronic, highly elevated, and overwhelming, however, it is toxic (Hobfoll 1998). Unmanageable stress, which interferes with work and daily living for a period lasting a month or more, is often the result of trauma (Davoine and Gaudillière 2004). Unlike triggers of stress in the workplace that can accumulate over time due to unhappiness, long work hours, uncertain employment, and poor management, trauma can be the apex of a good deal of suffering that ultimately follows a traumatic change in life (Caruth 2014). High on the list of trauma-provoking events that catalyze undo stress are death of a loved one, divorce, job loss and financial distress, chronic illness or severe injury (Van der Kolk 2014). Traumatic stressors, however, are very much in the eye of the beholder. Similar stressors can produce a variety of traumatic responses in individuals varying in intensity, duration, and potential for recovery. Resilience can be viewed as a positive response to a traumatic event in which the victim is rebounding or springing back towards recovery. Resilience is as psychological and behavioral process aimed at restoring the psyche and soma of an affected individual to its original, pre-traumatic status (Everly and Lating 2013).

Stimuli of traumatic events provoke a substantial level of fear, horror, and helplessness in response to a threat of injury or death (Golden and Bergo 2009). Natural disasters (e.g., floods, hurricanes, forest fires, etc.), terrorist attacks (e.g., Oklahoma bombing and 9/11 attacks), assault (especially rape), theft, or violence against a person or their loved ones constitute extreme stressors that readily do provoke post-traumatic stress disorder (PTSD). Trauma of this dimension represents an extraordinary challenge to coping with that which is perceived as overwhelming stress (Golden and Bergo 2009). As noted in the aftermath to the 9/11 terrorist attacks, traumatic stressors are not limited to those who directly experienced the initial insult, but also may include those who witnessed and confronted events that threatened death or serious injury to themselves or others. In the short term, symptoms of fatigue, sleep difficulties, lack of concentration, irritability, and GI disturbances are common for those suffering acute stress (Friedman 2015). In the absence of proper management, these symptoms are followed by more serious health conditions including depression, anxiousness that can be associated with cardiac arrhythmias, acute heart disease (including heart attacks), elevated blood pressure and hypertension, GI problems, and changes in body weight, either gain or loss. For most individuals, these symptoms and the difficulties of adjusting and coping can, with time and self-care, improve and eventually disappear (Bryant and Harvey 2000). In the case of people diagnosed with PTSD, these symptoms typically turn worse, last for months or even years, and interfere with work and daily living.

As the classic symptoms persist and worsen the victims of PTSD experience a constant degradation of their self-worth and personhood. As noted for other psychological disorders, PTSD is expressed in two domains: the inner "self" by a lack of understanding of what's happening to them; and, the "other" in the world who comments on or reacts negatively to behaviors of the victim that may now seem odd or threatening. Failing to understand this acute form of suffering in PTSD, the "other" questions the personhood of the victim and through such actions further marginalize them. In PTSD we observe an important maxim for recovery and resilience, that is, the healing of the "self" must precede the education of the "other." Absent any insight into the suffering and inner turmoil of people with PTSD, the "other" usually only exacerbates the symptoms, feeling of dread, depression, and anxiety. Because each person is unique, PTSD presents a myriad of signs and symptoms to the "other," that may be difficult to decode even for those whose true interest is empathetic and well wishing.

Most people suffering from stress or the extreme of PTSD seek help when their symptoms severely interfere in day-to-day life and present in combination with depression, fatigue, and/or irritability (Pierce 2019). For people suffering with PTSD, the fear, horror, and helplessness that characterized their response to an initial traumatic event often reappear in the form of flashbacks and/or intrusions, avoidance of reminders of the event, and *hyper*-arousal and reactivity (e.g., insomnia, irritability, hyper vigilance) that persists for more than a month. From my experience with people working through trauma and recovery, I conclude that trauma is in the "eye of the beholder/victim." Tragic, unexpected loss of a loved one may provoke a common response of grief and recovery that typically is resolved within six months, but in other cases may present with all of the symptoms of PTSD, although rarely diagnosed as such. The threshold for PTSD for some individuals with poor resilience may deserve closer scrutiny, especially when the long-term signs and symptoms include avoidance, flashbacks, and *hyper*-arousal. It is well known that loss of a long-term partner even to a predictable chronic disease process places the survivor at great jeopardy for death in the ensuing six months. Ample experience with death and bereavement confirms for me the extraordinary power of trauma to attack the personhood of even the seemingly most robust. Consider the facts that a normal and healthy elder survivor of a long-term marriage can decline to the point of death, the very loss of personhood, in such a short time. Such victims lose the power of self-preservation, become numb to life, and can seek death through intentionally refusing the medically advised provision of hydration and nutrient necessary for survival itself. These examples of what I would term the worst outcomes of "everyday PTSD" are hard to imagine. The narratives of the worst outcomes remain indelibly etched on my heart and can bring me back to an earlier situation. Through such experiences I am able to witness and positively intervene in a new episode of suffering, often followed by death, and its impact on the people left behind. One of my chaplaincy mentors rightly noted, after my suffering of a grievous loss, that these experiences expand your empathic grid and bring you new tools to help others struggling within the vicissitudes of life.

Individuals suffering from *stress-related disorders* often comment about feeling misunderstood and marginalized within their community. These victims may feel that "others" even within a community have discounted their personhood, unable to fully understand the grief that they experience. Their lives as victims of a trauma seems to them to be pushed to the margins. This marginalization of victims of trauma by the "other" often is felt within the earliest period after the trauma. Even close friends and associates can appear to grow numb to the very deep loss felt by the victims. Comments such as "you'll get over it," "time heals all wounds," or even "don't let it get to you" may reflect emotional exhaustion by even the most sincere well-wishers. Tone-deaf responses to traumatic events, even if delivered with good intention, deny or minimize the trauma felt by the victim, and further alienation often ensues. Officiating at wakes and funeral services, I am stunned that we as a society do not grow up with a better sense of how to encounter loss in the bereaved. Grief, on the other hand, especially grieving within a close community, is a hallmark of a healthy recovery process. The bereaved and survivors of other forms of trauma also need to have their loss acknowledged and validated within the community. Labeling the wounded victims of trauma as malingerers, sad sacks, and self-absorbed in their depression leads only to compounding the trauma and extending the recovery time to healing. Steeped in self-loathing and depression, traumatized individuals can turn to substance abuse (particularly alcohol) and isolation as their preferred therapy (Vujanovic and Back 2019). Ultimately, a sensed loss of personhood by a victim within the community spells a likely compound disaster. Alienation can culminate in the victim leaving the community, a loss to both the victim and to the community. In a community with true moral solidarity, our *Communio Sanctorum*, members would be aware of the potential extremes of a traumatic event and work towards inclusion of the recovery process within, rather than outside of, the community. Young people often learn about trauma, grieving, and recovery through social modeling. Sensitive sincere participation in a loss and proportionate grieving for the loss of a member of the community are important and perhaps life-long teaching moments, preparing all for the likely vicissitudes of life and death. These learning experiences provide a template for greater resilience in the face of real trauma, healthy for the individual as well as for the community.

VULNERABLE PSYCHE, ASSAULTED PERSONHOOD, AND RESILIENCE

Profiles in Courage and Resilience

Vulnerabilities of the psyche are quite common and often provoke assaults on the personhood of those suffering with these disorders. Perceptions about intelligence, mood, personality can create the "other," a person who seems odd, strange in behavior, and unlike "self." The forces that contest the personhood of the vulnerable are formidable and come from a diverse array of perpetrators. Equally formidable can be the forces "within," not the interpersonal, but the intrapersonal, the very "self" of the vulnerable. Embracing narratives that capture the suffering of the "other" in the hopes of generating a more inclusive and compassionate understanding of community is a good investment of our hearts and minds. More challenging are the efforts aimed at addressing the suffering of the vulnerable from "within" in the hopes of reducing or dispelling self-criticism and self-loathing of the victim. Treating the discounted self "within" requires greater patience, understanding, professional therapy, and often the judicious use of drug therapy. Importantly, it is proper to pause and reflect on the resilience displayed by a few individuals of historical note who suffered vulnerabilities of the mind, yet managed or overcame them. These victims of vulnerabilities of the mind flourished in an often unforgiving world, offering enormous gifts to the community, even communities that were not so inclusive, understanding, and empathetic at times. Like many, the struggles of the inner self, the intrapersonal, the ipseity, dominated their lives but eventually addressed therapeutically and in community. It cannot be said that these vulnerabilities were truly overcome, but rather that with empathy and unconditional love the vulnerabilities were managed as best possible at the time. In the inclusive *Communio Sanctorum* of individuals in moral solidarity, all people are valued for their unique special gifts as well as burdens, all bundled up in their humanity. It is intentional optimization of these gifts and welcomed sharing of the sometime considerable burdens of each other that fuse community into true moral solidarity.

Matt Savage, a Musician with Special Gifts

Matt Savage (b. 1992), an American savant musician, was diagnosed with what is now termed the autism spectrum disorder (see the DSM-5) when he was three years old. Savage's extraordinary career should heighten our awareness about the gifts that accompany human diversity. Absent early formal instruction in music, Savage taught himself to read piano music at age six, studied music at the New England Conservatory of Music in Boston at seven, eventually earning a B.M. in Performance (Piano) from Berklee College of Music in 2012. In 2015 Matt earned a M.M. in Jazz Performance from the Manhattan School of Music in the City of New York. His professional career includes rich experiences as a musician, composer, and bandleader. Matt has "jammed" with some of the biggest names in jazz, including Chick Corea, Wynton Marsalis, and others. Matt has released >10 albums and toured globally, including at Carnegie Hall, the Blue Note, the Kennedy Center, the Monterey Jazz Festival, and New Orleans Jazz Festival, to name but a few. In 2015, Savage opened for Neil Young, Stephen Stills, Shawn Colvin, and others at Autism Speaks "Light Up the Blues." His career now includes teaching at Bunker Hill Community College as well as conducting master classes worldwide.

In a 2015 in depth and powerful interview (available on YouTube), Matt Savage discussed freely the considerable obstacles that he had to overcome in the music world as well as in the business of composing, recording, and publishing music. His ASD includes hyperlexia as well as perfect pitch that have served him well in dimensions of his creative genius. These talents helped Savage in his pursuit of fullest personhood while embracing his being on ASD. He has been supported and largely embraced by his community. Yet, in some ways he is both an *exception* (based upon his truly extraordinary success) as well as the *rule* for the value of community inclusion of those diagnosed with ASD. His unique expression of ASD included extraordinary talents that were expressed and identified early. In this way he provides a model for early diagnosis and intervention. But in being embraced professionally and in the greater community, Savage offers the insight that for inclusive community to flourish, all members must be included and nurtured according to their own unique gifts and limitations.

Pablo Pineda, Gifted, but not "Special"

Pablo Pineda (b. 1974) is a Spanish actor with Down syndrome who speaks about his life as an on-going learning experience (Borsch et al. 2017). Pineda earned a BA degree in educational psychology and a diploma in teaching, making him the first European with Down syndrome to obtain a university degree. He starred in the film, *Yo También*, was nominated for a Goya Award (in the category of Best New Actor), and has participated in popular TEDx Talks. His interviews reflect Pablo's acute awareness of those who contest the personhood of people with vulnerabilities of psyche, like Down syndrome. He has offered, "I think that I'm at the front of the war, and this is inconvenient. You have to fight, get into society when the Down world usually tends to going a different direction. I stay with the "normal" ones, while others with Down go to their organizations, their parents, their little tiny world." Yet, Pineda frankly admits most of his success reflects the support of his parents. Pineda works with the Adecco Foundation, a foundation aimed at integration programs that fully include people with disabilities into the fullest social fabric. Inclusive community in moral solidarity with family and all members as well remains an invaluable element to assist those who seek to embrace *Communio Sanctorum.*

Pineda has expressed some anger at those organizations that seek to label him as a "special" case. He sees his approach as encouraging programs for improvement aimed at all people with Down syndrome and other vulnerabilities. He quipped, "I always tell parents not to pay attention to the fact that I've been in a movie and have a career. That is not important. What's important is that you can do it, and your parents have to teach you, and encourage you. After that, you can do anything." Herein Pineda rightly places emphasis on the need for community to be inclusive, that is, to welcome, accept, and support all people. True community enables the flourishing of all, each person displaying individual gifts and burdens to be shared. Full personhood cannot simply be claimed in the face of adversity, but rather must be earned through faith that fullest personhood of all people must be sought, as a basic human right.

John Forbes Nash, Possessing a Beautiful, if Imperfect, Mind

John Forbes Nash, Jr. (1928–2015) was born in Bluefield, West Virginia, educated at the Carnegie Institute of Technology, and earned at PhD at Princeton University. His contributions to mathematics in game theory, differential geometry, nonlinear partial differential equations, and the factors that govern chance and decision-making in complex systems were truly phenomenal. In 1994, Nash shared the Nobel Prize in Economic Sciences with John Harsanyi and Reinhard Selten. In 2015, the King of Norway awarded the Abel Prize in mathematics to Nash and Louis Nirenberg, recognizing their striking and seminal contributions to nonlinear partial differential equations and application to geometric analysis. When Nash was just thirty he developed symptoms later diagnosed as paranoid schizophrenia that would lead to his repeated hospitalizations. At a public lecture in 1959, rather than present a lecture aimed at a proof of the knotty Riemann hypothesis, Nash delivered a lecture that was incomprehensible, indicating quite publically that he was suffering from a severe mental illness. For a decade he spent most of his time hospitalized, treated with the then state-of-the-art therapies for schizophrenia. Nash's decline and eventual recovery were the core of Sylvia Nasar's biography, *A Beautiful Mind* (Nasar 1999), as well as a 2001 film of the same name directed by Ron Howard. John Nash was very fortunate, benefitting from deep support in the tight community of colleagues and friends of the mathematics department at Princeton University. According to his former wife Alicia De Larde, Nash's slow recovery was only made possible by a quiet existence supported by the local community and environment at Princeton.

The award of the 1994 Nobel Prizes had a special meaning for me. Drs. Alfred Gilman (University of Texas Southwestern Medical Center at Dallas) and Martin Rodbell (National Institutes of Health), two leaders, colleagues in my own area of research, and dear friends shared the 1994 Nobel Prize in Physiology or Medicine. In that same year the Nobel Prize in Chemistry was awarded to Dr. George Olah. Olah was on sabbatical at Case Western Reserve University where I met him in 1972 and received advanced training in organic chemistry. He was an extraordinary chemist, individual, and very kind. John Nash was to share the Nobel Prize in Economic Sciences that very same year! Both Gilman and Rodbell came to know much more about Nash's situation by participation in 1994 award meetings and public lectures. They shared with me their own recollections of John Nash, adding to my own. As a member of the faculty of Stony Brook University, I was thrilled when the university established a Center for Game Theory in Economics about 1989, which grew out of the former Institute of Decision Sciences (IDS). John Nash was a charter member of the center and frequent participant in their annual gatherings. My own introduction to Nash occurred when I was the Vice President of Research at Stony Brook University. I met Nash at a reception hosted by the Center for Game Theory. He was a frail, very quiet individual at that time. John was deeply admired and loved by the community of mathematicians who came to expound upon Nash's seminal work, especially at Princeton and Stony Brook. For Nash perhaps the most formidable assault to his personhood was again the intrapersonal, ipseity, that is, his "inner" world infused by paranoia and anxiety. The community in Princeton and the greater community of mathematicians/economists/decision scientists (including the Nobel committee) displayed a remarkable level of understanding, empathy and support that proved critical to his eventual partial recovery. These were truly communities with sustained inclusivity and moral solidarity for one who was made most vulnerable by a debilitating and severe illness of the psyche. In 2015, Nash and his former wife Alicia were killed in a car crash on Long Island, NY.

Isabella T., the Welcomed Stranger

On a Sunday morning, Isabella came to the church to which I had been Called. She did not introduce herself, but rather sat quietly in the front pew. Tears streamed down her comely face for the entire service! Each week women members of the congregation would invite themselves to sit with her, offering simply their presence and loving-kindness. Although composing herself for the beginning of each Sunday service, Isabella always dissolved into tears and soft weeping, but discernably by the time of the benediction and farewell. Striking up a simple conversation with Isabella was a challenge. In the first month, she departed abruptly at the close of the service, seeking to avoid social interaction. As a last resort I would depart from the service, exit the church sanctuary and walk briskly to the parking lot in the hopes of casually intercepting her. In the parking lot I discovered less resistance of simple conversation. There she felt less "closed in" and there we began our pastoral relationship. I was happy to have her later seek me out for counseling. Isabella was suffering deeply from old scars and new wounds of a challenging life, a life replete with vulnerabilities of mind. She had been treated professionally for ongoing major depression, anxiety disorder, and substance abuse, including abuse of illicit drugs and alcohol. She was in her thirties and was married. Only later, once she felt part of the church family, did she reveal that she had been forced to run away from her husband, a response to domestic abuse. Her lifelong challenge with depression, self-loathing, and suicidal ideation had rendered Isabella technically "disabled." As such, she received critical support by social services provided by the county. She was now living on her own in a small cottage near the church.

Isabella sought counseling with me, in addition to her ongoing psychiatric treatment and "talk" therapy. She asked for me to assist her in securing continued support from county social services, an essential stream of financial support for her that was continually being threatened. She recognized two things: in order to qualify for continued support she needed to "come clean" with social services; and, she needed a proxy to advocate for her. At that time, she was anxious, depressed, and had ongoing problems with sobriety. Consequently, she shared with me intimate details of her past and current life, authorizing me to share this background information on her behalf as needed with the county board that would approve or deny further social services support to her. At her hearing, she sat next to me, head bowed and reticent. The board had made a preliminary determination to terminate Isabella's disability support, based upon their ongoing impression that she was a malingerer, grifter, and "sponge" preying upon limited country resources. When I probed the board about the basis for the determination it became painfully clear to me that they knew very little about Isabella's life and circumstances. This lack of information was mostly a fault due to Isabella's shyness and desire to suppress details of her prior life. Through conversation with her estranged husband and acquaintances, I was able to eventually put together a Gestalt of Isabella's life and current challenges.

Isabella and her older sister were born into a family dominated by an abusive alcoholic father. When she was 14, her mother committed suicide by hanging. She and her sister discovered the body of their mother after returning home from school. Her father had physically abused his wife and their two daughters for years. He was an angry fellow, angry at the way he, an immigrant, was being treated. Not long after the death of their mother, the father's physical abuse expanded into sexual abuse. Along with sexual abuse was emotional abuse and forced isolation of the girls from their school friends by the father. He sought to keep from public knowledge the very nature of the girls' horrific life in the absence of their mother. This ongoing incest would create new problems for the family. Her older sister became pregnant, had an abortion, and left high school and the family home. Isabella was left to fend for herself. She turned to alcohol and illicit drugs to numb the pain of neglect, abuse, and feeling of abandonment by her sister. She felt only "like an object, not a person." Absent any voice, she remained an object of her father's various abuses. Her grades in school suffered. She withdrew into herself, filled with self-loathing. Eventually she began to seek solace in impulsive and dangerous behaviors, liaisons with strangers and prostitution.

Isabella lost contact with her sister, grieved for her mother, and unsuccessfully tried to fend off her father's assaults. Depression and anxiety dominated her life. Drugs, alcohol abuse, and prostitution offered no exit plans. In desperation she escaped her childhood home, marrying a man who, from what she shared with me, actually mirrored her abusive father. Her husband was a domineering man, who abused alcohol and displayed physically abusive tendencies aimed at Isabella. Their entertainment toggled between binge drinking and sadomasochistic behaviors. Eventually she was drawn to self-harming behaviors, including several unsuccessful attempts at committing suicide. Hospitalized on several occasions, Isabella eventually was diagnosed as suffering from major depression, anxiety disorder, and alcohol abuse. Isabella could no longer take care of herself. She became a ward of the county and landed in a small community where she lived inconspicuously in low-end housing assigned to her.

Attempts to find and sustain employment for Isabella were fruitless. The county's provision of short-term weekly talk therapy and periodic care by a psychiatrist in order to obtain her meds improved little in her life. The most important element to the recent improvement in her demeanor and life appeared to be the deep community in which the church embraced Isabella. Perhaps it was the community's non-judgmental loving-kindness that rekindled a new hope for her. Isabella longed for acceptance, for full personhood within a community that would not shun or judge her, but rather offer only unconditional love.

In the end, the county granted to Isabella a 6-month extension of benefits. In return, she promised to attend Alcohol Anonymous meetings every other day (offered at the church) and to strictly comply with the therapy plan agreed to with her mental health providers. Yet after four months of sustained, good faith efforts, Isabella failed to show up at church for service one Sunday. Her attendance at AA meetings had stopped. A member of the deacons tried in vain to contact Isabella by phone. Later the church leaders were informed that Isabella's estranged husband had turned up in the village. Not yet firmly planted in the new life that she professed to desire, Isabella had reverted to her former life of domestic abuse, drugs, and alcohol. Her story would end following a police report of a domestic disturbance involving alcohol abuse at her cottage. Isabella and her spouse were arrested for disorderly conduct, posted bail, and left the area. With her flight, I concluded with deep sadness and regret that Isabella likely would return to a life bereft of personhood. The traumas that Isabella sustained over the years had commodified her "self." Although she sought and found an inclusive community in moral solidarity, the prior wounds and scars were too much for Isabella to effectively overcome. For her, personhood had been assaulted throughout her life and perhaps now was irrevocably lost.

APPENDIX 2: FURTHER NOTES

Text in italics are callouts to places within the chapter.

"Not till we are lost, in other words not till we have lost the world, do we begin to find ourselves." This quotation taken from Henry David Thoreau's *Walden*, published in 1854 (Thoreau and Carew 1854), is an allegory. The complexity of the world in which we exist must be elevated to its proper transcendent place. Human beings, often seeking only the ends, often do not seek to embrace the means of human existence, with all of its complexities, nuances, shapes, and shades. It is our sensory perception and intellect that are challenged by this complexity. The ancient Greeks considered the mind to be so much more than a simple center of thinking. To them, the mind was the center of one's soul, that is, psyche, personhood, and emotive being. One's very being in all of the concrete complexity of life was contained by this soul, termed "psyche." The Greeks were quite right about the mind, it is often the platform on which personhood evolves and develops fullness. Assaults on personhood often target their victims making use of the portal of the mind and its complex and far reaching vulnerabilities. Thoreau was quite right also. To apprehend our *"inner* self," we must lose ourselves to the *"outer* world."

Few people are more vulnerable in 21st century America than those diagnosed with "mental illness." In advance, an apology must be made for the absence of a complete and exhaustive discussion of the broad set of disorders, disabilities, and vulnerabilities of the mind that assault personhood status in 21st century America. A brief perusal of the table of contents of the *Diagnostic and Statistical Manual of Mental Disorders* (*DSM-5*) (American Psychiatric Association DSM-5 Task Force 2013) or of the *Textbook of Psychiatry* (Hales et al. 2014) will reveal the rich complexity of vulnerabilities of the psyche. Two points deserve mention. First, a primary goal is to sample from the wide spectrum of mental disorders to gain specific insights into how such disorders can provoke assaults on personhood. Second, the intra-personal and inter-personal worlds contributing jointly to mental illness, disabilities, and vulnerabilities need to be introduced and explored around the issue of contested personhood (Black and Andreasen 2014). Personhood is shown to be vulnerable both from without (the "other") as well as from within (the "self," that is, ipseity), or some complex mixture of both operating in synergy. The citations provided are excellent, timely sourcebooks for those interested in further reading on the topics.

We observed that there is little doubt that children and adults with ASD are victims of discrimination, challenging the dimensions of their personhood in 21st century America and elsewhere. In 2005, Ms. Kathleen Seidel, the mother of a child with ASD exchanged correspondence with Dr. Thomas

Insel (then Director, National Institute of Mental Health, NIH). Ms. Seidel was reacting to an interview in which the Director is quoted as saying: "'(autism) really robs a child and a family of the personhood of this child.'" This exchange, correspondence between the two, is a powerful, candid and revealing insight on the challenges faced by parents of children with ASD. These challenges, Ms. Seidel offers, are often invisible to even the most learned experts in mental health. Perhaps, like much of life, you need to "live" it, to better understand it. One of the core tenets of the current book is that individuals often contest the personhood of someone else, simply by intentionally or inadvertently placing the victim outside of community. I encourage the interested reader to examine this correspondence and dwell upon Ms. Seidel's insightful primer for those who are little acquainted with ASD. The correspondence is available on neurodiversity.com: http://neurodiversity.com/autism_and_personhood.html (accessed May 30, 2020).

Fetal valproate syndrome remains a devastating and thankfully rare developmental disorder. Valproic acid (or the salt, sodium valproate) is prescribed widely in the United States. It effectively resolves and prevents epileptic seizures. Mood instability for patients suffering from bipolar disorder also responds well to valproic acid therapy. Women maintained of valproic acid to manage epilepsy and who are of childbearing age constitute a challenge in medical ethics as well as a challenge to personhood. The challenge to personhood is aimed both at the infant child as well as the mother. The nexus of the dilemma is that standard therapy with valproic acid incurs a considerable potential risk for the fetus. Fetal valproate syndrome (FVS) is a rare teratogenic disease capable of causing birth defects through embryo/fetus exposure to valproic acid. If a woman treated with valproic acid were to become pregnant unknowingly, normal development of the fetus would be at high risk. FVS is a rare situation in medical ethics, two lives are placed at risk due to the nature of the mother's need to manage the epilepsy and the sensitivity of the fetus to the teratogenic effects of valproic acid. Withholding valproic acid may provoke serious and potentially life-threatening seizures that place both lives in jeopardy. Successful management of the mother's epilepsy can provoke FVS and through unremitting feelings of guilt, degrade her personhood. Unfortunately, little is known about the underlying embryo-fetopathology of FVS. Common overt signs of FVS include distinct facial dysmorphism, varied congenital anomalies and delays in development, as well as marked effects on acquisition of language and communication that yield life-long deficits. For more information visit OrphaNet: https://www.orpha.net/consor/cgi-bin/OC_Exp.php?Lng=GB&Expert=1906 (accessed May 30, 2020).

The prevalence of diagnosed mental illness in the U.S.: statistics on mental health in the U.S. are not so hard and fast. Definitions of what constitutes mental illness, how mental illness is diagnosed, and limitations in understanding the full range of diseases of the mind preclude an accurate assessment for our purposes. In view of these limitations, readers are pointed to the best portals for the most recent mental health statistics regarding the United States. The three most up-to-date estimates on mental health statistics can be found at the following websites: Unnamed Author (2020), "Mental Health by the Numbers," Arlington, VA: *The National Alliance on Mental Illness*, https://www.nami.org/learn-more/mental-health-by-the-numbers (accessed May 30, 2020); Unnamed Author (2020), "Mental Health Statistics in the U.S.," Bethesda, MD: *The National Institute of Mental Health* (NIH), https://www.nimh.nih.gov/health/statistics/index.shtml (accessed May 30, 2020); Unnamed Author (2018), "The State of Mental Health in America 2018," Alexandria, VA: *Mental Health America*, http://www.mentalhealthamerica.net/issues/state-mental-health-america-2018 (accessed May 30, 2020).

The extraordinary and seminal contributions of John Forbes Nash to mathematics earned worldwide acclaim. Schizophrenia is a severe mental disorder that affects thinking, feeling, and behaviors of those afflicted with this chronic disease (Lieberman et al. 2020). John Nash wrestled with a particularly severe schizophrenia that disordered his thinking, altered his behaviors, and sporadically was resistant to medical intervention and so was disabling. His mental gifts were extraordinary and recognized widely with awards. For further information of two of the major awards earned by John Nash visit the following websites: The announcement of the 1994 Sveriges Riksbank Prize in Economic Sciences in Memory of Alfred Nobel can be viewed here: https://www.nobelprize.org/prizes/economic-sciences/1994/nash/facts/ (accessed on April 30, 2020). The announcement of the award of the Abel Prize for 2015 by the Norwegian Academy of Sciences & Letters can be viewed here: http://www.abelprize.no/nyheter/vis.html?tid=63693 (accessed on April 30, 2020).

Earlier we explored vulnerabilities of mind attendant to diagnosis of post-traumatic stress in the general population. Post-traumatic stress, within the domains of trauma, loss, and recovery, is encountered most often when average human beings traverse the normal vicissitudes of life and death (Walker 2013). Later, in Chapter 4, we revisit post-traumatic stress and its attendant disorder PTSD with the specific intention of probing it in the context of military and police service, a particular challenge to full personhood in 21st century America (Moore and Penk 2019).

REFERENCES

Abel, Ernest L. 1981. *Fetal alcohol syndrome*. 3 vols. Boca Ratan, FL: CRC Press.
Abraham, Suzanne. 2016. *Eating disorders: The facts* (7th ed.). Oxford, UK: Oxford University Press.

Amaral, David, Geraldine Dawson, and Daniel H. Geschwind. 2011. *Autism spectrum disorders*. New York, NY: Oxford University Press.

American Psychiatric Association., and American Psychiatric Association. DSM-5 Task Force. 2013. *Diagnostic and statistical manual of mental disorders: DSM-5* (5th ed.). Washington, DC: American Psychiatric Association.

Anderson, Leslie, Stuart Murray, and Walter H. Kaye. 2018. *Clinical handbook of complex and atypical eating disorders*. New York, NY: Oxford University Press.

Armstrong, Susan J., and Richard George Botzler. 2008. *The animal ethics reader* (2nd ed.). London, UK; New York, NY: Routledge.

Ashley, Mark J. 2018. *Traumatic brain injury: Rehabilitation, treatment, and case managemen* (4th ed.). Boca Rato, FL: CRC Press.

Balinson, Andrea. 2018. *Depression, anxiety, and bipolar disorders*. Broomall PA: Mason Crest.

Black, Donald W., and Nancy C. Andreasen. 2014. *Introductory textbook of psychiatry* (6th ed.). Washington, DC: American Psychiatric Association.

Booth, Janine. 2016. *Autism equality in the workplace: Removing barriers and challenging discrimination*. London, UK; Philadelphia, PA: Jessica Kingsley Publishers.

Borsch, Albert, María Sala, Silvia Alvarez, and Jon Brokenbrow. 2017. *Pablo Pineda—Being different is a value*. Madrid, Spain: Cuento de Luz.

Bryant, Richard A., and Allison G. Harvey. 2000. *Acute stress disorder: A handbook of theory, assessment, and treatment*. Washington, DC: American Psychological Association.

Caruth, Cathy. 2014. *Listening to trauma: Conversations with leaders in the theory and treatment of catastrophic experience*. Baltimore, MD: Johns Hopkins University Press.

Clarren, Sterling, Amy Salmon, and Egon Jonsson. 2011. *Prevention of fetal alcohol spectrum disorder FASD: Who is responsible?*. Weinheim, DRG: Wiley-Blackwell.

Davoine, Françoise, and Jean-Max Gaudillière. 2004. *History beyond trauma: Whereof one cannot speak, thereof one cannot stay silent*. New York, NY: Other Press.

DeRubeis, Robert J., and Daniel R. Strunk. 2017. *The Oxford handbook of mood disorders*. New York, NY: Oxford University Press.

Emanuel, Ezekiel J. 2008. *The Oxford textbook of clinical research ethics*. Oxford, UK; New York, NY: Oxford University Press.

Everly, George S., and Jeffrey M. Lating. 2013. *A clinical guide to the treatment of the human stress response* (3rd ed.). New York, NY: Springer.

Failer, Judith Lynn. 2002. *Who qualifies for rights?: Homelessness, mental illness, and civil commitment*. Ithaca, NY: Cornell University Press.

Frank, Justin A. 2018. *Trump on the couch: Inside the mind of the president*. New York, NY: Avery, an imprint of Penguin Random House.

Freedman, David, Robert Pisani, and Roger Purves. 2007. *Statistics* (4th ed.). New York, NY: W.W. Norton & Co.

Friedman, Matthew J. 2015. *Posttraumatic and acute stress disorders*. New York, NY: Springer Science+Business Media.

Gabbard, Glen O., Holly Crisp, and American Psychiatric Association Publishing. 2018. *Narcissism and its discontents: Diagnostic dilemmas and treatment strategies with narcissistic patients*. Washington, DC: American Psychiatric Association Publishing.

Golden, Kristen Brown, and Bettina Bergo. 2009. *The trauma controversy: Philosophical and interdisciplinary dialogues*. Albany, NY: State University of New York Press.

Goldstein, Sam, and Sally Ozonoff. 2018. *Assessment of autism spectrum disorder* (2nd ed.). New York, NY: The Guilford Press.

Goldstein, Sam, and Cecil R. Reynolds. 2011. *Handbook of neurodevelopmental and genetic disorders in children* (2nd ed.). New York, NY: Guilford Press.

Graham, James. 2008. *Autism, discrimination, and the law: A quick guide for parents, educators, and employers*. London, UK; Philadelphia, PA: Jessica Kingsley Publishers.

Grandin, Temple. 2011. *The way I see it: A personal look at autism & Asperger's* (revised and 2nd ed.). Arlington, TX: Future Horizons Inc.

Gupta, Ramesh C. 2017. *Reproductive and developmental toxicology* (2nd ed.). London UK: Elsevier, Academic Press.

Hales, Robert E., Stuart C. Yudofsky, Laura Weiss Roberts, and American Psychiatric Publishing. 2014. *The American Psychiatric Publishing textbook of psychiatry* (6th ed.). Washington, DC: American Psychiatric Publishing.

Harris, Michelle. 2019. Schizophrenia: When reality becomes distorted. In *Diseases and disorders*. New York, NY: Lucent Press.

Hobfoll, Stevan E. 1998. *Stress, culture, and community: The psychology and philosophy of stress* (The Plenum series on stress and coping). New York, NY: Plenum Press.

Höybye, Charlotte. 2013. *Prader-Willi syndrome* (Congenital disorders—Laboratory and clinical research). Hauppauge, NY: Nova Biomedical.

Jacob, Jen, and Mardra Sikora. 2016. *The parent's guide to Down syndrome: Advice, information, inspiration, and support for raising your child from diagnosis through adulthood.* Avon, MA: Adams Media.

Jeeves, Malcolm A. 2004. *From cells to souls, and beyond: Changing portraits of human nature.* Grand Rapids, MI: W.B. Eerdmans.

Jonsson, Egon. 2018. *Ethical and legal perspectives in fetal alcohol spectrum disorders (FASD): Foundational issues.* New York, NY: Springer Berlin Heidelberg.

Kaposy, Chris. 2018. *Choosing Down syndrome: Ethics and new prenatal testing technologies.* Cambridge, MA: The MIT Press.

Kerins, Marie R. 2015. *Child and adolescent communication disorders: Organic and neurogenic bases.* San Diego, CA: Plural Publishing.

Ketter, Terence A., and American Psychiatric Association. 2015. *Advances in treatment of bipolar disorders.* Washington, DC: American Psychiatric Publishing, a division of American Psychiatric Association.

Kittay, Eva Feder. 2019. *Learning from my daughter: The value and care of disabled minds.* New York, NY: Oxford University Press.

———. 2001. When caring is just and justice is caring. *Public Culture, 13*(3): 557–79.

Kittay, Eva Feder, and Licia Carlson. 2010. *Cognitive disability and its challenge to moral philosophy.* Chichester, West Sussex, UK; Malden, MA: Wiley-Blackwell.

Knauss, Andrea, and Elizabeth Martina. 2016. *Reasons to smile: Celebrating people living with Down syndrome.* Atglen, PA: Schiffer Publishing, Ltd.

Kulkarni, Shashikant. 2014. *Clinical genomics.* Boston, MA: Elsevier.

Lieberman, Jeffrey A., T. Scott Stroup, Diana O. Perkins, and Lisa B. Dixon. (2020). *The American Psychiatric Assocoiaiton publishing textbook of schizophrenia* (2nd ed.). Washington, DC: American Psychiatirc Association Publishing.

Livesley, W. John, and Roseann Larstone. 2018. *Handbook of personality disorders: Theory, research, and treatment* (2nd ed.). New York, NY: The Guilford Press.

Lynch, John. 2019. *The origins of bioethics: Remembering when medicine went wrong.* East Lansing, MI: Michigan State University Press.

Machan, Tibor R. 2004. *Putting humans first: Why we are nature's favorite.* Lanham, MD: Rowman & Littlefield Publishers.

Malbon, Craig C. 2013. *Abortion in 21st century America: A matter of life/lives and/or death.* North Charleston, SC: CreateSpace Publishing.

Marcsisin, Michael J., Jessica M. Gannon, and Jason Rosenstock. 2017. *Schizophrenia and related disorders.* New York, NY: Oxford University Press.

Marder, Stephen R., and Vandana Chopra. 2014. *Schizophrenia* (Oxford American psychiatry library). Oxford, UK; New York, NY: Oxford University Press.

McFarlane, Judy. 2014. *Writing with Grace: A journey beyond Down syndrome.* Madeira Park, British Columbia, CD: Douglas & McIntyre.

Mehler, Philip S., and Arnold E. Andersen. 2017. *Eating disorders: A guide to medical care and complications* (3rd ed.). Baltimore, MD: The Johns Hopkins University Press.

Mendez, Thomas. 2017. *Down syndrome (DS): Perspectives, challenges and management.* New York, NY: Nova Biomedical.

Mondimore, Francis Mark. 2014. *Bipolar disorder: A guide for patients and families.* Baltimore, MD: Johns Hopkins University Press.

Moore, Bret A. and Walter E. Penk. 2019. *Treating PTSD in military personnel* (2nd ed.). New York, NY: The Guilford Press.

Müller, Andreas, and Peter Schaber. 2018. *The Routledge handbook of the ethics of consent* (1st ed.). Abingdon, Oxon, UK ; New York, NY: Routledge.

Muneer, Ather. 2018. *Mood disorders: Practical issues in diagnosis and management*. New York, NY: Routledge.

Myers, Beth A. 2019. *Autobiography on the spectrum: Disrupting the autism narrative*. New York, NY: Teachers College Press.

Nasar, Sylvia. 1999. *A beautiful mind: A biography of John Forbes Nash, Jr., winner of the Nobel Prize in economics, 1994*. London, UK; New York, NY: Faber and Faber.

Nash, John Forbes. 2016. *Open problems in mathematics*. New York, NY: Springer Science+Business Media.

Nietzsche, Friedrich Wilhelm. 2006. *Thus spoke Zarathustra: A book for all and none*. Cambridge UK: Cambridge Univiersity Press.

Omnigraphics Inc. 2018a. *Anxiety disorders sourcebook: Basic consumer health information about mental health disorders and associated myths and facts, types of anxiety disorders, including general anxiety disorder, obsessive-compulsive disorder, posttraumatic stress disorder, panic disorder, social anxiety disorder, specific phobia, separation anxiety, illness anxiety disorder, somatic symptom disorder, and more; along with information about causes, risk factors, treatment options, including medications, psychotherapy, and complementary and alternative medications, financial assistance, tips for caregivers, a glossary of related terms, and a directory of resources for more information* (1st ed.). Detroit, MI: Omnigraphics Inc.

Omnigraphics Inc. 2018b. *Autism and pervasive developmental disorders sourcebook: Basic consumer health information about autism spectrum disorder, and pervasive developmental disorders such as asperger syndrome and rett syndrome, along with facts about causes, symptoms, assessment, interventions, treatments, and education. Tips for family members and teachers on the transition to adulthood, a glossary of related terms, and a directory of resources for more information*. Detroit, MI: Omnigraphics, Inc.

Pierce, Simon. 2019. *PTSD: Causes and care* (Diseases and disorders). New York, NY: Lucent Press.

Post, Stephen Garrard. 2000. *The moral challenge of Alzheimer disease: Ethical issues from diagnosis to dying* (2nd ed.). Baltimore, MD: Johns Hopkins University Press.

Prasher, Vee P., and Anisha Prasher. 2014. *The essential guide to health care for adults with Down syndrome*. Birmingham, AL: BILD Publications.

Pueschel, Siegfried M. 2006. *Adults with Down syndrome*. Baltimore, MD: Paul H. Brookes Pub. Co.

Rausch, Jeffrey L., Maria E. Johnson, and Manuel F. Casanova. 2008. *Asperger's disorder* (Medical Psychiatry series). New York, NY: Informa Healthcare.

Rawls, John. *A theory of justice* (revised ed.). Cambridge, MA: Harvard Universtiy Press.

Reinares, Maria, Anabel Martinez-Aran, and Eduard Vieta. 2020. *Psychotherapy for bipolar disorders: An integrative approach*. Cambridge, UK; New York, NY: Cambridge University Press.

Rodger, Ellen, and Rosie Gowsell. 2014. *Fetal alcohol spectrum disorder (Understanding mental health)*. St. Catharines, Ontario, CN; New York, NY: Crabtree Publishing Company.

Rose, Nikolas S. 1996. *Inventing our selves: Psychology, power, and personhood*. Cambridge, UK; New York, NY: Cambridge University Press.

Rothman-Kerr, Rachael. 2019. *Bipolar disorder: Dealing with mania and depression*. New York, NY: Lucent.

Russo, Jessica A., J. Kelly Coker, and Jason H. King. 2017. *DSM-5 and family systems*. New York, NY: Springer Publishing Company.

Ryder, Richard D. 1998. *The political animal: The conquest of speciesism*. Jefferson, NC: McFarland & Co.

Schmahl, Christian, K. Luan Phan, and Robert O. Friedel. 2018. *Neurobiology of personality disorders*. Oxford, UK; New York, NY: Oxford University Press.

Sharma, Sushil K. 2017. *Fetal alcohol spectrum disorders: Concepts, mechanisms, and cure*. New York, NY: Nova Biomedical.

Singer, Peter. 1975. *Animal liberation: A new ethics for our treatment of animals*. New York, NY: New York Review, distributed by Random House.

———. 2016. *Ethics in the real world: 82 brief essays on things that matter*. Princeton, NJ; Oxford, UK: Princeton University Press.

———. 2006. *In defense of animals: The second wave*. Malden, MA: Blackwell Pub.

———. 2011. *Practical ethics* (3rd ed.). New York, NY: Cambridge University Press.

Singh, Manpreet Kaur. 2019. *Clinical handbook for the diagnosis and treatment of pediatric mood disorders*. Washington, DC: American Psychiatric Association Publishing.

Skallerup, Susan J. 2008. *Babies with Down syndrome: A new parents' guide* (3rd ed.). Bethesda, MD: Woodbine House.

Soares, Jair C., and A. H. Young. 2016. *Bipolar disorders: Basic mechanisms and therapeutic implications* (3rd ed.). Cambridge, UK; New York, NY: Cambridge University Press.

Solomon, Andrew. 2012. *Far from the tree: Parents, children and the search for identity*. New York, NY: Scribner.

Sperry, Len. 2016. *Handbook of diagnosis and treatment of DSM-5 personality disorders: Assessment, case conceptualization, and treatment* (3rd ed.). New York, NY: Routledge, Taylor & Francis Group.

Stanley, Barbara, and Antonia S. New. 2018. *Borderline personality disorder*. New York, NY: Oxford University Press.

Thoreau, Henry David, and Thomas Carew. 1854. *Walden: Or, life in the woods*. Boston, MA: Ticknor and Fields.

Thoreau, Henry David, Horace Elisha Scudder, H. G. O. Blake, Ralph Waldo Emerson, and F. B. Sanborn. 1932. *Riverside edition. The writings of Henry David Thoreau, with bibliographical introductions and full indexes*. Boston, MA; New York, NY: Houghton Mifflin Company.

Tsuang, Ming T., Stephen V. Faraone, and Stephen J. Glatt. 2019. *Schizophrenia* (4th ed.). Oxford, UK: Oxford University Press.

Van der Kolk, Bessel A. 2014. *The body keeps the score: Brain, mind, and body in the healing of trauma*. New York, NY: Viking.

Van Herwegen, Jo, and Deborah Riby. 2015. *Neurodevelopmental disorders: Research challenges and solutions*. London, UK; New York, NY: Psychology Press/Taylor & Francis Group.

Vaughn, Jacqueline. 2003. *Disabled rights: American disability policy and the fight for equality*. Washington, DC: Georgetown University Press.

Vujanovic, Anka A., and Sudie E. Back. 2019. *Posttraumatic stress and substance use disorders: A comprehensive clinical handbook*. New York, NY: Routledge.

Wade, Tracey. 2017. *Encyclopedia of feeding and eating disorders*. New York, NY: Springer Berlin Heidelberg.

Walker, Pete. 2013. *Complex PTSD: From surviving to thriving: A guide and map from recovering from childhood trauma*. North Charleston, SC: CreateSpace Publishing.

Watkins, Christine. 2012. *Alcohol abuse*. Detroit, MI: Greenhaven Press.

Watson, Ronald R., and Sherma Zibadi. 2017. *Addictive substances and neurological disease: Alcohol, tobacco, caffeine, and drugs of abuse in everyday lifestyles*. London, UK; San Diego, CA: Elsevier/AP, Academic Press.

Whitaker, Robert. 2010. *Anatomy of an epidemic: Magic bullets, psychiatric drugs, and the astonishing rise of mental illness in America*. New York, NY: Crown Publishers.

Whittington, Joyce, Tony Holland, and Prader-Willi Syndrome Association. 2004. *Prader-Willi syndrome: Development and manifestations*. Cambridge, UK; New York, NY: Cambridge University Press.

Willemsen, Rob, and R. Frank Kooy. 2017. *Fragile X syndrome: From genetics to targeted treatment*. London, UK; San Diego CA: Elsevier/Academic Press, an imprint of Elsevier.

Wilson, Barbara A., Jill Winegardner, and Fiona Ashworth. 2014. *Life after brain injury: Survivors' stories*. Hove, East Sussex UK: Psychology Press.

Woo, Stephanie M., and Carolyn Keatinge. 2016. *Diagnosis and treatment of mental disorders across the lifespan* (2nd ed.). Hoboken, NJ: John Wiley & Sons.

Zanetti, Tatiana, Elena Tenconi, Angela Veronese, and Mariateresa Nardi. 2014. *Mirror mirror on the wall, who's the thinnest of them all?: Reflections on anorexia nervosa in adolescence.* New York, NY: Nova Biomedical.

Chapter Four

Special Challenges to Personhood in the 21st Century

CONTESTED PERSONHOOD IN THE NEWS

Current Overview

Twentieth century French philosopher Paul-Michel Foucault (1926–1984) observed in 1978, *"Where there is power, there is resistance."* The vulnerabilities of humans both in body (soma) and in mind (psyche) may become opportunities for conscious and unconscious challenges to full personhood, contesting being human in others. The two forces dominating in the assault on personhood are the "other" who constitutes those as dissimilar and strange to us, as well as the "self" which constitutes our own persona and identity that exist in opposition to the "other." As we observed earlier, the threats to personhood stemming from both without (i.e., the "other") and as well from within (i.e., the "self") may synergize and amplify the assaults. The fabric of contested personhood is as old as *Homo sapiens*, yet each epoch encounters manifestations of assaults on personhood that are unique to its own time and space. Twenty-first century America is no different!

We will sample from a range of unique and pressing examples of contested personhood that deserve further interrogation. The task is to seek to describe current day assaults on personhood in America, the perpetrator(s), as well as the victims of contested being. Not intending to be exhaustive, the topics to be explored below were selected because they chew on the very fabric of American life. Each topic spans the fullest range of discounted personhood and contested being human. Most assaults extend to the extreme of contested personhood, that is, death at the hand of the "other" and as we shall observe sometimes at the hand of the "self." The scourge of the opioid

131

epidemic that crosses America, for example, was a leading cause of death in America until the COVID-19 pandemic of 2019. Likewise, the 21st century American version of Jim Crow and the push back by the Black Lives Matter movement are worthy of greater analysis in the face of recalcitrant improvement in civil rights and absence of civil society. The threat of growing populations of adults with dementia, particularly those diagnosed with Alzheimer's disease, and the fate of the deeply forgetful in American life forces us to evaluate how dementia impacts personhood. Is personhood once assigned, unassailable? Is personhood status vulnerable to assault at the whim of changing social attitudes? Are barriers to full personhood only in the here-and-now? Do deeper "original sins" of the American story constitute a foundational source empowering attacks on the personhood of the "other"? Finally, we must evaluate how current 21st century views of death and dying impact our response to challenges to full personhood for the infirm and dying. How will America value the concept of the dignity of all people going forward in this century? Will the suffering masses mentioned above and those with vulnerabilities of soma and/or psyche remain helpless victims of assault on their personhood?

Opioid Addiction and Lost Personhood

Substance use disorders constitute a maladaptive pattern characterized by continued pathological use of a medication, non-medically indicated drug(s) whose chronic use leads to clinically severe impairment, distress, and addiction (Smith 2018a). Substance use disorders can negatively impact physical and/or psychological functioning and result in repeated adverse social effects in the workplace, school and/or home often provoking conflicts with others, self-loathing, or legal problems, including arrest and incarceration (Moore and Center for Substance Abuse Treatment [U.S.] 2002). Today, in America, the most serious outgrowth of substance abuse is that associated with opioid use, abuse, addiction, and overdose (Hampton and Foster 2018). For several years, the annual death toll from opioid overdose has exceeded the death toll of the entire Vietnam War! Each year, this toll increases at an alarming rate (Bisaga and Chernyaev 2018). In 2016, more than 170,000 people used heroin for the first time, 2.1 million had an opioid use disorder, 11.5 million misused prescription opioids. The sum of their loss to the economy was more than $500 billion (United States Congressional House Committee on Energy and Commerce 2015; United States Congressional House Committee on Oversight and Government Reform 2017; United States Congressional Senate Committee on Health Education Labor and Pensions 2018). The incidence of newborns experiencing withdrawal syndrome due to opioid use and misuse during pregnancy continues to rise. In some tertiary care hospitals, 1 in every 4 newborns suffers from opioid withdrawal. It is generally accepted that the misleading assurances by pharmaceutical companies in the 1990s as to the addiction potential of opioids led to increased rates of prescription (Courtwright 2001; Seppala and Rose 2010). Coupled with misuse, abuse, and ready non-prescription access, opioid addiction levels soared (Macy 2018). The founding premise that powerful opioids could be designed with high potency and little addiction potential was proven to be a disastrous overreach by companies reaping enormous profits and growth as America slid into a full blown epidemic of opioid use, abuse, misuse, and overuse (Shoham, Kett, and Addad 2010; Quinones 2016).

Opioid use disorders were not invented in the late 1990s. The U.S. "War on Drugs," initially launched in 1971, was the response to a Congressional report on the growing heroin use among U.S. servicemen in Vietnam (Caulkins and RAND Drug Policy Research Center 2005). In 1971, about ten to fifteen percent of the servicemen had a heroin addiction and President Nixon declared drug abuse as "public enemy number one." In the intervening years, the U.S. has spent more than a $1 trillion on the War on Drugs and nearly $40 billion each year since 2016. Excepting the last decade, the War on Drugs was being waged, absent an understanding of the nature of routine opioid addiction and its treatment. The U.S. government employed its power to control the narrative about drug addiction, demonizing those for whom addiction provided a temporary exit plan from lives of destitution, want, and frank oppression (Mallea 2014). Racial biases already operating within the U.S. conveniently dovetailed within the criminalization of drug abuse. Drug offenses accounted for two-thirds of the increase in federal inmate population (Quinones 2016). From 1985 to 2000, more than half of young African American men in the largest cities in the U.S. were being held under the Federal or state criminal justice system. In 2011, middle-aged Black Americans were more likely to been incarcerated in prison than admitted to the military or college (Quinones 2016). The U.S. criminal justice system had in fact reconstituted Jim Crow into a state-sponsored racial caste system (Alexander 2010). Thus, the government not only aided and abetted the "New Jim Crow," but also employed its power to shape "knowledge" about it and the narrative favoring the dominant White patriarchal ruling party (Alexander 2010).

Rather than attend to the true bases of drug abuse (e.g., powerlessness, hopelessness, lack of access to education and to employment opportunity), the U.S. narrative was heavily steeped in the "moral decline" of the targeted population, mostly Black and mostly lower-socioeconomic folks, that became a self-fulfilling prophecy serving U.S. politics particularly well, even though empty of evidence-based solutions to drug addiction (Zigon 2019). The demonization of the drug users was easy. They were the evil "other" in our orderly society who for historical, tradition, and some even added genetic bases were viewed as debasing American life. The "least of us" became the "other," a threat to the very fabric of society. Thus the stereotype promoted by U.S. interests for the "drug user" highlighted a double or in some cases triple jeopardy: color (i.e., race), gender, and addiction (Provine 2007). Projecting the self-serving "values" of a U.S. society that was largely White, patriarchal, Christian, and self-labeled "blemish-free," this America turned away from the radical love and inclusion proclaimed by Jesus of Nazareth to the radical abandonment and criminalization of the very least of us (Provine 2007, Zigon 2019).

We return to the French philosopher Michel Foucault. He insightfully recognized well the relationship between power and knowledge, formed in the neologism "power-knowledge." In the power-knowledge terminology, the "hyphen" highlights an inherent inextricability of the two (Foucault and Faubion 2000). We often consider knowledge to be "truth" in some form or other and fail to see that knowledge can be shaped by power for its own use (Foucault 1978). Cast in Foucault's paradigm, the drug abuse problem in America up until the 21st century might be considered a "Black Heroin" problem associated with people of color, people in lower socio-economic classes, and with abject moral decline (Fareed 2015; Walker, Spohn, and DeLone 2018). The American ruling class shaped the narrative to divert attention both from understanding what drives people to abuse drugs as well as from research into evidence-based medical therapies for addicts. Since the turn of the 21st century, American society was forced to confront the inconvenient truth about opioid use and abuse, (Meier 2003) a reality initially viewed, it proffered, as just an extension of the "Black Heroin" problem (Fernandez and Libby 2011). Opioid abuse had now infiltrated the White psyche, fueled by media images of middle-class White people overdosing on the broadcast news (Walker, Spohn, and DeLone 2018). In contrast to the existing "Black Heroin" problem was the "White Opioid" epidemic (Meier 2018). Realization that all people (e.g., White and Black, poor and rich) share that capacity to seek out drugs to alleviate not only pain, but also the ills of depression and anxiety, had emerged as an existential threat to the dominant White patriarchal ruling party in America (Hampton and Foster 2018; Schepis 2018).

Black and White Americans show the same propensity towards the use of illicit drugs (Hampton and Foster 2018). Yet, Black Americans are 6–10 times more likely to be subject to arrest and incarceration for the same drug offenses (Alexander 2010). The "prison industry" in the U.S. has been an area of rich profits and unparalleled growth. More than two million lives are under detention in the U.S. criminal justice system, most of them are Black or Hispanic (Alexander 2010; Forman 2017). When *de*criminalization of the drug laws created in the War on Drugs became a reality, the prison-for-profit industry census declined, provoking a political problem. The prison system in America is active in two efforts: incarceration of inmates in a "for-profit" model (Eisen 2018); and, substantial political donations to protect the growth of the "game." Biased drug enforcement practices and complicity within the justice system allow for continued disproportionate incarceration of people of color rather than Whites (Forman 2017; Eisen 2018; Walker, Spohn, and DeLone 2018). This disproportionality of criminalization of people of color in the U.S. feeds the decades-old narrative of moral decline linked to race and class. Drug addicts are both demonized and stigmatized in America. The penal system is merely a profitable way to marginalize these poor souls to places out of sight, out of mind (Wacquant 2001; Alexander 2018). A stark remnant of Jim Crow politics, Black Americans were precluded from cultural capital, social redistribution, and participating in the political process (Wacquant 2001, 2002). Loïs Wacquant proffered that 21st century America had transformed the Black "dark ghetto" to prison and the prison to the Black ghetto (Wacquant 2002). The intention was to embrace the concept of "out-of-sight, out-of-mind."

The White Opioid problem challenged the narrative of demonization and stigmatization of drug abusers with the uncomfortable and inconvenient truth that we all are no less immune to opioid addiction. One narrative showing the ability of the White ruling class to use power to shape knowledge towards a preferred narrative is that of the "treatment plan." Examination of the media's version of evidenced-based therapy for the celebrity "beautiful people" with an opioid addiction plan reveals as resort-like venue, a mansion replete with opportunities to confront one's addiction through yoga, inspirational meditation, specialized diets, and perhaps some prescription drug, for example, buprenorphine and naloxone (Brand 2017). This genre of constant episodic "news" acts to elevate our empathy for the "celebrity addict" and sanitize the public image of how simple drug addiction is to handle, especially if cost is no obstacle. Addiction to opioids may span all cultural and economic barriers, but the public image of treatment aimed at cultivating our empathy is the "celebrity addict." The media treatment of the so-called Black Heroin problem, in contrast, appears to be designed to provoke moral indignation, revulsion and fear, not love and empathy (Fernandez and Libby 2011). "Celebrity addicts" would be exalted and portrayed empathetically as victims of addiction, while addicts of color were ridiculed, abused, and incarcerated, not as victims of a medical condition, but rather as people bereft of moral fiber.

With this terse introduction to a major health epidemic in the U.S. what can we say about opioid addiction and personhood? The Black Heroin problem was presented to America as simply further proof that some Black Americans were not deserving of full personhood, dignity, and being. With a 400+ year of personhood deprived, discounted, stolen, and denied, Black Americans are familiar with such efforts engineered to contest their being human, their full personhood. Slavery, Jim Crow laws, the New Jim Crow of incarceration and oppression, all act to degrade Black people and people of color (Waquant 2002; Alexander 2010; Forman 2017). This potent discrimination has gained institutional power in America, simply disguised to reinforce the Black Heroin stereotype and warrant indentured servitude as prison laborers. The persistence of segregated road chain gangs fifty years after the book (Pearce 1965) and movie "Cool Hand Luke" (LC Purchase Collection [Library of Congress] 1967) is striking! The depiction of a chain gang in 1967 was politically corrected for the times, that is, in the segregated South the cinema relied upon chain gang members being mostly White. This distortion of the truth was necessary to appeal to the sensitivities of the moviegoers of those years. Who then would have had an appetite for a true depiction of mostly Black chain gangs, rather than one presented in which Paul Newman and George Kennedy were cast as central characters, both being White cinema stars of the 1960s?

Having a drug addiction in America clearly degrades one's personhood status. Contested-being obviously starts with and aims at the "other." Society has been conditioned by politics to view drug use as associated with marginalized people of color, people of lower socioeconomic class, people who are morally deficient or defective. Once made public through arrest, incarceration, or a poorly timed overdose, opioid addiction in 21st century America leads to labeling, stigmatization, and demonization for most (Redmond 2018). Equally challenged, the inner self, so too conditioned by the harsh social narrative, suffers from the consequences of disclosure. These negative forces are in addition to those that provoked the addiction, including prominently co-morbid disorders such as depression and anxiety (Redmond 2018). It has been estimated that about fifty percent of opioid overdoses admitted to hospital emergency departments are in fact attempted suicides provoked by depression (Lu 2017). About fifteen percent of opioid addicts treated for an overdose eventually succeed at suicide. The addict's own view of their personhood and self-image can be deeply discounted in response to judgment by both the "other" and inner world of "self." Personhood is a multidimensional aspect of living. Personhood encompasses the past, the present, and the anticipated life experiences, loved ones, study and work, family and community, relationships and sexuality, and the very dominion bequeathed to each of us over our bodies. Drug addiction can subsume and degrade personhood to the point of extinguishing the individual self (Hanson, Venturelli, and Fleckenstein 2018).

The need for community support and love, for evidence-based therapies, and for renewed efforts aimed at restoring the meaning of one's life must become overarching for America. This "not-so-silent-anymore" opioid epidemic only will be overcome by covenantal commitment to establishing a community in which all lives, as imperfect as they may be, are of worth and deserving love and understanding, rather than judgment and abandonment.

Moral solidarity in community compels us to accept and to embrace the knowledge that opioid addiction (and other form of drug addictions) constitutes a form of chronic, relapsing disease. Addiction is a medical condition requiring therapy, not a moral failing! If we embrace this knowledge of the medical basis of addiction we can disabuse ourselves of several fantasies. The first fantasy is that addiction simply is a moral failing and we good folks are not subject to its curse. The second fantasy is that, at the worst case, treatment and recovery from opioid addiction will require at the most only a few weeks and some suboxone therapy. The third fantasy is that opioid addiction can be overcome "cold turkey" simply by steely abstinence. A community in moral solidarity begins with the knowledge that all forms of chemical addiction and substance abuse are health issues not moral deficits (Foote et al. 2014). Thoughtful recovery programs to manage opioid addiction have been developed and employed with success. But such successful approaches are neither quick nor inexpensive of time or money. Particularly for physicians with substance abuse disorder (yes, physicians can become drug abusers), such programs have proven very successful. All are long term, 5-year protocols, including drug urine monitoring and comprehensive care (Grinspoon 2016). Our ethical foundations collapse when we ask why evidence-based therapies for addiction are made available for some, but not others? Are we to value the lives of one member of the community greater than that of another based upon level of education, vocation, earning potential, or privilege? In *Communio Sanctorum* such differences in people are not ignored, but the rights afforded to all members for love and support in the fight to overcome addiction cannot be withheld. The health and well-being of the entire community is dependent on covenantal responsibility for each and every member. If there is drug addiction, it is a problem for the entire community. The community needs to become fully informed about the medical condition of substance abuse and addiction, how to diagnosis and treat victims of opioid, and other, addiction disorders. The current criminal justice system's solution to the problem will be biased in application of the law and aiming to keep these folks out-of-sight, out-of-mind, while insuring fresh substrates for mass incarceration.

Discounted Personhood *in utero* (Fetus) and Pregnant Woman

The issues of double jeopardy for fetus and for pregnant woman with regard to personhood persist in 21st century America. Biologically, a fetus is human life from conception onwards (Malbon 2013). For women, full personhood and human rights always remain under attack in a patriarchal society replete with racism and classism (Malbon 2013). Child rights and fetal rights are not the same, although many states continue to intentionally blur the legal line of personhood between the born (i.e., a child) and the unborn (i.e., a fetus).

Based upon the influence that substances ingested by a pregnant woman may have upon the developing fetus, there is well-placed cautioning of pregnant women for avoiding alcohol and various prescription as well as illicit drugs, especially drugs of abuse (Solof 2013). In particular the effects of alcohol abuse upon fetal development is termed Fetal Alcohol Spectrum Disorder (see FASD above). In these cases the ultimate conflict is recast as "fetus *versus* pregnant woman" (Murphy and Rosenbaum 1999). Through continued drug abuse (e.g., alcohol. cocaine, opioids, etc.) the eventual personhood of the child who now is *in utero* can be placed at serious risk (Sherman, Sanders, and Trinh 1998). In this time of the opioid epidemic in America, the effects of opioid dependence and abuse has provoked a skyrocketing of births in which the newborn suffers from opioid withdrawal. This situation is categorically different from the earlier discussion of preimplantation genetic diagnosis (PGD) and early termination of pregnancy. Employed to identify genetic disorders that can be severe and even life threatening, PGD assesses risks quite apart from those discussed herein. Trisomy-21 (Down syndrome), for example, is readily diagnosed by PGD, although the diagnosis cannot predict with any precision where on a spectrum of mild-to-severe affliction the neonate will reside in development. With opioid addiction, the situation clearly distills to fetus *versus* pregnant mother with opioid dependence. The neonate of a mother with opioid addiction is at serious risk for a drug withdrawal syndrome, "neonatal abstinence syndrome" or "neonatal opioid withdrawal syndrome," that has both short-term and long-term negative effects on motor skills, behavior and cognitive development of the infant. This dilemma revisits how we view addiction and avoidable drug exposure *in utero* for a pregnant mother. Does drug use or abuse in response to a medical condition requiring therapy bias our thinking? Drug treatments for opioid addiction disorder may include methadone and buprenorphine, which also can expose the fetus to similar developmental issues. Will we label a pregnant recovering addict in treatment as a compliant patient or as a morally failed individual?

Regrettably, such tensions pit the personhood of the fetus against that of the pregnant woman. More worrisome is that such thick moral dilemmas largely have played out in legislatures and courts of individual states in America, often influenced more by theologically popular sentiment rather than compassionate justice. Making decisions around complex issues cast simplemindedly as pitting the personhood of a fetus against that of the pregnant woman has produced alarming outcomes! Such "justice" often is served up to restrict or preclude abortion under all conditions, thereby condemning the pregnant woman to either "coerced" forced childbirth or criminal prosecution for seeking an abortion, or both. Even where a potentially devastating genetic or chemically-induced birth defect can be diagnosed, hard line Pro-Life camps in some states seek to make abortion a criminal act. Although medically induced abortion is widely available and considered a low risk alternative to surgical abortions (Malbon 2013), choice can be usurped by the "state" and withheld from the pregnant woman. Harsh political strategies aim at erecting multiple spurious obstacles to freely available and legal abortion mandated at the Federal level, protected by U.S. Supreme Court decision in *Roe v. Wade*. The availability of medical abortifacients online as well as through women's rights group employing small drones to provide local deliveries of abortifacients offer potential relief. Such relief may be the only hope to preserving a woman's right to choose early termination to pregnancy in states hell-bent on abolishing abortion for any and all bases, even to spare the death of the woman experiencing a potentially lethal ectopic pregnancy. In seeking a legal medical abortion in the U.S. by making use of these newer routes of delivery, does a pregnant woman expose herself to additional risks? Would such an act be declared criminal? In some states, the answer rendered by legislatures is "yes." Women have been prosecuted for seeking and participating in self-induced abortions (Malbon 2013). As politically self-labeled "Pro-Life" states (e.g., Kansas, Louisiana, Mississippi, Oklahoma, et al.) become more imaginative in concocting legislative tools aimed squarely to close and to obstruct abortion clinics, new avenues to medical abortion undoubtedly will emerge. Will pregnant women lose their legally protected reproductive rights and subject to criminal prosecution in the effort to obtain a therapeutic abortion? When do ever expanding waiting periods, travel costs and time losses, and available access to abortion clinics pitched regularly by state legislatures constitute an "undue burden" as precluded by the 1992 Supreme Court decision *Planned Parenthood v. Casey*?

In 2020, the formidable obstacles encountered in obtaining an abortion in the U.S. reflect triple or quadruple jeopardy. This assault on personhood of many women is virtually unknown to any middle-class White woman in America. Triple jeopardy, for instance, starts for women residing in a state in which biblical patriarchy is embraced. So too is the additional jeopardy for a woman of color residing in a state that displays a long history of racism, White supremacy, and radical anti-abortion sentiment. Being pregnant and confronting dubious biblical warrants professed by anti-abortionists that are not theologically sound is anathema to liberty (Malbon 2013). More than thirty-five states place restrictions on abortion providers and hospitals, encourage medical personnel to refuse to participate in abortions, require parental involvement in a minor's decision to access abortion services, and strict non-deployment of states and Federal funds to pay for the medications or the procedure (Guttmacher Institute 2020). Keep in mind that abortion has been practiced globally for time immemorial and is not a *bona fide* topic touched upon in the Holy Bible. Yet early termination of a pregnancy for any reason has been cast as sinful, not legitimate, and unlawful at the state level. Add to this list of vulnerabilities that of being under the age of consent and you have quadruple jeopardy for some young, pregnant women of color, living states with vocal pro-life political influence. Interestingly, in several of these states child marriage (even at 13!) is legal with judicial or parental consent! This exception, reeking of hypocrisy in this current discussion, again reflects simple dominant patriarchy. Paradoxically, once such an underage female is married or gives birth (even as underage and unmarried) she becomes fully emancipated! In most states, such legal emancipation marks full personhood. Yet if a so emancipated woman seeks an abortion, assuming the service is available, she can expose herself to criminal prosecution under statutes in these same states! Historically throughout the U.S., White middle-class women of privilege and of means enjoy access to abortion services with little inconvenience (Malbon 2013). Close inspection of Guttmacher Institute data on abortion in America yields a profile of the most likely woman to seek an abortion in 21st century America as White, heterosexual, cohabitating with a male partner, adherent to a faith tradition (i.e., mainline Protestant, evangelical Protestant, and Roman Catholic), low-income to middle class, and with pre-existing children. The number one reason women seek early termination of a pregnancy remains economic insecurity. The inability to financially support an additional child in a preexisting family is a powerful deterrent to fulfilling a procreative event (Malbon 2013).

Pregnant women are victimized, denied full personhood, and the legal privileges granted to them under the Bill of Rights! If self-administered medical abortion (using abortifacients) is the only available option, should this act be criminalized? If unintentional, inadvertent maternal behavior can place the normal development of a fetus at risk, is it moral to deprive the mother of a legal remedy to avoid a birth defect that can cause great suffering for the infant? The case of Sherri Finkbine, a 1960s media star on *Romper Room*, wife, and mother of four, is pertinent here (Malbon 2013). Finkbine was prescribed thalidomide as a sleeping pill, before its powerful teratogenic effect on limb development was widely known. She was pregnant at the time and read with horror the reports of limbless children being born to mothers who used the same drug. Her odyssey from media voice about avoiding the drug to vilified *persona non grata* in the U.S. was the outcome of her seeking an abortion. Forced from the U.S. to obtain an abortion in Sweden, Finkbine and her family were ostracized, hounded, and unemployed simply to avoid the suffering of all that would have attended the birth of a child, who on post mortem was shown to lack both legs and one arm. Her exposure to thalidomide was inadvertent, but the hate and reprisals the family endured in response to a "therapeutic" abortion was most certainly not unintentional.

The American College of Obstetrics & Gynecology (ACOG) has provided a strongly worded position paper on the intentional shaming of women who simply are expressing their reproductive rights. It declares that criminalization of self-induced, medical abortion only intimidates and shames women unnecessarily. The ACOG professional position rightly notes that restrictive and punitive measures neither end abortions nor reduce unintended pregnancies. The pressure toward self-induced medical remedies really only reflects personal resolve and resistance to unbounded efforts by state legislatures to restrict women's reproductive rights. It is ironic that states seeking to criminalize a woman's choice for early termination of pregnancy actually may be fostering the very act that they seek to criminalize! Policies enacted mandating healthcare professionals, as "clandestine reporters," required to report to law enforcement women who may have attempted self-induced medical abortion are contrary to professional codes of privacy. They intrude upon and violate the very foundational privacy of the patient-physician relationship. Further debasement of women's personhood occurred in 2018, in which the Federal criminal justice system emerged as a formidable cudgel advancing extreme conservative views embraced by the Trump administration. Emblematic of this new role for the justice department was a decision to deny to pregnant women incarcerated in U.S. immigration detention centers the right to obtain an abortion. This policy was enforced in cases of professed or suspected incest and rape. No exceptions were made. Even when the rape of detainees occurred by prison personnel and reported to the authorities, requests for therapeutic abortions were denied. Women in the U.S. confront an ever-expanding reality of fewer reproductive choices, their personhood being subjected to denial, discount, and even loss.

Prevention of teen pregnancy, a hallmark of conservative law makers for decades, reveals itself to be a charade based upon the fantasy of unsubstantiated success of programs promoting "just abstinence." Consequently fewer insurance programs seek to cover necessary costs associated with birth control measures. Abortions that are legal become less available due to closure of clinics, harassment of those seeking abortion services, and sometimes-lethal assaults on abortion providers. The Fourteenth Amendment of the Bill of Rights makes use of the word "person" to guarantee that no state shall "deprive any *person* of life, liberty, or property, without due process of law; nor deny to any person within its jurisdiction the equal protection of the laws" (Malbon 2013). Although explicitly protected under the Bill of Rights, personhood for pregnant women remains under dire assault. The perpetrator of this loss of women's reproductive rights is not some hidden nemesis, but rather a White conservative, largely evangelical Christian minority of citizens in the U.S. hiding in plain sight! Consider this fact, less than 25% of voters of the states that legislate and enact the most restrictive access to abortion services are actually pro-life (Malbon 2013).

Fetal protection statutes and wrongful death actions on behalf of fetuses only aim to further diminish the human rights of women, reflecting a long history of bias by White conservative patriarchy in America. When the intimate biological relationship between a woman and a fetus is viewed merely as a target for fetal rights advocates, the goal simply is to create an adversarial position between woman and fetus. Women who were unaware of their pregnancy have been arrested, tried, and incarcerated for the inadvertent exposure of their embryo to chemical substances (e.g., alcohol). Criminalizing pregnancy to artificially address a whole host of "straw men" issues continues to assault, diminish, and deny full personhood to countless women in America. State laws ostensibly created to protect fetal rights wreak of misogyny, enacted simply to oppress and punish women. This is not to minimize the potential effects of a chemical such as alcohol on the normal development of a fetus. Fetal alcohol syndrome (FAS), discussed earlier, is a well-described entity in the medical literature. What is lacking in these state legislative efforts is recognition that substance abuse (i.e., think use/abuse of "alcohol, opioids, and cocaine") is a medical condition, not a character flaw. As politics, like any other profession, certainly is not devoid of practitioners who are suffering from substance abuse, the lack of compassion in their politics strikes one as cripplingly insensitive, hypocritical, and overtly self-serving. Naming the fetus entity as an "unborn child" in legal documents, for example, constitutes a disservice to a serious debate about how best to protect human development *in utero.* Rather it seeks to deflect the main issues around debates of pending laws to a wrongheaded polemic that professes to have established when personhood arises *in utero.* Philosophers, theologians, and ethicists have wrestled with this question for millennia. Do state legislators in their deliberations profess some new extraordinary insights on personhood and ensoulment that have been inadvertently overlooked for the past 4000 years? Wrongful death statutes that would permit civil suits against individuals who cause the death of a fetus actually work only to commodify and to objectify the very human life that they profess to hold so priceless? The legal tool then is relegated to the "tort" case in which injury or death of a fetus can be rectified only by a monetary award against a legal claim of loss, not life, not soul!

One wonders if there will come a time when not an immigrant in a U.S. detention center, but rather a visitor from Europe who does not share the ethos and ultraconservative leanings of various Bible-belt states may find herself incarcerated and criminally prosecuted for sharing a champagne toast at the news of a pregnancy? Should toasting the celebration of a new life commence with a nine-month detention in a parish jailhouse in conservative America? Will routine blood work in prenatal testing be employed not for gauging the health of the pregnant woman but rather employed as a toxicology screen for alcohol, opioids and stimulants, maybe even for caffeine and tobacco? Perhaps local traditions will offer a free pass on cannabinoids (i.e., marijuana) and tobacco (i.e., chew tobacco), while honing in upon conducting more sensitive surreptitious screens to detect users of cocaine or K2? Will pregnant women with chemical substance dependence or abuse be managed as medical cases with compassion or will they be prosecuted to the fullest extent of the law in local jailhouses? Is such misogyny and cruel treatment aimed to be protective of a pregnancy or act as a legal deterrent for some addictive behaviors labeled as sinful by some? Is not the echo of the failed Prohibition Era falling on deaf ears in America today? When others intentionally project their own religious, cultural, patriarchal impulses upon the "other," personal freedoms and personhood of all are placed at risk. Within our envisioned *Communio Sanctorum*, unconditional love and support embedded in moral solidarity would be inclusive, welcoming all, especially the less unfortunate souls who have developed a chemical addiction, pregnant or not. Welcoming all pro-creative events with the support for life long flourishing needs to commence with human conception. Community, in turn, requires loving-kindness aimed especially for those women suffering from chemical addiction who perhaps will procreate. Reassured that these women and their children are accepted into community and will be afforded resources necessary for them to flourish defines the solidarity of *Communio Sanctorum*.

Personhood at the Mercy of Narcan Rescue (or Not)

How do we assign the value of a human life? In a graduate ethics course, I lead students through the ongoing current debate engaging the question, what is the worth of a human life? The media is filled with possible insights into this area of human worth. Several instances are illuminating. A politically connected member of the White ruling class is moved to the very top of the waiting list for a *second* heart and lungs transplant, having rejected the first. People suffering from obesity and type-2 diabetes mellitus (T2DM) go on to kidney failure and now require hemodialysis every few days, probably for the rest of their lives. They are making use of a technology that initially was developed only to preserve patients with end-stage dialysis awaiting a kidney transplant. The cost of life-long hemodialysis per patient can be more than $70,000 per year. As a society we have afforded $20M to rescue two wealthy people who foolishly sailed their yacht into the likely path of a major hurricane, against the advice of the Coast Guard. Rescue efforts for miners trapped underground, therapy for small cohorts of children suffering with a rare disease, or aid to survivors of devastating earthquakes can cost staggering amounts of public wealth to ameliorate. Yet, on the flip side, sometime the "least of us" do not survive, will not be rescued at all, but rather will be abandoned and succumb to death owing to the lack of an immunization, antibiotic, or life-saving organ transplant. Of course, when the life of someone dear to us is threatened our instincts direct us towards sparing no expense, perhaps especially when the expense will be borne by the public at large. Death of the "other," occurring frequently outside the knowledge of the "self" within us, can be so distant as to not register in our everyday lives, let alone appear on our empathic grid.

Professional statisticians wrestle with the task of establishing the value of human life, seeking to estimate cost, benefit, and risks for insurance purposes (Mankiw 2012). Of import to our discussion is a key actuarial concept, "Value of Statistical Life" (VSL). VSL is calculated by experts intent on estimating the value of human life through understanding the benefit of reducing the risk of death itself (Viscusi 1992). If we can calculate the theoretical value of "statistical" life, an estimate can be made as to the real benefits of risk reduction gained by safety items such as mandatory seat belts in automobiles, crash helmet for motorcycle enthusiasts, etc. The Council of Economic Advisers, a U.S. agency in the Executive Office of the President, makes such calculations routinely. With regard to the topic of the opioid-crisis estimates this council advised that current assessments "vastly underestimate losses by undervaluing the fatalities that result from overdoses of opioids." VSL estimated for an individual human being range widely from $1.4 million to $8.9 million depending upon criteria unique to each individual life. In 2018, the Department of Health and Human Services preferred the estimate of $9.4 million per person for calculating the cost of the ongoing "opioid epidemic." The unofficial, but largely acknowledged, start of the opioid epidemic was in the 1990s. Since that start, the annual death toll due to opioid overdose has skyrocketed. In 2018, the daily death toll ascribed to the epidemic reached more than 175! These victims were shown to span 25–55 years of age, with 35–44 years of age for the median group. Financially speaking, the economic value lost incurred each day of the epidemic (in 2018 dollars) is more than $1.5 billion! If not mitigated, by 2022 the opioid epidemic will be responsible for the loss of more than one million lives! Calculated on this basis, the death toll to 2020 for the opioid epidemic would approximate that of all U.S. servicemen casualties in World War II!

With these data on the prevalence of opioid dependence and addiction as well as those on the death toll and cost of opioid overdoses, one can see why prevention, reversal, and the saving of lives in this opioid epidemic should constitute a national emergency. The expansion of the opioid crisis into a national epidemic was described earlier. Although the over-prescription, abuse, and misuse of ethical opioids all contributed to this epidemic, many of the current solutions to the epidemic offered are aimed not the underlying root causes, but rather at simply assuaging the acute symptoms derivative of the epidemic. Certainly one of the root causes per se is not the prescription drugs ethically used to treat pain resulting from either an medical procedure or injury such as a broken collar bone. Rather a root cause emerges well after the pain of the injury subsides and healing has ensued. Some cohort of patients treated with opioids for a legitimate and therapeutic trial discover that their lives were simply "better" (i.e., happier) during the interval when they were taking the pain killer (United States Congressional House Committee on Energy and Commerce 2019). This cohort of patients ethically prescribed short-term painkillers are likely to gravitate to opioid use, abuse, and addiction. The comorbidity of depression and of anxiety disorders observed with opioid abusers speaks clearly as to a driving force in what becomes self-medication to enjoy a better, happier, less depressing and anxious life (Compton, Manseau, and American Psychiatric Association 2019). With the advent of more powerful synthetic opioids in medical use and later abuse, so did the number of reported opioid overdoses in the U.S. Even long-term chronic abusers of common opioids (e.g., oxycontin, heroin) experienced more frequent episodes of overdosing, owing to the availability of newer more potent analgesics, like fentanyl which is 30–50 times more potent than heroin (Olsen and Sharfstein 2019).

Naloxone (commonly sold by the brand name Narcan or Evzio) is an opioid antagonist, acting to neutralize the effects of opioid drugs (Wilcox 2019). Narcan binds opioid receptors effectively blocking ingested opioids from binding to and activating their cellular receptors (Hilal-Dandan, Brunton, and Goodman 2014). Naloxone was playing a role in preventative measures aimed at those seeking to stop their addiction to opioids. It can be used in combination with other drugs (e.g., buprenorphine) employed in the treatment of opioid addiction. The best-known use of Narcan, however, is in rescuing someone actively overdosing in response to an opioid. Administered either intravenously (preferred, by auto-injector pen) or nasally (by spray), Narcan can rapidly reverse the opioid-induced respiratory depression that proves fatal (Hilal-Dandan, Brunton, and Goodman 2014). The early implementation programs designed to provide Narcan "take-home kits" available to addicts in communities-at-risk have saved countless lives from potentially lethal opioid overdose. Police and other first-responders were the first professionals outside of medical Emergency Departments permitted to carry Narcan. Many states have mandated that Narcan be made available for purchase over-the-counter, without prescription, for people who are or who know someone at risk for opioid overdose.

In spite of these obvious benefits and the countless lives saved by Narcan use, some have employed Narcan not to save, but to contest the very lives of people suffering from opioid dependence and overdose. First reported in Ohio and later Pennsylvania, Maine and other locales, police and first-responders have exploited the crisis in opioid overdosing, professing that withholding Narcan rescue from a person experiencing an opioid overdose might be justified on two accounts. The first would be that denying Narcan therapy is a stand against moral depravity. In their personal view, drug abuse is sinful and therefore should not be ameliorated when an overdose occurs. The death would be the just reward for living a sinful life, within the moral depravity of drug abuse. The second basis for denying Narcan rescue is to pushback against "economic extortion" by opioid abusers who simply would rather not purchase the antagonist on prescription at considerable cost to them. This kind of "thinking" is heartless, judgmental, and without moral foundation. Denial of Narcan rescue to a needy person assaults the very personhood of the victim. It renders the victim's being to the very limit, that is, life itself. In this case, the first-responder deprived their victims of the most basic human right, that is, not to be killed.

If a child in anaphylactic shock over a bee sting or peanut allergy required a stick with epinephrine, would any first-responder really contemplate that the rescue be withheld and the child left to die? Is there some limit as to the number of times first-responders could be called upon to administer life-saving epinephrine to children with life-threatening allergies? If the victim is an adolescent accidently ingesting or coming in contact with the powerful opioid fentanyl and now presents in respiratory depression, would there come a time when the life-saving antidote is considered to be too expensive or too inconvenient to use? The answer to these rhetorical questions is decidedly "No!" The very notion that anyone with the capacity to rescue another person from a fatal drug overdose would first stop to decide whether the victim's life is worthy of rescue patently is immoral! Again, the victims of drug abuse and overdose are just that, that is, victims, they are not criminals per se. They are suffering from a scourge most often not of their own doing. These people suffer from a well-known medical problem, chemical addiction, a problem often associated with other forms of vulnerabilities of the psyche. It is irrational to consider withholding Narcan as a tool to curb drug use. The willful withholding of Narcan most likely will provoke death rather than repentance. The high recidivism observed in opioid users seeking to "get clean" reflects more the serious challenges encountered in their search for a cure. Individuals suffering from alcohol abuse and addiction are far more numerous than people with opioid addiction disorder. Those who seek to kick alcohol dependence similarly display a high rate of recidivism. Abandoning someone in alcohol toxicity to die would be an analogous assault on the victim's personhood, threatening his or her very life. This kind of life-threatening alcohol abuse and toxicity is far more prevalent than commonly noted, occurring on college campuses in the form of young people binge drinking (Winograd and Sher 2015; Fitzgerald and Puttler 2018). Would we willfully attempt to teach youthful victims of ethanol intoxication, their family, friends, and society a moral lesson by withholding life-saving rescue? There is no evidence to support that encouraging preventable death is a tool with which to address perceived moral decay. Addiction is a medical disorder, not a moral failing.

How then do we meld these two propositions together as to whether there is a moral question about providing a life-saving opioid antagonist to some person who once again has overdosed, stopped breathing and is in acute respiratory distress? Will withholding the Narcan serve as a deterrent for this individual? This of course is unlikely since the victim is unconscious and if untreated certainly will succumb in response to the overdose. Will withholding Narcan from an overdose victim become a learning experience for others witnessing this scene? Overdosing, especially with the advent of fentanyl, clearly is more likely a matter of accidental overdosing due to its high potency in combination with a lack of knowledge of the victim about the high risk of death associated with use of such high potency opioids. The "therapeutic window" is quite narrow for opioid addicts experimenting with fentanyl or fentanyl-spiked drugs of abuse. Yet, one can understand that first-responders may grow weary of responding to repeated calls to 911 about an overdose by a recidivist abuser. In Butler County Ohio, a city councilman floated a "three-strikes-and-you're-out" policy, in which an ambulance would not be sent to resuscitate a "three-time loser." There are reports of several Narcan-based "resurrections" of the same addict in a single day, let alone in a week. Frankly, local efforts of first-responders to ameliorate drug overdoses can place a significant burden on personnel as well as the resources deployed by local authorities. As useful as naloxone is for rescue of a victim in respiratory depression, it is no panacea for the opioid epidemic in the U.S.

Recidivism is high and in the absence of an in depth psychological profile, the attending physicians frequently label opioid overdoses as "accidental." Once a victim of overdose is declared medically stable, Emergency Medicine physicians routinely simply discharge the patient suffering from opioid use disorder. Without some more long-term intervention aimed at addressing the underlying addiction, survivors most assuredly will return to the addictive behavior. For people with vulnerabilities of psyche, returning them to the same situation that led to a crisis will seldom, if ever, provoke a cure for untoward behaviors. The first step towards a long-term solution to this epidemic impacting all of America (especially people in rural areas) is to accept that opioid addiction (a.k.a., opioid use disorder) is a *chronic, relapsing disorder*. The disease is a complex medical disorder with psychological, behavioral, and medical dimensions not likely to be "cured" either by two weeks of suboxone therapy or by in-group therapy. The existence of such programs represents only the best approach available, even if it known to be woefully inadequate. If we are to build moral solidarity in *Communio Sanctorum*, all must be included in our sphere of unconditional love. Opioid use disorder must be approached as a chronic relapsing disorder that will require the investment of years of behavioral and drug therapy if victims are to kick the habit. Identifying the basic conditions of their lives that provoked the addiction is the best first step. The second step is aimed at correcting and improving the victim's living situation. This movement towards more positive outcomes will be time-consuming, expensive, and yet a wholly worthwhile effort to save these precious human lives at risk.

PERSONHOOD CONTESTED BY OLD GRUDGES

Race Always Matters in America

In 1993 Cornel West published a groundbreaking book simply entitled, *Race Matters*. It was a candid and biting critique of the social, economic, and moral dimensions of skin color in America (West 1993). A timeless read, *Race Matters* remains a powerful commentary on the lack of moral and ethical fiber in a country replete with racism. America displays only magical thinking purporting that the chronic issue of race has been solved and now is behind us. The American narrative on slavery and heroic efforts towards achieving equality among Black and White people has a long history, more than 400 years (Cone 1969; Kendi 2016). In 1790, along with 3,135,205 free White men and women enumerated in the U.S. census, were 694,280 enslaved Africans engaged in agricultural peonage by slavery and sharecropping. Ahead lay the start of the Civil War (1861), the Emancipation Proclamation (1862), the end of the Civil War (1865), the Reconstruction (1865–1877) and a series of state laws aimed at discounting Black personhood and re-enforcing racial segregation in the South.

Jim Crow Laws: Personhood Lost

The segregation and disenfranchisement laws to be labeled "Jim Crow" laws, first appeared in 1877 (Fremon 2015). The Great Northern Migration saw African Americans move to the North largely towards employment opportunities in industrial jobs. The hierarchy and dominant position of the Southern Whites would resist amendments to the U.S. Bill of Rights (especially those affording Blacks the right to vote) through harsh, state-sponsored Jim Crow laws that were designed to fortify a resurgent White supremacy (Mortensen 2015). In a landmark case of the U.S. Supreme Court of *Dred Scott v. Sandford* (60 US 393, 1857) (Fehrenbacher 1978), the Chief Justice Roger B. Taney spared no neutral language in declaring "no" to the foundational question of whether or not a "negro whose ancestors were imported into this country and sold as slaves become a member of the political community formed and brought into existence by the Constitution of the United States . . . ?" (Fehrenbacher 1981; Herda and Herda 2017). Clearly the *"we"* in *"We the people"* of the U.S. Constitution represented "self" only in the context of White Americans. The "other," being African Americans, would be precluded from all the rights, privileges, and immunities guaranteed under "We the people." During the Jim Crow era more than 2500 African Americans were stripped of all personhood and human rights and summarily lynched under the guise of maintaining the moral stability of the South states (Cone 2011; Smångs 2017). This era reinforced discrimination and flagrantly denied personhood to African Americans. The hatred and racial prejudice fueled by post-Reconstruction segregation and embodied in Jim Crow not only extended the tiered personhood of the Old South from 1870 to the 1960s, but also made such oppressive behaviors normative for racists throughout America.

The Reconstruction Amendments to the Bill of Rights were passed to extend and protect the civil rights of former slaves (Burgan 2006). The Thirteenth Amendment abolished slavery itself. The Fourteenth Amendment aimed at overturning the *Dred Scott v. Sandford* decision was passed in 1868. The Fifteenth Amendment of 1870 was passed to prohibit state and local governments from depriving citizens from voting rights based upon race, color, and prior condition of servitude. Yet state's rights continued to employ Jim Crow laws to oppress the civil rights of African Americans by placing a seemingly endless gauntlet of obstacles before them, nullifying all but the Thirteenth Amendment. The White patriarchal ruling class would continue to oppress and wrestle with African Americans who sought to reclaim and to secure their personhood status that the Civil War, its aftermath, and the Reconstruction Amendments gained on paper (Shanor 2017). In 1896, the U.S. Supreme Court decision *Plessy v. Ferguson* would become central to the institutionalization of the "separate but equal" doctrine, reversing hard won progress in civil rights gained by African Americans. This Supreme Court decision eroded the personhood and human rights of Black Americans not only in the South, but throughout the U.S. (Fireside and Rauf 2017). The Plessy decision acted to firmly institutionalize segregation of African Americans throughout America (Fireside and Rauf 2017). Efforts by the dominant White ruling class to abridge these basic human rights guaranteed by the U.S. Constitution would be repelled by the Civil Rights movement (1950s and 1960s). The Civil Rights movement would succeed in advancing and securing Federal laws aimed at restoring full personhood of all African Americans (Carson 1987).

The eventual product of resistance to racism in America was the Civil Rights Act of 1964. This United States landmark civil rights and labor law outlawed discrimination based upon race, color, religion, sex, or national origin. The Voting Rights Act of 1965 that followed sought to overcome legal barriers at the state and local levels. Such legal barriers precluded African Americans from exercising their right to vote as guaranteed under the Fifteenth Amendment (1870). Not to be outmaneuvered by these landmark acts, White conservative politicians created new means to render people of color (especially African Americans) as second-class citizens with heavily discounted personhood and rights. This new dimension, expertly documented by Michelle Alexander in her book entitled, *The New Jim Crow*, was aimed at exploiting the criminal justice system towards mass incarceration of Black Americans and minorities (Alexander 2010). Fortifying this new approach to power and control of minority people of color was aggressive racial profiling by police used in combination with mandatory sentencing that was disproportionate to the crime allegedly committed (Gilliard 2018). Like other public intellectuals had noted earlier, Alexander recognized that the incarceration of minorities exploited the victim's inability to secure quality lawyers, to make bail, and to seek redress of unjust sentencing on appeal (Alexander 2010). Additionally, mass incarceration of African Americans was a lucrative business supported by and supportive of conservative politicians running on a "law and order" platform almost anywhere in the U.S. (Alexander 2010; Forman 2017; Jeffreys 2018; Berger and Losier 2018). White anxiety surged in response to expanding racial diversity in America. White resentment also was fanned by continued immigration (legal or otherwise) to the U.S. As racial segregation expanded to levels as great or greater than prior to the Civil Rights Act of 1964, discrimination and hate speech towards minorities became normative for American society. The outcome was clear, that is, America's criminal justice system became an enabler for injustice towards people of color (Wacquant 2001, 2002). Persistent underrepresentation of minorities on juries prominent in the New Jim Crow are uncanny echoes to similarities common in the old Jim Crow days (Walker, Spohn, and DeLone 2018). Jim Crow laws not only resonate in the "new" Jim Crow (Alexander 2010), but also fueled analogous Jane Crow (targeting Black women) and Juan Crow (targeting Spanish-speaking, Latin American, and other people of color) efforts of the White ruling class in response to their growing anxiety to the changing complexion and womanist roles carried into the 21st century.

Contested Being Human Versus #BlackLivesMatter

Prompted by the acquittal of George Zimmerman in the horrific shooting death of a young Black unarmed man Trayvon Martin in 2013, the Twitter hashtag "#BlackLivesMatter" and the attendant activist movement BLM were born (Taylor 2016; Lebron 2017; Hillstrom 2018). The moral depravity of the shooting of Trayvon Martin coupled with the lack of justifiable public rage at the shooting and acquittal that followed were triggers for a movement whose time had come. The foundation of the movement, however, was latent, pent up rage and frustration created in response to decades of systemic oppression and violence born of the racism endemic throughout the U.S. Racial violence and oppression displays a long history in the U.S., from the immediate aftermath of the abolition of slavery following the Civil War through to 21st century America, well beyond the resurgence of both the old and the "new" Jim Crow laws (Alexander 2010; Taylor 2016; Forman 2017). In the eyes of the Black community, criminal justice in America was increasingly racist, unfair, and unjust, designed only to further the structural oppression of the Black "other." Exploiting a robust online campaign approach (Taylor 2016), the BLM movement showed remarkable agility and creativity in advancing the principles of this grass roots, group-centered model of activist leadership. The movement has succeeded in raising public awareness of the acute and ongoing level of violence that confronts the Black community, from without and within the criminal justice system in 21st century America (Stevenson 2014; Forman 2017; Ransby 2018).

Grounded in the recognition of the full personhood and rights of the "Black body," the BLM movement confronts the historical struggles of the Civil Rights movement, Black Panther and Black Power movements, anti-apartheid activism, and others. Acutely tied to the *Black Organizing for Leadership & Dignity* effort, BLM rejected two elements deemed essential to the success of the Civil Right movement. The first rejected the call for organization around charismatic leadership, whereas the second rejected an overarching role of the Black church (Taylor 2016; Lebron 2017; Hillstrom 2018). These former efforts might have been considered too middle-class and bourgeois for the needs of a new non-violent movement which placed the highest value on *inclusivity*. Absent were the lingering discrimination to the Civil Rights movement of some organizations (even internal) based upon gender, gender identity or sexual orientation, HIV status, and others potentially divisive positions. Over the intervening years, BLM has demonstrated adherence to these early principles and offers an outstanding model for activist groups seeking identity through true inclusivity (Hillstrom 2018). More importantly BLM has kept the media's feet to the fire on reporting the violence and predominant killing of unarmed Black people, metered out jointly by a racially biased criminal justice system, operating within sympathetic local, state, and Federal jurisdictions. In 2020, more than 200 Black people died at the hands of violence that many view as extrajudicial executions since the shocking murder of Trayvon Martin. The violent and untimely deaths of Jamir Clark, Jonathan Ferrell, Eric Garner (by NYPD police employing a "chokehold"), Freddie Gray, Akai Gurley, Antonio Martin, Tamir Rice, Walter Scott, and George Floyd ("Please, I can't breathe") to name but a few, provoked non-violent, high visibility protests that were amplified by BLM through national media. As the BLM movement ascended, works by Ta-Nehisi Coates highlighting the fearful existence that Black bodies encounter in daily living amongst a threatening police presence (Coates 2015) and by Ibram Kendi lifting up the manner in which Black people are "stamped" by racist views that require an "antiracism" response (Kendi 2016) offered broader and deeper interrogation of Black life in America. Black celebrities and public intellectuals (as well as their non-Black counterparts) have provided unbridled support to BLM and its guiding principles that includes non-violence, diversity, globalism, empathy, intergenerationality, and restorative justice (Hillstrom 2018). Clearly there is sense in the U.S. that extrajudicial killings of Black people by police are escalating. The use of such lethal force appears disproportionate to the situations encountered by many Black people living in cities (e.g., New York City, Chicago, Los Angeles, Minneapolis, Orlando, etc.) as well as rural and suburban regions (e.g., Ferguson, MO; North Charleston, SC; Waller County, TX; etc.) across the nation.

BLM resistance to police brutality begs the question why some cops treat people of color in such violent and demeaning ways? Is it simply fear of the "other"? or is it something much darker? The 2019 interaction between Iesha Harper, an African American mother of two, and an arresting Phoenix, AZ, police officer may be informative. Iesha's 4-year-old daughter was accused of stealing a doll from a Family Dollar Store. Iesha was ordered by the police to place her other child, a one-year-old daughter, on the pavement. Her refusal to physically abandon her youngest child provoked the arresting officer. The emotive content of the disagreement escalated, culminating with the officer drawing his gun, pointing it at her children, while trying to "rip the one-year-old" from Harper's arms. The police officer was reported to exclaim, "I could have shot you in front of your f#*king kids."

Whether it is fear of the "other" or simply an overreaction to an instinctive protective response by the mother (that most people would find justifiable), the policeman clearly overreacted. The officer displayed a behavior and response to Harper that some psychologists would label as "dehumanizing." As discussed earlier, assaulting someone's personhood, declaring their human rights null and void, and dehumanizing them are elements of a textbook response to rationalizing that can subsequently lead to oppression and to exploitation of the victims. Training of officers by superiors who may overtly (or inadvertently) display racial bias needs to be unearthed and stopped. For officers who embody duly sanctioned agents of power and control, use of that power in a manner that degrades and robs personhood of their wards is unconscionable. Behaviors and rituals of police that label people of color as "other" and "subhuman" may become normative in some jurisdictions. These negative models may constitute the earliest entry point for corrective measures. The sources of potentially deadly racist bias by those empowered to protect the public have been revealed to include hate groups. The number of hate groups in the U.S. compiled by the Southern Poverty Law Center (SPLC) was more than a thousand in 2018! Linkages and overlaps between hate groups (e.g., White nationalists, White supremacists) and those responsible for maintaining public order are no longer deemed speculative.

How to restore public trust and support of police by the Black community requires deep consideration. Examples of police using silhouette targets that clearly depict people of color and/or of Muslim faith became common in some locales after the terrorist attacks of September 11, 2001. On a local level, racial bias suspected by police and the criminal justice system must be unearthed and effectively disarmed. In Los Angeles, for example, the county's prosecutor, District Attorney Jackie Lacey, has succeeded in gaining death sentences for more than 20 defendants. *All* of the defendants sentenced to death are people of color, that is, none were White. California has a moratorium on capital punishment, yet this same district attorney continued to pursue death penalty sentences. BLM and others human rights movements continue to raise up the shocking racial disparity in both the police and criminal justice system throughout America. Although public disclosure of such injustice is an essential first step, vigilance and follow-through will be required to make real progress. Little will change for people of color unless the police and entire criminal justice system welcome, validate, and interrogate the personal narratives of people of color confronting racial bias by local authorities.

BLM, as would be expected, has not avoided criticism from both within and without the Black community (Gitlin 2018). *The Washington Post*'s extensive database of fatal police shootings, in fact, does not suggest that there is an epidemic of unjustified shooting deaths driven by race. The tactics of BLM, confrontational yet non-violent, have been labeled by some as "anti-police." Others accuse the BLM movement of lifting up extrajudicial shootings of Black Americans at the hands of the police, while ignoring "intraracial" violence, so called "Black-on-Black" deadly violence. Criticisms leveled at the BLM movement suggest that persistent levels of structural oppression and of racial bias confronting the Black community are often invisible to the average American. Police often are considered by many in the minority communities to represent the concerns of the White ruling class even if some of the officers are people of color (Forman 2017). People who are Black, Latin American, and others of color, in contrast, are often treated as a simple minority, even in locales where their numbers are in the majority. Yet they remain the substrate for chronic, historic oppression and exploitation. They remain people who largely are marginalized by socioeconomic forces that they cannot control. The intersection of these two groups creates the potential for either greater understanding or a flashpoint for racial violence.

Twenty-first century America is replete with examples of White asymmetric power assaulting the personhood and dignity of the oppressed (West 1993; Malbon 2013; Alexander 2010). The facts suggest, however, that these cases are not exceptions, but regrettably the rule. Each travesty of justice that degrades the personhood of the "other" must be justly received, lifted up and carefully interrogated. BLM continues to be a powerful platform aimed at justice, settling for nothing less. If the administration of President Barack Obama represented a high water mark in expanding the understanding of structural oppression for people of color, the Trump administration would mark a low point. Confronting White privilege and the products of several hundred years of structural oppression is a painful effort demanding of self-discernment and empathic understanding of the suffering of Black and other minorities on the receiving end of American oppression. Empires, like the Roman, Qing, Russian, Mongol, and British, historically are reluctant to expend the political currency and effort to embrace, validate, and seek solutions to long-term asymmetric suffering of peoples in their midst. The United States in the 21st century is no different. The historic record always remains at risk of selective "editing" by the White ruling class hegemonic forces operating in America today. This characteristic effort by empire, demands concerted pushback aimed at preserving the historical record of racism as an American "original" sin, expanded upon in the next chapter.

In life, for every "push," like that of the BLM movement, there is always a "pushback." So too did the hashtag campaign #BlackLivesMatter generate a robust pushback from several sources. "All Lives Matter," hashtag "#AllLivesMatter," emerged mostly as a political slogan aimed at pushing back ostensibly against a phantom (Meyer and Sanchez 2019). All Lives Matter interpreted the BLM movement as promoting "only" Black lives matter (Edgar and Johnson 2018). This interpretation is a "red herring," failing to recognize #BlackLivesMatter's laser-like focus not upon Black lives per se, but rather the disproportionate risk to Black lives at the lethal hand of racist America. The central aim of the BLM movement was to reiterate that something is gravely amiss morally in a nation where the violent deaths that BLM seeks to chronicle can be largely ignored as normative (Gitlin 2018). Media outlets like Fox News often promote stories of criminal acts when a face of color can be posted, as the perpetrator, while the face of the victim is predominantly White.

Emergence of a countermovement "Blue Lives Matter" (as #BlueLivesMatter or #BacktheBlue) was only a matter of time. Blue Lives Matter advocates that people prosecuted and convicted of killing law enforcement officers should suffer enhanced sentencing under hate crime statutes. Generated in response to what some right-leaning commentators labeled as the "anti-police" bias, Blue Lives Matter sought to include "career choice" (i.e., police) as one of the categories afforded special protection under hate crime statutes, that is, hate crime based dominantly upon race, sexual orientation, and gender identity. Blue Lives Matter promoted a "pro-police officer" effort, recognizing that indeed and regrettably police do lose their lives in the performance of their duty. Sources online and in print supporting Blue Lives Matter advertise gripping stories of "crimes against police officers" (CAPOs) that truly are heart rendering and powerful. Yet Blue Lives Matter is not a *bona fide* movement counter to #BlackLivesMatter. Rather, both occupy the same orbit of human suffering at the hands of violence. No assault on personhood is greater than one which robs a person, any person—either a Black youth or law enforcement officer—of their unalienable human right not to be killed!

Equally predictable was the emergence in 2015 of a "White Lives Matter" activist group advancing a more radical alternative to the "All Lives Matter" group. Itching to label the #BlackLivesMatter movement as an example of simple racial preference, favoring Black people, the White Lives Matter (WLM) pushed back as a countermovement. WLM, created primarily as a racist backlash to #BlackLivesMatter, was more right-wing leaning and racist. According to the Southern Poverty Law Center's (SPLC) annual listing of hate groups, WLM exists as a neo-Nazi hate group targeting not only Black people, but all people of color, especially immigrants. The WLM movement reinforces a central racist dogma embedded in the history of America, that White lives matter most (Meyer and Sanchez 2019). This dogma is the product of one of the two great "original" sins of America, that is, the assault on the personhood of African, African Americans, and their descendants brought to this country and born in this country as slaves to the dominant White ruling class (see Chapter 5). The WLM effort has been a touchstone and chant for the "Alt-right," that is, White supremacists who gather publically in the U.S. (Yiannopoulos 2017; Wendling 2018). Alt-right gatherings include the now infamous 2017 "Unite the Right" rally held in Charlottesville Virginia. This violent rally turned deadly with the killing of a non-violent activist protesting the Alt-right agenda (Kindinger 2019; Weinberg 2019). The seemingly quiet expansion of right-wing extremist groups promoting a "White nationalist supremacy," detailed by the SPLC, constitutes the greatest public threat to domestic peace and the personhood of all people of color (Crothers 2019). Breaking White supremacy is not a new effort, but rather one embedded in the roots of a "Black" Social Gospel, the work of African American Christian leaders, the emergence of Black Liberation theology, and many efforts aimed at securing racial justice in the context of social democracy of the 20th and 21st century of America (Dorrien 2015; Dorrien 2018) and elsewhere (Kindinger 2019). At a local level, signs supporting the #BlackLivesMatter movement have appeared on the lawns of predominantly White congregations, a clear and unmistakable sign of moral solidarity. Can White churches of the privileged more effectively lift up into the public square the inhumanity of racially biased oppressive police actions coupled with biased criminal justice system?

When considering the BLM movement in America, one must be impressed with their success to date as well as their methods. Nonviolent yet confrontational, decentralized and group-centered, agile and able to mobilize protests wherever necessary, strategic and adaptable, and most importantly inclusive, the BLM seems to have emerged as a powerful force aimed at forging true community based in moral solidarity. The very best qualities of the BLM movement engender a *Communio Sanctorum* articulated in the beginning of this book. An inclusive community in covenant where there can exist only "self" and no "other," in moral solidarity, and dedicated to the flourishing of all lives is a goal worthy of our nation's investment in social capital. Two essential questions about the BLM movement persist. First, is this community with moral solidarity and inclusivity capable of sustaining itself? Second, has the BLM movement successfully "moved the needle" of public opinion concerning the unjustified use of lethal force by police and the abject immorality of continued extrajudicial killings of Black Americans?

Personhood, Violence, and the Immigrant "Other"

The pattern of depersonalization and dehumanization has become all too common in assaults on personhood. Vulnerabilities of the body were detailed first. Early development (e.g., embryo and fetus) or delayed or inappropriate development of the neonate (e.g., vulnerabilities of soma and psyche) led the way. Analysis of the "other" who simply has a physical character or disability as unavoidable as old age next came into focus. Vulnerabilities of the psyche later assaulted the "other" who suffers from intellectual disabilities due to environmental factors, genetics, or trauma, as well as the "other" suffering with mental disorders of anxiety, mood, and psychoses. The opioid epidemic in America was shown to create "other" for those with chemical/ substance addiction disorders. Their personhood was assaulted even though the disorders are medical conditions, not lapses in moral character. Depersonalization based upon race and color is never far from any discussion of personhood in America. The legacy of the colonial empire, of 400+ years of slavery, the aftermath of the Civil War, the "old" as well as "new" Jim Crow, and the emergence of police violence and extrajudicial killings of Black people are deeply disturbing. Is it any wonder that the newest target of contested personhood paradoxically rests upon the birth of this nation, a so-called "nation of immigrants"? The foundational assault on personhood, oppression, and genocide aimed at the indigenous Native Americans who lived in the land of America some 30,000 years before invading "immigrants" arrived will be discussed in the next chapter. It is the first great "original" sin of American Empire. Suffice it to say, being human innately has a lot to do with freedom and movement of peoples. The movement of dissatisfied and exploited peoples to search for a better life exemplifies freedom in pursuit of a more safe and prosperous life. It is this agency in search of freedom and the necessary migration of peoples in its pursuit that create "immigrants." Immigration is a story as old as *Homo sapiens*. Freedom of movement is a human right, fueling the migration of tens of millions of immigrants in search of a better life often to escape violence, oppression, and lack of opportunities (Olson 2003; Brownell 2018).

Although age old, the question concerning whether human beings truly possess a negative right to move freely and to migrate remains controversial in the 21st century world. Historically, world religious traditions, including Judaism, Islam, Christianity, Hinduism, and the Buddhist tradition all provide "biblical warrants" in strong support of human migration. In the Hebrew Bible, for instance, God instructs the Israelites to respect the rights of the foreigner/alien in their midst (Leviticus 19:34). Further, the God of Abraham declares, "You must not mistreat or oppress foreigners in any way. Remember, you yourselves were once foreigners in the land of Egypt" (Exodus 22:21). "Do not take advantage of the widow or the fatherless. If you do and they cry out to me, I will certainly hear their cry. My anger will be aroused, and I will kill you with the sword; your wives will become widows and your children fatherless" (Exodus 22:22–23). In the Book of Numbers, God declares, "The community is to have the same rules for you and for the foreigner residing among you; this is a lasting ordinance for the generations to come. You and the foreigner shall be the same before the Lord: 'the same laws and regulations will apply both to you and to the foreigner residing among you' " (Num 15:15b). Most apropos, is the declaration "The foreigner residing among you must be treated as your native-born. Love them as yourself," (Lev 19:34).

In Christian traditions, Jesus of Nazareth offers, "Truly I say to you, as you did for the least of my brethren you did it to me" (Mat 24:40). In the Gospel according to Matthew (22:36–40), Jesus paraphrases the Torah, [36]"Teacher, which commandment in the law is the greatest?" [37]He said to him, "'You shall love the Lord your God with all your heart, and with all your soul, and with all your mind.' [38]This is the greatest and first commandment. [39]And a second is like it: 'You shall love your neighbor as yourself.' [40]On these two commandments hang all the law and the prophets." Islamic tradition offers, "But verily thy Lord,— to those who leave their homes after trials and persecutions,—and who thereafter strive and fight for the faith and patiently persevere,—Thy Lord, after all this is oft-forgiving, Most Merciful" (Surah An-Nahl, 110). Those of Hindu faith find God's presence permeating the cosmos. The presence of the stranger as well as the welcome encounter with the stranger constitutes "hospitality," which is one of the highest forms of Hindu worship. World religions generally express a common welcoming view of immigrant populations. Human beings reflexively react to the "stranger," the "other," often with fear, anxiety, and suspicion. Yet the human "self," most often through encounters with the "other" and self-discernment, comes to understand that all human beings are creatures of a common creation. All humans seek the same necessities to sustain life as well as to flourish. More importantly all people are just as deserving of full personhood as that enjoyed by the "self." All peoples with or without religious traditions generally will acquiesce to a moral imperative valuing the worth of every human being, even the stranger, even the immigrant.

In a nation that often aligns itself with Judeo-Christian teachings, the passage of the 14th Amendment to the Constitution could be viewed as canonization of the Greatest Commandment. The text of section 1 of this amendment is as follows: "All persons born or naturalized in the United States, and subject to the jurisdiction thereof, are citizens of the United States and of the State wherein they reside. No State shall make or enforce any law which shall abridge the privileges or immunities of citizens of the United States; nor shall any State deprive any person of life, liberty, or property, without due process of law; nor deny to any person within its jurisdiction the equal protection of the laws." This text commonly is interpreted as entitling all persons to equality under the law. Our discussion of Jim Crow laws demonstrates quite clearly this constitutional requirement for equality under the law is not immutable. Rather, states' rights can be readily amended to designate minority groups as "other," to deny equality under the law as well as access to housing, employment, education, healthcare, and social services. On the basis of being different from the dominant, historically White, ruling class of America, minorities are marginalized and deprived of personhood within their state of residence (Jardina 2019). The racial segregation plaguing America often is viewed as an unfortunate outcome of what topsiders consider to be no more that a "forced cohabitation" within a "nation of immigrants." Lurking under a false metaphor of the U.S. as a "melting pot" was the clear determination that some in this pot were more equal than others (Polakow-Suransky 2017).

Waves of immigrants have been "welcomed" to the U.S. throughout most of its brief history. The first waves of early merchants, theological purists, and separatists immigrated to America in the 17th century from 1720–1820, waves of mostly White migrants from England, Germany, the Netherlands, and Europe arrived on America's shores. White, Anglo-Saxon, Protestants constituted ~60% of the 1790 population. From 1820–1860, Irish (escaping poverty and famine), British, and German peoples (escaping economic and political pressures) constituted another, major second wave of immigration. A third wave of people, lasting from 1880–1914, was composed largely of Chinese, Japanese, and other Asians peoples immigrating to the U.S. in search of economic opportunities and religious freedoms. A fourth wave of immigration commencing ~1965 included more Europeans and Asian immigrants, and, for the first time, large numbers of Spanish-speaking people from Mexico (LeMay 2018).

Currently, the Spanish-speaking and Latin American population is the second largest ethnic group in the U.S. More than 57 million of these people live in the U.S. These immigrants are largely from Mexico (10% of U.S. population), the Caribbean (2.6%), Central (1.3%), and South America

(0.9%). The influx of immigrants and an attendant increase in the birth rate constitutes nearly two-thirds of the Spanish-speaking and Latin American population born in the U.S. By birthright, these children born in the U.S. are citizens endowed with full rights enjoyed under the 13th, 14th, and 15th Amendments to the U.S. Constitution. In the most recent decade to the existing immigrant masses was a newer, dominant wave of immigrants seeking political asylum. These people typically emigrate either in the aftermath of or during ongoing wars in the Middle East as well as political unrest that is ravaging Central and South Americas. These immigrants exercise their rights to seek legal asylum in the U.S., fleeing area bereft of safety, peace, freedom, and economic opportunity. Over the last several decades, the U.S. conservative right's response to immigration has soured and sharpened, even though the economic benefits of immigrant labor goes ignored but not uncontested (Swain 2018).

What is contested is the very personhood of these most recent and vulnerable immigrants, especially the so-called "undocumented illegal immigrants/ aliens." Is there really such a thing as an "illegal" person? Taking pages from the playbook of the Jim Crow South and a pushback to Federal court ordered desegregation throughout the nation, those who seek to diminish the personhood of the more recent immigrant "other" turn to state legislatures to create laws aimed at restricting immigrant rights, although strictly speaking, such laws remain within the Federal domain (Swain 2018). In so acting, states and municipal governments can effectively obviate and nullify the 14th Amendment. Enacting spurious local ordinances aimed at new immigrants, states assault the personhood of the immigrant "other." Fanning the flames of xenophobic fear of the "other," those in the White ruling class proffer notions that the very presence of these immigrant "aliens" destabilizes the fabric of the local communities through increases in crimes to persons and property, theft, delinquency, and moral turpitude (LeMay 2018). The second fear fanned by such harsh rhetoric aimed at contesting being human of Hispanic/Latino people is economic (Contreras, Cabello, and Raihan 2004). This fear is fueled by two arguments. The first is that the immigrant populations deprive the current "landed aristocracy" of job opportunities that should not be squandered to the "other." The second fear is that immigrant "aliens" drains community resources more rightly reserved for the "true" citizens of these locales (Chomsky 2007). These arguments aimed at assaulting the personhood of the more recent immigrants (both legal or illegal) are not new inventions, but rather have a long and successful history of fanning hate crimes to simultaneously oppress and yet further exploit the most recent waves of immigrants to America (Stein 2014).

Factually, the Spanish-speaking and Latin American community is heterogeneous, composed of groups of differing immigration history and/or status (Massey 2008). The dominant groups are natural born and naturalized citizens, but also including those who are legally admitted to the U.S., for example, permanent residents or conditional residents. In addition to these are those visitors with temporary legal status, for example, business visitors and students. Individuals granted temporary protected status (TPS, for example, Haitians following the devastating earthquake of 2010, and peoples escaping from conflicts in El Salvador, Honduras, Nicaragua, Somalia, South Sudan, Sudan, Syria and Yemen) are the final group of recent immigrants, representing about 30%. People in the U.S. lacking TPS status, permission and proper documents to support their presence are labeled "undocumented." They have no legal permission to reside in the U.S and often are labeled "illegal" immigrants (Massey 2008). Although public animus is aimed primarily at the undocumented/illegal immigrants, "all the above" immigrants (including all Hispanic/Latino people) have been merged into the crosshairs. States and local municipalities seeking to discourage this immigrant population target the undocumented immigrants as well as those deemed guilty through association. Restriction on access to social services, educational resources, and residential housing can effectively deny Hispanic/Latino peoples (and other desperate people) from public-needs programs in many communities throughout the nation. Cities and local activist groups have emerged that offer "sanctuary" to undocumented immigrants who become targeted for detention and then deportation. Typically, such immigrants are afforded little legal advice and representation. Intentionally placed outside of the social safety net afforded the "least of us," the undocumented immigrants are forced to seek sanctuary in houses of worship, cities and states offering "sanctuary."

The political Right has attacked the sanctuary movement and demonized "sanctuary cities," declaring them to be grave threats to public safety (United States. Congressional House Committee on Immigration and Border Security 2015; Lüsted 2019). Yet, most of the "evidence" offered in support of these claims and perceived threats is merely anecdotal, "Trumped-Up" to sensationalize and to embellish (Lüsted 2019). The denial or withdrawal of rental agreements as well as confiscation of personal properties (i.e., asset forfeiture) for those caught "harboring" illegal aliens are outrageous examples of local governments overreaching beyond Federal immigration law with regard to the definition of "harboring." The hypocrisy of the situation is that the exploitation of the labor of undocumented immigrants enables popular societal amenities such as cheap landscaping, childcare, and elder care, that is, essential needs of the White ruling class. Guilt-by-association remains a tool for separating the undocumented immigrants who are in desperate need of public welfare from the last source of help available to them, that is, family! The history of America is replete with charitable efforts created to help U.S. society adjust to and ameliorate the suffering of the "least of us." Only in the last decade (and in particular under the Trump administration) has the U.S.

vilified, demonized, and contested the very humanity of undocumented immigrants. Sanctuary cities may represent the last remnant of real hope for those weary people who seek to embrace the words on the Statue of Liberty, "Give me your tired, your poor, Your huddled masses yearning to breathe free, The wretched refuse of your teeming shore. Send these, the homeless, tempest-tossed to me, I lift my lamp beside the golden door (Delgado 2018)!" Trump administration officials have routinely mocked the very notion and meaning of the motto emblazoned on the base of the Statue of Liberty.

Biblical Emancipation Versus Mass Incarceration of the "Other"

Systemic racial injustice was the bedrock on which Jim Crow laws (both "old" and "new") flourished. With broadening application, White supremacy in the U.S. has assaulted being human not just upon race and color, but also ethnicity and nation of origin. Parallel systemic injustices termed "Juan Crow" (Casey and Watkins 2014; Bender and Arrocha 2017) and "Jane Crow" followed in the footsteps of Jim Crow (Azaransky 2011; Cooper 2017). These descriptors were advanced early in response to rampant fears of terrorism in the decade after the 9/11 terrorist attacks on U.S. soil. Later racial injustice worked diligently to repackage and propagate unfounded fears of lawlessness, economic rivalry, expansion of a "welfare" state, and displacement of members of the dominant White ruling class (i.e., the so-called "displacement theory"). "Juan Crow" is a neologism, which reflects not so much a redirection, but rather expansion of targets of racial segregation and diminished personhood first suffered by Black Americans, expanding to include Spanish-speaking and Latin American peoples in the U.S. (Bender and Arrocha 2017). San Bernardino (CA) provided a template for municipalities with the intention of exploiting unfounded criticism of peoples of color to conflate race and ethnicity with dire and unfounded threats to community safety and welfare of the White community. The goal in San Bernardino County was to avoid, "California from turning into a 'Third World cesspool' of illegal immigrants." Application of this prejudicial character assassination of whole communities by dominantly White ruling class enclaves was aided and abetted by virtually non-stop "news" coverage by Fox News and other conservative, right-leaning media outlets. Adoption of Juan Crow rhetoric in the aftermath of San Bernardino provided a vivid demonstration of how unfounded hate speech and fear mongering can easily morph from one target to another, always targeting the most vulnerable populations.

"Jane" Crow is another neologism, but one focusing upon the unique race-based experiences of African American women that extend from the post-Reconstruction era (1863–1877) all the way to present day (Azaransky

2011). Historically, Black women in America have encountered many assaults upon their personhood, beyond those of the old and the new Jim Crow laws. Maternal mortality and morbidity rates are much higher for Black women than those of White women (Cooper 2017). Lack of education, lack of employment opportunity, unequal pay, and structural poverty also are higher for Black women living in America. Susceptible to bias by Child Protective Services in custody matters, to inequality in a biased criminal justice system, to domestic violence, to rape, and to violent crimes in general, Black women often are forced to live within perilous, fragmented communities numbed by racial indifference (Rosenberg 2017). As the U.S. has become more conservative and right leaning, Black women (as all women of color) suffer greater risk of incarceration, of denial of their rights, and of assaults upon their personhood. Women of color face triple jeopardy in America, based on race, class, and gender. Racial subjugation of Black women deepens and perpetuates the fragmentation of the Black family and embodies the very label of the "New Jane Crow." Similarly, Juan Crow laws (such as California's successful referendum Proposition 187, "Save Our State," which was later struck down) aimed at denying social services and basic rights to Hispanic/Latino peoples abound across America. These discriminatory measures will continue to be challenged in the courts as divisive, inflammatory, and unjust. Clearly such laws fly in the face of the theological underpinning of how communities should embrace and help the "stranger," the "other."

Another deadly narrative has been the expansion of White ruling class efforts encouraging states to legislatively adopt so-called "stand-your-ground" (SYG) laws (Light 2017). These spurious "laws" exist in half of the states. Stand-your-ground laws find their origin in the ancient "castle doctrine," common law purporting to grant a right by which citizens may defend themselves or others against real or perceived threats with force, including lethal force (Light 2017). In such criminal cases, defendants often claim that the use of force (especially deadly force) was unavoidable, safe retreat was not an option, and the sole intent was ostensibly to protect and to defend themselves or others against a threatening person/people (Douglas 2015). The case of Trayvon Martin's killing by George Zimmerman (see above in #BlackLivesMatter) became a poster-boy for application of a SYG law in which racial bias was operating, although denied by the perpetrator (Light 2017; Douglas 2015). In 2018, Michael Drejka, a White man who fatally shot and unarmed Black man, Markeis McGlockton, in a Florida parking lot, was found guilty of manslaughter, after offering a SYG defense for his actions. Nearly a month lapsed between the killing and the arrest of Drejka. On February 23, 2020, Ahmaud Arbery, an unarmed Black man out for his routine morning jog in Brunswick GA, was gunned down in broad daylight by a White father and his son. The defense, suggesting SYG reasoning, was offered upon the arrest of the two, an arrest more than two months after the killing. In these cases, surveillance and cellphone videos established the truth, that is, brazen killing of the "other," by White ruling class members. The Rand Corporation suggests that there is some evidence that stand-your-ground laws actually may increase homicides ruled "justified." The jury is still out as to whether these SYG laws truly act as a deterrent to crime. Reports concluding affirmative as well as negative results of the value of SYG laws to public safety abound, results cast in the eye of the beholder on both sides of this contentious legal doctrine. Currently, there exists no data that SYG laws have increased the number of mixed race homicides.

Mass incarceration targets mainly the Black, Hispanic/Latino, and minority populations (Alexander 2010; Forman 2017; Hinton 2016). Such incarceration is an extension of an American criminal justice system that has morphed into an industry that is highly profitable, politically active, and being fed by a constant source of questionable government criminal and immigration efforts (e.g., Rockefeller drug laws, 1973; Three-Strikes law, 1994). When social costs of incarceration are included, the economic toll of mass incarceration in the U.S. has been estimated to be ~\$1 trillion (Stevenson 2014). Prison corporations, bail bond companies, phone companies, and commissary vendors are all part of a "deep state" system that leaves the taxpayer as well as the families of the incarcerated with enormous debt, but with little if any increased public safety (Stevenson 2014). James Forman (2017) rightly observed that the "new" Jim Crow is responsible for disproportionate Black over White rates of incarceration based in mostly drug law violations. In contrast, fifty percent of incarcerations of White, Black and people of color are jailed for committing violent crimes, which all communities, for example, Black, Brown, and White alike, abhor (Forman 2017). Forman noted that 60% of prisoners are not African Americans, and all convicts will lose the right to vote, jury participation, health and employee benefits, welfare benefits and food stamps, and access to public housing (Forman 2017). Two points emerge: mass incarceration at the hand of the White ruling class, no matter if drug-related (Alexander 2010) or due to violent crimes (Forman 2017), damage the psyche of the jailed. Echoing the words of Du Bois, Baldwin, Ellison, West, Cone and others, such damage to the psyche leaves scars and open wounds that likely will not heal. Maladaptive behaviors in response to structural oppression, social isolation, and self-loathing will not rescue the millions of young people cast off to the crucible of the criminal justice system in the U.S. Four centuries of oppression and assaults on personhood are prime accelerants to the fires of anger and violent tendencies of resistance and pushback against hopelessness.

Relaxation and decriminalization of various laws (e.g., Rockefeller drug laws 2004, 2009) provoked a drop in the census of the incarcerated in the U.S. Since 2016, efforts have aimed at rectifying this downward trend in

incarceration of the prison-industrial complex, aiming at immigrant populations, both legal (i.e., protected asylum seekers) and illegal (i.e., violators of
immigration laws), to swell the census. These interventions reversed the
decline in the mass incarceration census. Reinvigorated and refueled, the big
business of privately operated prisons enjoyed renewed life as cauldrons of
what Wacquant termed "prison ghettos" for the downtrodden and oppressed
who were best placed out-of-sight, out-of-mind. One must wonder how the
other countries of the modern world would judge the American empire with
regard to law-and-order versus human decency and empathy?

Recently the mercenary profits of forced labor by these pools of prison-
ers/detainees have been revealed by mass media, striking many as reminiscent of our deeply troubled history of indentured slavery. The 2017/2018
wildfires in the West were fought, in part, by conscription of people who are
inmates in U.S. prisons. Is compensation of 4 cents/hour considered to be a
"fair" wage for manual labor, let alone dangerous work associated with fighting wildfires? These revelations and those of "new" Jim Crow, Jane Crow,
and Juan Crow laws should provoke rage and moral consternation about the
moral trajectory of the Republic first envisioned by our Founding Fathers.
Even within structural White privilege and "status quo" economics, U.S.
citizens should be enraged by such clearly unconstitutional assaults of personhood, enabled by a biased criminal justice system. If communities across
the nation covenant in moral solidarity to embrace one another with respect
and love, to cherish and protect the men, women and children from harm and
exploitation, to extend empathy to the lowly captives, widows, and orphans,
and to optimize the gifts of the entire community, then *all* members of such a
Communio Sanctorum will flourish. Ancient biblical warrants aimed at protecting the lives of vulnerable strangers and of the "other" should not need
further explanation, especially in a country that displays such overt Christian
religiosity?

PERSONHOOD & DEMENTIA

The "Least of Us": Dementia, Alzheimer's Disease, and the Deeply Forgetful

There are more than 5.7 million people suffering from dementia in the U.S.,
most of the victims of this scourge are 60 years of age or older (Smith
2018b). First we must define what we mean by the medical term, "dementia."
Dementia is a chronic or persistent disorder/syndrome of mental processes
resulting from disease or injury to the brain that impairs reasoning, negatively affect memory, and can induce personality changes (Smith 2018b). There
are at least ten types of dementia. These commonly are associated with
Alzheimer's disease (AD), vascular dementia, Lewy body dementia, Parkin-

son's disease associated dementia, frontotemporal dementia, Huntington's disease and other less prominent mental diseases. The term "mixed dementia" recognizes that dementia can results from multiple diseases/insults (Smith 2018b). In the U.S., Alzheimer's disease (AD) accounts of a staggering 60–80% of dementia, is a progressive disorder, and a dementia most well-known by people, often through personal experience with an aging loved one (Sabat 2018). From initial diagnosis to death, from the "self" who initially senses the fading of mental capabilities to a "remnant self" whose self-identity becomes enigmatic, the personhood of the deeply forgetful is highly vulnerable to a myriad of assaults on personhood (Sabat 2018).

Searching for Personhood Among Those Suffering Dementia

Noted expert on dementia Stephen Post often lectures to caregivers encouraging them to be "open to surprises" that emerge in the deeply forgetful (Post 2000). As caregivers grapple with the overwhelming demands of caring for people with Alzheimer's disease, family members of loved ones who are progressing through dementia question what comes next? It is not within the scope of this discussion to delve either into the many signs and symptoms of dementia or to the probable causes, diagnostic criteria or potential therapies of Alzheimer's disease and other dementias. Our task simply is to answer for patients and their caregivers alike, on what basis does personhood status of a victim of dementia depend? Is modern day society all to ready to contest the very being of those suffering with dementia? For those whose prognosis remains grim from the standpoint of breakthrough therapy or drugs to stabilize, will personhood persist, be degraded, or even withdrawn? The resounding response today, absent a therapeutic miracle for the deeply forgetful, is largely indifference to their plight. As AD progresses, losses of personhood status can occur in small subtle steps or dramatic transitions, each victim's story is unique. We may ask why society now seems to judge dementia so harshly? Take a look around yourself, at your own day-to-day existence decorated with high-speed connectivity to your desktop, laptop, and "smart" phones. Just twenty years ago, such devices would be considered amazing computers! Today they are universal and essential to modern life. Sitting at a lab luncheon held at a hibachi-style restaurant, I noted a family dinner celebrating a birthday. Following the singing of "Happy Birthday," the faces of every one of the 14+ people seated around the hibachi returned to the faint glow of a smartphone and silence, while reconnecting with their high-speed world of communication. The "celebration" proceeded almost absent proximate family and mealtime conversation. This is not a criticism, merely an observation. Many have commented upon the same dominant theme of smart phone-induce isolation observed at social gatherings today. We live in a world that, in the term coined by Stephen Post, values "*hyper*cognition." Is it any wonder that our response to encounters with people suffering from dementia seems more or less disinterested, seeking avoidance rather than embrace? The mere presence of profound memory loss about us makes most feel very uncomfortable.

Alzheimer's disease is dominant in or co-morbid with most forms of dementia in 21st century America. Probing the impact of dementia on personhood status focuses on the specifics of AD, recognizing that it is a "gateway" to the existence of the deeply forgetful (Waldemar and Burns 2017). AD is not just a set of symptoms and limitations to cognition. Foremost, AD is a progressive and fatal disease (Sahyouni, Verma, and Chen 2017). Recent estimates have moved AD from sixth place to third in the ranking of leading cause of death in the U.S. (United States Senate Committee on Finance, Subcommittee on Health Care 2017) Beyond the loss to skills of thinking, reasoning, and remembering, behavioral deficits emerge in the progression of AD. Common behavioral symptoms of AD include anxiety, wakefulness, sleeplessness, agitation and increased physical aggression often targeting caregivers and other patients (Goldman 2017). Routine daily activities and self-care rituals become frustrating and confusing for those suffering this form of dementia. Managing a well justified frustration coupled with unfounded paranoia and enhanced aggression, most AD victims can tax even the most experienced caregivers and loving family members (Sloane 2017). The pathology of AD is focused in the brain, initially in the hippocampus, which is central to consolidating memory (Pluta 2019). With progression of AD, sometimes occurring faster than other brain diseases, the entire brain can become involved, leading to the loss of neurons, basic mental capabilities, and eventually life itself.

AD attacks the individual, but functionally morphs into a familial disease. Loss of brain function leads to behaviors such as repetitious questioning, displaying mild or severe confusion, wandering off, becoming "lost" in familiar surroundings, displaying progressive difficulty in managing a checkbook and handling money, and losing executive controls that can provoke abnormal behaviors (Brossard 2019). Loss of thought processing and memory continue to exacerbate cognition, negatively impacting the victim's ability to recognize family, caregivers, and familiar faces (Brossard 2019). The loss of familiar faces and surroundings in AD feeds into attendant paranoia and delusions. Victims often become suspicious of why their stuff is "missing"? Who are the thieves lurking in their midst? They may behave in a combative, impulsive manner that is very difficult to manage for either loved ones or caregivers alike. As AD worsens, language and communication skills deteriorate.

In most cases, people suffering AD will be unable to perform simple daily tasks and consequently will require considerable help from others. Ultimately, most AD victims cannot be maintained at home and must be provided skilled nursing care in specialized surroundings. Preferable is living in a specialized nursing facility well versed to cope with the challenges posed in caring for AD patients (Agronin 2016). Even with expert, loving care the prognosis for people suffering with end-stage AD is very poor. Most patients with severe AD will end up bedridden and largely uncommunicative. The world perceived about them increasingly becomes alien and anxiety producing. Caring for a loved one with AD is one of the most challenging situations in life. My father died as the result of AD. Like so many other families, ours was greatly impacted by the slow, predictably challenging and heart-wrenching course of AD. As a chaplain and the son of one who has died at the hand of AD I firmly believe that American society remains ill equipped to handle the looming bolus of people who will develop and succumb to AD by 2050. One of the stark challenges to personhood that lays ahead for the U.S. in attending to those suffering with AD is evaluation of victim's so-called "quality of life" (QoL). This calculus not only concerns the victim's QoL, but also that of the family and caregivers alike (Agronin 2014; Rizzo and Anderson 2018). Absent conscious thought and most sensory perception, people suffering with AD will retain a QoL that is a mere fragment of their former lives. In our *hyper*cognitive society, is interrogation of the QoL a moral imperative or a fool's errand regarding to the status of personhood of the deeply forgetful (Rizzo and Anderson 2018)?

Earlier the evolution of the philosophical term "personhood" was probed, including the works of René Descartes (1596–1650), John Locke (1631–1704), David Hume (1711–1776), Charles Taylor (b. 1931), and Harry G. Frankfurt (Farooq 2016; Foster 2017). Many have argued, with sound logic, that personhood is dependent on the capacity to think, reason, and recall, or upon a significance-based view which reflects higher ordering thinking and self-discernment, or on demonstration of the ability to act upon free will. Relationality, I offer, also is highly valued as a criterion for personhood. Foundationally, human beings are communal and have been so for at least the last 200,000 years of evolution by *Homo sapiens*. Living within communities with shared responsibilities was essential to the progress achieved by modern human beings. With such a significant number of well-defined properties assigned to those with "full" personhood, the question emerges whether or not people suffering with AD must voluntarily relinquish, or forcibly lose, or have significantly discounted personhood in 21st century America (Arstein-Kerslake 2017)? Many philosophers and ethicists have wrestled with the issue of personhood status of people with progressive AD. Assigning personhood for someone with a progressive disabling and ultimately fatal disease of the mind may be the single greatest challenge to ethics of the 21st century.

In the 1990s Thomas (Tom) Kitwood (b. 1951) offered a provocative paradigm that challenged what he labeled the "standard paradigm" for care of people suffering AD. Kitwood's proposal is captured in the title of the book in which he expounds upon his radical paradigm, *Dementia Reconsidered: The Person Comes First* (Kitwood 1997). Kitwood's central thesis is that the standard medical care for treating AD was deficient in *care* for the "person." In place of care, people suffering from dementia encounter a "malignant social psychology," replete with challenges to their personhood often launched by careworkers (Kitwood 1997). His proposal focused not on assessment of that which was lost, but rather on the "remnant being" of the person suffering from AD. Not unexpectedly, his more caring alternative therapy proved to be much more consuming of time and resources to deliver. It promulgated a comprehensive effort in patient care aimed towards sustaining the ever-declining remnant of the person suffering from AD (Kitwood 1997). There is general agreement that attendant to the course of AD certain faculties fade, skills diminish, and executive function will be lost. One rightly might query, what then remains as remnant, connected to the "person" severely afflicted by AD? Is there any "person" and personhood at all left to be considered? This questioning is aimed at the very heart of seeking to assess "personhood" in terms of interconnectedness. In a community with a moral solidarity for all, the "person" always remains, no matter how fragmented and diminished by mental disease (Jewell and Kitwood 2011). We cannot ignore what Jesse Ballenger (b.1961) characterized as the calling into question the "very personhood" of those exhibiting behaviors and symptoms of dementia (Ballenger 2006). In our *Communio Sanctorum*, Kitwood's "radical" proposal aimed at providing deep care for the mostly aged victims of AD would not be radical at all. Unconditional love truly must be expressed "unconditionally," irrespective of infirmity of the psyche or soma.

How then does our knowledge of AD inform our approach to assessing and assigning personhood status of victims who become deeply forgetful? Is personhood simply established at conception or at birth? Thereafter, is previously assigned personhood immutable, subject only to loss upon death? Operationally we have already traversed the landscape of those with vulnerabilities of the soma and those with vulnerabilities of the mind in which contested personhood is evident, almost wide spread and perhaps all too common. From our taxonomy, would we consider AD and similar disorders with chronic, progressive, and ultimately fatal diseases of the brain in some other category, that is, perhaps as disabilities of the mind? One might rightfully ask why we choose this more exhaustive treatment for the people and families who suffer from AD? The justification is simple. AD is a frightfully common cause of severe mental disability and ultimately death. In 2020, there are no new therapeutic drugs or protocols in clinical testing. This lack of 21st century medical "cures" for a prevalent and deadly disease process seems unfathomable. AD remains an irreversible, progressive brain disorder that robs its victims of mental skills and capabilities, ultimately assaulting personhood status in our *hyper*cognitive society. Honestly, AD should be labeled as a medical "epidemic" running rampant under the nose of the American health-care system. A progressive, disabling, and ultimately lethal disease on a rather long trajectory, AD will challenge our assumptions concerning the protected status of the personhood of the afflicted. The complexities of confronting personhood status in AD challenge us to address an profound ethical question, is assigned personhood immutable?

Is Personhood "All-or-Nothing"?

Francis Beckwith (b. 1960) does not view any key function as the determinant to assignment of personhood (Beckwith 2007). Rather Beckwith views an underlying "unity" of the person operating in each individual. Neonates lack many of the functions that are ascribed to adults, but few would argue that by their unity or future potential that they are not fully "persons." Beckwith propositions are consistent with the notion that there is a base human nature in every person, entitling them to full personhood, even if some of the attributes operate on a sliding scale (Beckwith 2007). This idea would be inconsistent with the notion that personhood is an all-or-nothing assignment. Is fulfilling all necessary requirements for thought, memory, executive function, possession of free will, and so on, the only path to assignment of full personhood? Can it be that diminishment or loss of one or more of these attributes would render assigned full personhood null and void? If all-or-nothing assignment is to be embraced, the "incomplete" individual would no longer be entitled to full "personhood." Beckwith's thesis argues that rights and privileges enjoyed with personhood reflect a Gestalt of a person's humanity, not the mere sum of performance against arbitrary criteria. James P. Moreland (b. 1948) and Scott B. Rae (b. 1954) assert that the mark of personhood is possession of a unity of skills and capabilities over a lifetime of existence that can help the individual navigate through change but still maintain identity personhood (Moreland and Rae 2000). This is an expansive and flexible assessment of personhood status. Although executive skills may be diminished, patients suffering from all but the end-stage of AD still are capable of making choices and exercising free will. We may not agree with their decisions and desires, but it is clear that the deeply forgetful respond well to attentive listening, love and affection. As further testament to Post's advice to caregivers of AD victims about making yourself open to surprise, victims will still express delight in favorite foods and visitors, while avoiding both foods and visitors that they detest! Striking is the remarkable response that AD victims display for music, especially music linked to a time/place of their past. Social worker Dan Cohen founded a nonprofit organization "Music and Memory" that advocates for use of music therapy for treatment of patients with dementia. His unforgettable 2014 documentary *Alive Inside—A*

Story of Music and Memory provides moving vignettes of people suffering with dementia living in nursing homes and healthcare facilities whose very being is brought to life by exposure to music! Minimally communicative patients, even with profound dementia, can display remarkable responses to music that brings back deep-seated memories dear to their hearts. Are these not examples of a *remnant* free will in action?

Stephen Post argues that sensing core self-identity of AD victims is essential to preserving and maintaining personhood (Post 2000). Aspects of self-identity will remain, even for the deeply forgetful. Consequently, our task is to increase our "gain" and amplify our ability to sense what core components remain for the deeply forgetful. These core aspects of personhood are accessible to reinforcement, especially through love and care. Visuals, music, photographs and pieces of memorabilia can be powerful triggers of fond memories for AD patients. With care and patient love, the deep meaning that may persist for some remnant of the past to a person suffering from AD can be decoded and revealed. Chaplains who visit patients in Veterans Administration hospital often note that for some veterans with dementia, the presence of "comrades, memorabilia, music, and iconography (e.g., the U.S. flag)" provides deep solace and promotes peace even in times of agitation. Much like children, people suffering from AD are always changing. Being on the lookout for new opportunities to enter into their world, which may retain important themes even through the chaos of declining mental skills, is essential to caring for AD patients (Post 2000; Bell and Troxel 2017). Thankfully, in some odd sense, there will come a time in the progression of AD that those afflicted no longer are racked by frustration. Their painful failures to recall names, faces and vocabulary fade into the mist, providing some welcome relief to the deeply forgetful as well as their caregivers. This exit from self-discernment about declining skills can be truly cathartic. There is an additional insight gained through experiencing the journey with someone in the throws of progressive loss of mental faculties. Intentionally gathering more information about the past life of a client with AD can be invaluable to discerning and preserving the remnant person inside (Bell and Troxel 2017). Finding the path to their continuing self-identity, the "person" within, opens new therapeutic opportunities for optimal care.

Another aspect of continuing self-identity in dementia is the remnant of spiritual practice and religious tradition (Jewell and Kitwood 2011). For many hospitalized patients and those in nursing care facilities, the mere presence of a clergy person, chaplain, or nun, can prove soothing, re-directing their attention to earlier deeply meaningful religious practice and rituals. I recall many occasions when in my clerical "tab-collar" and Black shirt uniform that folks suffering from dementia often would smile and mouth "Father." Still able to make the sign of the Cross on their chests, victims of dementia display the ability to reach through the mist into some deep recess of their remnant core of self-identity seeking renewed connection with the Holy. Communication is always difficult, but seldom impossible. My family learned this lesson well, through caring for my father who was well "churched" and succumbed to AD five years post initial diagnosis.

Through experience we learn that humans communicate on so many non-verbal levels. Non-verbally we are quite facile in expressing shared joy, care, and love. Conversations with the deeply forgetful that seemed one-sided and limited can expand, as we get better in touch with our non-verbal being. Such increased connectivity always was fortuitous, reflecting to me a blessing that warranted a parting moment ideal for sharing a thanksgiving prayer with people suffering for dementia. In such spiritual acts, many of the deeply forgetful would recall their past connections to what they deemed "holy," bowing their heads in reverence and quietly folding their hands. Within prayer a certain peace falls over the gathered, a serenity wholly different from their daily routine. Silence and patience will often provide the opportunity for folks with dementia to catch up with the theme, mouthing sacred words still embedded in their core identity. In this way, as a chaplain and as a pastor, I always connected with this "special congregation" suffering from AD, embracing each person as a unique collection of blessings and gifts. All of these precious souls confronted daunting levels of failing mental health and attendant suffering. With time, they felt comfortable and expressive enough to share their deep suffering with me, often non-verbally. Icons and items of worship from a faith tradition can provide a non-verbal reassurance to people suffering dementia. A set of rosary beads, a prayer shawl, a sacred text, all may impart deep meaning felt in the absence of rational thinking, memory, and executive function.

One of most powerful therapies for those suffering with declining mental abilities is community itself. All will pass along the aging path. Diminished abilities of soma and psyche will accompany us as we age. Within community, moral solidarity binds us together in anticipation of common joys as well as sorrows of life. Community reassures those facing the vicissitudes of life that we are not alone! In community, the shared experiences of caregivers provide an invaluable resource for those first encounters with suffering of a family member or friend with progressive dementia. Personhood resides in our continuing core of self-identity reflecting spirituality, religion, social memories, music and art, and the precious sacred text of "self" that is shared within covenantal community. Many changes in how one builds a physical community have emerged for folks with dementia. The large multistory buildings erected for long-term care of the elderly have been re-imagined in the context of organizing smaller, home-based facilities (Thomas 1994). The loneliness, helplessness, and boredom attendant to many long-term "facilities," can facilitate the decline in the QoL of the elderly and be especially damaging to people with AD (Thomas 1994). Community plays an essential role in long-term care for the elderly, with or without AD (Thomas 2006; Power 2017). There is much that sums up and synergizes within a person when embraced in community. Being human should not be consigned to performance on a Mini-Mental Status examination! Personhood cannot be cast as "all-or-nothing." We humans are too complex in body, spirit, mind, and connectedness with each other for simple altered capacity to contest, discount, or degrade personhood.

Loss *Versus* Concealment of Being?

Maintaining "personhood" in the face of those who contest a person's "being" is neither an academic nor theoretical exercise. Particularly when an assault on personhood may void the most basic human right, that is, the right not to be killed, it is important to explore how we as a society confront the moral questions attendant to end-stage AD. Decisions about life and death of the deeply forgetful are being made every day across 21st century America. Philosophers like Michael Tooley (Tooley 2009) and Peter Singer (Singer 2011) have articulated their moral logic on personhood being dependent largely upon cognition skills and intellectual performance. Although their logic may seem bulletproof, its relevance upon life and death decisions concerning the intellectually impaired with AD remains controversial. Discussions around life and death decisions of vulnerable people remains unavoidable today simply because there are very real costs associated with their care. If healthcare and its costs were not an issue I seriously doubt that there would much to discuss about whether or not an elderly person suffering with AD would be a candidate for either voluntary (according to early advanced directives) or involuntary (as directed by a healthcare proxy) "mercy killing," otherwise known as euthanization.

The involuntary, active form of euthanasia to most people constitutes an act of killing (Keown 2018). Michael Tooley argued persuasively that with respect to moral logic, intentionally killing a person and intentionally letting a person die (i.e., via withholding of necessary medications, or withdrawal of artificial hydration and nutrition) are indistinguishable (Tooley 2009). People suffering from moderate to severe AD and often lacking capacity obviously cannot consent to "voluntary" euthanasia, whether active or passive (Keown 2018). In dementia, recall memory can be severely impaired, while aspects of long-term memory, moral values, and selfhood still may be evident (Kastenbaum and Moreman 2018). Means capable of accurately assessing decision-making capabilities and selfhood for patients with dementia, however, are lacking. Consequently, people with AD can be negatively impacted, denied full personhood as well as the rights associated with determining the course of their care (Kastenbaum and Moreman 2018). In the modern world the single factor most pressing upon medical care of victims of dementia is time.

The time necessary for proper assessment of the needs of a patient with dementia may be prohibitive. For patients with AD, who can vary from mild to severe cognitive impairment, life and death decisions may prove particularly difficult to communicate to them, as well as to receive (Kastenbaum and Moreman 2018). Intact cognitive abilities are often "concealed" or masked by other dimensions of AD, making informed decisions difficult to coalesce (Johnstone 2013). Cognitive abilities are only some of the qualities of AD persons that may be concealed rather than lost (Johnstone 2013).

How well we in America treat our deeply forgetful aging population is a query particularly uncomfortable for most to confront. In 21st century America, the personhood of people suffering from dementia remains in grave risk. Often described as "ghosts," *un*beings," and victims of "social death," those suffering from dementia are most vulnerable in their personhood (Harper 2020). Harper notes in her book, *On Vanishing*, "when little is expected from persons with advanced dementia, little is given to or expected from them" (Harper 2020). We all have or will suffer vulnerabilities of psyche and/or of soma that might call into question our own personhood someday. Like pondering wills, we put off the painful, but necessary, discussion. Should personhood be viewed not as inviolate, but rather operating upon a "sliding scale," then we may face the unknown vulnerabilities ahead for us with anxiety and trepidation. Will there be a time when the "self," perhaps when one was 20, 40, or even 60 years of age, can no longer be guaranteed as "full"? Perhaps a future "self" will seem discounted and only a shell of what we were once? The autonomy and *hyper*cognition that our society values so much is clearly not sustainable for the populations naturally aging among us. In dementia, the autonomy from which we once executed decisions largely on our own may fail, requiring loved ones and trusted caregivers to stand in our place. If we convince the vulnerable that such attendant losses are no one's fault, but their own, we send a clear message that their needs and thoughts about care are no longer germane (Johnstone 2013). In early stages of dementia victims may sense well a pervasive atmosphere around them that makes them seem no longer like autonomous beings participating in life with full personhood. Their decline in autonomy may mirror a rise in the sense that they are merely "burdens" financially and emotionally, to their families. An inner sense of self-loss, that is, becoming "non-persons," only reinforces negative perceptions of "self." Even within close families, utilitarian ethos can degrade the personhood of a family member with AD as "burdensome."

Paradoxically, articles from the media tout an almost mythical celebration of the aged in America. Narratives about seniors of exceptional note distract us from the commonplace suffering that they experience in aging. Sadly, most families, cultures, and societies readily admit to some feelings of resentment when confronted with accepting the considerable emotional and financial burdens associated with caring for the deeply forgetful (Holstein,

Parks, and Waymack 2011). The prejudice and stereotyping of the aged is often conflated with the limitations derivative of increased memory loss, intellectual deficit, sadness and depression that routinely accompanies natural aging, let alone that attendant to AD (Holstein, Parks, and Waymack 2011). Many cultures today are grappling with contentious issues of "auto-thanasia" (Hooff 1990) as well as "senicide," that is, the killing of the elderly by involuntary euthanasia (Smeeding and the University of Utah Health Technology 1987). For those confronted with the care of an elderly family member suffering with AD, the ethical quandaries are serious. In the absence of a neutral advocate for the victim, that is, an advocate with no conflict-of-interest and concerned only in preserving the personhood and voice of the vulnerable, life-and-death decisions by the family-at-large may favor the survivors.

The number of the deeply forgetful in the U.S. is burgeoning. By 2025, those affected with dementia and/or AD will balloon to 7–8 million Americans? How will the personhood of these victims be preserved? First, recognition that core dimensions of personhood and self-identity continue throughout life, even in dementia. Second, discerning precious remnants of beings with dementia presents a formidable challenge to a society largely ill at ease with natural aging. Third, to optimize care of the deeply forgetful, core elements of psyche that persist and remain still accessible while AD progresses must emerge as the very foundation for caring for these infirm. As it stands in 21st century America, neither utilitarian discounts to nor dispensations for the burdens attendant to the cost of caring for deeply forgetful should be anticipated. Caring for the deeply forgetful places a real emotional and financial burden upon both on their families and society.

Are the deeply forgetful truly a "burden"? Or can we recast this seemingly insoluble conundrum in a new light? Personally, I confess that I embrace caring for the deeply forgetful not as a burden, but rather as "sacred opportunity" for building inclusive communities. Through engagement, working towards a deeper moral solidarity, we can enable people at all stages of life to flourish, even those suffering profound dementia. My experience among those suffering from AD, especially the more personal interactions with my beloved father, with members of my congregations and with chaplaincy clients, argues forcefully for the premise that people with AD retain "full personhood," just a more nuanced form. More importantly, the basic human rights afforded in personhood, most germane to the victims of progressive dementia is the inalienable right not to be killed! Through evolution, humans have emerged absolutely mutually dependent upon each other *en masse* to thrive from birth until death. We enter into a covenant of being! There can be no "sliding scale" or "partial discount" to personhood as we traverse the vicissitude of life, from womb until we live no more. Our role as caregivers is to give care and to love. Through such unconditional love and care we "mirror" a reflection of the core *curriculum vitae* (CVs) of all of those afflicted who now are in our charge. We then can anticipate and embrace the inevitable loss of autonomy of the wards of our hearts. Our understanding of autonomy should both anticipate as well as accommodate this eventual decline. Autonomy now is manifest by those who push onward through life, a life often burdened with declining intellectual skills and memory. Families can become the "living albums" of the loving memories. Such albums are the best source to enliven the being of the deeply forgetful, supplying to them past memories that can best reinforce their core CVs, now in decline. We work to help them to adapt, even though the deeply forgetful may seem to themselves as "strangers in an alien land." Our spiritual and religious traditions are replete with admonitions and instructions as to our sacred duty as humans to love and to care for the "least of us." Condensed into the Greatest Commandment in the Holy Bible, and echoed in virtually every sacred text is the dictum to "love one another" (Pojman, Vaughn, and Vaughn 2014). The Gospel of Matthew recounts the admonitions of Jesus of Nazareth, "Truly I tell you, whatever you did for one of the least of these brothers and sisters of mine, you did for me" (Matt 25:40).

AD, Freedom, and Privacy: The Story of Frank D.

I introduced myself to Frank D. in 2010. He was a patient in the Pulmonary ICU of a large metropolitan hospital in New York where I was assigned in chaplaincy training. Frank was in his early 80's and suffering from end-stage chronic obstructive pulmonary disease (COPD), a chronic and debilitative inflammatory lung disease. Like many people of his generation, he became a cigarette smoker as a GI during World War II. His three packs-a-day regimen lasted for more than five decades. The smoking ceased when early symptoms of COPD were manifest and Frank wholeheartedly kicked smoking cold turkey. Frank married young, prior to the war (WWII), raising a family on Long Island. His spouse Mabel was the love of his life. They shared a full life, raising three children and later enjoying their seven grandchildren, all who lived close by. When I met Frank he was still grieving the loss of his Mabel, who succumbed to the ravages of Alzheimer's disease (AD) in her seventies just a few years earlier. Frank enjoyed chatting about their marriage that spanned more than 60 years. He grew melancholic and anxious, however, when talking about how Mabel's AD changed their lives. His journey with a loved one, Mabel, traversing through the harsh landscape of AD was not atypical. The anger, frustration, depression, and exhaustion that he experienced in trying to manage her disease at home by himself were not unexpected. I had witnessed this draining scenario of loved ones trying valiantly to provide 24/7 care essentially on their own.

Now in the throes of his own impending death, Frank both sought out and yet first rejected deeper discussions with me around the topic of Mable and her AD. His anxiety in broaching the subject brought on respiratory decompensation and episodes of oxygen desaturation that only created more anxiety. Frank and I had a breakthrough a week after our first conversation at his hospital bedside, leading him to a confessional state about his very being. Slowly and deliberately Frank began to recount his last few years with Mabel, when she was suffering acute dementia and was deeply forgetful. Although it was clear from Frank's description that Mabel had been in dire need of skilled healthcare in a clinical setting designed for the deeply forgetful, Frank outright resisted the impulse to place her. For several years he valiantly managed her care, mostly alone, 24/7. Frank explained that it for him was never a money issue. He had the resources to place Mabel. He loved Mabel, in spite of the mountain of daily diapers needed, her combative and paranoid behaviors, and later painful lack of recognition for him. For Frank, it was an issue of love, protection, and very importantly "privacy." How could he place her into the care of strangers, he quipped? But this narrative was only the prelude to what was bugging Frank, provoking a heightened anxiety and deepening sense of guilt. A few visits later Frank would recount to me in vivid detail Mabel's final day living in their home. For Frank, it evolved into a day filled with Mabel's paranoia and aggressive behaviors towards him. She willfully had overcome the safety locks on the exterior doors and had broken free of the house. Frank realized that he needed to find her, and fast. He did not call the police, even after a few hours had passed. Calling the cops on his runaway wife would have provoked precisely what he had been trying to avoid at all costs. Later a former neighbor of theirs brought Mabel back home. Mabel had managed to escape Frank's protection and wander blocks away to a small shopping center where she weekly had bought groceries for years.

The "reunion" at the house was anything but a time for joy. Both Mabel and Frank were enraged, he for her breaking out, she for being returned to captivity with this guy whom she no longer knew. Mabel attacked Frank with a fury unknown to him. She beat him around the face, scratched his arms, and pulled his hair, threatening to strike him with a heavy bookend. Fearing for his safety, Frank physically "took down" Mabel to the floor and put her in a headlock, as she bit his forearm viciously. Unknown to Frank, a neighbor had heard the fracas next door and called the police. Frank was both bewildered and yet relieved when the police appeared. He had been the victim of a violent confrontation with Mabel. Mabel was taken into custody, transferred to a local hospital for observation, declared lacking capacity. With sound medical advice and Frank's acquiescence, Mabel was placed in a nursing facility offering a setting designed for patients with advanced stages of dementia. It would be only 8 months later that Mabel would pass, succumbing eventually to aspiration pneumonia.

In spite of the unconditional love and support Mabel received for over 63 years of a wonderful marriage, Frank could not escape his sense of self-recrimination and guilt for the "manhandling" to which he resorted on what was to be the last day of Mabel's life in their home. It was painfully cleat that Frank was visibly racked by guilt and anxiety. Both were chewing away on his mental health and precarious respiratory state in end-stage COPD. After our brief excursion into the private hell that imprisoned Frank for the past several years, we were able to talk openly and at length. I helped Frank to learn to focus his thinking on the kind of love and care that he displayed for Mabel over 63+ years. We did a graphic form of a life review on a small white board that allowed Frank to see his life with Mabel as a Gestalt of deep love and devotion that extended more than 60 years! I offered to Frank that Mabel, if she were here, would offer deep thanks to him for the care that Frank provided to her during her bout with AD. In the context of a life and marriage well lived, Frank finally could forgive himself and seek repentance, pardon, and adoption for his "sin" in accord with his Roman Catholic faith. Frank would succumb to pneumonia only four months later. I always will recall Frank and the lengths to which Frank's loving-kindness extended into his married life, preserving Mabel's personhood and dignity, even at great costs to his own sense of self-worth. Finally Frank had his redemption.

PERSONHOOD AND CONSCIOUSNESS

The Unconscious and Actively Dying (Especially the Aged)

In 21st century America, death is feared (Joralemon 2016). Not considered as a natural endpoint to the span of a human life, death is most often feared, rather than embraced, as an unacceptable and fearful failure of a world-class, but largely fragmented and unequally distributed healthcare. Although there is clear philosophical, moral, and legal certainty that "personhood" ends upon physical death, the extent to which personhood may be contested/discounted in the run up to death remains controversial. How we think about death, especially impending death (so-called, "active dying"), affects our decision-making (Institute of Medicine (U.S.). Committee on Approaching Death 2015). Most individuals think about death in concrete terms twice in their lives. The first exposure to death is when they personally confronted it, not their own demise, but most often in the context of a family member (e.g., an aging parent). The second discernment about death usually is encountered when we grapple with writing out a legal will and/or our preferences for healthcare in some future time of need, for example, advance directives, living wills, and healthcare proxies (Joralemon 2016). Advance directives are legal documents that state a person's decisions and wishes regarding medical treatment, sometimes in the form of a "living will." Such documents or proxies are designed to insure that the signatory's wishes will be honored should the individual be unable to communicate with a physician, EMT, and other healthcare staff (Thomas and Lobo 2011). Advance directives are best evaluated with sufficient time to investigate "when is a tube, not a tube?" and "who shall decide about my healthcare should I lose mental capacity?" In the U.S., advance directives are a domain of the state-of-residence and can be exceedingly detailed, for example, 100+ query boxes requiring a check mark response for each, or so sparse as to offer only the barest selection of "do-not-resuscitate" (DNR) order or "do-not-intubate" (DNI) order. The two most common forms of advance directives are the living will and the durable power of attorney for health care, sometimes termed "health care power of attorney" or "health care proxy." Generally speaking these advance directives are designed to offer choice, dignity, consideration around pain relief, and other extra instructions about topics such as organ donation, short-term versus long-term loss of capacity, and psychiatric health care directives (Thomas and Lobo 2011).

Consideration of a human being's personhood and all the rights guaranteed by personhood are front-and-center in the health care arena of modern life (Institute of Medicine (U.S.) Committee on Approaching Death 2015). Many of the choices may seem arbitrary. A moral underpinning may seem lacking foundation. At times, the decisions may be viewed cynically as mere products of fast-paced modern medicine. The availability of choice appeals to us, autonomous beings who seek reassurance that we know the future and wish to mold the future towards our own preferences. Yet, many of these choices may be illusionary. National polls concerning health care and individuals for the past twenty years have shown repeatedly that >85% of Americans seek to die in their homes, not in a hospital setting (Lichtman 2001). It may surprise you to learn that ~85% of all American still die in hospital settings? Simply making one's preferred choices known (either formally on paper or orally to a health care proxy or physician) does not insure that the choices will be honored. In my chaplaincy/pastoral life I constantly hear from folks who are dying or their loved ones and family members about seeking a "good" death (Neumann 2016). Although most can agree theoretically about what a "good death" might look like, executing a plan to achieve this end when death is virtually at the doorstep can be next to impossible in many cases. Patients bound for hospice care and their families typically are well informed about how hospice at home can achieve a "good death" in the caring presence of loved ones (Neumann 2016). There is forged an agreement among family about how hospice care will unfold in a home setting. Fragile patients, especially the elderly, seek at all costs to avoid chaos when death approaches at home. Yet, even well informed families can become understandably anxious as a death nears at home. Family members reflexively may do the wrong thing, that is, call 911 seeking EMT to confront an "expected" death, when death finally is close at hand. Observing the active dying of a loved one goes well beyond the dimensions of thoughtful advanced discussions with trained hospice personnel about what to expect. What was thoughtfully discussed as a hospice plan can devolve into a full-blown crisis of confidence in fulfilling dying wishes when death in imminent. Hospice patients at home may be forced to experience their worst-case scenario, that is, re-entering the health care system through the ER. In an ambulance or at the ER of a hospital, advances directives that once seemed clear, but lack a proper documentation at hand, may present as unclear and consequently may be ignored. All of these problems of dying are very real and make us wonder why we fear death so much?

The absence of cool heads in the midst of a medical crisis can provoke an assault on personhood and grave loss of autonomy. Robert Burns quipped, that the "best laid plans of mice and men often go awry." What people in the U.S. really want at the end of life has been studied recently in depth (Institute of Medicine [U.S.] Committee on Approaching Death 2015). Much has been learned also from the Education for Physicians on End-of-Life Care Project, first advanced by the American Medical Association in 1999. Less than half of the respondents to a recent survey ranked as extremely or very important "living as long as possible." Having "family not burdened by decisions" was extremely or very important to respondents, rising to 70%. Having "family not burdened financially" and "having your wishes for care followed" ranked at the very top of what people want at the end of life. More than 85% of respondents deemed these considerations either extremely or very important. We all seek to be comfortable and free from pain in our journey to death. We seek having loved ones around us when we die. We seek to die at home. Most importantly, we really desire to embrace death, but only on our own terms. Although three fourths of Americans have thought about their wishes for treatment if becoming seriously ill, only one-fourth have committed their end-of-life wishes to legal documents (Neumann 2016). It is this intrinsic autonomy of human beings that powers the desire to make our own decisions, especially about death. Challenges to full personhood encountered by the dying are of grave concern to most Americans. Failing to provide clear advance directives may discount the personhood of the dying. We can lose our autonomy as to how we wished to be treated in this most fragile state. What then challenges personhood as we embrace dying? The degree of consciousness, losses of capacity, and conflicts-of-interest can challenge autonomy. As these obstacles impact many right-to-die decisions (as well as organ donation) they need to be addressed.

States of Unconsciousness: A Sliding Scale for Personhood?

The hallmarks of being human include sensory perception, rationality, thinking capability, memory, and the communication skills demanded in our *hyper*cognitive modern world. We have observed that vulnerabilities in all of these properties lead to discounting of personhood and can enable others to contest our being (Chapter 3). The discounting of personhood can be minimal, serious, and at times even lethal, depriving us of our most basic human right, that is, the right not to be killed. Of all properties that constitute what it is to be human, the most overarching is consciousness (Fins 2015). Consciousness is best viewed as the quality of being "awake" and "aware" of one's self as well as one's surroundings. In spite of our analysis of the philosophical underpinning of being human, consciousness and its properties remain enigmatic. The extremes of consciousness are relatively clear. After awaking in the morning, showering, consuming breakfast and several cups of stimulant (i.e., the caffeine in coffee) we head off to work seemingly fully cognate and conscious. On the other end of the spectrum is the condition of unconsciousness, or lacking consciousness. We may know of, have read about, or encountered a poor soul who is "comatose." Comatose individuals exist in a state of deep unconsciousness often for long or indefinite periods of time. The most common cause of such deep unconsciousness is severe brain injury or illness (Fins 2015). Our moral medical, legal, and constitutional standard of the day help us to recognize that just being "alive" is not the same as being a "person" and possessing "full personhood." Consciousness has become almost synonymous with true absolute personhood and being fully human (Fins 2015).

Unconsciousness occurs on a temporal spectrum (Kandel 2013). Momentary loss of consciousness, or syncope, usually results from loss of adequate blood flow to the brain. Such fainting displays a rapid onset, is of short duration, and the victim recovers spontaneously. Anencephalic neonates lack a major portion of the brain (i.e., the telencephalon, which includes the neocortex) and skull (Wyszynski 2006). In humans, the neocortex is the major region of the brain responsible for sensory perception, spatial reasoning, language and cognition. Thus, anencephalic neonates lack both self-awareness and consciousness (Wyszynski 2006). Similarly, due to severe brain injury or illness, humans can suffer a loss of total consciousness, falling into a coma (Wijdicks 2014). While comatose, a person cannot be awakened, failing to respond to sensory inputs of painful stimuli, light, sound, and so on. Comatose patients cannot speak, hear, sense or move voluntarily. They display "eyes-closed" coma. An "eyes-wide open" presentation may occur for people suffering from persistent vegetative state, or PVS (Wijdicks 2014). PVS patients have suffered severe brain damage and although unconscious, may display a state of partial arousal. A diagnosis of PVS is classified as permanent if the PVS lasts more than 3 months following a non-traumatic brain injury (e.g., following near fatal drowning) or more than one year following a traumatic brain injury (e.g., combat-related, battle field skull wound). PVS may evolve from a coma, presenting as only wakefulness, not awareness. Permanently unconscious patients are the most vulnerable of all patients suffering from unconsciousness. The absence of a valid, reliable, and sensitive marker(s) of permanent unconsciousness constitutes a real and serious threat to these victims (Wijdicks 2014). There is yet no precise and expansive definition of consciousness, so diagnosing either its absence or presence is problematic. The presentation of wakefulness and eyes-wide open is challenging for most non-medically trained people to square with unconsciousness. As in the anencephalic neonate, neocortical function of PVS patients appears to be severely impaired or altogether absent. Whereas collateral loss of the gag and cough reflexes as well as of normal respiration in comatose patients is predictive of early demise of the victims in response to some attending medical complication, PVS typically does not display such losses.

The question of personhood for those in PVS is not a theoretical concern, but very real. Overarching concerns include the patient rights, availability of valid diagnostic criteria, substantial costs associated with the continuing medical care as well as the extraordinary emotional toll paid by loved ones and caregivers (Singer 1995). With respect to the diagnosis of permanent unconsciousness, we are forced to accept that a medical definition of unconsciousness is lacking (Wijdicks 2014). Yet, clinical data clearly demonstrate that although wakeful, PVS patients display no awareness to pain and consequently do not appear to be suffering. Retrospective data shows that on autopsy, PVS patients often display bilateral severe damage/atrophy of the cerebral hemispheres. Imaging studies by CAT, MRI, and more recently PET scanning can evaluate readily blood flow and metabolic activity of the neocortex presumed to be nonfunctioning or functioning below the level of consciousness (Wijdicks 2014). Although metabolic activity of the neocortex may be reduced to 50–60% of normal, activity may not be absent. Metabolic activity evaluated by PET scanning may better reveal changes in brain activity of victims with PVS. Their scans can show some similarities to scans of people in temporary deep sedation or deep coma. Yet importantly, people under heavy sedation (e.g., a medically-induced coma) will regain consciousness. Similarly, even if the diagnosis of PVS is supported by multiple diagnostic approaches, the real limitation of the diagnosis is its inability to guarantee that the loss of consciousness is truly permanent!

There are ample data to suggest that although of low probability, recovery from PVS into consciousness, but not perhaps fully functionality, occurs. Such partial recovery is a very low probability event, but certainly not a "zero" probability event. Herein lies the conundrum for depriving or contesting the personhood of someone diagnosed as suffering PVS. If restricted to labeling PVS as only "persistent," but not "permanent," physicians cannot declare the victim as absent personhood. Such a declaration must be considered both premature and immoral. Reports in reputable medical journals occasionally do include studies that purport some continuing brain function in patients declared to be medically dead (Singer 1995). Such "declarations" of medical death would legally preclude victims with PVS from their unalienable rights protected under the Bill of Rights and 14th Amendment to the U.S. Constitution. Does persisting (i.e., meaning "up until now") unconsciousness of a patient diagnosed with PVS then deprive them of their moral personhood and the most basic human right of all, that is, the right not to be killed? In chaplaincy I gained experience with patients suffering in a coma as well as from their families. For the hospital, the most common consideration raised about patients diagnosed with PVS was the "persistent" healthcare costs, not the persistent vegetative state of the patient. This is not to trivialize concern for health care costs. In the current climate of patchwork health insurance in the U.S., all such costs are borne by either the medically insured, the tax payer, or both. One does not need to resort to utilitarian modes of thinking to recognize that annual maintenance for a patient diagnosed with PVS (>$250,000/annually) is not inconsequential. If health care costs are a zero-sum game in the U.S., then Americans need some deep self-discernment around what types of medical care may be deemed as costing "too much" to be justified either on utilitarian moral grounds or financially?

Persistent Vegetative Status and Being Human: Personhood Lost?

We cannot escape the challenge of addressing personhood of minimally conscious people. We really have no rock solid definitions of consciousness to guide us, only anecdotal stories about PVS that highlight this thick dialectic. Anecdotes either support contested personhood for PVS patients or support the slim hope of a reversal and "resurrection" of the conscious state to afford a remarkable recovery. Even if absolutely assured that the PVS of a suffering patient was permanent, on what basis can we declare that the "mere" remnant life lacks moral and legal personhood (Singer 1995)? Declarations such as, "medicine cannot preserve and maintain health because there is no health for a patient in a persistent vegetative state, only life in terms of the most primitive vegetative functions" (Singer 1995), offer little insight, rather only reflect a frank frustration often times with ambiguity on the question of what constitutes "life." Who is to assign a concrete value to an autonomously functioning human being? Although unconscious (for some period of time), such patients benefit from immune systems that still fight infections, are in possession of heart, lungs, kidneys, and so on, that function well enough to make their owners prime candidates for possible organ harvest, and once were clearly individuals assigned personhood in full. The observation that a human fetus *in utero* can be normal and fully absent self-awareness, but still display some responses to external stimuli was explored earlier (Chapter 2). Is not a patient in a coma then analogous to such a fetus in development? Is personhood only preserved for the fetus, but not for a once fully autonomous human being? Does the presence of only the most "primitive vegetative functions" of an early-stage fetus deprive it of the human rights ascribed a "person"? With regard to being human, is the state of not yet fully realizing full potential the same as having reached full potential and then losing it? In not making the case for analogy between the rights of an early fetus and someone suffering from PVS, do we not suffer from a lack of moral consistency and logic? Regarding concern for pain and suffering of PVS patients Cranford and Smith (1987) stated, "Medicine cannot minimize disability because disability is maximal. Permanently unconscious patients are not weak, disabled, disadvantaged, handicapped, or helpless any more than someone who is dead." When lack of full consciousness is considered a simple "functional disability" and one that is "maximal," the discussion pivots from compassion for a person in need, to that of no person at all! Here again we encounter degradation of the personhood of one with a disability, minimizing the loss by comparison solely to a dead person, most certainly devoid of all personhood.

Organ Donation: The Dilemma of Personhood

A diagnosis of PVS with a high degree of certainty coupled with the patient's lack of self- and other-awareness, of pain perception, and of apparent suffering have prompted a proposal that moral, legal, and constitutional rights of such a patient should be amended. Proposed amendments include the following: weak presumption to medical treatment and preservation of life; autonomy, beneficence, and prior wishes of the patient and family are no longer relevant (except from a humanitarian perspective); the state's interest in preserving life is now less compelling for PVS patients; and, there is no more benefit from continued treatment of existence of these PVS patients than there is for patients who are dead (Caplan, McCartney, and Reid 2015). Such proposals, based solely upon assumptions not uniformly accepted within the medical community, suggest a clear moral and ethical overreach. Are patients suspected of suffering from PVS to be declared "dead" based solely upon their *un*consciousness? Can an early fetus lacking so-called consciousness likewise be so declared! As noted above, some patients diagnosed with PVS have recovered, albeit not all and not fully. Former PVS patients indeed have regained consciousness and awareness. Some, but not all, have regained considerable function. In making use of a diagnosis of "essentially dead," some adherents may presume equivalence with so-called "brain death" (Wijdicks 2014). Diagnosis of brain death, however, has a history of seeking greater precision, generated criteria and policies to guide diagnosis, and expert teams available nation-wide for assisting is a proper skilled diagnosis (Henderson 2011). Conflating the precision of declaring brain death with diagnosis of PVS is premature and unwarranted (Singer 1995). Contesting the personhood for patients diagnosed with brain death itself is not without controversy. Denial of the personhood of a PVS patient who, unlike the patient with declared brain death, actually may recover consciousness is a major moral conundrum. The question of personhood remains a lynchpin in deliberations of medical ethics, in no place more pressing than organ donation (Singer 1995; Henderson 2011).

A prominent source of ethical dilemmas continues to be the derivative of remarkable advances made possible by medical research. Organ transplantation is one such source of continuing research and derivative ethical dilemmas. The successful transplantation of a kidney between monozygotic twins in 1954 demonstrated feasibility of surgical approach, but raised the issue of "first, do no harm" with respect to the living donor. Deaths of living donors do occur and the real risk to the live donor can never be eliminated, owing to the unavoidable truth that such organ donation is surgically demanding. The unexpected death of a live organ donor casts a long shadow on the surviving recipient, the medical institution, surgeons, and society alike. Organ donation from living donors most often is considered to be morally justified, noble, and for the good of the recipient (Caplan, McCartney, and Reid 2015; Müller and Schaber 2018). Organ donation from a living donor may reflect filial love, *agape* (herein, the Greco-Christian term for the highest form of love and charity, perhaps exemplified in donation of a kidney to suitable match rather than family member), and selflessness, under the condition that the organ donor retains functional integrity. Human beings have two kidneys; donating one to a matched recipient is a selfless act and ideally does not jeopardize the functional integrity of a living donor. As mentioned above, organ donation from a live donor expected to survive the surgery carries with it risk to the very life of the donor. Major surgery entails risk. Although such risk can be reduced, the risk is never eliminated.

What about the case when the donation of an organ clearly will terminate the functional integrity of the donor, resulting in physical death (e.g., circulatory and respiratory collapse)? Heart transplant, the so-called "miracle of Cape Town, SA" reported in 1967, provided an example of a donation that guarantees the demise of a donor for the benefit of the recipient. The advent of heart and heart/lung transplants created a new set of ethical dilemmas about diagnosing death, selection of eligible recipients, and religious considerations. In the U.S. (as elsewhere), such quandaries led to the creation of Federal taskforces aimed at exploring the ethical considerations inherent with continuing advances in organ transplants. Ethicists consider a heart (or heart and lungs) transplant to be morally justified only in the event that the donor has succumbed to some other medical cause of death or will die imminently (Caplan, McCartney, and Reid 2015). With prior assent/attestation of the donor (i.e., the donor has expressed his/her participation in a registered organ donation program) or the fully informed consent of the next of kin, organs can be donated while the donor is being maintained singularly to preserve the value of the organs to be harvested (Müller and Schaber 2018).

There generally is agreement in the medical community that death, including brain death, can be diagnosed with some high level of confidence (Prokovyev 2010). The theological community has expressed its support for decision making by the medical community, even in the case of brain death. Yet, some controversy still remains over the "neurological criteria" required for moral certainty that death has occurred. The nagging paradox is this: if organs can only be preserved for transplant in life, how can the donor actually be dead? Media reinforces this conundrum by often referring to "brain dead" *patients* that continue to survive for various periods of time. Yet for some victims of catastrophic brain injury and particularly those who present with PVS, the complexities of determining consent (e.g., in the absence of organ donation declaration), establishing that the donor is actively dying (i.e., will not recover), respecting the wishes of the family and next of kin are formidable obstacles to obtaining true consent and cannot be minimized. Neonates suffering from anencephaly or cortical death of the brain fall into this dilemma of moral *versus* legal "life" of a potential donor (Singer 1995). Similarly, is the diagnosis of PVS in which unconsciousness seems irreversible equivalent to a medical declaration of "death"? Personhood demands respect for the most fundamental human right, that is, that of not being killed. Who will advocate preserving this precious negative right when the presumed organ donor is unconscious and lacks capacity? In the U.S. and elsewhere globally there is an acute need for transplantable organs. The shortage of donations for organ transplantation raises a serious ethical question. Should such justifiable need of a society trump the wishes of potential donors and their families? It seems likely that the absence of ethical answers exacerbates rather than ameliorates the shortage of organs for donation. Similarly, declarations that no financial compensation should be provided to donors for organs may seem ethically sound at first glance, but have exacerbated rather than remedied the shortage of donors (Satel 2008; Flescher 2018). The need for consent explicitly granted by the donor prior to death is well justified and intentioned (Jonsen 2003). Yet there likely will remain difficult situations of moral ambiguity that are not adequately addressed by application of such hard-and-fast principles.

Contested personhood of an organ donor may be best interrogated in the situation when the pressure to permit organ retrieval is at moral odds with the human rights of the candidate donor. Two such situations can be placed in conversation: the first, the case of the anencephalic neonate as donor; the second, the case of a person suffering in a PVS as donor. Each displays similarities with the other, yet also important differences. Both the anencephalic neonate and PVS patient suffer from an absence/loss of neocortical function. The prognosis for both is grim. For the anencephalic neonate, the neocortex is absent. In spite of the often "eyes-wide open" presentation, the anencephalic has a grim prognosis. Survival is limited to hours and days, less than a week in most cases. The PVS patient similarly is unconscious and may present with "eyes-wide open," falsely interpreted by some as a sign of awareness (Caplan, McCartney, and Sisti 2006; Goodman 2010). The neocortex of the PVS patient is functionally compromised, anatomically present, yet functioning below the threshold of detected consciousness. Statistically, anencephalic fetuses will not survive birth or are stillborn. Live-birthed anencephalic neonates, when they arise, typically will succumb to death shortly thereafter. Death from cardiorespiratory arrest frequently occurs in the first few hours or days. Exceptions can be found in the literature, where an anencephalic neonate survives for months and years. One such neonate survived to more than three years of age!

The issue of providing informed consent or being registered as an organ donor is applicable only to a PVS patient. Such documentation would clearly demonstrate voluntary assent to be an organ donor. Recorded prior to brain injury, when the patient's capacity was not in question, such documentation of assent as an organ donor is the gold standard. From a utilitarian perspective, organ retrieval from either the anencephalic neonate or the PVS patient would seem of great potential value to society. It could be claimed that such survival benefit to the recipient outweighs perhaps spurious claims of personhood and negative rights of a potential donor. Yet, the absence of a declaration of death in the cases of either potential donors makes retrieval of their organs, guaranteeing unequivocal death following organ harvest, a morally reprehensible act to most people, scholars, and ethicists (Singer 1995). The act of retrieval would be equivalent to involuntary euthanasia, active killing, legally tantamount to murder or manslaughter. Retrieval of heart, lungs, the entire liver, or both kidneys in either situation would be the proximate cause of death, even if "natural" death were lurking temporally close by. Absent informed consent and a declaration of death, organ retrieval thus constitutes homicide and moral turpitude violating the accepted standards of medical care. Herein the prime obstacle to organ "donation" is the fundamental human right of not being killed, even if a potential donor is actively dying or considered "dead" by some criteria other than circulatory or respiratory collapse. Additionally, there are other very real concerns. The cost of intensive medical care for patients for whom the prognosis for continued life is poor and indeterminate (i.e., for lingering anencephalic infants and PVS patients) or is non-existent will remain exorbitantly high, financially speaking. For a society already unable to adequately care for all of its members, how do we morally interrogate the "value of life" versus the real costs of preserving it in the face of PVS and unavoidable death, as in the case of the anencephalic neonate? Is *Communio Sanctorum*, with its foundational full moral solidarity for the flourishing of "all" members, ready and able to absorb such exorbitant healthcare costs with no concern for the utilitarian principle of seeking the greater good for the greatest number in healthcare?

There exists the added moral dilemma, introduced above, concerning the declaration of "brain death" itself for victims of catastrophic, but perhaps not fatal brain injury. The decision by loved ones to authorize organ donation of a person pronounced dead using neurological criteria often is no less agonizing. Questions often emerge casting doubts on how fully informed was the victim when he/she signed the organ donor authorization on the backside of a driver's license? Today, in the U.S., such "authorization" is recognized as legally sufficient. In these cases, informed consent by surviving family plays little role in organ donation from this source (Flescher 2018). Organ procurement organizations seeking to address the ongoing acute need for organs have worked to streamline procurement. When the wish to donate has been established (e.g., by signature on a driver's license or a living will), the organs can be removed. This protocol can provoke discussion about the rights of parents and loved ones to contest whether or not the earlier decision to be an organ donor was truly informed. Waived by a person who has authorized organ donation and is now declared "brain dead," personhood status would no longer seem relevant. Yet, can the trajectory of this voluntary altruistic act be declared null and void by loved ones who choose to ignore it? I can assure you that this is not a rhetorical question. The Uniform Anatomic Gift Act of 1968 (amended in 1987 and again in 2006) was enacted to avoid loss of organs from eligible donors. The 2006 version, however, has not been fully embraced in all fifty states in the U.S. Often times, considerate empathetic discussions with the parents, loved ones, or next of kin about the benefits and virtue of organ donation can assuage those who are conflicted. Understandably, some families may still seek to cling to the remnant personhood of one now lost to declared "brain death." In the presence of a damaged, but clearly organic, living and functioning physical body of a loved one, contesting the imminent loss of the victim's most fundamental right, to not be "killed," is as most human response. The thinking of those conflicted about organ donation is that this foundational right afforded by the U.S. Constitution and Bill of Rights to not be killed should remain sacrosanct. Does not full personhood guarantee the right not to be killed? Can a patient declared "brain dead" truly waive this fundamental human right? The challenge is that if we accept this foundational right for those deemed "persons," we are no further along in overcoming moral dilemma in those other than organ donation. Early termination of pregnancy, voluntary euthanasia, and organ donation remain final assaults on people, who have already sustained loss of personhood, including the incarcerated (i.e., prisoners), the marginalized and poor, and victims of vulnerabilities of soma and/or psyche (Chapters 2 and 3).

Organ Donation, the Last Act

I have a colleague at the medical school who is an experienced, board-certified anesthesiologist. His insights opened an entirely different perspective for me on contested personhood in the context of organ donation and retrieval. One afternoon in a small group, round discussion with medical students, my colleague recounted several challenges he confronts when called in to assist in organ retrieval from a patient declared "brain dead." He began by his retelling of the professional obligations as well as attendant feelings experienced following each episode in which he managed the sedation of a donor undergoing live organ retrieval. As anesthesiologist, he is solely responsible for keeping "alive" the organ donor throughout such long and complex medical procedures. Organ retrieval is often a long, methodical procedure involving several teams of specialists seeking to expeditiously and caringly harvest precious life-giving organs for transplant. Approaching the end of the "harvest" always proved to be a very difficult moment for my colleague. Post-surgery absent the usual recovery phase for the patient, it was his sole responsibility to shut off the ventilator and terminate the procedure. With deep sadness he shared with the group what he could describe only as a great weight upon him as he completed this final act. His entire career had been singularly devoted to the preservation of the life of the patients placed in his care. He queried the group, enthralled with his narrative, is this "living" body, now absent harvested organs a "patient" at all? It may be a challenge for us to understand emotionally how this act of mechanically terminating a process that kept this living body "alive" was so gut wrenching for him. Although the body had been declared "dead" on neurological criteria and the benefits that would accrue to recipient others by the donated organs were well known to him, he just could not shake this lingering moral conundrum posed by the unceremonious end to a "living" being placed in his care. For physicians who dedicate their professional careers to the care of the living, was a lingering emotive connection to "life" of an organ donor so odd?

Such candid testimony heightens awareness of the broader need for moral solidarity upon which community is built. How is moral solidarity possible when we have yet to address how organ donation from the "least of us" suffering in a permanent vegetative state reflects upon the lost personhood of the donor and not upon our own personhood? *Communio Sanctorum* constitutes a moral setting in which all are in covenant. In moral solidarity with one and other, community members seek that all pro-creative events (i.e., pregnancies), all lives, those of the robust and vulnerable alike, those of able and disabled, those of nascent and aged must be afforded *full* personhood. A community in full covenant must pledge to provide the resources required to ensure that all lives could flourish and reach their greatest potential. We can agree that such potential will never be quite equal for all. No fault of the individual (unless by free will), we all will suffer the vicissitudes of life and bad brute luck visiting upon humans in their common day-to-day existence. To be in true covenant is to willfully embrace the firm knowledge that we all shall share in the joys and disappointments, births and deaths, of a community so formed. Included in these pledges is the need to comfort and embrace those, like my dear colleague, who individually will be asked to carry unique and heavy burdens of the heart in seeking the greatest good of the community as a whole.

PERSONHOOD AND THE AFTERMATH OF CALL-TO-DUTY

Combat-Related Post-Traumatic Stress Disorder (PTSD)

Earlier we introduced post-traumatic stress as well as the disorder, commonly referred to as, "PTSD." In the military context, this psychiatric stress disorder is provoked by an experience, a "traumatic" event(s), such as war/combat itself, surviving a serious injury/accident, or witnessing a wide-scale unavoidable death, for example, world wars, regional conflicts, and the War on Terrorism (Friedman, Keane, and Resick 2014). The victims of this debilitating stress disorder may be either actively involved or witnessing the trauma (Felman and Laub 1991). Most commonly symptoms of combat-related PTSD are manifest within a few months of a traumatic event (Poole 2018). Yet, the onset of PTSD can be delayed and appear years after the trauma. Most commonly, evaluation for PTSD is sought when the symptoms become so severe as to create significant problems that make social interactions at the work place and/or play difficult (Van der Kolk 2014). The symptoms of PTSD can make normal daily living next to impossible and have been categorized into four types. Symptoms classified as intrusive memories find their way into everyday life, dreams, and nightmares, in which the triggering event is revisited repeatedly (i.e., flashbacks) provoking severe stress, emotion, and physical reactions. Avoidance is another common symptom of PTSD. People suffering in this way set their minds to avoid thinking, reliving, and talking about the triggering event. This is especially true for veterans of wars, following their military service. Habits, traditions, and settings that promote memory of the past "trigger" events are avoided at all costs. PTSD sufferers often experience dour moods characterized by anger, frustration, depression, irritation, melancholy, restlessness, and stress. Thinking and moods often turn very negative, numbing the individual with indifference and detachment from others, including loved ones, family, and friends. People suffering from combat-related PTSD often remark about feeling hopeless and unable to enjoy aspects of their former lives. Typically, PTSD leads to changes in emotional and/or physical reactions often termed "*hyper*aroused." Hyper-arousal places the victim on edge, on guard, unable to think, sleep, and rest. The response to this exhaustive hyperarousal often is abuse of alcohol, drugs (both licit and illicit), and acquisition of high-risk behaviors involving violence, firearms, and high-speed driving.

The early monikers for PTSD, such as "shell shock" (World War I) and "combat fatigue" (World War II and the Vietnam War) reveal the most commonly thought of trigger for the disorder, the stress of war/combat (Spiro, Settersten, and Aldwin 2018). As noted in Chapter 3, the association of war and the aftermath with experienced trauma held back public and professional awareness that war/combat were not the only triggers of PTSD. As readily accepted now, non-combat deaths due to accidents, fatal diseases, and the bad brute luck of life can be equally potent in traumatizing individuals (Alford 2016). About one in ten people in the U.S. will be diagnosed with PTSD in their lifetime. For combat-related PTSD in the military the prevalence is much higher. The connection between personhood status and PTSD is complex. Reaction of most individuals to people acting out in these manners is to simply take aim first at the person, later their personhood. In the past, PTSD-related behaviors and symptomology were viewed by the military as signs of either weaknesses or moral failings. Although it became clear that combat experiences could provoke abnormal behaviors, the military initially displayed little regard for understanding why these victims "acted out." Public shaming and humiliation of soldiers who could not return to the front was common. In a hospital scene from the epic biographical WWII film *Patton* (1970), General George S. Patton (portrayed by George C. Scott), while engaged in the campaign in Sicily, berated and then slapped a soldier suffering from "battle fatigue." Patton labeled the victim as suffering from malingering cowardice! As the result of the slapping incident, Patton lost his command and suffered America's harsh disapproval of his actions. It would not be until 1980 that PTSD was recognized as a psychiatric disorder, one with a symptomology that now could be diagnosed with some precision (Spiro, Settersten, and Aldwin 2018). In that year, PTSD was added to the American Psychiatric Association's Diagnostic & Statistical Manual of Mental Disorders, DSM-III (American Psychiatric Association 1982).

Even after a greater acceptance of PTSD as a true mental disorder, assaults on the person and personhood of victims of PTSD were common, especially in the military. Such attacks aimed at a victim suffering from PTSD usually arise out of ignorance of the disorder. For those who suffer PTSD, the ultimate damage is served on their person, both from without (e.g., social isolation and shaming) and more commonly from within (e.g., sense of self-loathing and guilt). For veterans of the Vietnam War and more recent conflicts in the Middle East public sentiment often remains ambiguous. Damage to their personhood first occurs from "without," among veterans and people in the service. Veterans who returned traumatized from combat experiences in Vietnam had to contend with harsh public sentiment. Not really aimed at the veterans, the negativity more reflected unpopularity and criticism about the U.S. role in the theater of war. Lacking positive reinforcement, veterans next would internalize external negative responses from without into negative feeling within. This transition is marked by increased feelings of guilt and self-loathing. Having spent time with veterans in a metropolitan VA, I was stunned by the physical and mental damage suffered by these mostly young men and women. I was immediately brought back to the poignant 1989 American biographical war drama *Born on the Fourth of July*. This movie, based on the 1976 bestselling autobiography of Ron Kovic, interrogates the transition of a patriotic veteran, paralyzed in Vietnam War combat, to that of a staunch anti-war activist (Kovic 1976). Evaluating their physical scars, the "open" wounds to their psyches, and then entering to their narratives of service, loss, and seemingly abandonment, one recognizes that these fine soldiers/veterans will require a lifetime of support, love and care.

Even if we disagree with the politics behind a military conflict like the Vietnam War, service in the armed forces deserves our deepest respect and compassion. Especially for Vietnam War veterans suffering from combat-related PTSD, research has revealed that the greatest single predictor of preoccupation with suicide (i.e., suicide ideation), attempted and successful suicides is combat-related *guilt* (Shapiro, Farrelly, and Curry 2018). For veterans of more recent military conflicts, PTSD remains a risk factor for suicidal ideation (Shapiro, Farrelly, and Curry 2018). Thus we observe again that personhood can be assaulted from without as well as within. In both cases the damage to personhood and self-image contributes to persisting and intensifying PTSD. The recognition of PTSD as a mental disorder rather than a flawed moral compass or innate mental weakness was essential to the development of long-term plans for the healing of veterans. Although only a small act affording veterans deep respect, in public and private events in which veterans are identified, I always take the time to chat with, listen to, and sincerely thank the men and women who have served in the military. Especially around holidays, a visit to a local veterans' home (e.g., the Long Island State Veterans Home on the campus of my medical school and hospital) or VA hospital, can connect our daily lives with those who gave so much for the many. Again, we may not agree with the politics of a military intervention, but we should always give thanks to those courageous and patriotic people who selflessly place themselves in harms way for the public welfare.

Public expression of sincere thanks for their military service can go a long way in restoring to greater personhood our U.S. combat veterans suffering from PTSD.

Non-Combat-Related Post-Traumatic Stress Disorder

PTSD is not limited to those who serve in the theaters of combat and war (see chapter 3). The fifth edition of DSM (i.e., DSM-5, 2013) reflects a broader understanding of the triggers of PTSD beyond war-related trauma, including trauma associated with acts of terrorism (e.g., attacks on the U.S. of 9/11/ 2001), gun violence-related mass murders, intimate partner violence, sudden and unexpected death of a loved one, diagnosis of a life-threatening illness such as cancer, and childbirth-related trauma such as miscarriage or stillbirth (First and American Psychiatric Association 2014). My pastoral and chaplaincy experiences forced me to conclude that "trauma (like beauty) is always in the eye of the beholder." Understanding that people can vary with regard to the robustness of their person/personhood itself in response to an assault on their personhood is critical for mental health counselors (Herman 2015). Unexpected death of a loved one always is traumatic. Yet, most of the bereaved will recover from a traumatic loss within six months; that is, they will be once again able to get out with friends and visit places shared with the person who has died. Others will experience "complicated grief," a bereavement persisting well beyond the typical six-month window of recovery. For some, the loss tragically will provoke the full-blown symptomology of PTSD, requiring long-term professional help for recovery. As the period of a victim's grief and the intensity of the symptoms of PTSD extends, so generally is the public less well prepared to embrace the proper diagnosis of PTSD. Failing to find continued support from "without," the bereaved begin to look "within." Failure to regain their former lives may be viewed internally by victims as a weakness or fallenness.

PTSD is a mood and/or anxiety disorder that can be healed over time with therapeutic intervention. PTSD is not a moral failing! Though perhaps not war-related, the internalized assault on personhood by the inner "self" of the traumatized is no different from that of combat-related service. Victims of PTSD, no matter the origin of the trauma, deserve our fullest support and compassion. A community seeking moral solidarity of all members in covenant should be prepared to embrace those suffering from PTSD. The damage inflicted by trauma and its aftermath to the victim, to their personhood and mental well-being is best addressable through sincere community embrace, empathy in abundance, and professional help. Untreated, isolation and self-loathing/guilt of PTSD can only fester, often to the point in which the victims extinguish their own lives. The 2019 National Veteran Suicide Prevention Annual Report of the U.S. Department of Veterans Administration reveals that the number of suicide of adults as well as veterans increased steadily from 2005 to 2017. In 2017, 6,139 veterans accounted for 6,139 of the 45,390 American adults who committed suicide. During the first year in VA treatment for the disorder, younger veterans suffering with PTSD were most likely to die of suicide or "accidental injuries," more than half of such injuries were poisonings (Forehand et al. 2019). Overall, PTSD affects approximately 8 million Americans a year. These data are stark reminders that there remains an unfulfilled need for effective therapeutic intervention for those at risk to the aftermath of trauma as well as the vicissitudes of life in 21st century America. When community fails to act to embrace all as "self," suffering, death, and suicide may ensue. Creating our *Communio Sanctorum* provides the best possible hope to addressing this ever expanding and deadly pestilence of suicide attendant to modern living.

THE QUEERING OF PERSONHOOD IN AMERICA

Gender Identity, Sexual Orientation, and "Sexual Preference"

Although the acronym "LGBTQI" firmly entered into the mainstream media in 21st century America to designate the inclusive product of human rights activists for Lesbian, Gay, Bisexual, Transgender, Queer (or questioning sexual identity), Intersex people, it reflects not an end-point, but rather points to a healthy, continued interrogation of the fundamental nature of being human. Like all human efforts to explore and then to label new discoveries, initial terms like "gay" and "lesbian" yielded over time to a more expansive inclusivity of gender identity, that is, the need to find greater definition for aspects, dimensions, and textures of human sexuality (Lehmiller 2017). This constant evolution and discovery speaks directly to our topic of personhood. To better understand the link between human sexuality and personhood or the being human in our complex world of sexuality, three rudimentary definitions are useful (Colker 2017). These terms are gender identity, sexual orientation, and sexual preferences. Gender identity, as defined by the Human Right Campaign, is the "innermost concept of self as male, female, a blend of both or neither—how individuals perceive themselves and what they call themselves." Gender identity for many people extends far beyond the gender assigned at birth on the basis of genitalia or genetic screening (Petrikowski 2017). Currently there are more than forty self-identifications related to gender identity. Additional self-identifications likely will follow.

Traditionally, sexual orientation allowed for four self-evident categories: heterosexuality, bisexuality, homosexuality and asexuality (i.e., lacking any sexual orientation). Ever evolving, the definition of "sexual orientation" has progressed to the inherent or immutable emotional, intimate and passionate, sexual attractions of one for others. Even these definitions may limit our understanding, since sexual orientation can be fluid rather than fixed and subject to change over a lifetime. Simply put into the current vernacular, sexual orientation reflects whom we are interested in romantically, whom we may wish to date, and with whom we desire to be intimate (Colker 2017). The potential paramour may be gay, bisexual, transgender, straight, asexual, or some complex mixture of these. Gender identity is expressed not only in the people we chose to love romantically, but also is expressed in our manners, behaviors, likes and dislikes, clothes, and personal appearance. Gender identity is a powerful dimension of the Gestalt of how we feel about ourselves as well as others.

The term "sexual preference" is included by intention. The most common usage of "sexual preference" was in conservative and right-leaning discussions aimed at defining sexual preference as a choice, clearly at odds with the definitions explored above. Just as the clinical term "homosexual" continues to be employed aggressively by anti-gay groups to suggest that gay people are suffering from some sort of disease or psychological disorder, "preference" is aggressively employed by similar groups to suggest that being LGBTQI is a "choice" (Burnett 2015), therefore it can be "cured." I vividly recall a conversation I had with an Anglican bishop in the, UK who shared with me proudly that he was chairing a synod conference on "Conversion Therapy." Conversion therapy includes a range of dangerous and discredited practices involving psychological or spiritual interventions aimed at changing an individual's sexual orientation from homosexual or bisexual to heterosexual. I challenged the Right Reverend's assertion by pointing out (as a teacher of medical students) that the term "therapy" was employed solely to describe a treatment of a well-defined, medically accepted "disease" state. I most emphatically was fully not aware of what disease state "conversion therapy" sought to "cure"? Following soul searching by the Anglicans, Christians, and adherents of other world religions, the tide for conversion therapy has turned. The Church of England later advocated that the UK government ban conversion therapy, condemning the practice in no uncertain terms. In 2018 all forms of "conversion therapy" were banned in the UK. Not unexpectedly and reflecting the disproportionate power of right-leaning orthodox Church leaders in 2020 U.S., less than a dozen states ban this psuedopsychological, pseudoscientific practice of attempting to alter an individual's sexual orientation or gender identity from other than heterosexual to heterosexual by psychological or spiritual methods. That conversion therapy continues to be permitted in the U.S. (even for minors) is an abomination, assaulting the fundamental personhood of the entire nation to accommodate theological leanings of the few.

I admit that I remain profoundly distressed when Christian clerics in particular seem to have no personal knowledge/sense of how damaging, demeaning, and hurtful such unenlightened thinking is to personhood as well as to the fuller dimensions of "all" of the children of God (Gaikwad et al. 2017)! Exploitation of the term "sexual preference" continues as a cudgel, disguised by those who employ it against the LGBTQI community. The perpetrators employ the term to assault the personhood of all LGBTQI people nationwide. We should be vigilant in ferreting out those who likewise employ "lifestyle" rather than "lives," "admitted" rather than "openly," and "special rights" rather than "equal/human rights." In a community of moral solidarity with all, we must act forcefully to protect the rights to flourish and to achieve fullest personhood. Community thrives in diversity and enjoys a robustness not found outside of true inclusivity. Assaults on personhood that go unchallenged threaten the very core existence of *Communio Sanctorum*.

Assault on the Personhood of LGBTQI People

Historically, discrimination and contested personhood have assaulted the existence of many, if not all, people who identify within the LGBTQI calculus. The assaults take place at several levels: personal, *en masse*, regionally, statewide, and federally. This listing is not inclusive. The dimensions of these assaults range from shunning by friends and family to the extremes of hate crimes, including physical attacks and the killing of members of the LGBTQI family. The legacy of discrimination, hatred and rejection is long, breeding fear and an inability to live into "life, liberty, and the pursuit of happiness" guaranteed by the U.S. Constitution. How does the desire to live, to love, to pursue employment, to marry, to have a family, and to pursue happiness for LGBTQI people provoke such extraordinary responses in America? The reality is that for the LGBTQI community at large, one in five will be the victim of a violent hate crime in their lifetime. Transgender people are viciously targeted, especially today. One in four transgender people are victims of violent assault (Gitlin 2017). The nature of such hate crimes seems generic. Crime statistics indicate that LGBTQI people suffer disproportionately more hate crimes, even though nearly half of such attacks go unreported for fear of further harassment and victimization (Gitlin 2017). Typically, hate crimes rightly provoke public outcry, enhanced criminal prosecution and harsh penalties. Yet at the state level, criminal treatment of perpetrators who assault the LGBTQI members typically fail to rise to the level afforded to other bias/hate crimes, for example, those aimed at religious minorities. Lack of prosecution, deterrent penalties, intentionally broad and watered-down statutes on bias and hate crimes foment assaults of the community. The very lack of enforcement of existing hate crime statues by police can provide a "green light" to perpetrators of hate crimes targeting the LGBTQI community. More than sixty members of the LGBTQI family have been murdered in the last decade!

We have interrogated the many populations vulnerable to contested personhood in 21st century America. Consistently we found the "other" differs on one or more dimensions of gender, race, color, class, religious affiliation, etc. What stands out in assaults on the personhood of the LGBTQI community is that many of these earlier discriminators seem no more relevant to the calculus. Targeted LGBTQI victims largely do not differ from the perpetrators on the basis of sex, race, color, class, etc.! LGBTQI folks often are assaulted as "other" simply on the basis of their more sweeping and inclusive sexual nature. This claim finds traction in the following sense. People often first encounter members of LGBTQI following the "coming out" of a family member, friends, or even celebrity. Flesh and blood family members of the LGBTQI community can be estranged, shunned, and separated. All other discriminators of otherness that are employed to discriminate are largely absent *en famille*. Even *en famille*, the revelation of a member "coming out" can present an existential threat to the individual. In 2020 U.S., adolescent LGBTQI kids constitute a large and growing population of the homeless! They can be denied shelter, education, and healthcare, leaving them "abandoned" to the streets where they are easily victimized (Meyer 2015).

The Federal government under the administration of the 45th president has sought to rollback even the most essential services from LGBTQI people, especially targeting transgender people. The "original sin" attached to the LGBTQI person is not a sin at all, but simply just people seeking to live into who they are. So-called religious "pronouncements" employ thin or baseless "biblical warrants" with which to grab authority and assault the personhood of LGBTQI. These "warrants" are theologically vapid and counter to the broader dictums of world religions to love one another (Copeland 2016). The truth is that for generations the U.S. has conditioned its citizens with bias and overt hatred of people heretofore little known to them. Media caricatures of gay men and lesbian women, off-color comedy derivative of a xenophobia targeting the LGBTQI community, and laying exclusive claim of dominance by the White "straight" ruling class patriarchs have left grave stains on America. Regrettably stains of bias, indifference, and hatred may be carefully hidden in plain sight. Perpetrators, most often White, young, "straight" males are the most likely to commit anti-LGBTQI crimes. When LGBTQI people are women, people of color, folks of differing socioeconomic class and country of origin or people of differing religious affiliation, the jeopardy to their physical well-being is amplified, often synergized. The precarious safety of a transgender woman of color in 2020 America is affirmed by the high frequency of hate crimes aimed at they/he/her (Meyer 2015). Herein, personhood is being multiply assailed, leaving scars and wounds on the soma and psyche on the vulnerable. In the extreme, anti-LGBTQI hatred can and does rob its victim of their most fundamental negative right afforded by the U.S. Constitution, namely the right not to be killed!

LGBTQI Community Resistance and Resilience

Up until the ascent of the 45th president of the U.S., generally speaking there was a renewed hopefulness for forming a more inclusive society in America. Efforts to insure that the Bill of Rights and the U.S. Constitution would blanket all Americans, especially members of the LGBTQI were gaining traction. The advent of right-wing extremists and so called conservatives hell bent on moving the clock back to the "good old days" of the 1950s was not so unexpected (Rozell and Wilcox 2018). What was unexpected from 2016 forward was the state and federal government in some cases becoming complicit in providing a "green light" for denying rights and privileges to LGBTQI people (Rozell and Wilcox 2018)! Under the guise of protecting "religious rights," but more honestly the "Religious Right" (Raja 2016; Rozell and Wilcox 2018)), the rights of the LGBTQI community came under fire (Meyer, Tarrow, and Hacker 2018). The forward progress of the community on same-sex marriage (Mazurek 2018; Paul 2018), both consolidated and affirmed by the courts, provoked a pushback as well as a rollback of LGBTQI rights. Same-sex marriage was viewed by the Right-Wing conservatives as a frontal attack on procreative heterosexual marriage, that is, the long-standing "gold standard" for many conservative religious and secular groups in the U.S. (Ball 2016).

These attacks on the LGBTQI family revealed two things: how perverse the Bully Pulpit can be when intent on bullying the LGBTQI; and, how fragile some advances can be when populist sentiment is inflamed and aimed at punishing those considered "other" by White ruling class, right-wing conservatives. The persistent and escalating attacks on the LGBTQI community have become "red meat" in conservative evangelical pulpits, right-wing political groups, White supremacists, and White nationalists. The din of these negative attacks by the conservative media damage American community *in toto*, but more troubling provokes bullying of the most fragile LGBTQI community. Paradoxically, we hear the administration of the 45th president professing concern around the problem of bullying and teen suicide, while actively participating in bullying of its own design. The "bully pulpit of the 45th president" itself now catalyzes enhanced bullying of the queer community! Yet, we should not lose sight of the amazing advances made by the LGBTQI community in the last 100 years (Brooks 2015). These advances will outlive the current scourge. Rights and privileges earned by LGBTQI community activists have accrued with advent of new labor laws, rights to marriage, rights to adoption, rights to not be denied healthcare, and family rights within couples and families. In 1973, lacking *any* data to suggest that "homosexuality" is no more than a natural, healthy, positive and normal sexual orientation, the American Psychiatric Association (APA) finally removed homosexuality from the DSM-II manual of disorders (1973)! The

APA (American Psychiatric Association 1982) and other professional psychiatric, medical, and psychological organizations have worked since to expunge the former and misplaced stigma of mental illness from the LGBTQI community. This affirmation of the LGBTQI community existing well within the nominative standard of human sexuality should assist in reducing the assault on the personhood of LGBTQI people from "without" and importantly "within." Unresolved feelings of self-loathing provoked by unfounded public discrimination, the denial of basic rights afforded in being human, and assault on a person-in-full have damaged the queer community. Thankfully the LGBTQI community flourishes, benefitting within its love, solidarity, and moral imperatives. It is a community of refuge, support and love for the assaulted/contested among them as well as all "other" (Brooks 2015). The many colors of human sexuality should allow us to paint a vivid portrait of uncontested human beings, just being human.

Thankfully, views about human sexuality in 21st century America (as elsewhere) are progressing, expanding, and informing the very society within which it evolves. The central message is that we are all part of the same Creation. We are co-travelers in this Creation, the seeds of a harvest yet to come. Our lives overlap deeply with a multitude of people who share so much more than mere social and political views currently being inflamed by some to divide us. We are witnesses to a natural, healthy and evolving process that yields a continual byproduct, that is, change. Regrettably, but unavoidably, some members of the society inevitably will find such evolution unpalatable, regrettable, and anxiety provoking. In a community of moral solidarity, our *Communio Sanctorum*, we should prepare to embrace both the change and the consequent dissention. Creating true inclusivity is hard, but essential to creating and maintaining a true flourishing community that is covenantal and bound by moral solidarity. The LGBTQI community is one that "lives into" the very nature of what we re-imagine as *Communio Sanctorum*.

APPENDIX 3: FURTHER NOTES

*Text in italics are callouts to places within the chapter.

The American College of Obstetrics & Gynecology provided a strongly worded position paper that declares criminalization of self-induced abortion only intimidates and shames women unnecessarily. For further details see: Unnamed Author (2018), "Criminalization of Self-Induced Abortion Intimidates and Shames Women Unnecessarily," Washington, DC: American College of Obstetricians and Gynecologists, published January 3, 2018 (accessed on April 30, 2020), https://www.acog.org/news/news-releases/2018/01/criminalization-of-self-induced-abortion-intimidates-and-shames-women-unnecessarily.

The Federal justice system in 2018 has exerted by force the conservative views of the Trump Administration by denying pregnant women incarcerated in immigration detention centers the right to an abortion. For details and specific state and Federal mandates see: Unnamed Author (2018), "State Standards for Pregnancy-Related Health Care and Abortion for Women in Prison," New York, NY: American Civil Liberties Union. Published online 2020 (accessed April 30, 2020), https://www.aclu.org/state-standards-pregnancy-related-health-care-and-abortion-women-prison.

Criminalizing pregnancy to artificially address a whole host of "straw men" issues has assaulted, diminished, and denied personhood to many women in America. For analysis of recent laws aimed a criminalizing pregnancy see: Lollar, Cortney (2017), "Criminalizing Pregnancy," *Indiana Law Journal, 92*(3), Article 3 (accessed online April 30, 2020), https://www.repository.law.indiana.edu/ilj/vol92/iss3/3.

The Council of Economic Advisers, a U.S. agency in the Executive Office of the President, has made such calculation and advised that the opioid-crisis estimates "vastly underestimate losses." For an in-depth examination of the true costs of the ongoing opioid epidemic in America, see: Unnamed Author (2017), "The Underestimated Cost of the Opioid Crisis," Washington, DC: *The Council of Economic Advisers to the White House*, published online November 1, 2017 (accessed on April 30, 2020), https://www.whitehouse.gov/sites/whitehouse.gov/files/images/The%20Underestimated%20Cost%20of%20the%20Opioid%20Crisis.pdf.

The early implementation programs making Narcan take-home kits available to communities have saved countless lives from opioid overdose. For a recent overview of the life-saving value of reversing opioid overdoses in Emergency Medicine, see: Vivolo, Alana M. et al. (2017), "Nonfatal Drug Overdoses Treated in Emergency Departments—United States 2016–2017," Atlanta, GA: *Morbidity and Mortality Weekly Report,* Centers for Disease and Prevention (CDC), published online April 3, 2020 (accessed on April 30, 2020), http://dx.doi.org/10.15585/mmwr.mm6913a3.

First reported in Ohio, Pennsylvania, and then in Maine and other locales, government units have used the opioid overdose crisis to suggest that it may be better to withhold Narcan rescue as a stand against moral depravity or even economic extortion. For a balanced narrative on the complexities of opioid overdose and naloxone rescue as well as the moral issues associated with rescuing repeat overdosing people, see: Unnamed Author (2017), "A Second Chance: Overdose Prevention, Naloxone, and Human Rights in the United States," New York, NY: Human Rights Watch, published online April 27, 2017 (accessed April 30, 2020), https://www.hrw.org/report/2017/

04/27/second-chance/overdose-prevention-naloxone-and-human-rights-unit-ed-states.

In Butler County Ohio, a city councilman floated a "three-strikes-and-you're-out" policy, where an ambulance would then not be sent to resuscitate the "three-times" loser. For the details about a controversial stance taken by Butler County (Ohio) police to not carry Narcan as well as consequent blowback against this police position, see: Richter, Ed (2017), "Sheriff's Decision to not Allow Officers to Carry Narcan Draws Protests: Others Came Out to Show Support for Butler County Sheriff Richard K. Jones," Dayton, OH: *Dayton Daily News*, published online July 15, 2017 (accessed on April 30, 2020), https://www.daytondailynews.com/news/local/sheriff-decision-not-allow-officers-carry-narcan-draws-protest/k7R9nzT89R2wiWTfXkD9JN/.

The efforts by the dominant White ruling class to abridge these basic human rights guaranteed by the U.S. Constitution would be repelled by the Civil Rights movement. In addition to the cited sources, there exist a series of video tapes (VHS, DVD formats) produced by Public Broadcasting Service and released from 1986–1991 entitled, "Eyes on the Prize- America's Civil Rights Years," "Eyes on the Prize- America at the Racial Crossroads," and accompanying texts and sources that should be required viewing for anyone seeking to truly immerse themselves in the extraordinary struggle, successes, and failures of this movement. In 1990, a second set of videos were released entitled, "Eyes on the Prize II" spanning years 1964 to the mid 1980's that are compelling, exposing interested viewers to the 1990's and examination of the aftermath of the Civil Rights Movement in America. For an overview on these invaluable resources, see: Unnamed Author (2006), "Eyes on the Prize," Arlington, VA: Public Broadcasting Service *American Experience,* aired online October 2, 2006 (accessed on April 30, 2020), https://www.pbs.org/wgbh/americanexperience/films/eyesontheprize/#cast_and_crew.

In the years since the killing of Trayvon Martin (2012) more than 200 Black people have died at the hands of violence, many viewed as extrajudicial executions. For more detailed information and graphic representations of killings of Blacks by police in America see: Lopez, German (2018), "There are Huge Racial Disparities in How US Police Use Force," New York, NY: *Vox Media*, published online November 14, 2018 (accessed on April 30, 2020), https://www.vox.com/identities/2016/8/13/17938186/police-shootings-killings-racism-racial-disparities.

At a local level, signs supporting the BLM movement have appeared on the lawns of predominantly white congregations, a sign of solidarity. In the June 18, 2019 issue of *The Christian Century* the Rev. Benjamin D. Wayman, pastor of a mostly White church congregation shares the church's experience of putting up a "Black Lives Matter" sign on the front lawn. For details, see: Wayman, Benjamin D. (2019), "What Happened after My Mostly White Church Put up a Black Lives Matter Sign," Chicago, IL: *The Christian Century*, published online June 18, 2019 (accessed on April 30, 2020), https://www.christiancentury.org/article/first-person/what-happened-after-my-mostly-white-church-put-Black-lives-matter-sign.

The police officer exclaimed, "I could have shot you in front of your f@#king kids." Assaults on personhood of people of color or other minorities are on the rise in 21st century America. For a look at how the dehumanization of Black people by law enforcement promotes a paradoxical increase in police brutality and even in death of victims, see: Butler, Paul (2019), "'I Could Have Shot You in Front of Your Fuck#&% Kids': How Cops Dehumanize Black People," London, UK: *The Guardian*, published online June 29, 2019 (accessed on April 30, 2020), https://www.theguardian.com/commentisfree/2019/jun/28/i-could-have-shot-you-in-front-of-your-fucking-kids-how-cops-dehumanize-Black-people.

All of the defendants sentenced to death are people of color, that is, none were "white." The story about LA county district attorney Jackie Lacey is emblematic of a criminal justice system that suffers from racial bias, sometimes in unexpected ways. For the full story, see: Levin, Sam (2019), "In Los Angeles, Only People of Color are Sentenced to Death," London, UK: *The Guardian*, published online June 18, 2019 (accessed on April 30, 2020), https://www.theguardian.com/us-news/2019/jun/18/los-angeles-death-penalty-sentences-jackie-lacey.

The Washington Post's database of fatal police shootings does not suggest that there is an epidemic of unjustified shooting deaths driven by race. The analysis of such data sets remains in the "eye of the beholder." To examine the database containing records of every fatal shooting in the U.S. by a police officer in the line of duty since January 1, 2015 complied by *The Washington Post* to delineate killings by police in the U.S., by year, and descriptors of the perpetrators and victims alike see: Unnamed Author (2020), "Fatal Force: 992 People Have Been Shot and Killed by Police in 2018," Washington, DC: *The Washington Post*, published online and update up to January 22, 2020 (accessed on April 30, 2020), https://www.washingtonpost.com/graphics/2018/national/police-shootings-2018/?utm_term=.cf5d2477c4de.

Restriction on access to social services, education resources, and residential housing can effectively deny Hispanic/Latino peoples (and other desperate people) from public-needs programs. Although a lower percentage of poor immigrants make use of public-needs programs than similar "native" populations, denial of such services has become another cudgel by which "conservatives" and right-wing groups seek to make worse the suffering of the "least of us." For more information on this political effort see: Samari, Goleen (2018), "Denying Legal Immigrants Medicaid and Other Social Services Won't Make the Rest of Us Any Safer," Miami, FL: *Miami Herald*, published online September 28, 2018 (accessed on April 30, 2020), https://www.miamiherald.com/opinion/op-ed/article219198090.html.

The denial or withdrawals of renting agreements as well as confiscation of personal properties (i.e., asset forfeiture) deserve prompt state and Federal investigation. The unconstitutional deployment of asset forfeiture is well known, but remains exploited in both penalizing the vulnerable as well as enriching local, state, and Federal coffers. For further reading on deployment of this reprehensible attack of the economically vulnerable see: Unnamed Author (2018), "How Crime Pays: The Unconstitutionality of Modern Civil Asset Forfeiture as a Tool of Criminal Law Enforcement," *The Harvard Law Review, 131*: 2387, published online June 8, 2018 (accessed April 30, 2020), https://harvardlawreview.org/2018/06/how-crime-pays-the-unconstitutionality-of-modern-civil-asset-forfeiture-as-a-tool-of-criminal-law-enforcement/.

The goal in San Bernardino was to avoid "California from turning into a 'Third World cesspool' of illegal immigrants." The story of Joseph Turner and of his creation of "Save Our State" movement exemplifies how a powerful xenophobia was fired up in response to undocumented immigrant populations in California. The thrust was to demonize a group of people who heretofore were welcomed into the agricultural business model in California (and elsewhere). In that model, undocumented immigrants were imported simply for exploitation as cheap labor to support the agricultural industry. For further reading on this topic see: Jordan, Miriam (2016), "In Immigrant Fight, Grass-Roots Group Boost Their Clout: Internet, Talk Radio are Used to Affect State, City Laws; Critics Slam 'Hate Groups,'" New York, NY: *The Wall Street Journal* published September 28, 2016 (accessed April 30, 2020), https://www.wsj.com/articles/SB115940950734176279.

Racial subjugation of Black women deepens and perpetuates the fragmentation of the Black family and has been labeled the "New Jane Crow." The aim of this assault on Black women is clear, that is, to deny them the fundamental human right of mothering their children and structuring a family life for them. This fragmentation of family system leads to a "staircase" effect insuring a never ending, intergenerational loss of family fabric and violation of a mother's right to guide her children. For further reading see the following accounts: Jones, Chenelle A. and Renita L. Seabrook (2017), *The New Jane Crow: Mass Incarceration and Denied Maternity of Black Women.* In *Race, Ethnicity and Law, 22*, available online May 25, 2017 (accessed on April 30, 2020), https://www.emeraldinsight.com/doi/full/10.1108/S1521-613620170000022011; and Clifford, Stephanie and Jessica Silver-Greenberg (2017), "Foster Care as Punishment: The New Reality of 'Jane Crow,'" New York, NY: *The New York Times*, published online July 21, 2017 (accessed April 30, 2020), https://www.nytimes.com/2017/07/21/nyregion/foster-care-nyc-jane-crow.html.

Another more deadly narrative emerges from the expansion of White ruling class efforts into state laws, legislatively adopting so-called "stand-your-ground" (SYG) laws. Like the case for the "Save Our State" movement, activism aimed at state legislatures has been revealed to be a particularly successful venue for scapegoating, demonizing, and degrading the personhood of the "other." Aimed a creating a hostile environment, fragmenting families, and sowing discontent among xenophobes of the White ruling class, these efforts can yield lethal outcomes. The "Stand Your Ground" movement employs discredited ancient "castle doctrine" as an excuse for the extreme degradation of personhood of the "other," literally aiming to deny a victim of the most fundamental human right, that is, the right not to be killed. For expanded reading on this effort to enable perpetrators access and use of deadly force in purported "self defense" (even when escape from a perceived threat is possible instead) see: Morral, Andrew R. (2020), "Effects of Stand-Your-Ground Laws on Violent Crime," Santa Monica, CA: *The RAND Corporation*, published online April 30, 2020 (accessed April 30, 2020), https://www.rand.org/research/gun-policy/analysis/stand-your-ground/violent-crime.html, and Unnamed Author (2020), "'Stand Your Ground' Laws," San Francisco, CA: *Giffords Law Center to Prevent Gun Violence*, published online April 30, 2020 (accessed on April 30, 2020), https://lawcenter.giffords.org/gun-laws/policy-areas/guns-in-public/stand-your-ground-laws/.

Incarceration is but one extension of the American criminal justice system that has become a highly profitable, politically active industry, fed by a constant source of government criminal justice and immigration efforts. Few people think of the criminal justice detention system as "big business," but it is. The business of mass incarceration and a criminal justice system that at all levels (e.g., local, state, Federal) aims at keeping prisons/detention centers "full and expanding" should be the object of public moral outrage in America. For more information see: Chen, Michelle (2018), "Who Profits From Our Prison System?," Washington, DC: *The Nation*, published online August 9, 2018 (accessed April 30, 2020), https://www.thenation.com/article/profits-prison-system/.

Recently the mercenary profits of forced labor by pools of prisoners/detainees in the U.S. have been revealed; they are painfully reminiscent of our troubled American history of indentured slavery. Although slavery in the U.S. was abolished in 1865, the practice employed in the prison system in America in the 21st century has enabled de facto slavery of the incarcerated to flourish. For more information on this troubling recent history see: Unnamed Author (2020), "Plantation to Prison," New York, NY: *The New York Times*, available online April 30, 2020 (accessed April 30, 2020), https://www.nytimes.com/paidpost/netflix-13th/plantation-to-prison.html; and Unnamed Author (2016), "Prison Labor and the Thirteenth Amendment," Montgomery, AL: *Equal Justice Initiative*, published February 1, 2016 (accessed April 30, 2020), https://eji.org/history-racial-injustice-prison-labor.

Visuals, music, photographs and pieces of memorabilia can be triggers for remnant memories of AD patients and the deeply-forgetful. Triggering seemingly lost memories in people with AD (and with other forms of memory loss) is a challenge, but can connect victims to their remnant core. This core personhood exists even in the shadow of AD. Dr. Dan Cohen, founder of the Music & Memory nonprofit provides a compelling set of testimonies by AD patients (and caregivers) about the therapeutic potential of music in the quality of life of the deeply forgetful. In *Alive Inside: A Story of Music and Memory*, a 2014 documentary film, we see the amazing results of music therapy provoking to consciousness some deeply concealed remnant memories dear to people suffering with AD and other types of dementia. For viewing these powerful videos, see: Unnamed Author (2020), "Bringing Music and Peace to Alzheimer's," New York, NY: *Alive Inside Coalition*, available online April 30, 2020 (accessed April 30, 2020), https://www.aliveinside.org.

Much has been learned from the Education for Physicians on End-of-Life Care Project advanced by the American Medical Association. For updated information related to efforts to train physicians in helping patients and families with end-of-life decisions and care see: Staff News Writer (2018), "End-of-Life Care: What's the Physician Role in Healthy Dying?," Chicago, IL: *The American Medical Association: Ethics*, published online August 9, 2018 (accessed April 30, 2020), https://www.ama-assn.org/delivering-care/ethics/end-life-care-whats-physician-role-healthy-dying.

There is yet no precise and expansive definition of consciousness, so diagnosing either its absence or presence is problematic. Defining consciousness has been a challenge for neural scientists and physicians alike. For further reading on this controversial area see: Koch, Christof (2018), "What is Consciousness?," New York, NY: *Scientific American*, published online June 1, 2018 (accessed April 30, 2020), https://www.scientificamerican.com/article/what-is-consciousness/?redirect=1; and Blain-Moraes, Eric Racine, and George A. Mashour (2018), "Consciousness and Personhood in Medical Care," *Frontiers in Human Neurosciences*, published August 2, 2018 (accessed on April 30, 2020), https://doi.org/10.3389/fnhum.2018.00306.

There are ample data to suggest that although low probability, recovery from persistent vegetative state (PVS) into consciousness, although perhaps not fully functional consciousness, occurs. There do exist case studies of patients diagnosed with PVS sustained in injuries involving the *substantia nigra* or ventral tegmental area who were treated successfully with L-dopa (a therapeutic agent employed to treat people suffering with symptoms of Parkinson's disease) and eventually regained consciousness. For further reading see: Matsuda, W., A. Matsumura, Y Komatsu, K. Yanaka, and T. Nose

(2003), "Awakenings from Persistent Vegetative State: Report of Three Cases with Parkinsonism and Brain Stem Lesions on MRI," *Journal of Neurology, Neurosurgery & Psychiatry* 74: 1571–1573, available online (accessed April 30, 2020), https://jnnp.bmj.com/content/74/11/1571.

Regrettably, deaths of "living organ donors" for organ transplant do occur and the risk to the live donor can never be eliminated, owing to the unavoidable truth that such organ donation is surgically demanding. Although rarely emerging into popular media, discussion of the real risks of organ transplantation from living donors is lacking. The risks are real and compel us to think more deeply in terms of the personhood of the live donor as well as the organ recipient. For and excellent discussion of the risks and obstacles to be overcome or at least minimized for organ transplantation from live donors, see: Ratner, L. E. and P. R. Sandoval (2010), "When Disaster Strikes: Death of a Living Organ Donor," *American Journal of Transplantation, 10*: 2577–81, available online (accessed April 30, 2020), https://onlinelibrary.wiley.com/doi/pdf/10.1111/j.1600-6143.2010.03341.x.

The theological community has expressed its support for decision making by the medical community, even in the case of brain death. Yet, there is no uniformity among world religions about the moral questions surrounding organ donation and transplantation. To address this issue a Federal web site was created providing "U.S. Government Information on Organ Donation and Transplantation" (see: https://www.organdonor.gov) and links providing up-to-date statements of various religious groups and denominations about organ donation and transplantation (see: Unnamed Author (2020), "Religion and Organ Donation," Washington, DC: *Health Resources & Services Administration*, available online April 30, 2020 (accessed April 30, 2020, https://www.organdonor.gov/about/donors/religion.html). These resources highlight rightly that all aspects of organ donation and transplantation are personal and require exploration for the parties involved. I recall a congregant who was placed on the top of the list for a heart transplant who wrestled with the very idea of navigating the linkage between his benefit versus the lost personhood of a donor. My experience tells me that discussions will be both theological and moral. Challenging questions will emerge as dialogue progresses. Why should I be the lucky recipient? What about others who also are waiting for a heart transplant? Interrogating the potential recipient's values and perspectives on good brute luck (i.e., for the recipient) and bad brute luck (i.e., for the unlucky donor) is a must. For those lucky individuals who float towards the top of a recipient transplant waiting list, there is a special need to explore these difficult questions in a timely manner and thoroughly. The consequences of refusing an organ donation and transplant (and it does occur) are equally daunting to "live into" for those few who decline the opportunity.

To better understand the link between human sexuality and personhood or being human in our complex world of sexuality, three rudimentary definitions are useful. For a more expansive source of definitions please see: Unnamed Author (2020), "Sexual Orientation and Gender Identity Definitions," Washington, DC: *Human Right Campaign*, published online April 30, 2020 (accessed on April 30, 2020), https://www.hrc.org/resources/sexual-orientation-and-gender-identity-terminology-and-definitions.

Gender identity, as defined by Human Rights Campaign is the largest LGBTQI advocacy group and political lobbyist for the queer community in the U.S. For more information on their history, issues, and advocacy see: Unnamed Author (2020), "Resources for the LGBTQ Community," Washington, DC: *Human Right Campaign*, published online April 30, 2020 (accessed on April 30, 2020) https://www.hrc.org.

The dimensions of these assaults range from shunning by friends and family to the extremes of hate crimes, including physical attacks and the killing of members of the LGBTQI family. For a more detailed analysis of statistics and data on sexual assault in the LGBTQI community see: Unnamed Author (2020), "Sexual Assault and the LGBTQ Community," Washington, DC: *Human Right Campaign*, published online April 30, 2020 (accessed on April 30, 2020), https://www.hrc.org/resources/sexual-assault-and-the-lgbt-community.

Under Administration of the 45th president of the U.S., the Federal government has sought to rollback even the most essential services from access by LGBTQI community members. The enhanced targeting and assaults on the personhood of transgender people cannot be ignored. For a powerful rebuttal to the unrelenting attacks on the personhood of the transgender by the Trump administration see this Op/Ed article in *The New York Times* by noted American author and transgender activist Jennifer Boylan. See: Boylan, Jennifer Finney (2018), "Trump Cannot Define Away My Existence," New York, NY: *The New York Times*, published online October 22, 2018 (accessed on April 30, 2020), https://www.nytimes.com/2018/10/22/opinion/trump-transgender-sex-policy.html.

More than sixty members of the LGBTQI family have been murdered in the decade since 2010. The level of hate crimes and violence against the LGBTQI family has "skyrocketed" in the past few years. To examine current statistics about this horrific trend in America see: Marzullo, Michelle A. and Alyn J. Libman (2009), "Research Overview: Hate Crimes and Violence against Lesbian, Gay, Bisexual and Transgender People," Washington, DC: *Human Right Campaign*, published online April 30, 2020 (accessed on April 30, 2020), https://assets2.hrc.org/files/assets/resources/Hatecrimesandviolenceagainstlgbtpeople_2009.pdf?_ga=2.160116221.1541658763.1558539863-633431175.1558539863.

Bullying of the queer community these days is from the "bully pulpit" itself! The LGBTQI community squarely rejects the hypocrisy of the Trump administration sheading crocodile tears for victims and families of teen suicide provoked by media and online bullying. For more on this topic, see: Michelson, Noah (2019), "If We Want to Stop Queer Kids From Dying By Suicide, We Need to Start at the Top: President Donald Trump's Administration has Worked Tirelessly to Terrorize Queer People, and the Consequences are Deadly," New York, NY: *Huffington Post: HuffPost Personal*, published online April 25, 2019 (accessed on April 30, 2020), https://www.huffpost.com/entry/queer-youth-suicide-donald-trump_n_5cc08040e4b0764d31db9a99.

REFERENCES

Agronin, Marc E. 2014. *Alzheimer's disease and other dementias: A practical guide.* New York, NY: Routledge, Taylor & Francis Group.

———. 2016. *The dementia caregiver: A guide to caring for someone with Alzheimer's disease and other neurocognitive disorders.* Lanham, MD: Rowman & Littlefield.

Alexander, Michelle. 2010. *The new Jim Crow: Mass incarceration in the age of colorblindness.* New York, NY; Jackson, TN: New Press, distributed by Perseus.

Alexander, Patrick Elliot. 2018. *From slave ship to Supermax: Mass incarceration, prisoner abuse, and the new neo-slave novel.* Philadelphia, PA: Temple University Press.

Alford, C. Fred. 2016. *Trauma, culture, and PTSD.* New York, NY: Palgrave Macmillan.

American Psychiatric Association. 1982. *Desk reference to the diagnostic criteria from DSM-III.* Washington, DC: American Psychiatric Publishing.

Arstein-Kerslake, Anna. 2017. *Restoring voice to people with cognitive disabilities: Realizing the right to equal recognition before the law.* Cambridge, UK; New York, NY: Cambridge University Press.

Azaransky, Sarah. 2011. *The dream is freedom: Pauli Murray and American democratic faith.* Oxford, UK; New York, NY: Oxford University Press.

Ball, Carlos A. 2016. *After marriage equality: The future of LGBT rights.* New York, NY ; London, UK: New York University Press.

Ballenger, Jesse F. 2006. *Self, senility, and Alzheimer's disease in modern America: A history.* Baltimore, MD: Johns Hopkins University Press.

Beckwith, Francis. 2007. *Defending life: A moral and legal case against abortion choice.* New York, NY: Cambridge University Press.

Bell, Virginia, and David Troxel. 2017. *The best friends approach to dementia care.* Baltimore, MD: Health Professions Press, Inc.

Bender, Steven, and William F. Arrocha. 2017. *Compassionate migration and regional policy in the Americas.* London, UK: Palgrave Macmillan.

Berger, Dan, and Toussaint Losier. 2018. *Rethinking the American prison movement.* New York, NY: Routledge, Taylor & Francis Group.

Bisaga, Adam, and Karen Chernyaev. 2018. *Overcoming opioid addiction: The authoritative medical guide for patients, families, doctors, and therapists.* New York, NY: The Experiment.

Brand, Russell. 2017. *Recovery: Freedom from our addictions.* New York, NY: Henry Holt and Company.

Brooks, Adrian. 2015. *The right side of history: 100 years of LGBTQI activism.* New York, NY: Cleis Press.

Brossard, Baptiste. 2019. *Forgetting items: The social experience of Alzheimer's disease.* Bloomington, IN: Indiana University Press.

Brownell, Richard. 2018. *Immigration in America*. Farmington Hills, MI: Gale, a Cengage Company.

Burgan, Michael. 2006. *The Reconstruction amendments*. Minneapolis, MN: Compass Point Books.

Burnett, Dean. 2015. Why would people "choose" to be gay? London, UK: *The Guardian*. published January 8, 1995. Accessed May 30, 2020. https://www.theguardian.com/science/brain-flapping/2015/jan/08/homosexuality-gay-choice-psychology.

Caplan, Arthur L., James J. McCartney, and Daniel P. Reid. 2015. *Replacement parts: The ethics of procuring and replacing organs in humans*. Washington, DC: Georgetown University Press.

Caplan, Arthur L., James J. McCartney, and Dominic A. Sisti. 2006. *The case of Terri Schiavo: Ethics at the end of life*. Amherst, NY: Prometheus Books.

Carson, Clayborne. 1987. *Eyes on the prize: America's civil rights years: a reader and guide*. New York, NY: Penguin Books.

Casey, Edward S., and Mary M. Watkins. 2014. *Up against the wall: Re-imagining the U.S.-Mexico border*. Austin, TX: University of Texas Press.

Caulkins, Jonathan P., and RAND Drug Policy Research Center. 2005. *How goes the "war on drugs"?: An assessment of U.S. drug problems and policy*. Santa Monica, CA: Rand.

Chomsky, Aviva. 2007. *"They take our jobs!": And 20 other myths about immigration*. Boston, MA: Beacon Press.

Coates, Ta-Nehisi. 2015. *Between the world and me*. New York, NY: Spiegel & Grau, an imprint of Random House.

Colker, Ruth. 2017. *Sexual orientation, gender identity, and the law in a nutshell*. St. Paul, MN: West Academic Publishing.

Compton, Michael T., Marc W. Manseau, and American Psychiatric Association. 2019. *The American opioid epidemic: From patient care to public health*. Washington, DC: American Psychiatric Publishing.

Cone, James H. 1969. *Black theology and Black power*. New York, NY: Seabury Press.

———. 2011. *The cross and the lynching tree*. Maryknoll, NY: Orbis Books.

Contreras, Raoul Lowery, Andrea Alessandra Cabello, and Sohaib Raihan. 2004. *The illegal alien: A dagger into the heart of America??* Mountain View, CA: Floricanto Press.

Cooper, Brittney C. 2017. Beyond respectability: The intellectual thought of race women. In *Women, gender, and sexuality in American history*. Urbana, IL: University of Illinois Press.

Copeland, Mychal. 2016. *Struggling in good faith: LGBTQI inclusion from 13 American religious perspectives*. Woodstock, VT: SkyLight Paths.

Courtwright, David T. 2001. *Dark paradise: A history of opiate addiction in America*. Cambridge, MA: Harvard University Press.

Crane, Ronald E., and David R. Smith. 1987. Consciousness: The most critical moral (constitutional) standard for human personhood. *Amer. Journal of Law & Med., 13*: 223.

Crothers, Lane. 2019. *Rage on the right: The American militia movement from Ruby Ridge to the Trump presidency*. Lanham, MD: Rowman & Littlefield.

Delgado, Melvin. 2018. *Sanctuary cities, communities, and organizations: A nation at a crossroads*. New York, NY: Oxford University Press.

Dorrien, Gary J. 2018. *Breaking White supremacy: Martin Luther King Jr. and the Black social gospel*. New Haven, CT; London, UK: Yale University Press.

———. 2015. *The new abolition: W.E.B. Du Bois and the Black social gospel*. New Haven, CT: Yale University Press.

Douglas, Kelly Brown. 2015. *Stand your ground: Black bodies and the justice of God*. Maryknoll, NY: Orbis Books.

Edgar, Amanda Nell, and Andre E. Johnson. 2018. *The struggle over Black lives matter and all lives matter*. Lanham, MD: Lexington Books.

Eisen, Lauren-Brooke. 2018. *Inside private prisons: An American dilemma in the age of mass incarceration*. New York, NY: Columbia University Press.

Fareed, Ayman M. 2015. *Heroin addiction: Prevalence, treatment approaches and health consequences*. New York, NY: Nova Publishers.

Farooq, Nihad M. 2016. *Undisciplined: Science, ethnography, and personhood in the Americas, 1830–1940*. New York, NY: New York University Press.

Fehrenbacher, Don Edward. 1978. *The Dred Scott case: Its significance in American law and politics*. New York, NY: Oxford University Press.

———. 1981. *Slavery, law, and politics: The Dred Scott case in historical perspective*. New York, NY: Oxford University Press.

Felman, Shoshana, and Dori Laub. 1991. *Testimony: Crises of witnessing in literature, psychoanalysis, and history*. New York, NY: Routledge.

Fernandez, Humberto, and Therissa A. Libby. 2011. *Heroin: Its history, pharmacology, and treatment* (2nd ed.). Center City, MN: Hazelden.

Fins, Joseph. 2015. *Rights come to mind: Brain injury, ethics, and the struggle for consciousness*. New York, NY: Cambridge University Press.

Fireside, Harvey, and Don Rauf. 2017. *Separate but equal: Plessy v. Ferguson*, US Supreme Court landmark cases. New York, NY: Enslow Publishing.

First, Michael B., and American Psychiatric Association. 2014. *DSM-5 handbook of differential diagnosis*. Washington, DC: American Psychiatric Publishing.

Fitzgerald, Hiram E., and Leon I. Puttler. 2018. *Alcohol use disorders: A developmental science approach to etiology*. Oxford, UK; New York, NY: Oxford University Press.

Flescher, Andrew Michael. 2018. *The organ shortage crisis in America: Incentives, civic duty, and closing the gap*. Washington, DC: Georgetown University Press.

Foote, Jeffrey, Carrie Wilkens, Nicole Kosanke, and Stephanie Higgs. 2014. *Beyond addiction: How science and kindness help people change*. New York, NY: Scribner.

Forman, James. 2017. *Locking up our own: Crime and punishment in Black America*. New York, NY: Farrar, Straus and Giroux.

Foster, Edgar G. 2017. *Contemplating personhood: A theoretical, analytical, historical and theological study of human nature*. Garden City, NY: Ettelloc Pub.

Forehand, Jenna A., Tayla Pelzman, Christine Leonard Westgate, Natalie B. Riblet, Bradley V. Watts, and Brian Shiner. 2019. Causes of excess mortality in veterans treated for posttraumatic stress disorder. *American Journal of Preventive Medicine, 57*: 145–52.

Foucault, Michel. 1978. *The history of sexuality*. New York, NY: Pantheon Books.

Foucault, Michel, and James D. Faubion. 2000. *Power* (Essential works of Foucault, 1954–1984, Vol. 3). New York, NY: New Press, distributed by W.W. Norton & Co.

Fremon, David K. 2015. *The Jim Crow laws and racism in United States history*. Berkeley Heights, NJ: Enslow Publishers, Inc.

Friedman, Matthew J., Terence Martin Keane, and Patricia A. Resick. 2014. *Handbook of PTSD: Science and practice*. New York, NY: The Guilford Press.

Gaikwad, Roger, Thomas Ninan, I.S.P.C.K. (Organization), and National Council of Churches in India. 2017. *A theological reader on human sexuality and gender diversities: Envisioning inclusivity*. Delhi, Nagpur, Maharashtra, ID: ISPCK; National Council of Churches in India (NCCI).

Gilliard, Dominique DuBois. 2018. *Rethinking incarceration: Advocating for justice that restores*. Downers Grove, IL: InterVarsity Press.

Gitlin, Marty. 2018. *Black lives matter*. New York, NY: Greenhaven Publishing.

———. 2017. *Transgender rights* (Issues that concern you series). New York, NY: Greenhaven Publishing.

Goldman, Marlene. 2017. *Forgotten: Narratives of age-related dementia and Alzheimer's disease in Canada*. Montreal CN; Kingston, London, UK; Chicago IL: McGill-Queen's University Press.

Goodman, Kenneth W. 2010. *The case of Terri Schiavo: Ethics, politics, and death in the 21st century*. Oxford, UK; New York, NY: Oxford University Press.

Grinspoon, Peter. 2016. *Free refills: A doctor confronts his addiction*. New York, NY: Hachette Books.

Guttmacher Institute. 2020. United States abortion. New York, NY: Guttmacher Institute Publishing.

Hampton, Ryan, and Claire Rudy Foster. 2018. *American fix: Inside the opioid addiction crisis—And how to end it*. New York, NY: All Points Books.

Hanson, Glen, Peter J. Venturelli, and Annette E. Fleckenstein. 2018. *Drugs and society* (13th ed.). Burlington, MA: Jones & Bartlett Learning.

Harper, Lynn Casteel. 2020. *On vanishing: Mortality, dementia, and what it means to disappear.* New York, NY: Catapult.

Henderson, D. Scott. 2011. *Death and donation: Rethinking brain death as a means for procuring transplantable organs.* Eugene, OR: Pickwick Publications.

Herda, D. J., and D. J. Herda. 2017. *Slavery and citizenship: The Dred Scott case.* New York, NY: Enslow Publishing.

Herman, Judith Lewis. 2015. *Trauma and recovery.* New York, NY: BasicBooks.

Hilal-Dandan, Randa, Laurence L. Brunton, and Louis S. Goodman. 2014. *Goodman and Gilman's manual of pharmacology and therapeutics.* Randa Hilal-Dandan and Laurence L. Brunton (Eds.). New York, NY: McGraw-Hill.

Hillstrom, Laurie Collier. 2018. *Black lives matter: From a moment to a movement.* Santa Barbara, CA; Denver, CO: Greenwood, an imprint of ABC-CLIO, LLC.

Hinton, Elizabeth Kai. 2016. *From the war on poverty to the war on crime: The making of mass incarceration in America.* Cambridge, MA: Harvard University Press.

Holstein, Martha, Jennifer A. Parks, and Mark H. Waymack. 2011. *Ethics, aging, and society: The critical turn.* New York, NY: Springer Publishing Co.

Hooff, Anton J. L. van. 1990. *From autothanasia to suicide: Self-killing in classical antiquity.* London, UK; New York, NY: Routledge.

Institute of Medicine (U.S.), Committee on Approaching Death: Addressing Key End-of-Life Issues. 2015. *Dying in America: Improving quality and honoring individual preferences near the end of life.* Washington, DC: The National Academies Press.

Jardina, Ashley. 2019. *White identity politics.* Cambridge, UK; New York, NY: Cambridge University Press.

Jeffreys, Derek S. 2018. *America's jails: The search for human dignity in an age of mass incarceration* (Alternative criminology series). New York, NY: New York University Press.

Jewell, Albert, and T. M. Kitwood. 2011. *Spirituality, personhood, and dementia.* Philadelphia, PA: Jessica Kingsley Publishers.

Johnstone, Megan-Jane. 2013. *Alzheimer's disease, media representations, and the politics of euthanasia: Constructing risk and selling death in an ageing society.* Farnham, Surrey, UK: Ashgate Publishing Limited.

Jonsen, Albert R. 2003. *The birth of bioethics.* New York, NY: Oxford University Press.

Joralemon, Donald. 2016. *Mortal dilemmas: The troubled landscape of death in America.* Walnut Creek CA: Left Coast Press Inc.

Kandel, Eric R. 2013. *Principles of neural science.* New York, NY: McGraw-Hill.

Kastenbaum, Robert, and Christopher M. Moreman. 2018. *Death, society, and human experience* (12th ed.). New York, NY: Routledge.

Kendi, Ibram X. 2016. *Stamped from the beginning: The definitive history of racist ideas in America.* New York, NY: Nation Books.

Keown, John. 2018. *Euthanasia, ethics and public policy: An argument against legalisation.* Cambridge, UK; New York, NY: Cambridge University Press.

Kindinger, Evangelia. 2019. *The intersections of whiteness.* London, UK; New York, NY: Routledge, Taylor & Francis Group.

Kitwood, Thomas M. 1997. *Dementia reconsidered: The person comes first* (Rethinking ageing series). Buckingham, UK; Philadelphia, PA: Open University Press.

Kovic, Ron. 1976. *Born on the Fourth of July.* New York, NY: McGraw-Hill.

LC Purchase Collection (Library of Congress). 1967. *Cool hand Luke.* Burbank, CA: Warner Bros. Pictures, Warner Home Video.

Lebron, Christopher J. 2017. *The making of Black lives matter: A brief history of an idea.* New York, NY: Oxford University Press.

Lehmiller, Justin J. 2017. *The psychology of human sexuality.* Hoboken, NJ: Wiley.

LeMay, Michael C. 2018. *U.S. immigration policy, ethnicity, and religion in American history.* Santa Barbara, CA: Praeger.

Lichtman, Richard. 2001. *Dying in America.* San Francisco, CA: Cadmus.

Light, Caroline E. 2017. *Stand your ground: A history of America's love affair with lethal self-defense.* Boston, MA: Beacon Press.

Lu, Da-Yong. 2017. *Suicide risks and treatments, new ideas and future perspectives.* Hauppauge NY: Nova Science Publishers, Inc.

Lüsted, Marcia Amidon. 2019. *Sanctuary cities* (Opposing viewpoints). New York, NY: Greenhaven Publishing.

Macy, Beth. 2018. *Dopesick: dealers, doctors, and the drug company that addicted America.* New York, NY: Little, Brown and Company.

Malbon, Craig C. 2013. *Abortion in 21st century America.* North Charleston, SC: CreateSpace Publishing.

Mallea, Paula. 2014. *The war on drugs: A failed experiment.* Toronto, Canada: Tonawanda Dundurn.

Mankiw, N. Gregory. 2012. *Principles of economics.* Australia: SOUTH-WESTERN CENGAGE Learning.

Massey, Douglas S. 2008. *New faces in new places: The changing geography of American immigration.* New York, NY: Russell Sage Foundation.

Mazurek, John. 2018. *The road to marriage equality* (The history of the LGBTQ+ rights movement). New York, NY: Rosen Publishing.

Meier, Barry. 2018. *Pain killer: An empire of deceit and the origin of America's opioid epidemic.* New York, NY: Random House.

———. 2003. *Pain killer: A "wonder" drug's trail of addiction and death.* Emmaus, PA: Rodale.

Meyer, David S., Sidney G. Tarrow, and Jacob S. Hacker. 2018. *The resistance: The dawn of the anti-Trump opposition movement.* New York, NY: Oxford University Press.

Meyer, Doug. 2015. *Violence against queer people: Race, class, gender, and the persistence of anti-LGBT discrimination.* New Brunswick, NJ: Rutgers University Press.

Meyer, Matt, and Sonia Sanchez. 2019. *White lives matter most: And other "little" white lies.* Oakland, CA: PM Press.

Moore, Dennis, and Center for Substance Abuse Treatment (U.S.). 2002. *Substance use disorder treatment for people with physical and cognitive disabilities.* Rockville, MD: U.S. Dept. of Health and Human Services, Public Health Service, Substance Abuse and Mental Health Services Administration, Center for Substance Abuse Treatment.

Moreland, James Porter, and Scott B. Rae. 2000. *Body & soul: Human nature & the crisis in ethics.* Downers Grove, IL: InterVarsity Press.

Mortensen, Lori. 2015. *Voices of the civil rights movement: A primary source of exploration of the struggle for racial equality.* North Mankato, MI: Capstone Press.

Müller, Andreas, and Peter Schaber. 2018. *The Routledge handbook of the ethics of consent* (1st ed.). Abingdon, Oxon, UK; New York, NY: Routledge.

Murphy, Sheigla, and Marsha Rosenbaum. 1999. *Pregnant women on drugs: Combating stereotypes and stigma.* New Brunswick, NJ: Rutgers University Press.

Neumann, Ann. 2016. *The good death: An exploration of dying in America.* Boston, MA: Beacon Press.

Olsen, Yngvild, and Joshua M. Sharfstein. 2019. *The opioid epidemic: What everyone needs to know* (What everyone needs to know series). Oxford, UK: Oxford University Press.

Olson, James Stuart. 2003. *Equality deferred: Race, ethnicity, and immigration in America since 1945* (Wadsworth books on America since 1945). Belmont, CA: Wadsworth/Thomson Learnng.

Paul, Darel E. 2018. *From tolerance to equality: How elites brought America to same-sex marriage.* Waco, TX: Baylor University Press.

Pearce, Donald. 1965. *Cool hand Luke.* New York, NY: Scribner.

Petrikowski, Nicki Peter. 2017. *Critical perspectives on gender identity.* New York, NY: Enslow Publishing.

Pluta, Ryszard. 2019. *Brain ischemia: Alzheimer's disease mechanisms.* New York, NY: Nova Medicine & Health.

Pojman, Louis P. and Lewis Vaughn. 2014. *The moral life: An introductory reader in ethics and literature.* New York, NY: Oxford University Press.

Polakow-Suransky, Sasha. 2017. *Go back to where you came from: The backlash against immigration and the fate of western democracy.* New York, NY: Nation Books.

Poole, Hilary W. 2018. *PTSD: Post-traumatic stress disorder* (Mental Illnesses and Disorders series). New York, NY: AV2 by Weigl.

Post, Stephen Garrard. 2000. *The moral challenge of Alzheimer disease: Ethical issues from diagnosis to dying.* Baltimore, MD: The Johns Hopkins University Press.

Power, G. Allen. 2017. *Dementia beyond disease: Enhancing well being.* Towson, MD: Health Professions Press.

Prokovyev, Luka. 2010. *Diagnosing death: Issues, ethics and questions in death determinations.* New York, NY: Nova Science Publishers.

Provine, Doris Marie. 2007. *Unequal under law: Race in the war on drugs.* Chicago, IL: University of Chicago Press.

Quinones, Sam. 2016. *Dreamland: The true tale of America's opiate epidemic.* New York, NY: Bloomsbury Press.

Raja, Masood A. 2016. *The religious right and the talibanization of America.* New York, NY: Palgrave Macmillan.

Ransby, Barbara. 2018. *Making all Black lives matter: Reimagining freedom in the twenty-first century.* Oakland, CA: University of California Press.

Redmond, Jodee. 2018. *The dangers of drug abuse* (Opioids and Opiates: The Silent Epidemic series). Broomall, PA: Mason Crest.

Rizzo, Matthew, and Steven W. Anderson. 2018. *The Wiley handbook on the aging mind and brain.* Hoboken, NJ: Wiley.

Rosenberg, Rosalind. 2017. *Jane Crow: The life of Pauli Murray.* New York, NY: Oxford University Press.

Rozell, Mark J., and Clyde Wilcox. 2018. *God at the grassroots 2016: The Christian right in American politics.* Lanham, MD: Rowman & Littlefield.

Sabat, Steven R. 2018. *Alzheimer's disease and dementia: What everyone needs to know.* New York, NY: Oxford University Press.

Sahyouni, Ronald, Aradhana Verma, and Jefferson Chen. 2017. *Alzheimer's disease decoded: the history, present, and future of Alzheimer's disease and dementia.* Hackensack, NJ: World Scientific.

Satel, Sally L. 2008. *When altruism isn't enough: The case for compensating kidney donors.* Washington, DC; Blue Ridge Summit, PA: AEI Press, distributed by National Book Network.

Schepis, Ty S. 2018. *The prescription drug abuse epidemic: Incidence, treatment, prevention, and policy.* Santa Barbara, CA: Praeger, an imprint of ABC-CLIO, LLC.

Seppala, Marvin D., and Mark E. Rose. 2010. *Prescription painkillers: History, pharmacology, and treatment.* Center City, MN: Hazelden.

Shanor, Charles A. 2017. *American constitutional law: Structure and reconstruction: Cases, notes, and problems* (6th ed.). St. Paul, MN: West Academic Publishing.

Shapiro, Shawna, Raichle Farrelly, and Mary Jane Curry. 2018. *Educating refugee-background students: Critical issues and dynamic contexts* (New perspectives on language and education). Bristol, UK; Blue Ridge Summit PA: Multilingual Matters.

Sherman, Barry Robert, Laura M. Sanders, and Chau Trinh. 1998. *Addiction and pregnancy: Empowering recovery through peer counseling.* Westport, CT: Praeger.

Shoham, S. Giora, Martin Kett, and Moshe Addad. 2010. *The insatiable gorge: An existentialist view of opiate addiction and its treatment.* Whitby ON: De Sitter Publications.

Singer, Peter. 1995. *Rethinking life & death: The collapse of our traditional ethics.* New York, NY: St. Martin's Press.

Singer, Peter. 2011. *Practical ethics.* New York, NY: Cambridge University Press.

Sloane, Philip D. 2017. *The Alzheimer's medical advisor: A caregiver's guide to common medical and behavioral signs and symptoms in persons with dementia.* Forest Lake, MN: Sunrise River Press.

Smångs, Mattias. 2017. *Doing violence, making race: Lynching and White racial group formation in the U.S. South, 1882–1930* (Routledge research in race and ethnicity). New York, NY; Abingdon, Oxon, UK: Routledge, Taylor & Francis Group.

Smeeding, Timothy M., and University of Utah. Health Technology and Environment Research Group. 1987. *Should medical care be rationed by age?* Totowa, NJ: Rowman & Littlefield.

Smith, Douglas C. 2018a. *Emerging adults and substance use disorder treatment: Developmental considerations and innovative approaches.* New York, NY: Oxford University Press.

Smith, Glenn E. 2018b. *APA handbook of dementia.* Washington, DC: American Psychological Association.

Solof, Barry. 2013. *The therapist's guide to addiction medicine: A handbook for addiction counselors and therapists.* Las Vegas, NV: Central Recovery Press.

Spiro, Avron, Richard A. Settersten, and Carolyn M. Aldwin. 2018. *Long-term outcomes of military service: The health and well-being of aging veterans.* Washington, DC: American Psychological Association.

Stein, Mark. 2014. *American panic: A history of who scares us and why.* New York, NY: Palgrave Macmillan.

Stevenson, Bryan. 2014. *Just mercy: A story of justice and redemption.* New York, NY: Spiegel & Grau.

Swain, Carol M. 2018. *Debating immigration.* Cambridge, UK; New York, NY: Cambridge University Press.

Taylor, Keeanga-Yamahtta. 2016. *From #BlackLivesMatter to Black liberation.* Chicago, IL: Haymarket Books.

Thomas, Keri, and Ben Lobo. 2011. *Advance care planning in end of life care.* Oxford, UK: Oxford University Press.

Thomas, William. 1994. *The eden alternative: Nature, hope, and nursing homes.* New York, NY: Eden Alternative Foundation.

———. 2006. *In the arms of elders: A parable of wise leadership and community building.* Acton, MA: VanderWyk & Burnham.

Tooley, Michael. 2009. *Abortion: Three perspectives* (Point/counterpoint series). New York, NY: Oxford University Press.

United States Congress. House Committee on Energy and Commerce: Subcommittee on Oversight and Investigations. 2019. *Combating the opioid epidemic: Examining concerns about distribution and diversion: Hearing before the Subcommittee on Oversight and Investigations of the Committee on Energy and Commerce, House of Representatives, One Hundred Fifteenth Congress, second session, May 8, 2018.* Washington, DC: U.S. Government Publishing Office.

———. 2015. *Combating the opioid abuse epidemic: Professional and academic perspectives: Hearing before the Subcommittee on Oversight and Investigations of the Committee on Energy and Commerce, House of Representatives, One Hundred Fourteenth Congress, first session, April 23, 2015.* Washington, DC: U.S. Government Publishing Office.

United States Congress. House Committee on Oversight and Government Reform. 2017. *America's heroin and opioid abuse epidemic: Hearing before the Committee on Oversight and Government Reform, House of Representatives, One Hundred Fourteenth Congress, second session, March 22, 2016.* Washington, DC: U.S. Government Publishing Office.

United States Congress. House Committee on the Judiciary: Subcommittee on Immigration and Border Security. 2015. *Sanctuary cities: A threat to public safety: Hearing before the Subcommittee on Immigration and Border Security of the Committee on the Judiciary, House of Representatives, One Hundred Fourteenth Congress, first session, July 23, 2015.* Washington, DC: U.S. Government Publishing Office.

United States Congress. Senate Committee on Finance: Subcommittee on Health Care. 2017. *Alzheimer's disease: The struggle for families, a looming crisis for Medicare: Hearing before the Subcommittee on Health Care of the Committee on Finance, United States Senate, One Hundred Fourteenth Congress, second session, July 13, 2016, S hrg.* Washington, DC: U.S. Government Publishing Office.

United States Congress. Senate Committee on Health Education Labor and Pensions. 2018. *Opioid abuse in America: Facing the epidemic and examining solutions: Hearing of the Committee on Health, Education, Labor, and Pensions, United States Senate, One Hundred Fourteenth Congress, first session on examining opioid abuse in America, focusing on facing the epidemic and examining solutions, December 8, 2015, S hrg.* Washington, DC: U.S. Government Publishing Office.

Van der Kolk, Bessel A. 2014. *The body keeps the score: Brain, mind, and body in the healing of trauma.* New York, NY: Viking.

Viscusi, W. Kip. 1992. *Fatal tradeoffs: Public and private responsibilities for risk.* New York, NY: Oxford University Press.

Wacquant, Loïs. 2001. Deadly symbiosis: When ghetto and prison meet and mesh. *Punishment & Society, 3*(1): 95–134.

Wacquant, Loïs. 2002. From slavery to mass incarceration: Rethinking the "race question" in the U.S. *New Left Review 13*: 41–60.

Waldemar, Gunhild, and Alistair S. Burns. 2017. *Alzheimer's disease* (Oxford neurology library). Oxford, UK: Oxford University Press.

Walker, Samuel, Cassia Spohn, and Miriam DeLone. 2018. *The color of justice: Race, ethnicity, and crime in America.* Boston, MA: Cengage Learning.

Weinberg, Leonard. 2019. *Fascism, populism and American democracy.* London, UK ; New York, NY: Routledge.

Wendling, Mike. 2018. *Alt-right: From 4chan to the White House.* Halifax, NS, Canada; Winnipeg, MT, Canada: Fernwood Publishing.

West, Cornel. 1993. *Race matters.* Boston, MA: Beacon Press.

Wijdicks, Eelco F. M. 2014. *The comatose patient.* Oxford, UK; New York, NY: Oxford University Press.

Wilcox, Christine. 2019. *Thinking critically: Opioid abuse.* San Diego, CA: ReferencePoint Press, Inc.

Winograd, Rachel P., and Kenneth J. Sher. 2015. *Binge drinking and alcohol misuse among college students and young adults.* Boston, MA: Hogrefe.

Wyszynski, Diego F. 2006. *Neural tube defect: From origin to treatment.* Oxford, UK; New York, NY: Oxford University Press.

Yiannopoulos, Milo. 2017. *Dangerous.* Miami, FL; Minneapolis, MN: Dangerous Books, Itasca Books.

Zigon, Jarrett. 2019. *A war on people: Drug user politics and a new ethics of community.* Oakland, CA: University of California Press.

Chapter Five

America's Great "Original Sins"

ORIGINAL SIN: A LEGACY OF GENOCIDE, SUBJUGATION, CONTESTED BEING

Introduction

American historian, activist, and writer Roxanne Dunbar-Ortiz confronts America with a painful truth: U.S. history would best describe settler colonialism as, "the founding of state based on the ideology of white supremacy, the widespread practice of African slavery, and a policy of genocide and land theft" (Dunbar-Ortiz 2014). The term "original sin" as employed herein is best understood in this harsh, but accurate context. Some may infer a reference to the "original sin" concept or as in Jonathan Edwards' 1758 Doctrine of Original Sin (Edwards and American Imprint Collection 1758) ascribed to the Book of Genesis in the Hebrew Bible. Foremost it is a "sin," that is, an immoral act often considered to transgress a divine law. It is "original," for this sin was the archetype, existing from the very beginning of American settle colonialism. In exploring manifestations of assaulted personhood in 21st century America, we seek to research the very roots from which these everyday assaults on the being of other humans arise, not in the personal, individual sense, but rather in the corporate historical sense.

We as Americans of all genders, races, colors, religious traditions, ethnicities and cultures possess the imprint of our past, including past wrongdoings, or "original sins." This "information" is past onto us, in some ways like genetic information, from generation-to-generation. Intergenerationally, our preferences, desires, taboos, and pasts are relayed forward to each new generation. This information is contained in oral traditions, shared stories, "histories" of one sort or other, and is framed within the sum total of our own experiences, education, and personality. We choose consciously (and some-times unconsciously) the stories that we share with others. What is learned and shared we assume to be a factual, neutral account of U.S. history. The expression that "history is written by the victors/survivors" has real traction in this regard. What we encounter in U.S. history, books and media is a concept labeled "American exceptionalism." It is most decidedly a highly distilled product of the victors/survivors. Accounts of "exceptional" perfor-mance, growth, and wonder produced through power and control abound in the topsiders' history of this nation. For the victims, for example, casualties, survivors, families and communities (e.g., Native American, Africans, and African Americans) it is four centuries of suffering at the hand of hegemony. The so-called "facts" and proffered perspective of American exceptionalism seem quite apart from their own undersiders' history (Van Engen 2020).

I offer this introduction only to heighten awareness that our treatment of one another, the dipole of "self" versus the "other," reflects our location. In brief, my location is as a male, white, Anglo-Saxton Protestant (Congrega-tionalist) product of a middle-class New England family with roots to Massa-chusetts and Maine immigrant settlers in a first wave that landed in Boston in the late 1620s. The Malbon family, finding much less than expected religious tolerance in New England, returned to Europe for several decades, pausing in the Netherlands and returning in the late 1600s, passaging in the company of French Huguenots as far as Massachusetts and then onto Maine. My entire exposure to U.S. history, both personal and in the classrooms of New Eng-land public schools was absolutely from the "topside." My learning and teaching in university and seminary, coupled with exposure to and serving the "least of us" changed my perspective on my own location. Readings like that cited by Roxanne Dunbar-Ortiz and others reaffirmed two notions for me. First, in spite of my transformation through seminary and ministry, I cannot escape my "topside" location. At first encounter, most will consider me clearly to be aligned with the victors. This labeling I cannot escape and must accept. However, my hermeneutic, how I interpret information, now is one of deep suspicion. A hermeneutic of suspicion has afforded me a new perspective, one working daily to better welcome and live into the suffering of the "underside." I see things much differently now. My own guilt and complacency about the "original sins" of my forbearers coupled with my own complicity in such sins must be confessed.

Viewing from a perspective of the "underside," the reader is encouraged to develop a hermeneutic of suspicion. With it, the central thesis of this book, that is, assaults on personhood today are toxic legacies of our inability to embrace, confront, and address the two damning original sins initiated upon the founding of America. This thesis will be interrogated. The first, treated below, is the assault on indigenous Native Americans and their descendants. This history is not filled so much with American exceptionalism, but rather the workings of a dominant White ruling class calculus of oppression that includes genocide, subjugation, dispossession and continued assaults on the being of Native Americans who were "in the land" 30,000 years prior to the European explorers and later immigrants like my family. It is a history of intentional neglect, abuse, and contested personhood. The overarching design was and is to achieve the single calculus of "victory" over those whose rightful claim to occupy the land is unambiguous. The second original sin, presented later in this chapter, is a horrific assault upon African slaves, their families and African American descendants that powers White supremacy, a byproduct of the White ruling class responsible for four centuries of slavery, displacement, dispossession, subjugation, and contested being of Black folks in America. A detailed history of each of these original sins is not possible within the scope of the current work. The primary focus must be recast to teasing apart how a dark, deadly and stained history of original sins contributes ultimately to condoning, empowering, and enlivening everyday and sometime deadly assaults on the personhood of peoples in the United States in the 21st century.

Assault on Indigenous Native Americans and Descendants

Few chapters of United States history are as dark as those disclosing the "treatment" of the indigenous Native Americans by immigrant explorers and settles to the U.S. Truthfully speaking I confess that attempting to compress more than a half millennium of dispossession, genocide, subjugation, and displacement to a mere "chapter" of American history serves only to victimize again peoples who were in the land for 30,000 years before European invaders arrived. Many outstanding sources of my knowledge will be referenced, each worthy of a deep read. Since the exploration and colonization of Native American lands commenced in the late 15th and early 16th centuries, the assault on personhood of the indigenous peoples by the U.S. has been unrelenting and continues in full, even today! The earliest (by a century) claimants to "America" were crowns of Spain and Portugal, whose combined population approached 450,000 when the Pilgrims landed in Plymouth Massachusetts in 1620. Unlike the newest immigrants to America, the Spanish and Portuguese cohabited peacefully for some time in regions of the East Coast with the indigenous "peoples in the land."

A precise account of the population of Native Americans existing in what is today the United States of America prior to the arrival of European explorers and settlers is not possible. Estimates ranging from a low of ~2 million up to ~18 million reflect the unavoidable variance in starting assumptions and extrapolations in calculations based in population dynamics (Thornton 1987). By the advent of the 19th century, more precise estimates made by head counting revealed the Native population had declined to ~0.6 million.

By the end of the 19th century, less than 250,000 indigenous Native Americans remained in the U.S. (Thornton 1987). There are many explanations offered for this precipitous decline in Native populations, including infectious diseases, violence and death at the hands of irregular armies of settler colonists, intertribal warfare, internal violence, enslavement, and death resulting from tribal displacement from shelter and food sources. Epidemics of smallpox, measles, and chicken pox depopulated large swaths of Native tribes and lands in Eastern and Central regions of North America, in some places almost to extinction (Mann 2009). Dominating the narratives of the Native American peoples was unbridled assaults on their very being, on their personhood, often to the extreme, depriving them of the basic negative human right to not be killed. Various terms have been proposed to characterize the violent and deadly treatment of the Native Americans at the hands of the European immigrants to North America. These descriptors include a "holocaust" or frank "genocide," although the use of these hot button terms remains controversial (Thornton 1987; Osborn 2000; Dunbar-Ortiz 2014). Although smallpox vaccination was introduced to the U.S. in 1801, the Indian Vaccination Act aimed to establish vaccination for all Native Americans was launched more than three decades later, in 1832!

The scale and scope of the wars, attacks, and raids upon the indigenous Native Americans by governments as well as irregular armies composed of White settler-rangers (i.e., full-time soldiers employed by colonial authorities), activist colonists, and other local militia is well known (Kidd 2016; Calloway 2016; Small 2018; Healey, Stepnick, and O'Brien 2019). Equally well known is the extreme violence with which these White militia attacked the indigenous peoples, seldom differentiating between resistance combatants and helpless civilian non-combatants who included women, children, and the aged (Dunbar-Ortiz 2014; Smith 2015). Borderland confrontations were the crucible of interactions between colonist settlers versus indigenous people (Frank and Crothers 2017). The "unlimited war" waged by the immigrant colonists, their militia, and eventual regular military of the U.S. employed tactics that would be considered war crimes today. The Rome Statute of the International Criminal Court (1998) established four core criminal actions: genocide, crimes against humanity, war crimes, and crime of aggression. War crimes include the intentional killing of civilians (or prisoners), torture, destruction of civilian property, hostage taking, performance of perfidy, rape and sexual crimes, recruitment of child soldiers, pillage, and so on. The practice of beheading Native Americans for bounty payments ultimately was replaced by simple scalping in order to reduce the sheer volume of evidence required for bounties. Bounty payments for dead Native Americans, including civilian noncombatant children, women and the elderly, created an industry of death. Vigilante groups composed of professional scalp hunters roamed the American frontier in search of bounties (O'Brien 2008). Based upon documented history and classification of the tools of war employed by the colonists, settler-rangers, and irregular and regular militia against the Native Americans (Dunbar-Ortiz 2014), a "war crimes" label seems well deserved. Murder, killing, and death by neglect, aimed at indigenous Native Americans, were complemented by enslavement of their young children, burning of their shelters, and the intentional deprivation of land and food sources for the indigenous people (Dunbar-Ortiz 2014; McCormick 2015). In light of the wanton demonstration of toxic White xenophobia aimed at indigenous Native Americans that succeeded in yielding a complete loss of their personhood, their ancestral lands and lives, one must explore the stimuli fueling such criminal and unconscionable behaviors of colonial settlers.

This Land is Whose Land?

Folk singer Woody Guthrie (1912–1967) captured the ethos around the American claim to the land in his 1944 recording "This Land is Your Land," which displays exuberant patriotism and libertarian virtues. The original 1940 lyrics, ending each verse with "God blessed America for me" were eventually struck out. For most Native Americans, the 1940 or 1944 lyrics would provoke a deep pathos. Whose land was America? For Native Americans "ownership" of land itself was a foreign idea. Human beings and the land lived in interdependent harmony, necessary for flourishing. Land was sacred, to be shared *not* owned. In light of the Native Americans' belief system about the sacred nature of the land, what warrant gave European colonial settlers to the U.S. a "green light" for a grab of Native American lands? Virtually precluded from inheriting property in Europe, colonial settlers were enticed to take a chance at settling the "new world." Land, it was advertised, was for the taking and natural resources were in abundance. It is estimated that from 1776–2018 indigenous peoples of North America forcibly lost 1.5 billion acres of land (Saunt 2014)! The vast ancient homelands shared by indigenous Native Americans would be supplanted with contrived, severely downsized "reservations." Treaties and executive orders were engineered to continue dispossession and displacement of Native Americans from their lands, offering only ambiguous language that insured future *re-negotiations* and consequent further downsizing (Saunt 2014; Dunbar-Ortiz 2014).

Historically, indigenous peoples of America displayed a high religiosity, centered upon animistic beliefs about the land and their spirituality as peoples in the land (Gill 2005). Furthermore, land was not considered just a resource, but intimately connected to religious ceremonies and traditions performed by Native Americans intergenerationally transmitted generationally by oral traditions for more than 30,000 years. The theological linkage of the land to the indigenous peoples' spirituality eventually led to the U.S.

setting aside small tracts of lands that were held to be sacred as tributes or monuments. Even the smallest most sacred ancestral lands were assaulted through broken treaties and consequent downsizing. Assaults of this nature continue to this day (e.g., Dakota Access Pipeline protests, *Washington v. United States*, *#StandWithBearEars* protests).

Has God but One Blessing?

Perhaps one of the greatest paradoxes in American history is the degree of religious intolerance leveled at the indigenous Native Americans by the settler colonists who immigrated to North America commencing in the 16th century. Catholic and Protestant denominations alike launched missionaries to "convert" the indigenous peoples in the land. Labeled generally as "heathens," indigenous Native Americans were targeted for conversion to Christianity. Driven by a fervor that resonated with core teachings of the Old Testament (i.e., the Hebrew Bible) on Israelites commanded by God to dwell in Canaan, missionaries and common settlers professed that the indigenous peoples must be converted to Christianity. The conversion of the "heathens" became essential, in the eyes of the settler clergy, to secure the blessings of being in covenantal communion, that is, within the community of saints insuring life hereafter (Gaustad and Schmidt 2002). The harsh, violent, and fervent practice aimed a converting of the heathens finds little support in the New Testament. Included in the synoptic Gospels (i.e., Mark 12:28–31; Matthew 22:35–40; Luke 10:25–28; and John 13:31–35), the Greatest Commandment argues for compassion and *agape*, rather than force and violence against the neighbor. The Greek term *agape* refers to a special, self-sacrificing love and charity displayed in John 3:16. The verse is "[16]For God so loved the world that he gave his one and only Son, that whoever believes in him shall not perish but have eternal life." In Mark's Gospel we read: [28]One of the scribes came near and heard them disputing with one another, and seeing that he answered them well, he asked him, "Which commandment is the first of all?" [29]Jesus answered, "The first is, 'Hear, O Israel: The Lord our God, the Lord is one [30]you shall love the Lord your God with all your heart, and with all your soul, and with all your mind, and with all your strength.'[31]" Jesus' continues, "The second is this, 'You shall love your neighbor as yourself.' There is no other commandment greater than these." Echoes from the Old Testament books of Deuteronomy (Deut 6:4–5) and of Leviticus (Lev 19:17–18) fortify the Greatest Commandment declared by Jesus of Nazareth. In Leviticus 19, we read: "[17]You shall not hate in your heart anyone of your kin; you shall reprove your neighbor, or you will incur guilt yourself. [18]You shall not take vengeance or bear a grudge against any of your people, but you shall love your neighbor as yourself: I am the Lord."

The Greatest Commandment is regarded as bedrock to living a Christian way of life as preached by Jesus of Nazareth. Yet killing, starving, enslaving, and maltreatment of the indigenous Native American were widespread and at the hands of colonial settlers professing Christian faith. Considered merely as "interlopers" by the indigenous people in the land, the settlers would confront the Native Americans as "other," not with *agape*, but with xenophobia and fear. Was not this wanton culture of violence and hatred anathema to Christian dogma and living a Christian life? How could it be that these indigenous peoples were considered outside of "your people," as delivered in Lev 19:17? This glaring paradox provokes a fundamental theological question concerning the personhood status of the "stranger" or "other." Does God have but one blessing, bestowed solely upon Christians, or more precisely White Christians of the dominant ruling class of colonial times or the modern age?

Striking is the false narrative that indigenous Native Americans deserved designation as "heathens." This moniker, attached to those who did not acknowledge the God of the Holy Bible, assaulted the Native Americans, declaring them immoral, uncivilized, and "beast-like." Did a failure to acknowledge God in the context of the Holy Bible establish a people to be bereft of faith and religion? The answer to this query is "no." Confronted with the very same vicissitudes of all human beings, for example, strife, birth, life, sickness, and death, the indigenous Native Americans had developed rich religious beliefs and rituals, including a complex and coherent system of animist cosmology that addressed their existence in the universe (Gaustad and Schmidt 2002; Gaustad and Noll 2003). A systematic theological analysis of major Native American religions, such as crafted by the leading theologian Paul Tillich (Tillich 1967), would reveal many intersections of the beliefs of indigenous Native Americans with Christian dogma, albeit monotheism and the theology of the Trinity would not be among them. Like early Christian missionaries that sought to degrade what was considered "pagan" practices rather than work towards assimilating such "heathens" towards Christian theology, the success of efforts at conversion of Native Americans were mixed as best. It was proffered that Christianity of the White invading missionaries and settlers was superior to the spiritual traditions of the heathens. There exists little evidence to support this proposition. Many Christian observers of Native American religious faith and rituals were deeply moved by the profound spirituality and practice of these "heathens." Clergy would remark on the religiosity of the "Indians." Unlike the settlers who rarely could be coerced into Sunday church services, the indigenous Native Americans daily displayed devotions, water rituals, and a reverence for the Creator, the natural world, its creatures, and the land. For Native Americans land was considered sacred and a shared resource (Dunbar-Ortiz 1984). The commodification of land as property was a notion alien to these "people in the land," introduced by colonial settlers whose only opportunity to own land would be derivative of brazen, wanton theft of the land from those who occupied it for 30,000 years.

Three elements largely determined the view espoused by American history about the adoption of Christianity by indigenous Native Americans. First, local and eventually federal governments crafted policies designed to insure "conversion" of the "Indians" to Christianity (Gaustad and Noll 2003). These policies were employed to enforce a standard of theological adherence to Christian dogma, one which produced much blunt force trauma to the Indians' spiritual well-being (Gaustad and Noll 2003). For more than 80 years, federal policies were designed to suppress and extinguish rather than protect and preserve Native American religious practices and culture (Gaustad and Schmidt 2002). In spite of clear parallels to Creation stories (including the presence of a central "Creator"), deep respect for the dead and their everlasting spirits, and being of no existential threat to Christianity itself, Native American religions were perceived as a grave threat to the dominant White ruling class. The deep reverence of the Native American religions for the natural world and sacred lands would be denigrated simply to advance sinister plots to acquire (i.e., "grab") land as well as to despoil the environment (Gaustad and Schmidt 2002). This policy of religious intolerance and forced cultural annihilation came to a close only in *1978* with the signing into Federal law of the "American Indian Religious Freedom Act" (Tavares, Berryhill, and National Public Radio 1979)! Thus the indigenous peoples in the land for 30,000 years and who first welcomed the European explorers and settlers would endure more than three centuries of forced indoctrination and suppression of their religious freedom (Shally-Jensen 2017a).

Second, the resilience of Native Americans to successfully shield, self-protect, and preserve their religion and cultural practices was largely underestimated. Peoples oppressed by a dominant White ruling class are often dehumanized, labeled as non-White, of color, and "other." These assaults on the peoples labeled "other" sought to weaken Native American resolve, but more often than not provoked unexpected resilience, aiming to find legislative remedies or justice in the courts. There was an unmistakable lesson to be learned by the Civil Rights movement in America. Legislation in the mid-1960s succeeded in enacting laws aimed at remedying centuries of racial discrimination (United States Commerce Clearing House 1964). The lesson learned well was that signing legislation into law alone does not magically achieve, in a step-like function, the lofty goals of the laws. Rather, for every such action, that is, the eventual enactment of the American Indian Religious Freedom Act, there would be pushback, foot-dragging and efforts to minimize impact of U.S. Federal law. To this day there still abounds chronic, remnant efforts aimed at revitalizing and eventually regaining the former status quo of the dominant White ruling class in order to oppress the indigenous Native American peoples. Monuments on lands that are eternally sacred to Native Americans remain under constant attack by mineral developers and politicians alike. These perpetrators of assaults on indigenous people's personhood intentionally and with malice employ legislative tricks aimed at redesignating the status of and reducing the footprint of sacred ancestral lands. Evolving from earliest exploitation of the populous Native Americans by the few, White ruling class always seeks to perpetuate and expand true American hegemony (Hixson 2013). Such contemporary, thoughtless and punitive reprisals seek continually to intentionally denigrate the seminal role of the "people in the land." Indigenous Paleo-Indian peoples were in the land for more than 30 millennia prior to the arrival of Christopher Columbus (1451–1506) in 1492!

Third, the effort to evaluate the success of the "conversion" of indigenous Native Americans to Christians, presented the clergy and settlers with a problem. Failure to be converted to Christianity brought punishment or death to the indigenous people. Limiting the options to either proclaiming Christian conversion or suffering punishment and death, the choice of the Native Americans largely was nuanced. Accepting Christ in the face of coercion provoked empty promises, not a change in spiritual heart. Native Americans were more curious than concerned about Christianity. Tolerant of Christian rituals, Native Americans proved resilient in preserving their own ancient religious traditions and practices. Theologically speaking, Native Americans clearly posed no threat to Christendom. In some cases Native Americans were reported to have truly "converted" to Christianity not through coercion, embracing Christ Jesus as Lord and Savior. Did the success of so coerced conversions guarantee covenantal union of the indigenous people with their Christian overseers? The value of a newly professed "life in Christ" would be short-lived, discounted for the "Indian converts." Bringing indigenous people to Christianity, of course, created the dilemma. How to Christianize Native Americans and then successfully attack their personhood and declare them as "*sub*human" would be a challenge. Ultimately, "Christianized Indians" would fare no better at the hands of the White ruling class. Christianity would not immunize the converts from exploitation, oppression, dispossession and killing. Failure of the overseers to extend to these "other" the Christian bedrock of the Greatest Commandment preached by Jesus of Nazareth only canonized the asymmetric interactions between the dominant White ruling class and their powerless wards, the indigenous Native peoples of America.

Metastasis and Subjugation: Lost Personhood

The inevitable Western expansion of the United States exposed increasing numbers of indigenous Native American peoples to the tyranny of oppression first demonstrated East of the Mississippi River (Meinig 1986). The Revolutionary War brought independence to the nascent United States, creating an entity that now by necessity had to negotiate treaties with tribes of indigenous Native Americans. The foremost aim of such treaties was to codify the Federal government's authority over all the Native Americans east of the Mississippi river and to employ this as a template for what would emerge as a "sea to shining sea" manifest destiny of the dominant White ruling class over indigenous peoples and their lands (Greenberg 2018). In exchange for acknowledging U.S. dominion over the peoples and land, Native American tribes sought money, goods, medicines, and protection through the Federal government. Peace was essential for trade, expansion, and further subjugation of indigenous people by the young nation (Meinig 1986). The Louisiana Purchase opened the West like no other single event. Lewis and Clark would encounter many indigenous peoples and tribes, most of who posed no threat. Rather, many Native Americans would assist the Lewis and Clark expedition in the remarkable mapping of an expansive largely unknown region of North America. At the age of sixteen, the Lemhi Shoshone woman, Sacagawea, and her French husband trader Toussaint Charbonneau joined the expedition and provided invaluable assistance to the Corps of Discovery Expedition traverse from North Dakota to the Pacific Ocean (Berne 2010).

During the War of 1812 some Native American tribes aligned with the British in the hopes of reversing the settlers' advance in the East. Absent a victor with whom to rest power from the embedded settlers, the Native Americans saw their future as a metastasis, a virulent cancer that would continue to eat away at their ancestral land rights, religious practice, culture, and very being. In the 19th century, the White ruling class introduced "blood quantum" into Federal Indian laws (Spruhan 2006). An "Indian" was defined by the fractional amount of "Indian" blood in a clear effort to attack their personhood as Native Americans and thereby repudiate their land claims. The commodification of blood quantum assaulted the personhood of all indigenous Native Americans, increasing their vulnerability to denial of property rights as well as human rights (Ratteree and Hill 2017). Wars and conflicts provoked by this pressure resulted in death, destruction, and further westward migration of Native Americans (Tucker, Arnold, and Wiener 2011). By treaty, millions of Native Americans were eventually forced from their ancestral lands, relocating to reservations, that is, relatively small pieces of Federal lands (Coates 2014). The governing White ruling class often broke treaties with tribes. The goal being to force a re-negotiation of land claims with the aim of containing the indigenous peoples to smaller and smaller reservations. Reservations were intentionally relocated to areas distant from sacred tribal lands and traditional food sources. When confronted with no remaining theological basis to justify such horrific denial of personhood of millions of Native Americans, the White ruling class would choose first silence and then judicial remedies concocted to favor continued subjugation of indigenous people. Forced migrations, death walks, and harsh subjugation of indigenous peoples was not new to history, but nearly perfected in the U.S. It signaled a turning point, away from a theologically based, moral compass touted as guiding the relationship of American colonialism with indigenous peoples in the land. It was tantamount to a forced exile of Native Americans to a challenging, hostile, new world dominated by harsh, oppressive, and murderous overseers.

Doctrine of Discovery: Land Grab, Genocide, and Lost Souls

With respect to loss of tribal lands, the plight of Native Americans can be traced back to Constantine the Great (272–337) (McGuckin 2004). Baptized on his deathbed by Eusebius of Nicomedia, Constantine was the first Roman emperor to convert to Christianity. He heavily promoted Christianity throughout the Roman Empire, called the First Council of Nicaea in 325 CE, and was declared (erroneously) as the source of the Papal claim to power in the Middle Ages. Church and the Empire became a defacto "Christian Empire." Later, Saint Augustine (354–430) declared "just war" theories to promote Christianity at the very same time he discounted the personhood of the religious "other," for example, Muslims (Brown 2000). Ultimately these threads of Christian belief converged under Papal authority in an enunciation of what was termed the "Doctrine of Discovery" in the mid-15th century. This seminal doctrine privileged the White ruling class explorers, providing to them with a Papal "legal" cudgel with which to claim title to billions of acres of ancestral land of indigenous peoples around the world simply on the spurious claim that land could be "owned" solely by Christian monarchies! Remarkably, it would take three centuries after the first crimes against Native Americans were waged for the principles of this Papal Doctrine of Discovery to emerge in the legal question of to whom does land in the U.S. rightly belong? This ancient Papal Doctrine of Discovery would eventually be seized upon and amended by the U.S. Supreme Court for a single dark purpose, to declare that a Eurocentric papal doctrine could be sourced as the legal foundation to justify the unprecedented land grab from indigenous peoples native to North America. Colonial powers could lay claim to lands of foreign sovereign Native American nations whose peoples were not subjects to a European Christian monarch. Paradoxically, the United States of America was lacking sovereign rule by a Christian monarch. Theoretically, colonial settlers and Christianized Indians would have equal legal footing under this doctrine. Finally, the separation of church and state under the U.S. Constitution precluded the U.S. from declaring itself a "Christian nation." In spite of these obvious contravening legal issues, the Doctrine of Discovery was embraced enthusiastically in the U.S. as a means to support its nascent hegemony over Native lands (Miller 2010; Watson 2012; Newcomb 2008). This slight-of-hand trick simultaneously sought to repudiate Papal supremacy (forbidden in the U.S. Constitution) while still advancing the notion that as a self-proclaimed Christian nation, the U.S. was destined to fulfill a divine covenant with the colonists to seize land. Seizure of Native tribal lands became the overarching pillar of the Protestant wing of the American colonists. The theft was steeped in profits rather than theology. Enforced by an iron hand in the seizure of indigenous tribal lands, the Doctrine of Discovery was propped up as some kind of "biblical" warrant. It was implied that only God could author such a biblical warrant! After all, through "analogous" divine intervention, so the colonists would purport, did the Jewish people through Joshua seize the lands of Canaan (Joshua 24:13). The Papal See, the Bishop of Rome and ruling Pontiff of the Catholic Church likewise made exceptional use of analogous "biblical warrant" to expand Christendom to vast swaths of the New World. Lacking such compelling warrants, the young "Christian" nation implemented the Doctrine of Discovery by fiat (Dunbar-Ortiz 2014, Miller 2010).

Was there, in fact, a warrant in the Holy Bible that would justify the sequestration of Native American lands, dispossession and subjugation of these indigenous peoples, and their internment on reservations that constituted less than 2% of their ancestral home? The Holy Bible lacks such a warrant! There exists *no* direct covenant of God with America providing justification for the seizure of the lands of indigenous Native Americans or for that matter, any other indigenous peoples. Then, from what source have generations of Americans acquired a strong unshakable sense that a biblical warrant from God underwrote their seizure of tribal lands? The answer is simple. The true source is a mythology commonly termed, "American exceptionalism" (Van Engen 2020). Cobbled together from bits and pieces of the American history favoring the dominant White ruling class engaged in the vigorous exploitation of the "new" world, the political concept of American exceptionalism has captured the hearts of many Americans (Wallis 2016; Söderlind and Carson 2011). John Winthrop delivered the first bit in 1630 (Bremer 2003). As the Governor of the Massachusetts Bay Colony, Winthrop charged the English settlers with a mission cast in "providential" and "covenantal" dimensions. He invoked the Old Testament prophet Micah (6:8) for the settler colonists to "do justly, to love mercy, and walk humbly with our God" (Bremer 2003). Later, the mythology would expand and be transformed into frank "manifest destiny," that is, the notion that America ought to overspread the continent allotted to it by divine Providence (Democratic Review, 1845).

The value of such a divine commission would wilt with time, but was resurrected repeatedly during the "Great Awakenings" in America (circa 1730s, 1790s, 1850s–1900s, and 1960s–1970s). Each of these "great awakenings" proclaimed that the United States was to play some ineffable, divine role in the cosmos through fulfilling its manifest destiny (Greenberg 2018). The mythology revisited John Winthrop's 1630 treatise, "A Model of Christian Charity" that enjoined the Puritans to recognize that their community would be "as a city upon a hill," borrowing heavily from Jesus' Sermon on the Mount in Matthew 5:14 (Bremer 2003; Van Engen 2020). Therein Jesus of Nazareth preaches, "you are the light of the world. A city that is set on a hill cannot be hidden." This mythology of a "city on a hill" most likely is alluding to the city of Jerusalem, which is perched ~2500 feet above the Judean desert. Along with the notion of America being a "New Jerusalem" comes the analogy of Americans as "chosen", as were the Jewish people "chosen by God to be God's treasured people from all the nations that are on the face of the earth" (Deut 14:2). It is no coincidence that leading clergy as well as prominent politicians, not the least of which includes U.S. Presidents John F. Kennedy, Ronald Reagan, and Barack Obama, have borrowed the phrase "a [shining] city upon a hill" to allude to the parable of Salt and Light in Jesus's Sermon on the Mount. The intersection of this imaginary biblical warrant with self-dealing manifest destiny is nationalist, patriotic fervor (Van Engen 2020). A current day by-product of this mythology is a cultural "White nationalism" and political "White supremacy," that most of the public view as toxic to living into the rights and guarantees afforded to all Americans by the U.S. Constitution (Swain and Nieli 2003; Fletcher 2017; Saslow 2018; Dorrien 2018). The mythology of American exceptionalism with a biblical warrant both has fueled and been further inculcated into White nationalism by a strong military presence that some argue is the sole protector of democracy and freedom for the entire world. Others may view this practice as unadulterated, bare-knuckles American "gun boat" imperialism driven by White, Neoliberal patriarchy (Söderlind and Carson 2011).

Even if accepting the Doctrine of Discovery, the mythology of American exceptionalism, biblical warrant and manifest destiny, we fall short of explaining how these "givens" from the topside, dominant White ruling class justify the grievous outcomes for indigenous Native Americans as viewed from their decidedly underside location. How can such suffering, displacement from ancestral lands, violence, and killings possibly be viewed as "providential"? The situation for the Native Americans seems more like a forced exodus *and* exile within their own former tribal lands!

Colonial settlers and their governments proclaimed what the indigenous people in America needed first was "conversion" to Christianity. Christian faith was a dominant theme of colonialism, although adherence to Christian principles was spotty at best (Tinker 2004). Certainly there exist numerous case studies in which some level of conversion of the Native Americans to Christianity was achieved. Adherence and true personal attestation to Christ as Savior for such native indigenous peoples so "converted" was impossible to gauge, as discussed above. If conversion to Christianity truly was the goal, then the land grabs and genocide aimed at these potential fellow Christians don't ring true with this lofty goal. Remarkably, American history highlights many atrocities aimed at Native Americans, including at "Christianized Indians," by colonial settlers, in addition to revocation of their most fundamental right to not be killed. The expansion of the colonies and later of the U.S. created continued pressure for land. Aimed first at Native Americans labeled as "heathens" simply to justify land seizures in the name of a Christian nation, the Doctrine of Discovery encountered a formidable obstacle confronting the rights of Christianized Indians. Not to be neutered by the increased success of apparent Indian conversions to Christianity, the doctrine continued unabated to afford the necessary "biblical warrant" for application to later, larger land seizures from Native Americans (Tinker 2004).

The dark side of the manifest destiny threatened the immigrant colonists in America, pitting them against Christianized Indians (Greenberg 2018). For the sake of argument, first imagine an outcome in which all of the indigenous people of North America were successfully converted to Christianity. Once conversion of Native Americans to Christianity was complete, how could such Christianized indigenous peoples be separated from their ancestral lands? What warrants theologically or legally could deprive indigenous Christian peoples from their rights as espoused by the Doctrine of Discovery? Devout Christians, both the settlers and the Christianized indigenous peoples, by oath would be disciples of Christ. They would have constituted a *Communio Sanctorum* in Christian moral solidarity with Jesus as the body and head of the Church! Would the Doctrine of Discovery be legal and enforceable if applied to a Christian community whose monarch, King, and Prince of Peace was Christ Jesus? Could the sovereignty of Christ acting in this world be declared unassailable by the White ruling class in order to seize tribal lands, while at the same time be declared null and void for Christianized Indians in covenantal community with their overlords? It would not take Clarence Darrow to argue compellingly that in a world in which you cannot "have your cake and eat it too," the United States would be unable to mount a claim that indigenous people who have come to Christ and professed Jesus Christ as their King, would *not* be included in and protected by the Doctrine of Discovery!

Confronted with this considerable moral impediment to expansionist hegemony (Hixson 2013), the default position of the White ruling class was predictable. Subjugation of indigenous native peoples required that these peoples once again be declared as "heathens" or "false Christians." Only by declaring the indigenous peoples as "heathens," by separating them from the Greatest Commandment, and by ignoring with intention the biblical admonition to "love the stranger" (Deut 10:19) could the dominant White ruling class resume subjugating the "heathens" with impunity. No longer restrained by Christian principles, manifest destiny in American colonialism simply became a declaration of White supremacy precluding all indigenous Native Americans and peoples-of-color from their ancestral rights to the land (Greenberg 2018; Wallis 2016). The bastardized biblical warrant was narrowed. The goal simply was to deprive indigenous peoples of personhood and their human rights! This declaration of "otherness" for native indigenous peoples would prove both necessary and invaluable to excusing ongoing American expansionist hegemony. This original sin continues unabated, to rob people-of-color of personhood under the label of American exceptionalism and White nationalism (Swain and Nieli 2003; Saslow 2018; Van Engen 2020). It emerged in parallel with the earliest efforts of creating an American empire. In 2020 and hidden in plain sight, American empire at the hands of the White ruling class targets various citizens by color, gender, race, religious traditions, ethnicities, and cultures, depriving them of their rights guaranteed under the Bill of Rights and U.S. Constitution. The callous treatment of the people of Puerto Rico following the devastation caused by the Category 5 hurricane "Maria" in 2017 is but one example how U.S. citizens of color, like the indigenous Native Americans, remain subject to harsh assaults on their personhood by 21st century American empire.

With full personhood, the indigenous Native Americans would be immune to the loss and destruction of their lands, cultures, and privileges. Personhood guarantees the most basic of human rights, that is, the right not to be killed. Full legally protected personhood in the U.S. would engender the unfettered right to life, liberty, and the pursuit of happiness, absent any worry of being subject to killing! So how did the colonial expansionists of American empire devolve from seeking to "convert" the Native Americans to exterminating them as a preferred tool to unleash an unprecedented grab of indigenous peoples' lands? The mythology of American exceptionalism and providential covenant again afforded the necessary warrants. In the Holy Bible, similar wars of extermination (Joshua 11:11) were waged to enable a "chosen people" to occupy an already inhabited land that was promised by God to Abraham (Joshua 24:13). In a like manner, the American mythology was dependent on labeling the indigenous peoples as "heathens," "idolaters," and "subhuman." Yet, neither Canaan nor America was functionally *terra nullius*, that is, lands devoid of people, uninhabited. Both Canaan and America were inhabited and thus had to be officially declared *terra nullius*, meaning "nobody's land" rather than uninhabited. For the Hebrew "chosen people" the declaration of their promised lands in Canaan was by God (Joshua 24:13). For the American "self-chosen" immigrants, there was no declaration by God, just a preferred narrative of exceptionalism. For the indigenous peoples in both cases, the outcome was the same, that is, displacement, destruction, and enslavement (Joshua 17:12–13). The key to the success of American hegemony herein was denial of the very personhood of the indigenous Native Americans (Hixson 2013). The loss was nearly complete, achieving the goals by proclaiming that indigenous inhabitants were not human and therefore no longer protected either through acquired Christian conversion or the basic tenets of Jesus of Nazareth professed in the faith attributed to their White Christian occupiers.

Once declared "heathens" or "subhuman" by the White ruling class, indigenous Native Americans transitioned from persons (with innate personhood) to chattel, not being people any longer, but rather property, degraded and enslaved by the "victors." Biblical verses such as "You shall also love the stranger" (Deut 10:19), "You shall love your neighbor as yourself" (Matt 22:39), and "to do justly, to love mercy, and walk humbly with our God" (Micah 6:8) did not apply to chattel. Once deprived of personhood, indigenous peoples became the targets of biblical "dominion" by humankind (Gen 1:26–28). The "human" kind of the White ruling class no longer afforded personhood to indigenous native inhabitants of color. Genesis 1:26 reads, then God said, "Let us make humankind in our image, according to our likeness; and let them have dominion over the fish of the sea, and over the birds of the air, and over the cattle, and over all the wild animals of the earth, and over every creeping thing that creeps upon the earth." By now the use of "dominion" should activate your hermeneutic of suspicion about who claims dominion and who is being dominated! In Genesis 1:28, it states further, "God blessed them, and God said to them, 'Be fruitful and multiply, and fill the earth and subdue it; and have dominion over the fish of the sea and over the birds of the air and over every living thing that moves upon the earth.'" Thus, the essential step towards realizing the profligate goals of American colonialism (and imperialism) was assuring the loss of personhood for the indigenous inhabitant. Sub- and de-humanized Native Americans could now be subdued, made vulnerable to separation from their ancestral lands, deprived of their freedom (i.e., some were enslaved or conscripted), deprived of their children who would be taken away to be "re-educated," and in the case of millions deprived of their very lives (Dunbar-Ortiz 1984, 2014; Wallis 2016). Native ancestral lands then could be declared truly *terra nullius*, available for legalized theft, occupancy, and exploitation. At this juncture, we should be beginning to ask ourselves how it was possible for a horrific set of events, involving the lives of *millions* of Native American men, women, and children, involving the loss of more than 1.5 billion acres of Native American ancestral lands, and involving the subjugation/dehumanization of a people in the land for 30,000 years could continue into today, some five centuries after European explorers encountered North America? The inescapable horrific trauma endured by our indigenous Native Americans requires further interrogation to understand how it shapes assaults on personhood today.

Resistance, Trauma, and Resilience

Confronting whole-scale killing, displacement, destruction of culture, or dehumanization is deeply traumatizing. For indigenous Native Americans, the colonial world from the 17th century forward was replete with each of these assaults, most of which continue today in some covert manner (Estes 2019; Weaver 2019). Yet, within this horrific first "original sin" of America, is a core narrative about being human and how trauma of this scale is confronted. Over five hundred years of oppression, subjugation, and dehumanization, indigenous Native Americans displayed remarkable and unyielding "resistance" (Churchill 2002; Dunbar-Ortiz 2014; Hämäläinen 2019). Bereft of support from outside their communities, Native Americans looked to their core values of life, their long history of survival and flourishing, and their spiritual enlightenment to survive again, this time against a thoroughgoing onslaught of assaults on their very persons. Resistance, which can take on many forms, is a powerful essential response of oppressed peoples (Chomsky et al. 2010; Fletcher 2017; Simpson 2017). Their narratives of remarkable resistance included those of outstanding, majestic leaders, "patriot chiefs," whose leadership helped preserve their peoples, their heritage and culture, through mobilization of resistance (Josephy 1993). Sadly and predictably local historians worked diligently to extinguish such Native American narratives (O'Brien 2010). Precious few records around Native American resistance and resilience remain. Historically, from a perspective of half of a millennium, the resistance of indigenous Native Americans to unrelenting assaults by America's White ruling class hegemony remains a truly impressive narrative of human resolve (Churchill 2002; Tinker 2004; Petersen 2016; Simpson 2017; Weaver 2019).

By itself, resistance cannot preclude trauma. Rather resistance acts to confront trauma! Resistance reestablished the victims' identity, individually and as a cohesive community (Grounds, Tinker, and Wilkins 2003). Resistance is a defense mechanism that aims to recapture the narrative from those who assault personhood and give it back to the victims who need to regain personhood (Grounds, Tinker, and Wilkins 2003; Weaver 2019). Trauma resides in the psyche of individuals, but collectives of peoples traumatized acutely can provoke creation of cohesive community of victims all suffering from the aftermath of trauma. These people exist not in the Promised Land, but rather are forced to accept an "exilic" existence. The destruction of Jerusalem (587 BCE) and the Babylonian Exile of the Jews (608–538 BCE) constitute a prime example of severe trauma extending more than seventy years and an eternal legacy thereafter. This corporate trauma yielded resistance and fomented a powerful restorative resilience that would follow (Carr 2014). In modern times, we encounter compelling testimony of living victims, witnesses to the horrors of the Holocaust (Dwork and Pelt 2002). World history is replete with deeply traumatic events, some lasting but moments (e.g., mass shootings in Las Vegas in 2017 and 9/11 attacks), whereas others can span years and decades (e.g., World Wars I and II, the Vietnam War, and the ongoing U.S. War on Terror). There is an important distinction to be made here when we place into conversation the traumas of modern times versus those experienced by indigenous Native Americans over more than 500 years. The similarity of these traumatic events is that there exists an oppressor. This was not a cataclysmic "natural" event such as in response to floods, earthquakes, famine, and plagues. There was a perpetrator! The oppressor is responsible for the assault. The most common and clearest example emerges as standard for military conflicts and wars. Of the combatants, who is cast as the aggressor versus the defender/victim often is biased by the observer's perspective? All parties in these modern conflicts will suffer trauma, victor and victim alike. The aftermath of such horrific violence is never to be viewed as "natural" or normative, even in war. For the indigenous Native Americans the aggressor/oppressor remains the dominant White ruling class who created apocalyptic events for Native Americans. Eventually succeeding through "victory," the White victors also created a lopsided self-congratulatory narrative from the topsiders' perspective.

Witnessing, remembering, and testimony are key elements in how humans constructively respond to trauma, in the best of cases (Smith 2015; Felman and Laub 1991). When trauma remains buried within the self, quarantined to a less accessible space of one's psyche, resolution is not possible. The loss of personhood, sense of individual being, and tribal identity can be precipitated by the trauma of displacement and violence. A sad example of intergenerational trauma, relived through preservation of oral narratives of Native Americans involves the children. Witness extends back to earliest times when Native American children at 6 years of age were taken from parents to boarding schools to "educate" them in European ways. The overarching goal of destroying Native American language, traditions, and culture was never in doubt (Adams 1995; Child 1998). Childhood trauma was intentional. The boarding schools to which the children of the oppressed relocated were built intentionally hundreds of miles away from their ancestral tribal homes (Bensen 2001). Only in recent years have the long lasting horrors of the Federal boarding home program targeting Native American children been shown to include neglect, physical and sexual abuse, and attendant trauma. Testimony of Native Americans about the loss and trauma, as well as witness, memory, and resilience in the aftermath are an indispensible part of the American narrative (Nabokov 1991; Weaver 2019; Pembert 2019).

In my counseling work as clergy I often have been startled when people, in response to some triggering event, reveal almost by accident the videotape-like details of repressed sexual abuse, of witnessing the aftermath of suicides, or of surviving abandonment. Memories of the horrors of the Holocaust reverberate in our time and remain essential to gaining a deeper under-standing of trauma. Testimony by witnesses has been indispensable, reveal-ing much about how victims can go on to recover from trauma (Frankl 1946; Felman and Laub 1991; Herman 2015; Laub and Hamburger 2017). When untreated, trauma can manifest itself years and decades later, morphing into full-blown PTSD, as discussed earlier. The intrusions and flashbacks often attendant to traumatic events can reappear. For victims these psychological insults can constitute a continual source of horror, bearing witness again and again to the original trauma (Felman and Laub 1991). In rare instances, extraordinary self-discernment about experienced trauma and later recovery have proven deeply therapeutic to the victim as well as insightful to society (Frankl 2017).

The overarching lesson learned from the aftermath of the Holocaust was that of "remembering" (Jilovsky 2015). Remembering the horrors of the Holocaust creates an unavoidable, thick dialectic for deeper understanding. On the one hand, humans may seek to avoid or to dispel such a deeply troubling trauma. Perhaps we hope that the memory of the trauma might recede back into our minds and eventually with enough time that we might forget. This hope is generally magical thinking. On the other hand we cannot dismiss the ultimate hope of eventually creating a therapeutic narrative, one with the possibility of providing a path to the future, rather than one confined to the shadow of the past. In this foundational sense, Holocaust memorials are both places and experiences (Young 1993). Memorials are designed to facilitate remembrance and pathos, grief and hope. Throughout the world, art and sculpture have sought to capture the trauma, loss, grief, survival, and hope sustained through the Holocaust. These are symbolic tools aimed at repentance and reconciliation, that is, teaching tools for generations that follow. I argue that embracing the fullest depths of the Holocaust as well as the comparatively small lesser everyday traumas we encounter among life's vicissitudes, no matter how painful, is essential to sustaining the human soul. The Holocaust remains a profoundly relevant modern time example of the horrors of human fallenness. In error, some may consider such memorials and the keeping alive of the horrors of the Holocaust to be strictly initiatives of the Jewish community. This notion is wrong-headed. Such narrow think-ing defeats the greater narrative and an essential element of our *Communio Sanctorum*, that is, inclusivity! In true community in which there is no "oth-er," only "self," we all stand in moral solidarity and embrace the sufferings of all. The trauma and recovery experience of this trauma remains to be shared, taught, remembered, and never forgotten (Jilovsky 2015).

As survivors who bear witness to the horrors of the Holocaust age and die, their narratives, faces, and humanity in the face of such trauma must be retained, remaining etched on our hearts and minds (Moscovici 2019). It is essential for community to search out and interrogate, rather than to either ignore or forget, such past atrocities, to seek deeper understanding of how these atrocities arose, to share a sincere corporate guilt for permitting the conditions under which members of our human community can befall such horrors, and finally, to seek repentance of the perpetrators and eventual reconciliation. The communal need to give testimony, bear witness, and interrogate each human atrocity is essential. Remembering and lifting up horrors of the Holocaust provide a prime example, one that remains uniquely relevant to developing a greater understanding of the first "original sin" of America. The killing, displacement, dehumanization, and demonization of the millions of indigenous Native Americans who lived in the land for 30,000 years compels us to confront a tragic pathos-filled shared past. The overarching goal to seek truths about the scale of the human horrors, to validate and to embrace findings, and to work earnestly towards repairing the breach in our American narrative concerning its first "original sin" remains lofty, but achievable (Weaver 2019).

Repairing the Breach: Guilt, Repentance, and Reconciliation

How do we confront the first original sin of the founding of America? New challenges arise in trying to apply that which has been learned from the Holocaust experience directly to the genocide and mass destruction aimed at indigenous Native Americans, their history and culture. There are several formidable obstacles. First is the time frame for America's first original sin. The duration of America's assault on its indigenous Native Americans is shocking! Few mass traumas extend intergenerationally for over five hundred years! The Holocaust extended over a period of 12 years (1933–1945). For the Native Americans their horrors extended from the late 15th century and continue to this day, a period of more than 530+ years! It is hard to conceive of the sum total of suffering, killing, and debasement endured by these indigenous people summed up over half a millennium! Second is the obstacle of insuring the preservation of intergenerational memory. Lifting up and embracing the Holocaust intergenerationally has proven challenging. The Holocaust ended in 1945. What of an "original sin" of America that spans 8–10 generations and continues into the present day? Third is the length of the so-called "look back." The Holocaust ended 75+ years ago. A look back at America's first original sin is a distant 500+ years to its origin, marked by the earliest conquests by explorers to the New World. In today's digital world, yesterday news cycle can seem stale, as if like it happened long ago. How do we wrap our heads around an unprecedented horror that started in America half a millennium ago and continues into today? Fourth is the issue posed by accurately identifying both the perpetrators as well as the victims, 500+ years after the initial assault commenced?

For the Holocaust there has been an exhaustive and thoroughgoing effort to document the victims and perpetrators. Some perpetrators of the Holocaust with direct connection to the horrors of 1933–1945 were placed successfully in the dock and tried for crimes against humanity. The end of WWII and the prosecution of prominent members of Nazi Germany who participated in the Holocaust concluded at the Nuremberg Trials (1945–1949). The end of the trials demarcated an end to the acute horror and fostered nascent efforts towards a new narrative. For the indigenous Native Americans, there has never been a serious effort at unearthing the grim facts attendant to the 500+ year assault on their personhood. Historical records may lift up individual conflicts, massacres, and begin to capture the horrific crimes against humanity endured by the indigenous people at the hands of the dominant White ruling class. Incredibly, over the last five centuries, there has not been empaneled a single tribunal, criminal justice review, or fact gathering aimed at identifying those responsible for the American assault on the indigenous peoples in the land! Perhaps, this profound question is criminally rhetorical? Do we not know whom the perpetrators, enablers, and their descendants are?

The haunting truth is that many Americans would like to mislead themselves, thinking that the past is dead. But as noted American author William Faulkner (1897–1962) quipped, "The past is never dead. It's not even past." This quotation declares as most "alive," the core claim for denied justice by the indigenous Native Americans who have endured five centuries of horrific treatment. This "original sin" perpetrated by the White ruling class against the personhood of indigenous Native Americans is not dead and it most assuredly is not even past! It should be painfully apparent that in choosing to overlook, ignore, and minimize the dimensions of the first original sin of America we shackle ourselves to a false narrative (Smith 2015). Such avoidance denies the victims their rights to claim their horrific traumatic treatment at the hands of the White ruling class and to have these claims validated by the U.S. public and judiciary. A denial to a just consideration of these claims only succeeds to further dumb down our moral selves to continuing assaults on Native Americans (and others) ongoing in everyday life in the U.S. We have self-anesthetized and sought to sanitize our complicity and active participation in the longest lasting and most horrific atrocity upon which the American empire was founded. Unwilling to confront the atrocities of our making, Americans distort and sanitize local histories, seeking to erase Native Americans from the narrative.

The overarching goal of revisionism was and remains simply to try to forget our complicity. Erasing this complicity only further debases the identity, human rights, and full personhood of indigenous Native Americans and, frankly, all Americans (O'Brien 2010; Weaver 2019)! This, we shall see, is not the only great sin of America, but is more assuredly our *first* original sin! Applauding the spiritual and moral doggedness of America's indigenous peoples in face of asymmetric assaults by the Doctrine of Discovery, manifest destiny, efforts to "convert" the indigenous Native Americans to Christianity, and horrific crimes against humanity cannot absolve us of individual and corporate guilt (Tinker 2004). To seek the truths of the past, to validate such truths, to offer sincere repentance and to work towards reconciliation of our original sin all will be required to regain our moral standing. Thankfully, our indigenous fellow Americans still live among us, in the broad community of humankind, truly deserving of the honor of being considered our "first" Americans! Their presence affords us a precious, but fleeting opportunity to seek amends toward our first great sin, to offer contrition and to seek forgiveness from a people who even today find their personhood under attack. The reclamation of Native American personhood, restoration of their well-being, and insuring justice for their community (and so thereby to *Communio Sanctorum*) are essential (Weaver 2019). America has gone to great lengths to marginalize rather than to lift up and revere the true forefathers of the land. This window of opportunity remains to confront our sins, seek forgiveness, justice, and reconciliation with our indigenous Native American sisters and brothers still in the land.

How then do we rationally review the prospects for reconciliation and eventual just reparations (Cunningham 2017)? If there is any real progress being made in these efforts, most of it reflects the efforts of local activists. Living among the peoples in the land might be the best manner to explore these tough questions of sin, repentance, forgiveness, and reconciliation (Weaver 2019; Hämäläinen 2019). Truth and reconciliation tribunals have shown some success in reconciling the aftermath of traumatic conflicts among peoples. Yet, there seems to be little interest in either the U.S. Congress or the Federal administration to take on what is cast as a divisive and politically charged issue. Rather, as noted, the U.S. has made use of flawed legal thinking to disparage any notion that indigenous American Natives can seek just restitution for individual and corporate injuries sustained over 500+ years of assault by the White ruling class. The history of negotiations between the U.S. and its indigenous Native Americans repeatedly displays all the trappings of how American Empire does business with the "other." Personhood is assaulted, claims are delegitimized, and past atrocities are either minimized or ignored entirely by promulgation of topsider-driven narratives.

In late December 2009, President Barack Obama signed the Senate Joint Resolution (S.J.Res.14, 111th United States Congress), a Congressional Resolution of Apology to Native Peoples of the United States replete with a litany of twenty "Whereas" and seven "findings" within the "apology." The absence of "Native Americans" is both offensive, yet anticipated in such a dilute, corporate *mea culpa.* The document lists many contributions of Native Peoples that assisted the survival of a fledgling republic and later United States, glossing over and sanitizing the killing of ("perished"), the lying to

("Federal Government violated"), dispossession of ("United States forced"), ethnocide of ("Federal Government condemned the traditions, beliefs, and customs of Native Peoples") indigenous Native Americans, and forced removal of and boarding of Native children at schools distant from their homes. The final "whereas," states "Native Peoples are endowed by their Creator with certain unalienable rights, among those are life, liberty, and the pursuit of happiness:" It took 233 years for the Declaration of Independence to be resolved to apply also to the indigenous people of America, in the land for 30 centuries! The crass intentional *mis*labeling of Native Americans to "Native Peoples" is outdone only by two other points of interest. The first is that these "heartfelt" apologies by Congress included a prominent disclaimer that "Nothing in the resolution authorizes or supports any claim against the United States." The final indignity was the manner in which this resolution was *enacted* on December 19th, 2009. The President signed the joint resolution. He neither publicly read it nor signed it in the presence of any tribal leader or official representatives of more than 560 federally recognized tribes in the U.S.! Subsequent to the signing, the resolution was folded into the unrelated 2010 Defense Appropriation Act (H.R.3326, 111th United States Congress) signed the same day.

California's governor Gavin Newsom formally apologized to Native Americans in June 2019. The governor acknowledged the White ruling class' use of "war of extermination," that is, "genocide," as declared policy by the state's first governor in 1851! California, for example, employed extermination, displacement of indigenous Native Americans from their ancestral land, physical separation of Native American children from their families, forced destruction of Native culture and languages, wrong-headed plans calling for Native peoples to "assimilate" to the White ruling class expectations, and created an insidious system fomenting dependence of Native Americans on State/Federal custody to insure permanent denial of full personhood for these indigenous peoples. Although such public contrition for passed sins may be viewed as a milestone for a state with more than 100 federally recognized tribes of Native Americans and three-quarters of a million Native Americans, an apology for past original sin is simply not enough. Such longstanding horrific injustice perpetrated by the White ruling class and endured by indigenous peoples commonly were only "sweep under the carpet," absent public scrutiny. Confession is good for the soul, even the corporate soul. Yet, truly public apologies replete with sincere contrition are essential, but only the first steps. They alone are not pathways aimed at achieving restorative justice for claims by injured indigenous people.

Seeking justice requires revelation of the nature of the crimes, suffered and endured by the Native Americans. We must "come clean" about the truth of America's "original sin" against the Native Americans. The topsiders' history of recasting brutal exploitation as a benign product of simple, national exceptionalism must not persist. This false narrative must be rectified for the record. A dead reckoning of all land claims and investigations of all claims of broken treaties are essential to the eventual success of any effort to achieve reconciliation. American indigenous peoples were in the land for 30,000 years before European explorers sought to exploit the Americas! This fact, above all others, justifies the march towards consideration of reparations.

What is to be gained by efforts at reconciliation and reparations? First, only by accepting responsibility for discounting personhood and deprivation of human rights can a "perpetrator" ruling class seek repentance. I would speculate that few of the hegemonic White ruling class would have the fortitude and moral fiber to accept with grace any responsibility suggesting complicity in an "original sin" against the Native Americans. American exceptionalism affords little space for guilt and apologies (Van Engen 2020). This stiff-necked behavior must change if we are to evolve into the community of moral solidarity. Second, a Federal effort to empanel a truth and reconciliation tribunal must be charged with unearthing the true greater dimensions of original sin. A serious effort might require a decade-long analysis, covering an original sin persisting for more than 500 years. The goal would to be to begin a process to rectify the historic narrative and to work towards healing its derivative and long history of wounds. Third, the Doctrine of Discovery must be set aside as unlawful. International law and expert opinion declare this U.S. doctrine null and void, lacking legal foundation, only magical thinking (Wilkins and Lomawaima 2002; Wilkins 2013; Dunbar-Ortiz 2014). The U.S. discovery doctrine has been declared, "a clear legal fiction that needs to be explicitly stricken from the federal governmnet's political and legal vocabulary (Wilkins and Lomawaima 2002). Only such just action will permit an unbiased and accurate accounting of the claims of atrocities, genocide, dispossession, starvation and displacement of Native Americans. In possession of these new facts, Americans may begin to understand better the vast dimensions, long history, and horrific scale of this original sin perpetrated against indigenous Native Americans. Equally necessary is a cost accounting of what economists expect to be a staggering financial loss endured by the indigenous Native Americans over 500+ years. Some level of reparations deemed reasonable will need to weigh the historic losses against possible financial remedies within the scope of the U.S. economy (Sargent and Samanta 2016). Finally, what must not be lost in the details is that truth and reconciliation tribunals exist primarily as an opportunity for the dominant ruling class to admit guilt, display contrition, and seek forgiveness of the aggrieved as partial restitution for original sin. Such acts of contrition and repentance must precede a request for forgiveness. Forgiveness would be the only viable start of a healing process in America. Americans must admit a guilt, complicity, and vulnerability to valid and uncontested claims of the indigenous American Natives. It is not only for the sake of restoring the dignity and place of peoples dehumanized and marginalized, but also for the creation of a new American community. Let us embrace our true "founding fathers" and "founding peoples" whose rich heritage and customs may be mutually embraced by all Americans. For these people must be "self" for us, they cannot be "other." This *Communio Sanctorum* must be inclusive, in moral solidarity, and acknowledge the essential role that indigenous Native Americans and their cultures have played in the founding and success of American enterprise. Reparations, when granted as redistributive justice, may be best directed at the building of community—that is, *Communio Sanctorum*—that will be essential to the true flourishing of all indigenous Native Americans.

A Personal Confession: Original Sin and Guilt

My family's ancestry in America reaches back to 1627 when George Malbon and family left Nantwich England and sailed to the New World. The family has ancient roots in Nantwich dating back to the Battle of Hastings (1066 CE). This history has been explored in some detail (Lynch 2005). The trip to America was more of a "visit." The immigrant family griped publically that religious tolerance in the colony was less than they expected, returning to England in the mid-17th century. A New England source quoted in the family history saying only, "It would have been better for all if the Malbons had never left England!" The family now in Europe eventually made their way to the Netherlands where they billeted with French Huguenots. Eventually they received a land grant in "New France" from the Monarchy. The Malbons returned to America with the French Huguenots, settling on 650+ acre lands in Maine, earlier claimed by France (Allen 1931, Groves 1977). Both the English and French had claimed this area of Maine, an ancient tribal land of the indigenous Abenaki Native Americans. This ambiguity of land claims would provoke several violent and deadly conflicts, attacks of the colonial settlers upon their Native American neighbors.

Members of the "clan" (as my father referred to the family) still reside in Maine on the same large tract of land, at the junction of the three streams of the Wesserunsett River, fed by the Kennebec River. At the juncture of the Wesserunsett stream there are ~40 foot waterfalls that once powered successful saw milling. The family eventually bought a large local lumber mill. Some histories reference the town in which the mills emerged as "Malbons' Mills." Later after a devastating fire at the mills, the local name was changed to "Milburn." Eventually an earlier Native American name "Skowhegan," meaning a watching place for fish, was readopted. Most of my own narrative was acquired through an oral tradition, absent much authentication. The matriarch of the family in Skowhegan, however, maintained an extensive family history supported by a large "family" Holy Bible (including genealogy), the original land grant from France inked onto animal skin delineating all natural boundaries of the land granted and embossed with a red wax seal of France, as well as handwritten accounts of deadly skirmishes over the years between the Malbons and the Native Americans indigenous to the area. The Abenaki tribe, declared adversaries in these family narratives, is both a Native American tribe as well as one of Canadian First Nation tribes. The Abenaki are one of Algonquian-speaking peoples of North America and considered a linguistic and geographic tribal grouping. The family took great pride in their history of overcoming challenges, especially those posed by conflicts with the indigenous Abenaki. Colonial settlers frequently were planted in specific areas to provide buffers among Native American, Spanish, and English interests. The hand-written accounts of conflicts were read and regaled as reflecting on the courage and valor of the family.

Oddly coincidental, I grew up in a small town in Massachusetts (Oxford) that also had a long history of Huguenot immigrants. Thirty Huguenot families established a settlement and fort there in 1686. My Easter sunrise services with the town Protestants routinely was held in a field at the top of a plain where stood a very large stone Christian Cross. The cross was erected at the hilltop of the fort to memorialize the arrival of these Calvinist Protestant early Huguenot settlers. In fact each day on my way to school I passed a second stone monument, this one erected in 1930 to memorialize the so-called "Johnson Massacre" of local folklore. The inscription reads: "John Johnson and three children were killed by Indians in his house on this spot August 25, 1696." Only after college did I encounter and converse with Native Americans, living on reservations in Maine (Penobscot tribe) and at a second larger reservation in the Four Corners region, home to semi-autonomous Native American nations including the Navajo, Hopi, Ute, and Zuni. My topsider location, however, rendered me poorly prepared to listen attentively and with empathy to the gravity of their personal narratives and suffering.

The past and present suffering of indigenous peoples at the hands of dominant White ruling class members had been rendered "invisible" in my world. Only through immersions into Native American histories gained at Union Theological Seminary in the City of New York were my heart and mind made open. Those learning experiences, especially dialogue with Native American theologians, exposed me to their deep suffering. The potential of liberation theology for indigenous peoples to emerge in the U.S. and elsewhere was palpable. I was transformed by 21st century voices of indigenous people, replete with the 500+ years of suffering, killing, and debased treatment of the Native Americans. Over the intervening decade I have searched my soul while trying to gain perspectives of the "oppressed" against a larger picture about my own family's history and complicity. I confess that

I offer only my own perspective on how I try to recast the history of my family with my knowledge of the mistreatment, death, and displacement of the indigenous Abenaki people in the land. This transformative journey gained though attentive listening to the Native American voices and my own more detailed research of my family history in Maine has left an indelible mark on my heart and soul.

In particular I was moved by the accounts of what is termed, the "Norridgewock Massacre," that occurred in August 1724 in close proximity to family land (Hanson 1849). The focus of massacre was reported to be the presence of a French Jesuit priest, Father Râle, whose flock was the Abenaki people in Maine. The attack by 200+ settler "raiders" was conducted with fierce "barbarity" upon an unsuspecting Abenaki group. I quote a first-hand source: "They [we] slaughtered women and children indiscriminately, and after Father Râle was slain, he was scalped and shockingly mutilated. Those who coolly shot little children and women, as they were seeking safety by swimming, could not with great propriety charge cruelty upon French priests or savage Indians" (Hanson 1849). Whatever Doctrine of Discovery, European colonialism, and some historians may offer as counterclaim, my hermeneutic of suspicion sadly came to rest upon me, ancestors of my family, and the compelling local history. Deprivation of the personhood of indigenous Native Americans of human rights, loss of their ancestral lands, and ultimately denial of the basic human right to not being killed constitute for me a deep and lasting scar of guilt. Having conducted this investigation, I cannot choose to gaze away from historic complicity in the matter, no matter how distant I might seek to place the atrocity. The Maine Indian Claims Settlement Act, signed into Federal law in 1980, eventually provided $81.5 M in restitutions/reparations to the Passamaquoddy, Penobscot, and Maliseet tribes, all members with the Abenaki of the old Wabanaki Confederacy (Wilkins 2013). Although driven from their ancestral lands in Maine, the Abenaki Native Americans live nearby, on two reservations in Quebec and small tracts of land scattered around New England. Repentance seeking forgiveness and reconciliation with the Abenaki for those who suffered and died in skirmishes in Maine remains for me a life-long moral imperative.

ORIGINAL SIN: ASSAULT ON AFRICAN, AFRICAN AMERICANS, AND DESCENDANTS

Legacy of Displacement, Commodification, and Contested Being

The overarching thesis offered on assaulting personhood in 21st century America finds its roots and was enabled by two originals sins: the genocide, subjugation and dispossession of the indigenous Native Americans from their ancestral lands (above); and, the displacement, commodification, and enslavement of Africans, African Americans, and their descendants (below). The tendency of Americans to discount, degrade, and withhold personhood in present time, I offer, reflects the callous way in which we ignore these two original sins. As just recounted, the treatment of the Native Americans, indigenous to North America for 30,000 years, continues to be abhorrent, dehumanizing, and intentionally degrading of their full personhood. These people were in the land for 300 centuries before European explorers and settler colonists commenced grievous assaults upon them. When claiming that these deeply religious natives were "heathens" did not work, when Christianity was enforced upon them and its Greatest Commandment then ignored, when land and later mineral claims were scurrilously and perpetually set aside by courts, and when near genocide failed to wipe out the Native Americans, the United States regrouped to deprive them of their tribal heritage by claiming that current members of the tribes had been assimilated into the common pool by "outbreeding." Thus Native Americans were deprived claim to their ancestral lands and to basic human rights protected under the U.S. Constitution!

For African and African American slaves the assault on personhood was in many ways different, but yet fundamentally similar. Being declared anything less than 100% Native American was enough to challenge the legal personhood of indigenous people, denying them "Indian rights" and land claims, by the so-called "blood quantum" test (Spruhan 2006; Ratteree and Hill 2017). For the enslaved African and African American people, in contrast, the presence of "one drop of black blood" in their veins became a social and legal principle in the U.S. for racial discrimination (Sweet 2005). Simply interpreted, the presence of even one drop of "black" blood was sufficient to assign children of mixed background to be "black" or "colored." Unlike Native Americans who were placed at risk to lose their claims of heritage as their peoples mixed, the Black enslaved stood virtually no chance of escaping their indentured status. Colonial settlers in America were threatened by the very presence of indigenous people who first occupied the lands. Slavers and slaveholders, in contrast, would be most threatened by abolitionists who sought to break the "commodification" of Black slaves and their descendants. Fundamentally, both are systems of oppression, both are grave "original" sins. These sins share the most profound bond, being based in racism rooted in the dominant White ruling class that immigrated to North America in the 15th and 16th century. It is racism that fueled the dehumanization of both the Native Americans and Black slaves in America, then and now. Without such dehumanization, the horrific treatment of both groups presumably would have violated public sensitivities of White folks. With such dehumanization, people assigned the status of chattel, subjected to dominion, and overt racist treatment could be ensnared into slavery (Davis 2006; Franklin and Higginbotham 2010). The divine dominion as biblical warrant was created expressly and solely for the White ruling class to label Blacks as chattel and exploit their labor through slavery (Baptist 2014).

Commodification as employed to assault the personhood of African and African Americans is the action or process of treating or labeling someone as a mere "commodity," bereft of human dignity and rights. Slaves were commodified to property, deprived of their human being entirely as "wards" with no legal status. The principles of property law, not human rights, became the legal framework that enabled slave owners to own, buy, and sell human beings (Berry 2017). As valuable property, Black slaves (unlike their Native American counterparts) were not targeted for genocide. The Black slaves owned no property, had no legal rights, not even the basic right to be accepted as human. Custom and prevailing auction pricing established their value. Values of slaves in the American colonies were carefully assigned and dynamic in character. Calculation of Black slave value took into consideration many factors, including gender, age, age to-and-from "prime" value, fecundity, general health, and history of behavior (Berry 2017). Even after death, slaves were not free! The "ghost" values of dead slaves were calculated to support insurance claims. Their value in death, based upon a slave's potential as a cadaver for dissection by medical students in training, also was subject to calculation and negotiation (Berry 2017).

Setting aside the mechanism by which Africans were enslaved and commodified to fuel economic interests of nascent American commerce, did there in fact exist a biblical warrant concerning slavery? Slavery was a common aspect of life in the Ancient Near East (Tsai 2014). The Book of Genesis of the Hebrew Bible (Gen 9: 18–27) includes the story of the nakedness of Noah and the cursing of Ham and the Canaanites. The story concludes with the "Curse of Ham" in which servitude is declared for Ham and the Canaanites. In modern times Genesis 9 has been referenced as a biblical warrant justifying slavery, particularly for enslavement of Black peoples throughout the centuries. This version of the biblical "curse" casts Ham as "black" and his descendants as "African." A more expansive set of additional texts employed to justify slavery referenced Exodus 21, Leviticus 25, and Deuteronomy 15. The complex and synergistic role of these biblical texts is not our focus. The basic feature they all share is that each of these texts has been adopted and rationalized to justify and perpetuate the institution of slavery. Such servitude and dominion under the White ruling class empowered centuries of domination of Black people (Baptist 2014). Domination of Black slaves was not restricted to labor, but expanded to include sexual exploitation and conjugal slavery (Jennings 1990).

One prominent theme of Mosaic Law concerning slavery demanded that such servitude be subject to legal manumission (i.e., release from slavery) at the end of 6–7 years of service (Exo 21:2–11; Lev 25:39–55; Deut 15:12–18). This bedrock of slavery as practiced in the Ancient Near East found no traction in colonial America. Most Africans in the Virginia colony, for example, were held for a lifetime of indentured servitude, not 6–7 years (Morgan 1975). Deuteronomy (23:16–17) concludes with a petition seeking to protect the lives of escaped slaves. Humane and ethical treatment of slaves is proffered throughout the Pentateuch, the first five books of the Hebrew Bible ascribed to Moses. For their part, the English colonists brought with them no legal foundations for either the practice of slavery or the ownership of human beings. English Law was bereft of any rules regarding the ownership of human beings! The explanation for these apparent paradoxes in biblical warrant of the Ancient Near East versus colonial America is simple. In ancient times, slavery did not deprive the slave of personhood, that is, slaves were still regarded as human beings. To address the labor needs of a nascent American Empire, slavery was cast not as indenturing human beings into servitude, but rather exercising biblical dominion over the chattel of African Blacks. This posture was the single foundational assault on African and African American personhood that would be the hardest to shake. The everyday racist behaviors aimed at Black people and at people of color can trace their lineage to a biblically warrant justifying harsh and expansive dominion over African Blacks cast, through the Curse of Ham, as chattel, "beasts" rather than humans, whose labor and sexual being was to be exploited. First came the necessary dehumanization and commodification of Black bodies, followed thereafter by life terms of harsh slavery.

Christian slavers in America created their own justifications for slavery while readily ignoring true biblical injunctions in the Old Testament that placed limitations on terms of indentured slavery (Schaff 1861; Warren and Confederate States of America Collection, Library of Congress 1864). Broad concepts of true biblical warrants were ignored. Slavers could find sufficient justification for enslaving Blacks by simply referencing short snippets of the biblical texts. The topic of slavery was not confined to the Hebrew Bible. The New Testament mentions slavery, but often only metaphorically. Jesus of Nazareth uses a metaphor referencing master and slaves to explicate the relationship of God and humankind, respectively (Matt 18:21–35; 24:36–51). In the Epistles, codes of behavior are proposed referring again to necessary obedience of slaves to their master. This metaphor crafted to explicate the relationship of God to humankind is based, however, on a paradigm in which a master (representing God) loves and cares about the well-being of their wards (slaves), rather than of masters who exploit slaves through physical abuse and coercion (Eph 6:5–8; Col 3:22–24; 1 Tim 6:1–2; Titus 2:9–10; Philemon).

In America, Southern slave owners drew upon the Holy Bible as providing an ex post facto endorsement for enslaving Africans and for perpetuating slavery as an institution for African American descendants of slaves. In this manner, slaves and their progeny generation to generation for their entire existence constituted property of the slaver. The distinction often lost in the haze of American Empire is that the core message of the Holy Bible around slavery was that slaves remain people. Slaves still retain unalienable rights, obligations, as well as privileges of personhood. In America, the institution of slavery rests upon the notion that slaves have no personhood. Slaves are dehumanized, labeled as *sub*human. Slaves are mere chattel; best placed under the "dominion of man," or more accurately under the dominion of White ruling class patriarchs! This Anglo-Saxon myth enabled the preclusion of Black bodies from natural law, creating a *"theo*-ideology" rendering Africans and African Americans devoid of citizenship as well as being human (Douglas 2015). Furthermore, as chattel, female slaves were preyed upon freely by white men (Jennings 1990; National Humanities Center 2007). Liken to livestock, the offspring of the female slave was legally "owned" by the slaver. Procreative products of the sexual abuse and rape of female slaves constituted a valuable, renewable source of labor for commerce. Denial of personhood precluded American slaves of virtually all human rights (Douglass 1855). Laws were crafted to deny slave women the right to control their bodies, reproductive capacity, as well as their role as mothers. The harsh treatment of Black women in 21st century America remains a toxic remnant of abusive White patriarchy seeking dominion over Black bodies, whether slaves or emancipated descendants of slave women.

Historically, the Hollywood film industry sanitized the institution of slavery with films like *Gone With the Wind* replete with sets of nearly bucolic living conditions, compassionate and humane masters, and patriarchal loving-kindness of the masters for the hard working "chattel." The adaptation of Solomon Northup's riveting memoir as a freeman who was kidnapped, enslaved, and rescued in 1853 in *Twelve Years a Slave* (Northup and Wilson 1859) eventually would dispel this Hollywood haze. The depiction of the true horrific brutality and indifference of slavery underscored the dehumanized role cast for the African and African American (*12 Years a Slave* 2013; McQueen et al. 2013). The book and film adaptation portray a profound truth, an "original sin" in America that persists long after its 1619–1865 institution! When slavery is cast as a mere period of 246 years within American history, the subjugation, commodification and denied personhood of millions of Africans, African Americans, and their descendants is trivialized. The legacy of slavery did not term in 1865. The legacy of assaulted personhood did not term in 1865, nor a hundred and fifty years later. The toxic legacy of American Empire inflicted upon Blacks persists robustly in 21st century America. For a hundred and fifty years and counting, since the Emancipation Proclamation signed by President Abraham Lincoln, the legacy of slavery birthed in 1619 remains a horrific scar on the psyche of the United States. Estimates of modern-day slaves, a grim reminder of the "original sin" of America, were pegged at 403,000 people, mostly of color, in the U.S. as of 2018!

Souls of Black Slaves

Slavery in America raised the same moral issues as did the displacement, cultural degradation, and genocide of indigenous Native Americans that preceded it. Unresolved concerns around race, ethnicity, and religion in the treatment of indigenous peoples applied equally to Black "strangers" forcibly kidnapped in Africa and brought to North America as slaves. The first strategy exploited religion. In order either to kill Native Americans or enslave Black Africans, the White ruling class needed to declare these "other" bereft of Christian religion. Once labeled as "heathens" and subhuman, Native Americans and Black African slaves could be deprived of human rights. This strategy was essential to successful seizure of indigenous Native American tribal lands. Once declared lacking personhood and legal status on religious grounds, "Indians" were precluded from claiming right to ancestral lands, subjected to exclusion under the Doctrine of Discovery, and declared "wards" of the U.S. Federal government. Being in the land for 30,000 years, Native Americans threatened the land needs of the nascent American Empire. The Black African slaves, in sharp contrast, posed no threat to the land needs of America. Black Africans were not "in the land", but rather had been kidnapped and forcibly brought to American shores. These dark-skinned "strangers" brought nothing of value with them, only their bodies now property for sale in an alien world. Justification of freedom denied (Black Africans) was adapted from the justification applied for the taking of lands (Native Americans), that is, absence of Christian faith. The same biblical warrant alleged to justify labeling Native Americans as "less-than-human" and therefore bereft of intrinsic human rights could be neatly applied to Black Africans. The logic of Christian evangelism, earlier explicating European colonialism on religious grounds and justifying need for "missionaries," professed that coming to Christ Jesus was the only means to insure salvation for the heathens. Yet there was an inherent paradox to this fevered evangelism. In the case of land claims, once the Native Americans were Christianized, how could their lands be seized? In the case of slavery, once the souls of Black Africans are "saved" by the Christian slavers, how could the servitude of these nascent fellow Christians be justified? There were some European Christians who expected that conversion of the Native Americans would end deprivation of their human rights by colonial settlers (Davis 2006). Similarly, these European Christians expected that coming to Christ by Black Africans would be the catalyst for their manumission or emancipation in America. This magical thinking most assuredly did not bring to full personhood either the indigenous people or their Black African brothers and sisters kidnapped and enslaved in the American colonies. Christian or not, African slaves were forced from a one-way voyage to America to a lifetime of harsh servitude (Franklin and Higginbotham 2010; Paquette and Smith 2016).

How were such well-intentioned Christian impulses of some Europeans distorted to permit Christian souls and bodies of Black Africans to be shackled by the institution of American slavery? Deprived by evangelical success of biblical warrants and the Curse of Ham, slavers turned to legislative and judicial remedies. Declarations were formulated that ancestry of Blacks, even distant, would remain "African" and thereby considered de facto "non-Christian." A slave would remain a slave, Christianized or not (Finkelman 2003). Reformulations of these declarations continued into the 17th century. Legally enforceable justifications for enslavement were crafted to embrace other criteria unique to an individual, their ancestors, as well as the actual port of their entry into America. Entering America through Slave States by ship versus land, for example, afforded justification of enslavement and denial of their personhood (Finkelman 2003). Victims would continue to be declared "chattel," thereby denied personhood and attendant rights. Loss of the most basic of all human rights, that is, the right not to be killed, placed slaves under the constant threat of punishment, even punishment to death! Atrocities committed upon slaves by their masters could not be prosecuted. For the slaves, deprived of personhood, there existed no justice or legal remedies when targeted in criminal acts or abuse by their master. These victims were voiceless. Death of a slave as the result of punishment by his master, even if intentional, would not rise to the grounds for criminal charges of murder or manslaughter (Finkelman 2003). The American Revolution, the enactment of the U.S. Constitution and Bill of Rights, would provoke soul-searching and increased self-discernment by many citizens about the morality of the institution of slavery.

The question of the innate personhood and presence of Black peoples' souls was debated during deliberation on the "three-fifths" amendment offered at the 1787 U.S. Constitutional Convention (Paquette and Smith 2016). The question of representation of slave state populations ended in a compromise. Only three out of every five slaves in slave states would be counted as a "person"! Was it possible that some Black slaves had no souls or that slaves in general had only 3/5ths of a soul apiece, after their personhood had been declared null and void? The moral issue of slavery continued in a fog. U.S. Supreme Court decisions, such as *United States v. The Amistad* (Freedman 2000) and *Groves v. Slaughter* (Shally-Jensen 2017b), both in 1841, had a great impact on the ongoing controversy (Davis 2006; Franklin and Higginbotham 2010; Paquette and Smith 2016). These cases popularizing two competing narratives. The first case, *United States v. The Amistad,* concluded that Africans indeed were persons. The second case, *Groves v. Slaughter*, reversed the decision of *United States v. The Amistad* that Africans indeed were people. *Groves v. Slaughter* declared once again that Africans were mere "commodities." The decision in the case of *United States v. The Amistad* exonerated Amistad's African crew and its use of force to secure their freedom. This decision advanced anti-slavery sentiment of the time, but had failed to yield legal clarity about the personhood of Blacks at the Federal level. The U.S. Supreme Court landmark decision in *Dred Scott v. Sandford* in 1857 aided sentiment for slavery, declaring that the Constitution did not provide for automatic American citizenship for Black people, whether their status be enslaved or free (Van Zee and Maltz 2013). As the American West was expanding, the economic and political implications of the *Dred Scott v. Sandford* decision were dire, eventually polarizing the country and provoking the Civil War in America (1861–1865). By 1857 the Slave States of the U.S. included Alabama, Arkansas, Florida, Georgia, Kentucky, Louisiana, Maryland, Mississippi, Missouri, North Carolina, South Carolina, Tennessee, Texas, and Virginia. The status of the souls of African and African American slaves and their descendants remained amorphous in the crucible of state and Federal jousting over the fate of slavery in the U.S. up to and well beyond the American Civil War (Franklin and Higginbotham 2010).

Christian Words, but Not Deeds

How were African slaves who were brought to America by force received by a nascent and self-described Christian nation? Africans kidnapped and forced to America in the 17th century were not atheists. African spirituality and other religious traditions were transplanted to the New World with kidnapped Black slaves (Stewart 1999). Some slaveholders proclaimed that a Divine hand had brought the hardworking Black Africans to labor in the fields and homes of colonists (Baptist 2014). In so doing, the ultimate goal of the divine intervention was to save the souls of these Black folks. In return for "conversion" to the Christian faith, slaves would yield better to the slaveholders' preferred biblical message, obedience to one's master (Noll 2002). The slaveholders' assumption that an African slave's eternal soul was at risk was never seriously questioned. Ferreting out a biblical warrant to enforce submission and obedience gave a Christian imprimatur to the institution of American slavery. Yet, the injunction in the Apostle Paul's Letters to the Ephesians (6:5) and to the Colossians (3:22) "slaves, obey your earthly masters" could be viewed not as a call for obedience to masters, but rather a metaphor. The Apostle Paul simply may have been following the lead of Jesus of Nazareth who employed the relationship between slaves and masters as a metaphor to guide the relationship between humankind and their Heavenly Master.

There are several colonial period, Christian churches in the Northeast whose very structure addresses the complex relationship between slavers and their "chattel." High-minded slave owners of the period made accommodations to their churches to enable their slaves to attend religious services. One wonders what kind of Gospel message the slavers hoped to hear from the pulpit on Sundays? Would the readings endorse the radical love of Jesus and his message of freedom to the enslaved? Or was the intention to display Christian charity to the "least among us," that is, indentured slaves? Or did settler colonial pressure welcome only sermons that preach on the Christian virtues of obedience of women, children, and servants alike? Many churches from the colonial period retain the legacy of embraced slavery, retaining the hardware and shackles that were installed to secure the slaves to the lesser spaces of the balconies, out of sight from their Christian White ruling class "benevolent" owners! This legacy lived on in the Old North Church in Boston's North End, where even today the congregation seeks to confront its early ties to the slave trade. Performed in a sanctuary, the practice of shackling slaves to pews in some Christian churches revealed a brutal paradox. In such services did pastors forego the liberation and freedom themes in Exodus to focus rather upon Israelites practicing slavery, the curse of Ham upon Africans, and the Christian message of an eventual heavenly reward that awaits slaves who are dutiful and obedient in their earthly work (Noll 2002)? Where were the stirring stories of liberation fueled by God, the Gospel message of the Greatest Commandment, and the injunction of Paul's Letter to the Galatians (4:4–7)? Paul offers, "'But when the set time had fully come, God sent his Son, born of a woman, born under the law, ⁵to redeem those under the law, that we might receive adoption to Sonship. ⁶Because you are his sons, God sent the Spirit of his Son into our hearts, the Spirit who calls out, 'Abba, Father.'" ⁷So you are no longer a slave, but God's child; and since you are his child, God has made you also an heir." In Galatians 5 (v. 1) Paul asserts, "It was for freedom that Christ has set us free." The clear premise advanced by many readings of the New Testament at the time of slavery would be that for a Christian, being bound to God through Christ Jesus brings liberty. The innate desire for freedom from bondage and from oppression of Black African slaves would be enlivened by the Gospel message. Improvement in their literacy and reading skills in tandem with the availability of unedited Holy Bibles fanned the flames of liberation preached by Jesus of Nazareth. Some "slave versions" of the Holy Book were prepared in which such stirring words and images of Christian freedom were excised completely (Noll 2002). Ultimately Christian words of liberation (e.g., John 8:31–36) would empower a fusion of Black spirituality, culture, and courage to counter oppression and the losses of liberty, dignity, and identity. To the ears of the enslaved, selective parsing of words of obedience and of earning the promise of a heavenly reward through suffering in the world, absent the love and freedom of which Jesus speaks, would reflect only upon Christian words, but not upon Christian deeds of slavers in their world of a nascent racist America.

Biblical Injunction and the "Stranger"

Considering the world of the 17th century, few visitors to the shores of North America would appear more like "strangers" than the Black Africans. We would be remiss to overlook the Holy Bible's injunctions of concern for the "immigrant" stranger. The earliest and most direct codes concerning the status of the stranger (i.e., foreigner, migrant, alien, *ger*) are found in the books of Exodus and Deuteronomy of the Hebrew Bible (Hepner 2010; Awabdy 2014). Clearly there is a differentiation between the stranger, who passes through or resides for some time in the community, and a slave in the Ancient Near Eastern context. We have pointed out the application of Noah's Curse as an often used and early justification of the institution of American slavery (Haynes 2007). Yet, it is clear from readings of the Hebrew Bible that outsiders, no matter as either stranger or slave, receive blessings from God designed to protect them. Exodus 23:9 reads, "⁹Do not oppress a foreigner; you yourselves know how it feels to be foreigners, because you were foreigners in Egypt." This biblical warrant extends the Covenant Code (i.e., the second law given to Moses by God at Mount Sinai, Exo 20:22–23 and 21:1–22), protections, and responsibilities to all foreigners. For the true stranger, as would have been the case for the widow and for the orphan, the absence of the traditional family unit makes each one vulnerable. God addressed their acute vulnerabilities. Equally clear, the stranger would be expected to share in meals, ritual celebrations, and holy worship. The newcomer would participate, as any Israelite, in community-based religious obligations (Deut. 14:29, 16:14). By Mosaic Law, the community harvesting also must intentionally overlook some of the harvest, enabling the time-honored grace of gleaning of the fields and vineyards by vulnerable groups, including the foreigner. For the churched, devout Christians of the 17th and 18th century in America, the presence of the Black African, as slave or freeman, created a moral dilemma. God sought to protect the vulnerable foreigner, granting rights and responsibilities that included being "in community" with those with whom they reside. In the 21st century, historical-critical reading of the Hebrew Bible has lifted up numerous counter readings of the Bible that effectively push back against Noah's curse as a moral justification for slavery (Haynes 2007). Yet even today, immigrant populations to the U.S. often are cast as "foreign" and "criminal," subject to incarceration, and thereby existing as little more than modern day slaves.

Reading from the book of the prophet Isaiah, Jesus provoked his rejection at the synagogue of his hometown of Nazareth in the very launch of his earthly ministry. In Jesus' own words (according to the Gospel of Luke, Chapter 4) echoing those of Isaiah 61:1, "Jesus said, [18]'The Spirit of the Lord is on me, because he has anointed me to proclaim good news to the poor. He has sent me to proclaim freedom for the prisoners and recovery of sight for the blind, to set the oppressed free, [19]to proclaim the year of the Lord's favor.'" Freeing the oppressed may raise up the notion that all are oppressed by their individual sins. The Good News of the Gospel proclaimed by Jesus was that through forgiveness and the love of God, all penitent sinners are released from the bondage of sin. In quoting Isaiah and examining the socio-economic conditions of those looking from the underside, Jesus shines a particularly harsh light upon human bondage. The institution of subjecting humans to bondage was immoral, becoming a core target of social justice and activism. In the Apostle Paul's most theologically developed Epistle to the Romans, the universal nature of God's liberation is cast in sharp contrast to the moral decay of human bondage (Rom 8:20–21). In Romans 8 Paul informs us, "[20]For the creation was subjected to frustration, not by its own choice, but by the will of the one who subjected it, in hope [21]that the creation itself will be liberated from its bondage to decay and brought into the freedom and glory of the children of God." Bondage to sin, like the practice of slavery, reflects moral decay, a decay that can be extinguished only by embracing the message of the Good News!

Christian impulses of liberation and freedom, not shared with inclusivity by 17th century colonists, ultimately would provoke American Black slaves to resist the tyranny of slavery and to demand freedom in a long-term corporate effort. The 1739 armed insurrection against the White ruling power, called the "Stono Rebellion" in South Carolina, was led by a literate Christian slave named "Jemmy" (Wood 1974). With loss of life on both sides, the militia effectively suppressed the rebellion by Blacks. Slaves not killed in the battle were later executed or sold to the West Indies. Such overly zealous reactions to the fear of armed rebellions by slaves were not confined to the South. New York City, plagued by suspicious fires and eager to find a scapegoat to assuage the fears of the city dwellers, rounded up 200 slaves and accused them of a conspiracy and of setting the fires. The New York Conspiracy Trials held in 1741 resulted in the execution of seventeen New Yorkers (Horsmanden and Zabin 2004). The sentencing included death by burning at the stake (leveled at thirteen Black African slaves) and hanging (leveled at four Whites). It is likely that the local histories written by the dominant White ruling class grossly distorted the racial sentiments fueling this massacre. The deeply felt yearning for liberation inspired in slaves by biblical texts aimed at seeking justice and freedom for those shackled in human bondage would be met with violence and even death of these "strangers," mostly at the hands of "Christian" White people.

In the 17th and 18th century, the sharp dichotomy between interpretation of the biblical warrants employed to justify rather than vilify the slavery of Black Africans (as well as the harsh mistreatment of freeman "strangers") resulted in the emergence of houses of Christian worship largely segregated by race. The legacy of divergent biblical interpretations about slavery and covert racism against the Black stranger by the dominant White ruling class persists into the 21st century. The practice of segregation continues in Christian churches long after the end of the American Civil War, Reconstruction, and the success of the Civil Rights and Voting Rights movements of the 1960s. Although the demonstrably greater penetration of Black Americans in local, State and Federal politics is cause for celebration, the greater specter of continuing racism in the U.S. remains in 2020. The churching of America appears to reveal much about the true legacy of fear and trepidation of the dominant White ruling class in response to the "rising tide" that also lifts the boat of African Americans in society. Demands for social justice for Blacks continue to fuel racism and White nationalism in America. The Southern Poverty Law Center tracks the emergence of hate groups across America over time. Racist White Nationalism and White Supremacy hate groups are on the rise. Blacks, people of color, and many Whites in the U.S. rightly heralded the enactment of the Civil Rights and Voting Rights Federal legislation as well as the election of Barrack Obama as U.S. President as clearly reflecting "success" and racial progress. Yet, the persistence of overt and covert racism in America continues, even today within our houses of worship!

Waves Crashing Upon Black Personhood

An exhaustive history of the violence, oppression, exploitation and toxicity of White racism is beyond the scope of our efforts to probe the "original sin" perpetrated in the U.S. throughout its history against Africans, African Americans, and their descendants. Slavery became a long-lived institution of power and control by the dominant White ruling class (Paquette and Smith 2016). The institution of slavery in North America commenced in 1619. Unrelenting measures aimed at exacting power and control over Black lives and bodies occurred like waves crashing upon the shore. Relentless, no two alike, but fueled by the same racist impulses, these waves demonized African and African American slaves and their descendants. The enslaved and eventually freed witnessed the Civil War (1861–1865), the Emancipation Proclamation (1862), the Reconstruction Era (1863–1877), attempts at reconciliation and peace-making (1865), the Black Codes (1865, 1866) and Jim Crow laws offering up policies of harsh segregation (late 19th and early 20th century, up until 1965). In a landmark decision of civil rights, the U.S. Supreme Court declared segregation of public schools to be unconstitutional (*Brown v.*

Board of Education 1954). The success of the Civil Rights Movement culminated in the Civil Right Act of 1964 and the Voting Rights Act of 1965 aimed to extinguish forms of endemic, institutional and functional discrimination. Pushback against such progress in civil rights continues today as the lasting legacy of racism perpetuated by the dominant White ruling class in America.

One effort cut short by the silencing of the prophetic voice of the Rev. Dr. Martin Luther King Jr. following his assassination in 1968 was the Poor People's Campaign. This grass roots campaign sought to raise public awareness to the often minimalized, oppressive economic conditions endured by poor people (especially Black Americans) over centuries (Baptist 2014). Poverty remains endemic in America today, that is, 30–40 million people live below the Federal poverty level (Laurent and Wilson 2018). In his 1967 address "Beyond Vietnam" delivered at The Riverside Church in the City of New York, Dr. King illuminated the toxic linkage between hegemonic, ill-advised and expensive wars waged by America and the absence of economic opportunity for poor peoples in the U.S. Following King's assassination, Ralph Abernathy and the Southern Christian Leadership Conference (SCLC) sought to leverage momentum of the Poor People's Campaign from the earlier nascent War on Poverty launched in 1964 by President Lyndon Johnson (1908–1973). Having been trained at Union Theological Seminary in the City of New York, I welcomed the opportunity to learn about the revival of Dr. King's Poor People's Campaign. The seminary spearheaded a National Call for a Moral Revival as the core to advance the Poor People's Campaign redux. Fellow Union aluma, Rev. Liz Theoharis, organized this effort as a seminary student. The effort was fortified by the energy of the Rev. William J. Barber II (b. 1963), a prominent Protestant minister and social justice activist who co-leads this movement and Repairers of the Breach (Barber and Wilson-Hartgrove 2016).

The waves crashing against the oppressed masses of Blacks and other peoples of color in America did not cease magically in the mid-1960s. Rather, the waves persisted in the aftermath of radical racial tensions and riots that overlapped and provided violent blowback to social justice movements. The U.S. criminal justice system would contribute to further waves of oppression aimed at the "least of us." Racist politics were fueled by toxic White racism and resentment aimed at countering political "wins" of Black Americans. Prospects of the underprivileged victims of structural oppression gaining full personhood and guaranteed human rights threatened the status quo of the White ruling class. Advances in civil and voting rights would prop up flagging personhood of the oppressed, assaulted for 400+ years in America. Full personhood, especially the most basic right, that is, the right not to be killed, would remain out of reach. The so-called criminal "justice" system in America had never been designed to promote the peace and well-being of people of color and minorities. It was aimed directly at promoting and protecting the liberty, wealth, power and lives of the White ruling class. The history of America's two original sins, one against the indigenous Native Americans and the other against African slaves and their descendants, involved the killing of millions of people of color. The harsh subjugation and oppression of millions of Americans extends from the earliest days of the European exploitation of North America and continues well into the 21st century. The horror of extra-judicial lynching of predominantly African American men in the South, of Latinos in California of the Old West, as well as of Native Americans and Asian Americans, including some women, is but another example of "crimes against humanity" perpetrated by White nationalist fervor within the U.S. and against its citizenry (Cone 2011; Bohm and Lee 2018). That the criminal justice system would become the flag bearer for oppression and White nationalism rather than for protection of the people of color in the U.S. was both awful and yet not unexpected.

In the aftermath and loss of lives of ongoing 1967 "race riots" in Detroit and earlier elsewhere (e.g., Los Angeles, Chicago, Newark), President Lyndon Johnson established the Kerner Commission to investigate the root causes of the civil strife (Vargus, Indiana University Bureau of Correspondence Study and Indiana University Bureau of Public Discussion 1968). Justifiably, the final report of the commission had harsh words for state and federal government highlighted failures to provide adequate housing, education, and employment opportunity programs for people of color steeped in abject poverty. The media was pilloried in the 1968 final report of the Kerner Commission entitled, *The Report of the National Advisory Commission on Civil Disorders.* The Commission declared, "The press has too long basked in a white world looking out of it, if at all, with white men's eyes and white perspective." In retrospect, the final report failed at focusing public attention on the root causes of the poverty and disadvantage of Black people in America, culminating in 400+ years of oppression. Rather it catalyzed further victimization of the oppressed! The first assault on the oppressed would be spuriously termed a "war on crime" (Stevenson 2014; White 2019). Later, a second assault would be declared as a "war on drugs" (Alexander 2010; Forman 2017). Both efforts seeking to further victimize the poor were designed simply to placate the anxiety of the dominant White ruling classes. The race riots and public discord of the late 1960s had destabilized and offended the sensitivities of the White ruling class. Such domestic "wars" would prove to be anathema to the compelling argument advanced by Dr. King and made infamous to the White folks in his candid "Beyond Vietnam" speech. The military adventures engaged by the U.S. and called to public attention by "Beyond Vietnam" would provoke large, ineffective para-military and *in country* policing expenditures by the federal government aimed largely at the very people who were the victims of poverty. What they needed most of all was better housing, improved education, employment opportunities, and effective social services! And just as night follows day, the wars on domestic crime and on drugs sought most of all to display actions that would be most welcomed by the White ruling class as "tough on crime." Tough on crime propelled the criminal justice system towards harsher and longer sentences, even for lesser crimes (Alexander 2010; Stevenson 2014; Forman 2017).

The once more compassionate perspective, that is, that drug abuse was a medical, not criminal, problem was promptly discarded in the 1970s. Governor Nelson Rockefeller introduced drug laws to New York created intentionally to be the "toughest" laws of its kind in the U.S. The "Rockefeller" drug laws became a paradigm and the preferred model for toughening up the criminal justice system across the U.S. Ostensibly the Rockefeller drug laws constituted one launch of what would be many "new Jim Crow" laws (Alexander 2010; Foremen 2017). These laws, aimed at longer sentences, succeeded in increasing the population of the incarcerated, a group of people predominantly of color (Alexander 2010; Wallis 2016). The Controlled Substance Act (1971) statute in the "war on drugs" enacted under President Richard Nixon (1913–1994) led to further criminalization of drugs other than cocaine and heroin, including suspected "gateway" drugs opening a straight path to drug abuse and addiction. The NAACP reported that from 1980–2015, incarceration of Americans increased from 0.5 to >2.2 million! African Americans were incarcerated at more than five times the rate of Whites (Alexander 2010). Although the use of illicit drugs shows no racial disparity, African Americans continue to be imprisoned on drug charges at a rate many folds greater than that of Whites. Poverty, lack of education, lack of employment opportunity, and absence of effective social services remain the root causes of much Black suffering as well as of incarceration of Black bodies at the hands of the criminal justice system (Childs 2015; Forman 2017).

Shamefully, hundreds of billions of dollars have been expended to fund increased criminalization of drug use and an enhanced criminal justice system. Both outcomes largely are viewed as robust expenditures fueling failed policies (Angeulov and McCarthy 2018). The *Terry v. Ohio* U. S. Supreme Court ruling of 1968 allowed police the ability to stop and frisk a citizen based upon "reasonable suspicion" that a crime had been committed. From the late 1960s and onward implementation of so-called "stop-and-frisk" programs by police emerged in America, popularized by Mayor Michael Bloomberg (b. 1942) in New York City. In the "stop-and-frisk" efforts, police would temporarily detain, question, and often search civilians in an effort to seize weapons and contraband without the same probable cause historically employed heretofore. Initially, White and Black politicians alike welcomed virtually all "get tough on crime" programs offered up by the criminal justice system (Forman 2017). The public, especially in high-crime metropolitan neighborhoods, were hopeful that aggressive "stop-and-frisk" sweeps in cities would result in a precipitous decline in crime and drug abuse. Yet time revealed that the heart of such programs was "racial profiling." In 2017 New York City, 90% of those people subjected to "stop-and-frisk" were African Americans or Latinos, between 14–24 years of age. More than 70% of the thousands stopped and detained later would be declared innocent of the suspected charges. To what extent these harsh procedures aimed largely at young men of color were effective as deterrents of crime and drug abuse is not settled. The legal basis for such stops versus the violation of people's rights through racial profiling led to the eventual abandonment of "stop-and-frisk" policies in New York City. Reversal of such harsh policies, decriminalization of the use of drugs such as marijuana, and the consequent decline in the numbers of people incarcerated in the U.S. occurred under the Obama administration. In more recent years, under the Trump administration, there has been aggressive movement of the criminal justice system to once again get "tough on crime," a tried and tested panacea at least for White ruling class anxiety fueled by the very racism it chose to overlook (Angeulov and McCarthy 2018). Remarkably, the systemic and sustained trauma absorbed by African Americans in their lives in the U.S. has been consistently met with robust, but largely peaceful, Black resistance. Black Americans likewise continue to demonstrate astonishing resilience of spirit and a robustness of character. The psychology of the persistent racism in the U.S. that confronts Black Americans everyday requires further interrogation.

Psychology of Racism in America: An Exilic Existence

Racism in America has a long and far reaching history. The hypothesis that the assault on personhood today in the United States is a first derivative of the "original sins" of America's founding finds traction in the history of the psychology of racism in America. In particular, racism aimed at African Americans has been interrogated by many who lifted up the challenges to Black people living under a dominant White ruling class. As discussed, early prejudice and discrimination of Black people in America historically was rooted in the Bible. Genesis texts have been distorted to provide two false pillars of racialized America, that is, dominion theology (Gen 1:26–28) and the Curse of Ham (Gen 9:20–27). Perpetuated by dominant White ruling classes over millennia, these often cited biblical pericopes are employed as warrants enabling exploitation of marginalized peoples. Historically the targets are people of color and foreign origin, declared inferior or even subhuman. Noted author W.E.B. Du Bois espoused the complexity of the psychology of racialized oppression and devaluation experienced by Blacks in a society dominated by White patriarchy. His 1903 reflection, *The Souls of*

Black Folks, proved to be a landmark, seminal writing in the nascent field of sociology (Du Bois 1903). To social philosophy Du Bois ascribed a "double-consciousness" or a "twoness" of inner being experienced by Black people. According to his observations, Blacks are precluded from true self-consciousness. Consequently they are forced to rely upon the eyes of the "other", that is, a dominant White ruling class, to enable formation of images of Black self. Du Bois' development of a concept of double-consciousness for Black American echoed prominently an earlier work of G. H. F. Hegel (1770–1831) entitled *Phenomenology of Spirit (Hegel and Williams 2007)*. Hegel's work dealt with an analogous dialectic of humans caught between their material being and an ineffable transcendence of God (Adell 1994). Du Bois described such "twoness" as a dialectic operating between two souls, one Negro and the other "American." Each acts striving mightily towards establishing *détente* between two forces that can tear apart the soul. There can be no healthy "coming-into-being" for a soul taut with tensions of devaluation and ambiguous personhood. The need for self-identity and personhood as a Negro/Black person is essential for survival in an unsympathetic society. Du Bois, in his classic essay "The Souls of White Folk" (Du Bois 2016) proffered, "racial injustice originates with the godlike power of whiteness to possess the earth exclusively." Whether or not invocated as biblical warrant, Du Bois sensed a world for Black folk only seen through White dominion. Blacks are reduced to "chattel" labeling them as "things," but not people, absent personhood. For centuries, American politics of Whiteness and White dominion have preyed upon economic insecurities of White that were real (Allen 2012; Fletcher 2018), but labeled "anti-Black racism." The fictional work *Invisible Man* by Ralph Ellison (1913–1994) attempts to interrogate the complexity of Black life in America through tragic-comedy. The creative narrative dwells in a 20th century world of an America still in the toxic throws of deep Jim Crow racism. More than a century has past since Du Bois articulated the concept of "double-consciousness." The Jim Crow era as well as its newest edition (i.e., termed the "new" Jim Crow) would emerge and reinvigorate the "twoness" felt by Black Americans as they navigate in the 21st century within a racist landscape still dominated by a White ruling class (Gooding-Williams 2009; Alexander 2010).

The psychology of racism interrogated largely within the context of Black Americans offers insights into the destructive forces unleashed by the dominant White ruling class upon the Black psyche. The works of Frederick Douglass, Martin Luther King Jr., Malcolm X, Cornel West, James Cone, Ibram Kendi, and Ta-Nehisi Coates, to name but the headliners, helped to detail these destructive forces that distorted the Black experience in contemporary America, alluded to earlier. The exploitation and devaluation of Black personhood reflects objectification by the dominant White ruling class. Cornel West, in *Race Matters* (West 1993), highlighted that objectification and devaluation yields only toxic "disintegrated selves" for Blacks. Absent true self-consciousness building, Black Americans turned to nihilism, which Cornel West insightfully termed a "disease of the soul." Nihilism precludes any real self-discernment and identity formation. Nihilism suffocates the self, placing it outside the reach of tacit awareness and the necessary grasping of one's self and self-worth. The trauma of being unable to discern, receive, and interrogate one's self renders an individual defenseless, bereft of the tools necessary for mending one's psyche. Contrary to many leaders of the civil rights movement in America, Malcolm X presciently argued against one alternative, "white assimilation," as a path to Black identity and dignity (Cone 1991; Marable 2011; Harris 2013; Kendi 2016). Absent the tools necessary for healthy self-discernment, objectified and devalued, Blacks in racialized America remained shackled to a default program characterized by varied degrees of self-hatred and profound feelings of "otherness." The constant threat of police violence and a criminal justice system operating as an extension of the White ruling class likewise contributed to a fearfulness for black bodies. Few contemporary works capture the dimensions of fearfulness encountered by black people, parents and children, as does Ta-Nehisi Coates autobiographical personal letter to his adolescent son (Coates 2015).

The seeds of "otherness," intergenerational nihilism and anxiety included an additional trauma, unique for Black Americans. This element deserves consideration as it differentiates the trauma endured by the Africans, African Americans, and their descendants from those of the indigenous Native Americans. This is the issue of not "being in the land." The indigenous Native Americans were in the land of the Americas for 300 centuries before European settlers arrived. Even today, indigenous Native Americans remain deeply connected to their sacred ancestral lands spread throughout the U.S. The major driving force for the colonist settlers was access to land, a land that they could call their "own," by whatever means necessary. Earlier we discussed the genocide, displacement, dispossession and cultural annihilation that enabled the confiscation of ancestral lands from Native Americans by White Christian European interlopers. But still, for the Native Americans, there remains this unbreakable linkage to the land, reaffirmed by their continued presence in the same land to this day. For Blacks in America *no* such ancestral claim to the land existed in the U.S. Africans, African Americans and their descendants were confronted with this other unavoidable toxic obstacle, that is, the traumatic awareness that their existence had no anchor to the land in which they dwelled. No Doctrine of Discovery would be developed for those brought by slavery to this New World. For Black Americans, embedded in their foundational narrative, theirs was an "exilic" existence.

A deep-seated trauma of exile and living the exilic existence may be manifest for slaves, their descendants as well as modern day immigrants. A diaspora of biblical proportions may be forced upon exilic peoples, even migrants who have no other viable option. Waves of refugees, enduring horrific passage both to escape, yet often only to re-encounter violence, death, and discrimination, crashed upon the shores of America and the entire globe. This violence, loss and death seem almost routine in the 21st century world. The situation of Black Americans differs. Even after 400 years in America, an empathetic and therapeutic path to self-awareness, identity, and dignity is sadly anemic for many Black Americans. Exilic peoples, Africans and African Americans alike, suffer from a base lack of certainty, familiar rules, traditions, and faces. Seldom does a dominant ruling class welcome the exilic "other." Rather, the ruling class most readily holds the exile at a safe distance (sometimes incarcerated in cages), fearful of the strange exiles that they reflexively label simply as "other." In contrast, a community in moral solidarity includes the exilic strangers. Such empathic welcoming and inclusion receives and validates the traumatic narratives of the exilic stranger. Empathetic engagement is the necessary first step on a path to healing the traumatized "other." For Black Americans, few resources were available and allocated to help them in this process of healing their wounds of exilic trauma. It is no coincidence that Black Americans often have identified with and acculturated the exilic narrative of the Jews forced to Babylonian exile and the diaspora. Black American found real hope and inspiration in the post-exilic narratives in the Bible of a Messiah who "walks with them in their suffering."

Absent healthy character formation in their exilic existence, some Black Americans suffer the trauma of objectification, eventual self-loathing and lost personhood. These default forces often become externalized, reinforced in a racialized criminal justice system (Alexander 2010; Stevenson 2014; Kendi 2016; Forman 2017). Through favoring social indifference and malignant projections, the White ruling class precluded health formation of self-image by the modern day "remnant" of a displaced exilic Black people. The society, dominating their very lives, remains White, patriarchal and persistently racist. This process, steeped in nihilism, would seem an insurmountable obstacle to recapturing full personhood, dignity, and rights afforded to peoples in this land for more than 400 years. Remarkably, there continues to be a robust resistance within the Black soul, capable of pushing back in large and small everyday ways against the tides of racism that characterize the exilic lives of Black Americans in the United States. Black activists, Gospel music, theology in search of ameliorating Black suffering, Black prophetic voices, and indefatigable persistence to demand their God-given human rights has enabled African Americans to overcome their sense of exile, but not yet to fully flourish while in the shackles of structural oppression endemic in the U.S.

Resistance, Resilience, and Black Theology of Liberation

The dimensions of the trauma endured by Africans and African Americans and their descendants in the U.S. are horrific and breathtaking. Slavery, subjugation, and denial of personhood continue as themes of oppression that scar the very soma and psyche of Black people in America. The objectification, extrajudicial lynching and killing, dehumanization, and denial of the rights of full personhood never seem to stop, only to "pause" now and again. I was in training at Union when the first Black American president, Barack Obama, was elected. Seminarians displayed an air of jubilation and celebration as they reflected on what was hoped to be "social justice in the making," a turning point for people of color in America. Yet in the midst of such joy there emerged an air of caution. Professor James H. Cone, founder of black liberation theology and appointed the Bill and Judith Moyers Distinguished Professor of Systematic Theology at Union, paused and wagged his finger at us saying, "with regard to Black people in America, don't read too much into the outcome of this election!" Growing up in the South, Cone as a boy had witnessed the aftermath of a lynching in his hometown in Arkansas (Cone 2011). Cone knew all too well that the election of a Black man as president was a "pause," not a permanent "step function" upwards towards equality for all people of color in the U.S. (Cone 2018). In his signature course entitled, "Martin & Malcolm: A Dream or a Nightmare," Cone highlighted and contrasted the lives, writings, and views of Martin Luther King Jr. and Malcolm X. The former viewed America as an unfulfilled dream, while the latter viewed American society as a nightmare for Black people. Based upon Cone's best-selling book, *Martin & Malcolm & America: A Dream or a Nightmare* (Cone 1991), the course made use of scenes and interviews from the Civil Rights era from a powerful documentary television series "Eyes on the Prize" (DeVinney et al. 1986). The horrific graphic details of the inhumanity and trauma endured by everyday Black people in the U.S. in that era were largely unknown to most twenty-something seminary students as well as to me. The shock, horror, and sadness catalyzed by the viewings often resulted in fundamental questions around Black personhood. How did Black people survive, endure, and preserve their identities and personhood in the face of centuries of such hostility, violence, indifference, and racism? Attentive viewing of the documentary, "Eyes on the Prize," had a profound effect on all of Cone's students. The reliable witness of little-viewed news footage from the Civil Rights era depicted brazen and horrific racism and brought sighs and tears to the audience.

One essential element to confronting trauma for the Black person in America has been a robust resistance. Contrary to the pro-slavery writings that sought to infantilize and dehumanize the African American slaves, the history of slavery in America is replete with slave rebellions (Aptheker 1983;

Higginson 1998; Walters 2015)! As introduced earlier, the Stono Rebellion in 1739, the New York City Conspiracy of 1741, and Nat Turner's Rebellion of 1831 were but a few of more than thirty rebellions and uprisings by Black Americans. Historians disagree on the precise number of revolts and conspiracies that were fueled by slave resistance, but clearly the number was hundreds. Perhaps less easy to document was the day-to-day resistance of African Americans designed to jab a stick in the spokes of American slavery at the homestead and plantation. Work stoppages, sabotage, foot-dragging, and malingering are powerful tools of resistance and also help the personhood-of-self flourish in the face of oppression. Cotton was "king" throughout industrialized America (Baptist 2014). Purposefully putting the brakes on commerce was an effective tool of resistance, but not without consequences (Baptist 2014). One of the best-known anti-slavery responses was the Underground Railroad established in early 19th century. This network of abolitionist-supported safe houses and routes evolved to help African American slaves to escape to free states and Canadian provinces in search of freedom (Bordewich 2005; Still and Finseth 2007). Born into slavery, Harriet Tubman became a political activist set on rescuing other slaves and their families by making good use of the Underground Railroad (Clinton 2004). The effect of stories of the successes of Harriet Tubman and other abolitionists in striking a blow for freedom and against slavery helped to fortify Black resistance (Sawyer 2010).

In the 1960s and 1970s, the Black Power Movement emerged into the mainstream of American politics (Van Deburg 1992). Malcolm X vigorously advocated for black independence, black pride, and robust black masculinity (Cone 1969, 1991; Marable 2011). Replete with a revolutionary theme of increased racial pride, empowerment aimed at economic equality, and promoting distinctly African American culture and politics, Black Power was unique. Black Power highlighted not the political achievements of the Civil Rights Movement, but rather the movement's failures to adequately address and confront the raw racism of the White ruling class. Daily, racism was degrading the very lives of Black people throughout America (Joseph 2006)! The Student Nonviolent Coordinating Committee (SNCC) that played such a pivotal role in the Civil Rights Movement emerged as a source of many spokespeople for Black Power, for example, Stokely Carmichael, a.k.a. Kwame Ture and H. "Rap" Brown (Carmichael et al. 1987; Bell 2014). Black public intellectuals like Robert F. Williams (Williams and Schleifer 1973; Tyson, Boehm, and Lewis 2001) and Malcolm X (X 1964; X 1966) reframed the racist oppression of Black people. The Black Panther Party was an activist group with deep philosophical beliefs of the freedom of Black people, nationally and globally (Jones 1998; Bloom and Martin 2013). Although suffering from declining popularity, the Black Power movement would be followed by other activist groups, including the Black Radical

Congress, Black Riders Liberation Party, and the most contemporary Black Lives Matters movement, discussed earlier. Promoting Black identity and resisting the toxic legacy inflicted upon Black bodies by White racism would become a two-pronged core sustaining Black resistance in America.

Resilience also is essential to preservation of identity, personhood, and culture in the crucible of traumatic oppression (Johnson 2015). Resilience is the capacity to preserve oneself in the face of challenges, stress, trauma, and adversity (Greitens 2015). In the absence of such resilience, trauma often leads to debilitating and sometime fatal outcomes, like PTSD, self-loathing, and suicide. Resilience results from basic self-defense mechanisms aimed at avoiding, defusing, disarming, reframing, and coping with harsh adversity. These skills are learned behaviors. For African Americans, resilience in the face endemic daily racism is acquired intergenerationally. In my experience, Black elders, matriarchs and patriarchs alike, display extraordinary resilience, empathy, and love to all. The elders offer a model to youth, guiding them as they journey through the crucible of racism in America in their time. Stories of elders around Black resilience forged in the face of harsh adversity are intergenerational, that is, extending to children, to grandchildren, and sometimes to great grandchildren, becoming organic to their very being.

The character of such Black resilience has several features of note. Resilience offers a positive outlook engrained in the Black perspective. It displays hopefulness and optimism in the face of disappointment and disillusion that have persisted, even over many generations. Rather than giving into hopelessness and depression, Black resistance and resilience promotes a "cognitive reframing" of the adversary as well as the adversity. This reframing of adversity provides an invaluable tool with which to better understand the meaning of the challenge. Like Victor Frankl's approach to finding meaning in one's life (Frankl 1946), African Americans sought not merely to react to adversity, but rather to discern what is the meaning behind the assault. Everyday racism is common to Black people in the U.S. Insecurities promoted by toxic White resentment find subtle and persistent reinforcement in everyday life. Reframing the "racism-du-jour," approaching adversity with hopefulness, overcoming disillusionment about the slow pace of progress against racism are key strategies shared by parents and grandparents with their children. The details of the insults may vary over time, but the gut reaction to racist insults and acts still requires reframing and renewed hopefulness that such obstacles can be understood and thereby overcome.

Coping skills are a mainstay for avoiding everyday trauma of being Black (or of color) in America. Humans have evolved many coping strategies with which to manage anxiety, stress, and traumatic situations (Hanson and Hanson 2018). The situation for the African American slaves and their descendants is not, however, generic. One major obstacle is the persistence of racism in America. When trauma becomes chronic and long-standing, the most common response is despair (Case and Deaton 2020). The long history of racism encourages its victims to accept that its assault on their personhood is unlikely to be resolved any time soon. Many defense mechanisms that operate well in acute, short-term trauma, such as the loss of a loved one, cannot be engaged in a predicament in which the trauma seems endless. Although releasing pent-up emotions is cathartic for the short-term management of trauma, for management of a long-standing trauma, like the racist legacy of slavery, it adds a positive, but limited capacity to coping. Distracting oneself from the adversity also can be more cathartic in the short, rather than the long-term. The knowledge of being embedded in a thoroughgoing institution of oppression and lost personhood requires more robust tools. In the past, active coping skills for the African American slave would include managing chronic hostile feelings aimed at the slaver.

Day-to-day resistance offers a simple but therapeutic tool. Meditation and exercise for the enslaved was possible at work, which typically was hard labor over long hours. Spiritual songs reflecting the anguish of intergenerational oppression became a voice of resistance for the oppressed. Such songs of pathos would not transform the heart of the slaver, but did decant a hopelessness that could not go unchallenged by the victims. Singing spirituals became a powerful pro-social tool aimed at maintaining and building community. Within all communities elders emerged who could offer advice on exercising self-control and finding meaning in life, especially when spirits were low. The Black church remained for many the true "beloved community" for Africans, African American, and their descendants (Cone 1989; Wilmore 1998). The Black church arose in reaction to the segregated Christian churches built by the White ruling class (Cone 1970; Wilmore 1998). For Blacks in America their church became the dominant source of resistance and resilience for African Americans (Cone 1989). Each active coping mechanism employed in the Black community was aimed at understanding and transforming the stressor, deflecting its path, and diminishing attention away from it. Emotion-focused coping skills empowered those who, as slaves or their descendants, could no longer tolerate their lack of power and control. It was an antidote to their oppressed lives that they found impossible to simply "live into." These active coping skills emerged and were tested in real time. To the extent to which the skills provided some relief to cope with the daily trauma, they would be adopted, adapted, and sustained going forward in the Black community.

Negative coping skills emerge from hopelessness and are acquired passively. Maladaptive responses include avoidance of the trauma, that is, talking oneself out of the current intolerable reality. Passive tools of coping are most often detrimental. Included in the repertoire of passive tools is abuse of alcohol and drugs, as well as self-destructive behaviors. The profound suffering of the slave would collide with any effort by Whites to Christianize the

African Americans. Indigenous Native Americans suffering displacement and genocide under dominant White rule had confronted similar efforts to Christianize the "heathens." Both evangelical efforts would provoke a profound theological question. With regard to African slaves and their descendants, the question posed was, what kind of message of hope and justice was there to be found in Christianity? Exodus 21:20–21, the holiness codes of Leviticus and of Deuteronomy in the Old Testament all were interpreted as biblical warrants condoning slavery, extolling submission to dominion by the "master," and in place of justice on earth offering a reward deferred to the afterlife. In 1 Peter (2:18–29) the Christian message offered by the ruling class to their slaves seemed straightforward, that is, all earthly just rewards earned in labor would be found in heaven (Whitford 2009). The extent to which this self-serving rationalization proffered by the slavers had resonance with their slaves is hard to gauge. Criticism has been leveled at the Black church for its subordination of earlier burning zeal for freedom subsumed by giving in to the trappings offered by the White ruling class (Cone 1989). The thick dialectic of suffering by enslaved and oppressed Black bodies viewed in the light of the Cross called again the same question, what kind of message of hope and justice was there to be found in Christianity? Belief in the power of redemption through Jesus Christ would be cast as a new coping tool. The answer to this fundamental, nagging theological question would be formulation of a Black "theology of liberation."

The power of the logic of a Black theology of liberation for America, formulated by James Cone, is irrefutable (Cone 1970). Simply put, there exist two dipoles in the dialectic of the Black theology of liberation: the oppressed; and the oppressors. For Cone, the oppressed in America are the African Americans slaves and their descendants, constituting a mass of people subjugated, dehumanized, and marginalized for more than 400 years. The suffering of the oppressed includes lost personhood, deprivation of basic human rights, lack of education and economic opportunities, and chronic hopelessness cast around a future bereft of freedom and dignity. The other dipole represents the oppressors in America. The oppressors declare dominion over objectified Black bodies, secure power and control over Black people by racist acts, and seek to insure their continued dominance by ruthless and violent hegemony. The reach of the oppressors in America extends beyond Blacks to all people of color, women, and marginalized people labeled as "other." Placed in oppositional conversation, the theologically question distills to, what is the position of God in the dialectic of privileged *versus* oppressed? Is there but one blessing of Almighty God solely for the privileged? Theologians assume the role of the inquisitor, asking further, on whose behalf will God act in this world of asymmetric wealth, control, and power?

"On whose 'side' should the blessing of God rest?" is both an overarching question as well as the destination for deep discernment. Jesus, I offer, is the compass for this journey. Rather than reference the Holiness Codes that canonized slavery in the Ancient Near East, Jesus set his face to Jerusalem and lifted up the core theme of the Hebrew Bible, that is, freedom! The God of Moses, Isaac, and Jacob freed the ancient Hebrews from slavery by Egyptian rulers. The Pharaohs symbolized the privileged ruling class, exercising unparalleled power and control in this world. In so acting against the interests of Egyptian slavers and for the Hebrew slaves, Cone declares that God is revealed as the "God of the Oppressed" (Cone 1975, 1997, 2010). God made flesh and dwelling among us is Jesus of Nazareth, who suffers death on a cross to liberate people from bondage and suffering (Cone 1997, 2010). Jesus is the compass, pointing to the Way, the Light, and freedom for the oppressed masses.

Cone's Egypt for Black people is the United States! The oppressed are Black people and people of color all of who suffer under the toxic bondage of "whiteness" (Cone 1989, 1997, 2010; Wallis 2016; Cone and West 2018). African Spirituals that infuse the hymns and anthems of modern Christian churches are replete with the imagery of God's power and authority based in justice. Abrahamic religions and virtually all world religions are based in a theology in which God is the source of justice. Without justice, God could not exist; without God (or Creator), justice cannot exist. It is the asymmetry of wealth, power, and control that generates want, suffering, and oppression. Black theology of liberation follows the theme of freedom as a means to strike down asymmetric power and wealth. Cone's Black theology of liberation flies in the face of the "prosperity gospel," favored especially by some Protestant Evangelical Christians who view financial blessings, power, and well-being as the products of God rewarding their faith (Bowler 2013). Perhaps the prosperity gospel is best viewed as simple "contractual theology" between humans and God (Hinn 2019). In this "contract," one's pledged faith to God is reflected in proportion to the prosperity granted in return by God. Unlike divine grace that is freely and lavishly given by God to all people, wealth and power becomes "coin of the realm" granted in kind by God to the most zealous adherents of the prosperity gospel (Hinn 2019).

Critics of the Black theology of liberation (as well as of other theologies of liberation) view any goal of *redistributive justice* aimed at remediating the suffering of the oppressed and neutralizing both the asymmetric power and control of the oppressors in the world as Marxist in character (Gutiérrez 1973). As noted earlier, if you are on the topside of life, the most important goals often is maintaining the status quo (Gutiérrez and Müller 2015). Black theology views this topside perspective as idolatry of wealth and power, unrelated to the grace of God (Cone 2010). From the underside of life, bereft of full personhood and opportunities, liberation remains the only path to self-empowerment (McMickle 2006). My years as a pastor, chaplain, and professor of ethics have only reaffirmed the power of a theology of liberation, as founded by Gustavo Gutiérrez (Gutiérrez González 1977; Gutiérrez and Müller 2015) and by James H. Cone (Cone 1970; Cone 2018). Black theology of liberation is not only a redemptive road map for people of color suffering horrific oppression in this world, but also, perhaps paradoxically, for the topsider people of privilege who seek to embrace true justice and seek personal redemption. As long as want and oppression remain a luxury of those who seek to exploit their power and control upon the marginalized "other," the justice inherent in God will remain out of reach. Only the scourge and legacy of the "original sin" of America will be immanent.

Confronting the Breach: Guilt, Repentance, and Reconciliation

In 21st century America, no assault on personhood is more pervasive than racism, especially that aimed at Black people. Racists assault personhood employing a variety of tools. Personhood of Black Americans is routinely degraded and demeaned in public. The goal of the unrelenting assault is to deny the descendants of African and African American slaves full personhood and the human rights guaranteed under the Constitution and U.S. Bill of Rights. The oppressors continue to highjack local, state, and Federal laws, and judicial decisions that affect where Black people live (or cannot), are educated (or not), express their right to vote (or not), and are employed (or not). In the extreme, the assaults can target a Black person's most basic human right, that is, the right of not being killed (Cone 2011; Cone 2018; Stevenson 2014; Taylor 2016). How do Black people in the U.S. view the racism that they encounter every day? Is it possible to gauge the sum magnitude of these unyielding assaults on personhood, both small and large bore? Historically, Black authors, theologians, politicians, and activists have offered their own testimony, bearing witness to the assaults that they endure. The "double consciousness" described by W.E.B. Du Bois captured the internal conflict of Black people finding themselves forced to look at themselves simultaneously through their own eyes as well as those of their White oppressor (Du Bois 1996). Speeches by Malcolm X sought to raise the self-esteem of Black Americans and to reach back to their African heritage for self-identity (X 1966; Cone 1969, 1991). Malcolm X's voice was quite different from that of Martin Luther King Jr. (Cone 1991). Malcolm focused on the scourge of economic inequality and what I would term "lost personhood." These are but two derivatives of more than three centuries of brutal oppression at the hands of the dominant White ruling class (Terrill 2010). Malcolm X's teachings were considered radical and militant for the times, breaking through an old calculus and nucleating new efforts like the Black Power movement (Cone 1991; Marable 2011). Martin Luther King Jr.'s non-violence black protest movement offered a starkly different but equally compelling response of the Black American to White racism (King and Washington 1991). Both Malcolm and Martin, highly revered for their intellect and dedicated efforts in the Civil Rights era, were complex individuals whose life experiences in White racist America were quite different, often antagonistic, but eventually complementary in the march for Civil Rights (Cone 1991).

The witness of those who shaped the Civil Rights movement in America is a powerful source of testimony. But what of the "average" people in America, what were their views on structural oppression and racism? Watching the 14-hour epic documentary of Harry Hampton's "Eyes of the Prize" left me with two new insights. First for me was an "eyes-wide-open" broadened aperture of the Civil Rights movement in America. The movement was composed of countless hundreds of thousands of average Americans, Black and White, who supported, marched, and suffered to advance the progress of Civil Rights. Best known were the luminaries who led the various groups (NAACP, SCLC, SNCC and CORE) that eventually congealed into the movement. Often overlooked, however, were the masses of everyday Americans fed up with racial inequality and chronic White patriarchal hegemony. By the thousands, these civil rights activists constituted the life's blood of the many protests and marches. Second is an appreciation for the contextual character of racism lifted up in the Civil Rights era. The suffering of Blacks in the Deep South, in the Watts district of Los Angeles, in the Hough district of Cleveland, and in major cities such as Chicago and Detroit was not uniform. Although the discrimination, marginalization, and indifference of the oppressors to the plight of Blacks across America were common, the context of the racism was not. Leaders of the Civil Rights movement found it impossible to scale the success in opening lunch counters and public spaces for Blacks in the South to the context of Watts where unemployment, rather than segregation, dominated. Methods proven so useful in attacking racism in Selma Alabama under Mayor Joseph Smitherman proved ineffectual in attempts to outsmart Mayor Richard Daley and the racial context of Chicago's size and complexity.

The Pew Research Center published a report entitled, "Race in America 2019." The expansive report revealed stark, negative views of the public with regard to real racial progress in America. Worrying trends have emerged suggesting that race relations were worsening rather than improving in America. On the average, most people noted that racist language and public displays of racism, if anything, are far more common in 21st century America. More than 50% of Blacks opined that being black hurts their ability to "get ahead," an opinion that is less prevalent for Whites viewing Black progress. Striking are data that reveal 8 in 10 Blacks feel maltreated by police, the criminal justice system, and employment practices. Half of American adults would agree with Black sentiment on this issue. More broadly, more than half of Americans again declare that being Black/Hispanic, poor, or of Muslim faith disadvantages people in society. This research illuminates a core set of American beliefs that recognize well the discrimination, racism, and loss of personhood suffered by Blacks. These outcomes, I offer, are a legacy of the great "original sin" of slavery that pervades society today and constitutes a scourge. Importantly, only 1 in 5 of Blacks declare all/most Whites as prejudiced against Blacks. So it would seem that racism in America is sustained through a fervent but diminishing number of people who avidly support White patriarchal hegemony more like a religion than a political platform.

The higher profile of the chronic injustices served upon Blacks and the degradation of their personhood seems to be gaining traction. Loss of, delay of, or denial of protections and rights afforded by the U. S. Constitution and laws may enliven empathy of 21st century Americans for the plight of lost personhood in Black America! Opposing these trends aimed towards racial progress is the belief of the ruling White class that too much attention is paid to race. Clearly Blacks and other minorities feel issues of race are being overlooked entirely or at least minimized. A common White response to failures in racial progress is that "assimilation" is succeeding, lifting up increased commonalities among Blacks and Whites perceived only by Whites. Many people view this default towards increased assimilation arises mostly from a desire by White Americans to minimize the stark racism assaulting Blacks and people of color. More than 80% of Blacks say America needs to work harder at providing full personhood and equal rights to Blacks. Although legislation is essential, legislating the heart and souls of Americans to rampant racial inequality is a formidable obstacle to achieving a common hope for racial equality and community in 21st century America. Are racial harmony and creation of an inclusive community a "dream," or the product of simple "magical thinking"? Perhaps any progress towards true racial equality will exact a price from the privileged, constituting for some a "reverse oppression" aimed at the White ruling class. This very real phenomenon of the White ruling class sensing and objecting to the tables being turned on them has been labeled "White Fragility" (Brown 2018; DiAngelo 2018).

Disadvantages encountered by Black Americans in the criminal justice system, lack of access to quality education, and poor employment opportunities are pervasive and damaging to the whole of society. Lost in the discussions of the economics of racial oppression and of denial towards full personhood is another pillar of American life in which Black are held back, that is, wealth. Wealth is measured for individuals or for families by their financial "net worth." A 2018 report on systematic inequality in America by The Center for American Progress reveals the dire financial consequences to Black families today who possess only a small fraction of the wealth of White families in America. Much like the 2019 Pew Research Center report on racism, this report also lifts up lesions in education, upward mobility, and employment derivative of maldistribution of wealth suffered by Blacks as well as people of color. Lacking equivalent wealth, Black families do not prosper by access to preferred mortgage markets, tax benefits, and retirement benefits. In 2016, the median wealth of White families was $171,000, whereas that for Black families was $17,600! Focusing only upon the top fifth of income levels, Black families' wealth is $234,500, compared to $785,250 for White families. The Black families with one-tenth of the wealth of their White counterparts still proved far more resistant to the recovery following the 2007/8 Great Recession than families with no wealth. Recovering from the Great Recession and managing many of the same needs but with less wealth shackled Black families, however, to more costly instruments of borrowing, for example, predatory banks as well as "payday lenders" charging an annual rate of interest of 400%!

The Center for American Progress report showed that inequality in wealth for Black Americans is clearly systemic. Today for Black households on par with White families for education, age, marital status and employment income, wealth remains disparate. All other things considered, the wealth of Black households remains only a fraction of their White counterparts. The continuing disparity in family wealth based upon race should dispel from current thinking the probable success of any "simple" solution that does not include redistributive justice. The systemic nature of the asymmetry of wealth in America cannot be overemphasized. Any economic stimulus simply applied to both white and black families equally will only perpetuate and aggravate the wealth gap. Slavery, reconstruction, emancipation, Jim Crow laws, mass incarcerations, and the "new" Jim Crow (Alexander 2010) all exacted a severe blow to Black wealth and future opportunities to "get ahead" (Wallis 2016). Such maldistribution is not confined to wealth, but also to basic elements of personhood, such as freedom from incarceration, access to adequate healthcare, access to suitable affordable housing (Forman 2017), as well as avoidance of chronic diseases like chronic obstructive pulmonary disease (COPD), obesity, and type-2 diabetes mellitus (Barr 2019). The ability of White racism to target Blacks and to create barriers to an inclusive economy provided not only a legacy, but also a blueprint for insuring this long-standing suffering, economic and otherwise, of Black families in America (Baptist 2016; Flynn 2018). Creating *Communio Sanctorum* and a just economy will require strategies that recognize and seek to ameliorate past wrongs that persist in holding back Black families in America (Powell 2012; Baptist 2016). Rectifying asymmetric income *and* wealth will require implementation of thoughtful and insightful solutions that take into account not the status quo alone, but also the four centuries of victimization Black people endured as a result of the "original sin" foundational to the success of American Empire (Baptist 2016).

Inclusivity of *Communio Sanctorum* ensures that all with be "self," there can be no "other." The inequities shouldered by the Black community reflect the iniquities of the White ruling class and its desire to maintain a topsider *status quo*. In covenantal community with moral solidarity, all will work to redress past wrongs and ensure the ability of all to flourish going forward. Simple "fixes" of income disparity will not correct asymmetric wealth distribution. Empty gestures of Congressional resolutions of past wrongs will not resolve ongoing issues of inadequate opportunities for education, employment, and healthcare. Critically, absolving oneself of moral responsibility or proclaiming the challenge of reconciliation and reparations for past original sins is too great or onerous just will not cut it! Only within *Communio Sanctorum* will dignity become universal and integrity essential. Reconciliation, restitution and reparations should target community building, aiming to create an American *Communio Sanctorum*. In 1897, W.E.B. Du Bois wrote in *The Atlantic* about the black in America who "stands helpless, dismayed, and well-nigh speechless; before that personal disrespect and mockery, the ridicule, and systematic humiliation." The "problem" then, as now, is not Black people. There is nothing "wrong" with Black people, but rather there is something very wrong with the dominant White ruling class that imprints its failings at forming inclusive community in moral solidarity upon people of color (Coates 2015, 2017; Kendi 2016, 2019). Black community is rich, organic, thick with unconditional love and acceptance. This is true not due in any part to support by the White ruling class, but rather in spite of White ruling class indifference to the historic aspirations of the Black community. To this I personally can attest with deep thanks and humility to my beloved community. Black America does not need a lesson in building *Communio Sanctorum*, it only needs to be fully embraced for its beauty, redressed for its inhumane treatment, and afforded its just rights and deserts.

Do toxic White privilege, the *status quo* for wealth distribution, and the racism suffered by Blacks exist outside of the realm of discernment, repentance, search for forgiveness, and self-redemption by the American public? Is this great "original" sin perpetrated against Africans, African Americans, and their descendants also on par with the "original" sin of killing and displacing the indigenous Native Americans discussed earlier? The context of our greatest sins can only be apprehended if we understand how events in the 17th to 19th centuries of American history led to economic hegemony at an enormous and continuing cost to our moral character (Baptist 2014; Dunbar-Ortiz 2014). The silent suffering derivative of American original sins should echo loudly in our moral ears. It is altogether too easy for Americans then and now to view these earlier formative centuries of our country as "distant." Have so many years passed that our original sins can be ignored, while their toxic legacy remains hidden in plain sight? Is America's past only brought to consciousness by annual celebrations like Columbus Day and Thanksgiving?

The answer seems obvious, as the very nature of such holidays themselves celebrate an intentionally self-serving, self-dealing topsider history. Is "patriotism" a panacea designed to dull our memories of horrors and crimes truly perpetuated against humanity?

At the very first mention of possible "reparations" for past original sins, the most common response we Americans offer proclaims our immunity to original sins attached to the 17th and 18th centuries. Convinced that the country has rectified the injustices in the intervening 300–400 years through periodic proclamations and legislation, we judge ourselves to be "off the hook." It was so easy to declare the past as dead and move on. Recall that the past is never really dead, nor is even past! Paradoxically, Americans typically do not shrug off the idea that there is no moral responsibility to make or to exact reparations from others as a consequence of either war or military conflicts. The record on the U.S. accepting moral or financial responsibility for atrocities is checkered at best. The U.S. displayed a frank reluctance to make reparations to Japanese-American victims for their internment during World War II, although some reparations were offered in 1948. This same reluctance and foot-dragging was on display when the U.S. was directed to make reparations to victims and families of the horrific 1932–1972 Tuskegee experiments. This "clinical research" included intentionally infecting of Black Americans with syphilis and then depriving the victims of standard medical care in order to study disease progression. Reparations for the Tuskegee victims finally were awarded in 1974! In the 20th century, most U.S. states practiced some form of eugenics, that is, especially the forced sterilization of "unfit," mostly disadvantaged women of color. North Carolina was the only state to apologize eventually to the victims and families. North Carolina has earmarked $10 million to compensate *living* victims of the state-sponsored, forced sterilization program. About 7,600 North Carolinians (mostly women and 39% Black) were victimized. Considering that the sterilization was performed on some very young (age 14 and up), one wonders how this level of compensatory payments solely to the victims still living could be considered "just." The state of Florida agreed to reparations of several million dollars to remaining survivors (10 survivors remained in 2014) of the Rosewood race riot in 1923. The race riot resulted in the killing of at least six Black residents and the forced escape of the injured survivors from the town.

A more proper moral posture for accepting responsibility and eventual payment of just reparations was provided by West Germany (and later other nations) in the aftermath of the Holocaust. This example, I offer, is just and applicable to addressing the losses suffered through slavery in America as well as in the aftermath of crimes against indigenous Native Americans over 400 years. On June 19th ("Juneteenth"), 2019, journalist Ta-Nehisi Coates (Coates 2017) testified at a U.S. House of Representative hearing on H.R. 40.

This House bill is designed to establish a commission to examine the case for reparations, that is, a national discussion about debts owed in compensation for slavery and discrimination against black Americans. Careful documentation of the historical, plantation-based economics (Baptist 2016) as well as current individual stories of theft of Black people's property by tax-sale laws are compelling. These data and narratives illuminate how the legacy of an "original sin" first committed in the 17th and 18th centuries enables ever-morphing Jim Crow laws to re-victimize Black people, robbing them in the 21st century of their personhood and human rights! The denial of economic justice to Black people over four centuries provides the explanation for Black family average wealth being but a fraction of that of White families in 21st century America. The call for a national discussion on reparations, in my view, should be expansive and inclusive, interrogating the two "original sins" of the founding of the American enterprise owed to indigenous Native Americans and black Americans. Details of how best this goal may be accomplished are discussed later. The jaundiced eye of the Trump Administration towards efforts aimed at social and redistributive justice for Native Americans and African Americans paradoxically has raised the profile of these original sins.

The 2016 election of Donald J. Trump to the U.S. presidency has had a predictable and dramatic effect on conversations about America's "Original Sins." Heated conversations about race and class dominate the media. The Trump administration publically favors the dominant White ruling class and is an adherent to a far right-wing perspective that they alone built an "exceptional" America (Van Engen 2020). Few economists would argue that absent the land grabs and genocide aimed at the indigenous Native Americans (Dunbar-Ortiz 2014) and the labor robbed from millions of African and African American slaves for centuries (Baptist 2014), America would be considered so "exceptional." The furor over New Deal-era mural art installed in George Washington High School in San Francisco is quite telling of this point. The 1936 mural by Russian émigré Victor Arnautoff (1896–1979) features American exceptionalism in terms of exploitation of murdered Native Americans and Black slaves. In 2019, the local school board voted to paint over the murals depicting settler colonists' violence aimed at indigenous people and African slaves, 83 years after the mural was installed! In 2019, GOP member of the U.S. House of Representatives Steve King of Iowa lost his congressional committee assignments following a series of comments viewed by most as racist and consistent with the rebounding perspective of White supremacists. Later Steve King doubled-down on his professed views on race, by claiming "if we presume that every culture is equal and has an equal amount to contribute to our civilization, then we're devaluing the contributions of the people who laid the foundation for America, and that's our Founding Fathers. . . ." The aim is clear, that is, to whitewash American history of the horrific stains from centuries of mistreatment of the indigenous peoples and Black slaves.

The *modus operandi* of revisionists is to draw attention away from the original sins and recast them into simple differences in "culture." This well-worn tactic, borrowed from the playbook of White supremacists, is incapable of submerging the heights of human rights violations and crimes against humanity leveled at the indigenous people and Black folks in America since the 17th century. The Trump administration continues upon a path of fortifying White nationalism (Acosta 2019; Kendi 2019). It announced the launch of a new "human rights panel" entitled, the "Commission of Unalienable Rights." The members were to be handpicked by the Administration. Its stated purpose was to aim at re-thinking "natural law and natural rights." The recent taunting (by Trump on Twitter) of four U.S. Congressional women of color to "go back" to their countries of origin has resurrected the idea of America again being is a "White man's country." The racist motive of this Administration to make America a whiter Christian-like nation (i.e., to *Make America Great Again*) was not so oblique. There have been few parallels of such overt racism expressed in the 21st century. The revival of "White man's country" rhetoric, however, should not be viewed as an isolated post-modern expression of cultural differences. In 2020, the Trump administration continues to stoke racial fear and resentment. The death of George Floyd, a black man who was killed during an arrest in Minneapolis MN by a white police officer was exploited by the Trump administration in its run up to the election. President Trump, with Holy Bible in hand and exercising disproportionate military force to clear his path through people protesting the death of George Floyd in order to stage a photo op in front of a Episcopal Church in Washington, DC, left little to the imagination about the health of White nationalism in 21st century America. Rather it is coded rhetoric that echoes back to America's two great "original sins," which continue to feed racism in America. This persistence resonates with our obstinacy and inability to interrogate, validate, receive, repent, and seek forgiveness for these on-going atrocities embedded in the very foundation of the U.S. narrative.

A Personal Reflection James H. Cone, My "Professor"

I was in my mid-50s when I sought post-graduate training in ethics at Union Theological Seminary in the City of New York. In my admission interviews, some seminary faculty forewarned me of the very progressive atmosphere at Union. In the midst of some of the brightest, twenty-something activist students I might be viewed as an "outsider," that is, a topsider, who was older, White, Anglo-Saxon, and likely patriarchal. Initially their cautions seemed prophetic. The warnings were spot on. I began my journey feeling "put upon," especially by my brilliant, truth-telling African American and Spanish-speaking Latin American classmates. I was ill prepared at first for their pithy, brutally honest critiques of me and of what I seemed to represent to them. These courageous and candid classmates correctly diagnosed the symptoms of my "disease," white, patriarchal, and privileged. I clearly was not prepared, however, for what emerged in tandem. What moved me were the simultaneous love, empathy, and desire they displayed aimed to foster my growth in understanding of their prescient diagnosis of my condition. What emerged in that first semester (and thereafter) was a necessary cycle of what seemed initially harsh critique, followed by loving-kindness, reaffirming my moral and spiritual growth and worth. I would experience a transformation that only accelerated throughout years of seminary, chaplaincy training, and my ongoing life as a pastor. Quite honestly, my seminary classmates succeeded at this critical effort in which my own life, up to then, had not.

One of my professors at Union, Dr. James H. Cone, would play a prominent role in my transformation. It was my very first full week as a seminarian and Professor Cone was the instructor of record for Systematic Theology (ST103). The course was a detailed and rigorous examination of the foundations and evolution of Christian theology. The syllabus was detailed, listing "assigned readings," "suggested readings," and a category of "optional readings." We learned very quickly that Cone expected us to consume *all* of the readings listed in the syllabus. The class was fast-paced. Keeping up with the lectures required annotated schemata of timelines, theologians, premises, logic, and relationships critical to our nascent understanding. Cone's reputation was well known. Upper classmates rated Cone as "tough," "fair," and "illuminating." For me, Cone's teaching method was all of these, but more importantly it was "transformative." In the very first ST103 lecture, systematic theology clearly was in the foreground, but something much deeper emerged in the background. Beyond Systematic Theology, there were two fundamentals to be apprehended in Cone's ST103 class: the evolution of Black Liberation Theology that he founded; and, frank advice that we all must learn to tell "our own story." He touched upon the suffering of the oppressed Black African and African American slaves and their descendants. He touched upon "whiteness," "white privilege," and "being blind to the suffering around you." Honestly, the first lecture wounded me, wounded me deeply, in a way that was both new and odd to me. In some way, the classroom seemed at times more like a church and the lecture more like a sermon offered by a preacher rather than a teacher. Professor Cone was drilling into my very being! His words caught me off guard and seemed to be directed to me. I had a deeply visceral response to his speaking a "truth" I had to hear.

At the end of the lecture I raced down several flights of stairs, picked up a coffee in the place called "the Pit," and started to exit in the direction of my next class. As I was leaving the Pit, Cone crossed the doorway in front of me. He paused and looked me in the eye. We both stopped dead in our tracks. I assumed that my wounded persona was clear to Cone's perceptive eye. He said to me, "Well Malbon, how did you like the first lecture?" Again, I was caught off guard and simply had no choice but respond honestly. "It hurt me. I really felt that my person was being drilled." After a brief pause and silence, Cone cocked his head to one side and with a broad smile uttered, "That's gooood!"

In response to his lectures I read Cone's works, starting with *Black Theology & Black Power*, published in 1969 (Cone 1969). Cone and I bumped into each other many times thereafter, even sharing a coffee break near the end of my very first semester. As I listened to his "own story," Professor Cone was sowing seeds about how an academic theologian can approach the ineffable Almighty God. His perspective and insights were unlike anything encountered in my decades of churching. Cone argued persuasively to the need to understand with whom God's agency in the world aligned. The overarching tenet he preached was that through Jesus, Almighty God aligns with the oppressed (Cone 1997). Cone expanded upon seminal work of others about the relationship between God and the oppressed (Thurman 1949; Gutiérrez 1973). Jesus was not simply being "inclusive" of the poor and oppressed. Jesus was God's answer to the lamentations of the poor and dispossessed! Cone raised up a Jesus who could identify with, walk with, and demand justice for the oppressed peoples of the world, especially for the Black African and African American slaves and their descendants. Professor Cone told "his own story" and encouraged all of his students to do the same. Self-discernment was essential to unearth in each of us our "own story." It would be this innermost reflection that would empower witness and testimony on behalf of the voiceless.

Late in my seminary training I was fortunate enough to attend Cone's signature course, "Malcolm [X] & Martin [Luther King, Jr.], a Dream or a Nightmare." These three-hour lectures were the most transformative of my training. To qualify for a seat in the limited, small group enrollment of another signature class offered by Cone on Reinhold Niebuhr, prospective students needed to read a number of Niebuhr's books over the summer and then qualify for a seat in the class. To qualify, a perspective student's performance would be judged by Cone through an oral exam on the pre-assigned readings! The assigned readings were demanding, but wholly worthwhile. I passed the "qualifier!" In the end my medical school teaching responsibilities conflicted with the timing for Cone's course. What a disappointment! In his teaching and in his book *The Cross and the Lynching Tree* (2011) Cone argued that Reinhold Niebuhr, a giant in the field of Christian Realism who taught at Union, had "eyes to see" black suffering, but yet lacked the "heart to feel" (Cone 2011). Prior to my Union experience, the very same critique could have been leveled at me. I had eyes to see, but did not see, being blind in my heart. In the years that followed, whenever I returned to Union, I always made sure to sit and chat with Professor Cone. Yes, we were both professorial in rank, but for me, James H. Cone would always be "Professor Cone." Near the end of his life, still actively writing and teaching, Cone always found time for my visits. He was generous with all of his students and former students. In the high tower of the medical school and hospital complex where I work, all photos and awards reflecting decades of effort devoted to research by my lab group eventually came down. Now there hangs but a single black and white framed photograph on the ivory painted walls of my private office. It is a splendid portrait of "Professor Cone." In that photo he displays that same provocative smile he cast upon me on my first day in seminary. Perhaps he had called out, "Follow me."

APPENDIX 4: FURTHER NOTES

*Text in italics are callouts to places within the chapter.

The history of the United States is a history of settler colonialism-the founding of state based on the ideology of white supremacy, the widespread practice of African slavery, and a policy of genocide and land theft. Roxanne Dunbar-Ortiz's *An Indigenous Peoples' History of the United States* captures the "original sin" of colonial settlers exacted upon the indigenous Native Americans who were in the land for 30,000 years before their European thieves and murders (Dunbar-Ortiz 2014). This book, winner of the 2015 American Book Award is an outstanding example of a book bringing truth to power. In sharp contrast of U.S. history's perspective from the "topside," this work offers the reader an invaluable and moving historical perspective from the "underside." For this quotation and a more detailed perspective on mythology surrounding American empires, see: Dunbar-Ortiz, Roxanne (2014), "America's Founding Myths," Brooklyn, NY: *Jacobin*, War and Imperialism, published online November 27, 2014 (accessed on April 30, 2020), https://www.jacobinmag.com/2014/11/americas-founding-myths.

The earliest (by a century) claimants to "America" were crowns of Spain and Portugal, whose combined population approached 450,000 when the Pilgrims landed in Plymouth Massachusetts in 1620. The dimensions of the first "original sin" perpetrated against the indigenous Native Americans in the founding of America can best be apprehended by analysis of the population dynamics of indigenous peoples "in the land" versus those people who invaded America in the 16th and 17th century. For an excellent historical introduction to the concept of "Spain's America" and review of two recent histories, see: Elliot, J. H. (2019), *Spain's America.* New York, NY: *The New York Review of Books*, published May 9, 2019 (accessed on April 30, 2020), https://www.nybooks.com/articles/2019/05/09/spains-america/.

The first original sin is that of the assault on indigenous Native Americans and their descendants. Use of an appropriate and respectful terminology for the indigenous peoples of the Western hemisphere, in North America and restricted to those whose native lands would eventually be considered within what is now called the United States of America is essential. Henceforth the preferred terms "Native Americans," "American Indians," and on occasion "Indian" (adopted from the invading settler-rangers) are employed in reference to the indigenous Native American peoples and their tribes, often in concert to material referenced in the text.

Various terms have been proposed to characterize the violent and deadly treatment of the Native Americans at the hands of the European immigrants to North America, including "holocaust" and "genocide." The proposition that treatment of indigenous Native Americans can be characterized to some extent, as "genocide," remains highly controversial. For an excellent and balanced treatment of the topic see: Ostler, Jeffrey (2015), "Genocide and American Indian History," Oxford, UK: T*he Oxford Research Encyclopedia of American History* (accessed on April 30, 2020), https://oxfordre.com/americanhistory/view/10.1093/acrefore/9780199329175.001.0001/acrefore-9780199329175-e-3.

This policy of religious intolerance and forced cultural annihilation came to a close only in 1978 with the signing into Federal law of the "American Indian Religious Freedom Act" (Tavares, Berryhill, and National Public Radio 1979)! This landmark Federal legislation was a significant step in halting many of the abuses aimed at degrading the personhood status of the indigenous Native Americans. It should not be lost upon the reader that religious freedoms of indigenous Native Americans only came to be protected in 1978, more than 200+ years following the founding of the Republic. For more details please see: Unnamed author (1979), *"We Also Have a Religion": The American Indian Religious Freedom Act and the Religious Freedom Project of the Native American Rights Fund*, Boulder, CO: Native American Rights Fund (accessed on April 30, 2020), https://www.narf.org/nill/documents/nlr/nlr5-1.pdf.

Land was considered sacred and a shared resource. The concept of land as property was alien to the indigenous people in the land. For a better understanding of the nature of sacred lands of indigenous Native Americans to the practice of their religion, see: Trope. Jack F. (1995), "Existing Federal Law and the Protections of Sacred Sites: Possibilities and Limitations," *Cultural Survival Quarterly Magazine* (accessed on April 30, 2020), https://www.culturalsurvival.org/publications/cultural-survival-quarterly/existing-federal-law-and-protection-sacred-sites.

Remarkably, American history highlights many of the atrocities at the hands of the expansionists involving Native Americans, including those of killing "Christianized Indians." A recent story by Donald L. Fixico on this critical topic deserves a careful read, see: Fixico, Donald L. (2020), *When Native Americans Were Slaughtered in the Name of Civilization*, New York, NY: A&E Television Networks, LLC (accessed on April 30, 2020), https:// www.history.com/news/native-americans-genocide-united-states.

No longer restrained by Christian principles, manifest destiny in American colonialism simply became a declaration of White supremacy pre-cluding all indigenous Native Americans and nonwhite peoples from their ancestral rights to the land. For an excellent and more detailed development of this topic, see: Hayman, Christine Leigh (2020), *Native American Religion in Early America*, Research Triangle Park ,NC: National Humanities Center (accessed on April 30, 2020), http://nationalhumanitiescenter.org/tserve/ eighteen/ekeyinfo/natrel.htm.

The Holocaust remains a profoundly relevant modern time example of the horrors of human fallenness. There are many powerful tools available online to assist readers to interrogate, better understand, and memorialize the Holo-caust and its meaning going forward. For a comprehensive site on the Holo-caust, see the two sources listed below: Laughlin, Estelle (2020), *Why We Remember the Holocaust*, Washington, DC: United States Holocaust Memo-rial Museum (accessed on April 30, 2020), https://www.ushmm.org/remem-ber/days-of-remembrance/resources/why-we-remember; and see Unnamed Author. (2020), "What Was the Holocaust?," Jerusalem, IS: *Vad Vashem*: The World Holocaust Remembrance Center (accessed on April 30, 2020), https://www.yadvashem.org.

These boarding schools were intentionally set hundreds of miles away from their tribal homes. Only in recent years has the horrors of the Federal boarding homes for Native American children been shown to include ne-glect, physical and sexual abuse, and trauma. To gain a better understanding of the horrors of these boarding schools for Native American children and for a discussion of their lost personhood and human rights see the following three sources: Peterson, Rebecca (2012), "The Impact of Historical Boarding Schools on Native American Families and Parenting Roles," *The McNair Scholars Journal of the University of Wisconsin Superior*, https:// minds.wisconsin.edu/bitstream/handle/1793/66821/Peter-son.pdf?sequence=8&isAllowed=y; Davis, Julie (2001), "American Indian Boarding School Experiences: Recent Studies from Native Perspectives: *OAH Magazine of History, 15*: 20–22 (accessed on April 30, 2020), https:// doi.org/10.1093/maghis/15.2.20; and Smith, Andrea (2004), "Boarding School Abuses, Human Rights, and Reparations," *Social Justice, 31*(4): 89–102 (accessed on April 30, 2020), https://www.jstor.org/stable/pdf/ 29768278.pdf?refreqid=excelsior%3A3b13b686bff804a6e2111ab023c067b 1.

A note about the nouns "African," "African American," "Black," and derivative adjectives employed in this writing project. One of the challenges in interrogating the original sin of slavery in America is respectfully and properly naming the victims. For "African," the noun is employed to name a person from Africa, especially a black person, whereas the adjective simply connotes relating to Africa or people of African descent. "Black,' employed as a noun refers to a member of a dark-skinned people, especially one of African or Australian Aboriginal ancestry. In the current work, the use of these appellations is intended in the following manner: "African" as a noun for black people born in Africa who were brought to America as slaves starting in 1619; "African American" as a noun for black people who are decedents of African slaves, but were born in America; and "Black" as a noun for dark-skinned people originally born either in Africa or in America. In many cases the choice of the appellation is contextual, based upon the time in history under discussion or their usage in the sources referenced in the current work. People who are forced today to self-identify as one of these three nouns justly may be upset by such a request. Some dark-skinned Americans may either welcome or shun the noun "African American" or question its relevance to native-born black Americans who have never been to Africa at all. Finally, there are instances wherein the broader, more inclusive term "people of color" is employed to recognize the growing diversity of people in America with varying degrees of skin pigment as well as with differing ancestry. The author apologizes in advance if the usage of one of these nouns, adjectives, or single phrases is a source of discomfort for the reader.

For the African and African American slaves the deprivation of personhood was in many ways different, but yet fundamentally the same. In August 2019, "The 1619 Project" was published in *The New York Times*. This major initiative was prepared in an effort to observe the 400th anniversary of the American slavery. The goal of the article is to truthfully tell the story of the institution of American slavery and how it shapes the lives of Black people today as well as conversations about racism and White ruling class hegemony in 21st century America. For an overview of this expansive 400-year history see: Silverstein, Jake (2019), "Why We Published the 1619 Project," *The New York Times Magazine*, December 20, 2019 edition and "The 1619 Project" in its entirety (accessed on April 30, 2020), https://www.nytimes.com/interactive/2019/08/14/magazine/1619-america-slavery.html.

Recent study of the legacy of divergent biblical interpretations about slavery and covert racism against the Black stranger by the dominant white ruling class reveals persistence in the 21st century. The Pew Research Center finds that the public does not view racial progress in the U.S. so glowingly. For the most current data, please see: Horowitz, Juliana M., Anna Brown, and Kiana Cox. "Race in America 2019." Washington, DC: *The Pew Re-*

search Center: Social & Demographic Trends (accessed on April 30, 2020). https://www.pewsocialtrends.org/2019/04/09/race-in-america-2019/.

Estimate of modern-day slaves in the U.S., a legacy of this original sin of America, was 403,000 in 2018! For a perspective on modern day slavery in developed countries (including the U.S.), see: Tutton, Mark (2018), "Modern Slavers in Developed Countries More Common Than Thought," Atlanta, GA: *The CNN FREEDOM PROJECT* (accessed on April 30, 2020), https://www.cnn.com/2018/07/19/world/global-slavery-index-2018/index.html.

The NAACP reports that from 1980–2015 the incarceration of Americans increased from 0.5 to >2.2 million. African Americans are incarcerated at more than five times the rate of whites; and, although use of drugs shows no racial disparity, African Americans are imprisoned on drug charges at a rate six times greater than whites. For further data and analysis see: "Incarceration Trends in America," *Criminal Justice Fact Sheet*, Baltimore, MD: NAACP (accessed on April 30, 2020), https://www.naacp.org/criminal-justice-fact-sheet/.

The legal basis for such stops versus the violation of people's rights through racial profiling led to the eventual abandonment of stop-and-frisk policies in New York City. For a more nuanced analysis of the stop-and-frisk policy in New York City see: Unnamed Author (2013), "US Crime: Federal Appeals Court Upholds Rulings that Stop-and-Frisk is Unconstitutional," *The Guardian* U.S. Edition, published online November 22, 2013 (accessed on April 30, 2020), https://www.theguardian.com/world/2013/nov/22/federal-appeals-court-upholds-rulings-stop-frisk-unconstitutional.

Work stoppages, sabotage, foot-dragging, and malingering are powerful tools of resistance and also help the personhood-of-self to flourish in the face of oppression. The National Museum of American History and the National Museum of African American History & Culture offer invaluable perspectives on slave resistance. See the following two sources: "We Have as Much Right to Fight for Our Liberty as Any Man: Testimony of 'Sam,' Richmond Virginia October 29, 1800," Washington, DC: The National Museum of American History (accessed on April 30, 2020), https://americanhistory.si.edu/changing-america-emancipation-proclamation-1863-and-march-washington-1963/1863/resistance; and "Resistance," Washington, DC: The National Museum of African American History & Culture (accessed on April 30, 2020), https://nmaahc.si.edu/blog/series/resistance.

The effect of the stories of the success of Harriet Tubman and other abolitionists in striking a blow for freedom and against slavery on the resistance movement was considerable. The legacy of Harriet Tubman to our understanding of African American resistance to slavery and oppression was reflected, in a small way, in the 2015 Treasury Department announcement that Harriet Tubman would replace Andrew Jackson on the U.S. currency $20 bill in 2020. How befitting! In 2019, the Trump administration announced that the début of the Tubman $20-bill would be deferred until 2026, in order to develop more "security" features? To learn more of this announced delay, see: St. Félix, Doreen (2019), "The Haunted Image of Harriet Tubman on the Twenty-Dollar Bill," New York, NY: *The New Yorker*, June 18, 2019 edition (accessed on April 30, 2020), https://www.newyorker.com/culture/cultural-comment/the-haunted-image-of-harriet-tubman-on-the-twenty-dollar-bill.

The power of James H. Cone's logic in formulating a Black theology of liberation in the United States is irrefutable. As a former student and later dear friend of Professor James Cone, I recommend the YouTube video created by Democracy Now! It examines the rich life and legacy of James H. Cone, the founder of Black Liberation Theology. Professor Cone died in 2018 (accessed on April 30, 2020), https://www.youtube.com/watch?v=8duS8kTf8Z8.

As long as want and oppression remain a luxury of those who seek to exploit their power and control upon the marginalized "other," the justice inherent in God will remain out of reach. For an excellent article with insights into the maladaptive principles of America's worship and idolatry of wealth, power and control by the dominant White ruling class, see: Reich, Robert (2019), "Forget China—It's America's Own Economic System That's Broken," London, UK: *The Guardian* (U.S. edition) June 23, 2019 edition (accessed on April 30, 2020), https://www.theguardian.com/commentisfree/2019/jun/23/china-america-economic-system-xi-jinping-trump.

How exactly do Black people in the U.S. view the racism that they encounter every day? For an excellent example of testimony on the topic of "everyday racism" in America, see: Jones, Brian. 2018. "Growing Up Black in America: Here's My Story of Everyday Racism," London, UK: *The Guardian* (U.S. edition) June 6, 2018 edition (accessed on April 30, 2020), https://www.theguardian.com/us-news/2018/jun/06/growing-up-black-in-america-racism-education?CMP=share_btn_link.

The Pew Research Center published are report entitled, "Race in America 2019," that revealed negative views of the public with regard to racial progress and some worrying trends suggesting race relations were worsening. This 2019 report offers an exhaustive analysis of public opinion on race relations in the United States from the perspectives both of the victims and of the perpetrators. The report including insights about the effects of age, color, ethnicity and politics on how Americans view the role of race in the personal lives of Americans. For the full report, see: Horowitz, Juliana M., Anna Brown, and Kiana Cox (2019), "Race in America 2019," Washington, DC: *The Pew Center* (accessed on April 30, 2020), https://www.pewsocialtrends.org/wp-content/uploads/sites/3/2019/04/PewResearchCenter_RaceStudy_FINAL-1.pdf.

Lost in the discussions of the economics of racial oppression and of denial of full personhood is another pillar of American life in which Black are held back, that is, wealth. In 2018, the Center for American Progress published a data-laden analysis of wealth in America. Wealth is as an essential element to people transiting through life to new locations, moving up to owning a house, paying for education and training, building a retirement, and meeting unforeseen financial emergencies. Entitled, "Systematic Inequality: How America's Structural Racism Helped Create the Black-White Wealth Gap," it is a thoughtful and provocative study of wealth acquisition and of obstacles encountered by Black people. For details, graphs, and tables, see: Hanks, Angela, Danyelle Solomon, and Christian E. Weller (2018), "Systematic Inequality: How America's Structural Racism Helped Create the Black-White Wealth Gap," Washington, DC: Center for American Progress, posted online February 21, 2018 (accessed on April 30, 2020), https://www.americanprogress.org/issues/race/reports/2018/02/21/447051/systematic-inequality/.

On June 19th ("Juneteenth"), 2019, journalist Ta-Nehisi Coates testified at a House of Representative hearing on H.R. 40–116th Congress (2019–2020). This U.S. House bill was crafted to establish a commission to examine the case for reparations. This article updates earlier published work of Coates on the case for reparations over debts owed to African and African American slaves and their descendants for maltreatment, discrimination, and exploitation since the 17th century (Coates 2015). To read on this further, see: Paschal, Olivia and Madeleine Carlisle (2019), "Read Ta-Nehisi Coates's Testimony on Reparations," Washington, DC: *The Atlantic*, published June 19, 2019 (accessed on April 30, 2020), https://www.theatlantic.com/politics/archive/2019/06/ta-nehisi-coates-testimony-house-reparations-hr-40/592042/.

Careful documentation of the historical, plantation-based economics (Baptist 2016) as well as current individual stories of theft of Black people's property by tax-sale laws provide a compelling case. This narrative illuminates how the legacy of an original sin perpetrated in the 17th and 18th centuries can enable ever-morphing Jim Crow laws to rob Black people of their personhood and human rights! For an excellent in-depth analysis of how the legacy of the original sin of slavery is being manifest in 21st century lives of Black people, see the following Op/Ed piece: Kahrl, Andrew W. (2019), "Black People's Land was Stolen," New York, NY: *The New York Times,* published June 20, 2019 (accessed on April 30, 2020), https://www.nytimes.com/2019/06/20/opinion/sunday/reparations-hearing.html.

Conversations about race and class predominate in the media, with the Trump administration publically favoring the dominant White ruling class, right-wing perspective that it alone built an "exceptional" America. For an oral history describing the evolution of the views of Donald J. Trump on race and immigration, see: Graham, David A., Adrienne Green, Cullen Murphy, and Parker Richards (2019), "An Oral History of Trump's Bigotry," Washington, DC: *The Atlantic*, published June 2019 (accessed on April 30, 2020), https://www.theatlantic.com/magazine/archive/2019/06/trump-racism-comments/588067/.

The school board voted to paint over the murals of settler colonists' violence aimed at indigenous people and African slaves, eighty-three years after the mural was installed! For the full story on the "white-washing" of U.S. history and desecration of American art, see the full store here: Arnautoff, Victor (2019), "Life of Washington," Washington, DC: *Public Art and Architecture from Around the World*, released online April 28, 2019 (accessed on April 30, 2020), https://www.artandarchitecture-sf.com/life-of-washington-by-victor-arnautoff.html.

The Trump administration continues upon a path of fortifying White nationalism. It announced the launch of a new "human rights panel" entitled, the "Commission of Unalienable Rights." Each of the members of this "human rights commission" will be hand-picked by the Trump administration with the specified goal aimed at re-thinking "natural law and natural rights." The formation of this committee on "natural law and natural rights" has been widely denounced as an effort to employ the assets of the U.S. federal government towards politicization of right-wing hate and ignoring international agreements, such as the Universal Declaration for Human Rights, supported by the U.S. for more than seven decades. For the full story, see: Unnamed Author (2019), "Trump Administration Commission on Unalienable Rights Politicizes Human Right for Hate," *Amnesty International*, published online July 8, 2019 (accessed on April 30, 2020), https://www.amnestyusa.org/press-releases/trump-administration-commission-on-unalienable-rights-politicizes-human-rights-for-hate/.

The recent taunting (by Twitter) of four U.S. Congressional women of color to "go back" to their countries of origin has resurrected the idea of America again being a "White man's country." For more perspectives of the "Go Back" rhetoric by Trump and the history of this racist rhetoric aimed at assaulting the personhood and human rights of the oppressed peoples of color and especially women of color, see: Montanaro, Domenico (2019), "Trump's 'Go Back' Rhetoric Is Sign of a Racially Divisive and Turbulent Year to Come," *National Public Radio*, aired July 19, 2019 (accessed on April 30, 2020), https://www.npr.org/2019/07/19/743310472/trumps-go-back-rhetoric-is-sign-of-a-racially-divisive-and-turbulent-year-to-com; and, Painter, Nell (2019), "Trump Revives the Idea of A 'White Man's Country,'" London, UK: *The Guardian* U.S. edition, published July 20, 2019 (accessed on April 30, 2020), https://www.theguardian.com/commentisfree/2019/jul/20/as-donald-trump-revives-racism-struggle-against-it-gathers-momentum.

President Trump, with Holy Bible in hand and exercising disproportion-ate military force to clear his path through people protesting the death of George Floyd in order to stage a photo op in front of an Episcopal Church in Washington, DC. Little was left to the imagination about the health of White nationalism in Trump's 21st century America view. For the details of President Trump's controversial and militaristic foray to St. John's Episcopal Church on June 1, 2020, see: Chappell, Bill (2020), "'He Did Not Pray': Fallout Grows from Trump's Photo-Op at St. John's Church," *National Public Radio*, Politics, aired on June 2, 2020 (accessed June 3, 2020), https://www.npr.org/2020/06/02/867705160/he-did-not-pray-fallout-grows-from-trump-s-photo-op-at-st-john-s-church.

In my office high in a tower of the medical school and hospital complex, photos and awards reflecting upon my life and as a research scientist have been removed. For a profile of the author's multi-vocational career as a scientist, ethicist and pastor, see the two following websites: https://www.pharm.stonybrook.edu/faculty/m/malbon (accessed on April 30, 2020) and https://www.stonybrook.edu/commcms/bioethics/people/malbon.php (accessed on April 30, 2020).

REFERENCES

Acosta, Abilio James. 2019. *The enemy of the people.* New York, NY: HarperCollins Publishers.

Adams, David Wallace. 1995. *Education for extinction: American Indians and the boarding school experience, 1875–1928.* Lawrence, KS: University Press of Kansas.

Adell, Sandra. 1994. *Double-consciousness/double bind: Theoretical issues in twentieth-century Black literature.* Urbana, IL: University of Illinois Press.

Alexander, Michelle. 2010. *The new Jim Crow: Mass incarceration in the age of colorblindness.* New York, NY; Jackson, TN: New Press; distributed by Perseus Distribution.

Allen, Charles Edwin. 1931. *History of Dresden, Maine: Formerly a part of the old town of Pownalborough, from its earliest settlement to the year 1900.* Augusta, ME: Kennebec Journal Print Shop.

Allen, Theodore. 2012. *The invention of the White race.* New York, NY: Verso Books.

Angeulov, Nikolay, and Michael H. McCarthy. 2018. *From criminalizing to decriminalizing marijuana: The politics of social control.* Lanham, MD: Lexington Books.

Aptheker, Herbert. 1983. *American Negro slave revolts.* New York, NY: International Publishers.

Awabdy, Mark A. 2014. *Immigrants and innovative law: Deuteronomy's theological and social vision for the [rg].* Tübingen, DE: Mohr Siebeck.

Baptist, Edward E. 2016. *The half has never been told: Slavery and the making of American capitalism.* New York, NY: Basic Books.

Barber, William J., and Jonathan Wilson-Hartgrove. 2016. *The third reconstruction: Moral Mondays, fusion politics, and the rise of a new justice movement.* Boston, MA: Beacon Press.

Barr, Donald A. 2019. *Health disparities in the United States: Social class, race, ethnicity, and the social determinants of health.* Baltimore, MD: Johns Hopkins University Press.

Bell, Joyce Marie. 2014. *The Black power movement and American social work.* New York, NY: Columbia University Press.

Bensen, Robert. 2001. *Children of the dragonfly: Native American voices on child custody and education*. Tucson, AZ: University of Arizona Press.

Berne, Emma Carlson. 2010. *Sacagawea: Crossing the continent with Lewis & Clark*, Sterling Biographies. New York, NY: Sterling.

Berry, Daina Ramey. 2017. *The price for their pound of flesh: The value of the enslaved from womb to grave in the building of a nation*. Boston, MA: Beacon Press.

Bloom, Joshua, and Waldo E. Martin. 2013. *Black against empire: The history and politics of the Black Panther party*. Berkeley, CA: University of California Press.

Bohm, Robert M., and Gavin Lee. 2018. *Routledge handbook on capital punishment*. New York, NY: Routledge, Taylor & Francis Group.

Bordewich, Fergus M. 2005. *Bound for Canaan: The underground railroad and the war for the soul of America*. New York, NY: Amistad.

Bowler, Kate. 2013. *Blessed: A history of the American prosperity gospel*. New York, NY: Oxford University Press.

Bremer, Francis J. 2003. *John Winthrop: America's forgotten founding father*. New York, NY: Oxford University Press.

Brown, Austin Channing. 2018. *I'm still her: Black dignity in a world made for whiteness*. New York, NY: Convergent Books.

Brown, Peter. 2000. *Augustine of Hippo: A biography*. Berkeley, CA: University of California Press.

Calloway, Colin G. 2016. *First peoples: A documentary survey of American Indian history*. Boston, MA: Bedford/St. Martin's, a Macmillan Education imprint.

Carmichael, Stokely, Malcolm X, James Baldwin, and James L. Bevel. 1987. *A new Black consciousness*. Staten Isalnd, NY: Blackside, Inc., (sound recording).

Carr, David McLain. 2014. *Holy resilience: The Bible's traumatic origins*. New Haven, CT: Yale University Press.

Child, Brenda J. 1998. *Boarding school seasons: American Indian families, 1900–1940*. Lincoln, NE: University of Nebraska Press.

Childs, Dennis. 2015. *Slaves of the state: Black incarceration from the chain gang to the penitentiary*. Minneapolis, MN: University of Minnesota Press.

Chomsky, Noam, Lois Meyer and Benjmain Maldonado. 2010. *New world of indigenous resistance*. San Francisco, CA: City Lights Book.

Churchill, Ward. 2002. *Struggle for the land: Native North American resistance to genocide, ecocide, and colonization*. San Francisco, CA: City Lights.

Clinton, Catherine. 2004. *Harriet Tubman: The road to freedom*. Boston, MA: Little, Brown.

Coates, Julia. 2014. *Trail of tears* (Landmarks of the American Mosaic series). Santa Barbara, CA: Greenwood.

Coates, Ta-Nehisi. 2015. *Between the world and me*. New York, NY: Spiegel and Grau, an imprint of Random House.

———. 2017. *We were eight years in power: An American tragedy*. New York, NY: One World, an imprint of Random House.

Cone, James H. 1969. *Black theology and black power*. New York, NY: Seabury Press.

———. 1989. *Black theology and black power*. San Francisco, CA: Harper & Row.

———. 2010. *A black theology of liberation*. Maryknoll, NY: Orbis Books.

———. 1970. *A black theology of liberation* (1st ed.). Philadelphia, PA: Lippincott.

———. 2011. *The cross and the lynching tree*. Maryknoll, NY: Orbis Books.

———. 1975. *God of the oppressed*. Maryknoll, NY: Orbis Books.

———. 1991. *Martin & Malcolm & America: A dream or a nightmare*. Maryknoll, NY: Orbis Books.

———. 2018. *Said I wasn't gonna tell nobody: The making of a black theologian*. Maryknoll, NY: Orbis Books.

Cone, James H., and Cornel West. 2018. *Black theology and black power*. Maryknoll, NY: Orbis Books.

Cunningham, Anne C. 2017. *Reparations* (Opposing viewpoints series). New York, NY: Greenhaven Publishing.

Davis, David Brion. 2006. *Inhuman bondage: The rise and fall of slavery in the New World.* New York, NY: Oxford University Press.

DeVinney, James A., Callie Crossley, Henry Hampton, Bernice Johnson Reagon, Michael Ambrosino, Judith Vecchione, Jon Else, Steve Fayer, Julian Bond, Blackside Inc., PBS Video., LC Collection (Library of Congress), and Copyright Collection (Library of Congress). 1986. *Eyes on the prize—America's civil rights years, 1954–1965. No easy walk, 1961–1963.* United States: Boston, MA: WGBH, PBS Video, 14 hour playtime.

DiAngelo, Robin J. 2018. *White fragility: Why it's so hard for white people to talk about racism.* Boston, MA: Beacon Press.

Dorrien, Gary. 2018. *Breaking white supremacy: Martin Luther King Jr. and the Black social gospel.* New Haven, CT: Yale University Press.

Douglas, Kelly Brown. 2015. *Stand your ground: Black bodies and the justice of God.* Maryknoll, NY: Orbis Books.

Du Bois, W.E.B. 2016. *Darkwater: Voices from within the veil.* New York, NY: Verso Books.

———. 1996. *The souls of black folk.* New York, NY: Modern Library.

———. 1903. *The souls of black folk: Essays and sketches.* Chicago, IL: A. C. McClurg & Co.

Dunbar-Ortiz, Roxanne. 1984. *Indians of the Americas: Human rights and self-determination.* London, UK: Zed Books.

———. 2014. *An indigenous peoples' history of the United States.* Boston, MA: Beacon Press.

Dwork, Deborah, and R. J. van Pelt. 2002. *Holocaust: A history.* New York, NY: W. W. Norton & Co.

Edwards, Jonathan, and American Imprint Collection (Library of Congress). 1758. *The great Christian doctrine of original sin defended; evidences of it's truth produced, and arguments to the contrary answered. Containing, in particular, a reply to the objections and arguings of Dr. John Taylor, in his book, intitled, "The Scripture-doctrine of original sin proposed to free and candid examination," & comp.* Boston, MA: S. Kneeland.

Estes, Nick. 2019. *Our history is the future: Standing Rock versus the Dakota Access Pipeline, and the long tradition of indigenous resistance.* London, UK; New York, NY: Verso.

Felman, Shoshana, and Dori Laub. 1991. *Testimony: Crises of witnessing in literature, psychoanalysis, and history.* New York, NY: Routledge.

Finkelman, Paul. 2003. *Defending slavery: Proslavery thought in the Old South: A brief history with documents* (The Bedford series in history and culture). Boston, MA: Bedford/St. Martin's.

Fletcher, Jeannine Hill. 2017. *The sin of white supremacy: Christianity, racism, and religious diversity in America.* Maryknoll NY: Orbis Books.

Flynn, Andrea. 2018. *The hidden rules of race: Barriers to an inclusive economy* (Cambridge studies in stratification economics: Economics and social identity). New York, NY: Cambridge University Press.

Forman, James Jr. 2017. *Locking up our own: Crime and punishment in Black America.* New York, NY: Farrar, Straus and Giroux.

Frank, Andrew, and A. Glenn Crothers. 2017. *Borderland narratives: Negotiation and accommodation in North America's contested spaces, 1500–1850* (Contested boundaries). Gainesville, Tallahassee, Tampa, Boca Raton, FL: University Press of Florida.

Frankl, Viktor E. 1946. *Man's search for meaning: An introduction to logotherapy.* New York, NY: Simon & Schuster.

Franklin, John Hope, and Evelyn Higginbotham. 2010. *From slavery to freedom: A history of African Americans* (9th ed.). New York, NY: McGraw-Hill.

Freedman, Suzanne. 2000. *United States v. Amistad: Rebellion on a slave ship* (Landmark Supreme Court cases). Berkeley Heights, NJ: Enslow Publishers.

Gaustad, Edwin S., and Mark A. Noll. 2003. *A documentary history of religion in America* (3rd ed.). 2 vols. Grand Rapids, MI: W.B. Eerdmans Publishing Co.

Gaustad, Edwin S., and Leigh Eric Schmidt. 2002. *The religious history of America* (revised ed.). San Francisco, CA: HarperSanFrancisco.

Gill, Sam D. 2005. *Native American religions: An introduction* (2nd ed.). Belmont, CA: Wadsworth Thomson.

Gooding-Williams, Robert. 2009. *In the shadow of Du Bois: Afro-modern political thought in America*. Cambridge, MA: Harvard University Press.

Greenberg, Amy S. 2018. *Manifest destiny and American territorial expansion: A brief history with documents* (2nd ed., The Bedford series in history and culture). Boston, MA: Bedford/St. Martin's, Macmillan Learning.

Greitens, Eric. 2015. *Resilience: Hard-won wisdom for living a better life*. Boston, MA: Houghton Mifflin Harcourt.

Grounds, Richard A., George E. Tinker, and David E. Wilkins. 2003. *Native voices: American Indian identity and resistance*. Lawrence KS: University Press of Kansas.

Groves, Marlene A. 1977. *Malbon genealogy: Ancestors and descendants of Daniel Malbon of Montbéliard, France and Dresden, Maine*. Rockland ME: Groves.

Gutiérrez, Gustavo. 1973. *A theology of liberation: History, politics, and salvation*. Maryknoll NY: Orbis Books.

Gutiérrez, Gustavo, and Gerhard Ludwig Müller. 2015. *On the side of the poor: The theology of liberation*. Maryknoll NY: Orbis Books.

Gutiérrez González, Juan. 1977. *The new Libertarian gospel: Pitfalls of the theology of liberation*. Chicago IL: Franciscan Herald Press.

Hämäläinen, Pekka. 2019. *Lakota America: A new history of indigenous power*. New Haven CT: Yale University Press.

Hanson, J. W. 1849. *History of the old towns, Norridgewock and Cannaan: Comprising Norridgewock, Canaan, Starks, Skowhegan, and Bloomfield, from their early settlement to the year 1849; including a sketch of the Abnakis Indians*. Boston, MA: By the author.

Hanson, Rick, and Forrest Hanson. 2018. *Resilient: How to grow an unshakable core of calm, strength, and happiness*. New York, NY: Harmony Books.

Harris, Robert L. 2013. Malcom X: Critical assessments and unanswered questions. *Journal of African American History, 98*(4): 595–601.

Haynes, Stephen R. 2007. *Noah's curse: The biblical justification of American slavery*. Oxford, UK; New York, NY: Oxford University Press.

Healey, Joseph F., Andi Stepnick, and Eileen O'Brien. 2019. *Race, ethnicity, gender, & class: The sociology of group conflict and change* (8th ed.). Los Angeles, CA: SAGE.

Hegel, Georg Wilhelm Friedrich, and Robert R. Williams. 2007. *Georg Wilhelm Friedrich Hegel: Lectures on the philosophy of spirit 1827–8*. Oxford, UK; New York, NY: Oxford University Press.

Hepner, Gershon. 2010. *Legal friction: Law, narrative, and identity politics in biblical Israel*. New York, NY: Peter Lang.

Herman, Judith Lewis. 2015. *Trauma and recovery*. New York, NY: BasicBooks.

Higginson, Thomas Wentworth. 1998. *Black rebellion: Five slave revolts* (1st Da Capo Press ed.). New York, NY: Da Capo Press.

Hinn, Costi W. 2019. *God, greed, and the (prosperity) gospel: How truth overwhelms a life built on lies*. Grand Rapids, MI: Zondervan.

Hixson, Walter L. 2013. *American settler colonialism: A history* (1st ed.). New York, NY: Palgrave Macmillan.

Horsmanden, Daniel, and Serena R. Zabin. 2004. *The New York conspiracy trials of 1741: Daniel Horsmanden's Journal of the proceedings: With related documents*. Boston, MA: Bedford/St. Martin's.

Jennings, Thelma. 1990. "Us colored women had to go through a plenty": Sexual exploitation of African American slave women. *Project Muse, Journal of Women's History, 1*(3): 45–74.

Jilovsky, Esther. 2015. *Remembering the Holocaust: Generations, witnessing and place*. New York, NY: Bloomsbury Academic, an imprint of Bloomsbury Publishing Plc.

Johnson, Cedric C. 2015. *Race, religion, and resilience in the neoliberal age*. New York, NY: Palgrave Macmillan.

Jones, Charles E. 1998. *The Black Panther party (reconsidered)*. Baltimore, MD: Black Classic Press.

Joseph, Peniel E. 2006. *The black power movement: Rethinking the civil rights-Black power era*. New York, NY: Routledge.

Josephy, Alvin M. 1993. *The patriot chiefs: A chronicle of American Indian resistance* (revised ed.). New York, NY: Penguin Books.

Kendi, Ibram X. 2016. *Stamped from the beginning: The definitive history of racist ideas.* New York, NY: Nation Books.

Kendi, Ibram X. 2019. *How to be an antiracist.* New York, NY: One World, an impring of Random House.

Kidd, Thomas S. 2016. *American colonial history: Clashing cultures and faiths.* New Haven, CT; London, UK: Yale University Press.

King, Martin Luther, and James Melvin Washington. 1991. *A testament of hope: The essential writings and speeches of Martin Luther King, Jr.* San Francisco, CA: HarperSanFrancisco.

Laub, Dori, and Andreas Hamburger. 2017. *Psychoanalysis and holocaust testimony: Unwanted memories of social trauma.* London, UK; New York, NY: Routledge/Taylor & Francis Group.

Laurent, Sylvie, and William J. Wilson. 2018. *King and the other America: The Poor People's Campaign and the quest for economic equality.* Oakland, CA: University of California Press.

Lynch, Barbara. 2005. *The Malbons: Eight hundred years of family history.* Vancouver, BC, Canada: Fernleigh Publications.

Marable, Manning. 2011. *Malcolm X: A life of reinvention.* New York, NY: Penguin Publishing Group.

Mann, Charles C. 2009. *Before Columbus: The Americas of 1491.* New York, NY: Atheneum Books.

McCormick, Anita Louise. 2015. *The Native American struggle in United States history.* Berkeley Heights, NJ: Enslow Publishers, Inc.

McGuckin, John Anthony. 2004. *The Westminster handbook to patristic theology* (1st ed.). Louisville, KY: Westminster John Knox Press.

McMickle, Marvin Andrew. 2006. *Where have all the prophets gone?: Reclaiming prophetic preaching in America.* Cleveland, OH: Pilgrim Press.

McQueen, Steve (Director), et al. 2013. *12 years a slave* [film]. Los Angeles, CA: Twentieth Century-Fox Film Corporation.

Meinig, D. W. 1986. *The shaping of America: A geographical perspective on 500 years of history.* New Haven, CT: Yale University Press.

Miller, Robert J. 2010. *Discovering indigenous lands: The doctrine of discovery in the English colonies.* Oxford, UK: Oxford University Press.

Morgan, Edmund S. 1975. *American slavery, American freedom: The ordeal of colonial Virginia.* New York, NY: W. W. Norton & Co.

Moscovici, Claudia. 2019. *Holocaust memories: A survey of holocaust memoirs, histories, novels, and films.* Lanham, MD: Hamilton Books.

Nabokov, Peter. 1991. *Native American testimony: A chronicle of Indian-white relations from prophecy to the present, 1492–1992.* New York, NY: Viking.

National Humanities Center. 2007. On slaveholder's sexual abuse of slaves: Selections from the 19th & 20th century slave narratives. In *The making of African American identity: Vol. 1, 1500–1865.* Washington, DC: National Humanities Center.

Newcomb, Steven T. 2008. *Pagans in the promised land: Decoding the doctrine of Christian discovery.* Golden, CO: Fulcrum Pub.

Noll, Mark A. 2002. *The old religion in a new world: The history of North American Christianity.* Grand Rapids, MI: Eerdmans.

Northup, Solomon, and D. Wilson (Eds). 1859. *Twelve years a slave. Narrative of Solomon Northup, a citizen of New-York, kidnapped in Washington city in 1841, and rescued in 1853, from a cotton plantation near the Red River in Louisiana.* New York, NY: C.M. Saxton.

O'Brien, Cormac. 2008. *The forgotten history of America: Little-known conflicts of lasting importance from the earliest colonists to the eve of the revolution.* Beverly, MA: Fair Winds Press.

O'Brien, Jean M. 2010. *Firsting and lasting: Writing Indians out of existence in New England.* Minneapolis, MN: University of Minnesota Press.

Osborn, William M. 2000. *The wild frontier: Atrocities during the American-Indian War from Jamestown Colony to Wounded Knee*. New York, NY: Random House.

Paquette, Robert L., and Mark M. Smith. 2016. *The Oxford handbook of slavery in the Americas*. Oxford Handbooks. Oxford, UK; New York, NY: Oxford University Press.

Pember, Mary Annette. 2019, March 8. Death by civilization. *The Atlantic*. https://www.theatlantic.com/education/archive/2019/03/traumatic-legacy-indian-boarding-schools/584293/.

Petersen, Tore T. 2016. *The military conquest of the prairie: Native American resistance, evasion and survival, 1865–1890*. Brighton, UK; Chicago, IL: Sussex Academic Press.

Powell, John A. 2012. *Racing to justice: Transforming our conceptions of self and other to build an inclusive society*. Bloomington, IN: Indiana University Press.

Ratteree, Kathleen and Nobert Hill Jr. 2017. *The great vanishing act: Blood quantum and the future of native nations*. Golden, CO: Fulcrum Publishing.

Sargent, Sarah, and Jo Samanta. 2016. *Indigenous rights: Changes and challenges for the 21st century*. Buckingham, UK: The University of Buckingham Press.

Saslow, Eli. 2018. *Rising out of hatred: The awakening of a former white nationalist*. New York, NY: Doubleday.

Saunt, Claudio. 2014. *West of the Revolution: An uncommon history of 1776*. New York, NY: W.W. Norton & Co.

Sawyer, Kem Knapp. 2010. *Harriet Tubman* (1st American ed.). New York, NY: DK Publishers.

Schaff, Philip. 1861. *Slavery and the Bible. A tract for the times*. Chambersburg, PA: M. Kieffer & Co.'s Caloric Printing Press.

Shally-Jensen, Michael (Ed.). 2017a. *Defining documents in American history: Native Americans (1451–2017)*. Ipswich, MA; Amenia, NY: Salem Press, a division of EBSCO Information Services, Inc., Grey House Publishing.

———. 2017b. *Defining documents in American history: Supreme Court decisions (1803–2017)*. Ipswich, MA; Amenia, NY: Salem Press, Grey House Publishing.

Simpson, Leanne Betasamosake. 2017. *As we have always done: Indigenous freedom through radical resistance*. Minneapolis, MN: University of Minnesota Press.

Small, Cathleen. 2018. *Colonial interactions with Native Americans*. New York, NY: Cavendish Square Publishing.

Smith, Page. 2015. *Tragic encounters: The people's history of Native Americans*. Berkeley, CA: Counterpoint.

Söderlind, Sylvia, and James Taylor Carson. 2011. *American exceptionalisms: From Winthrop to Winfrey*. Albany, NY: State University of New York Press.

Spruhan, Paul. 2006. A legal history of blood quantum in federal Indian law to 1935. *South Dakota Law Review, 51*(1). Published online January 7, 2007.

Stevenson, Bryan. 2014. *Just mercy: A story of justice and redemption*. New York, NY: Spiegel & Grau.

Stewart, Carlyle Fielding. 1999. *Black spirituality and black consciousness: Soul force, culture, and freedom in the African American experience*. Trenton, NJ: Africa World Press.

Still, William, and Ian Frederick Finseth. 2007. *The underground railroad: Authentic narratives and first-hand accounts*. Mineola, NY: Dover Publications.

Swain, Carol M., and Russ Nieli. 2003. *Contemporary voices of white nationalism in America*. Cambridge, UK: Cambridge University Press.

Sweet, Frank W. 2005. *Legal history of the color line: The notion of invisible blackness*. Palm Coast, FL: Backintyme.

Tavares, Frank, Peggy Berryhill, and National Public Radio (U.S.). 1979. *The American Indian Religious Freedom Act* [sound recording]. Washington, DC: National Public Radio.

Taylor, Keeanga-Yamahtta. 2016. *From #BlackLivesMatter to Black liberation*. Chicago, IL: Haymarket Books.

Terrill, Robert. 2010. *The Cambridge companion to Malcolm X*. Cambridge, UK; New York, NY: Cambridge University Press.

Thornton, Russell. 1987. *American Indian holocaust and survival: A population history since 1492* (1st ed.). Norman, OK: University of Oklahoma Press.

Thurman, Howard. 1949. *Jesus and the disinherited*. New York, NY: Abingdon-Cokesbury Press.

Tillich, Paul. 1967. *Systematic theology*. 3 vols. Chicago, IL: University of Chicago Press.

Tinker, George E. 2004. *Spirit and resistance: Political theology and American Indian liberation*. Minneapolis, MN: Fortress Press.

Tsai, Daisy Yulin. 2014. *Human rights in Deuteronomy: With special focus on slave laws*. Berlin, DE: De Gruyter.

Tucker, Spencer, James R. Arnold, and Roberta Wiener. 2011. *The encyclopedia of North American Indian wars, 1607–1890: A political, social, and military history*. 3 vols. Santa Barbara, CA: ABC-CLIO.

Tyson, Timothy B., Randolph Boehm, and Daniel Lewis. 2001. *The Black power movement. Part 2, the papers of Robert F. Williams*. Bethesda, MD: University Publications of America.

United States., and Commerce Clearing House. 1964. *Civil rights act of 1964, with explanation, as passed by the Congress and sent to the president*. Chicago, IL: Commerce Clearing House.

Van Deburg, William L. 1992. *New day in Babylon: The Black power movement and American culture, 1965–1975*. Chicago, IL: University of Chicago Press.

Van Engen, Abram C. 2020. *City on a hill: A history of American exceptionalism*. New Haven, CT: Yale University Press.

Van Zee, Amy, and Earl M. Maltz. 2013. *Dred Scott v. Sandford: Slavery and freedom before the American civil war*. Minneapolis, MN: ABDO Pub.

Vargus, Brian S., Indiana. University. Bureau of Correspondence Study., and Indiana. University. Bureau of Public Discussion. 1968. *The Kerner Commission report: Black and white in America; a study guide*. Bloomington, IN: Indiana University.

Wallis, Jim. 2016. *America's original sin: Racism, white privilege, and the bridge to a new America*. Grand Rapids, MI: Brazos Press.

Walters, Kerry S. 2015. *American slave revolts and conspiracies: A reference guide*. Santa Barbara, CA: ABC-CLIO, an Imprint of ABC-CLIO, LLC.

Warren, E. W., and Confederate States of America Collection (Library of Congress). 1864. *Nellie Norton: Or, Southern slavery and the Bible. A Scriptural refutation of the principal arguments upon which the abolitionists rely. A vindication of Southern slavery from the Old and New Testaments*. Macon, GA: Burke, Boykin & Company.

Watson, Blake. 2011. The doctrine of discovery and elusive defonition of Indian title. *Lewis & Clark Law Review, 15*: 995.

Watson, Blake A. 2012. *Buying America from the Indians: Johnson v. McIntosh and the history of native land rights*. Norman, OK: University of Oklahoma Press.

Weaver, Hilary N. 2019. *Trauma and resilience in the loves of contemporary native Americans: Reclaiming our balance, restoring our wellbeing*. New York, NY: Routledge.

West, Cornel. 1993. *Race matters*. Boston, MA: Beacon Press.

White, Christopher M. 2019. *The war on drugs in America*. New York, NY: Routledge.

Whitford, David M. 2009. *The curse of Ham in the early modern era: The Bible and the justifications for slavery*. Farnham, UK; Burlington, VT: Ashgate Pub. Ltd.

Wilkins, David E. 2013. *Hollow justice: A history of Indigenous claims in the United States*. New Haven, CT: Yale University Press.

Wilkins, David E., and K. Tsianina Lomawaima. 2002. *Uneven ground: American Indian sovereignty and federal law*. Normal, OK: Oklahoma University Press.

Williams, Robert F., and Marc Schleifer. 1973. *Negroes with guns*. Chicago, IL: Third World Press.

Wilmore, Gayraud S. 1998. *Black religion and Black radicalism: An interpretation of the religious history of African Americans*. Maryknoll, NY: Orbis Books.

Wood, Peter H. 1974. *Black majority; Negroes in colonial South Carolina from 1670 through the Stono Rebellion*. New York, NY: Knopf, distributed by Random House.

X, Malcolm. 1966. *The autobiography of Malcolm X: With the assistance of Alex Haley*. London, UK: Hutchinson.

————. 1964. *Ballots or bullets.* Speech delivered on April 3, 1964 at the Cory Methodist Church, Cleveland, OH: Philadelphia, PA: First Amendment Records; Jamie/Guyden Distributing Corp., (sound recording).

————. 1990. *Malcolm X speaks: Selected speeches and statements.* George Breitman (ed.). New York, NY: Grove Weidenfeld.

Young, James Edward. 1993. *The texture of memory: Holocaust memorials and meaning.* New Haven, CT: Yale University Press.

Chapter Six

Understanding Those Who Attack the Being of the "Other"

Who Decides?

Up to this point, our discussions have necessarily focused upon a working contemporary definition of "personhood" and upon those for whom personhood is never firmly established, discounted, extinguished, or systematically degraded. Ample evidence is provided both historically as well as contemporaneously that people with vulnerabilities of the soma and in particular those with vulnerabilities in the psyche are major targets for those contesting their personhood. We have exhaustively interrogated the qualities of the physically disabled, the mentally disabled and special people in our times (e.g., people of color, people with chemical dependence and drug abuse, as well as the deeply forgetful) whose vulnerabilities have laid them waste to racism, discrimination, and lost personhood, even to the point of being killed. We now pivot our hermeneutic of suspicion from the victim to the perpetrator. Here we must keep in mind that, not unlike victims, perpetrators may constitute a broad spectrum of individuals, including sadly even ourselves at some times to some extent. As we interrogate this difficult landscape, it would be best if we commit ourselves to self-discernment about those times (and I believe that everyone has them) when we feel empowered to discount the personhood of people whose "otherness" challenges, destabilizes, or overcomes us.

Although physically and mentally disabled people often are categorically deprived of full personhood, the most common trigger for a more common form of contesting personhood resides in our own sense of identity ("self") with respect to those that seem, as we discussed earlier, "other." Nations can contest the personhood of entire peoples. Since 2016, Myanmar's armed forces have enforced persecution of the Rohingya, a stateless, Indo-Aryan-speaking people whose population is estimated to be >1 million (Farzana 2017). These persecuted peoples have suffered military crackdown for more than four decades and in recent years have been subject to what Human Rights Watch term "genocide" (United States Congress, House Committee on Foreign Affairs 2018). This is but one example of the full loss of person-hood, to the extend that the basic human right of "not being killed" has been suspended by those considering the Rohingya as "other." Similarly, the Mid-dle East is beset with the more than fifty year occupation of the West Bank and Gaza. This forced occupation, according to Human Rights Watch, has led to systematic human rights abuses of the Palestinian people by the state of Israel. For 2017, Amnesty International lists China, the EU and Australia, Saudi Arabia, Russia, Syria, Turkey, Yemen, Venezuela, and the U.S. with violations in which sovereign governments promote hate-filled speech that fuels persecution of people around the globe.

Front and center in contesting personhood of the "other" is the broad topic of the plight of people suffering outside of their home country as "immigrants." More than 244 million people were classified as international immigrants in 2015. Although surveys of leading economists show repeated-ly that the influx of refugees to destinations in the EU and elsewhere (e.g., the U.S.) will generate "net economic benefits" over succeeding decades (Bansak, Simpson, and Zavodny 2015), the visibility of these "others" within more homogenous national populations promotes negative appraisal of the immigrant populations. Historically, nations that prospered by colonialism fail to see themselves as "immigrants" to new lands. Earlier waves of immi-grants who themselves largely are assimilated into their new land actively seek to preclude later waves the "other" from enjoying the same benefits, that is, movement to safer, more prosperous countries. Accepting the immigrant "other" then is cast as a violation of the sovereignty of the countries to which the "other" seeks to immigrate. In some cases, the immigrants' physical appearance within the context of more homogenous pre-existing groups can mark them immediately for discrimination and oppression. Recently in the U.S., purported to be a "nation of immigrants," international immigrants have been denunciated openly and come under savage attacks. Led by con-servative, right-leaning groups of self-styled "populists," the drumbeat of anti-immigration has found resonance worldwide as the populace of interna-tional immigrants surpasses a quarter of a billion people (Nicholls 2019)! Lost, perhaps intentionally, in this discussion is a frank understanding of why there are so many people on the move globally? The never ending foray of nations (e.g., the U.S. and the UK in recent times) venturing out to produce "democracy," "regime change," and a new political world order is a dominant driving force for most of the tension. Later, as was the case in Iraq and Syria, came the destruction and ultimate displacement of people seeking to simply live a life absent of war by proxy at the hands of global powers and to embrace a life with a future in which their children can flourish (Hosein 2019). Although the defense of such harsh treatment of immigrants (both legal or undocumented) is always purported to be economic, the data clearly show that people moving from areas of low-productivity to higher-productivity yield the most efficient path to marked reductions in global poverty (Bansak, Simpson, and Zavodny 2015).

Regionalism constitutes another powerful basis for identity politics that results in depersonalization of others, even though these "others" reside within the region and may be legal citizens. Herein we all can envision ourselves either as victims or perpetrators, or both. Having been brought up in Massachusetts and imprinted with the Boston Red Sox, Bruins, Celtics, and the New England Patriots (the most regional of all the sports teams), I often found myself the victim of apparent "otherness" when living in Cleveland and later again in New York. This type of regionalism is seemingly innocent (which often it is). I employ it to aid in our understanding of the feelings that "otherness" stimulates within us and within those "others" viewing our patterns of likes, dislikes, and behaviors. Regionalism within the United States, China, Russia, and other large countries is unavoidable and again often is innocent. But cool embers of difference can be inflamed by harsh rhetoric and hatemongering, provoking assaults on personhood, exploitation by a dominant regional group, and maybe even violence and loss of life. The existence of Southern versus Northern discrimination and animus may seem preposterous in light of the 150+ years that has passed since the end of the Civil War in the U.S. Yet, on both sides, the flames of discrimination, bigotry, racism and overt hatred can flare up almost without notice and with alarming outcomes. The Civil Rights era in the 1950s and 1960s was played out in the midst of tinderbox-like conditions of social unrest, ripe for exploitation (Szczesiul 2017). More recently the "Unite the Right" rally held in Charlottesville, North Caroline in 2017 brought together protest and hate groups of the far-right (e.g., alt-Right, neo-Confederates, neo-fascists, neo-Nazis, White Nationalists, and others)! The rally became violent, provoked a state of emergency, and resulted in injuries, including the death of a counter protestor to the hate groups, Heather Heyer. As we shall discuss later, the politics that we use to identify ourselves and differentiate ourselves from "others" is a very human character, but can feed assaults on the "other," sometimes seemingly innocent, but still sourced to the great "original sins" festering in America for four centuries. The history of humankind begs a question. Is there something intrinsic to humans and their fallenness fueling discrimination that in the extreme can provoke hatred and killing of the "other"?

There is an old (and perhaps wise) aphorism to the effect, "Never talk about religion or politics." Identity of self is often cast in an amorphous mixture that includes religion and politics. The two elements converge in our own person, although the overlap is seldom unity. Political party platforms can be broad, forcing one to accept the entire menu even if it is only a few appetizers or main courses that one finds compelling or at least appealing. Likewise, world religions are seldom monoliths of anything, but do profess a core dogma. Adherents may hold fast to that which seems "correct" to them. Yet, adherents can veer away from core dogma at junctures in which the dogma just does not sit well in their gut. This practice may be termed "faithful disbelief." Although developed in a Christian context (Morse 2009), faithful disbelief suggests that even the faithful may have a sense of disbelief about some aspect of the interpretation of sacred texts or of an action purported to be in keeping with their faith. The history of world religions clearly is one replete with acts of faithful disbelief. Such disbelief can create tension leading to fragmentation of religious groups. Reconstitution of faith in an amended form typically follows, often constituting a new growing edge for a people of faith. For example, some members of the Roman Catholic faith may accept theoretically the church's dogma in a general broad sense, but find the church's position on women's reproductive rights to be archaic and paternalistic to the point patriarchy (Ruether 2013). Many Protestant denominations may adhere to core principles of Christian dogma, but still reject progressive views on topics such as gender equality and same-sex marriage (Wilson 2018). The Haredi, Judaism's steadfast adherents to Mosaic, Talmudic, and rabbinical Law, may well consider themselves the most authentic group of Jewish people, but offering little consideration to the political leanings of Conservative, Reform, or secular Jews on women's reproductive rights (Kasstan 2019). Today, adherents of Islam suffer disunity due to sectarianism, yet continue to strive towards a more homogeneous Muslim community centered about The Holy Qur'an (Ali 2018). Smaller populations of adherents of all faiths often can achieve a level of unity that simply is out of reach for sects and groups that number in the thousands or millions. Thus, from the perspective of religion, it is easy to identify with a group of adherents that appear as "self," which automatically renders the outsiders as "other." More often than not, collections of the "self" in religious or political groups can act to demean and therein to assault the personhood of those who fail to blindly affirm their core dogma or fail to meet strict criteria governing inclusion in the group.

Political groups may coalesce around a set of religious beliefs, principles, or experiences that bond and inform them as a group. Faith-based groups offer communities services and charitable giving typically consistent with a religious set of preferences and principles. Although charitable efforts may be restricted to "self-serving" targets (e.g., either for or against abortion), these groups often display great generosity and kindness to others. Charitable giving in 2018 surpassed $400B and is propelled also by tax policy in the U.S. (Fack and Landais 2016). Such truly charitable groups contrast sharply with what the Southern Poverty Law Center designates as "Hate Groups." Hate groups are social groups that advocate and practice hatred, hostility, and often violence aimed at "others" who differ from them (Southern Poverty Law Center 2018). Categories of the "other" are cast not only in religion, but more broadly in terms of race, class, gender, sexuality, as well as religious dogma, changing and evolving with the current times (Ore 2019). These days, hate groups in America use criteria such as skin color, national origin, ethnicity, religion, race, gender, gender identity, sexual orientation, and other considerations on which to judge "others." Hate speech and writings are designed to attack the personhood and basic rights of people who differ from the "base" identity of such hate groups. People can suffer multiple jeopardies at the hands of hate groups, for example, the personhood of a Muslim woman may be in grave triple jeopardy on the basis of color, gender, and religion (Southern Poverty Law Center 2018). Similarly, Americans who embrace gender rights and preferences of LGBTQI people may be subject to harassment in person, in writings of a hate group, or by Internet online harassment. Racism still dominates the Knights of the Klu Klux Klan (KKK) and other derivative groups that openly dismiss the personhood and rights of people of color (Bartoletti 2010). In the reverse, the Nation of Islam promotes a set of beliefs professing innate black superiority over whites (rejected by mainstream Muslims), anti-Semitism and anti-LGBT rhetoric (Gibson and Berg 2017). Self-proclaimed Christian Identity hate groups, export hatred towards progressive Christian denominations (e.g., the United Church of Christ) as well as world religions outside of Christianity (Southern Poverty Law Center 2018). White nationalists Neo-Nazi groups targeting women's rights as well as progressive Christians, non-Christians, and Jews are on the rise and again constitute an extreme example of hate groups that contest, degrade, or entirely deny the personhood and human rights of many people in the U.S. (Robbins and Crockett 2018). Mass shootings in the U.S. reflect the varied targets being threatened by far-right extremists with their fervent hatred. In many of these mass shootings, the "assault" upon the "other" is literal, that is, the perpetrators employ semiautomatic black "assault-like" rifles, derivatives of true weapons of war intentionally designed to inflict mass killings of labeled "others." Social unrest and upheaval often is employed as a foil to advance the agenda and membership of hate groups and typically is mirrored by increased purchases of handguns, shotguns, and "black" rifles in America.

Through self-discernment we may come to the conclusion that we all, every last one of us Americans, contest/assault the personhood of other people at some time, perhaps mostly in subtler manners. The infirm, the old, the deeply forgetful "other" always can be simply ignored. Is not intentionally ignoring another human being a form of assault on their personhood? Whether wheel chair bound navigating a parking spot, helplessly trying to manage a flight of stairs, or even panhandling on a subway or walkway, the "other" by virtue of their visual differences from us can be simply ignored. Yet, if these suffering humans were members of our family or community would not we be loath to simply ignore them? Can we somehow come to see through the veil of apparent "other" to a familiar face? These daily decisions to label people as "other" or as "self" constitutes an important element of what we call "identity politics" in America (Jardina 2019). Yes, it can be said that America is unique in having forged a national identity that does not preclude the emergence of derivative identity politics. We are happy to announce that we are Native American, African American, Italian American, Irish American, Lebanese American, and so on, and to label ourselves based upon ancestry, history, tradition, and religion. In so doing we are announcing to those not in our tribe that we are different from others. Toxic nationalism, in contrast, aims to erase the identities and being of competing groups of "other." Thankfully, it is a fool's errand. Asian and European nations, perhaps based upon their greater racial homogeneity, would think it odd if their citizens were to label themselves with a modifier indicating a nationality, for example, Irish Dutch, Italian Norwegian, English Chinese, or Lebanese Japanese! With respect to identity politics, Americans seem to want to have their cake and eat it too? If it is our preferred identity group, we are "all for it." If it is an identity group coalesced about the "other," however, we may be against it!

Identity politics can fuel national pride! In our nation with its checkered legacy of forced displacement, dispossession, and genocide of indigenous peoples, slavery of Blacks, a violent Civil War, rampant Civil Rights and Voting Rights violations, and continued suffering of marginalized peoples, do not these identities fragment the Great Society (Jardina 2019)? The violent death of Heather Heyer, a counter protester in a "Unite the Right" rally in Charlottesville, NC, in 2017, deeply stunned the nation (Acosta 2019). Chaotic rallies of White supremacists and White nationalists were propelled by a sharp rise in Neo-Nazi and white supremacist hate speech that placed identity politics front and center in the minds of Americans (Acosta 2019). Such hate rallies collectively bring together people whose hatred mostly is not targeted and monolithic, but rather scatted, amorphous, vile, and ill defined. The overarching content of these hate groups remains clear, it is racism. Racism in America now targets virtually all peoples of color, ethnic minorities, immigrants, and the historically marginalized. The images from the Charlottesville 2017 rally hark back to early days of the KKK in the South, as well as Nazi Germany and Fascist Italy of the 1930s and 1940s. In the last two centuries, torches in America have been deployed as a symbol of power and racial superiority. The assault on the basic human rights of fellow citizens and neighbors provokes the foundational question, what is driving such hatred and divisiveness?

What Drives Assaults on Personhood?

Based upon experiences as a senior academic administrator, pastor, and chaplain, I suspect that *fear* is the dominant catalyst in assaults on personhood. For someone attacking the personhood of another, it is the "fear of the other" that is the main driver of the calculus. Discounting the personhood of another often provides a cathartic response to the elements of fear. Fear is first provoked when "strangers," that is, the "others" whose appearance differs from one's own, confront us. Clothing, speech, and mannerism may suggest a different or unknown geographic ancestry and/or heritable phenotype. Such personal traits of the "other" often are lumped together with or simply labeled "race." Yet, skin color can vary naturally within races as well as ethnic groups. Skin color is the product of two genetic factors controlling the capacity for skin to form pigments, reddish yellow pheomelanin and brownish black eumelanin, in response to sunshine (Jablonski 2012). Human hair color also provides a wide range of colors and hues that can be quite striking when reflecting the relative absence of pigment (i.e., low levels of pheomelanin and eumelanin) in blond hair, to eumelanin-rich black hair (Gray 2000). Brown, auburn, and red hair actually are due to a recessive variation of the MC1R gene (encoding the melanocortin 1 receptor involved in normal pigmentation) yielding increased expression of pheomelanin (Gray 2000). The Norse Vikings may have introduced the MC1R hair color gene to their conquered peoples. The presence of MC1R gene likely provided the Vikings with a considerable advantage. Imagine the alarm and fear provoked in the "other" by Viking invaders sporting heads and faces thick with bright red hair, unknown to the inhabitants being invaded! Grey and white hair is often associated with aging humans. Not unexpectedly, the appearance of white hair and baldness in the "other" can generate significant anxiety. Those subconsciously fearing the inevitable creep of greying hair and/or baldness attendant to their own aging may feel strangely uncomfortable with elders. Yet, these physical characteristics, as striking as they may be, are not the only cause for fear and alarm among human beings.

Differences in religious creeds can be potent catalysts for fear and loathing among groups (Melton 1991). These factors are often conflated with ethno-nationalism (e.g., White supremacy), threats to community social identity (e.g., in Northern Ireland), and large-scale social-psychological trauma (e.g., forced migrations of people escaping wartime danger). Within this amalgam of fear, emotions, and the reaction to perceived change, the apparent provocateurs (e.g., immigrants, vagrants, and visitors) can be transformed in our minds to the "other," to be feared, despised, and discounted as being human according to our own context. A critical act and essential component to assaulting personhood is identifying and then actually affixing the label "other" (Morgan 2019). But rather than provoking empathy as Lévinas' ethics suggests (Morgan 2019), "otherness" can be the overarching basis on which inherent human rights of the other are contested, often to the extreme of discounting their being altogether. History has repeatedly shown the need of perpetrators to declare the "other." In order to achieve control over, forced migration of, or large-scale killing of the fear-promoting strangers, the humanity as "other" must first be steeply discounted or denied entirely. We are loath to act so upon those we consider as "self." Yet we have little problem ramping up our visceral response to those whom we hold accountable for either threats to our current state of affairs or bad brute fortune. People, we observed earlier, value freedom and autonomy, avoiding threats to either. The current ruling class with the greatest power and control at times may sense a withering away of their privileged status and autonomy. Such loss typically provokes an almost "*hyper*immune" response aimed at preserving "self," while attacking those who are "other." Physiologically we are conditioned to respond by either "fight-or-flight" when confronted with the challenge. Attendant with this fight-or-flight response is a state of "*hyper*arousal." Perceived as a threat to status, power, and especially survival, otherness provokes *hyper*arousal.

Lessons From Psychology: Understanding Fear and Hatred

How we manage fear of the stranger will determine how and to what extent we place at risk the human rights of the "other." The pursuit of understanding what drives human behaviors is timeless. Leading figures in psychology have each offered insights into human drives, which obviously would be operating in the confrontation of "self" with "other." Sigmund Freud (1856–1939) was the founder of the First Viennese School of Psychotherapy, proffering that pursuit of pleasure and avoidance of pain, or the "will to pleasure," was a dominant force behind all human behaviors (Freud and Brill 1930). According to Freud, deep sexual drives, the desire to procreate, and immediate gratification were central to "normal" desires. The Second Viennese School founded by Alfred Adler (1870–1937) stressed the basic drive of self-actualization, that is, a desire to fulfill our potential and overcome inherent limitations (Adler 1924). Adler's individual psychology was influenced by the "will-to-power" concept of the philosophy of Friedrich Nietzsche (Adler, Glueck, and Lind 1917). Noted neurologist and psychiatrist Viktor Frankl (1905–1997) founded the Third Viennese School of Psychology. A survivor of the Holocaust, Frankl proffered that no matter what the circumstance confronting humans, humans can choose how to respond to them (Frankl 2017). For Frankl, the basic freedom that enables humans to choose was man's "search for meaning," his dominant driver of human behavior (Frankl 1946, 1988; Redsand 2006). Modern psychology has expanded enormously in the 21st century, yet it is clear that drivers of human behavior, especially those driving the response of "self" to "other," are complex, multifactorial, and beyond the scope of our discussion.

The landscape of fear of "other"—especially in response to physical and mental disabilities, race, color, gender and gender identity, faith system and creeds, ageism, and identity politics—are front and center to interrogating innate fears. This litany of discriminators represents only some of the many and varied labels that can be embraced to contest another's personhood, yet it hardly defines underlying motives. The assault on being human can manifest in a wide range of manners. Some are disingenuous (e.g., intentionally mislabeling misogyny simply as the more innocuous "sexism"). Others may avoid any label at all, yet be dominant (e.g., excusing overt racism by White supremacists simply as reflecting "cultural anomalies"). Our own psychology of mistrust, animus, and fear of "other" is seldom a robust varietal; rather it is a complex blend of psychology that is often incompletely known to us. In a knee-jerk manner we may reject a claim that we are racist, homophobic, or xenophobic in our dealings with the "other," ascribing our behaviors as innocuously based in some religious or political beliefs. In the absence of truly significant exposure to and covenant with the "other," our mistrust and hatred can be submerged by sheer ignorance of how our "location" in life shapes our worldview on whom we label "other" rather than "self." An important first step in the direction of understanding our basis for how we contest the personhood of others is self-discernment. Self-discernment can be a misnomer. Our unassisted ability to spot our base fears, biases, mistrust, and perhaps hatred at times is poor (Dunning 2005). Community provides a place in which we can engage the "other" through authentic joint interests, fellowship, and the sharing of daily experiences of life. Community enables self-discernment. When we react to the "other" in a familiar tolerable discomfort we avoid self-discernment. Painfully, we often can recognize immediately in someone else hateful behaviors that we ourselves display subconsciously. Recall times among "friends" when the conversation may morph into racist memes or identity politics? Such public displays of discrimination and loathing of the "other" makes us uncomfortable, wishing that we could vanish and leave the setting. Yet, viewing bad behaviors in others may offer us a unique lens enabling self-discernment.

We may ask ourselves why public acts of discrimination makes us feel uncomfortable. We ask, "Am I like those of whom I now sit in judgment?" The psychologies of Freud, Adler, Frankl, Jung and others all operate, to some extent, within our being and explain, in part, our need to contest the being of the "other" whose simple presence can make us feel distressed, strange, fearful or angry. The inability to find a single paradigm of human behavior to explain this common unease is not so important. Being unable to discern our own inner self and our motivation to rush to judgment of the "other" is far more problematic. The daily media is filled with stories of folks "dropping a dime" on some other person, calling 911 to report a "suspicious" person to the police. By using the term "suspicious," we often are simply labeling the "other" and "otherness." We have learned that the response of the police at times also can be disproportionate to the initial uneasiness of a caller and provoke a sometimes lethal outcome for the innocent, often marginalized victim (Taylor 2016; Hillstrom 2018). High-visibility assaults on the personhood of the "other" may provoke widespread condemnation, as they should. Yet, on a smaller scale and daily, are not we all guilty of the same sins aimed at the "other" whose mere existence simply challenges our sensibilities or preferences?

BUILDING RESISTANCE TO THE AGGRESSORS: THEOLOGICAL PRESCRIPTS

Confronted with the face of those who seek to discount, degrade, and marginalize the personhood of others, are there ways to resist? The fallenness of humans, which I consider the basis for such ill will towards others, has been evident since the dawn of human interactions. The fight-or-flight response or a keen sense of "self" from "other" likely were selected by evolution to preserve an individual or tribe (Csermely et al. 2007). The fear and trepidation provoked by those that objectively present as "different" in skin color, race, ethnic origin, gender, and so on, are common and perhaps universal (Everly and Lating 2013). Nietzsche's will-to-power (like the fight-or-flight response) points to the resolution of the fear provoked by the "other," seeking to "power over" those who are not viewed as self (Nietzsche and Ludovici 2019). Such universality of human behavior would lead us to believe that throughout history, civilizations and empires (like people) must have developed defense mechanisms for the corporate as well as individual response to threatened being. Sensing that executive control of the will-to-power in fearful situations could provoke chaos and disharmony within groups, ancient as well as modern day rulers and their governments have turned to theological resources and common sense to combat such assaults. Typically, this option is selected only when it benefits the dominant ruling class. The legacy of theological principles and their eventual canonization in law and moral thinking is rich, definitively dated back to about 4,000 years ago. Such guiding moral principles most certainly evolved within conversations between secular ruling classes and the theological milieu in which they were embedded at the time. Herein we shall lens back in search of theological foundations for these moral leanings. Our first stop is ancient Mesopotamia. Current social mores constitute a fusion of secular and religious responses to fallen behaviors of humankind. They aim to neutralize uncontested "will-to-power" that both threatens and assaults the personhood of those deemed unlike us.

Hammurabi's Code and *Lex Talionis* (~1754 BCE)

Hammurabi, the sixth Babylonian king, codified a litany of 282 rules (and punishments) operating largely on the *lex talionis*, that is, "an eye for an eye, a tooth for a tooth" tradition (Hammurabi and Johns 2000). As punitive as this law of retaliation and retribution seems, *lex talionis* also offered the nucleus of the eventual Golden Rule, declaring, "do unto others as you would have them do unto you." Categorically, Hammurabi's admonition is a negative rule; the Golden Rule is positive (Gensler 2013). The Golden Rule does not proffer going beyond the requirements of duty. Actually, it does not declare that you should "love thy neighbor," rather it is more like a proverb or maxim encouraging social reciprocity along lines of socially accepted standards of behavior. The Golden Rule could be cast as a Categorical Imperative according to the moral prescripts of Immanuel Kant, for it would truly be better if we did unto others only that as we would have them do unto us (Gensler 2013). From an operational standpoint Hammurabi's version of *lex talionis* is most effective in face-to-face interactions among members of a familial group. Therefore it does imply an unstated need for proximity among the parties. It is doubtful that *lex talionis* alone would have been effective if presented to the people as some "motto" or "analect" handed down by some distant ruler (Gensler 2013). *Lex talionis* provided rather both moral direction and a proactive perspective that proved useful in many circumstances. At its worst, "eye for an eye" thinking only perpetuates similar acts of retaliation, politely termed "retributive justice."

As a tool to promote equanimity and avoid assaults on personhood, the Golden Rule proved valuable mostly in the context of homogenous tribes and clans in which the rule evolved. In seeking equal treatment, punishment as accorded under the Rule was seldom necessary, especially amongst members of society possessing roughly equivalent wealth and power. Application of the Golden Rule among families, tribes, and clans demands little moral investment other than peer-conventions aimed at optimizing harmony among "relevant" members (Gensler 2013). Full membership in familial groups would virtually guarantee seamless application of the Golden Rule to address disputes among all the male adults with wealth, property and power. Historically, women and children, widows and orphans, did not enter into the calculus in such patriarchal, patrilineal societies. Virtually all ancient civilizations and empires considered the Golden Rule more as a privileged principle to be shared among members of the ruling class males. In the margins of society life was different. Marginalized groups, such as women, orphans, freemen, and slaves alike simply were denied personhood. On the one hand, the Golden Rule evolved from the "eye for an eye" to "do unto others." On the other hand, application of the Golden Rule was *not* universal, it was made available only to a privileged class of powerful men. Absent membership in this privileged ruling class automatically discounted one's personhood to some low standard or to no personhood at all. Thus the tension between "self" and "other" at this level was not solved. At its best, the Golden Rule only guided in a prescribed manner interpersonal tensions that arose among the "topsiders" for whom it was crafted. There was no intention to be inclusive in the application of the Golden Rule at this time in history.

World Religions and Encountering the Marginalized "Other"

Forming a basic love and respect for someone other than you, another person, the "other" by definition, is a core prescript of world religions. Within family groups, clans, tribes, and some communities that are more or less homogenous in skin color, race, creed/faith, and moral agreement there is little disagreement that we must "do unto others, as we would have them do unto us" (Gensler 2013). The term "other" in some cases must be applied to those whose lives fall outside of the norm. Examples are the widows, orphans, the broader class of the "poor," as well as the "*goyem*" or heathens. For the Jewish people in ancient times, the Book of Moses (e.g., Exodus 23:9 and Leviticus 19:9, 18) included what could be best characterized by the concept of a "preferential option for the poor." This concept does not guarantee full personhood of all "other," but rather seeks to make amends to people for whom bad brute luck has discounted their lives. Such "cutouts" for the widows, orphans, and destitute reaffirmed the victims' core identity as "Jews" and reinforced peerage, but yet fell short of demanding full personhood for all Jews. Among people of the Jewish faith, in its many forms, there is great tension even today as to who is worthy of the designation of the fullest personhood among the Jewish people? Is it the Ultra Orthodox (Haredi), Reformed, Conservative, or Orthodox Jews who are to be included in "self," or not? The emergence of the Jewish diaspora virtually insured that Jews could no longer be considered a uniform, homogeneous group, but rather more a rich tapestry of distinctive communities found within the global ethnically Jewish population. *Eudemonia*, like *Shalom*, are terms calling for peace, harmony, and "wholeness" for all in community. Benevolence, which extends beyond the Golden Rule, is central to Jewish people, focusing proximally upon family and neighbors of the same sect. Leviticus 19:18 reinforces this point by proffering a need for altruistic reciprocity. Yet, the intent of Lev 19:18 is aimed squarely to operate solely within the concept of "kinsfolk." Providing hospitality to the stranger or alien was an act designed to remind the Jews that once they too were slaves in a foreign land. Such acts of charity (see Leviticus 23:22; 25:25–35) are to be lauded. They reveal, however, little about the broader question of who is declared eligible for these charitable acts? Importantly, the act of not judging the "other" should not be equated with acting in true community with the "other," embraced as "self" (Plaut and Stein 2015). Beneficence is put to the test of inclusivity when the spheres of "self" come into contact and consequent tension with those of the "other" who may not be family, tribal cohort, or kinsfolk.

The Analects of Confucius (551–479 BCE) included additional variation of the Golden Rule stating, "that which you do not want done to yourself, do not do to others" (Analects 15:23) (Confucius and Dawson 2008). Yet, what emerged from Confucian thought was a broader, deeper, and more altruistic prescript than simply "doing unto others." Confucius introduced a core principle of "*ren*." *Ren*, considered to be an essential virtue, is derived by altruistic thought and action (Confucius and Dawson 2008). *Ren* is an extension of Confucian inner ideals to the outward world, that is, to the "other." Embedded in this Confucian practice is basic human compassion, humanness, or human-heartedness. For example, *ren* is expressed naturally in the care of children and aged family. Confucius extended these principles to all, a remarkable achievement within an ancient China that displayed a rigid clan system. Yet, like the restrictions of earlier patriarchal belief systems, inclusion of women and children under the care of *ren* was not clearly affirmed. In his time, Confucius would likely not have considered patriarchy as anything more than a long-standing and venerable tradition. In practice, Confucianism was more than a religion or philosophy of ideals, it was a path to living a simple life that was humane and compassionate. It displays an ideal well beyond the Golden Rule aiming obliquely to achieve base equivalence for the personhood for all human beings.

The practice of Buddhism (considered by many as a "religion") is infused with the Golden Rule. "Hurt not others with that which pains you," found in the Udanavarga (5:18) was preached by Gautama Buddha (~563/480 to ~483/400 BCE). This concept is the basis of the Buddhist Three Pure Precepts, simply put, to not create evil, to practice good, and to actualize good for others. Importantly, the Third Pure Precept (a.k.a., Third Noble Truth), sometimes is translated as "living to benefit *all* beings," is clear as to inclusivity. Consequently, compassion of a Buddhist adherent is to be extended to all beings, true inclusiveness (Nhât 1999). As we have observed, such inclusivity is a radical departure from most belief systems. Buddhism encourages compassion to be extended to all beings, including humans. The fullest personhood of the "other" is never in doubt. In Buddhist tradition, compassion extends beyond inclusivity for human beings to *all* beings! In today's lexicon, Buddhist practice of compassion extends to the entire "biome," the community of animal life, flora, and fauna. Although not steeped in the metaphysical, Buddhism also extends its belief system to a life hereafter. For

Buddhists, the hereafter creates an opportunity for continued practice. These pillars encourage deep compassion for all people, effectively extinguishing the notion of "other." There is only that "self" extending outwards enveloping all that lives. The practice extends from what one simply knows, to how one is to live one's life in harmony, with life itself. Discrimination aimed at peoples of different skin color, creed/religion, gender, age, and so on, finds no place in the Buddhist heart. Compassion remains as the dominant force of avoiding evil, of doing good, and of saving all beings. Assaults on personhood aimed at peoples with vulnerabilities of body, or mind, or soul are anathema to Buddhism. The very act of contesting the being of anybody would violate each of the Three Pure Precepts of Buddhism (Nhât 1999).

The "eternal" tradition of Hinduism has many ancient roots that coalesced in 500 to 300 BCE in the absence of a founder. Rich in diversity, Hinduism is a hybrid of traditions constituted as a foundational spirituality. The essence of the Golden Rule also can be captured in the sacred writing Mahabharata (5:1517), "this is the sum of duty: do nothing that would cause you pain if done to you." Early Vedas and later Upanishads, considered the most sacred texts of Hinduism, focus primarily on the "first do no harm" aspect of morality (Jacobsen et al. 2009). Neither the active aspects of helping others nor an overarching compassion for all are emphasized in these writings. Compassion remains a virtue and a philosophical core in *dharma*, that is, the way of righteous and ethical living (Jacobsen et al. 2009). *Daya* is the desire to mitigate the troubles and sorrows of the "other." *Karuna*, also translating as "compassion," is placing one's mindset into that of the "other," in order to gain insights into the suffering of the "other." *Anukampa* is the compassion learned through empathetic support of one suffering (Jacobsen et al. 2009). Most of all, Hinduism seeks self-discernment in the context of "learning through sharing" the pain of the "other." In spite of the long and noble traditions, inclusivity in the sense that all people are deserving of full personhood has had to push mightily against the considerable social ethnographic discrimination embedded in the caste system in India. Whether the caste system truly can be considered a Hindi tradition or a remnant imposed upon India by British Empire in the collapse of the Mughal era remains controversial (Bayly 2001). Thus, what is encountered again is an insuppressible human fallenness that restricts one's compassion to only a peer-relevant group, family, clan, or tribe. To what extent the Hindu practice extends beyond and crosses boundaries such as those of the castes is beyond the scope of our discussion.

Islamic tradition is infused with the content of the Golden Rule. "None of you has faith until he loves for his brother or neighbor what he loves for himself" (Sahih Muslim, Book 1, Number 72). The ethics of reciprocity is a fundamental pillar of Islam (Al-Faruqi and International Institute of Islamic Thought 1992). Not unlike other world religions, the principle of reciprocity in Islam was early on largely confined to the "relevant other," not to *all* people. What is universal is the pillar of compassion delivered by the Islamic prophet Muhammad in the Holy Qur'an. Tawhid, or the principle of "oneness" or unity, espoused in the Holy Qur'an opens the aperture of the principle of reciprocity and compassion to all (Al-Faruqi and International Institute of Islamic Thought 1992). "Truly those who believe, and the Jews, and the Christians, and Sabeans—whosoever believes in God and the Day of Judgment and act virtuously will receive their reward from their Lord," (2:62). Furthermore the Holy Qur'an encourages compassion, "whoever saves the life of one human being, it shall be as if he had saved the whole of humankind" (5:32). The works of Islamic writers like Jalâl al-Din Rumi (1207–1273 CE) still resonate with those seeking to understand the essential role of compassion in all human interactions (Jalâl al-Dīn and Barks 1995). Thus, assaulting the personhood of the "other," the stranger, the widow, the orphan, and poor finds abundant pushback in Judaism, Confucianism, Buddhism, Hinduism, and in Islam. These are powerful theological tools that can be mobilized to advance the argument for the fullest personhood of all human beings, regardless of how they differ from one's self.

The Christian faith likewise is replete with biblical verses and theological dogma encouraging compassion for the "other." Morphing well beyond the reciprocity principle and injunctions for fairness and compassion found in the Hebrew Bible, the message promoted by Jesus of Nazareth (circa 4 BCE–circa 30–33 CE) expanded the Golden Rule in response to pressing questions. Who is one's neighbor? How is the "other" to be embraced? The Gospel according to John informs us of a new dictum offered by Jesus of Nazareth (13:34) "A new command I give you: Love one another. As I have loved you, so you must love one another." A second example borrows heavily from Deuteronomy (6:4–7) of the Torah. The Gospel according to Matthew (22:34–40) recounts an interaction between Jesus of Nazareth and Temple scribes. The scribes are seeking to entrap Jesus. "Hearing that Jesus had silenced the Sadducees, the Pharisees got together. One of them, an expert in the law, tested him with this question: 'Teacher, which is the greatest commandment in the Law?' Jesus replied: 'Love the Lord your God with all your heart and with all your soul and with all your mind.' This is the first and greatest commandment. And the second is like it: 'Love your neighbor as yourself. All the Law and the Prophets hang on these two commandments.'" Today, such love proffered by Jesus often is labeled as "radical" love. The aim is simple, to create true inclusivity. This pronouncement, however, falls short. Although commonly interpreted as inclusive language, the text fails to firmly establish if every "stranger" is to be declared truly one's neighbor or not? This begs the question, to whom does Christian "humanism" extend? It is a critical question for 21st century followers of Jesus to ask themselves (Zimmermann 2017).

A deeper meaning of the intention of this "radical" love is found elsewhere in the New Testament. Blessings recounted by Jesus in the Sermon on the Mount appear in the so-called "Beatitudes." Eight of beatitudes appear in the Gospel of Matthew (5:3–11). Four appear in the blessings recounted by Jesus in the Sermon on the Plain in chapter 6 of the Gospel of Luke (Hunsinger 2015). The final blessing of the Sermon on the Plain (Luke 6:22) expands the domain of "neighbor," intentionally reaching out to embrace those who hate, exclude, insult, and reject you (McKenna 1999). The Gospel of Luke continues with more explicit advice aimed at embracing so-called enemies, into which category we may include the "other," the "stranger," the "foreigner" and the *provocateur* of fear. Luke 6 (vs. 27–31) reads: "But I say to you that listen, Love your enemies, do good to those who hate you, bless those who curse you, pray for those who abuse you. If anyone strikes you on the cheek, offer the other also; and from anyone who takes away your coat do not withhold even your shirt. Give to everyone who begs from you; and if anyone takes away your goods, do not ask for them again. Do to others as you would have them do to you." Herein we hear a clear echo from the Hebrew Bible, absent earlier demands for reciprocal justice, *lex talionis*, the call for "eye for an eye" retribution. According to this amendment, violent acts and assaults call the victims to offer greater understanding, compassion, and "yes" even Christian love (i.e., *agape*) for the perpetrator. This advice truly is "radical!" It requires restraint of the "fight-or-flight" response hardwired into our psyche and physiology. Rather we are encouraged to embrace a "tolerance-and-love" response. Practically speaking, this recipe is much "easier said than done."

Jesus of Nazareth offers a rationale for radical love towards the "other," especially one's enemy. In Luke 6 (31–36) Jesus instructs: "Do to others, as you would have them do to you. If you love those who love you, what credit is that to you? For even sinners love those who love them. If you do good to those who do good to you, what credit is that to you? For even sinners do the same. If you lend to those from whom you hope to receive, what credit is that to you? Even sinners lend to sinners, to receive as much again. But love your enemies, do good, and lend, expecting nothing in return. Your reward will be great, and you will be children of the Most High; for he is kind to the ungrateful and the wicked. Be merciful, just as your Father is merciful." Justification fueling such radical love is consolidated and amplified in these final pronouncements. Theologically, Jesus invokes the foundational need for thanksgiving for the mercy that is found in the grace of God. As Christians adhere to the belief that humans receive divine grace freely and without regard to merit (or absence of merit), so ought they extend mercy and love to all others, especially the displaced, marginalized, often despised "other."

Two principles emerge in our search for theological tools with which to understand and then overcome those who assault the personhood of the "other." First, our understanding and compassion should not be restricted to those who love us, for example, our family, our tribe, clan, or nation. Jesus of Nazareth encourages all people to a broader, deeper inclusivity of humankind. Christians view each other first as members of God's community, benefitting from the grace of God, the love of Jesus, and community of the Holy Spirit. In so embracing this dogma, we are encouraged to love those who love us and as well those who hate us. Such love is not self-seeking, but rather self-denying. Furthermore it is an invitation to voluntarily enter into the suffering of the "other." The suffering of the "other" may not be obvious to us. Our perception of someone else's hatred or dislike of who we are, what we represent, or how we behave can shield our eyes and hearts to their suffering. Our psyche's immune system is set to high gain for ourselves and loved ones, but often is "turned down" or "off" to the suffering of the "other."

Discrimination, hunger, food insecurity, homelessness, and fear of the "other" continue to climb in the U.S., as identity politics gains ever-increasing traction in the public square. Do we intentionally turn down the gain of our compassion to those in need simply if they are different from us? Do we withhold compassion from victims and their suffering when they present to us as unlike our family, clan, or tribe? What is necessary to overcome our innate fear or contempt of the "other" is simple, just mercy. If divine mercy operates in our lives, how can we ignore the suffering for others, especially if there is something that we can do to mitigate it? In the Gospel of Matthew (5:44–45), Jesus of Nazareth reminds his audience that God causes the sun to rise on the evil as well as the good. God sends the rain to the righteous and the unrighteous. Who are we to deny the benefits of divine grace and just compassion to other human beings who are suffering? Can we profess allegiance to freedom and the flourishing of all, if the "other" among us are suffering from insults or injury that we can prevent? Or rather do we seek to offer only "fake" solace? Is our true *modus operandi* simple, unadulterated hypocrisy? Does the suffering of the "other" provoke kind, but only empty words and gestures, bereft of compassion and action?

A more detailed road map towards greater understanding the pronouncements of Jesus of Nazareth on radical love is found in the Gospel of Matthew 25 (34–45). This pericope provides rich examples on being hypocritical in our valuing of the personhood of the "other." The Gospel recounts Jesus telling of a parable about a king, " Then the king will say to those at his right hand, 'Come, you that are blessed by my Father, inherit the kingdom prepared for you from the foundation of the world; for I was hungry and you gave me food, I was thirsty and you gave me something to drink, I was a stranger and you welcomed me, I was naked and you gave me clothing, I was sick and you took care of me, I was in prison and you visited me.' Then the righteous will answer him, 'Lord, when was it that we saw you hungry and gave you food, or thirsty and gave you something to drink? And when was it that we saw you a stranger and welcomed you, or naked and gave you clothing? And when was it that we saw you sick or in prison and visited you?' And the king will answer them, 'Truly I tell you, just as you did it to one of the least of these who are members of my family, you did it to me.' Whereas, for those at his left hand Jesus recounts this same King saying, 'You that are accursed, depart from me into the eternal fire prepared for the devil and his angels; for I was hungry and you gave me no food, I was thirsty and you gave me nothing to drink, I was a stranger and you did not welcome me, naked and you did not give me clothing, sick and in prison and you did not visit me.' Then they also will answer, 'Lord, when was it that we saw you hungry or thirsty or a stranger or naked or sick or in prison, and did not take care of you?' Then he will answer them, 'Truly I tell you, just as you did not do it to one of the least of these, you did not do it to me.'" This parable is a powerful injunction against displays of false Christian love and inaction. After digesting this parable, should we not plumb our own being, interrogating how we truly respond to the "other," the least of us, those "strangers" in dire need among us? Do we value their being as humans? Will our efforts selflessly advocate for their full personhood and well-being? Would we love them as family, or rather are we repelled by their strangeness and cast them as "other"? The poor, sick, needy, shelterless, and marginalized who challenge our sensibilities, would they not cast us in the role as the hypocrites at the left hand of the King?

REIMAGINING PERSONHOOD

Why Reimagine?

Instead of confronting the many ways, both large and small, that we all are capable of discounting/degrading the personhood of others, perhaps we should seek to *reimagine* personhood? Most of the time only the obvious symptoms of assaults on personhood are in our mind's eye. Racism, identity politics, anti-Semitism, and a multitude of common sins in our society are manifest in both small and large ways. But the underlying disease that allows us to discriminate, demean, and discount another's personhood often is far from the view of both the observer as well as the perpetrator. In my experience, people who carry out every day racist acts seldom consider themselves racists at all. Harsh public assaults aimed at the personhood of transsexual and LGBTQI people, for example, are far more common than thought. Yet, the perpetrators would likely deny what they do as "hate crimes." The complexity of the human psyche does not render it accessible to detailed analysis of either the source or the amplifiers that drive inhumane acts and criminal behaviors. Such assaults are well documented in the annals of humankind, past and present. In the absence of any good data suggesting major progress in addressing the roots of deep-seated fear and loathing of the "other" in U.S. society, a new approach seems necessary and a worthwhile investment!

Beings Within Creation

A "creation myth" is a foundational sacred element of many religious traditions. Creation myths are rich and diverse, drawing from cultural, religious, and oral traditions that hold great meaning for adherents (Sproul 1979). A central theme permeating many such myths is that of a creation "event" either bringing cosmic order to chaos or establishing being from *ex nihilo* (i.e., out of nothing). Creation myths seek to pose as well as to answer queries about the source and meaning of life, extending from the broadest reaches of the cosmos to reflection upon self-identity (Sproul 1979). By necessity, creation narratives are human attempts to discern in their time, oral traditions, and symbols passed on by countless prior generations of humans. By definition, such narratives are imaginative, offering clues as to how the cosmos/world was formed, from what source(s), and most importantly about the role of human beings in Creation. Creation from nothing (*ex nihilo*) is common to some ancient creation myths as well as to the "Creation *Ex Nihilo*" theory of multiverse creation (Sproul 1979). The Hot Big Bang theory of the universe is not theological, but rather is a product of research in physics and cosmology that supports the general "out of nothing" origin (Gorbunov and Rubakov 2017). In the presence of substance and energy, the chaos myth of creation suggests in contrast, that the cosmos was formed and ordered by some supernatural force or being (Leeming and Leeming 2010). The creation narratives of the Hebrew Bible (e.g., Genesis chapters 1:1 to 2:3 of the Pentateuch) best resemble a "chaos" myth. Chaos is then brought into order by "In the beginning God created the heaven and the earth" from the Book of Genesis. In this mythology, order and form are products of the hands of God. For some traditions, the present-day inhabited world represents the emergence or reemergence from a former world. This mythology imagines the "womb" of an earth "mother" who enables the "birth" or "emergence" of the current world. Thus there exist many rich and imaginative myths about creation (Farmer 1978). Of these varied cosmic creation narratives, only the Big Bang can be viewed as supported by compelling physical analysis and data (Keranen 2017). As impressive as the physical data set supporting the Big Bang theory is, it neither precludes nor dispels other creation myths and narratives. Creation narratives remain a source of great spiritual meaning for many people.

One singularly essential character of creation narratives has been largely overlooked. Creation commonly is viewed as a singular event that occurred in a very distant past. Whether 6,000 to 12,000 years ago accorded by some religious sources or the 13.5 billion-year timeline approximated by the Big Bang theory, creation is cast as an "event in the past." Overlooked is fact that whenever commenced, creation is a dynamic, *ongoing* process not a singular event in the past. By any account, the grand dimensions and expanding nature of creation is thoroughgoing, limitless, and outside of time itself! The American astrophysicist and astronomer Carl Sagan (1934–1996) offered a poignant humility about the "pale blue dot" called "Earth." In his popular book *Pale Blue Dot: A Vision of the Human Future in Space* Sagan wrote, . . . "Look again at that dot. That's here. That's home. That's us. On it everyone you love, everyone you know, everyone you ever heard of, every human being who ever was, lived out their lives. The aggregate of our joy and suffering, thousands of confident religions, ideologies, and economic doctrines, every hunter and forager, every hero and coward, every creator and destroyer of civilization, every king and peasant, every young couple in love, every mother and father, hopeful child, inventor and explorer, every teacher of morals, every corrupt politician, every 'superstar,' every 'supreme leader,' every saint and sinner in the history of our species lived there—on a mote of dust suspended in a sunbeam (Sagan 1994)." The point that Sagan makes is this, within a vast cosmic arena, creation has played out and *is playing out* each and every day of our existence. We humans simply are called into being, into whatever Creation narrative we prefer. We are parts of the ongoing vast cosmic story. Put simply, we are the existing seeds of the harvest to come. Only in this context as being part of the ongoing creation can we begin to reimagine personhood.

Suppose we reimagine the significance of the concept of "called into being" in this world. "Called into being" is an event over which we each have no control. Typically, reflection on this phrase encourages enumeration of contextual markers in a human life, for example, birthdate, place of birth, birth parents, and data obtained from family ancestry. In the context of our reimagined "call into being" and Creation, such hallmarks are of little consequence. The details of our birth parents shrinks in importance when compared to the enormity of realizing that we fully cohabit this singular time and space, each of us being seeds sown of a harvest yet to come within Creation itself. Consider a process initiated billions of years ago. More importantly, this process is *ongoing* in our own time. In this new context of understanding, creation is expressed in our *own* being. When we reflect about Creation, casting it as a singular ancient event, we lose perspective on the essential feature, that is, our own "being" is part and parcel of the cosmic process! Creation is unfolding through us in our time. Rather than simple observers, we are *participants* actively contributing in ongoing creation. Creation continues with us and within us! *Homo sapiens* have been called into being on Earth for only the last 50,000 years. Already a 13.5 billion year timeframe (and counting), Creation continues in our existence! The formation of the stars, continuing expansion of the multiverse, evolving infinite number of solar systems, and "yes" each of us together constitutes Creation *in progress*. Most human beings would hardly consider their very existence as indispensable to *ongoing* Creation, but it is so. In this *ongoing*, creative, billions-of-years Creation, every person whom you know, everyone whom you have loved, everyone whom you have heard about, and everyone whose life has overlapped with your existence are truly "*co-travelers*" on this journey.

Co-Travelers Within a Community of Being

How should we reimagine our new relationship to each other? On a numerical basis, how might our interactions with co-travelers in Creation stack up with members of our family of origin? At the present time, it has been calculated that more than 110 billion of humans (i.e., *Homo sapiens*) have lived or are living on Earth. This number is staggering on all counts! First, ten thousand years ago only ~5–10 million people were alive, or about 0.0000005% of all human beings ever called into being to date. Second, by the beginning of the Common Era (i.e., year 1, Anno Domini + AD) the number of humans in existence had increased to 150–300 million, that is, 0.00027% of all humans called into being. Third, by 1650, the population of what would emerge as the United States of America was estimated to be ~6.05 million, indigenous Native Americans constituted more than 99%, or ~6 million! Fourth, the ~330,000,000 Americans alive at the beginning of the 21st century constitute less than 0.3% of all humans ever called into being on Earth! Thus, we the current co-travelers in Creation are but a tiny sliver of humanity, less than 0.5%, following thousands of generations of humans called into being before us. By such metrics, our relationality to "co-travelers" at this very moment in Creation is far greater than with that of members of the former generations that have preceded us, our family included!

As co-travelers in this very thin slice of Creation, how do we interact spatially? For adults emancipated from their childhood home, the bulk of their existence is *not* spent with siblings, parents, and second and third degree family relatives. Rather, our existence is spent among those "others" who simply were coincidentally called into being, that is, co-travelers in our own time and space. In the most populous state of the U.S. per unit area (i.e., New Jersey), the average density of humans is a scant 2 people per acre of land (U.S. Census, 2017)! In Alaska, the population density of Americans declines precipitously. On average there is but one human being for every 830 acres of land in Alaska! In view of these data it is clear that we embrace the humanity about us most regularly and intimately in our homes, work places, schools and shopping centers. Yet, such a congregation of people does not a community make. The concept of "community" most often conjures up visuals of residential areas. Residences (e.g., "bedroom communities") and places set aside for commerce, communal worship, and sports facilities rather are meeting places. They are where we congregate, but are they "community"? The ancient tribal and family-based community was essential to flourishing of early hominids. Such tightly functional communities have been lost or fragmented by modern life and increased mobility (Block 2018). The ancient tribes did not need to overtly claim to be "in community," their survival was dependent upon it. Today collections of humans congregating together often do not constitute true "community," in the ancient sense.

True communities are founded through forming covenantal ties that bind us with our co-travelers. In 21st century America, seldom are these co-travelers first or second degree family. Covenant-based true community of "self" and "other" (i.e., co-travelers) emerges only gradually. In community, each new member voluntarily swears by oath (typically before God for adherents of the Abrahamic religions) that they will love, care for, and commit their time, concern, and blessings to the community for the greater good (Horsley 2009). In community, relationships emerge in which genetically unrelated (i.e., not blood kin) members assume new roles as surrogate family members, committed to the common good and needs of all. In true community, moral solidarity is present and essential. The personhood of all members of such a community is embraced as "full." Full personhood is insured through the covenantal relationship, founded in community through moral solidarity. The fallenness of community members can continually challenge moral solidarity. In such cases, conviction of unethical or criminal behavior made public damages both the individual as well as to the corporate community. A community in moral solidarity, however, will neither cast out nor shun the fallen individual. Rather the community understands, anticipates, and accepts that human fallenness cannot be abolished, only overcome with unconditional self-sacrificing love, *agape*. Working together in the wake, the community seeks not to judge, but only to assist in the redemption of a genuinely repentant, fallen member. Such forgiveness can extend well beyond community.

An extraordinary example of forgiveness overcoming abject fallenness of the "other" was displayed in the aftermath of the West Nickel Mines School shooting in 2006. An outside gunman confronted the Old Order Amish community in Pennsylvania, executing a horrific mass shooting of Amish children at school. In a series of shooting, five children (ages 7 to 13) were murdered in the community's meetinghouse. Shortly after and in a remarkable display of community, the Old Order members who suffered the losses paid a visit to the shooter's family to embrace the tragedy and to offer forgiveness (Kraybill, Nolt, and Weaver-Zercher 2010). Martin Doblemeier's movie entitled *The Power of Forgiveness* (2007) provides a deeply moving analysis of forgiveness and magnanimity that overcame this tragic loss in the Amish community. The capacity of the Amish survivors to embrace and defend the personhood of the shooter and his family remains unimaginable for most people. This capacity to forgive and overcome evil with loving-kindness is the product of true community with moral solidarity. In this case the Amish community was in fact "closed." However, its moral solidarity clearly extended outside of its community to the greater world.

If the aim is to create community that commits to the full personhood of all, how might it form? The example from the Old Order Amish community in West Nickel Mines is extraordinary, but exemplary behavior of other communities abounds in the everyday world in which we live. For the Old Order Amish, moral solidarity by covenant resides within the community, but reaches beyond, to the outside world. "Outsiders" are operationally labeled as "other." The outsiders benefit from the moral solidarity of the community, but remain outside of the community. As noted for the application of the Golden Rule or the Greatest Commandment, a key limitation was inclusivity and who could be a member of the community. Herein is where the definition of community deepens. Is the community inclusive of all, in which there is only "self," there can be no "other"? This lack of inclusivity in our examples harkens back to the analysis of theological tools available to facilitate creation of true community. The overarching theme remains inclusivity, for only in true community will moral solidarity extend to all. Theoretically, the logic of Jesus of Nazareth enveloping unconditional and self-sacrificial love, emerges as a worthwhile paradigm to building true community, that is, a personhood for all (Lohfink 1984). Yet, in most cases, the Christian message as practiced in the 21st century America remains bereft of true inclusivity, including the Old Order Amish. The theoretical power and logic of the Greatest Commandment can be viewed as a roadmap to true community in moral solidarity. It remains at best a hope, lingering at the narrow gate of "already, but not yet" (Lohfink 1984). If our lived humanity rests upon community that can emerge in many "flavors," how do co-travelers in Creation build one with true inclusivity and moral solidarity?

The Protestant German Lutheran pastor and theologian Dietrich Bonhoeffer proposed a theological model termed *Communio Sanctorum* (a.k.a., *sanctorum communio*), a "communion of saints," as a paradigm for Christian inclusivity within the body of Christ (Bonhoeffer and Green 1998). In our diverse and non-ecumenical 21st century nation, can we reimagine a similar, but irreligious path towards the lofty goal of creating moral solidarity in the U.S. in the 21st century? In a nation of dynamic diversity of races, cultures, traditions, and beliefs can a template arise for inclusive community in moral solidarity found within the logic of Jesus of Nazareth, but absent Christian dogma? Dietrich Bonhoeffer analyzed the requirements for inclusive community bonded in covenant, in his 1927 doctoral dissertation (Bonhoeffer 1931). As emphasized herein, achieving formation of *Communio Sanctorum* requires above all other criteria, the *singular need for moral solidarity in covenantal relationship among all*. Reimagining personhood in 21st century America in concert with the desire to create of inclusive community free of contested personhood is benefitted by this earlier work of Bonhoeffer (Bonhoeffer and Brocker 2006).

REIMAGINED *COMMUNIO SANCTORUM* OF 21ST CENTURY AMERICA

Why is Community Essential?

Reimagined community embracing full personhood, is it simply "fantasy"? In our context, reimagination is taking stock in what we know and more importantly extending it imaginatively into the future. It is not fanciful, empty, baseless, or childlike to employ our powers of analysis based upon that which we see about us in 21st century America extended into the future. This future that we imagine is not tomorrow. Yet, more importantly, the time-frame should not be reduced to the "distant" future, decades, or even centuries ahead. If we can agree on the first principles that guide our reimaging America, the implementation only will be limited by our resolve to bring this reimagined society into being. We have lifted up the deep relationships that exist among co-travelers in Creation. Relationality with co-travelers in our existence is greater than with those ascribed to family and tradition. We have noted that examples of this reimagined future already exist in some small communities, distributed throughout the nation. Emergence of such covenantal communities may be idiosyncratic at times, yet these covenantal communities display many of the features necessary to forming *Communio Sanctorum*. We shall incorporate those features which we have discerned as essential to forming true community into our final reimagined planning documents.

It behooves us to take stock in former and existing covenantal communities, distilling the principles that are *writ large* and propel our imagination. Likewise we must be vigilant for untoward properties of communities, for example, lack of scalability, that would prevent success. Scalability is essential. What succeeds in a small community may be unworkable in efforts aimed at creating an inclusive American community in moral solidarity. The Old Order Amish Mennonite Church displays an emblematic character of humility, forgiveness and reconciliation (Niemeyer and Kraybill 1993). Yet, the Old Order remains a "closed community." It is estimated that the Order has permitted less than a hundred new outside "seekers" to join since 1950. Its moral solidarity and inclusivity are attractive and worth emulating, but the "closed" nature of its covenant is not. Likewise, similar efforts of the Shakers succeeded in generating harmonious community steeped in communalism, pacifism, and equality of the sexes in 18th century America (Stein 1992), but ultimately were doomed to fail on other accounts. In their case, the Shakers suffered through adherence to celibacy. Lacking a sufficient and constant stream of new adherents ultimately placed sustainable of formerly vibrant Shaker communities throughout America out of reach (Stein 1992). By 2017, all but a handful of the Shakers remained at its last site, the Sabbathday Community in Maine. Most exemplary movements enjoyed success, but almost universally on a small scale. These communities were not created as a template for society-at-large in mind. Success of community building on a larger scale is most often enabled within homogenous populations, already sharing common beliefs and traditions (e.g., Japan and South Korea). As a society rich in diversity and frank heterogeneity, the U.S. exhibits formidable obstacles to creating inclusive community, for example, racism, poverty, and classism. Thus properties of sustainability and of scalability remain essential to forming *Communio Sanctorum* in America. Overarching with regard to obstacles to formation of inclusive community in moral solidarity, I profess, is intentionally overlooking the legacy of "original sins" upon which American empire was built. The true test of any community that we reimagine for the U.S. is the moral fiber to address original sins. For addressing and redressing the legacy of these profound original sins is the only path to overcoming deeply felt animus that fuels assaults on personhood every day, throughout the U.S.

"Self," There Can Be No "Other"

The first step would be to embrace the fundamental truth that all human beings possess high relationality with each other, products of a thorough going, progressive Creation. This gesture is essential to building a reimagined community. As such, we share a "call into being," that is, a short-lived lifetime of shared existence on Earth less than a blink of an eye contrasted with the 13.5 billion year age of Creation. As co-travelers, fellow travelers in Creation, we are reduced to the foundational knowledge that we arose from the same ancient genetic lineage. All are "self." In accepting this truth, by definition then there can be no "other." Interrogating secular, theological, and philosophical drivers that elevate "self" over "other" is essential. Such drivers impair forming a true community. *Communio Sanctorum* cannot be actualized if self-discernment of the intrinsic value of community of all over "self" has been intentionally ignored or postponed. Reimagined community must be absolutely inclusive, from the start, and at any cost. Theological "believers" as well as "non-believers" must be accommodated, willing to enter into covenant that does not demean or disparage religious traditions. Covenant is this sense is not theological. Professing an oath of moral solidarity among members creates covenant supplanting theological differences and limitations. This proposal is not premature. In modern day versions of the

Hippocratic Oath, for example, our medical students swear an "oath" absent of any theological element. It is not an oath in which medical students swear by the Gods of Apollo, Asclepius, Hygeia, Panaceia, and "all the gods and goddesses" as did the ancient Greeks. Absent is the phrase "swear before God." Yet they will swear publically their lives to the service of all, including the "other," taking the "oath" in deep solemnity and humility. Oath taking in 21st century medicine offers a prime modern-day example of being in covenant with others outside of theological constraints. Let the doctor-patient covenant, preserved and valued by all, offer a model for oath taking in reimagined community. Differences in religion, politics, and identity are not lost, only set aside in pursuit of a loftier goal, inclusive community. The "oath" now required by the courts for people giving testimony has this same solemn character sought among members in *Communio Sanctorum*. Our newly recast covenantal "oath" avoids individual belief systems, deities and sacred books. Rather, the "oath" morphs into a deeply valued public affirmation of an inclusive moral and just community wherein all are "self," there can be no "other."

Abiding by such an affirmation requires deeply committed community. The pressure test of commitment to the community, I offer, remains directly proportional to the degree of its heterogeneity. The more heterogeneous the population, the greater are obstacles to forming community accommodating to all. Coincidentally called into being in the same thin slice of Creation, a true community of co-travelers cannot but embrace the totality of humanity. The community that we declare exists solely on one affirmation, that is, our brothers and sisters who are co-travelers in Creation with us are precious to all. Setting aside limits as to whom we choose to embrace, whose bad brute luck and suffering we accept and share, and with whom we share our spaces, resources, and *agape* positions community towards growth and away from decay. Community only begins by embracing the recurring core concept that by definition all are "self," there can be no "other."

History only reaffirms that achieving unconditional self-sacrificial love for all in community is easier said than done. Moral impulses sourced upon justice and lovingkindness are never wrong, no matter how difficult realizing them may seem. The recent fervent yet unsuccessful push to guarantee universal healthcare in the U.S. is but one recent example. What largely has "worked" for decades in Scandinavian countries, Japan, and the United Kingdom indeed was heavy lifting for the U.S. Congress. Passage of the Affordable Care Act (ACA, signed into law by President Obama in March, 2010) was just the beginning of a contentious and acrimonious test of the resolve of the U.S. to view the "least of us," that is, those lacking healthcare, as the "rest of us" (Patel and Rushefsky 2019). Nearly a decade later, the ACA remains the target of fierce discontent and vicious partisan political attacks by right-wing political groups. Not unexpectedly, racists and robust libertarians would have us believe that healthcare for all is of no moral concern to us all (Morris et al. 2019). How can universal healthcare be a moral issue among the nations of the modern world, but not for the U.S.? A partial answer to this query is that most countries with universal healthcare are more homogenous than the U.S. "Otherness" in America, I offer, persists in the shadow of the inability of the U.S. to confront and then embrace its original sins. As discussed earlier, "otherness" was the essential cudgel employed by American Empire to execute its founding original sins upon the indigenous Native Americans as well as African and African American slaves for more than four centuries. Does "otherness" need to stalk American wholeness in the 21st century?

The saga of the ACA is not unlike that of the Civil Rights Act of 1964 and the Voting Rights Act of 1965. Although each was codified into U.S. law, simply passing this legislation and obtaining the signature of the president does not guarantee successful implementation. Structural oppression and privilege fueled by a "will-to-power," oppose such change. This was never truer than in the preservation of asymmetric benefits of the status quo that favor the White ruling class in America. In our reimagined community of "self," when there can be no "other," we must freely admit to the fallenness and failings that permeate our very checkered history as a nation. A nation founded upon two original sins is unable to embrace universal human rights, even those enumerated and codified in the U.S. Constitution and Bill of Rights! In our reimagined future, the failings of the past should not shackle us to either determinism or fatalism. Even when we work at a problem for the long-term without the benefit of a final solution, progress is achieved. By such work, we better discern how a failed solution can be re-engineered and eventually implemented towards success. Sustained commitment to the overarching goal of building an inclusive American community in moral solidarity must be our mantra!

The triad of psychological impulses of pleasure (Freud), control (Adler), and search for meaning (Frankl) illuminated by the Viennese School of Psychotherapy contributes to everyday tensions in our lives. Such impulses will remain formidable obstacles to creating core affirmation for a new covenantal community in which there are only "self," there can be no "other." The historian and moralist Lord John Dalberg-Acton reiterated a central element that opposes creation of any new, inclusive community. He said, "power tends to corrupt, and absolute power corrupts absolutely." Asymmetric power and control (e.g., America commerce and politics past and present) encourage corruption, whereas structural privilege and oppression manifest by corrupting absolutely (Chadwick 1998). America persists in oppression of people's legal right to vote, to benefit from education, to access healthcare, to find gainful employment, to expect clean air and water, and finally to secure a humane future free from the threat of killing and an inability to flourish.

The greatest of these denials is that precluding flourishing. All of the other slights and crimes of structural oppression can be folded into one, that is, denied the human right to flourish. The inability to flourish not only denies universal personhood, but also makes opaque the suffering of those on the underside of America. In the U.S., "underside" people persist in that oppressed location due to persistent asymmetric wealth and structural privilege of the "topsiders." The underserved and oppressed masses not only includes the historical targets of American hegemony, that is, indigenous Native Americans and enslaved Africans and African Americans, but today is expanded to include marginalized people of all types who are displaced by economic disadvantage, denied justice, precluded from adequate healthcare, stigmatized socially, and victimized by bad brute luck not of their own doing.

Have we not as a nation become "desensitized" to the acute suffering of vulnerable and marginalized groups shouldering the burden of structural oppression? Do we simply rationalize their suffering versus our privilege as unfortunate, but "structural" and leave it at that? John Rawls called for a "veil of ignorance" in our moral decision-making, to preclude our own self-interest from dominating the very real ethical pressures of inequality (Rawls 2005). American empire abhors and precludes any "veil of ignorance" that would level the moral playing field. Asymmetric power perpetuates monolithic paradigms in all too familiar ways. Oppressed peoples may be forced to rash ends simply in order to survive. Yet, we often blame the exploited as if their lack of flourishing was a deliberate choice on their part rather than a product of bad brute luck. Lack of full employment (e.g., in response to production automation) and the shift of people towards living in metropolitan rather than rural communities caused an exodus from rural America that has devastated the futures of many Americans. Especially for rural areas bereft of voice and absent a path to better outcomes has despair and rage been ameliorated by use of drugs of addiction, especially alcohol and opioids (Olsen and Sharfstein 2019; Case and Deaton 2020). In small, homogenous communities that once flourished, such dead-end futures, despair, and wasted human capital would not have been tolerated (Case and Deaton 2020). Rather, unconditional love and empathy of small town communities provided the only sure therapy for their chronic suffering and hopelessness. If it is to offer a viable paradigm for living in this harsh new world, reimagined community must insure inclusivity, that is, that all are "self." In solidarity, we accept that harsh realities can befall anyone. Bad brute luck is never judged to be a moral failing, only bad luck. Drug dependence, abuse and addiction disorders are to be viewed as bad brute luck. They do not signal moral failings, but rather are *bona fide* medical conditions requiring attention and community support to be overcome. In community, such calamities are anticipated and treated in stride. The same unconditional love that enables families to work through trauma towards recovery *is* scalable. In covenantal community, moral solidarity empowered by unconditional love will exist as "already here, but not yet" fully realized.

Nietzsche's "will-to-power" may explain the push towards domination and control that underlies structural privilege in America as well as U.S. domination of global economics and politics (Alexander 2018; Nietzsche and Ludovici 2019). Is it possible to reimagine this primal impulse playing some positive role in *Communio Sanctorum*? Nietzsche's concept of the *übermensch* (i.e., "overman") will be explored in our current brainstorming on community (Nietzsche and Kaufmann 1992). Nietzsche envisioned an optimal society in which human beings were constantly evolving. The product of human evolution as it progressed in real time was the emergence of the "*übermensch*," also known as the "overman," "superman," or "superhuman" (Nietzsche and Kaufmann 1992). The Overman concept pushed against the theological supernatural dimensions of Christian faith, offering in its place a "this-worldliness" in which society must view one of its critical functions as the continual launch of a small class of Overmen (Nietzsche and Kaufmann 1992). These Overmen seek no answers to the concrete problems and suffering of humans in the current world from otherworldly place, such as heaven or through Christian salvation. They are pragmatic, placed in the "here-and-now," "this-worldliness," thoroughly convinced of their superhuman capacities to overcome the present and glide into the future. The robust will-to-power exuded by Nietzsche's Overman in tandem with unbridled confidence makes the Overman particularly worthy of embrace by society (Nietzsche and Kaufmann 1992). In our imaging an inclusive community, bounded by deeply seated affirmation of full personhood for all, wherein all belong, none are "other," we too may need to embrace an adaptation of Nietzsche's "Overperson," a goal to which humanity should strive for a product who creates new values.

Nietzsche introduced the concept of the "*übermensch*" in *Thus Spoke Zarathustra*, in the main character (Nietzsche 1883; Nietzsche and Kaufmann 1992). According to Nietzsche's later view, Overpersons have emerged throughout history as people willing to stake all in pursuit of enhancement of human society. In *Beyond Good and Evil*, Nietzsche identifies Alcibiades, Julius Caesar, and Frederick II as potential "*übermensches*" (Nietzsche 1886; Nietzsche and Kaufmann 1992). Although Nietzsche would deny to "*übermensch*" any idealism, humanitarian motives, or necessary moral values (Nietzsche 1908; Nietzsche and Ludovici 2019), he viewed the *übermensch* as truly beyond good and evil. As such, the *übermensch* could act beyond evil and not necessarily without good. I will highjack this opening in Nietzsche's operating system and adapt the concept of the *übermensch* acting beyond evil as to form inclusive community with true moral solidarity. As such I offer up for consideration the extraordinary Martin Luther King Jr. as an *übermensch* acting beyond good and evil to gain civil rights against enormous odds. An ordained minister whose powerful faith was an essential element of his push for civil rights and voting rights for all in America, the Rev. Dr. Martin Luther King displayed a mixture of goodness, humility, will-to-power, and self-confidence which one could view as emblematic of an "American Overperson." America has had its share of outstanding individuals who would have earned the designation "Overperson." Their will-to-power and self-confidence allowed them to risk all for the sake of enhancement of humanity, a core effort of Nietzsche's *übermensch*. U.S. presidents George Washington, Abraham Lincoln, and Franklin D. Roosevelt as well as people like John R. Mott, Elizabeth Cady Stanton, Harriet Tubman, Sandra Day O'Conner, Elie Wiesel and Sacagawea, are but a few figures whose imprint on the nation's humanity at personal risk remains indelible. For the task of creating an inclusive society perhaps the task is too great for any one person, but a true American Overperson? Perhaps achieving *Communio Sanctorum* will require a collection of such extraordinary people, "American Overpersons"? The path towards a true community of self in which personhood by affirmation is full and considered an unalienable human right certainly will require substantially increased self-discernment. In the past, Overpersons have encouraged greater self-discernment and spiritual formation for people as well as for their governments. These efforts aimed at solving crises in finding faith and hope for the future, as during world wars and civil conflicts, demanded much from all. The good news is that the energy and commitment necessary for such undertakings is insured by the intrinsic worth of American human capital. With deeper understanding of the base principles for creating an inclusive community, demanding full personhood, as well as greater self-discernment, we must turn attention to the very nature of a reimagined inclusive community in which our Overperson(s), society-at-large, and all human beings gain and retain full personhood can be realized. This goal can be realized only within our reimagined and formed *Communio Sanctorum*.

True *Communio Sanctorum*

The term "*Communio Sanctorum*" was appropriated and expanded from its original theological context explicated by Dietrich Bonhoeffer's seminal thesis work (Bonhoeffer 1930). The goal is to explicate just what is envisioned for a community so reimagined. We first reimagine a community wherein personhood in full and not assaulted, degraded or discounted for any American. This remains the core principle that cannot be violated without collapse of the overarching concept. We should divorce ourselves from any restrictive, exclusive connotation of the term "*Communio Sanctorum*." It is no longer to be embraced as a theological construct in which we only achieve being human within what Bonhoeffer envisioned as a "communion of saints." Saints are not just Overpersons who dedicate their exceptional talents and drive towards "moral perfection." Most are/were exceptional leaders and teachers, living lives of high risk to inspire and motivate others to enhance humanity. Moreover, "saints" are the co-travelers who in their own time established relationality with people that extended beyond themselves and their families to all, achieving inclusivity. For Dietrich Bonhoeffer all of humanity, past and present, were saints and remained in "communion." His theological construct of communion is unworkable for our current purposes. Constituting a solemn Christian ritual at which bread and wine is consecrated and shared, "communion" to Bonhoeffer was exclusive to Christian congregations sharing the body of Christ Risen. We, however, continue to intentionally break out from the theological exclusivity of the term to an intentional irreligious context. We expand "saints," by radical inclusivity to all people, irrespective of religious tradition or no tradition at all! We all are saints, now sharing in a true communion aimed at sharing our thoughts, hopes, and efforts insuring inclusive community, in which all are "self," there can be no "other." In this way our inclusive community composed of all (i.e., the "saints"), share a truly unique property. Our "communion" necessarily embraces our steadfast knowledge that all have been called into being, all are the precious seeds being sown into community, and all constitute a future harvest in ongoing Creation. In such an expansive communion, we share intimate thoughts, hope, and desires that encourage a singular vision of our new deeper relationality to one another as co-travelers in Creation.

The *logic* of the teachings of Jesus of Nazareth remains paradigmatic for creating our new inclusive community of saints (Meyers and Bergel 2002). Rather than invoking theology *per se*, we recall and lift up the fundamental teachings of Jesus, calling us to love one another. According to Nietzsche's criteria, Jesus of Nazareth can be cast in the role as an Overperson in our community, both then and now! Rather than shackled by the theological, we focus on the "logic" of Jesus in teaching and demanding inclusivity. In this manner, we are liberated to more fully embrace a set of teachings that focus on human relationality, rather than theological dogma. We cannot aim to achieving inclusivity for the fullest house of humanity, if we demand theological adherence to Christ (or any world religion or dogma) at the front door. Community must be formed around inclusivity. As such we embrace a pillar of our new community, that is, all people past, present, and future as "saints." We are blessed simply by our acquiescence to this new and profound knowledge: we are bound first and foremost as co-travelers existing contemporaneously in Creation, companions called into a common being, into the thoroughgoing Creation for only a infinitely small, but precious time. We are vaulted into sainthood in each other's presence through inclusivity. We all are "saints" in this usage, an appellation that reflects upon a special "holiness" of shared being in ongoing Creation. Beyond the shared being of existence in this moment, we are bonded through creation to the 100+ billions of "saints" who were called into being before us. With humility and wonder, we embrace the shared knowledge of our being, current "seeds" of a harvest yet to come in this cosmic ongoing Creation.

We share in sainthood with co-travelers and past travelers alike! All are bound into a communion as beings called into this ongoing ineffable Creation. Anthropological genetics support our newfound knowledge. Although diverse and unique co-travelers in Creation, we all share this undeniable, physical and spiritual common heritage. Genetically we share the same ancient history of each generation of beings, derivative of earlier generations extending to more than 10,000 generations! We share the same remnant genetic material (Rutherford 2017), an ever-evolving blueprint of our being as part and parcel of ongoing Creation. At the extreme, we all are unique (in psyche), but yet fundamentally so much the same (in soma). Importantly, we now can appreciate more readily the continuing bonds that link us to the past as well as to those within Creation that have yet to be called, that is, the seeds of a future harvest. Collectively, these future saints will be our children, grandchildren, great-grandchildren, and so on, and the generations of humans yet to be called into being, co-travelers in Creation. Though not yet called into being, they too will be saints with whom we will share communion. Conceptualized in the wondrous blessing of shared being, these were, are, and will be the persons whose "personhood" we struggle to protect herein. Not just our children, grandchildren, as so forth, but all of Creation's beings who exist now as well as those to follow us in future generations. There is no "other," only "self" in our *Communio Sanctorum* forming and expanding about ongoing Creation!

The overarching principle of *Communio Sanctorum* to embrace social justice and to distain structural oppression deserves a second visit. The shared being in community is a blessing that must confront and defeat our innate human tendencies to privilege ourselves and those we choose to label as "self." In real time, we must reaffirm our commitment to avoid with intention identity and theological politics, racist tendencies, and will-to-power in search of becoming a dominant ruling class. Historically, these evils of "self" constitute the single greatest threat to inclusivity and the communion of the saints. Stretching back we see the European empires whose explorers invaded the lands of the indigenous Native Americans (Dunbar-Ortiz 2014; Hämäläinen 2019). What resulted from their self-vaulted position of power and control was the genocide, dispossession of indigenous peoples, and appropriation of their lands. The Native Americans were in the land more than 10,000 years before the Akkadian Empire in Mesopotamia existed (2300 BCE)! Equally horrific was the introduction of slavery in America in the 17th century, constituting the second original sin (Baptist 2014; Paquette and Smith 2016). Through corporate discernment, we are compelled to view such theologically based "politics of empire" as a scourge that degrades and defaces *Communio Sanctorum*. Americans long have picked and chose elements of theological politics that enable celebration of an adulterated version of "Thanksgiving" as well as the "victory" of Christopher Columbus! Yet, sadly we have chosen to close our eyes to the fact that theological practices predating the creation of the "American Dream" were centered about worship and discernment of one's inner world, not building empires.

When confronted with theological friction and clashes in dogma, the earliest Americans simply moved away from and avoided theological politics. This tendency was obvious even before colonizing settlers set foot in America! It was a vision of community in which all theological practices could be carefully amalgamated, fused into mottos and acts of civic strife appealing to those who sought "religious freedom." Sadly, the theological practices and cultural traditions of those who prospered in the Americas for 30,000 years prior to the "landing at Plymouth Rock," that is, the indigenous Native Americans, were suppressed and denied by pious, self-righteous invaders. Theological and identity politics, bastardized by U.S. Supreme Court chief justice John J. Marshall (1755–1835), explicated a spurious and legally dubious tool, termed the "Discovery Doctrine." For America this doctrine only reinforced the worst impulses of empire-building from lands and resources expropriated from those with rights deeded by an ancient "call into being" predating the founding of America by 30,000 years! This revisionist doctrine (first declared law in 1823) has been roundly condemned as unjust, racist, and in violation of basic human rights. As a false but indispensible tool of empire building in America, this doctrine remains unlikely to be amended or rendered null-and-void any time soon. Social justice and confronting the original sins on which American empire emerged and prospered can no longer tolerate either structural privilege or oppression of human rights.

Communio Sanctorum promotes inward spiritualty and worship, not externalized identity and theological politics. Theological "dogma du jour" only politicizes and fuels divisive efforts in America. Aimed at denying legal standing of Native Americans, degrading the personhood of African slaves and their descendants, and demonizing the most recent immigrants to America populist notions of White supremacy and nationalism remain formidable threats to the core principle that all are welcome, there is no "other." Identity and theological politics typically seek only to distract our attention away from the shared humanity foundational to *Communio Sanctorum*. Reimagining the fullest potential of our blessings and gifts, our shared call into being, our present, past, and future life in communion will provide a powerful source of continued inspiration, especially when community is threatened. Indeed, we can reengineer the current world to make straight our path to the world to come. Through placing the highest value on sharing rather than hoarding in the abundance of thoroughgoing Creation, all can fully participate as the seeds being sown for a harvest yet to come. The harvest in ongoing Creation is a bounty that must be shared among all of its co-travelers, current and future generations. Through affirmation of social justice and of the preferential option of the poor, the harvest will be shared among the fullest communion of saints.

Reimagining the flourishing for all (i.e., *eudaimonia, shalom,* peace, and well-being) is not an exercise in magical thinking. Flourishing of all in community is part and parcel of ongoing Creation. Recall that theological elements for the flourishing of all exist in Abrahamic religions (Judaism, Christian, Islam) and virtually all theologies. Exclusivity imposes limitations around who is judged to qualify as "self" in family, tribe, or nations. Such exclusive tendencies are anathema to the principle of inclusivity, our communion of the saints. Two Buddhist individuals heavily influenced my views on social justice and the preferential option of the poor. It is worth recalling a Buddhism metaphor of life, that is, a large ship envisioned to provide the only means by which the entire community can cross the sea of suffering. Within such a ship of the communion of saints, all rise together. In the late 1980s and early 1990s it was my good fortune to work with the Buddhist Compassion Relief "Tzu Chi" Foundation in the Far East (O'Neill 2010). It was there in Hualien Taiwan that I first encountered Dharma Master Cheng Yen. The Master Cheng Yen is a diminutive Buddhist nun whose vision and teachings made a lasting impression upon most people, including me. Initially her ministry was organized around mobilizing a group of thirty housewives to donate and to collect small daily contributions for the poor and needy families (Cheng, Sharifah, and Tang 2015). Today, the Tzu Chi Foundation is one of the largest international, non-governmental humanitarian organizations in the world. It has more than 10 million avid followers whose charity and daily devotions center about the teachings of Master Cheng Yen. I was invited to advise the Master about her visionary hopes to build a large hospital and local clinics to serve healthcare needs of the very poor. As a senior administrator at a major new health sciences center and medical school, I was keen to assist Master Cheng Yen. Our meeting place was a large rural compound in Hualien. There her work included not only international outreach in humanitarian aid, but also a deep caring for the needs of hundreds of orphan children who lived on the compound. Our conversations informed my mind and fed my spirit. The work of Tzu Chi knew no bounds, focusing simply upon the suffering of the "least of us." Master Cheng Yen displayed a boundless inner peace and visionary soul, capable of overcoming enormous obstacles in this world to help people in the thousands. For me in the 1990s, Tzu Chi resonated with my growing ideal of *Communio Sanctorum.*

The second Buddhist whose teaching informed my evolving perspectives of community was the foremost spiritual leader of Tibetan Buddhism, Tenzin

Gyatso, the 14th Dalai Lama (Nagle 2017). Although well read in the spiritual writings of the Dalai Lama, it would be in the early 1990s that I would have the opportunity to meet His Holiness Tenzin Gyatso. Stony Brook University had developed a special relationship with the Tibetan government in exile, enabling Tibetan students to pursue graduate education in New York. In person, the Dalai Lama was very impressive, possessing great humanitarian and spiritual insights. Many found his lectures transformative, down to earth, and spiritually enlivening. I could not but note similarities between Master Cheng Yen and His Holiness the 14th Dalai Lama. Both of these Buddhist leaders possessed religious authority and spiritual vision that reached well beyond spiritual and sectarian boundaries. Both lifted up the essential nature of community and the central function of unconditional self-sacrificial love necessary to the healing of suffering and overcoming human fallenness. Each of these leaders effused deep understanding of the dimensions of abject suffering in the world, coupled to boundless compassion and optimism for healing the world. The vision of compassionate and inclusive community espoused by both resonates deeply with my goals in authoring this work. The content of my relationship with each, now years later, still informs my understanding of the power of *Communio Sanctorum*. Remarkably, I remain unable to fully apprehend the power of their mere presence as well as the unmistakable divine quality of their very being.

Building inclusive *Communio Sanctorum* in which all are "self," there are no "other," cannot be predicated on a goal of simple flourishing. Even our shared being as co-travelers in Creation, an enormously important pillar to our relationality with one another, is not enough to empower the building of true community. Simply declaring that we are "all in this together" ultimately will fail in achieving lasting communion among the saints. Simply offering a "free pass" for past sins, misdeeds, and ongoing assaults on personhood that fuel structural oppression cannot provide a path forward. Simply choosing to ignore the original sins of a nation that continue a 400-year legacy that intentionally denied, discounted, and degraded the being of victims past and present is unacceptable and immoral. Formidable challenges posed by past failures, shortcomings, and ongoing sins ought not to shackle and doom us to simply repeat them. What has changed is our understanding and awareness of the brutal forces operating then and now aimed at the personhood of the "other." Inattention to rooting out the wrongs that must be righted for a truly just society, however, threatens to doom the future health and well-being of Americans. The persistent and sinful inequities of asymmetric wealth and power are intolerable within a community seeking to advance moral solidarity and social justice.

I proffer a simple but hard solution to this dilemma threatening social justice as well as moral solidarity in *Communio Sanctorum*. The solution will require public "kenosis." In theology, *kenosis* describes the kind of "self-emptying." The earthly life of Jesus of Nazareth provides a compelling narrative of kenosis. According to the description in the Apostle Paul's Letter to the Philippians (Phil 2:5b-8), Jesus displayed a kenotic ethic of life. Paul recorded, "[5b]. . . have the same mindset as Christ Jesus: [6]Who, being in very nature God, did not consider equality with God something to be used to his own advantage; [7]rather, he made himself nothing by taking the very nature of a bond servant, being made in human likeness. [8]And being found in appearance as a man, he humbled himself by becoming obedient to death—even death on a cross!" By intent, Jesus of Nazareth, although free of blemish, sacrifices his divinity to the very level of extinction, wherein he dies on a cross as a common criminal. This voluntary selflessness was poured out publicly in order to help us all to self-discern the good, the bad, and the ugly of our innermost beings. This soul-searching is not just good for community building. This act is essential to truly entering within *Communio Sanctorum*.

Adopting a true kenotic ethic is life-long and demanding task for all comers. The individual practice of the kenotic ethic is a necessary prelude to a corporate, national kenosis aimed to confront, accept, and seek forgiveness for complicity in America's original sins. Structural privilege and the suffering it provokes especially for the "least of us" most often seems invisible to human beings. Yet, in the absence of frank and deep kenosis, all efforts aimed at fulfilling the fullest personhood for all will remain out of reach, impossible to achieve. Self-discernment of the health of the soul within is absolutely necessary. Lack of self-discernment, in sharp contrast, will rob any community not in moral solidarity of its capacity to insure the flourishing of all! Our path forward, within a call to embrace kenosis and self-discernment, includes concrete steps toward unearthing, confronting, taking responsibility, and seeking forgiveness for our sins, current and past. Foremost among these are the two great "original sins" of America. Large and small, sinful acts fuel the degradation, contestation, and loss of personhood for our community of saints who co-journey with us in ongoing Creation. Receipt and validation of the suffering of others at our hands, true repentance in search of justice for all and attendant reconciliation, as well as the courage to make amends and to embrace all as "self," are essential to the ultimate goal. Steps taken toward living the kenotic ethic embodied by Jesus of Nazareth offers a prescriptive strategy for the transformation of U.S. society. It will be essential to reinvent U.S. society towards inclusive community. Once retrieved in earnest, the moral compass of the U.S. will enable the nation to truly transform from mythological empire to a beacon for peace, hope, and joy for all. The path to achieving true community remains steep and perilous. The endpoint will be moral solidarity in *Communio Sanctorum*, our community in which all are "self," there can be no "other."

APPENDIX 5: FURTHER NOTES

*Text in italics are callouts to places within the chapter.

Similarly, the Middle East is beset with the 50+ year occupation of the West Bank and Gaza which, again according to Human Rights Watch, has led to systematic human rights abuses of the Palestinians by Israel. For more information on the Israel and Palestine conflict from Human Rights Watch, Amnesty International as well as the United Nations, see: Roth, Kenneth (2019), "Israel and Palestine: Events of 2018," Human Rights Watch: World Report (accessed on April 30, 2020), https://www.hrw.org/world-report/2019/country-chapters/israel/palestine; Nebehay, Stephanie and Dan Williams (2019), "Israel Should Face Justice for Unlawful Gaza Protest Killings: U.N.," *Reuters World News*, published February 28, 2019 (accessed on April 30, 2020), https://www.reuters.com/article/us-israel-palestinians-un/israel-should-face-justice-for-unlawful-gaza-protest-killings-un-idUSKCN1QH14J; Unnamed Author (2019), "Israel and Occupied Palestinian Territories," *Amnesty International*, published online September 30, 2019 (accessed on April 30, 2020), https://www.amnesty.org/en/countries/middle-east-and-north-africa/israel-and-occupied-palestinian-territories/report-israel-and-occupied-palestinian-territories/; and Unnamed Author (2018), "Amnesty International Report 2017/2018: The State of the World's Human Rights," *Amnesty International*, published online February 22, 2018 (accessed on April 30, 2020), https://www.amnestyusa.org/files/pol1048002017english_0.pdf.

Although unresolved, if the Vikings actually introduced the MC1R hair color gene to their conquered peoples, the alarm and fear provoked by such wild invaders is easy to imagine! For insights into the MC1R gene and its role in determining human hair color, see: Unnamed Author (2020), "MC1R gene: Melanocortin 1 Receptor," Washington, DC: *Genetics Home Reference*, U.S. National Library of Medicine, available online April 30, 2020 (accessed on April 30, 2020), https://ghr.nlm.nih.gov/gene/MC1R; and Unnamed Author (2020), "Is Hair Color Determined by Genetics?," Washington, DC, *Genetics Home Reference,* U.S. National Library of Medicine, available online April 30, 2020 (accessed on April 30, 2020), https://ghr.nlm.nih.gov/primer/traits/haircolor.

The response of the police at times can be disproportionate to the initial uneasiness of the caller and provoke a sometimes-lethal outcome for the innocent, marginalized victim. For a recent publication on the overrepresentation of people of color in violence of police in the U.S. see: Bui, Anthony L., Matthew M. Coates, and Ellicott C. Matthay (2017), "Years of Life Lost Due to Encounters with Law Enforcement in the USA, 2015–2016," *Journal of Epidemiology & Community Health*, published online May 7, 2018 (accessed on April 30, 2020), https://jech.bmj.com/content/72/8/715; and more recently Harris, Adam (2020), "Racism Won't Be Solved by Yet Another Blue-Ribbon Report," *The Atlantic*, published online June 4, 2020 (accessed June 30, 2020), https://www.theatlantic.com/politics/archive/2020/06/george-floyd-racism-police-brutality/612565/.

By 1650, the population of United States of America is estimated to be ~6.05 million. Of this, indigenous Native American constituted ~6 million! Census population data and demographics see: Gibson, Campbell and Kay Jung (2005), "Historic Census Statistics on Population Totals by Race, 1790 to 1990, and by Hispanic Origin 1970 to 1990, for Large Cities and Other Urban Places in the United States," U.S. Department of Commerce: *United States Census Bureau*, published online February 2005 (accessed on April 30, 2020), https://web.archive.org/web/20120812191959/http://www.census.gov/population/www/documentation/twps0076/twps0076.html.

The true test of any community that we reimagine for the U.S. is the moral fiber to address original sins. English philosopher John Locke (1632–1704) offered this insight about "community" from his *Second Treatise of Civil Government* (1690, Chapter 8, Section 95), "The only way whereby any one divests himself of his natural liberty, and puts on the bonds of civil society, is by agreeing with other men to join and unite into a community for their comfortable, safe, and peaceable living one amongst another, in a secure enjoyment of their properties, and a greater security against any, that are not of it." Such collections of human beings offer a sense of community that includes a sense of belonging, a sense that *in toto* the group has more influence, a sense of "self" that resonates throughout the community and reinforces its needs, and a shared sense of emotional connection. For more on these qualities of community see: McMillan, David W. and David M. Chavis (1986), "Sense of Community: A Definition and Theory" *Journal of Community Psychology, 14*(1): 6–23, available online April 30, 2020 (accessed on April 30, 2020), https://onlinelibrary.wiley.com/doi/abs/10.1002/1520-6629(198601)14:1%3C6::AID-JCOP2290140103%3E3.0.CO;2-I.

REFERENCES

Acosta, Abilio James. 2019. *The enemy of the people: A dangerous time to tell the truth in America*. New York, NY: Harper, imprint of HarperCollinsPublishers.

Adler, Alfred. 1924. *The practice and theory of individual psychology*. London, UK: K. Paul, Trench, Trubner & co. ltd.; New York, NY: Harcourt, Brace & Company, Inc.

Adler, Alfred, Bernard Glueck, and John E. Lind. 1917. *The neurotic constitutional outlines of a comparative individualistic psychology and psychotherapy*. New York, NY: Moffat, Yard and Company.

Alexander, Estrelda Y. 2018. *The will to power: Confronting ideologies that dismantle Christian community*. Bowie, MD: Seymour Press.

Al-Faruqi, Isma'il R., and International Institute of Islamic Thought. 1992. *Al Tawhīd: Its implications for thought and life* (2nd ed.). Herndon, VA: International Institute of Islamic Thought.

Ali, Muna. 2018. *Young Muslim America: Faith, community, and belonging.* New York, NY: Oxford University Press.

Bansak, Cynthia, Nicole B. Simpson, and Madeline Zavodny. 2015. *The economics of immigration.* London, UK; New York, NY: Routledge, Taylor & Francis Group.

Baptist, Edward E. 2014. *The half has never been told: Slavery and the making of American capitalism.* New York, NY: Basic Books.

Bartoletti, Susan Campbell. 2010. *They called themselves the K.K.K.: The birth of an American terrorist group.* Boston, MA: Houghton Mifflin Harcourt.

Bayly, Susan. 2001. *Caste, society, and politics in India from the eighteen century to the Modern Age.* Cambridge, UK: Cambridge University Press.

Block, Peter. 2018. *Community: The structure of belonging.* Oakland, CA: Berrett-Koehler Publishers, Inc.

Bonhoeffer, Dietrich. 1930. *Sanctorum communio: A theological study of the sociology of the church.* Translated from German, edited by Joachim von Soosten. Berlin, FRG: Trowlitzsch & Sohn.

Bonhoeffer, Dietrich, and Mark S. Brocker. 2006. *Conspiracy and imprisonment, 1940–1945* (1st English-language ed.). Minneapolis, MN: Fortress Press.

Bonhoeffer, Dietrich, and Clifford J. Green. 1998. *Sanctorum communio: A theological study of the sociology of the church* (Dietrich Bonhoeffer works). Minneapolis, MN: Fortress Press.

Case, Anne and Angus Deaton. 2020. *Deaths of despair and the future of capitalism.* Baltimore, MD: Princeton University Press.

Chadwick, Owen. 1998. *Acton and history.* Cambridge, UK; New York, NY: Cambridge University Press.

Cheng, Willie, Mohamed Sharifah, and Cheryl Tang. 2015. *Doing good great: Thirteen Asian heroes and their causes.* Singapore, SG: Epigram Books.

Confucius, and Raymond Stanley Dawson. 2008. *The analects* (Oxford world's classics series). Oxford, UK; New York, NY: Oxford University Press.

Csermely, Peter, Tamás Korcsmáros, Katalin Sulyok, and New York Academy of Sciences. 2007. *Stress responses in biology and medicine: Stress of life in molecules, cells, organisms, and psychosocial communities* (Annals of the New York Academy of Sciences). Boston, MA: Published by Blackwell Publishers on behalf of the New York Academy of Sciences.

Dunbar-Ortiz, Roxanne. 2014. *An indigenous peoples' history of the United States.* Boston, MA: Beacon Press.

Dunning, David. 2005. *Self-insight: Roadblocks and detours on the path to knowing thyself* (Essays in social psychology). New York, NY: Psychology Press.

Everly, George S., and Jeffrey M. Lating. 2013. *A clinical guide to the treatment of the human stress response* (3rd ed.). New York, NY: Springer.

Fack, Gabrielle, and Camille Landais. 2016. *Charitable giving and tax policy: A historical and comparative perspective* (1st ed.). Oxford, UK; New York, NY: Oxford University Press.

Farmer, Penelope. 1978. *Beginnings: Creation myths of the world.* London, UK: Chatto & Windus.

Farzana, Kazi Fahmida. 2017. *Memories of Burmese Rohingya refugees: Contested identity and belonging.* New York, NY: Palgrave Macmillan.

Frankl, Viktor E. 1946. *Man's search for meaning* (German ed.). Vienna, AT: Verlag für Jugend und Volk.

———. 1988. *The will to meaning: Foundations and applications of logotherapy.* New York, NY: New American Library.

Freud, Sigmund, and A. A. Brill. 1930. *Psychopathology of everyday life.* New York, NY: The Macmillan Company.

Gensler, Harry J. 2013. *Ethics and the golden rule.* New York, NY: Routledge.

Gibson, Dawn-Marie, and Herbert Berg. 2017. *New perspectives on the nation of Islam.* New York, NY: Routledge, Taylor & Francis Group.

Gorbunov, D. S., and V. A. Rubakov. 2017. *Introduction to the theory of the early universe: Hot big bang theory*. Singapore, SG: World Scientific Publishing Comp.

Gray, John. 2000. *Human hair diversity*. Abingdon, Oxon, UK: Blackwell Science.

Hämäläinen, Pekka. 2019. *Lakota America: A new history of indigenous power*. New Haven, CT; London, UK: Yale University Press.

Hammurabi, and C. H. W. Johns. 2000. *The oldest code of laws in the world: The code of laws promulgated by Hammurabi, King of Babylon, B.C. 2285–2242*. Union, NJ: Lawbook Exchange.

Hillstrom, Laurie Collier. 2018. *Black Lives Matter: From a moment to a movement*. Santa Barbara, CA; Denver, CO: Greenwood, an imprint of ABC-CLIO, LLC.

Horsley, Richard A. 2009. *Covenant economics: A biblical vision of justice for all*. Louisville, KY: Westminster John Knox Press.

Hosein, Adam. 2019. *The ethics of migration: An introduction*. Abingdon, Oxon, UK; New York, NY: Routledge.

Hunsinger, George. 2015. *The Beatitudes*. New York, NY: Paulist Press.

Jablonski, Nina G. 2012. *Living color: The biological and social meaning of skin color*. Berkeley, CA: University of California Press.

Jacobsen, Knut A., Helene Basu, Angelika Malinar, and Vasudha Narayanan. 2009. *Brill's encyclopedia of Hinduism* (Handbook of oriental studies, section 2). 6 vols. India. Leiden, NL; Boston, MA: Brill.

Jalāl al-Dīn, Rūmī, and Coleman Barks. 1995. *The essential Rumi*. San Francisco, CA: Harper.

Jardina, Ashley. 2019. *White identity politics*. Cambridge, UK; New York, NY: Cambridge University Press.

Kasstan, Ben. 2019. *Making bodies kosher: The politics of reproduction among Haredi Jews in England* (1st ed.). New York, NY: Berghahn Books.

Keranen, Rachel. 2017. *The big bang theory* (Great Discoveries in Science series). New York, NY: Cavendish Square Publishing.

Kraybill, Donald B., Steven M. Nolt, and David Weaver-Zercher. 2010. *Amish grace: How forgiveness transcended tragedy*. San Francisco, CA: Jossey-Bass.

Leeming, David Adams, and David Adams Leeming. 2010. *Creation myths of the world: An encyclopedia*. 2 vols. Santa Barbara, CA: ABC-CLIO.

Lohfink, Gerhard. 1984. *Jesus and community: The social dimension of Christian faith*. Philadelphia, PA; New York, NY: Fortress Press, Paulist Press.

McKenna, Megan. 1999. *Blessings and woes: The Beatitudes and the Sermon on the Plain in the Gospel of Luke*. Maryknoll, NY: Orbis Books.

Melton, J. Gordon. 1991. *American religious creeds*. New York, NY: Triumph Books.

Meyer, Marvin and Kurt Bergel. 2002. *Reverence for life: The ethics of Albert Schweitzer for the twenty first century*. Syracuse, NY: Syracuse University Press.

Morgan, Michael L. 2019. *The Oxford handbook of Levinas*. New York, NY: Oxford University Press.

Morris, John C., Martin K. Mayer, Robert C. Kenter, and Luisa M. Lucero. 2019. *State politics and the Affordable Care Act: Choices and decisions* (Routledge research in public administration and public policy). New York, NY: Routledge.

Morse, Christopher. 2009. *Not every spirit: A dogmatics of Christian disbelief*. New York, NY: Continuum.

Nagle, Jeanne. 2017. *The 14th Dalai Lama: Spiritual leader of Tibet* (1st ed., Spotlight On Civic Courage: Heroes of Conscience). New York, NY: Rosen Publishing.

Nhất, Hạnh. 1999. *The heart of the Buddha's teaching: Transforming suffering into peace, joy & liberation: The four noble truths, the noble eightfold path, and other basic Buddhist teachings*. New York, NY: Broadway Books.

Nicholls, Walter. 2019. *The immigrant rights movement: The battle over national citizenship*. Stanford, CA: Stanford University Press.

Niemeyer, Lucian, and Donald B. Kraybill. 1993. *Old Order Amish: Their enduring way of life*. Baltimore, MD: Johns Hopkins University Press.

Nietzsche, Friedrich Wilhelm, and Walter Arnold Kaufmann. 1992. *Basic writings of Nietzsche* (Modern Library ed.). New York, NY: Modern Library.

Nietzsche, Friedrich Wilhelm, and Anthony M. Ludovici. 2019. *The will to power*. Mineola NY: Dover Publications, Inc.

O'Neill, Mark. 2010. *Tzu Chi: Serving with compassion*. Singapore SG: John Wiley.

Olsen, Yngvild, and Joshua M. Sharfstein. 2019. *The opioid epidemic: What everyone needs to know*. Oxford, UK: Oxford University Press.

Ore, Tracy E. 2019. *The social construction of difference and inequality: Race, class, gender, and sexuality* (7th ed.). New York, NY: Oxford University Press.

Paquette, Robert L. and Mark M. Smith. 2016. *The Oxford handbook of slavery in the Americas*. Oxford, UK: Oxford University Press.

Patel, Kant, and Mark E. Rushefsky. 2019. *Healthcare politics and policy in America* (5th ed.). New York, NY: Routledge.

Plaut, W. Gunther, and David E. S. Stein. 2015. *The Torah: A modern commentary* (revised ed.). New York, NY: Reform Judaism Publications Central Conference of American Rabbis.

Rawls, John. 2005. *A theory of justice*. Cambridge, MA: Belknap Press.

Redsand, Anna. 2006. *Viktor Frankl: A life worth living*. New York, NY: Clarion Books.

Robbins, Jeffrey W., and Clayton Crockett. 2018. *Doing theology in the age of Trump: A critical report on Christian nationalism*. Eugene, OR: Cascade Books.

Ruether, Rosemary Radford. 2013. *My quests for hope and meaning: An autobiography*. Eugene, OR: Cascade Books.

Rutherford, Adam. 2017. *A brief history of everyone who ever lived*. New York, NY: The Experiment.

Sagan, Carl. 1994. *Pale blue dot: A vision of the human future in space*. New York, NY: Random House.

Southern Poverty Law Center. 2018. *Active hate groups in the United States in 2017*. Montgomery, AL: Southern Poverty Law Center.

Sproul, Barbara C. 1979. *Primal myths: Creating the world*. San Francisco, CA: Harper & Row.

Stein, Stephen J. 1992. *The Shaker experience in America: A history of the United Society of Believers*. New Haven, CT: Yale University Press.

Szczesiul, Anthony. 2017. *The Southern hospitality myth: Ethics, politics, race, and American memory*. Athens, GA: The University of Georgia Press.

Taylor, Keeanga-Yamahtta. 2016. *From #BlackLivesMatter to Black liberation*. Chicago, IL: Haymarket Books.

United States Congress. House Committee on Foreign Affairs. 2018. *Genocide against the Burmese Rohingya: Hearing before the Committee on Foreign Affairs, House of Representatives, One Hundred Fifteenth Congress, second session, September 26, 2018*. Washington, DC: U.S. Government Publishing Office.

Wilson, Robin Fretwell. 2018. *The contested place of religion in family law*. Cambridge, UK; New York, NY: Cambridge University Press.

Zimmermann, Jens. 2017. *Re-envisioning Christian humanism: Education and the restoration of humanity*. Oxford, UK: Oxford University Press.

Chapter Seven

Prescriptions (Rx)

Hard Truths, Contrition, and Metanoia

FIRST RX: SELF-DISCERNMENT AS A NATION

For America to nucleate and strive towards creating a *Communio Sanctorum* in the 21st century will require moving the boundaries beyond those in which most of us find a "comfort zone." For those few on the topside and privileged the effort will require much more. Lensing back to sacred scripture in the Gospel of Mark we read, [17]As he was setting out on a journey, a man ran up and knelt before him, and asked him, "Good Teacher, what must I do to inherit eternal life?" [18]Jesus said to him, "Why do you call me good? No one is good but God alone. [19]You know the commandments: 'You shall not murder; You shall not commit adultery; You shall not steal; You shall not bear false witness; You shall not defraud; Honor your father and mother.'" [20]He said to him, "Teacher, I have kept all these since my youth." [21]Jesus, looking at him, loved him and said, "You lack one thing; go, sell what you own, and give the money to the poor, and you will have treasure in heaven; then come, follow me." [22]When he heard this, he was shocked and went away grieving, for he had many possessions (Mark 10:17–22). This parable, often termed, "The Rich and the Kingdom of God" demonstrates two things. First, the issue of asymmetric wealth and power and its consequences on the lives of the "other" has dogged human civilization since time immemorial. Second, the solution to accumulation of wealth in the face of dire need and want of the "other" constitutes a harsh challenge to achieving full personhood for all. Inclusivity that extends beyond blood, family, tribe, culture, and all other identity qualifiers is a state in which all are "self" and there can be no "other." Structural privilege viewed alongside of structural oppression focuses upon the untoward suffering and death derivative of lost personhood.

The advice of Jesus of Nazareth to the young ruler went further (Mark 10:23–27), [23]Then Jesus looked around and said to his disciples, "How hard it will be for those who have wealth to enter the kingdom of God!" [24]And the disciples were perplexed at these words. But Jesus said to them again, "Children, how hard it is to enter the kingdom of God! [25]It is easier for a camel to go through the eye of a needle than for someone who is rich to enter the kingdom of God." [26]They were greatly astounded and said to one another, "Then who can be saved?" [27]Jesus looked at them and said, "For mortals it is impossible, but not for God; for God all things are possible." The metaphor of the camel passing through the eye of a needle is appropriate. Virtually all religious traditions, philosophers, and ethicists would agree that asymmetric wealth, that is, possession of wealth in times of great want, creates a thick almost insoluble dialectic for those with excess. Wealth and power in abundance contrasts sharply with poverty and suffering, even if the linkage is viewed by the wealthy *through a glass, darkly* (1 Corinthians 13:12). In our time, Neoliberal *laissez-faire* capitalism in tandem with postmodern thinking often minimizes to obscurity the real suffering of the oppressed on the underside (Gutiérrez and Müller 2015) . This is not to vilify prosperity and the just fruits of hard work and good fortune. Yet, like Gautama the Buddha, only when the suffering and plight of the poor is encountered first hand, do we begin to appreciate the depths of our crime of professed ignorance. In such circumstances we lack discernment of the suffering of the "other" as well as lack self-discernment of our complicity in creating such suffering. If we sincerely seek to build a true community in which the basic needs of all are provided, greater "sacrifice" by those of wealth and privilege to fight poverty and suffering will be required. This commitment to redistribution of abundance must be the very first step of our plan. Through greater self-discernment of our bonds to our co-travelers in Creation, former empty gestures of caring for the "other" absent shared resources will give way to a new generosity, but only when a community achieves moral solidarity and there no longer is "other," only "self." Jesus' parable rightly encourages generosity for the poor, but points out that the remedy can only flow from one's heart. Attempts to legislate empathy and social engineering aimed at poverty that develop bereft of deep discussion of the suffering inherent of asymmetric wealth and power will not transform the hearts and minds of the wealthy. Answering this call for redistributive justice for the impoverished is a "Calling" (Rawls 1972; Mau and Veghte 2007). Answering this calling will require self-discernment, kenosis, several concrete steps towards actualizing full personhood for all, and a commitment to a *preferential option for the poor*.

A concrete thickness of embracing co-being of those with whom we share on-going Creation evades most of our daily thinking. Yet, as discussed, we have so much for which to be thankful as humans, in just being essential and privileged co-travelers in ongoing Creation. Considering our infinitesimally thin slice of the arc of history, we should bond together with our co-travelers and bear witness that the thoroughgoing pro-creative future absolutely is dependent upon each and every one of us. We are the seeds of the harvest to come. This is a truth above all truths. Our focus cannot be constrained by the present, as if structural privilege and oppression are only a matter of historical note, unchangeable, and irrelevant to 21st century America. As racism, identity politics, and White privilege plague our people, we must dispel the notion that structural privilege and oppression cannot be ameliorated. We do not lack resources. We only lack sufficient resolve to deploy some of that rich abundance towards economic justice for all Americans. In 2018, the United States had the 8th highest GDP per capita and wealth, but this is an average. The GDP per capita is the total GDP of the nation divided by all the people of the nation, for example, workers and non-workers, young and elderly alike. If calculated upon the basis of those engaged in producing the GDP (i.e., workers), the average would be nearly $100,000 annually per worker! These data from the World Bank, International Monetary Fund, and the United Nations demonstrates that the U.S. has *no* wealth problem! Rather the U.S. suffers from an acute and far-reaching maldistribution of income and wealth. Herein lays the thread that reaches back to a historical past replete with indifference, oppression, corruption, and abject denial of personhood. Within only four centuries of genocide and dispossession of indigenous peoples and the introduction of the original sin of slavery, the U.S. has launched an accelerating arc of asymmetric wealth steeped in human rights violations of breathtaking dimensions.

In spite of tremendous and unrelenting efforts to whitewash over the horrific sins of empire, American Empire remains founded upon and prospering in the wake of its two great original sins: genocide and dispossession of indigenous Native Americans and the introduction of slavery of Africans, African Americans and their descendants. In both cases, the personhood of the indigenous Native American and the African slaves as well as the descendants of both peoples was assaulted. The very being of these victims, numbering in the *tens of millions* was degraded, effectively sacrificed to serve the economic aspirations of a nascent empire. These sins of empire were never successfully expunged from the history or memory of Americans. Concerted ongoing efforts to repudiate culpability of topsiders for the suffering and deaths of millions of Americans aim to sweep individual and corporate responsibility for these sins into the dustbin of American hegemony. Yet, these original sins and their derivative suffering persist in the 21st century, "hidden in plain sight." The history of brutal oppression is never intentionally relegated to the past. The brutality is retained as an unmistakable warning sign to dissuade those who seek "truth-telling." The goal of empire is to insure that Americans become desensitized to the many faces of denied personhood, especially the loss of the most basic right to not be killed. Steeped in news cycles replete with unjustified harsh treatment and killing of the "other," we become deaf, dumb, blind and depraved in moral character. We prefer to be made ignorant of the toxic and tragic products of asymmetric wealth and power that grip this nation. Is there no path towards confronting original sin and accepting responsibility of the two great sins on which the nation was founded? Truth telling is the only path forward for a nation confronted with these past original sins. Without truth telling, these great sins shackle the entire nation to depravity and promote an ongoing desensitization to injustice offered up as an elixir for national guilt.

The United States is not the only empire to commit such great sins. Historically, most empires committed similar horrendous acts: killing of indigenous populations; killing and enslavement of conquered peoples; and depriving large swaths of peoples of their ancestral lands and innate human rights. Personhood is discounted, partially withdrawn, or totally denied in order to fuel the growth of empire (Moses 2008). A list of more than 175 self-proclaimed historical "empires" of the world (Morris and Scheidel 2009) includes: the oldest, that is, the Akkadian Empire, 2300–2200 BCE; the longest, that is, the Pandyan Empire of ancient India, 500 BCE to 1350 CE, lasting 1850 years (Thinakaran 1987); the newest, that is, the Pahlavi Dynasty of Persia, from 1925–1979 CE (Fardūst 1995); and the shortest, that is, the First Mexican Empire, 1821–1823 (Deeds, Meyer, and Sherman 2018). Is there truly an American Empire? The answer remains controversial (Schlesinger 2005), at least in the context of former imperial empires of Rome, Britain, and France. President James Polk was said to have first employed the term "American Empire" during the Mexican-American War. Today, "American Empire" refers to the United States and its perceived sphere of "imperial" influence throughout the globe (Burns 2017). Client states of American Empire do not fear military invasions, but rather withdrawal or discount of American support.

Detailing of atrocities at the hand of empire by the victors customarily is omitted, rather taking on the disguise in the language of the overcoming the "other," who by failing the "self" test administered by empire is stripped of virtually all human rights, including the most basic right of being spared from killing. Yet, over the last hundred years, a new paradigm for dealing with the internalized guilt and self-loathing that virtually always accompanies excursions into human mass atrocities has emerged. This new paradigm is that of truth and reconciliation ("T&R") commissions, aimed at uncovering violations of human rights, crimes against humanity, and a path forward to eventual reconciliation (Hayner 2011; Bstan 'dzin rgya and Tutu 2016).

Lingering hatred for unpunished sins and lack of due process for past wrong-doings can "freeze" both the victims as well as the perpetrators in a quagmire. T&R commissions emerged and were constituted to free all complainants from a quagmire of untreated and toxic trauma. Large-scale trauma, when untreated, precludes regeneration of community that is essential to regaining the mental health of victims and perpetrators alike (Herman 1997). Festering with time, the sins of empire often become the seeds of its eventual collapse. Seeds of discontent laying dormant throughout and in the aftermath of a trauma committed at the hands of empire eventually will germinate. Ongoing civil unrest and disobedience are fed by boundless hatred of peoples assaulted as "other" and deprived of personhood by actions of a hegemonic ruling empire. The goal of T&R commissions is not to minimize or dismiss such trauma, but rather to invite, receive, and validate testimony of victims that bears witness to atrocities exacted by empire (Felman and Laub 1992).

The truth about America's great original sins need not be restricted only to a truth-telling and reconciliation framework. In many cases, the heavy lifting of truth telling needs to focus upon seeking justice, rather than simple reconciliation. Distillation of empire's great sins can reveal derivative criminal acts that only further provoke trauma. Criminal trials often set a more limited goal of seeking justice rather than truth *and* reconciliation. When the crimes exceed the high bar of those labeled "war crimes" and "crimes against humanity," truth, justice, and reconciliation needs to be sought. The historic Nuremberg War Crimes Trials in Germany at the close of World War II is a well-known example of truth-seeking, including testimony of both victims and defendants (under oath) in pursuit of justice (Marrus 1997). In Nuremberg, the war crimes laid out by the prosecutors were so atrocious and grotesque that reciprocal justice was impossible. How does one meter out punishment for the death of millions of people? The remedy is beyond reciprocal justice. Truth telling encourages acceptance of responsibility and contrition, essential elements of eventual reconciliation. Would not the adoption of the truth-seeking model of the Nuremburg trials provide a useful template for interrogating the long-standing crimes against humanity perpetrated against the indigenous Native Americans as well as the African slaves and their descendants? Regarding America's first great sin, that is, its subjugation, dispossession and decimation of indigenous Native Americans, who were depopulated by European conquest, war, and massacres, forced displacement from homelands, and intentional exposure to deadly pestilence (Dunbar-Ortiz 2014), would not these actions fulfill the criteria for the war crime termed "ethnic cleansing"? In 2000, the U.S. Bureau of Indian Affairs made history in this regard. The Bureau of Indian Affairs formally apologized for its participation in "ethnic cleansing of the Western Tribes." As remarkable as this single event was, one must wonder whether it was truth telling fortified with a good measure of "truth-avoidance," designed to whitewash, minimize, and deflect from the sheer magnitude of almost 400 years of crimes against humanity?

The original sin of slavery in America follows the same general playbook of American imperialist empire, but with important distinctions. First, unlike the Native Americans, Africans and later African Americans were forced into enslavement as human chattel. Legal as a colonial and later U.S. institution, slavery and involuntary servitude was prohibited only in 1865 by adoption of the 13th Amendment to the U.S. Constitution. Unlike the Native Americans who presented as a persistent "nuisance" to the hegemonic acquisition of Native lands and resources, the American slave was treated as a beast of burden to be exploited. The dominant ruling White class laid claim to Black bodies as chattel under White dominion as alleged to be sourced to the Book of Genesis. Slaves were merely resources exploited to underpin economic development and expansion in the 18th and 19th century. Slaves were an essential substrate to support the building of the American empire under a cloak of capitalism (Baptist 2016). American slavery deprived millions Africans and African Americans of their human rights, dignity, and sometimes even their lives. Documenting the size and scope of the inhumanity of slavery in America will require perseverance and long-term analysis. The marking of the 400th anniversary of introduction of slavery into the English colony in Virginia offers an opportunity to look back at four centuries of the legacy of slavery and its hegemonic horror. Most shocking, these irrefutable facts about American slavery and its current legacy still largely remain "hidden in plain sight."

Remarkably, within a list of more than forty instances of "atrocities and high crimes against humanity" that demanded the use of T&R commissions in modern times, the inhumane and criminal treatment of the Native Americans and of the Africans/African Americans by the U.S. are absent! In this list of "atrocities and high crimes against humanity," under the heading of "U.S.," there are *no* Federal declarations, no T&R commissions! There do exist two examples, at the state level, of such commissions having been established. The first was established in North Carolina, regarding the horrific Greensboro massacre by the Klu Klux Klan and American Nazi Party occurring on November 3, 1979. The second was established in Maine in 2012 (i.e., Maine Wabanaki-State Child Welfare T&R Commission) to unearth the truth, to promote healing, and to effect corrective change about the horrific maltreatment of Native American children as an aftermath to the passage of the 1978 Indian Child Welfare Act. The most well-known of such commissions occurred outside of the U.S. Notable were the National Truth & Reconciliation Commissions established to address human rights violation in Chile (created 1990), El Salvador (established by the United Nations in 1992), Rwanda (established in 1990), and South Africa, which was authorized by South Africa President Nelson Mandela in 1995 and led by Anglican

Archbishop Desmond Tutu (Hayner 2011; Bstan 'dzin rgya and Tutu 2016). Each of these remarkable commissions sought a noble outcome, that is, to share the truth (truth-telling), to seek accountability and responsibility for the crimes, and to achieve "restorative justice." It is important to note the period of time that elapsed from when the atrocities and crime against humanity occurred to when these high-profile T&R commissions were convened. Most contemporary T&R commissions were created within a few decades of the primary assault on personhood. The most powerful truths established by truth telling remain sourced to living eyewitnesses. Living eyewitnesses can provide corroborating first-hand testimony about crimes committed against humanity.

What about establishing T&R commissions tasked with addressing America's crimes against humanity? Is it possible to address an "original sin" first committed in the 16th and 17th century? This seemingly insoluble obstacle often is employed as a "straw man" erected to deflect accountability of the White ruling class for past sins. The obstacle may be more easily overcome than one might think. First, the intervening four centuries of the history of the founding of the republic has enabled accumulation of facts, including transcripts and recordings of eyewitness testimony. Without credible challenge, the assaults on the personhood and human rights of indigenous Native American and African/African American slaves are justifiably regarded as horrific crimes against humanity. With the passage of time, the facts and testimony have accumulated and scholarly research is ongoing. Though irrefutable, newer research of additional crimes simply is appended to an existing large corpus of information. This tradition guarantees that most documentation of original sins will remain largely hidden in plain sight. In the absence of proper respect and public disclosure, apathy and intentional disregard will dominate, preventing America from the opportunity to confront the full horrors of its two great original sins.

Confronting the two great original sins of American may be viewed as a crucial starting point for a path forward to truth telling. Ultimately confronting crimes derivative of original sins affords to us additional opportunities to better discern both past and current day assaults on personhood. A product of *self-discernment* would be a third opportunity to confront deep-seated and unresolved guilt. For many today, America continues as a place in which the "other" are marginalized and suffer double or triple jeopardy with regard to assaults on their human rights. An Iraqi woman seeking a new life in the U.S. may find obstacles based in her gender, race, and country of origin as well as faith tradition (e.g., adherent to Islam). People with physical and/or mental disabilities may be labeled as "invalids," their personhood and suffering discounted in a no less similar manner. For people of color, female gender, and targeted by populist identity politics, the burden on personhood is compounded. Truth telling is not only bearing eye-witness to current sins, but also sharing the facts about miserable behaviors and indeed atrocities perpetrated against the "other" every day in the name of "self."

For truth telling, the singular goal of the U.S. Congress must be to craft legislation aimed at creating unbiased and unimpeachable fact-based analysis of the four hundred year products of these two original sins. On-going derivative sins present in American culture today will emerge through increased discernment and self-awareness. Ignoring complicity only enables continued assaults on those who are the "least of us." The current suffering of these victims, I offer, finds its headwaters in a 400-year history of mistreatment and degraded personhood. With the combined expertise of the U.S. National Academy of Sciences and of other academic experts whose credentials and history of gathering truths is unimpeachable and well known, the U.S. Congress can delegate the essential task of truth gathering. Similarly, academic institutions that have invested heavily in Black Studies, Studies of Indigenous Peoples, and Social Justice could well lend an expert hand to the deployment of their specialists whose thoughtful reports and recommendations would be welcomed. A fresh starting point is needed. Unearthing and decoding narratives spanning four centuries of structural privilege and oppression in America must remain the task assigned to unimpeachable academic researchers. A country shackling itself to the guilt and self-loathing of great and small sins that tear at the fabric of everyday society will have but a limited future. If we truly seek a future in which all can flourish, all are welcome, and there is no "other," then we need to empower Congress to create a T&R commission tasked with truth gathering and truth telling of our painful history. Only such a commitment will provide the unvarnished and miserable facts about our inhumanity towards each other in the past and present. Only with a corpus of truth expertly assembled and validated can the nation begin the more challenging steps of discernment, that is, self-discernment, contrition, and eventual search for reconciliation between the victims and perpetrators whose past and future is inextricably shackled to our original sins. Only with a nation of people listening attentively to the expansive painful truths embedded in a history of sins against humanity that reach back four centuries in America will the next step of this redemptive journey come into focus.

SECOND RX: SEARCHING FOR, RECEIVING, AND VALIDATING HARD TRUTHS

A foundational theme of chaplaincy training is "self-discernment." Self-discernment enables a process seeking to understand what shapes the ability of one's self to listen attentively to others, especially those who are suffering. Often we learn to filter out that with which we have no context or that with which we disagree. Attentive listening requires people to concentrate both on the content and on the delivery of someone else's witness and testimony. While listening attentively we can begin to understand and contextualize the concrete details of the lives, living, and current suffering of the "other." Although this effort alone may be therapeutic and soothing to those afflicted, it is not enough. Attentive listening, a necessary initial step, requires two additional responses on our part: receipt of the narrative and validation of its content. Once the act of attentive listening invites the afflicted to share with us, we must receive their content. Then there must be acknowledgement that the content of the communication, at least the basic content, has been received. This act of acknowledged receipt is essential to encouraging further active dialogue. Further and deepening knowledge about the suffering of the "other" depends upon this simple candid sharing. Simple acknowledgement, along the lines of "I am beginning to understand what you are sharing with me," engenders trust for an empathetic listener. The content of the suffering is simply received and acknowledged, importantly *without* prejudice. Receipt and acknowledgement often reduces the anxiety of the afflicted. In some small and very real manner, this deeper sharing is cathartic to one who suffers. Without reassuring victims of assaulted personhood that we have received the sacred shared content of their suffering, very little can be accomplished going forward in search of truth telling.

As cathartic as truth telling can be to a victim of assault, it will be a short-lived catharsis without proper validation. Validation is the sincere and empathetic response to the victim's sharing of the small sacred text of his/her suffering at the hands of structural forces that have robbed her/him of personhood, basic human rights and dignity. Validation of suffering is never simply response of "I see" or "I know what you mean." Such off-the-cuff responses can spontaneously roll off our lips when we are confronted with the acute suffering of the "other." This point is best demonstrated by "normal" routine response metered out about a death at a wake or funeral service. Poorly prepared, we are left to only muster an often trivial and off the mark response to the bereaved. Any pastor or chaplain attending to the aftermath of a child loss has witnessed countless seemingly well-intentioned but decidedly empty gestures. Well-wishers may attempt to reassure the grieving parents that they "can have more children" or "another child." Similarly, death of an elderly spouse can provoke superficial responses such as "well, she/he had a long life" or "he/she looked good for their age," and "now he/she is at peace." Common is the unhelpful response to death that offers only reciprocal suffering. These responses include, "yes, I lost a friend last year, so I know what you are going through" and "I know how hard this is for you." Really? These hurtful responses are both unintentional yet common. The responses neither receive nor validate a deep loss for the surviving victims. Lacking sufficient sincerity and empathic content necessary to connect with the victim and the dimensions of her/his suffering, such empty words and gestures are best avoided and replaced by simple quiet presence.

It is far better to search oneself and respond to a victim with candor, "I really cannot imagine how much suffering this situation has brought you." Sharing the sadness, melancholia, and disappointment of loss, requires deep empathy, that is, the ability both to understand and to share in the suffering of the "other." The goal becomes to deploy empathy and unconditional love to dissolve "otherness" and embrace the "self" in the "other." The loss of a loved one, a friend, or an acquaintance is unparalleled. More common, victims can suffer from "ambiguous" loss. Absent death, separation from a loved one who has left in the aftermath of a broken relationship (often accompanied by lost personhood) can manifest itself as ambiguous loss. In ambiguous loss, the magnitude of loss to personhood and emotional well-being remains difficult to discern for victim and active listener alike. Current victims sharing a legacy of four centuries of assaulted personhood, genocide, and denied human rights also may suffer ambiguous loss, that is, a profound yet intangible sense of the suffering of the millions that preceded them to this same hegemonic America. We can fail to apprehend the dimensions of another injury, "structural victimization." Derivative of ongoing intergenerational suffering attendant to original sins of America, victims can suffer structural victimization in which the loss of personhood is profound, but the perpetrators remain enigmatic, in a fog of centuries past. Small children of color often sense structural oppression obliquely through trying to understand glaring eyes and faces of seemingly disapproving Whiteness. In their mind's eye they see all people as "self," there are no difference. No difference, that is, until forced to discern that their appearance actually does differ from Whiteness amongst them. Eventually, a mirror reflection corrects their mistaken belief that they simply are like everyone else. This visual revelation will neither dispel nor explain the root source of the structural victimization that they sensed acutely in disapproving White faces.

In the absence of truth telling, the burden of centuries of victimization of the "other" that resulted from the deaths/killings of millions of people, in deprivation of basic liberties for those existing in a "free nation," and in the continuing silencing of the wailing voice of past generations can become an unbearable burden for those labeled as "other." Voices of human suffering derivative of assaults on personhood have been silenced systematically. In Genesis 4, for example, we read that Cain murdered his brother Able. The Lord quizzes Cain. The dialogue (Genesis 4) is as follows: [9]Then the Lord said to Cain, "Where is your brother Abel?" "I don't know," he replied. "Am I my brother's keeper?" [10]The Lord said, "What have you done? Listen! Your brother's blood cries out to me from the ground. [11]Now you are under a curse and driven from the ground, which opened its mouth to receive your brother's blood from your hand. [12]When you work the ground, it will no longer yield its crops for you. You will be a restless wanderer on the earth." Is not the blood of four centuries of systematic and structural killing of the "other" crying out to us?

Are not the deeply emotive African American spirituals speaking to us today about the hardship, brutality, and suffering at the hand of slavery in America crying out to us? Do not cries of victimized Black folk emanating from the underside today find voice of resistance and resilience in both spirituals as well as American jazz (Rappaport and Evans 2002; Horne 2019)? Racism flourishes in 21st century America. The voices of Black, brown and of all people of color are no longer silenced and rise up like the "blood of Abel," crying out for justice for lost generations. Similarly, music of the Native American diaspora echoes lamentations of voices long since silenced. In a plaintive voice Native American songs express the horror of killings and of forced relocations inflicted upon these indigenous peoples by the dominant White ruling class launched in colonial settler America. The personhood of the indigenous Native Americans continues to be assaulted. Exploitation and sacrilege of Native American ancestral lands, water, and their ways of life continues unabated. Assaults occur with increased frequency, especially since 2016 when the Trump administration took office (Klein 2017; Acosta 2019; Estes 2019). How can we not receive and validate the sorrow and losses of so many precious lives? They are still speaking to us, like the blood of Abel, in a haunting voice of countless millions lost and degraded. Cannot our hearts hear such wailing from the blood in American soil crying out to us?

Today, indigenous Native Americans search for justice to prevail against the Discovery doctrine of the U.S. Supreme Court, advanced by Chief Justice John Marshall in 1823. Entitling the acquisition of native tribal lands (i.e., most of the U.S.) to colonial powers of foreign nations during the Age of Discovery (i.e., the so-called, "Discovery doctrine" explored in Chapter 5) was arbitrary and capricious, invalidating indigenous peoples' human rights as well as rightful claims to ancestral tribal lands of peoples in the land for more than 30,000 years (Kukathas 2008; Weaver 2019). We should listen attentively! When African Americans seek to redress the horrors of the slavery in America that left not only the blood of Abel, but additionally the lost personhood of an entire population of more than 10 million Africans (including their descendants) derived from peoples captured and then forced into slavery (Armstrong 2015), we should listen attentively! This "blood of Abel," from an estimated 4 million Africans whose demise in capture, Middle Passage to America, and premature deaths calls out to us here and now (Thomas 1997). Their voices compel us to a full hearing. We should listen attentively! When peoples in this nation suffer from assaults on their personhood solely on the basis of race, gender, identity politics, immigration status, religious preferences, sexual preferences, both physical and mental vulnerabilities (Caruth 1995), we should listen attentively! Our quest to create a nation in which all are welcome, all can flourish, and there can be no "other" compels us to listen attentively, receive, then validate and embrace the suffering, both past and present. We must listen attentively!

Attentive listening and revisiting past inequities with honesty, truth, and empathy for the truth tellers start with each of us. It is both the "I" and "we" together. Tackling the two great original sins on which the founding of America was launched as well as the plethora of derivative current day examples of the intentional exploitation of identity politics to advantage White ruling class "self," while disadvantaging the "other," will be a formidable task. One wonders if such a Herculean task can be assigned to any nation? On a small scale, the on-going efforts of the non-profit organization "StoryCorps" to capture and share intimate stories of Americans from all backgrounds and beliefs already have provided one workable template. The oral narratives of everyday people who reflect upon hardships and joy, gains and losses in their American lives often transfix listeners to StoryCorps. In the U.S., recording oral history interviews began in the 1930s with the efforts of the Works Progress Administration (WPA). From 1936–1938, the WPA created the first series of recorded narratives recounting the histories of former slaves in America. The power of oral narratives cannot be denied. Attentive listening of personal narratives relaying small sacred texts of our history remains an integral and essential part of truth telling and bearing witness. Detailing the historical background of current day American society by such narratives is invaluable. Yet the narratives cannot replace fundamental and more expansive work of a Federal T&R commission empowered to collecting, verifying and validating an essential history of human fallenness in America, of both the corporate and the individual sins aimed at the "other."

At every step, the long arc of American hegemony, structural privilege, and White ruling class power enjoyed by the few at the expense of the many, will challenge progress toward capturing the fullest dimensions of assaulted personhood. The purpose of exposing the dialectic about wealth and power asymmetry in America is not to castigate the economics of capitalism per se. Capitalism has been an impressive engine of economic growth (Friedman 1968), but unchained capitalism has proven to be anathema to forming a society that cares for its members (Piketty 2014), especially the "least of us." Rather, interrogating this dialectic knot seeks to unpack how the enormous asymmetries in wealth, income, power, and privilege in America's past emerged, with eyes wide open. The legacy of asymmetric power and wealth of capitalism favoring the ruling White class precluded those victimized by 400-years of structural oppression from just benefits that should be afforded to all peoples, especially to those whose lands and resources were stolen (Dunbar-Ortiz 2016; Saunt 2020) as well as to those whose labor established the U.S. as a world economic power (Baptist 2016; Case and Deaton 2020).

In fact, the U.S. remains able to create a truly "great society" with ample capacity to provide for all of its members the ability to flourish *en masse*. Recall the overarching aim of our effort is to reimagine a new path to creating true *Communio Sanctorum*. Only therein will all be welcome, formed into a true community displaying moral solidarity, where all are "self" and there can be no "other." Generations before often express community composed for "me and my own." We must look beyond the bonds of blood to the broader, deeper bonds of those who with us co-journey in this thin slice of being, in a thoroughgoing Creation. We, the seeds of the harvest to come, are essential to the present as well as to the future. We must act, accepting our roles and agency as "called into being," into Creation, for the well-being of all our fellow co-travelers. The intention is clear, to address past and current inequities in which all Americans have complicity. In the absence of true contrition for both passive as well as active complicity, Americans will only persist in the *status quo*, that is, privileged existence for the very few at the incalculable expense of the oppression of the many.

THIRD RX: ACCEPTING RESPONSIBILITY AND SEEKING FORGIVENESS

Authorizing, organizing, and empowering an independent U.S. National Truth and Reconciliation Commission (i.e., hereafter the "Commission") is the cornerstone to our redemption and a truly formidable task. The model for this Commission already exists, derivative of similar efforts of other nations to address violations of human rights and crimes against humanity. The efforts of the Commission would be fact-finding, creating a sustained purposefulness, and establishing a broad variety of media venues by which its findings are to be collected, organized, vetted, and published on an annual basis. Key to the success is the requirement for continuous amendment of the corpus of the Commission in response to new findings. Through detailed referencing, annotation, amendment, and constant oversight a dynamic and inclusive U.S.-based history of assaults on the personhood of Native Americans, African Americans and their descendant peoples can emerge. Wikipedia may provide a useful model, employing juried oversight by unimpeachable experts appointed by the Commission. Such a living corpus prepared by the Commission will encounter controversial data and generate contentious viewpoints. Its findings inevitably might well become a source of some public consternation. Seeking truth telling rather than revisionist tripe, the Commission will need unfettered authority and unwavering Congressional support to bring forth the truth necessary for eventual reconciliation. A dominant ruling class steeped in privilege and power will not sit by idly. The ruling White class in America can be expected to act in self-interest seeking to maintain and protect a *status quo*, insuring their privileged position as topsiders.

Frankly speaking, the scale of America's original sins and a plethora of everyday sins assaulting the personhood of the "other" are without parallel. Tackling the inequity while seeking true and just redress will be a formidable challenge. Yet, the task is doable, worthy of any nation seeking moral standing among its citizens as well as those of the world. Achieving full public agreement on all the fine features of such a living document of original sins is magical thinking. Achieving a plurality of support for the Commission's ongoing effort, in contrast, is not outside of the possible. The current asymmetry of access to education, income, wealth, and justice both privilege and sustain the ruling White class while oppressing people of color is as plain as the nose on your face. We all see it, every day. Will compelling disclosures of past wrong doing force society to accept both corporate and individual guilt by complicity in enabling extension of 400-year old original sins into everyday lives of 21st century Americans? Pulling back the "green curtain" to a four hundred year old history of hegemony and privilege is only the first step, but it is foundational to further steps on the journey to forming an American community bound together in moral solidarity.

Ameliorating the inhumane treatment and injustice derivative of four centuries of structural oppression constructed on such a grand scale in America will require a sustained commitment to the Commission's project, from start to finish. The success of the Suffrage Movement, the Civil Rights and Voting Rights movements, and the American Indian movement offer hope for the success of a Federal T&R Commission tasked with addressing original sins. The keystone to the success of a T&R Commission in the U.S. is utter faith in the process that it can transcend the fallenness replete in the *status quo*. Imagine the Native American and Black and brown bodies whose personhood was extinguished all standing together as a "cloud of witnesses" demanding that the millions of their souls be lifted up to full personhood. This cloud of witnesses to America's original sins is an integral concept to covenantal communion among a community of saints. These witnesses cannot speak to us of assaulted personhood of centuries past, so we must be their voices. Only we co-travelers in this thin slice of Creation can demand the truth which encourages acceptance of guilt by complicity, discloses past and current iniquities, and demands justice and redemption from past sins. We make this demand on behalf of the cloud of witnesses past and present. A dedicated, balanced analysis of collected corpus of American original sins must emerge from the Commission. With a full disclosure of centuries of assaults on personhood of the "other," the next step looms large. Will simple disclosure and delineation of original sins expunge continued structural privilege of the ruling White class? Will disclosure of horrific oppression of the "other" in the history of the U.S. drive a spoke into the wheels of *in*justice?

For the greater good of the U.S. people, responsibility-taking rather than denial of culpability for the harsh inequities of the *status quo* will be necessary for individuals, organizations, as well as corporate American.

The corporate response to the Commission's corpus is highly predictable. The corporate goal is simple, that is, to protect the *status quo* for those people and organizations that have benefitted by structural privilege, a privilege that was centuries in the making. The "landed aristocracy," the banking industry, and trade groups will demand protection. It is the overarching knee jerk response of corporate America to perceived liabilities and threats of their guilt and complicity. Embracing the corpus crafted by a national T&R Commission with exuberance while welcoming an airing of the horrific assaults on personhood associated with two original sins would be anathema to corporate ethos. In many cases, corporate empire would likely cast itself as a "victim" of misplaced and unfounded anti-capitalist social engineering.

Native Americans, African Americans and their descendants assaulted by structural oppression suffer from an intergenerational, long-term trauma much like PTSD. The collective trauma from four centuries of assault as well as from the everyday trauma of living on the underside replete with racism, identity politics, gender bias, and so on, has few parallels around the world. Impaneling a T&R Commission will reinvigorate organizations whose charters are aimed at protecting and providing for basic human rights and services to the oppressed. The ACLU, labor unions, Human Rights Watch, NAACP, Native American Rights Fund, and Southern Poverty Law Center are but a few of the non-governmental organizations (i.e., NGOs) deeply committed to creating a more just society. Detailed annual progress reports by the T&R Commission and creation of a living history documenting America's original sins are not to be used as cudgels for activist fervor. Neither assaults on personhood nor denial of human rights and dignity of the oppressed should be adopted to create harsh rhetoric around retribution, but rather as a platform on which to engage deep dialogue. As Cornel West chides his students, remember "race matters, always matters." Launch of the version 101 T&R Commission report would herald into being a new, fact-based, truth-telling platform for continuing dialogue on these very large and contentious issues. Few feel comfortable taking about race in America. In fact, we seek to avoid the topic, but it is the most necessary conversation for the U.S. to embrace. The version 101 launch would not signify the conclusion of a commission's work, but rather a true beginning of a new reimagined America.

Forces that actively promote acts to nullify, vilify, and bury the Commission's corpus critical of structural privilege and asymmetric wealth and power undoubtedly will resist dialogue about the factors, like race, gender, sexual preference, and alike that fuel structural oppression and poverty. The pillar of structural oppression based in identity politics, racism, classism, and so on, aimed at the least of us, created through denial of personhood, will always haunt the privileged. Jesus of Nazareth offered, "The poor you will always have with you" (Matt 26:11). The Book of Deuteronomy (15:11 Hebrew Bible) acknowledged, "There will always be poor people in the land." The scale of the poverty and of asymmetric wealth that now exists between the rich and the poor has never been greater (Piketty 2017). The dimensions of both structural privilege *and* poverty in the U.S. continue to outstrip all predictions (Case and Deaton 2020).

We cannot conclude that this expansion of the poor, indigent and immigrant populations among us is simple fulfillment of a biblical prophecy employed to suggest divine warrant of White dominion over peoples of color. It is the unjust distribution of opportunity, a "rigged" system of acquisition of wealth, income taxation evasion, and banking interests that punish the poor and insure that they stay poor (Case and Deaton 2020). It must be highlighted that beyond the derivatives of the two original sins of America is the ongoing daily assaults on personhood. These assaults occur often outside the simple boundaries either of income or of wealth. They are all too common. Everyday assaults upon those viewed as "other" or "different" threaten and intentionally target human rights, personhood and dignity of the oppressed. Those with physical and/or mental disabilities, those suffering from ageing, chronic diseases, abandonment, addiction, and lack of human compassion and empathy outnumber those who have been oppressed economically. For the economically impoverished, the hope for raising themselves out of poverty depends upon the implementation of a fair and equitable economic system (Baptist 2016; Piketty 2017; Case and Deaton 2020). Today in America, the economics for the underprivileged "other" remain shackled to an unbridled capitalism advanced by cronyism rather than competitive creativity (Piketty 2017). For the least of us, daily suffering in the crucible of identity politics, religious intolerance, racial discrimination, gender bias crimes of large and small dimensions, corporate/legislative/legal solutions offer no promising way forward. The sorry history of Native American rights, civil rights and voting rights, legislation failing to overcome Jim Crow laws (both "old" and "new"), racism and discrimination are cases in point. The human heart, I proffer, will remain the most formidable challenge to change when confronting truth and reconciliation on the issues of America's original sins.

Historic past and current crimes against the "least of us," against indigenous Native Americans, African slaves and their descendants cannot be addressed without individual, self-discernment. Accepting responsibility for past assaults on personhood and human rights ultimately emerges as a personal issue of conscience and morality. Avoiding responsibility by suggesting that the past is "dead" is a non-starter in the ascent to redemption. William Faulkner reminded us, "The past is never dead. It's not even past." In many ways our ability today to continually assault the personhood of the "other" draws its water from the headwaters of indifference that first enabled and then submerged acts of original sin in America. Seeking moral personhood and justice in our time cannot constrain us to "our time" alone. Morally we are compelled to follow this river of hatred and debasement to the headwaters of this Nation's past. For more than four hundred years we have proffered and perhaps embraced the notion that indeed *the past is dead*.

One look at the character of the assaults upon least of us today with those of centuries past will disabuse one of the false narrative that the present is unrelated to the past. By definition, we expect structural privilege to fight tooth and nail against distributive and redistributive justice as methods to address past sins. The privileged simply feign culpability, that is, the past is past. But our argument regarding the toxic history of structural privilege is not simply economic. Our argument seeks to address assaults on human rights and personhood of all the members of the American society, co-travelers in this thoroughgoing continuing roll-out of Creation. The ties that bind us existentially to one another are deep, anthropological, and for some biblical in origin. Whether from a discussion of the Big Bang Theory on the origin of the cosmos or a reading from a sacred text (e.g., Genesis 1:1–2:3 and 2:4–2:25 of the Hebrew Bible), we readily accept our profound shared humanity in this time and space. We share a common past within the founding of this nation. Only within the perspective of such shared humanity can we practice the self-discernment aimed primarily at opening our hearts. Can the search for accountability, the seeking and affording forgiveness for historic, long-lived, and continuing assaults on the personhood of our fellow co-travelers in Creation find a home beyond understanding in the mind to a pathos in our hearts?

Accountability and accepting responsibility for one's own role in assaults on personhood and losses of human rights and lives is the necessary step towards moral duty. In light of new information from a T&R Commission or in response to personally gaining greater insights into the many ways that structural evils of the past are degrading the lives of the "other" today, we are compelled to be accountable and take responsibility. Lacking adequate discernment around our feelings about the sorrowful fate of victims of structural oppression, we are unlikely to be able to make the essential step towards accountability. We accept accountability when we move from simply being appraised of prior assaults on peoples' human rights to offering testimony and joining the "cloud of witnesses" past and present. We transform ourselves when we move from the role of "passive bystander" to "active witness." We transform others by bearing witness. Those, whose complicity is no longer denied, now know, speak, and are compelled to bear witness that reflects accountability.

Through increased awareness and candor we are compelled to proclaim that the past and current fallenness simply is not okay! This transformation from bystander to witness occurs when we understand that our *in*action as well as action can harm. When offering sympathy rather than empathy, we reveal that we know not and remain distant from the suffering of the "other." Sympathy is offered to the "other." Empathy, in contrast, invites us to extend our very selfhood to entering into the suffering of the "other." Those for whom personhood has been denied for generation upon generation, century after century in America seek the bystander to embrace their suffering and thereby to transform into a witness. Now we can apprehend how our action (i.e., preserving the *status quo* and asymmetric privilege) as well as *in*action (i.e., feigning ignorance in the face of structural oppression) fuels a future shackled to two original sins and a plethora of everyday sins degrading the personhood of all. Intentionally overlooking privilege and economic benefits accrued by the few preclude us from any community of moral solidarity. We must expose our true complicity, accept accountability, and bear witness to the structural oppression from which many of us, including myself, have benefitted! Absent accountability and contrition for our complicity blocks us from embracing our co-travelers in communion through our ongoing Creation. We embrace a new knowledge, that is, as co-travelers in Creation, we are bound to each other through covenant in ways deeper than those of familial and tribal bonds.

Accepting accountability and responsibility for past and current assaults on personhood is not only an essential step towards moral personhood for America, but it is the straight path towards seeking forgiveness. Seeking forgiveness is a matter of the heart not the intellect. Instinctively almost everyone knows this truth to be self-evident. Shallow apologies littered with insincerity and an overarching desire to simply "get over this harm" can be deciphered by young and old alike. Deciphering authentic apologies is probably an adaptation favoring survival. Sincere apologies effectively can reduce the "otherness" of the perpetrator felt by the victim. Seeking forgiveness is never a negotiation, but rather an act of contrition seeking to reveal acts of complicity for which we take full responsibility. Past and current assaults aimed at the personhood of the "other" are substantive, not to be discounted. We do not apologize in order to negotiate forgiveness! Seeking forgiveness and apologies require self-discernment squarely aimed at repentance. We apologize in the hope, not the knowledge, that forgiveness may be possible. Absence of forgiveness does not discount the sincere apology. An act of contrition is noble, even if initially not well received by the victim. Traumatic injury to the person of the "other" will not likely be resolved quickly by apologies, no matter how well intentioned. Victims may require and even request a pause in response to an apology. It is said, "time heals all wounds." Undoubtedly, this is true. The length of the pause in receiving the apology, however, is likely proportional to the trauma ascribed to the perpetrator.

We cannot offer an apology, if and only if, we seek to advance the surety of a "guarantee" of forgiveness. Adopting such an ill-conceived, contractual strategy behind making an apology precludes forgiveness. Most often the perpetrator employs this tactic only to save face. Lacking heartfelt repentance, we condemn ourselves to guilt without the possibility of asking for and then receiving forgiveness. Yet contrition is the only path towards redemption for America's original sins. In my own complicity with original sin of the killing of Abenaki Native Americans and of unlawful land seizure in the late 17th century, I have come to discern the fallenness that these sins entail. Land settlements to the Native American nations may or may not properly attend to the illegal land grab. What of the killing of Native American men, women, and children? My complicity in the assault on the personhood of Black and brown, people of color, remains more challenging to apprehend. Lessons learned from my beloved classmates at Union Theological Seminary in the City of New York were transformative as were lessons learned from James Cone. How does one seek to address such grievous sins? For me, I continue to seek forgiveness in actions large and small, never turning away from responsibility and the heartfelt search for forgiveness and mercy. It has become a kenotic journey that leads me back to reconnoiter my past sins in an effort to prepare me better for a future that I believe still awaits 21st century Americans.

FOURTH RX: REPENTANCE, FORGIVENESS, ACTUALIZING CHANGE, AND METANOIA

Repentance best can be defined as a sincere feeling of regret and contrition for past wrong doings following disclosure of sins that have harmed others. Repentance is most often sought in response to recent sin(s). It can be sparked also by disclosure or recollection of great earlier sins that were either ignored or unknown prior. The two original sins of America often do provoke an outpouring of repentance when the structural nature of the assaults on the personhood of indigenous Native Americans and African slaves and their descendants is revealed. In the U.S., however, heightened aware of original sins is sporadic at best, fading fast into the public memory, too uncomfortable to be sustained for long. Recent, high-visibility public tribal confrontations with the energy industry and interests of the American empire, for example, the Dakota Pipeline protest (Estes 2019; and #*NoDAPL* movement), make all too real the linkage of current assaults to past sins. The vast four-century history of assaults and genocide were directed against indigenous peoples who were here in the land for 30,000 years. They greeted the invading immigrants settlers of European empires and were rewarded with assaults, killing, dispossession, and displacement. Simply pushing these sins against humanity aimed at Native Americans from our conscience does not and cannot dismiss such horrendous acts.

What of confronting the original sin of slavery against humanity aimed at Africans, African Americans, and their descendants? How do we measure true repentance and contrition for a four hundred year assault on people of color? Declaration of a national day of remembrance for the Rev. Dr. Martin Luther King and a tribute to his life, work, and devotion to civil rights was necessary, but incomplete if lacking self-discernment of all Americans. King's memorial in West Potomac Park next to the National Mall should encourage us daily to pause and to reflect upon the toxic chronic legacy of slavery in America and a formidable structural oppression of more than 400 years in the making. Americans welcomed the National Museum of African American History & Culture of the Smithsonian Institution in Washington, DC. Are they thereby better able to enter into the vast suffering and lost personhood of people of color in the U.S. today? Empathetic embrace of deep suffering of the "other" can be a profound teacher, but the lesson must be absorbed internally, not learned intellectually. When one considers the dimensions of suffering, depersonalization, death, and destruction to African American people inflicted by the dominant White ruling class over all these centuries, personal sorrow should be unavoidable. The plight of indigenous Native Americans, in contrast, still remains largely outside of the national consciousness about structural oppression, lost personhood, and lost lives! Sadly this oppression, fueled by identity politics and raw racism is all too palpable today among many American people. The behavior of the administration of the 45th president of the U.S. goes well beyond ignoring these original sins, reveling in the myth of American exceptionalism and brutal hegemony (Acosta 2019).

We must work to envision an effort great enough to overcome these times, characterized by bigotry and racism. Establishing a U.S. Commission on Truth & Reconciliation affords just such a path. Over time, the Commission can unshackle all, perpetrators and victims alike, from the chains of denied personhood and human rights violations aimed at tens of millions of innocent people. We must insure that any emergent documentation of assaults on personhood crafted in 21st century America is historically accurate, wide angle in nature, and inclusive. We must act with the utmost intention to embrace the fullest dimension of these assaults on personhood! The treatment of the Black and Native Americans, that is, our original sins, spills over into our everyday lives targeting a variety of peoples labeled as "other." As we canvassed earlier, the assault on personhood in America casts a broad and fine net to capture the vulnerable, the least among us. Victims of assaults on personhood include not only people of color, but also those that may be labeled as "other" due simply to ageism, Alzheimer's and deeply forgetfulness, drug addiction, mental disability, physical disability, gender, gender orientation, racism, sexual preference, and identity politics of the White ruling class. In the 21st century, millions of American are suffering deeply within this void of "self" versus "other." The suffering of this plethora of victims of assaults on personhood cannot go unnamed and unrecognized. The only monolith that can ameliorate this history of suffering is truth itself. For only the truth can set us all free (adapted from John 8:31). Following disclosure of the details of foundational "original sin" and persistent, pervasive sins of everyday U.S. life, no American should be able to turn their gaze away from assaulted personhood. The product of a Federal T&R Commission must aim to defeat those who either deny or ignore personal culpability. Rarely is repentance the product of accidental disclosure. Rather, repentance is an essential and intentional product of concerted discernment around moral judgment and how we choose to live our lives.

If we accept responsibility for the historic sins of America, how then do we repent? What are the signs and symptoms of sincere repentance? What will help us to discern our individual responsibility for assaults on personhood both present and past? Earlier (see Chapter 6), we explored theological resources from the Abrahamic religions, most world traditions and philosophies that display concordance about gestures necessary to signify true repentance. When confronted with past histories of corporate culpability, we first must acknowledge, receive, and validate that such acts constitute a corpus that we can neither ignore nor dismiss. We must examine these lessons of suffering through the lens of our hearts, not our heads. The horrid sight of the products of assaulted personhood, if internalized through the eyes of the victims embraced as "self" rather than "other," provokes deep inner sorrow, a cause for further self-discernment.

Discernment is aimed at acknowledging not only the veracity and scope of the sins, but also personal culpability. Although we may need to work hard at making connections to the original sins in our nation's past as well as to our sin of complicity, everyday life offers us opportunities toward greater moral duty demanded of us in light of such disclosures. Moral duty includes bearing witness to sin, so others may hear and be moved to contrite repentance. People of color, people who are in double and triple jeopardy by gender, race, identity politics in America (e.g., a Muslim woman of color) know these assaults on their personhood all too well, as do the perpetrators of the everyday assaults. These victims not only observe the assaults, but also *live* them every day. If we view such behaviors only to ignore them, our acts of repentance are empty, bereft of moral standing in community! By need and intention, the act of repentance must generate a greater sense of shared identity that all are welcome, there can be no "other." Our accountability includes the responsibility to speak up, demanding justice. In bearing moral witness, rather than being a bystander, we begin early nascent steps on the path of repentance. Admitting responsibility for structural oppression current and past is foundational. We cannot be true to our moral witness if we remain bystanders to the ongoing oppression nested in the original sins of America. Denial of personhood and attendant basic human rights to the least of us should fill all with guilt and then just rage! Need we be shamed before we commit ourselves to repentance and to greater moral courage? For life to flourish in *Communio Sanctorum*, all are "self." There can be no "other" in the communion of the saints that we seek to build.

The nature of repentance is such that we cannot limit our response just to sorrow and to confession of our complicity. Repentance requires of us to bear moral witness. Our inner sense of responsibility, sorrow, and shame should engender greater moral witness. We cannot tolerate yet another example, another moment, or another assault on the "other" go unnamed and ignored. Repentance can *re*sensitize our being to discern ongoing assaults on personhood in our everyday world. As all are "self," assaults on an aged person, a person suffering from deep forgetfulness, a person with physical or mental disabilities, a person struggling with drug addiction, a person whose gender, sexual orientation and preferences may not be shared should provoke an inner rage against the assault as well as the perpetrators. Paul Monette (1945–1995), a prescient American author, poet and activist entreaties us, "Go without hate, but not without rage (Monette 2014)." Heal the world! Thoughtful intervention to call out a perpetrator "caught in the act," makes headlines in the media. Why? The frequency and amplitude of assaults on personhood in everyday America has displayed robust growth in 21st century. Calling out a perpetrator is not to be confused with retaliatory aggressive acts buying into the perpetrators' world of assault and violence. Calling attention to the act, invites two outcomes, broader intervention to stop the behavior and hopefully education of a perpetrator. The immorality and reprehensibility of the assault as well as of its perpetrator(s) can no longer go ignored by our mind's eye. Calling out a perpetrator should not be advanced to attack someone or as a ploy aimed at elevating oneself to position of seemingly superiority, power, control or morality. Highlighting such assaults on personhood and calling attention to the perpetrator, quite to the contrary, more importantly signifies that we truly are sharing in the vulnerability of the victim. The goals of intervention should include being constructive not destructive, educating not judging the perpetrator, seeking not notoriety but just mercy, and reflecting moral solidarity as one who bears witness.

The overarching lesson illuminated up to this point is the knowledge that we all have vulnerabilities that make us vulnerable to everyday assaults on our personhood. In American society we often avoid acknowledging any vulnerability. Humility and professed vulnerability are anathema to the very ethos of American exceptionalism. Exceptionalism displayed by Americans seeks to lift up a "special character" of the U.S., its citizenry, and its divinely guided destiny to be the biblical "City on the Hill" first preached in a 1630 sermon to the Massachusetts Bay colonists (Van Engen 2020). Yet, such "exceptionalism," when fueled by braggadocio at the expense of the least of us, is no more than exceptional fallenness. Only when we see ourselves in the faces of those suffering in calamities and crimes of lost personhood do we connect to their sorrow, with our confession and shame. Let us be clear, assaults on any one of us, especially the least of us, truly hurt everyone. In a letter from the Birmingham jail, Martin Luther King Jr. scolds, "Injustice anywhere is a threat to justice everywhere (King 2018)." We would not tolerate abuse and assaults upon family and loved ones, would we? Yet, if we seek to protect only our children or grandchildren from such abuse, who will protect the children and grandchildren of others?

Let's look at a specific situation. You come upon a swaddled infant resting upon the edge of a well. The baby begins to roll, inching towards an abyss of certain death. Will we intervene only if the child or grandchild is our "own"? Moralists argue that most any human being will intervene in this case of a young life at risk. Life's trial and tribulations thankfully do not place us in such dire and dramatic settings filled with potentially fatal outcomes. With American children dying from lack of healthcare, proper nourishment, and parental care, is their suffering of no less concern if they are not family? If our hearts compel us to intervene for all children, adults, and the otherwise vulnerable people, we dedicate ourselves to building *Communio Sanctorum*. If we seek to create and invest in covenantal community in which all are "self," there can be no "other," the impetus to intervene and to counter hatred and fallenness of perpetrators must be viewed as moral duty, a pursuit of virtue.

In the final analysis, it will be our learned intolerance of assaults on personhood fueled by past original sins that will fuel our own capacity to embrace the suffering of all who labor under structural oppression and vulnerability. Exposure to life's brute bad life can educate our hearts. People with beloved aging parents or grandparents are far less likely to ignore the needs of the aged in general. They reflexively offer seating to the aged on a subway or bus. They are loathe to tolerate verbal abuse often aimed at the aged and vulnerable. When you welcome the hardship of life endured by caring for someone who is deeply forgetful, a greater inner compassion emerges. Compassion for other people's suffering, those neglected or abused in response to their mental afflictions or disabilities, emerges collaterally. In gospel singing, American jazz, and the "Blues" do we not begin to discern in our souls the echoes of centuries of suffering and oppression at the hands of the dominant White ruling class in America? Or perhaps in reciting the writings of early Native Americans like the author Mourning Dove we discern and keep alive precious oral narratives and texts linked to the suffering of America's indigenous peoples (Mourning, Sho pow, and McWhorter 1981). Loss of ancestral lands and forced assimilation of "White man culture" provoke the wailing of indigenous people in the land who are under assault. Or maybe it is the voice of homeless panhandlers wandering through the cities of America (Phillips 2016). Or yet maybe it is the moaning lamentation of the elderly populations displaced from homes to impersonal and derelict nursing facilities that overmedicate them to make them docile (Flamm and Human Rights Watch 2018). These are not "nursing" homes, but rather are holding pens for the elderly awaiting death out of sight, out of mind. The aftermath of COVID-19 pandemic in 2020 exposed our complicity in gazing away as disease and death ravaged the elderly in America! Who emerged to protect these most vulnerable people from the pandemic?

As a pastor, chaplain, and New Yorker I can bear witness to the destitute, overlooked, infirm, and displaced masses that exist for many Americans only in a foggy, distant peripheral place. These overlooked people too were once beloved children with a future, now seemingly bereft of care and concern. All too common, these are victims of vulnerabilities or structural oppression, deprived of personhood and shamefully blamed for their brute bad luck! Yet in many cases rather than brute bad luck, the culprit really is intentional exploitation, an extension of the original sins of America replayed in the 21st century. The root cause of their existential suffering is the absence of community that can bear witness to their plight, embrace their deep suffering, and make room for their needs on our social empathic grid. Desensitized by intentionally not seeking to know of our complicity, do we prefer now to gaze away from their suffering as if making it disappear?

Seeking forgiveness for current sins as well as for those overlooked from the distant past is heavy lifting for most. The act of repentance naturally flows into searching for the opportunity to disclose one's true remorse. In current times, this search for forgiveness may aim directly towards the victims. Seeking forgiveness requires a committed heart, full of contrition and one not seeking instant redemption, fishing for a "that's OK, I know that you did not mean it." An apology is an act of repentance intrinsically seeking forgiveness. As noted above, an apology is not a facile "escape mechanism," offered to terminate an uncomfortable situation created around an uncomfortable truth about our identity politics, racism or the like. Too often an apology is "set" more like a contractual trap meant to ensnare the victim into a quick pardon. Terminating discussion of the offense ends the discomfort. Pastoral settings are replete with people suffering from the slings and arrows of "family, friends, and loved ones." A discord or the inadvertent revelation of harsh bias aimed at the victim is so very uncomfortable that often both victim and perpetrator often seek the nearest exit door marked "forgiveness." This strategy, whether unintentional or not, yields little closure or lasting peace. It may well only provide an entry point revealing a greater sin, perhaps disclosing only the mere tip of the iceberg of identity politics, racism, bias, and structural privilege.

The insincere apology offered in pursuit of forgiveness is a fool's errand. Humans readily detect the vapid apology. You may not have a PhD in psychology, but your gut can tell you when an apology is bereft of true sorrow, repentance, and self-discernment of the perpetrator. In spite of this, the act of apology, no matter how vapid the first volley, is worthy of note, receipt, and some form of validation. This pause affords both parties time for reflection and further self-discernment. Apology and granting forgiveness may well be a process that requires multiple attempts before the summit is reached. In response to the nation's two great sins foisted upon millions of indigenous Native American and African slaves and their descendants, what apologies are due?

The stunning and horrific dimensions of America's two great sins exacted upon indigenous Native Americans and African slaves and their descendants require a more robust understanding, internalization, and actualization towards the act of repentance and eventual the search for forgiveness. Even with the derivatives of these two great sins hiding in plain sight throughout America today there seems little appreciation of the culpability of the historic White ruling class for hegemonic actions. Most White people, including my former self, fail miserably to comprehend the dimensions of structural oppression afflicting the "other" sourced to one's own intrinsic "self"-directed privilege. Resensitizing ourselves to the profound evils of discrimination that assault, diminish, and deprive personhood must become an inextricably a part of a new daily American narrative. Within a mixed audience, ask people of color how structural oppression and racism affects their everyday being? Emotive, thoughtful, and soul-searching responses will be voiced. Victims need not try to recall slings and arrows of a distant past, they are *living and suffering* in the shadow of assaulted personhood every day. African Americans continue to live today within a narrative shackled to the past. The legacy of Jim Crow laws, that is, the "old" and "new," have roots stretching back four centuries of slavery to today! Racism remains an enduring "original sin" of America.

Indigenous people in the U.S. remain deprived of basic human rights. These indigenous people in the land for 30,000 years are living within dialectic of being considered by race-baiters to be "wards of the Federal government" on the one hand *versus* being indigenous people with sovereign rights on the other. In accord with the U.S. Constitution, Native American tribes are sovereign nations that lay outside of plenary power of the Congress! How can we hope to adequately and sincerely repent and seek forgiveness for original sins that we perpetuate today through complicity? The first means is to *re*sensitize our hardened hearts to the plight of these people. The history of U.S. structural oppression already has been documented. By supporting a Truth and Reconciliation Commission empowered by Congress to consolidate the narratives, validate, publish and bear witness to the sins, a process of healing can commence. Broad-based support will entail efforts to properly educate children now and henceforth in a U.S. curriculum that "corrects" the record.

Collectively we take responsibility, act accountably, and bear witness to the assault on personhood that has permeated the American culture. We must invite the sincere and candid conversation on the unavoidable and controversial topic of *reparations*. Such lofty consideration constitute a "to do" list for the nation. It is a prescription for a people who are robust enough in their moral thinking to commit to fair play and democracy for all. It is folly to seek face-saving, to merely deflect the arc of justice within American history towards a partial or unjust solution. We must seek a new corrective narrative, one fulfilling the arc of compassion and just virtue for America. Forces pushing back against these imperatives will be fierce, but will vanish with time and the passing of generations. If we convince ourselves that this task is too great for us to overcome, we lack sincere hearts and resolve. If we convince ourselves that the totality of these assaults on personhood for more than four centuries are someone else's doing and therefore not our responsibility, we shall be remembered for our depravity. If we convince ourselves that establishing *Communio Sanctorum* is "a bridge too far" for our energies as a people, we diminish past progress and our demonstrated ability to overcome evil with goodness. This is not to say that we can abolish such evils. Rather, we acknowledge that we can overcome evil through provision of an abundance of unconditional love, compassion, and goodness. Intrinsic to real progress will be acts of repentance and seeking forgiveness. Reciprocity of contrition by forgiveness remains essential to healing the nation.

Ultimately, how do we achieve "forgiveness"? Is there a "tipping point" when seeking forgiveness and the granting of forgiveness reach equilibrium? An example from the discipline of redistribution justice offers some insights. The question is cast in the following moral conundrum. How do we know when we have given enough to compensate for an earlier injustice in distribution? Virtue ethics provides the answer. Only when the suffering that we can ameliorate in others by actions of beneficence creates an equivalent amount of suffering in our own lives do we approach the moral "tipping point." Bias in assigning degrees of someone else's suffering compared to that of our own is predictable, but the approach has merit. After all we are only human. But the principle is clearly of some value in our desire to seek, receive, and grant forgiveness. Only when the content of an apology overcomes the injury and needs of those who we have injured may we achieve equilibrium. Greater apology would be superfluous; lesser would fail to meet the need. Remarkably, victims of assaults on their personhood often display the ability to genuinely forgive, even when the suffering that they endured is unlikely ever to be overcome by an apology. This kind of self-sacrificing forgiveness offers real hope for America to succeed in confronting and overcoming the fallenness derivative of original sin. Forgiveness received in this case is a blessing that enables a dialogue to new possibilities. It is unlikely to achieve full restoration for all sins past due, but it is a necessary step in the direction of hope. Those, like me, in the vocation of seeking reconciliation among warring parties on topics small and large, past and present, concerning assaults on the person of the "other" can bear witness to the power of granting forgiveness.

Withholding forgiveness precludes closure as well as creation of a new path forward. When our personhood is degraded, we may initially seek vengeance, turning our backs to apology and gestures of forgiveness. Failing to receive and validate genuine apology and willfully withholding forgiveness to a truly sorrowful, repentant sinner may yield some self-catharsis, but it will be short-lived and unsatisfying. In the long run, withholding forgiveness is not salvific either for the target of the transgression or for the perpetrator. Mental, spiritual, and physical health and well-being of the assaulted cannot heal within a stew of anger, hatred, and feelings of vengeance. Likewise reciprocal, *lex talionis* or "eye-for-an-eye" justice seldom leads to closure and healing. More often reciprocal justice begets only further trauma. The ongoing contentious wrestling of the U.S. with the moral issue of the death penalty and capital punishment argues that vengeance offers little in the way of closure (Banner 2002; Bedau and Cassell 2004). Healing requires the art of forgiveness as a solemn dialogue of contrition, sincere repentance, and eventual forgiveness.

The benefits of granting forgiveness include a kind of self-preservation and self-care enabled by letting go of the angst and pain of past sins. Benefits accrue both to the victim and to perpetrator alike. We all face times when asking for forgiveness as well as the granting forgiveness are essential. Seeking and granting forgiveness are never an "event," rather it is the beginning of a process that proceeds on its own timeframe. As we enter into personal truth telling and reconciliation, Jesus of Nazareth provides a paradigm for our kenotic journey. In ministerial life and death, Jesus was ever seeking to work towards self-discernment. The destination was to gain full reconciliation of human fallenness directed at the "other." Included in this falleness were both assaults from the outer world of the "other," as well as the inner world of the "self." Practicing the art of seeking and granting forgiveness is an effective and well-known skill for addressing assaults by those who label us as "other." This will require that we constantly reset the "gain" on our sensitivity setting to better embrace the suffering of the "other." Daily we must work to debride the wounds and scars of suffering around us that can overwhelm our lives with despair (Case and Deaton 2020). At some point, assaults can manifest in our inner-world, "self" targeting "self." Giving in to despondency is self-defeating, cutting us off from acts of kindness and forgiveness that we need to give and to receive.

Learning how to forgive ourselves is no less important than forgiving others. Forgiveness leads us toward greater moral personhood. Expanding moral personhood is the ultimate personal action item aimed to unearth, receive, validate, and forgive iniquities heaped upon us through assaults on our person. As much as we must invite, internalize, and reflect upon the products of truth telling unearthed and validated by a T&R Commission, we cannot and should not seek to avoid our duty to self-discern about individual complicity and to provide an apology. Simple acceptance of culpability, apology, and seeking forgiveness, however, will not be enough. To achieve moral growth will require a final and essential act, namely, *metanoia*.

For the ancient Greeks, the term "*metanoia*" was employed to mark a "change, changing one's mind; a transformative change in a person; a change of heart; in some cases perhaps a spiritual transition or conversion." The transliteration of the Koine Greek term to English is "metanoia." Theological sources largely employ the term "metanoia" to describe a "lasting change, a reorientation of the self, a change of mind and heart, etc." Such a change would encompass the whole being, not just the mind, nor just the heart, nor soul. For our efforts, metanoia becomes an essential ingredient to creating *Communio Sanctorum*. Metanoia demands a change of mind and heart in which there can be no "other," only the "self," in which *all* are in communion. Our reimagining of *Communio Sanctorum* hangs upon the Greatest Commandment, manifest in community through metanoia! It requires renunciation within oneself of the "old" self. In concert, metanoia demands the creation of a "new" self. The new self commits its being to reimaging and making real human community as it best might exist. By definition and covenant, the new community is unabridged and inclusive of all. Through metanoia, the exclusive, identity politics-based, racist, homophobia, and superior-"self" is banished, forever. Through metanoia a new communion of saints is emerging. It is committed to reaching out, without exception, to all, with an unwavering inclusive outlook. Original sins and the plethora of everyday assaults on personhood and human rights against the "other" can no longer be sustained. If in this new community there exist only "self," and there are no "other," all of the past suffering of discounted and lost personhood is revealed, embraced, and absorbed by the whole community. Included in this community is the cloud of witnesses, that is, past saints in communion with us. Past sins are lifted up, not pushed aside. Through sharing in the suffering of the entire community, the fallen seek forgiveness. The community recognizes fallenness, past and present, as simply life "as good as it gets." Accepting the byproducts of free will gone bad, those in community do not respond with judgment, but rather with empathy. They expect acts of fallenness to occur, preparing in advance ways to avoid, mitigate, and overcome their toxic effects on the life in community. In *Communio Sanctorum* the expectation is this, through self-discernment, accountability, contrition and repentance, and forgiveness, a new being who is bound by covenant and communion in moral solidarity will emerge.

A just community with intrinsic trust and love among its people is not out of reach. Sacrifices will be required by all, greater for some than others. Through "living into" the suffering of others, not avoiding it, asymmetries will be avoided or mitigated. Those who have been blessed with more will gain community though the act of sharing within community. This is not only an economic remedy. The same approach would be true for ameliorating physical and mental limitations of those in need. The Gospel of Luke (12:48b) recounts the logic of Jesus of Nazareth in the Parable of the Faithful Servant, "From everyone who has been given much, much will be expected; and from the one who has been entrusted with much, much more will be asked." Through enhanced self-discernment, those with greater insights into the understanding of chemical addiction will be entrusted to help care for those suffering in addiction. Those with greater insights to the understanding of the deeply forgetful will be entrusted to help care for those suffering with dementia such as Alzheimer's disease. Those with greater insights to the understanding of the physical disabilities will be entrusted to help care for those suffering with impaired mobility, such as those suffering from diabetes-related amputations. The parable reveals a powerful and bulletproof logic. In our times the example of *L'Arche* deserves mention. *L'Arche* is an international movement aimed at integrating people with intellectual disabilities into lives with caregivers and people who commit to an ethic of care and unconditional love. *L'Arche* offers a compelling story of human empathy and compassionate personal action, aimed to lift up the lives of the "least of us." It is a journey of deep commitment, filled with unexpected benefits and joy for all in the community (Whitney-Brown 2019).

Moral solidarity enables a communion of "being in covenant." Such moral solidarity remains the ultimate source for bearing witness to the world. Solidarity demands all to seek, receive, validate, and finally amend our shared history of America. The U.S. is a dominant world power, a nation of great potential good, but one beleaguered and shackled by two great original sins. We have interrogated a plethora of everyday sins degrading the personhood of those labeled as "other." Our ability to so freely assault the personhood of others, I offer, reflects a chronic debilitating refusal to confront, receive, and redress original sin. The essence of *Communio Sanctorum* is its laser-like focus towards achieving true moral solidarity. A society is truly moral only to the point that each of its members seeks to achieve moral personhood and solidarity with and for all members. Moral solidarity calls us to reckon with the sins against personhood both present and past, both small and large, aimed at all or more commonly at the "least of us" in community. Our moral precept remains that all are "self" and there can be no "other."

Only in self-actualized community, fortified with the strength and conviction required to confront and redress past and present sins can America move forward. Equating the hegemony and horrific suffering of "other" at the hand of a dominant White ruling class as the work of a righteous and Christian nation is a dangerous distortion of the truth and must be abandoned. The current history, one steeped in America exceptionalism, is but the product of self-serving recollections of the "top-siders," whose structural privilege, power and control over the narrative was absolute. The lived experiences of those viewing life from the bottom side, from beneath, with their dreams marginalized by White privilege must now be heard. The history must be amended to reflect the greater truths (and sins) on which American empire prospered for some, but not all. We anticipate that in response to gathering truth excising the mythology of White supremacy, a large breach will emerge in the American narrative. Former baseless and self-serving myths will need to be expunged and replaced with a dark and deeply troubling but honest account of original sin. The emergence of this breach is painfully necessary and ultimately healthy. Changing the arc of the U.S. experience, towards a new trajectory, one untethered from mistruths, lies, and self-congratulatory myths remains the only one true path to redemption and to full personhood for all Americans.

APPENDIX 6: FURTHER NOTES

*Text in italics are callouts to places within the chapter.

The data from the World Bank (WB), International Monetary Fund (IMF), and the United Nations (UN) demonstrates that the U.S. has not a wealth problem per se, but rather one of asymmetric distribution of the wealth. These data are derived mostly from the year 2019, complied by the WB, IMF, and U.N. A consolidated report by "country" can be viewed here: Unnamed Authors (2019), "Report for Selected Countries and Subjects," *The International Monetary Fund,* Washington, DC: *IMF Reports, 2019* (accessed April 30, 2020), https://www.imf.org/en/Publications.

In 2000, the U.S. Bureau of Indian Affairs (BIA) formally apologized for its participation in ethnic cleansing of the Western Tribes. To examine the apology of the BIA regarding the ethnic cleansing and cultural annihilation of indigenous Native Americans see: Darling, Nedra (2000), "Gover Apologizes for BIA's Misdeeds: Agency's 175th Anniversary Occasion for Reflection," Washington, DC: *U.S. Department of Interior: Indian Affairs* (accessed April 30, 2020), https://www.bia.gov/as-ia/opa/online-press-release/gover-apologizes-bias-misdeeds.

Today, music of the Native American diaspora captures the forced relocations inflicted upon these indigenous peoples by the White ruling class empire launched in America. The 21st century continues a history of assault on indigenous Native American sacred lands and customs as evidenced by Native American protests of the Dakota Access Pipeline that culminated with a 2016 legal action *Standing Rock Sioux Tribe v. U.S. Army Corps of Engineers.* Resistance in the form of music has raised public awareness. For an example, featuring work of Lyla June in tandem with Chloe Smith and her band Rising Appalachia, see: Getz, B. (2017), "Resistance Movements in Music: On the Ground at Standing Rock and Beyond With Chloe Smith and Lyla June," London, UK: *The BBC Live4LiveMusic* (accessed April 30, 2020), https://liveforlivemusic.com/features/resistance-movements-music-ground-standing-rock-beyond-chloe-smith-lyla-june/.

On a small scale, the on-going efforts of the non-profit organization StoryCorps to capture and to share stories of Americans from all backgrounds and beliefs already has provided a working template. For poignant recollections of assaulted personhood see two particular episodes of Story-Corps. The first podcast looks back on events from the Civil Rights Era. The second examines America's complex relationship with its Native Americans. Both episodes reflect upon the courage, sacrifice, and resilience of the folks whose personhood remains challenged. Garofalo, Michael (2017), "We Came Through," Washington, DC: *National Public Radio StoryCorps podcast #491* (accessed April 30, 2020), https://storycorps.org/podcast/story-corps-491-we-came-through/; and Warren, Mia (2018), "A Native American Railroad Worker on His Complex Relationship With His Work," Washington, DC: *National Public Radio StoryCorps podcast aired December 14, 2018 on NPR's Morning Edition* (accessed April 30, 2020), https://story-corps.org/stories/a-native-american-railroad-worker-on-his-complex-relationship-with-his-work/.

From 1936–1938, the WPA created the first series of recorded narrative recounting the histories of former slaves in America. To hear the recordings and gain insights from the personal perspectives of slaves in America, see: Unnamed Author (2000), "The WPA and the Slave Narrative Collection," Washington, DC: *U.S. Library of Congress series, Born in Slavery: Slave Narratives From the Federal Writers' Project, 1936 to 1938* (accessed April 30, 2020), https://www.loc.gov/collections/slave-narratives-from-the-federal-writers-project-1936-to-1938/articles-and-essays/introduction-to-the-wpa-slave-narratives/wpa-and-the-slave-narrative-collection/.

Avoiding responsibility by suggesting that the past is "dead" is a non-starter for redemption. In 2019, the issue of the U.S. paying reparations for slavery reemerged. The Majority Leader of the U.S. Senate Mitch McConnell was quoted as offering opposition, saying "I don't think reparations for something that happened 150 years ago for whom none of us currently living are responsible is a good idea." The Kentucky Republican told reporters in response to a question about whether reparations should be paid or Congress or the President should make a public apology, "We've tried to deal with our original sin of slavery by fighting a civil war, by passing landmark civil rights legislation. We elected an African American president." These comments have been placed in utter contrast to global protests stirred by the killing of George Floyd in Minneapolis in May of 2020. The lethal product of racism for Blacks and people of color finds its headwaters in the original sin of slavery in America. For a transcript see: Barrett, Ted (2019), "McConnell Opposes Paying Reparations: 'None of Us Currently Living are Responsible' for Slavery," Atlanta, GA: *CNN Politics,* aired on June 19, 2019 (accessed April 30, 2020), https://www.cnn.com/2019/06/18/politics/mitch-mcconnell-opposes-reparations-slavery/index.html.

Sadly this oppression, fueled by identity politics and raw racism, is all too present among the American people today. The year 2019 will be remembered for the a U.S. House of Representatives resolution condemning the 45th President's racist remarks aimed at four minority congresswomen whom he told to "go back" to their "crime infested places from which they came." All four congresswomen are U.S. citizens, three being born in the U.S.! For details see: DeBonis, John Wagner, and Rachel Bade (2019), "A Divided House Votes for Resolution Condemning Trump's Racist Remarks," Washington, DC: *The Washington Post: Politics*, aired on July 17, 2019 (accessed April 30, 2020), https://www.washingtonpost.com/politics/trump-lashes-out-again-at-minority-lawmakers-as-house-prepares-to-condemn-his-racist-tweets/2019/07/16/bca3afa4-a7b3-11e9-a3a6-ab670962db05_story.html?utm_term=.7cafc05bc38c.

REFERENCES

Acosta, Abilio James. 2019. *The enemy of the people.* New York, NY: Harper, an imprint of HarperCollins Publishers.

Armstrong, Julie Buckner. 2015. *The Cambridge companion to American civil rights literature.* New York, NY: Cambridge University Press.

Banner, Stuart. 2002. *The death penalty: And American history.* Cambridge, MA: Harvard University Press.

Baptist, Edward E. 2016. *The half has never been told: Slavery and the making of American capitalism.* New York, NY: Basic Books.

Bedau, Hugo Adam. 2004. *Debating the death penalty: Should America have capital punishment? Experts on both sides make their best case.* Oxford, UK; New York, NY: Oxford University Press.

Bstan 'dzin-rgya-mtsho, Dalai Lama XIV, Desmond Tutu, and Douglas Abrams. 2016. *The book of joy: Lasting happiness in a changing world.* New York, NY: Avery, an imprint of Penguin Random House.

Burns, Adam D. 2017. *American imperialism: The territorial expansion of the United States, 1783–2013.* Edinburgh, UK: Edinburgh University Press.

Caruth, Cathy. 1995. *Trauma: Explorations in memory.* Baltimore, MD: John Hopkins University Press.

Case, Anne and Angus Deaton. 2020. *Deaths of despair and the future of capitalism.* Oxford, UK; Princeton, NJ: Princeton University Press.

Deeds, Susan M., Michael C. Meyer, and William L. Sherman. 2018. *The course of Mexican history* (11th ed.). Oxford, UK; New York, NY: Oxford University Press.

Dunbar-Ortiz, Roxanne. 2014. *An indigenous peoples' history of the United States*. Boston, MA: Beacon Press.

Estes, Nick. 2019. *Our history is the future: Standing Rock versus the Dakota Access Pipeline, and the long tradition of indigenous resistance*. London, UK; New York, NY: Verso.

Fardūst, Ḥusayn. 1995. *The rise and fall of [sic] Pahlavi dynasty: The memoirs of General Hossein Fardoust*. Tehran IR: Institute for Political Studies and Researches.

Felman, Shoshana and Dori Laub. 1992. *Testimony: Crises of witnessing in literature, psychoanalysis, and history*. New York, NY: Routledge.

Flamm, Hannah, et al., and Human Rights Watch (Organization). 2018. "They want docile": How nursing homes in the United States overmedicate people with dementia. New York, NY: *Human Rights Watch*. Published online February 5, 2018 (accessed online May 30, 2020).

Friedman, Milton. 1968. *Capitalism & freedom: A leading economist's view of the proper role of competitive capitalism*. Chicago, IL: University of Chicago Press.

Gutiérrez, Gustavo, and Gerhard Ludwig Müller. 2015. *On the side of the poor: The theology of liberation*. Maryknoll, NY: Orbis Books.

Hayner, Priscilla B. 2011. *Unspeakable truths: Transitional justice and the challenge of truth commissions* (2nd ed.). New York, NY: Routledge.

Horne, Gerald. 2019. *Jazz and justice: Racism and the political economy of the music*. New York, NY: Monthly Review Press.

Herman, Judith. 1997. *Trauma and recovery*. New York, NY: Basic Books.

King, Martin Luther, Jr. 2018. *Letter from Birmingham jail*. New York, NY: Penguin Random House.

Klein, Naomi. 2017. *No is not enough: Resisting Trump's shock politics and winning the world we need*. Chicago IL: Haymarket Books.

Kukathas, Uma. 2008. *Native American rights* (Issues on trial series). Detroit, MI: Greenhaven Press.

Marrus, Michael Robert. 1997. *The Nuremberg war crimes trial, 1945–46: A documentary history* (The Bedford series in history and culture). Boston, MA: Bedford Books.

Mau, Steffen, and Benjamin Veghte. 2007. *Social justice, legitimacy and the welfare state*. Aldershot, UK; Burlington, VT: Ashgate.

Monette, Paul. 2014. *No witnesses: Poem*. New York, NY: Open Road Integrated Media. pp 126.

Morris, Ian, and Walter Scheidel. 2009. *The dynamics of ancient empires: State power from Assyria to Byzantium* (Oxford studies in early empires). Oxford, UK; New York, NY: Oxford University Press.

Moses, A. Dirk. 2008. *Empire, colony, genocide: Conquest, occupation, and subaltern resistance in world history*. New York, NY: Berghahn Books.

Mourning, Dove, tan Sho pow, and Lucullus Virgil McWhorter. 1981. *Cogewea, the half blood: A depiction of the great Montana cattle range*. Lincoln, NE: University of Nebraska Press.

Phillips, Joshua Daniel. 2016. *Homeless: Narratives from the streets*. Jefferson, NC: McFarland & Company, Inc., Publishers.

Piketty, Thomas. 2014. *Capital in the twenty first century*. Cambridge, MA: Harvard University Press.

Rappaport, Doreen, and Shane Evans. 2002. *No more!: Stories and songs of slave resistance* (1st ed.). Cambridge, MA: Candlewick Press.

Rawls, John. 1972. *A theory of justice*. Oxford, UK: Clarendon Press.

Saunt, Claudio, 2020. *Unworthy republic: The dispossession of Native Americans and the road to Indian territory*. New York, NY: W.W. Norton & Company.

Schlesinger, Arthur. 2015. The American empire? Not so fast. *World Policy Journal, 22*(1): 43–46

Thinakaran, A. J. 1987. *The Second Pandyan empire, A.D. 1190–1312*. Madurai, IN: A.J. Thinakaran.

Thomas, Hugh. 1997. *The slave trade: The story of the Atlantic slave trade, 1440–1870*. New York, NY: Simon & Schuster.

Van Engen, Abram C. 2020. *City on a hill: A history of American exceptionalism*. London, UK; New Haven, CT: Yale University Press.

Weaver, Hilary N. 2019. *Trauma and resilience in the lives of contemporary Native Americans*. New York, NY: Routledge.

Whitney-Brown, Carolyn. 2019. *Sharing life: Stories of L'Arche founders*. Mahwah, NJ: Paulus Press.

Epilogue

All non-fictional writing projects include "turning pages," a term meaning that we discover what we thought were our "original" observations have been observed by others earlier. As we gain information new to us and deeper understanding through our interrogations, earlier works can speak to us with an amplified voice and novelty that are unexpected. For more than a decade I have been studying the concept of the "soul." As a scientist, pastor, and chaplain, this pursuit seemed a fool's errand with regard to the wealth of writings on this seemingly ineffable object of attention for millennia. Working with people wrestling with abortion, the moral hot button issue of our time, I devoted three years to develop the topic of abortion from a seminary thesis to a full-length book. The product entitled, *Abortion in 21st Century America* (Malbon 2013) renewed and expanded my interest in the topic of "personhood," how it is assigned, valued, and lost. In the intervening years, working in my Calling I noted the frequency at which personhood of the "other" was under assault in 21st century America. Work within communities of faith and the evolution of my concept of *Communio Sanctorum* refined and focused my attention upon two derivative questions. First, who are the victims and perpetrators of the assaults on personhood? Second, what is the root source in the American experience empowering such crass, damaging, and sometimes-violent assaults on the personhood of the "other"? The current book entitled, *Assaulted Personhood*, provides data, interpretation, and insights into the behavior that enables these assaults, or the answer to the first question.

Answering the second question, that is, what are the headwaters of the anxiety and hatred aimed at the "other" in 21st century America required a reach back of more than four hundred years of history. The thesis I offer in answer to the second question is simply that we in the U.S. have ignored the two great original sins on which the American empire prospered and grew. Baptist's work, *The Half has Never Been Told (Baptist 2014)*, speaking truth to power, revealed slavery not as some primitive cottage industry, but rather as a large-scale capitalist hegemony benefitting all but the slaves! Baptist makes a compelling case that North or South, all Americans prospered by the success of slavery to power "King Cotton." It is the revealed truths of such sin that will horrify. The unrelenting effort to displace, dispossess, and eliminate Native American claims to theirs lands, history, and traditions is another original sin, all to obvious, even to the most imperialist of Americans. The horrific dimensions of such original sins cost the personhood and lives of millions (Dunbar-Ortiz 2014). These sins truly *live on* in our everyday attacks on personhood of the "other" in 21st century America. Turning from the truth enabled our conditioned, intentional desire to remain silent about complicity that fuels a plethora of everyday sins attacking the "other."

Although consistent with a linkage existing between original sins and the making of everyday assaults on the "other," I readily admit that the current data, neither proves nor disproves the central theme posited herein. More tangibly, this writing project provides a template enabling a thoughtful and definitive test of the hypothesis. The core need is for a platform capable of seeking truth and reconciliation through an honest effort devoted to unearthing a historically faithful and verifiable corpus of documents tracing the impact of the original sins to everyday 21st century America. In *The Half has Never Been Told*, Baptist has done just that, that is, unearthed compelling data and narratives casting slavery and the cotton industry in a sharp new focus on how this sin powered American enterprise on the backs of millions of slaves. Beyond interrogating original sin, what potentially positive outcomes can be proposed as a solution? My own data gathering among the "least of us" coupled with years of pastoral work and chaplaincy compels me to advocate for a core tool, that is, building a more inclusive and just community, a *Communio Sanctorum*. Human interactions rooted in true community and moral solidarity offer a path forward to reimagining American community. What remains unknown is whether the U.S. can mobilize its soma and soul on a gamble. Can redressing the original sins fueling assaults on personhood succeed to regain for the U.S. the moral high ground? Can the linkage to past original sins provoke current day metanoia justifying a "preferential option" for the oppressed, marginalized, poor, destitute, different, and vulnerable among us?

Many of the books I reference herein have had a lasting powerful effect upon my own kenotic journey and metanoia. While at seminary I was fortunate to learn from Cornel West who was a visiting scholar. Like James Cone, Cornel West encouraged further readings to help me gain insight into the plight and suffering of those forced into the crucible of American empire (Bailey 2015). West also suggested music that might help me to sense the voice of sorrow extending back four centuries for African and African Americans slaves and their descendants. In particular, he lifted up the works of John Coltrane, Miles Davis, Thelonious Monk, and some newer Hip-Hop artists (Winters 2013). My assignment was simple: listen to the music, examine biographical matter, and engage the music from the "underside." Prime videos of these Jazz and Blues legends reaching back to African musical traditions, spirituals, and African-American songs of labor, informed me. Documentaries such as *I am Not Your Negro, 12 Years a Slave, The African Americans: Many Rivers to Cross*, and *Eye on the Prize*, as well as movies like *Selma* constitute a compelling visual history that would benefit all Americans. The core significance of these works was driven by oral traditions, perhaps best captured in spirituals conveying an intense ongoing struggle for freedom and dignity. W.E.B. Du Bois, James Baldwin, Martin Luther King Jr., Malcolm X, and others carried these laments forward and help us to understand their suffering in the context of our times.

In my travels to Maine as well as to the Great Southwest I first encountered indigenous Native Americans, who welcomed discussion about their situation and plight. In seminary, I encountered writings by Vine Deloria, Jr. (1933–2005), works such as *Nations Within: The Past and Future of American Indian Sovereignty* (Deloria and Lytle 1984). Deloria was a Native American author, theologian, and activist who left a deep imprint about the genocide and abuses endured by Native Americans at the hand of American expansionism. Similarly, in seminary I was exposed to the work of George E. Tinker, *American Indian Liberation: A Theology of Sovereignty* (Tinker 2008), who encouraged Native American Christians to banish colonial settler perspective from their theology and rather draw from their deep Native American spirituality for growth. Indigenous Native Americans also made use of songs of lament to fortify their everyday lives in the midst of grave historic suffering. Like that of the African and African American slave, the Native Americans endured forced migrations, dispossession, and exilic life fraught with misery, dislocation, and death (e.g., Trail of Tears and the Massacre at Sand Creek). This exilic existence forced upon them by the White ruling class of America separated them from sacred ancestral lands where for generations, since the time of *Paleo*-Indians, they buried their dead. Sorrowful music of the Native Americans preserves the voices of the suffering masses, sourced from resistance and resilience of more than four centuries (Carnevale 2020). Not well known to most Americans was the 1971 re-release of a song written by John Loudermilk and recorded by Paul Revere & The Raiders (Columbia Records) entitled, "Indian Reservation (The Lament of the Cherokee Reservation Indian)." The recording topped the Hot 100 and went on to sell more than a million copies! Few Native American laments have resonated in Pop culture like this hit. Documentaries such as *We Shall Remain: America Through Native Eyes* (PBS), *Native*

America: Tales of a Proud People (Mill Creek), and *Trail of Tears* (Mill Creek) also graphically explore the great "original sin" perpetrated against indigenous people by the U.S government. Recently, two important books were published that powerfully lift up the existential suffering of the Native Americans, namely Pekka Hämäläinen's *Lokota America: A New History of Indigenous Power* (Hämäläinen 2019) and Claudio Saunt's *Unworthy Republic: The Dispossession of Native Americans and the Road to Indian Territory* (Saunt 2020).

The Administration of the 45th president has provoked a backsliding of reforms and progress aimed at protecting the personhood of the vulnerable, marginalized, "least of us." More than any other lesson to be learned from the period of 2016–2020 is that efforts aimed at restoring and protecting the personhood of the "other" can be far more fragile than most would have imagined. The anger and hatred that fuels growing numbers of assaults on the personhood of people in America is a classic sign of self-loathing. Unable to either redress or dismiss the horrific original sins on which America was founded, the U.S. now is locked in a retrograde, self-loathing which provokes anxiety, fear, and a toxic blend of White nationalism and White supremacy. The book entitled, *Deaths of Despair and the Future of Capitalism* (2020), by Anne Case and Angus Deaton provides an invaluable capstone to my thesis (Case and Deaton 2020). Among middle-aged white people in America, Case and Deaton reported that not only suicide, drug and alcohol-related deaths were rising, but all deaths! This rising mortality of middle-aged whites contrasts markedly with the falling global death rates observed for most people over the last twenty years (Siddiqi et al. 2019). Rising white mortality cannot be adequately explained by changes in their social and economic health indicators. Threat to perceived social status is offered as an explanation for the rise in mortality among whites (Siddiqi et al. 2019). I proffer that anxiety and fear rises in any group that shies away from taking responsibility for past horrific original sins perpetrated against the personhood of the "other." The Civil Rights and American Indian movements transformed many Americans. These ongoing movements lift into stark view the horrific history of oppression and exploitation that is the undercurrent of attacks on the "other" in 21st century America. Regretfully, many others steeped in the myth of American exceptionalism developed a contextual understanding of structural privilege, but not of structural oppression. Failure to confront traumatic and painful foundational truths provokes self-loathing. Self-loathing provokes drug and alcohol abuse, risky behaviors, and suicide. Does this not contribute to a perceived loss of relative status for members of the White ruling class? Are these white people reacting to a perception that the social distances between them and those they oppress historically as "other" are fading away? Will the crucible of oppression, racism, and hatred consume them also? Or will White nationalism and White supremacy provide a balm for their anxiety and fear of losing social status to people of color whose "otherness" remains threatening to their being? I proffer that self-loathing and fear are predictable responses of ruling class white people opting to willfully ignore a four hundred year degradation of the personhood of millions of Americans, that is, Native Americans, Black Americans, Americans of color, and the "very least of us." As Frederick Douglass noted, "power concedes nothing with a demand. It never did and never will" (Douglass and Frederick Douglass Historical and Cultural League 1857).

The collision between the personhood status of all Americans with the populist, White nationalism and supremacy movements was a long time in the making. Hate Groups in the U.S. have grown larger and more vocal. They respond with enthusiasm to oblique encouragement by a "bully pulpit" whose very "success" in 2016 would have been impossible without the fervor and vitriol of those who professed the need "to make American great again!" Perhaps a more truthful motto for the Trumpist Republicans would be "to make America White, Christian, and great again." To the average citizen, the violence, hate, and perfidy for authority displayed by the right-wing extremists are alarming. Once viewed as the single greatest threat to America's future (since the September 11, 2001, attacks), terrorism from outside the nation is waning. The homegrown version of domestic terrorism "inside" has largely displaced terrorist threat posed by the "outside." The sources of this violence and anarchy, I argue, source back to the two great original sins aimed at the indigenous Native Americans and the enslaved Africans, African Americans and their descendants.

Without full disclosure, wide acceptance, truth telling and reconciliation, the U.S. will continue to suffer from these original sins. The legacy of these two sins only perpetuates new forms of assaults on the personhood of vulnerable people. High value targets for assault are those with vulnerabilities of body and mind, including assaults aimed at chemical abuse and addiction, age, Alzheimer's, gender, identity politics, racism, religious orientation, and sexual identity, as well as any outgrowth of frank xenophobia. The solution outlined herein, to create a platform for truth telling and reconciliation, is the only way out. Searching for and labeling new scapegoats (e.g., immigrants and those seeking legal asylum at our shores) to assuage American self-loathing treats only one symptom of a deep infection (i.e., the symptom *du jour*), but not the infection itself.

If there was any question about a 2020 legacy of personhood assaulted, discounted, or denied in the past, the aftermath of the COVID-19 pandemic in the U.S. reaffirmed the sorrowful state of the nation's healthcare system, especially for the "least of us." The two prominent examples of vulnerable populations disproportionately infected and killed by COVID-19 are Black Americans and Native Americans! Longstanding health and socio-economic disparities have made African Americans (and other peoples of color) more vulnerable to COVID-19 (Laughland 2020). The Navajo Nations continues to suffer some of the highest rates of infection with COVID-19 recorded in the U.S. (Morales 2020). Although deemed "curious" and "unanticipated" revelations by the media, to those of us in healthcare and ethics, the underlying basis for this increased vulnerability of both marginalized groups to the pandemic was not news. Health disparities between White America and these two longstanding vulnerable groups are well known (Kawachi et al. 2005). Denial of personhood and consequent *in*adequate healthcare for African Americans and Native Americans is not unintentional. It is habitual! Poor and inadequate diets, limited access to proper foods and nutrition, absence of routine healthcare, increased cigarette smoking and chronic obstructive pulmonary disease, increased consumption of alcohol and alcoholism, increased prevalence of diabetes and hypertension, target vulnerable people for increased infection and poor outcomes for COVID-19. In 2020, suffering from assaulted personhood can be traced back to the headwaters of two 17th century original sins aimed at power and control over groups labeled "other" simply to promote an agenda of Americans exceptionalism and hegemony. Confronting our history of denying personhood to millions of Americans will require talking truth to power. It is the only path forward to redemption and reconciliation, freeing us from bondage to original and everyday sins. For four centuries and for millions of oppressed Americans, the once popular notion of an "American dream" remains illusionary. For many, daily life will be lived not as an American "dream," but rather as a "nightmare." Reimaging community, a community in covenant and with moral solidarity, in which everyone is "self," and there can be no "other," may hold the only key to unlock the door of justice and economic promise to all in America.

REFERENCES

Bailey, Wilma A. 2003. *Lamentations, songs of songs.* Harrisburg, VA: Herald Press.

Baptist, Edward E. 2014. *The half has never been told: Slavery and the making of American capitalism.* New York, NY: Basic Books.

Carnevale, Jennifer. 2020. Trail of Tears: Music of the American Indian diaspora. Washington, DC: *Smithsonian FolkWays Recordings.*

Case, Anne and Angus Deaton. 2020. *Deaths of despair and the future of capitalism.* Princeton, NJ: Princeton University Press.

Deloria, Vine, and Clifford M. Lytle. 1984. *The nations within: The past and future of American Indian sovereignty.* New York, NY: Pantheon Books.

Douglass, Frederick and Frederick Douglass Historical and Cultural League. 1857. The significance of emancipation in the West Indies (a speech delivered on August 3, 1857). In *Life and times of Frederick Douglass.* New York, NY: Pathway Press.

Dunbar-Ortiz, Roxanne. 2014. *An indigenous peoples' history of the United States.* Boston, MA: Beacon Press.

Hämäläinen, Pekka. 2019. *The Lakota: A history of Native American power.* New Haven, CT: Yale University Press.

Kawachi, Ichirō, Norman Daniels, and Dean E. Robinson. 2005. Health disparities by race and class: Why both matter. *Health Affairs, Race & Ethnic Disparities, 24*(2), published online https://doi.org.10.1377/hithaff.24.2.343.

Laughland, Oliver and Lauren Zanolli. 2020. Why is coronavirus taking such a deadly toll on Black Americans? *The Guardian,* U.S. edition, published on April 25, 2020.

Malbon, Craig C. 2013. *Abortion in 21st century America.* North Charleston, SC: CreateSpace Publishing.

Morales, Laural. 2020. Navajo nation sees high rate of Covid-19 and contact tracing is a challenge. *NPR, Morning Edition,* aired April 24, 2020.

Saunt, Claudio. 2020. *Unworthy republic: The dispossession of Native Americans and the road to Indian territory.* New York, NY: W. W. Norton & Company.

Siddiqi, Arjumand et al. 2019, December. Growing sense of social status threat and concomitant deaths of despair among Whites. *SSM-Population Health 9.*

Tinker, George E. 2008. *American Indian liberation: A theology of sovereignty.* Maryknoll, NY: Orbis Books.

Winters, Joseph. 2013. Contemporary sorrow songs: Traces of mourning, lament, and vulnerability in hip hop. *African American Review, 46*(1): 9–20.

Index

Abenaki Native Americans, 239–241

Abernathy, Ralph, 253

abortifacient drugs, 39, 40, 139

abortion, xii, xiv, 138, 369; abortifacient drugs for, 39, 40, 139; biblical warrant for, 139; criminalization of self-induced medical, 140–141, 198; D&C, D&E, IDX for, 41; defined, 40; economic concerns and, 47–48; emancipation and, 140; ensoulment and, 44; of Finkbine and thalidomide, 140; Harrison two lives linked in, 45–46; Hippocratic Oath and, 39; as human right, 20; immigration detention centers and rights of, 141, 199; morality of, 39, 44, 45–46, 72; MVA for, 41; patriarchy and, 140; Pope Francis on, 44, 50, 73; procedures of, 40–41; Roman Catholic Church on, 73; therapeutic, for DNS, 89; universal rule of exceptions for, 45; U.S. decline in, 46–47; Western world and, 3; WHO and, 39

ACA. *See* Affordable Care Act

accountability, for National T&R Commission, 351

ACOG. *See* American College of Obstetrics & Gynecology

actively dying personhood, 177; advance directives and, 177–178; Education for Physicians on End-of-Life Care Project, 179, 204

AD. *See* Alzheimer's Disease

ADA. *See* Americans with Disabilities Act

addiction: described, 132; FASD and, 94–96, 138; heroin, of veterans, 133; as medical condition, 146; thoughtful recovery programs for, 137; trauma and, 119–121. *See also* drug abuse; opioid addiction

Adecco Foundation, 117

Adler, Alfred, 300, 319

advance directives, death and, 177–178

Affordable Care Act (ACA), 318–319

Africans and African Americans: author reflection on, 273–276; biblical warrant of dominion of, 19, 26, 250–252, 257; black liberation theology, of Cone, 264–266, 281; Black personhood, 252–256; Christianity and, 248–250; Coates on reparations for, 271–272, 282; commodification, 243–246; contested being of, 243–246; displacement legacy, 241–243; documentaries on, 371; exilic life of, 256–259; freedom denial, 246; incarceration and, 21, 133, 163–164, 255, 280; original sin and, 27, 241–276, 282, 324, 337, 340; otherness of, 258; repairing the breach for, 266–273; resilience of, 262–264; resistance of, 260–262, 280; slavery of, 4, 246–248, 324; term description, 278. *See also*

Blacks
disabilities and withdrawal from, 67–68
ageism, xiv, 25, 173–174
AQ. *See* autism-spectrum quotient score
Age of Enlightenment, 9
Aquinas, Thomas, 20, 47; on faith and
AI. *See* artificial intelligence
reason, 7; on *hyper*cognition, 8; reason-
Alexander, Michelle, 27, 149–150
based natural theology of, 7; on *sacra*
All Lives Matter, 154, 155
doctrina, 7; on soul and body, 7
all-or-nothing personhood, 169–172
Aristotle: on causality, 5; hylomorphism
ALS. *See* amyotrophiclateralsclerosis
of, 7–8; Nicomachean ethics of, 6; on
alterity, Lévinas on, 18, 300
soul, 5–6
Alzheimer's Disease (AD), xi, 164, 204;
Arnautoff, Victor, 272, 283
brain pathology of, 166; death and, 166;
artificial intelligence (AI), 3, 14
as familial disease, 166–167; Frank D.
ASD. *See* autism spectrum disorder
example, 175–177; freedom and,
assaulted personhood: ancient roots for,
175–177; Kitwood on care for,
15–17; driving forces for, 7, 43, 258,
167–168; Locke on consciousness and,
299–300; fear as catalyst for, 299;
10; QoL and, 167, 171
history of, 26–28; intolerance of,
ambiguous loss, 344
357–358; on LGBTQI people,
American College of Obstetrics &
195–196, 285; otherness concept and,
Gynecology (ACOG), on reproductive
17–19, 131–132; pastor personal
rights, 140–141
reflections, 29–33; postmodernism and,
American Dream or nightmare, 374
14; power-and-control and, 28, 281;
American exceptionalism, 32, 216–217,
self and, 131–132; by Trump, 345, 372;
356–357; Arnautoff mural on, 272, 283;
victims of, 23–25
with biblical warrant, 227, 229–230;
atrocities: of empires, 338; T&R on high
Bill of Rights and, 229; Native
crimes against humanity and, 340
Americans ancestral land taking and,
attentive listening, for truths, 343;
226, 230, 238; people of color
StoryCorps and, 346, 365; WPA oral
personhood and, 229
history interviews, 346, 365
American Indian Liberation (Tinker), 371
Augustine of Hippo, 6; Manichaeism
American Indian Religious Freedom Act
conversion by, 6
(1978), 222, 277
autism spectrum disorder (ASD), 84; AQ
Americans with Disabilities Act (ADA)
scores for, 85, 86, 87; discrimination of,
(1990), 69; bipolar disorder and, 104
85; IQ and, 85; of Savage, 116–117;
amyotrophiclateralsclerosis (ALS or Lou
Seidel and Insel on, 122–123
Gehrig's disease), xii–xiii; of Hawking,
autism-spectrum quotient score (AQ), 85,
83
86, 87
ancestral lands, of Native Americans, 23,
awareness, Locke and, 10–11
219–220; American exceptionalism
and, 226, 230, 238; Doctrine of
Baldwin, James, 371
Discovery to support taking of,
Ballenger, Jesse, 168
225–226, 236, 246
Baptist, Edward E., 370
anencephalic neonates, 19, 54–55
Barber, William J., II, 253
anorexia nervosa, 107–109
A Beautiful Mind (Nash), 82–83, 118
Anthony, Susan B., 16
Beckett, Samuel, 14
anti-apartheid activism, 151
Beckwith, Francis, 169
anti-immigration, 29; xenophobia and, 28
bereavement: complicated grief, 192;
anti-racism and slavery, 248
PTSD and, 114–115
anxiety disorders, 101–102, 119–121;
Beyond Good and Evil (Nietzsche), 321
opioid addiction and, 145; physical

"Beyond Vietnam" speech, of King, 253, 254–255

BIA. *See* Bureau of Indian Affairs

Biblical approach, Western world influenced by, 3

biblical warrant of dominion, 30; for abortion and pregnant women, 139; of Africans and African Americans, 19, 26, 250–252, 257; American exceptionalism with, 227, 229–230; of Doctrine of Discovery, 226, 228; in Genesis story, 31; of indigenous Native Americans, 19, 229, 246; against LGBTQI people, 196, 206; slavery and, 242–245, 248–250, 279–280

Big Bang theory, 311, 312, 351

Bill of Rights (U.S.): American exceptionalism and rights of, 229; Black rights and, 148; DNS personhood and, 93; fetal rights and, 50; human rights and, 319; LGBTQI people and, 197; pregnant woman and, 140; PVS and, 182, 187; Reconstruction Amendments to, 149

binge-eating disorder, 107

bipolar disorders, 103–105

Black Heroin problem, 134, 135

black liberation theology, of Cone, 281; contractual theology and, 265; on freedom, 265; Jesus and, 265, 275; oppressed and oppressors in, 264; redistributive justice and, 265–266

Black Lives Matter (BLM, #BlackLivesMatter) movement, 150, 152, 153–155, 200, 262; criticism of, 153; inclusivity and, 151; methods and success of, 155–156; police brutality and, 151–152, 201; violence against Blacks, 151

Black-on-Black violence, 153

Black Organizing for Leadership & Dignity effort, 151

Black Panther and Black Power movements, 151, 261, 266

Black personhood, 252–256

Black resistance, 27

Blacks, 278; Bill of Rights and, 148; death sentences of, 153; dehumanization of, 152; deprived personhood of, 135–136;

disintegrated selves of, 257; financial inequality of, 268–269, 282; health disparity, 269; Obama on oppression of, 153; resilience perspective of, 262; slaves, commodification of, 242–243; Trump and oppression of, 153; Wacquant on, 135; White ruling class and, 30–31

Black Theology & Black Power (Cone), 275

BLM. *See* Black Lives Matter

blood quantum, White ruling class and Federal Indian laws on, 224, 242

Blue Lives Matter (#BlueLivesMatter), 154–155

body (soma), 4; being human and, 41–44; Butler on mind and, 10; emerging life basics, 39–41; *in utero* development and other life, 44–49; neonate/infant and, 51–62; personhood and physical disabilities, 69–71; physical disabilities and, 66–69; stillbirth and, 49–51; vulnerabilities of, xiv, 62–66

Boethius, 20

Bonhoeffer, Dietrich, 8, 315–316, 322–323

borderline personality disorder, 110–111

Born-Alive Infants Protection Act, 2002, 21

Born on the Fourth of July (Kovic), 191

brain death, 205; moral dilemma of, 187; organ donations and, 183–184, 185

brain pathology, of AD, 166

Breaking White Supremacy (Dorrien), 27

Brown, H. "Rap," 261

Brown v. Board of Education (1954), 252

brutality, of oppression, 337–338

Buddhism, 305–306

bulimia nervosa, 107

bullying, Trump and, 197, 207

Bureau of Indian Affairs (BIA), ethnic cleansing formal apology of, 339, 364

Bush, George W., 41

Butler, Joseph, 10

called into being, 312–313, 347

capacity, informed consent and, 97–99

Caplan, Arthur L. (ethicist), 183

caregiving burden, for dementia, 173–174

Carmichael, Stokely (Kwame Ture), 261

Case, Anne, 372
causality, Aristotle on, 5
Center for American Progress, on Black
    financial inequality, 268–269, 282
change of heart. *See metanoia* (change of
    heart)
chaos myth, 311
chaplaincy training, on self-discernment,
    342–343
Cheng Yen, 326, 327
child-loss v. fetal-loss, 49
children: corporal punishment of, 21;
    indigenous Native Americans removal
    to boarding schools, 232, 237, 278;
    moral solidarity and, 93; rights, fetal
    rights and, 137–138; T&R commission
    on maltreatment of indigenous Native
    Americans, 340
Christianity: Africans, African Americans
    and, 248–250; Christian slavers
    justification, 244; classical Greek
    philosophy influence on, 6; of colonial
    settlers, 221; on freedom, 249–250,
    251; hope and justice in, 264;
    indigenous Native Americans
    conversion to, 220, 221–222, 223,
    227–228, 242; otherness and, 307–309;
    Roman Empire promotion of, 225
City on a Hill, 32, 227, 356–357
civil rights, 30
Civil Rights Act (1964), 26, 149, 252, 253,
    319
Civil Rights movement, 27, 149, 151, 197,
    252–253, 258; participants of, 267; on
    racial discrimination, 222–223; racism
    acknowledgment in, 267
Civil War, 252
classical Greek philosophy, on spiritual
    world, 6
clinical research trials: benefits, on
    intellectual disabilities, 97–98;
    informed consent for, 96–99;
    intellectual disabilities and, 96–99;
    justification for, 98–99
closed communities, 316
Coates, Ta-Nehisi, 151, 257, 258; on
    Africans and African Americans
    reparations, 271–272, 282
coercive childbearing, 46

cognitive ability, 80
Cohen, Dan, 169–170, 204
colonial settlers: Christianity of, 221;
    Dunbar-Ortiz on, 215, 276; on
    indigenous Native Americans
    Christianity conversion, 227–228;
    Native Americans population before,
    217; original sin of, 215
combat-related PTSD, 189–192
commodification: of Africans and African
    Americans, 243–246; of Black slaves,
    242–243; fetal death and, 141; savior
    siblings, 59
Communio Sanctorum: for Africans and
    African Americans, 269; Bonhoeffer,
    315–316, 322–323; community and,
    136–137, 143; community of being and,
    315–316; Doctrine of Discovery and,
    228; on flourishing for all, 326;
    inclusivity in, 60–61, 90–91, 270, 323,
    327, 370; indigenous Native Americans
    and, 239; Jesus Christ and, 323; kenosis
    required for, 327–328; LGBTQI people
    and, 198; moral solidarity in, 72,
    317–318, 363; Nietzsche and, 321;
    physical disabilities and, 68–69;
    prescriptions for building in, 270; social
    justice and, 324–325; on spirituality and
    worship, 325; in 21st century, 316–328;
    universal healthcare and, 318–319;
    will-to-power and, 319
community: closed, 316; *Communio
    Sanctorum* and, 136–137, 143;
    dementia and importance of, 171–172;
    importance of, 316–317; LGBTQI
    resistance and resilience, 197–198;
    Locke on, 330; opioid addiction support
    in, 136–137; Shaker, 316–317
community of being: Bonhoeffer and,
    315–316; *Communio Sanctorum* and,
    315–316; covenantal ties in, 314;
    definition of, 313–314; forgiveness and,
    314–315; moral solidarity in, 314, 315;
    otherness and, 313–316; population in,
    313, 330
complicated grief, 192
concealment of being, loss versus,
    172–175

Cone, James H., 257, 260; author personal reflection on, 273–276; black liberation theology of, 264–266, 281

Confucius analects, 305

Congressional Resolution of Apology to Native People of the United States, 236–237

connection, for dementia, 171

conquest myths, 32

consciousness, 180, 204; defining, 42–43; Locke on, 10–11

Constantine the Great, 31, 225

Constitution (U.S.): Thirteenth Amendment, 149; Fifteenth Amendment, 149; Fourteenth Amendment of, 21, 141, 158, 159; human rights and, 319; immigrants rights and, 159; Nineteenth Amendment, 16, 21

contested being, of Africans and African Americans, 243–246

contractual/prosperity theology, 265; Constantine the Great use of, 31

contrition, xiv; forgiveness and, 347–353

control, eating disorders and loss of, 109

Controlled Substance Act (1971), 255

conversion therapy, for sexual preference, 194

Copernicus, Nicolaus, 9

coping skills, of Blacks, 262; negative or passive, 263–264; for resistance, 263

corporal punishment, of children, 21

corporate response, to National T&R Commission, 349

co-travelers in Creation, 198, 316, 317–318, 323–324, 326, 327, 336

covenant, 317–318

covenantal responsibility, 136

covenantal ties, in community of being, 314

COVID-19 (2019), 19; abortion and economic concerns for, 47–48; death from, 132; least of us health disparities, 373–374

Creation *Ex Nihilo* theory, 311

creation myth, 311

creation narratives and theories: Big Bang theory, 311, 312, 351; called into being, 312–313, 347; chaos myth, 311;

creation as dynamic, ongoing process, 311–312; Creation *Ex Nihilo* theory, 311; creation myth, 311; human superiority and, 92; indigenous Native Americans and, 222; otherness and, 311–313, 355

crimes against humanity, of White nationalism, 254

criminalization: of drug abuse, 133, 134, 255–256; of people of color, 135; of self-induced medical abortion, 140–141, 198

criminal justice system: Blacks death sentences, 153; Jim Crow laws and, 133; least of us oppression by, 253–254; profit in, 163, 200; racial bias of, 201; tough on crime of, 255. *See also* prison industry, U.S.

CRISPR-Cas9 genome editing capability, 60

The Cross and the Lynching Tree (Cone), 275

Curse of Ham, racism and, 243–254, 256

Dakota Access Pipeline protests, 220, 353, 364

Dalai Lama, 72, 326–327

D&C. *See* dilation and curettage

D&E. *See* dilation and evacuation

death: actively dying personhood, 177–179; AD and, 166; advance directives and, 177–178; brain, 183–184, 185, 187, 205; from COVID-19, 132; definitions, 344; fetal, xi, 141; of *in utero* being, 49, 72; PTSD and, 114–115

Deaths of Despair and the Future of Capitalism (Case and Deaton), 372

Deaton, Angus, 372

decriminalization of laws, 163–164

deeply forgetful. *See* dementia and deeply forgetful

Defense Appropriation Act (2010), 237

dehumanization: of Blacks, 152, 242; slavery and, 244–245

Deloria, Vine, Jr., 371

dementia and deeply forgetful, 164; caregiving burden for, 173–174; Cohen music therapy for, 169–170, 204;

community importance for, 171–172; connection for, 171; Harper on, 173; loss versus concealment of being and, 172–175; personhood search in, 165–169; Post on, 165, 170; self-identity in, 170–171; types of, 164–165. *See also* Alzheimer's Disease

Dementia Reconsidered (Kitwood), 168

dental abscess, xiv

dependent personality disorder, 112

depersonalization, of physical disabilities, 63

depression, 119–121; mood disorders and, 102–103; opioid addiction and, 145

Descartes, René, 1, 9, 92–93, 167

designer babies, 60

despair, 361

DiAngelo, Robin, 30, 268

dilation and curettage (D&C), for abortion, 41

dilation and evacuation (D&E), for abortion, 41

disability rights movement, 93

discounted personhood, for physical disabilities, 66

Discourse on the Method (Descartes), 1

Discovery Doctrine. *See* Doctrine of Discovery

discrimination: of ASD, 85; fear as basis of, 301; physical disabilities soft, 69; racial, Civil Rights movement and, 222–223

disintegrated selves, of Blacks, 257

displacement theory: Africans and African Americans and, 241–243; White ruling class and, 161

dispossession: of indigenous Native Americans, 217, 219, 226, 238, 241–242, 258, 298, 324, 337, 339, 371; of White ruling class, for Blacks, 217

distributive justice, 90

DNR. *See* do-not-resuscitate (DNR) order

DNS. *See* Down syndrome

Doblemeier, Martin, 314–315

Doctrine of Discovery, 345; biblical warrant of, 226, 228; *Communio Sanctorum* and, 228; human rights violation of, 32, 325; indigenous Native Americans and, 225–230, 236; Native

Americans ancestral lands rights and, 225–226, 236, 246; Supreme Court decision and, 225; unlawful, 238; of White ruling class, 32

Doctrine of Original Sin, of Edwards, 215

documentaries: on Africans and African Americans, 371; "Eyes on the Prize," of Hampton, 260, 267; on indigenous Native Americans, 371–372

domestic terrorism, 373

dominion theology, 256–257

do-not-resuscitate (DNR) order, 178

Dorrien, Gary J., 27

double-consciousness, 256–257, 266

Douglas, Kelly-Brown, 162

Douglass, Frederick, 257, 373

Down syndrome (DNS), 89; human rights advocacy for, 90; IQ and, 88; personhood challenges for, 93; PGD diagnosis of, 138; of Pineda, 117–118; therapeutic abortions for, 89

Dred Scott v. Sandford (1857), 148, 149, 248

Driver, Deamonte, xiv

driving forces, for assaulted personhood, 7, 43, 258, 299–300

drug abuse, xiv; criminalization of, 133, 134, 255–256; of fentanyl, 146–147; morality and, 133–134, 137; pregnant woman and, 138, 142–143

dualism, 43, 72

Du Bois, W.E.B., 270, 371; double-consciousness and, 256–257, 266; on racial oppression, 256

Dunbar-Ortiz, Roxanne, 215, 216, 276

eating disorders: anorexia nervosa, 107–109; binge-eating disorder, 107; bulimia nervosa, 107; hospitalization for, 108, 109; inner self and, 107–108; loss of control in, 109; statistics on, 107

Ecce Homo (Nietzsche), xi

Education for Physicians for End-of-Life Care Project, 179, 204

Edwards, Jonathan, 215

Ellison, Brooke, xiii–xiv, 71, 74

Ellison, Jean, xiii–xiv, 71

Ellison, Ralph, 257

emancipation, abortion and, 140

Emancipation Proclamation (1862), 26, 245, 252
empathy, National T&R Commission and, 351–352
empires, atrocities of, 338
ensoulment, 16–17, 43, 61, 73; abortion and, 44; pregnancy quickening and, 44
epistemology, 5; Descartes and, 9
equality: Jim Crow laws and, 158; racial, 268–269
ethics: of care, Kittay and, 90–91; of human stem cell biology, 1–2; on intellectually disabled clinical trials, 96–97; organ donations and PVS, 184–185
ethnic cleansing formal apology, of BIA, 339, 364
ethnic conflicts, 24
euthanasia: for least of us, 56; for lethal birth defects, 55; non-voluntary, 56; for terminal childhood diseases, 55
exceptionalism. *See* American exceptionalism
exilic life, 259; of African Americans, 256–259; of indigenous Native Americans, 231–232
"Eyes on the Prize" documentary, Hampton, 260, 267

faith: Aquinas on reason and, 7; -based groups, 296–297
faithful disbelief, 296
familial disease, AD as, 166–167
FAS. *See* fetal alcohol syndrome
FASD. *See* Fetal Alcohol Spectrum Disorder
Faulkner, William, 235, 350
fear: as assaulted personhood catalyst, 299; as discrimination basis, 301; fight-or-flight response to, 302; hate groups and, 299; hatred and, 300–302; otherness and, 301
femicide, 53, 54
fentanyl drugs, 146–147
Fetal Alcohol Spectrum Disorder (FASD), 94–96, 138
fetal alcohol syndrome (FAS), 141
fetal death, xi; commodification and, 141

fetal rights, 50; child rights and, 137–138; women human rights and, 141–142
fetal valproate syndrome (FVS), 95–96, 123
fetus: pain perception of, 45; viability of, 40
Fifteenth Amendment, 149
fight-or-flight response, to fear, 302
financial inequality: of Blacks, 268–269, 282; redistributive justice and, 269, 336
Finkbine, Sherri, 140
flourishing for all, *Communio Sanctorum* on, 326
Floyd, George, 273, 284, 366
FMR1 gene, fragile X syndrome and, 83–84
forced labor, in mass incarceration, 164, 203
forced sterilizations, reparations for, 271
forgiveness, 353–364; achievement of, 360–362; contrition and, 347–353; insincere apology and, 359; National T&R Commission seeking of, 352–353; West Nickel Mines School shooting, 314–315
Forman, James, Jr., 163
Foucault, Paul-Michel, 131, 134
Fourteenth Amendment, 21, 141, 158, 159
fragile X syndrome, 83–84
Francis (pope), on abortions, 44, 50, 73
Frankfurt, Harry G., 167
Frankl, Victor, 262, 319; on freedom, 300–301; on search for meaning, 300–301
frank xenophobia, xiv
freedom, 28; AD and, 175–177; Africans and African Americans denial of, 246; black liberation theology on, 265; Christianity on, 249–250, 251; denial of indigenous Native Americans, 230; Frankl on, 300–301; immigration pursuit of, 156, 158; indigenous Native Americans religious, 222, 277; patriarchy and, 143; religious, 222, 277, 325; rights to, 62, 109
free will, 7; Nietzsche on, 12–13
Freud, Sigmund, 300, 319
Fukuyama, Francis, xv
FVS. *See* fetal valproate syndrome

Game Theory, 30
gatekeepers of personhood, 19–22, 24
gendercide, 53–54
gender identity, 25, 206; sexuality and, xiv, 193–195
gender-selective reproductive techniques, 54
Genesis story, biblical warrant of dominion in, 31
genocide, 22; of indigenous Native Americans, 218, 228, 229, 234, 235, 242, 277, 324, 359; in Rohingya, 294; Rwanda, 340–341
"Genocide and American Indian History" (Ostler), 277
gestational surrogacy, 60
Geulincx, Arnold, 10
Ghost in the Machine, Ryle and, 11
Global Slavery Index, 2018, on modern slavery, xiv, 22
Golden Rule, 303–304
Gone With the Wind (film), 245
Gonzales v. Carhart (2007), 41
"Great Awakenings," in U.S., 226–227
Greatest Commandment, 315; African, African Americans and, 249; indigenous Native Americans and, 220–221, 242
Great Lockdown, of COVID-19. *See* COVID-19
Great Northern Migration, 148
Great Recession, 47–48, 269
Greensboro massacre, T&R commission on, 340
Groves v. Slaughter (1841), 247–248
Gutiérrez, Gustavo, 266

The Half has Never Been Told (Baptist), 370
Hämäläinen, Pekka, 372
Hammurabi's Code, 303–304
Hampton, Harry, 267
Harper, Lynn, 173
Harrison, Beverly, 45–46
hate groups, 373; fear and loathing of, 299; against LGBTQI people, 195, 206; otherness and, 297; SPLC on, 24, 152, 155, 297; White nationalism and White supremacy, 252, 297

hatred, fear and, 300–302
Hawking, Stephen, 83
health disparities: Black, 269; for COVID-19, 373–374
Hegel, Georg Wilhelm Friedrich, 257; on otherness, 18
Herman, Judith, 192, 233, 339
hermeneutic of suspicion, 92, 216–217, 230, 293
heroin addiction: Black Heroin problem, 134, 135; of veterans, 133
Heyer, Heather, 298
Hinduism, 306
Hippocratic Oath, 39, 72, 318
HLA. *See* human leucocyte antigen (HLA) compatibility
Holocaust, 278; documentation of, 235; duration of, 234; reparations for, 271; trauma and, 231–233
holy interrogation. *See sacra doctrina* (holy interrogation), Aquinas on
homogeneity, of social groups, 27
homosexuality, APA on, 197–198
human leucocyte antigen (HLA) compatibility, 58, 59–60, 61
human rights: abortion as, 20; Bill of Rights and Constitution on, 319; DNS advocacy for, 90; Doctrine of Discovery violation of, 32, 325; fetal rights and women, 141–142; to flourish, 320; indigenous Native Americans genocide and, 229, 359; U.S. wealth violations, 337; violations of, 22; White ruling class and, 200
Human Rights Watch, 329
humans: being of, 41–42; creation narratives and superiority of, 92
human stem cell biology, 1–2, 71
Hume, David: personhood and, 11, 167; on self sensory perception, 11, 14
Husserl, Edmund Gustav Albrecht, 18
hylomorphism, of Aristotle, 7–8
*hyper*cognition, 91; Aquinas on, 8; Post on, 165–166; society value of, 173; Western world and, 3–4
*hyper*violence, 31

identity politics, xiv, 30, 325; otherness and, 295, 298, 309

IDX. *See* intact/intrauterine dilation and extraction (IDX), for abortion
immigrants: constitutional rights of, 159; depersonalization of, 28; otherness of, 294–295; overview of U.S., 158–159; TPS for, 160; undocumented illegal, 159, 160–161; White ruling class and, 159
immigration, 24; freedom pursuit of, 156, 158; religious traditions on, 157–158; violence and, 156–161
immigration detention centers, abortion rights at, 141, 199
immigration politics, 21–22, 201–202
incarceration: of Africans and African Americans, 21, 133, 163–164, 255, 280; mass, 163–164, 203
incest, 120
inclusivity: BLM and, 151; in *Communio Sanctorum*, 60–61, 90–91, 270, 323, 327, 370
Indian Child Welfare Act (1978), 340
"Indian Reservation" (song), by Loudermilk, 371
indigenous Native Americans: Abenaki, 239–241; American original sin toward, 4, 26, 74, 217–241, 276–277, 337, 339–340; ancestral lands and freedom of, 23, 32, 219–220, 223; author confession for, 239–241; biblical warrant of dominion of, 19; children removal to boarding schools, 232, 237, 278; Christianity conversion of, 220, 221–222, 223, 227–228, 242; dispossession of, 217, 219, 226, 238, 241–242, 258, 298, 324, 337, 339, 371; Doctrine of Discovery and, 225–230, 236; documentaries on, 371–372; exilic life of, 231–232; genocide of, 218, 228, 234, 235, 242, 277, 324; Greatest Commandment and, 220–221; human rights and genocide of, 229, 359; intergenerational trauma of, 232; killing of Christianized Indians, 277–278; land treaties for, 224; metastasis and subjugation of, 223–225; narrative records destroyed of, 231; Newsom apology to, 237; population, before colonial settlers, 217; population

decline of, 218; religiosity of, 219–220, 221, 222; religious freedom, 222, 277; religious intolerance toward, 220; repairing the breach for, 234–239; reparations to, 236, 238; resilience of, 222–223, 231–234; revisionism of, 235–236; on sacred nature of land, 219–220, 277; scalping of, 218–219; structural oppression acknowledgement, 354, 359–360; trauma of, 231–234; T&R commission on children maltreatment, 340; war crimes against, 218–219; White ruling class and, 74, 228–230, 235; writings on, 371; xenophobia against, 219, 221
indigenous people, 22
An Indigenous Peoples' History of the United States (Dunbar-Ortiz), 276
infanticide, xiv, 54–58; morality and, 56–57
informed consent: capacity and, 97–99; for clinical research trials, 96–99; organ donations and, 186
inner self, 79–80, 122; eating disorders and, 107–108
Insel, Thomas, 122–123
insincere apology, forgiveness and, 359
intact/intrauterine dilation and extraction (IDX), for abortion, 41
intellect, xiv; personhood and, 92; Singer on personhood and, 172; Tooley on personhood and, 172
intellectual disabilities, 80–83; clinical research benefits, 97–98; clinical research trials and, 96–99; ethics on clinical trials of, 96–97; Willowbrook State School and, 97
intelligence quotient (IQ), 87; ASD and, 85; DNS and, 88; normal distribution of, 80–83
intergenerational trauma, 232
intersubjectivity, Husserl on, 18
intolerance: of assaulted personhood, 357–358; religious, toward indigenous Native Americans, 220
intrinsic value, Kant on, 59
in utero being: death of, 49, 72; development and other life of, 44–49; ensoulment and, 44; malformations of,

55; pregnant woman and, 137–143
Invisible Man (Ellison, R.), 257
in vitro fertilization (IVF), 60
ipseity, 106; of Nash, 119; personality disorders and, 112
IQ. *See* intelligence quotient
Islam, 306–307
IVF. *See in vitro* fertilization

Jane Crow, 161–162, 164, 202
Japanese-American internment, 271
Jesus Christ: black liberation theology and, 265, 275; crucifixion of, xi; kenosis of, 328; otherness and, 308–310; personhood and nature of, 20; on self-discernment parable of, 335–336
Jewish religion, 304–305
Jim Crow laws, xiv, 21, 26, 148, 149–150, 161, 164, 272; background on, 148; criminal justice system and, 133; equality and, 158; White supremacy and, 148
Johnson, Lyndon, 253
Juan Crow, 161, 164
Judeo-Christian traditions, in Western world, 3
justice: redistributive, 239, 265–266, 269, 272, 336, 351; retributive, 303

Kant, Immanuel, 303; on intrinsic value, 59; on life value, 55; on means to an end, 97
Kendi, Ibram, 151, 257
kenosis required, for *Communio Sanctorum*, 327–328
Kepler, Johannes, 9
Kerner Commission: on civil strife, 254; *Report of the National Advisory Commission on Civil Disorders*, 254
King, Martin Luther, Jr., 23, 27, 257, 266–267, 354, 357, 371; "Beyond Vietnam" speech of, 253, 254–255; übermensch concept and, 321–322
Kittay, Eva Feder, 90–91
Kitwood, Thomas "Tom," 167–168
Koch, Christof, 72
Kovic, Ron, 191

Labeling Theory, 30; deviance judged in, 29; on labeled individuals, 29
labor exploitation, of undocumented illegal immigrants, 160
Lakota America (Hämäläinen), 372
land treaties, for indigenous Native Americans, 224
Lange, Friedrich Albert, 12
least of us, 61; COVID-19 health disparities for, 373–374; criminal justice system oppression of, 253–254; defective label for, 82; drug abuse and, 133–134; euthanasia for, 56; gendercide and, 53–54; *in utero* malformation, 55; patriarchy and, 53
Lesbian, Gay, Binary, Transgender, Queer, Questioning, and Intersex (LGBTQI), 25; assault on personhood of, 195–196, 285; Bill of Rights and, 197; community resistance and resilience, 197–198; gender identity and, xiv, 193–195, 206; hate groups against, 195, 206; otherness of, 297; Trump and biblical warrants against, 196, 206; White supremacy and, 197
Lévinas, Emmanuel, 18, 300
Lewis and Clark expedition, 224
lex talionis, 303–304
LGBTQI. *See* Lesbian, Gay, Binary, Transgender, Queer, Questioning, and Intersex
life and ensoulment, 16–17, 43, 44, 61, 73
Lincoln, Abraham, 26, 245
Liu Xiaobo, 22
Locke, John, 167; on AD and consciousness, 10; awareness and, 10–11; on community, 330; on consciousness, 10–11; Reid on, 11; on self consciousness experience, 10; on self sensory perception, 14
loss, concealment of being versus, 172–175
Loudermilk, John, 371
Lou Gehrig's disease. *See* amyotrophiclateralsclerosis (ALS or Lou Gehrig's disease)

major depressive disorder, 102

Malcolm X, 27, 257, 261, 266, 371; on White assimilation, 258

Malebranche, Nicholas, 10

Mandela, Nelson, 22, 340–341

Manichaeism, Augustine conversion from, 6

manifest destiny: indigenous Native American ancestral lands and, 228; U.S. nationalism and, 227; White supremacy and, 278

manual vacuum aspiration (MVA), for abortion, 41

Marshall, John J., 325, 345

Martin, Trayvon, 150, 162, 200

Martin & Malcolm & America (Cone), 260, 275

mass incarceration, 163; decriminalization of laws and, 163–164; forced labor in, 164, 203

MC1R hair color gene, of Norse Vikings, 299, 329

McConnell, Mitch, 365

means to an end, Kant on, 97

mental disorders/disabilities: ASD, 84–87, 116–117, 122–123; DNS and, 88–90; FASD and, 94–96, 138; fragile X syndrome, 83–84; FVS, 95–96, 123; inner self and, 79–80; intellectual disabilities, 80–83, 96–98; PWS, 87–88

mental health, in U.S., 99–101

mental illness, 122; anxiety, 67–68, 101–102, 119–121, 145; bipolar disorders, 103–105; described, 123–124; eating disorders, 107–109; Herman on, 192, 233, 339; inner self and, 101; mood disorders, 102–105; personality disorders, 109–112; schizophrenia, 82–83, 105–106, 118–119, 124; stress-related disorders, 114–115; vulnerabilities in U.S. and, 99–101. *See also* post-traumatic stress disorder

metanoia (change of heart), xiv–xv, 353–364, 370

metaphorical dualism, Ryle on, 12

Middle East, occupation of, 329

mind (psyche), 4; Butler on body and, 10; Descartes on soul and, 9

mind (psyche) vulnerabilities, xiv, 62, 115; courage and resilience profiles, 115–116; Isabella T. trauma and mental illness, 119–121; Nash schizophrenia and, 118–119; Pineda DNS and, 117–118; Savage ASD and, 116–117

"A Model of Christian Charity" (Winthrop), 227

modernism, 13–15

mood disorders: bipolar disorder, 103–105; depression and, 102–103; major depressive disorder, 102; seasonal affective disorder, 102; U.S. prevalence of, 102

morality: of abortion, 39, 44, 45–46, 72; drug abuse and, 133–134, 137; infanticide and, 56–57; of PGD, 60; repentance and, 356; of slavery, 247

moral responsibility, 270

moral solidarity: children and, 93; in *Communio Sanctorum*, 72, 317–318, 363; in community of being, 314, 315; DNS and, 93; exilic strangers inclusion, 259; upon people of color, 270; physical disabilities and, 68–69; Scheler and, 58, 60

moral value, of otherness, 7

Moreland, James P., 169

music: of Africans and African Americans, 345, 365, 370–371; of indigenous Native Americans, 345, 364–365; of Savage, 116–117; therapy, for dementia, 169–170, 204

MVA. *See* manual vacuum aspiration (MVA), for abortion

Narcan: opioid overdose rescue with, 145–147, 199; take-home kits of, 145; withholding of, 145–146, 199–200

narcissistic personality disorder, 110

Nash, John Forbes, 82–83, 118–119, 124

National Institute of General Medical Sciences, NIH, 2

National Institutes of Health (NIH): human stem cell biology of, 1; National Institute of General Medical Sciences of, 2

nationalism, 22; toxic, 298; U.S. manifest destiny and, 227. *See also* White

nationalism
National Truth and Reconciliation
Commission, U.S., 341; accountability
for, 351; challenges for, 348; corporate
response to, 349; efforts of, 347–348;
empathy and, 351–352; forgiveness
sought by, 352–353; organizations
support of, 349; original sins disclosure
by, 348–349; otherness and, 350; self-
discernment for, 350–351; on structural
oppression, 348, 349; structural
privilege and, 349–350, 351
Nations Within (Deloria), 371
Native Americans. *See* indigenous Native
Americans
nativist movements, 28
Nat Turner's Rebellion, of 1831, 260
negative coping skills, of Blacks, 263–264
neonatal euthanasia, 54–58
neonatal intensive care unit (NICU), 52
neonate/infant: anencephalic, 54–55;
coming into being of, 51–52; CRISPR-
Cas9 genome editing capability, 60; full
personhood and, 53–54; gestational
surrogacy, 60; infanticide, 54–58;
neonatal euthanasia, 54–58; NICU and,
52; opioid addiction and, 138;
personhood lacking of, 52; savior
siblings for spare parts, 58–62
neurofibromatosis (NF), 67
The New Abolition (Dorrien), 27
New Gospel, 29
New Jim Crow, xiv, 27; on Black financial
inequality, 269; Rockefeller drug laws
and, 255; White ruling class and, 133
The New Jim Crow (Alexander), 27, 149
Newsom, Gavin, 237
Newton, Isaac, 9
New York City Conspiracy, of 1741, 260
NF. *See* neurofibromatosis
Nicomachean ethics, of Aristotle, 6
NICU. *See* neonatal intensive care unit
Nietzsche, Friedrich Wilhelm, xi; on free
will, 12–13; on selfhood, 12–13; on
übermensch concept, 12–13, 321–322;
will-to-power and, 13, 300, 302, 319,
321
NIH. *See* National Institutes of Health

nihilism, 259; Beckett on, 14; Nietzsche
on, 14; West on, 258
Nineteenth Amendment, U.S. Constitution,
16, 21
Nixon, Richard, 255
non-combat-related PTSD, 192–193
non-voluntary euthanasia, 56
Norridgewock Massacre, 241
Norse Vikings, MC1R hair color gene,
299, 329
NYSTEM stem cell science program, 2

Obama, Barack: Black oppression and,
153; Congressional Resolution of
Apology to Native People of the United
States signed by, 236–237; pro-choice
and, 50; racism and election of, 252,
260
objectification: of Blacks, White ruling
class, 257; patriarchy and, 15; trauma
of, 259
obsessive-compulsive personality disorder,
112
Olah, George, 118
On Vanishing (Harper), 173
opioid addiction, xiv, 132, 133–134, 199;
as chronic, relapsing disorder, 147;
community support for, 136–137;
depression and anxiety disorders of,
145; Narcan rescue and, 145–147;
newborns incidence of, 132; overdoses
in, 136, 144; pregnant woman and, 138;
statistics on, 132; VSL and, 144; War
on Drugs and, 133; White ruling class
narrative on, 135
oppression, 15–16, 281; of Africans and
African Americans, 260; brutality of,
337–338; criminal justice system least
of us, 253–254; Du Bois on racial, 256;
race and White, 253–254; resistance to,
231; of White ruling class, 31, 217
organ donations, 205; brain death and,
183–184, 185; example, 188–189;
informed consent and, 186; PVS and,
183–188
original sins: African and African
Americans, 27, 241–276, 282, 324, 337,
340; of colonial settlers, 215;
indigenous Native Americans, 4, 26,

74, 217–241, 276–277, 337, 339–340; introduction to, 215–217; National T& R Commission disclosure of, 348–349; racism and, 32, 74; Trump White ruling class and, 272, 282–283, 354; U.S. continuation of, 373

original sins thesis, 23, 132

Ostler, Jeffrey, 277

otherness, 293, 329–330; of Africans and African Americans, 258; assaulted personhood and concept of, 17–19, 131–132; *Communio Sanctorum* in 21st century, 316–328; community of being and, 313–316; creation narratives and theories, 311–313, 355; fear and, 301; Hammurabi's Code, 303–304; hate groups and, 297; Hegel on, 18; identity politics and, 295, 298, 309; of immigrants, 294–295; Jesus Christ and, 308–310; Lévinas on alterity and, 18, 300; of LGBTQI people, 297; moral value of, 6; National T&R Commission and, 350; personhood reimagined, 310–311; regionalism and, 295; tribalism response to uncertain, 19; vulnerabilities and, 293, 300–302; world religions and, 304–310

overdoses: Narcan rescue for, 145–147, 199; opioid addiction, 136, 144

overman. *See* übermensch ("overman") concept

Pale Blue Dot (Sagan), 312

Partial-Birth Abortion Ban Act (2003), 41

passive coping skills, of Blacks, 263–264

patriarchy, 16, 137; abortion and, 140; freedom and, 143; gatekeepers of personhood and, 19; least of us and, 53; objectification and, 15; unborn fetuses and, 17; White, of Black slaves, 245

people of color, 278; American exceptionalism and personhood of, 229; moral solidarity upon, 270

persistent vegetative state (PVS), 204; Bill of Rights and, 182, 187; ethical dilemmas for, 184–185; organ donation, 183–188; overview of, 181; personhood loss from, 182–183; postmodernism and, 15; recovery from,

181–182; unconsciousness and, 180–181

personality disorders: borderline, 110–111; dependent, 112; description of, 109; ipseity and, 112; narcissistic, 110; obsessive-compulsive, 112; schizoid and schizotypal, 111

personhood: all-or-nothing, 169–172; fluid character of, xii; Hume and, 11, 167; literature on, 1; loss narratives of, xi–xii; nature of Christ and, 20; nonhuman, 3; properties of, 2–3; rational soul and, 20

personhood challenges, in 21st century: all-or-nothing, 169–172; #BlackLivesMatter, 150–156; combat-related PTSD, 189–192; concealment of being and, 172–175; dementia and Alzheimer's Disease, 164–169, 204; Frank D. AD example, 175–177; of *in utero* fetus and pregnant woman, 137–143; Jim Crow laws, 148–150; LGBTQI, 193–198; mass incarceration, 163–164, 203; Narcan rescue, 143–147; non-combat-related PTSD, 192–193; opioid addiction, xiv, 132–137, 199; organ donation example, 188–189; overview of, 131–132; PVS and, 182–183; PVS and organ donation, 183–188; race in U.S., 148; unconscious and actively dying, 177–179; unconsciousness states, 180–182; violence and immigration, 156–161

Personhood Movement, 50

Pew Research Center, "Race in America 2019" report, 267–268

PGD. *See* preimplantation genetic diagnosis

Phenomenology of Spirit (Hegel), 257

physical disabilities, xiv; beauty and, 64–66; depersonalization and, 64; discounted personhood for, 66; experience of, 66–69; marginalized existence from, 68; moral solidarity and, 68–69; NF, 67; soft discrimination of, 69; vulnerabilities and, 62–64, 74; withdrawal from anxiety of, 67–68

Piketty, Thomas, 346, 350

pineal gland, Descartes on, 9
Pineda, Pablo, 117–118
Planned Parenthood v. Casey (1992), 139
Plato, on soul, 4–5, 6
Plessy v. Ferguson (1896), 149
police brutality, 258, 329; BLM and,
　151–152, 201
political groups, 296–297
politics: identity, xiv, 30, 295, 298, 309,
　325; immigration, 21–22, 201–202;
　racist, 253; self-identity and, 296;
　theological, 325
Polk, James, 338
Pontius Pilate, xi
Poor People's Campaign, 253
Post, Stephen Garrard: on dementia, 165,
　170; on *hyper*cognition, 3–4, 165–166
postmodernism: assaulted personhood and,
　14; intrinsic self-worth and, 14; on
　personhood, 13–15; PVS patient and,
　15
post-traumatic stress disorder (PTSD),
　112–113, 124; combat-related,
　189–192; death, bereavement and,
　114–115; domains of, 113–114; non-
　combat-related, 192–193; suicides and,
　192–193; Vietnam War and, 191
power-and-control, 15–16; assaulted
　personhood and, 28, 281
power-knowledge, of Foucault, 134
The Power of Forgiveness (film), of
　Doblemeier, 314–315
Prader-Willi syndrome (PWS), 87–88
preferential option of poor, Gutiérrez on,
　266
pregnant woman: biblical warrants and,
　139; Bill of Rights and, 140; drug abuse
　and, 138, 142–143; *in utero* being and,
　137–143; teen pregnancy prevention,
　141
preimplantation genetic diagnosis (PGD),
　58, 61, 138; morality of, 60
prescriptions for building, in *Communio
　Sanctorum*, 270
prison industry, U.S.: African, African
　Americans and, 134; Wacquant on
　prison ghettos, 164
pro-choice, 73; Obama and, 50
profit, in criminal justice system, 163, 200

pro-life groups, 19–20, 45–46, 49, 50–51
proprioception, 9
prosperity gospel, 29, 31–32
Proteus Syndrome, 67
prudential unity, 48, 57
psyche. *See* soul (psyche)
psychological vulnerabilities: Adler and,
　300, 319; fear and hatred, 300–302;
　Frankl and, 300–301; Freud and, 300;
　Nietzsche and, 300
PTSD. *See* post-traumatic stress disorder
PVS. *See* persistent vegetative state
PWS. *See* Prader-Willi syndrome

QoL. *See* quality of life (QoL), AD and
quadriplegic child, Ellison, B., as, xiii–xiv,
　71, 74
quality of life (QoL), AD and, 167, 171
quickening, in pregnancy, 44

race, xiv; financial inequality and,
　268–269; riots, in 1967, 254; in U.S.,
　148; White oppression and, 253–254;
　White ruling class on, 268
"Race in America 2019" report, of Pew
　Research Center, 267–268, 281
Race Matters (West), 26, 148, 257–258
racial bias, in criminal justice system, 201
racial discrimination, Civil Rights
　movement and, 222–223
racial equality, 268–269
racial profiling, 256, 280
racial violence, 150–151
racism, xiv, 152–153, 281, 298–299;
　Africans and African Americans exilic
　life and, 256–259; Black slaves
　dehumanization and, 242; Civil Rights
　movement acknowledgment of, 267;
　Curse of Ham and, 243–254, 256;
　Obama election and, 252, 260; original
　sin and, 32, 74; Trump overt, 273, 283,
　366; in 21st century, 345
racist politics, 253
Rae, Scott B., 169
Rawls, John, 90, 320
reason, Aquinas on faith and, 7
reciprocal justice, 361
reconciliation: for Africans and African
　Americans, 266–273; for indigenous

Native Americans, 234–239; slavery and, 252

Reconstruction Amendments, to Bill of Rights, 149

Reconstruction Era, 1865–1877, 21, 252

redistributive justice, 351; black liberation theology and, 265–266; financial inequality and, 269, 336; reparations as, 239; Trump and, 272

Reed v. Reed (1971), on Fourteenth Amendment, 21

regionalism, otherness and, 295

Reid, Thomas, 11

reimagining personhood, 310; community of being and, 313–316; creation narratives and theologies, 311–313; reason for, 310–311

religion: Greatest Commandment in, 220–221, 242; Self-identity and, 296; slave resistance through, 263; world, otherness and, 304–310

religiosity, of indigenous Native Americans, 219–220, 221, 222

religious affiliation: Buddhism, 305–306; Christianity and otherness, 307–309; Confucius analects, 305; Hinduism, 306; Islam, 306–307; Jewish, 304–305

religious freedom, 222, 277, 325

religious intolerance, toward indigenous Native Americans, 220

Religious Right, 197

religious traditions, on immigration, 157–158

Renaissance, 3, 42

Repairers of the Breach, 253

repairing the breach: for Africans and African Americans, 266–273; for indigenous Native Americans, 234–239

reparations, 360; to Africans and African Americans, 271–272, 282; for forced sterilizations, 271; for Holocaust, 271; to indigenous Native Americans, 236, 238, 241; for Japanese-American internment, 271; McConnell on, 365; as redistributive justice, 239; for Tuskegee experiments, 271

repentance, xiv, 353–364, 358; for indigenous Native Americans, 234–239; morality and, 356

Report of the National Advisory Commission on Civil Disorders, Kerner Commission, 254

reproductive rights, ACOG on, 140–141

resilience: of Africans, African Americans, 262–264; Black perspective of, 262; coping skills for, 262–264; of indigenous Native Americans, 222–223, 231–234; of LGBTQI community, 197–198; mind vulnerabilities profiles of courage and, 115–116

resistance: of Africans and African Americans, 260–262, 280; Black, 27; Blacks coping skills for, 263; of indigenous Native Americans, 231–234; LGBTQI community, 197–198; to oppression, 231; slave day-to-day, 263; slave rebellions, 251, 260–261; trauma confronted by, 231, 262; Underground Railroad, 260

responsibility, 57–58, 238, 271, 338; covenantal, 136; moral, 270

retributive justice, 303

revisionism, indigenous Native Americans and, 235–236

Revolutionary War, 224

Rockefeller, Nelson, 255

Roe v. Wade, 50–51, 73, 139

Rohingya, genocide in, 294

Roman Catholic Church, on abortion, 73

Roman Empire, Christianity promotion during, 225

Rome Statute of the International Criminal Court, 218

Rwanda genocide, 340–341

Ryle, Gilbert: Ghost in the Machine and, 11; on metaphorical dualism, 12

sacra doctrina (holy interrogation), Aquinas on, 7

Sagan, Carl, 312

same-sex marriage, 197

Saunt, Claudio, 372

Savage, Matt, 116–117

savior siblings, 61–62; HLA compatibility and, 58, 59–60, 61; human life commodification and, 59; PGD and, 58, 60, 61

scalping, of indigenous Native Americans, 218–219
Scheler, Max, 58, 60
schizoaffective disorder, 105
schizoid personality disorder, 111
schizophrenia, 105–106; of Nash, 82–83, 118–119, 124
schizophreniform disorder, 105
schizotypal personality disorder, 111
Schopenhauer, Arthur, 12
SCLC. *See* Southern Christian Leadership Conference
seasonal affective disorder, 102
Second Treatise of Civil Government (Locke), 330
segregation, 252
Seidel, Kathleen, 122–123
self: assaulted personhood and, 131–132; sensory perception of, 11
self-actualization, Adler on, 300, 319
self-discernment, 363; of brutality in oppression, 337–338; chaplaincy training and, 342–343; empire atrocities, 338; Jesus Christ parable of, 335–336; National T&R Commission and, 350–351; of structural privilege, 337; T&R commissions for, 340–341; of U.S., 335–342; U.S. Congress on, 342; of U.S. wealth, 337; war crime trials, 339
selfhood, Nietzsche on, 12–13
self-identity, 293; in dementia, 170–171; religion and politics for, 296
self-loathing, 372–373
sensory perception, of self, 11, 14
sentience, 42
sexuality, gender identity and, xiv, 193–195
sexual orientation, 25, 193–194, 206
sexual preference, 194–195; conversion therapy for, 194
Shaker community, 316–317
Silber, John, 67–68
Singer, Peter, 172
slave rebellions, for resistance, 260–261; Nat Turner's Rebellion, 260; Stono Rebellion, 251, 260
slavery, 26–27, 148, 279, 340; Africans and African Americans, 4, 246–248,

324; armed rebellions and, 251; biblical warrant of dominion for, 242–245, 248–250, 279–280; Black slaves value calculation, 243; Christian slavers justification for, 244; dehumanization and, 244–245; estimates for, 280; films depiction of, 245; legal justifications for, 247; modern day, xiv, 22; morality of, 247; reconciliation and, 252; Three-Fifths Compromise and, 16, 247–248
SNCC. *See* Student Nonviolent Coordinating Committee
social groups, homogeneity of, 27
social justice, *Communio Sanctorum* and, 324–325
society, *hyper*cognition value by, 173
Socrates, personhood and, 4–5, 6
soft discrimination, for physical disabilities, 69
soma. *See* body (soma)
soul (psyche): Aquinas on body and, 7; Aristotle on, 5–6; of Black slaves, 246–248; Descartes on mind and, 9; over body, Plato on, 4–5, 6; Socrates on, 4, 6; trauma in, 231
The Souls of Black Folks (Du Bois), 256–257
"The Souls of White Folk" (Du Bois), 257
Southern Christian Leadership Conference (SCLC), 253
Southern Poverty Law Center (SPLC), on hate groups, 24, 152, 155, 297
specieism, 91–92
spiritual world, classical Greek philosophy on, 6
SPLC. *See* Southern Poverty Law Center (SPLC), on hate groups
Standing Rock Sioux Tribe v. U.S. Army Corps of Engineers (2016), 364
#StandWithBearEars protests, 220
stand-your-ground (SYG) gun laws, 162–163, 203
Stanton, Elizabeth Cady, 16
Stenberg v. Carhart (2001), 41
stillbirth, 49–50
stomach cancer, xi–xii
Stono Rebellion, of 1739, 251, 260
stop-and-frisk police programs, 255–256, 280

StoryCorps, 346, 365
stress, response to, 112–113
structural oppression, 344; of indigenous
Native Americans, 359–360;
indigenous Native Americans
acknowledgement, 354; National T&R
Commission on, 348, 349
structural privilege, 346, 364; National T&
R Commission on, 349–350, 351
structural privilege, self-discernment and,
337
Student Nonviolent Coordinating
Committee (SNCC), 261
subjugation, of indigenous Native
Americans, 223–225, 228–229
suicides, PTSD and, 192–193
Supreme Court (U.S.) decisions: *Brown v.
Board of Education* (1954), 252;
Doctrine of Discovery and, 225; *Dred
Scott v. Sandford* (1857), 148, 149, 248;
Gonzales v. Carhart (2007), 41; *Groves
v. Slaughter* (1841), 247–248; *Planned
Parenthood v. Casey* (1992), 139;
Plessy v. Ferguson (1896), 149; *Reed v.
Reed* (1971), 21; *Roe v. Wade*, 50–51,
73, 139; *Standing Rock Sioux Tribe v.
U.S. Army Corps of Engineers* (2016),
364; *Stenberg v. Carhart* (2001), 41;
Terry v. Ohio (1968), 255; *United
States v. The Amistad* (1841), 247–248;
Washington v. United States, 220
SYG. *See* stand-your-ground gun laws

Taylor, Charles, 167
teen pregnancy prevention, 141
teleology, 5
temporary protected status (TPS), for
immigrants, 160
Terry v. Ohio (1968), 255
thalidomide, Finkbine abortion and, 140
Theoharis, Liz, 253
theological politics, 325
A Theory of Justice (Rawls), 90
Thirteenth Amendment, 149
Thoreau, Henry David, 79, 122
thoughtful recovery programs, for
addiction, 137
Three-Fifths Compromise, slavery and, 16,
247–248

Thurman, Howard, 275
Thus Spoke Zarathustra (Nietzsche), 321
Tinker, George E., 371
Tooley, Michael, 172
tough on crime, of criminal justice system,
255
toxic nationalism, 298
TPS. *See* temporary protected status
trauma: addiction and, 119–121; of
Africans and African Americans, 260;
defense mechanisms of, 263; Holocaust
and, 231–233; of indigenous Native
Americans, 231–234; intergenerational,
232; mental illness and, 119–121; of
objectification, 259; in psyche, 231;
resistance confrontation for, 231, 262;
response to, 232. *See also* post-
traumatic stress disorder
tribalism, 22; uncertain otherness response
of, 19
Trinity, 6, 7
Trump, Donald: assaulted personhood by,
345, 372; biblical warrants against
LGBTQI people, 196, 206; Black
oppression and, 153; bullying and, 197,
207; hate groups and, 373; overt racism
of, 273, 283, 366; pro-life and, 50;
redistributive justice and, 272; on
Tubman, 281; on undocumented
immigrants, 160–161; White
nationalism support by, 273, 283;
White ruling class original sins and,
272, 282–283, 354
truth and reconciliation (T&R)
commissions: on atrocities and high
crimes against humanity, 340; examples
of, 340–341; on Greensboro massacre,
340; on Native American children
maltreatment, 340; for restorative
justice, 341. *See also* National Truth
and Reconciliation Commission, U.S.
truths: attentive listening for, 343, 346,
365; searching for, 342–347; validation
of, 343–344; on victimization, 344–345
Tubman, Harriet, 260, 280
Ture, Kwame. *See* Carmichael, Stokely
(Kwame Ture)
Tuskegee experiments, reparations for, 271
Tutu, Desmond, 340–341

Twelve Years a Slave (film), 245
two lives linked in abortion, Harrison and,
    45–46
Tzu Chi Foundation, 326
übermensch ("overman") concept: figures
    of, 322; King and, 321–322; narcissistic
    personality disorder and, 110;
    Nietzsche on, 12–13, 321–322

unborn fetuses, patriarchy and, 17
unconsciousness, 204; actively dying and,
    177–179; PVS and, 180–181; states of,
    180–182
Underground Railroad, 260
undocumented illegal immigrants, 159;
    labor exploitation of, 160; Trump on,
    160–161
United States (U.S.): abortions decline in,
    46–47; Great Awakenings in, 226–227;
    human rights wealth violations, 337;
    immigrants overview, 158–159; mental
    health and vulnerabilities in, 99–101;
    mood disorder prevalence in, 102;
    nationalism and manifest destiny in,
    227; original sins continuation in, 373;
    prison industry in, 134, 164; race in,
    148; self-discernment of, 335–342;
    wealth distribution asymmetry in, 282,
    337, 364. *See also* Bill of Rights (U.S.);
    Constitution (U.S.); National Truth and
    Reconciliation Commission, U.S.;
    Supreme Court (U.S.) decisions
United States v. The Amistad (1841),
    247–248
Unite the Right rally, 295, 298
universal healthcare, 318–319
universal rule of exceptions, for abortions,
    45
Unworthy Republic (Saunt), 372
U.S. *See* United States

validation, of truths, 343–344
value: Black slaves calculation of, 243; of
    human life, 143–144; Kant intrinsic, 59;
    Kant on life, 55; moral, of otherness, 7;
    society, of *hyper*cognition, 173; VSL
    for human life, 144
Value of Statistical Life (VSL), 144
veil of ignorance, Rawls on, 320

veterans: combat-related PTSD, 189–192;
    heroin addiction of, 133
victims, of assaulted personhood, 23–25
Vietnam War, PTSD and, 191
violence: Black-on-Black, 153; against
    Blacks, BLM and, 151; *hyper*violence,
    31; immigration and, 156–161; police
    brutality, 151–152, 201, 258, 329;
    racial, 150–151
Voting Rights Act (1965), 26, 30, 149,
    252, 319
VSL. *See* Value of Statistical Life
vulnerabilities, 357–358; of body, xiv,
    62–66; of mind, xiv, 62, 115–121;
    otherness and, 293, 300–302; of
    physical disabilities, 62–64, 74

Wacquant, Lois: on Blacks, 135; on prison
    ghettos, 164
Wagner, Richard, 12
Walden (Thoreau), 122
war crimes, against indigenous Native
    Americans, 218–219
War of 1812, 224
War on Crime, 254
War on Drugs, 134, 254, 255; opioid
    addiction and, 133
War on Poverty (1964), 253
War on Terrorism, 19
Washington v. United States, 220
wealth distribution asymmetry, in U.S.,
    282, 337, 364
West, Cornel, 26, 148, 257–258, 349, 370
Western world: abortion and, 3; Biblical
    approach influence on, 3;
    *hyper*cognition and, 3–4; Judeo-
    Christian traditions in, 3
West Nickel Mines School shooting,
    314–315
White assimilation: Malcolm X on, 258;
    White ruling class on, 268
White fragility, of DiAngelo, 30, 268
White Lives Matter (WLM), 155
White nationalism: crimes against
    humanity of, 254; hate groups, 252,
    297; LGBTQI people and, 197; people
    of color personhood and, 229; Trump
    support of, 273, 283
White Opioid problem, 134–135

White oppression, race and, 253–254
White ruling class: Black Americans and, 74, 256; Blacks dispossession, 217; Blacks objectification by, 257; displacement theory and, 161; Doctrine of Discovery of, 32; Federal Indian laws blood quantum, 224, 242; human rights and, 200; immigrants and, 159; indigenous Native Americans and, 74, 230; indigenous Native Americans subjugation, 228–229, 235; New Jim Crow and, 133; opioid addiction narrative of, 135; oppression of, 31, 217; on race, 268; SYG laws, 162–163, 203; Trump and original sins of, 272, 282–283, 354; on White assimilation, 268
White supremacy, 26, 27, 155, 161, 364; hate groups, 252; Jim Crow laws and, 148; LGBTQI people and, 197; manifest destiny and, 278
WHO. *See* World Health Organization (WHO), abortion and
Williams, Robert F., 261

Willowbrook State School, intellectual disabilities and, 97
will to pleasure pursuit, Freud on, 300
will-to-power, Nietzsche and, 13, 300, 302, 319, 321
Winthrop, John, 226, 227
withholding, of Narcan, 145–146, 199–200
WLM. *See* White Lives Matter
women: equal rights, 21; fetal rights and, 141–142; Jane Crow, 161–162, 164, 202. *See also* pregnant woman
Works Progress Administration (WPA), oral history interviews, 346, 365
World Health Organization (WHO), abortion and, 39
world religions, otherness and, 304–310
WPA. *See* Works Progress Administration (WPA), oral history interviews

xenophobia, 29; anti-immigrant sentiment and, 28; frank, xiv; against indigenous Native Americans, 219, 221

Zimmerman, George, 150, 162
zygote, 40, 41, 43

About the Author

The Rev. Dr. **Craig C. Malbon** grew up and was educated in New England. For more than 30-years he led a successful research laboratory on signaling and human disease, culminating with more than 250 publications and numerous national and international awards, including election to rank of Fellow in the American Association for the Advancement of Science, to the Royal Society of Medicine (London), and recipient of the Goodman & Gilman lifetime achievement award from the American Society of Pharmacology & Experimental Therapeutics (USA). He trained in ethics at Princeton Theological Seminary, received a master's in divinity at Union Theological Seminary in the City of New York, and trained in chaplaincy in the Catholic Healthcare Services of Long Island, NY. He is an ordained and authorized minister in the United Church of Christ. He holds the academic title of leading professor and ethicist. He divides his time between Long Island and Manhattan.